The Development of Secularism in Turkey

Africa

The
Development of
Secularism in
Turkey

NIYAZI BERKES

MONTREAL

McGill University Press

1964

preface

THE OBJECT of this work is to acquaint the English-speaking reader with the evolution of the Turkish transformation whose beginning goes back as far as the early part of the eighteenth century. A study of this transformation may contribute to an understanding of present-day political conditions in many Muslim countries; but, apart from this, it will be helpful to those who are interested in the comparative study of political and religious transformations in non-Western societies.

The discussion is focused on the question of the relationship between religion and state, but the scope of the work is broader for two reasons: first, in order to present the context of the processes affecting relations between state and religion, and, second, because those relations had a wider connotation in the case of Islam than in that of Christianity. Thus the process of secularization has been examined here as it affected many aspects of society. This examination leads to the discussion of a doctrine of secularism that emerged on the eve of World War II as the basis of a policy of government and religion.

The survey will deal largely with the development and changes in ideas and values rather than with economic, demographic, or other material conditions of change although references will be made to them when necessary. It should not, however, be taken as a history of religious, scientific, political, educational, or legal ideas in Turkey. These have been described only insofar as they serve as indices of social change and the evolution of views, especially in the secularization of thought.

v

Readers unacquainted with the technicalities of Islamic and Turkish history and institutions are cautioned against conceiving these as analogous to those of the modern West. Terms for institutions such as the state, religion, and law, which are basic to our survey, should not be interpreted in their present Western sense. It is to avoid such associations that Islamic or Turkish words have frequently been used, although an effort has been made to limit their number. The concepts and institutions to which these terms refer have been described briefly in the Introduction. The reader, however, will best understand their original meaning in the medieval pattern by seeing them challenged by forces of change—just as one can see how a pattern was woven by watching the fabric being unravelled. Although most of the Islamic and Turkish terms used in the text are defined either directly or contextually, and in many cases used as indices showing the changes in institutions and ideas, some which have not been so defined are grouped into a glossary at the end of the book.

Modern Turkish orthography has been used for words that are now a part of the Turkish vocabulary, irrespective of their origin or original spelling. (The following letters in modern Turkish are pronounced as indicated: *c*, English *j*; *ç*, English *ch*; *ğ*, almost English *y*; *ö*, German *ö*; *ü*, German *ü*; *ş*, English *sh*; and *ı*, the actual sound value given to the vowel in English *tion* in ac*tion* or *ton* in car*ton*. The mark ^ indicates where a syllable contains a long vowel; in most cases these are found in Arabic words or those derived from Arabic.) Very frequently used words like "Ulema" and "Tanzimat" have not been italicized or given in Arabic transliteration. The Arabic *Sharî'a* has, for the most part, been used in the Turkish form "Şeriat" to mean a body of traditional religious rules (it has been rendered *şeriat* in such contexts as "*şeriat* courts" to avoid an overlapping of unfamiliar words such as the adjective şer'î). "Ulema" (which is *'ulamâ* in Arabic, and the plural of *'âlim*, a learned man) is used as a generic name for a class of people who constituted a corporate body in the Ottoman-Turkish polity; *ulema* has been used to denote a number of persons having had the traditional Islamic religious education but not necessarily belonging to the Ulema organization, which disintegrated and disappeared imperceptibly from the middle of the nineteenth century and parallel to the gradual transformation of the medieval polity into a new order. Three persons representing three important institutions have been designated by their Turkish rather than their Anglicized or original Arabic or Persian titles: "Padişah"

vi

rather than "Sultan"; "Sadrazam" (the contracted form of *sadr-i a'zam*) rather than "Grand Vizir"; and "Şeyhul-Islâm" rather than "Shaykh ul-Islâm." The English "caliph" and "caliphate" are generally used, but their Arabic equivalents *khalîfa* and *khilâfat* are preferred where the reference is meant to convey the peculiarly Islamic qualities of the institution.

One difficulty likely to confuse some readers is the transposition of Islamic and Turkish dates. The Muslim or *Hijrî* calendar (designated by A.H.) dates from A.D. 622, the year of the Prophet Muhammad's emigration (*hijra*) from Mecca to Medina; but its equivalents in the Gregorian calendar cannot be found simply through arithmetical addition because the *Hijrî* calendar is a lunar calendar. To make matters worse, the so-called *Malî* (fiscal) calendar, having a Julian base with *Hijrî* numerals, was used in Turkey in the nineteenth and twentieth centuries until the adoption of the Western calendar in 1926. To avoid the confusion of three systems of dates and to relieve the reader from using conversion tables, all dates have been given according to the Gregorian calendar; the dates of the Turkish writings referred to in the notes have, therefore, been converted to that calendar as closely as possible.

The writing of this work was completed before the publication of three books, one by Professor Bernard Lewis entitled *The Emergence of Modern Turkey* (London, 1961) and the other two by Dr. Şerif Mardin on *The Genesis of Young Ottoman Thought* (Princeton, 1962) and Robert Devereux on *The First Ottoman Constitutional Period* (Baltimore, 1963), and it has not been possible to benefit from their contributions. The latter two will be particularly useful to readers of this work as they deal in greater detail with the material covered in Chapters 7 and 8, respectively.

I am deeply grateful to many persons whom I cannot enumerate here. I owe special gratitude to the authorities of McGill University and to the Institute of Islamic Studies of McGill University for encouragement and support as well as for the grant made by the latter for the publication of this work. My thanks are due to Mr. William J. Watson, the librarian of the Institute, and Miss Margery E. Simpson of McGill University Press for their invaluable suggestions for the improvement of the text. Above all, I feel a particular debt of gratitude to my wife without whose constant help this work would not have been completed.

Niyazi Berkes

THE STRUGGLE FOR ESTABLISHMENT OF A SECULAR NATION-STATE 1919-39

INTRODUCTION

A STEADY TREND toward secularization in traditional institutions is a feature of Muslim societies facing the impact of modern civilization. The Muslim peoples have different ethnic origins, geographic situations, historical backgrounds, and present-day conditions; the changes occurring among them differ in scope, intensity, and velocity. Still, one cannot avoid noting certain similarities in their experiences of social change.

The disparity between the new and the old is perhaps to be found nowhere so clearly as in the lives of these peoples. Traditional patterns are in the process of dissolution, and new forms have not yet become established. There are cleavages in almost every department of life—in ideas, in institutions, between generations, and among classes and communities. Such a condition of flux is an unmistakable sign of internal change in the value system of a society; and this change is unavoidably followed by some degree of secularization.

The process is universal, but the attitude towards the problems created by it differs in every case. The acceptance of a secular outlook on religious, political, social, and cultural matters is far from universal. That such an outlook is warranted or even relevant under the present conditions of flux is far from being generally recognized, let alone accepted.

It will be useful to make a distinction between the process of secularization and the doctrine of secularism. Secularization is a sociological process which takes place as a result of factors beyond the control of individuals. A doctrine of secularism involves indi-

3

vidual ideas, attitudes, beliefs, or interests. The two are often interrelated, but the latter is not a necessary accompaniment or a necessary product of the former.

Among the Muslim countries it was in Turkey that, prior to World War II, a secular concept of state, religion, law, education, and economy was first promoted, and a definite doctrine of secularism implemented as a political, constitutional, educational, and cultural policy. This policy has not, however, won the approval of all Muslim nations or of most individual Muslims. The doctrine is being challenged even in Turkey. Many claim that Islam is incompatible with such an attitude. Although such claims are based on differing considerations, all amount to the belief that Islam cannot be merely a faith for the conscience of the individual, that it is, on the contrary, the foundation of an entire social system, and that in Islam religion is so fused to every social institution that the existence of any one is endangered by the attempt to separate it from religion.

The opponents of secularism are made up of two equally opposed groups: the traditionalists, who look back to medieval Islam as the one true polity, and the modernists, who reject medieval Islam in favour of a "real" or "pristine" Islam. This modernist view arose as a reaction to a clear policy of secularism and drew much of its inspiration from the desire to develop a totalitarian ideology that would serve as a substitute for European forms of totalitarianism.

The anti-secularist view represents a challenge to modern trends in all Muslim countries and invites objective study of secularization as it involves fundamental changes in society as well as minds. It will be our object to survey the rise and development of secularism in Turkey in order to evaluate the policy on factual grounds and to see what are the implications of secularism for the social and, especially, the religious and moral values in Muslim society.

We shall do this in terms of the transformation of the social context provided by Turkish history. We shall examine historically the process of secularization which reached its clearest culmination as a result of the radical reforms undertaken between 1927 and 1937. These reforms were the definite signs of a final rupture with the basic institutions of medieval Islamic tradition as manifest in the history of the Ottoman-Turkish state from the fourteenth to the twentieth centuries.

Two Concepts of Secularism

The use of the term "secularism" in connection with the determination of relations between spiritual and temporal authorities gives the impression that the condition to which the term refers is found only where such distinctly institutionalized authorities coexisted. In this narrow concept, secularism appears to be merely a matter of separating the respective areas of jurisdiction of two institutions of authority.

From the middle of the nineteenth century, the term was used in the West to refer to a specific policy of separating church from state. The word was derived from the Latin *saeculum*, which meant originally "age" or "generation" but which came to mean in Christian Latin "the temporal world." The word "secular" has been used with this meaning in all the major Protestant countries. The policy of secularism in Catholic countries is more often expressed by the term "laicism," which derives from the Greek *laos* (the people) and *laikos* (the lay). While the underlying emphasis in the word "secularism" is on the idea of worldliness, the term "laicism" emphasizes the distinction of the laity from the clergy. Both terms, however, refer to two aspects of the same thing. They were used in connection with the problems of duality, opposition, or separation of church and state. The church represented the highest authority over the spiritual sphere and the state the highest authority over temporal matters. Secularization or laicization meant the transformation of persons, offices, properties, institutions, or matters of an ecclesiastical or spiritual character to a lay, or worldly, position. It has been usual to designate as "secularized" or "laicized" any institution withdrawn from the jurisdiction of the religious authority.

In Christianity, the two realms, spiritual and temporal, were separate from the beginning. However, relations between the two, or attitudes of one towards the other, varied with time. Christian thinking had to cope with the difficulty of maintaining relations between two established institutions and authorities. The solution in Eastern Christianity was found in the creation of a state church. Western Christianity aspired to a universal Christian civilization in which the church would be ascendant over temporal authorities. After the Reformation the universal supremacy of the church was denied. In modern times, keeping the two spheres apart has become a more or less established principle in Western Europe and North

America, although the mechanisms developed for the maintenance of a modus vivendi between the two vary from one political regime to another.

Owing to unique historical circumstances, the establishment of a church above, or subordinate to, or parallel with, the state was peculiar to Christianity; it constituted an exception rather than the rule in relations between the state and religion. This existence of the Christian church as a political power in its own right has tended to focus attention mainly on the political aspects of secularism. In a non-Christian state such political considerations are not necessarily of primary importance.

To understand the process of secularization in a non-Christian society, one must examine the extent of the domination of religious rules over all areas of life and discover whether or not this domination is either implemented or supported by the state. Further, one must estimate the extent of this domination and also try to ascertain the degree of separation between the religious life of the people and the other aspects of their lives. In this matter of separation, the relationship of religion and economic life is often of primary importance.

The basic conflict in secularism is not necessarily between religion and the world, as was the case in Christian experience. The conflict is often between the forces of tradition, which tend to promote the domination of religion and sacred law, and the forces of change. Such a struggle can take place in a society where there is no organized church authority. Perhaps the best example will be found in this work.

In a society governed by a tradition which carries the sanction of the dominant religion, secularization will inevitably involve a major upheaval. Yet once the tradition has been challenged and new conditions result, the traditional order often faces an increasing number of such challenges. In such a process the emancipation of political institutions has tended to appear the most vital, but there are cases in which secularization has appeared first in other areas with startling results. The process may lag behind in various areas, including the political, and there is no evidence to support the view that secularization occurs proportionately in every area of social action. The term "secular" is currently used in sociological literature for the state of a society that is normally capable of maintaining a degree of differentiation and flexibility in its value system. In this wider concept of the term, "secularism" can include the behaviour of individuals and groups within the state and can be manifest in economic and other major fields of social action as well as in the political sphere.

From a sociological viewpoint, secularization may be observed in the differentiating of social values into areas removed from the authority of tradition. Changes take place in the relationship between what is "sacred," or "unchangeable," and what is taken to be "profane," or neutral to tradition. In the non-secular or traditionalist system, there is no room for the idea of change through the agency of state or any organ of society or individuals, whether by legislative or by other means independent of the fixed traditional prescriptions. Stability and order are given the highest value. Change is associated with disorder and evil. The absolute principles of the tradition are not subject to fundamental modification; they can only be interpreted by definite groups of men in accordance with definite rules. In contrast to this type of traditionalist society, secular societies exhibit greater dynamism, by which various sectors of social life are freed from the domination of sacred rules. This condition emerges in all major social institutions; it is particularly manifest in economic and scientific-technological behaviour. Rational behaviour, as the epitome of secularism, seems to appear in these areas first. The religious system of the society ceases to be the supreme provider of values, or a greater degree of freedom is recognized to individuals or groups to interpret these values in terms of exigencies.

In the present work, "secularization" and "secularism" will not be used in the narrower sense, referring merely to the relationship between the church and temporal authorities; at times they will have connotations transcending the purely political. This broader use of the terms is necessitated by the nature of the case under investigation. The core of the tradition which we find being challenged in Islamic countries by the forces of modern civilization (by no means unrelated to the rise and development of Western secularism) was Islam. One of the distinguishing marks of this tradition was the relation of religion and state. In Islam there were no concepts of church and state as specifically religious and political institutions. Religion and state were believed to be fused together; the state was conceived as the embodiment of religion, and religion as the essence of the state.

It is this feature, partly misinterpreted under modern conditions by certain modern Muslims, which has given rise to the opinion that the concepts of secularism and secularization are irrelevant to the study of Muslim societies. There is not even any term, it is claimed, to express these words in the languages of the Muslim peoples. We shall see in this work how far the assertion is tenable; but we would like here to note the fact that even in the West the term 'secularism" has a history of barely a century.

The modernist Islamic view, valid if secularism is understood in its more limited meaning, does not bar the study of secularization in Muslim societies when the process is understood in its broader sense. The distinction between the Christian and Islamic experience lies in the differences in the institutions and hierarchies within the religion, which influenced the relationship between the religious and political authorities. Despite the differences, however, there were common features in the medieval development of both Christianity and Islam when each showed tendencies opposed to secular conditions. Both religions were conceived as systems striving to include the spiritual and the temporal, and within which the two spheres would be subordinated to the rules of tradition. This similarity did not exist simply because a religion was involved in each case. Just as in Islam, so in Christianity, secularism remained irrelevant as long as the religious outlook remained loyal to the medieval view of life. This was true even when the claim of the Universal Church was rejected by the leading representatives of the Reformation. Secularism within Christendom came in its real sense, not with the separation of state and church, but with the collapse of the medieval concept of society. There was no secularism so long as the medieval concept continued, although in Christianity church and state existed side by side while in Islam one stood inside the other. In either case, the church or state, or amalgam of the two, found it hard to co-exist with the political, economic, scientific, and cultural institutions produced by a secular view of society.

The Medieval View of Society

Like all medieval societies, the Ottoman-Turkish polity differed fundamentally from modern political systems. Perhaps the most striking point of contrast is in their views of society as a whole.

The first distinguishing mark of the medieval outlook was its all-pervasive religious spirit. This spirit even affected those areas that were not governed directly by religious injunctions or beliefs. Because of the deeply religious colouring of medieval Christian and Muslim societies, each saw the other primarily as a religious community. For both there were only Christians, Muslims, Jews, idolators, and heretics. A Turk of medieval times never called himself a Turk, and when a European used this word, he meant, in fact, a "Mahometan", or "infidel"—just as the Turk used such non-religious terms as *Rûm* (Roman) for a Greek Orthodox Christian and *Frenk* (Frank) for a Latin, or Western European, Christian. As a corollary, all Muslims who were not excluded as heretical were thought of as constituting a community called in Arabic *umma*. In Turkish usage this was *ümmet*, the community of Islam or of Muhammad. For one to be considered a part of this community, it was sufficient not to be a Christian, a Jew, or a heretic, and to bear witness as a Muslim. The fact that an individual's national beliefs, practices, customs, and institutions were quite different and on some points even contrary to the Turks' did not disqualify him from the Islamic community in the medieval outlook, when the interplay among the various Muslim societies was limited.

No distinctions were made between the religious and non-religious in the present understanding of the terms. The distinctions were made among what conformed to the *Shari'a*, that is, to the body of rules regulating the conduct of the Muslim, what deviated from it, and what was irrelevant to it. An aspect of life had religious significance only if it had traditional recognition according to this body of rules, which covered not only belief and ritual but also matters of custom and law. These rules were studied, administered, watched over, and, especially when new situations arose, interpreted by a specially trained body of academicians called Ulema. Their ultimate aim was to achieve harmony, and even unity, between the provisions of this system of rules and the conduct of worldly affairs.

Traditional Ottoman polity was fashioned essentially by a patrimonial authority called Sultanate, Islamized by recognizing the *Shari'a*, which the Turks spelled as Şeriat, as the sacred law of the Muslims, and by assuming the charismatic title of Caliphate, which was believed to be a succession to the Prophet's headship of the community of Islam. More than any other medieval Islamic polity, the Turkish one, headed by the Ottoman dynasty, characterized that combination of temporal and religious attributes implied in the combination of the words Sultanate and Caliphate— a combination believed to be typical of the Islamic form of polity. In Turkish history, the concept of unity of state and religion (*din-u-devlet*) was applied through an imperial system which gave unity and order to a great multiplicity of religions, sects, professions, and social classes. However, this system reflected a different understanding of the unity between religion and government than that implied in the classical Islamic theory of *imâmah* which simply meant, to the exponents of this theory, leadership or headship of the community of believers. In the medieval concept, headship shifted from the leader of the community, conducting the religious acts of the believers, to a sovereign ruler whose chief function was to maintain unity and order through the application of power.

The medieval Muslim political view, like the Christian, was permeated by belief in a social structure based on distinct orders and estates. Unlike the *ümmet* in which all Muslims were brothers and equals, a polity composed of these orders was seen as an organism pyramidally stratified and hierarchically arranged, fashioned and governed by the Creator. Important elements in this view were the emphasis on non-equality, on a rigid differentiation according to economic and political functions and religious differences, and on the need for a power with which to oversee and hold the separate units together. Naturally, just as the view of society differed from that of the modern world, so the concept and mode of applying justice differed from those generally followed today.

The Ottoman-Turkish Hierarchy

According to the Ottoman-Turkish view, the ruler, known in the West as the Sultan and commonly called by the Turks Padişah, was appointed by God to hold together the estates of the society which constituted its order. Directly under him came his vicar called Sadrazam (a contraction of *sadr-ı a'zam*, the highest rank) known in Europe as Grand Vizir. He was the chief of the ruler's administrative, military, and judicial staffs. Beside these stood the Ulema, the corps of the learned, distinct from the military and civil estates. Finally, there was the great bulk of the body politic, the common people (*'awâmm*), the ruled. The most important part of the people was the *ra'iyya* (known in Turkish by its plural, *raâya* and in English as *rayah*, which latter term was applied by the Europeans only to the Christians under Turkish rule). These were the primary producers, most of them peasants. The artisans and traders constituted another category and the least worthy in the eyes of medieval writers. Besides this differentiation by economic function, the *raâya* were also differentiated into Muslims and non-Muslims. While the first constituted a politically amorphous community, the second (Jews and Christians) were differentiated according to their ecclesiastical affiliations and not according to their ethnic or national differences) in spiritually autonomous religious communities called *millets*. The function of the ruling estates (the administrative, the military, and the learned, including the judiciary) was to maintain the order as an unalterable tradition by securing to each category of the ruled no less and no more than it deserved according to its function or station. This was the meaning of justice.

Through the application of certain principles implied in this concept of society, a great degree of unity was realized over a long period of time. Disorder broke out only when the principles ceased to be applied or to be applicable and the various groups began to develop tendencies that were incompatible with these principles. In the following chapters we shall see how some of these groups disappeared, some were transformed into occupational groups or social classes, and some developed into nationalities.

Since God created every particle of the social universe for specific purposes and, thus, every individual should remain as God willed, the first principle was traditionalism. Anything deviating from the established tradition, whether or not it was derived from religious sources, was contrary to a supposed Ancient Law (*kanûn-u kadîm*), which the Şeriat was invoked to sanctify. Many ordinary practices became not only lawful but also religiously sanctioned by becoming a part of the tradition.

The second principle was that each group should be protected from influences which might upset the order. This was applied in the policies of segregating a group by assigning to it a separate status. These policies encouraged corporate groups which sometimes enhanced communal or "national" differences and sometimes emphasized the inter-confessional or international nature of the Turkish empire. Each was recognized by the ruler and possessed privileges granted by his favour. In each there was some authority recognized as partial delegate of the supreme holder of power. For example, heads of the guilds or of the Christian and Jewish *millets* had administrative and juridical rights and duties. (The Turkish system found a place for the non-Muslim communities in its medieval structure, without segregating them into ghettos or resorting to expulsion or extermination, by according right of jurisdiction to their respective ecclesiastical authorities—a method which invited praise from Arnold J. Toynbee.) Each group had traditions as to titles, grades, recruitment, ceremonies, discipline, but absolute loyalty to the supreme ruler. Shifts from one to another were rare (proselytization was not normally encouraged). Remuneration for duties was only partially monetary—in many cases prebends or benefices were assigned to a position as a source of income to its holder.

Since there was no equality among the various orders and groups and since each had a separate function and status, each tended to form a closed group. This led to the third principle according to which each individual and category should remain where and as it traditionally was. To discourage discontent and migration each individual was accorded the means best suited to his function and station. No one was assigned, or allowed to perform, the functions of another category. For example, tillers were not expected to be soldiers and soldiers were not intended to possess artisan skills. No lower order was permitted to arouse discontent by encroaching upon the rights and prerogatives of a higher order. Above all, the privileges granted to the ruling estates were not available to the lower orders. The moralists and the writers of books on statecraft were particularly concerned with this last point and warned the rulers of the evil consequences of possible changes.

One exception was made to the third principle and this exception itself became another ruling principle. It was that while all other orders had roots in their group, religion, family, and occupation, the military and administrative orders of the central government should possess no roots in society and should bear allegiance only to their ruler. The respective positions of and relations between the rulers and the ruled differed from modern conditions. While in a modern democracy the aim is to make the political authorities of the state as accessible to the bulk of the people as possible with no demarcation between the rulers and the ruled, in the medieval system the ideal was exactly the opposite. The rulers were supposed to be separated from the ruled. They could be recruited from among certain categories of the ruled, but the recruits were detached from their original social classes. The system was believed to have collapsed when the common people entered the ranks of the administrative, military, and clerical orders, and when they were no longer divested of their original social identity.

The fifth ruling principle, the "law of nature" of this system, was the preservation of order, called *nizâm*. This meant maintaining a proportional distribution and, hence, a balance among the various status groups. This principle derived from the belief that all the prerogatives and privileges granted to the groups were bestowed by the grace of God for the sake of the happiness and order of the world (*nizâm-ı âlem*). The modern concept of natural rights and equality of citizenship had no place in the medieval system since there was no idea of individual freedom or popular sovereignty. Since each order had its unique function and position, like the organs of a body, there was no equality among them. The relative status assigned to a particular category was dictated not by the utility of the function performed, but by the value of that function, that is, by the assumed proximity of the category to God.

The sixth principle, therefore, was the maintenance of order and the distribution of prerogatives according to a hierarchy of values. Value was vested not in the individual but in his position. The value was designated not according to rational norms but according to the moral and religious purposes of the order created by God.

Padişah and Ulema: Temporal and Spiritual Authority

Naturally, the position of the Padişah ranked highest in the hierarchy. He was the direct representative or shadow of God in the world. The title Khalîfa (Caliph) was understood in this sense; in other words, it did not imply successorship to the Prophet who was never imagined as a ruler. The Ottoman ruler did not claim divine nature or any prophetic attribute; but he was viewed as being different from other mortals since he held the highest position in the divine arrangement of the world. Here also not the person but the position was invested with value. The Padişah had no personal charisma, and when he was deposed (a number of them were deposed and one killed) he simply did not exist socially.

How far the Padişahs, before the eighteenth century, were absolute and their rule autocratic or theocratic may be judged by considering the nature of the relationship between the temporal authority and the Şeriat as the supreme manifestation of the religion, because this relationship was believed to have expressed

14

the unity between the two areas of life and formed the link across the gulf between the ruler and the ruled. Since the rulers and the Ulema as the representatives of the Şeriat played great roles in the entire course of the transformation from this traditional system which we shall survey, we shall dwell a little more upon both.

The area left to the will (*irâde*) of the ruler was free from the limitations of the Şeriat. He could enact laws (*kanûn*) in various forms, according to, but outside the realm of, the Şeriat on the basis of his right (recognized by the Şeriat) of discretion and censure (*takdîr* and *ta'zîr*). The discretionary prerogative of the ruler was not subject to legislative or legal control on the part of the ruled. There was no conception of legislation as distinct from the administrative and judicial branches of government. Legislative, executive, and judicial powers belonged to the ruler who delegated these to his vicar, the Sadrazam, from whom all functionaries in these fields received their authorities.

In theory, applicable in other Muslim states as well, the ruler was limited in the exercise of his authority only by the Şeriat. In reality, threats to his power came from his temporal officials. There were three principal means by which the Padişah protected his unique authority from division: (*a*) through an administrative staff called the "servants of the porte" (*kapı kulu*), which was bound unconditionally to the ruler, and detached or uprooted from social classes; (*b*) through a military force called Janissaries (Yeniçeri, new soldiers) also completely detached from their social origins and directly bound to the ruler; and (*c*) through the granting of fief benefices (*timar*) for tested service in war; the holders of these grants were called *sipahî*, the cavalry men; they too were subject to the favour of the ruler; they did not constitute a feudal class. By these methods a highly centralized power was established. As long as these institutions continued to function, the ruler held onto his power; feudal tendencies were kept under control.

The Ulema, the corps of the learned men of religion or of the Şeriat, maintained the continuity of law and tradition and combatted the anti-authoritarian, anti-traditionalist religious tendencies which manifested themselves, particularly in the seventeenth century, either in the form of the fundamentalism of the pious or the antinomianism of the mystic (*sufî*). Occasionally fundamentalists and antinomians were sentenced as heretics; but moderates in both groups were tolerated when they formed religious or spiritual orders. Particularly, the mystic orders were favoured by the official Ulema and were influential in tempering the zeal of the fundamentalists or popular fanatics.

The unique feature of the pre-modern Turkish policy of *din-u-devlet* can be understood more clearly by noting the function of the Ulema in this polity. The word is the plural of *âlim* which itself derives from the Arabic *'ilm* (knowledge), presumably religious knowledge. The sum total of the men having acquired this knowledge does not, however, signify Ulema in the Turkish sense of the term. A man might be erudite in religious knowledge and yet not be a member of the Ulema estate. Members of the Ulema were drawn from institutions of education called *medreses*; these were not monastic or cathedral or guild schools but colleges founded and financed by the rulers. The emphasis in the curricula was on law and theology. Graduates holding various degrees were registered in official Ulema ledgers as soon as they received appointments; one might be appointed as a minister of religion (*imâm*), as a juristconsult (*muftî*), or as a judge (*kadı* or Arabic *qâdî*). The last constituted by far the most important category in the Turkish system in so far as the administration of justice, according to Şeriat and kanûn, served the maintenance of order.

However, the second of the three groups mentioned above had greater significance as it played a special role in maintaining the link between *din* (religion) and *devlet* (state). Its function was to interpret the Şeriat when new cases arose. This interpretation was called *iftâ*, and the statement in which an interpretation was given was called a *fetva* (from Arabic *fatwâ*). When a statement concerned a technical legal matter, the *muftî* who passed the judgment was nothing but an ordinary juristconsult, advising the judge as well as the public. But when the case involved something which had special religious or political import, the *muftî* assumed an unusual importance. Because of this, the highest ranking *muftî*, called the Şeyhul-Islâm, became the highest religious authority, almost equal in power to the Sadrazam in state affairs. His official statements related not only to matters of religious policy, but also such major concerns of the state as declarations of war, relations with non-Muslim states, taxation, and innovations such as the use of coffee or tobacco and the introduction of inventions such as the printing press.

While originally a *fetva* had no official authority, the Turkish system gave to it an official political sanction. Still, the office of Şeyhul-Islâm remained somewhat ambiguous in the political structure. The Şeyhul-Islâm was appointed by the Padişah from among

16

the highest ranking Ulema and could be dismissed by the ruler's will, but a *fetva* of the Şeyhul-Islâm could depose the Padişah. However, the Şeyhul-Islâm had no power to carry out his judgement and, therefore, had to rely upon the administrative and military orders. As long as he and the Ulema sided with the ruler and legitimized his decisions, other holders of power were kept at bay. When the Padişah attempted to introduce an innovation not supported by the Ulema he was powerless and in most cases lost his sovereignty.

The Ulema order differed from the Christian clergy in its nature, function, and organization. The hierarchy which developed within that order bore no resemblance to the Catholic or Orthodox clerical hierarchy. They did not constitute a spiritual corps organized through a church. Religious matters were organized not through an autonomous church but by the state through the order of Ulema which constituted an official and temporal body. Only the mystic orders, referred to above, remained outside this regimentation and close to the artisan corporations and to the people. Only these constituted specifically religious institutions indifferent to temporal affairs. The Ulema's specific concern was to see that the ruler's legislation, administration, and justice agreed with the Şeriat. As such their supreme aim was the preservation of the traditional order, not change or reform. Their emphasis on order (*nizâm*) was so influential that eventually those attempting reforms (for which no generally established term came into being) were forced to claim that they were attempting to restore the *nizâm*. As we shall see later, the major reform attempts were called by such terms as *New Nizâm, Tanzimat, nizâmat-ı esasiye*, which were all cognates.

Political power was completely detached from all social strata. The peasantry, artisans, and merchants were outside the élite (*khawâss*). Not only the masses of people (*'awâmm*), but even the élite had no legally defined position in the constitution of the state; their status was held only by tradition. The doctrine of election (*bai'a*, or in the Turkish form *bîat*) of the Padişah by the "men of binding and loosening" (*ahl al-'aqd wa al-hall*) was maintained only as a traditional ceremony of allegiance. There is no evidence to show that those in attendance at the ceremony represented the people or the estates; the people played no role in the appointment of the electors. The exclusion of the people from the government was not incompatible with the Şeriat. Long before the establishment of the Ottoman-Turkish state at the end of the fourteenth century, conditions had tended not only to systematize the Şeriat as a private law based on the tradition of the Islamic community sanctified by the authority of the Kur'an, the holy scripture, and Sunna, the tradition of the Prophet, but to further a political authority that did not derive from the religious tradition. The acceptance of the Sultanate, the patrimonial rule, as the legitimate state authority with the Şeriat as a non-political law ruled out the possibility of legislating political constitution.

Thus, neither the Ulema and the ruling orders nor the social classes such as peasantry, artisans, and merchants developed constitutional rights to limit the ruler's power or to extend their own. This did not mean, however, that the Padişahs became more autocratic or absolute with the disruption of the traditional order and balance. Had this been the case, there might have been better chances for modern reforms in the military, political, fiscal, commercial, and scientific fields such as occurred earlier under the absolute monarchs of some Western European countries. Apart from a few capable rulers who tended to become absolute autocrats, the actual power of the Padişah had almost entirely disintegrated by the end of the eighteenth century. By then the struggle for power was waged among groups that were traditionally subservient to the ruler and detached from the social classes and knew no law other than tradition, whose sanctity was waning.

Breakdown of the Traditional Order

When the traditional order reached the stage of complete disorder at the end of the eighteenth century, as we shall see later in more detail, there were some efforts to establish a legal definition of the relationship between the Padişah and the Ulema, the army and the feudalized landed power holders. The aim was never to limit or alter the supreme authority of the Padişah. Therefore, while a document of 1809 defined contractual relations between these groups in legal terms, the Padişah was not seen as a party to the pact. The document, thus, in no way resembled a constitution, nor did it ever serve as a step in the development of constitutional government.

It is, therefore, not possible to see a genuine transformation from a traditional to a legal constitutional system until much later

18

times. We shall trace the steps in this direction during the nineteenth century. Any such transformation is usually initiated by the disintegration of the medieval estates and their evolution into social classes. In Turkey this pattern, common in Western Europe, was missing largely because of the continued existence of a tradition of sovereignty based on the unity of religion and state.

How far can a traditionalist system allow change? Although anything which deviated from the Sunna, referred to above, was considered a novelty (*bid'a* or in Turkish *bid'at*) and rejected, the Ulema were free to accept what they regarded as "good or praiseworthy" innovations. Many such innovations which had become part and parcel of the medieval order and civilization were approved by the Ulema as necessities of the time. They exhibited a good degree of elasticity within the limits of the order and tradition. From the beginning of the seventeenth century, when the order began to feel that it was being shaken, there developed the type of fundamentalists, referred to before, who regarded any innovation as contrary to the Şeriat. These came mostly from the lower ranks of the Ulema or outside that order and regarded it as a mere interest group, corrupt, mundane, and no longer genuinely representative of religion. These fundamentalists opposed not only all contemporary and future changes but even those innovations introduced in the past. They no longer cared for the temporal *nizâm* of the Ulema and the kanûn of the rulers; they preached a return to the pristine injunctions of the Kur'an and the Sunna of the Prophet.

The opposition of the fundamentalists to any form of innovation drove a wedge into the medieval union of religion and state and contributed to the rupture between the two, which finally occurred in the nineteenth century. But already at the end of the seventeenth century, no level of religiosity remained untouched by the effects of the disruption of the traditional order. While the fundamentalist upsurge agitated popular fanaticism, the religious life of the urban and rural masses turned increasingly to magic and superstition. The mystic orders, which so far remained outside the influence of the political powers, skidded more and more towards antinomianism and free-thinking, and this, in turn, furthered the fundamentalist reaction against rational or spiritual liberalization.

The earliest symptoms of the disruption of the traditional order coincided with the approach of the Muslim millenium (corresponding to 1590 A.D.). Its coming had long been anticipated with grave apprehension. Many expected the event to signal the end of the world. The signs of disorder following the turn of the millenium confirmed such fears and produced a psychological state which lasted far beyond the event itself and hampered all ideas of reform or progress. These were looked upon as vain and doomed.

In the seventeenth century, Turkey began to be exposed to the early effects of the changes occurring in the Western economy, and contemporary Turkish statesmen and writers were able to note down the political symptoms of these effects upon basic institutions of the traditional order.[1] Unaware of the novelty of the new forces from which the influences originated, they made a series of recommendations for political reform. These invariably insisted upon the retention or the restoration of the traditional institutions.

---

[1] Most famous of these were *Kavanîn-i Âl-i Osman* by Ayn-î Ali written about 1607, *Risâle* of Koçi Bey written about 1630, *Düstûr-ül Amel* by Kâtip Çelebi written about 1652. But there were others written both before and after these. See A. C. Barbier de Maynard, "Considérations sur l'Histoire Ottomane, d'après un document turc," *Nouveau Mélanges Orientaux, Mémoires et Textes et Traductions* (Paris, 1886), pp. 51-75.

THE GLIMMERINGS 1718-1826

Silhouette of a Renaissance *chapter 1*

THE EMERGENCE in the early eighteenth century of the idea that it would be necessary to reform the existing organization by introducing new methods marked a turning point and the beginning of the modern era in Turkish history. In this chapter, covering the fifty years 1718-68, we shall review the events that conditioned the emergence of the new attitude. We shall also consider certain economic, social, and cultural trends having relevance for the earliest reform efforts.

Turkey and the Powers of Europe

The political and administrative disintegration observed by the seventeenth-century statesmen was basically nothing but a product of a gradual economic transformation bearing striking resemblance to that which accompanied the collapse of medieval Europe in the previous two centuries. Probably the decline in the medieval Turkish economy was caused by the same factors that had affected the West. However, this decline was not followed by the emergence of new economic forces and institutions as had been the case in Western Europe.

The difference was due largely to the effects of the pre-eminent modern Western economy. It was through the mechanism of capitulations that the new European economy played its role in the Ottoman Empire. These were originally grants accorded to the mercantile European powers and covered commercial, legal, and religious exterritorial privileges.

A number of internal conditions also served to inhibit new economic development. These were the lack of a national homogeneity, the persistence of medieval status groups, the unmercantilistic policies of government, and the monetary and fiscal measures necessitated by economic decline in the commercial, industrial, and rural sectors.

Economic decline had pushed the fiscal-administrative-military institutions basic to Ottoman rule out of gear. This was reflected in internal and external failures—military, economic, etc. The vicious spiral of decline that seals the doom of a system was in its last coils by the end of the seventeenth century. The statesmen of that century were sucked into the vortex at each attempt to make reforms. The eighteenth century was to face the task of deciding at which point the spiral could be broken and turned into a linear path towards a new order.

The Ottoman Turks had numerous contacts with the new Western world. In fact, they were never out of contact with the West. They were aware of the rise of a new civilization, but they steadfastly remained aloof from Western developments because they were convinced of the superiority of their own system. It was only in the wave of doubt occasioned by certain events in the early eighteenth century that they began to realize that their assumptions were no longer absolute truths. They began to realize that they had been overwhelmed by a superior military power. The acknowledgement of defeat became the stimulus for the rise of a new attitude.

Once its military power threatening Central Europe had been broken after 1700 the Turkish state could expect to face the challenge of a united European Christian world.[1] But the new powers of the West were not interested in proposals to unite in a Holy War against the Turks. Turkey had no military conflicts with Western Europe until Napoleon invaded Egypt. There was, on the other hand, a new power emerging in Eastern Europe. This was destined to cause Turkey to seek closer contact with the West during the eighteenth century.

Modern Russia, as shaped by the Westernizing reforms of Peter the Great, who had escaped annihilation at the hands of the Turk-

[1] Cf. F. L. Baumer, "England, the Turk, and the Common Corps of Christendom," *American Historical Review*, L (1944), 48.

ish army in 1711 at the Pruth, was the force turning Turkey to the West. Also, its challenges led the West, whose imperceptibly gradual economic penetration was providing a milieu congenial to the germination of the new reform attitude, to extend help in modernizing the Turkish military institutions.

25

The period following the Treaty of Passarovitz (1718) is called the Tulip Era. It was characterized by a great desire to realize peace. The ruler, Ahmed III, and his chief minister, the Sadrazam Ibrahim Paşa, decided to avoid war at all cost. At the same time the Ottoman Turks began to look outside, more particularly to the West, for new inspiration.

It became clear in the Tulip Era that the Islamic East had been exhausted of what the Ottoman Turks required, and that the West had entered into a new phase of economic wealth, scientific progress, and military might. Reviving the heritage of the Islamic East could reinforce and keep alive the traditional values; but, as was shown by the failure of several attempts at reform, this heritage provided no solution to the pressing needs under new conditions.

Among the Western powers of the eighteenth century, France alone would capture the focus of the outward looking Turks. She was the most formidable continental power of the century and represented the most advanced civilization on the Continent. Her diplomatic relations with the Turkish government were the most ancient and were also, on the whole, satisfactory. She shared as her own the two principal adversaries of the Turkish Empire: Austria and Russia. Her trade relations with the territories of the Empire were extended and exceeded those of the other powers. During the early part of the century, French diplomacy recognized that the collapse of the Turkish Empire would create a political vacuum inimical to French interests.[2]

---

[2] See Paul Masson, *Histoire du commerce français dans le Levant au xviiie siècle* (Paris, 1911), for the development of French commercial relations with Turkey. The commercial interests of France and of England were reflected in the political attitudes of these powers towards this region. England was pursuing a policy of hostility towards France and of friendship towards Russia and Austria, both of which were adversaries of France and Turkey. See *ibid.*, p. 367; A. C. Wood, *A History of the Levant Company* (London, 1935), pp. 141 ff., 106 ff., 174-75; M. S. Anderson, "Great Britain and the Russian Fleet, 1769-70," *Slavonic and East European Review*, III (1952-53), 148 and 161-63. France's diplomatic and commercial status rose markedly, especially during Cardinal Fleury's administration, from 1726 to 1743. It was during this period that France took an active interest in the internal conditions of the Ottoman Empire.

The apparent mutuality of French and Turkish interests determined where the Turkish statesmen would look for inspiration.
It is worth noting that France continued to represent the West
in Turkish eyes until the present century in spite of her disappoint-
ing performance in later eras and the practical ascendancy of
Britain in the nineteenth century.

26

New Worldliness

Meanwhile, changes were occurring in Turkish social, cultural,
and moral life. Although we can be sure that neither the whole
society nor all strata were affected, still the indications are sufficient to be taken as indices of an impending social transformation.
Whatever its extent, this transformation facilitated the acceptance
of a new reform concept and helped to determine the directions it
would take.

The period displayed certain features which might have been
the signs of a renaissance had they been accompanied by favourable material conditions. The most remarkable characteristic of the
time was the rise of a spirit of worldliness. This spirit was manifested in numerous aspects of life; it does not appear to have been
confined to the prosperous classes.

In sophisticated circles, the new spirit of worldliness was manifest in, for example, literature. E. J. W. Gibb characterizes this
period of Ottoman literature as one of transition from Persianism
to Westernism; he even finds expressed in it the first rudiments of
a national spirit.[3]

The new secular spirit manifested itself also in the sudden rise
of an interest in secular learning. We may note at least two important developments in this connection: the translation of foreign
works and the introduction of the printing press. As Gibb stated,

the Grand Vizir [Sadrazam] encouraged letters by every means in
his power. On at least two occasions he formed committees consisting
of the most learned and accomplished men in Constantinople for
the purpose of translating some of the great Arabian and Persian
classics which had hitherto never appeared in a Turkish dress.[4]

[3] E. J. W. Gibb, *A History of Ottoman Poetry* (London, 1905), IV,
4, 12-13.

[4] *Ibid.*, 13.

It is also reported that there were some Western works among the books to be translated. This is significant because, just a few years earlier, a Şeyhul-Islâm had issued a *fetva* against endowing the library of a deceased Sadrazam because it contained books (possibly some of them in European languages) dealing with astronomy, philosophy and history.[5] As the literature of the transition period represented a turn from Persianism, so this new scholarly interest marked a transition from interest in the religious to interest in the mundane; all of the books translated were on non-religious subjects.

We find examples of parallel trends in music and architecture. Oriental music found its characteristically Turkish forms of expression from this period to the end of the century. This music was an indispensable part of the literary revival described by Gibb and had essentially the same spirit. The main concern of earlier Turkish patrons of architecture had been to build mosques, buildings of religious endowments, and the like. The taste of the Tulip Era in architecture showed itself in small palaces and pleasure houses (*köşks*—the origin of the English word kiosk), pools, fountains, and gardens. A touch of French design was apparent in these. It was in this period that the first items of European furniture began to appear in the miniature palaces of the rich.

We find other indications of the loosening of the traditional patterns of behaviour. One source of information in this respect is the chronicles of foreign observers. These writings abound in prejudices and errors in interpretation; their authors were not aware that they were observing symptoms of the disintegration of an older system, and they thus accepted what they saw as part of what they called the "Turkish character"; they presented their observations as a natural product of the Turkish or Muslim culture which, for them, was inherently "wicked." And yet, read with care, these sources show that there were unmistakable signs of a breakdown in traditional values. They depict this period as one of cynicism, moral turpitude, selfishness, and materialism on the part of the higher classes. It was also a time when moral restrictions among the common people were greatly relaxed. The coffee house, the tavern, and the brothel appear to have become established places of pleasure. The time was gone when even coffee drinking and coffee houses had been resisted severely. Public houses were still repressed, but, none the less, they existed.

[5] Adnan-Adıvar, *Osmanlı Türklerinde İlim* (Istanbul, 1943), pp. 139 ff.

Other types of behaviour indicative of laxity in observing religious prohibitions appear to have been seen openly; for example, the rulers felt it necessary to issue *fermans* from time to time prohibiting changes in women's attire and their appearance in public places.

28

The foreign observers of the age were prone to pass harsh judgments on the people about whose history they knew so little. Sir James Porter, a relatively careful and fair observer, who describes with astounding frankness the immoral means used by the European diplomats and traders to obtain their aims and profits, makes a number of generalizations which, although incorrect, may be taken as indices of the decline of traditional values among the officials.[6] The following generalizations of a former Greek dragoman are too sweeping, but may be taken as indicative of striking features of the Turkish scene:

Notwithstanding the great appearance of devotion amongst the Turks, the principle of whose religion is *Deism,* yet its very opposite, *Atheism,* has generally prevailed of late years. Let this be a lesson for deists in Christian countries. . . . As no people on earth entertain such doubts of their religion as the Turks do of theirs, it is not in the least surprising, that they have proceeded one step farther, and embraced Atheism. This fundamental error has penetrated the most private recesses of the Seraglio, and infected all parts of the empire. . . . We are now to mark the decline of the empire. . . .

All these circumstances seem to denote an approaching revolution in the Turkish system of religion and civil government, or a total subversion of the once formidable empire of the Ottomans.[7]

Lady Mary Wortley Montagu, who lived in Turkey during 1716-18 and whose *Letters on Turkey* became classic in English literature, says in one of her letters:

The Turks are not so ignorant as we fancy them to be. . . . They have no more faith in the inspiration of Mahomet, than in the infallibility of the Pope. They make a frank profession of Deism

---

[6] Sir James Porter, *Observations on the Religion, Law, Government and Manners of the Turks* . . . (2nd ed.; London, 1771), particularly p. 123.

[7] Elias Habesci, *The Present State of the Ottoman Empire* (London, 1784), pp. 135-41.

among themselves, or to those they can trust; and never speak of their law but as of a political institution. . . .[8]

All the above tend to show that there was an incipient crisis in moral life alongside the changing economic conditions, the declining military organization, and the transformation in administrative and political practices. The new interest in material life was in sharp contrast with the old Ottoman rigourism, which had been the dominant Ottoman ethos in the military and religious zeal of the past. It was also in sharp contrast with another and rival tradition—mysticism and unworldly asceticism. The old morality was under the onslaught of new forces; it was proving itself inadequate to the challenge.

Concomitant with the changes in the religiously oriented outlook there was an observable change in attitude toward the European, designated by the term Frenk. To call this a softening would be erroneous because one could argue readily that the attitude towards the European became more unfriendly from this period onward and that the relations between Turks and Europeans became increasingly bitter, especially as the latter became more widely identified as a factor of change in social life, or of economic impoverishment. The point that should be noticed here is that the European began to gain importance in the eyes not only of government officials, but also of the people. The European could no longer be ignored, or looked upon with contempt.

Theretofore, the dealings of Muslims with Europeans were carried out only at the levels of warfare, diplomacy, and trade. Religion was the creator of the iron curtain which neither the necessities of common diplomatic interests nor the lures of commercial profit could remove. This curtain barred all exchange on a cultural level. The European resident in the Turkish territories did not provide an important vehicle of cultural contact. No Muslims resided in any European country, either for the purpose of carrying on trade or as diplomatic representatives. No need was felt to have permanent representatives at the European capitals although Western European nations had representatives of their trade companies and governments not only at the Turkish capital, but also in the major commercial towns. It was only in the eighteenth century that the Turks began to send special envoys to visit

---

[8] "Original letter said to be wrote by L-y M-y W-t-y M-t-ge, from Constantinople to a Venetian nobleman, translated from the French," *Annual Register, Year 1766* (London, 1767), pp. 216-18.

European countries. Also Europeans began to visit the Turkish territories in greater number and to enjoy greater freedom of movement.

30

Recognizing the Necessity of Change

The earliest documentary clue to the realization that something new should be done comes from the year of the Treaty of Passarovitz, 1718. It was a clear reaction to the tested and proven inadequacy of the traditional military institution in the face of the modern European military techniques already in use by the Russians.

The document is a record of a real or imaginary conversation between a Muslim and an unnamed "Christian officer."[9] The question put to the Christian was simple and direct: What is the reason for our defeats? The Christian's immediate response was: First of all, your failure to observe the prescriptions of the Şeriat, and secondly, your ignorance of your traditional laws. He continued, however, to describe the decline of the old military organization and the use of outmoded methods of warfare and concluded that it was mandatory for the army to be reformed and for new officers to be trained. Since the training of officers in modern sciences and techniques was a time-consuming process, it would be permissible temporarily to employ Christian officers.

The Muslim conversant stopped agreeing with the Christian after the latter's introductory remark. The Muslim continually defended the traditional institutions against criticism. He frequently reaffirmed his conviction that, "perfection and truth are on the side of the Muslims," an opinion which the Christian critic did not contradict.

This document contained in embryonic form the whole eighteenth-century debate on reform. The two conversants symbolized the eighteenth-century reformer and the conservative or traditionalist. As the discussion indicates, the reformer had no doubt that there was anything amiss in the basic Islamic-Turkish economic, political, social, religious, and cultural institutions. He recognized only that new techniques of military art needed to be

---

[9] Published by Faik Reşit Unat, "Ahmet III Devrine Ait Bir İslâhat Takriri," *Tarih Vesikaları*, I, No. 2 (Ankara, Aug. 1941), 107-21, from Vol. III of the MSS of "Vekayiname" by Mehmed Esad.

introduced. He perceived this to be a simple matter and not one implying widespread consequences. As we shall see later, the boldest project of reform produced during the eighteenth century, by Ibrahim Müteferrika, was nothing more than an elaboration on this theme. The conservative, on the other hand, seems to have realized intuitively, as traditionalists everywhere and at all times apparently do, that even a seemingly insignificant innovation would destroy the harmony of the whole. Hence, he only conceded the desirability of polishing up the traditional system.

31

We cannot help but be interested in the sources of inspiration for, and authors of, this document. A nineteenth-century historian says, "it seems to have been written by a foreign officer,"[10] whereas an earlier chronicler presents it as "a document written in the form of a discussion by certain thinking men and submitted to Sultan Ahmed III through the Sadrazam Ibrahim Paşa."[11]

The document does not seem to have been written by a foreign observer. However, we can safely guess that it was inspired by the recommendations of some European observers who happened to be in Turkey at the time. According to von Hammer, one of them was a French officer named De Rochefort who submitted to the Ottoman government in 1717 a report entitled "Projet pour l'éstablissement d'une troupe d'ingénieurs au service de la Porte."[12] This project seems to have constituted the second part of a larger project which is worthy of description because its basic ideas were revived some twenty-five years later.

De Rochefort visited the Ottoman capital with a group of French Protestants to seek the Turkish government's permission to settle a Huguenot colony in the European territories of the Empire. In order to show the reciprocal advantages of having such a colony admitted to Turkey, he proposed certain undertakings for the economic and military benefit of the country. He suggested

---

[10] Mustafa Paşa (1824-89), *Netayic-ül Vukuat* (Istanbul, 1879), III, 31.

[11] Mehmed Esad (1785-1847), author of the three-volume chronicle "Vekayiname"; quoted by Unat, "Ahmet III," p. 107.

[12] Joseph von Hammer, *Histoire de l'Empire ottoman*, trans. J. J. Hellert (Paris, 1839), XV, 68. A letter (*ibid.*, 348-56) written to the Austrian Emperor concerning Count de Bonneval's activities in Turkey (cf. *infra*, pp. 47-48) gives some details of De Rochefort's earlier mission. It was written by one Chénier (probably Louis Chénier, father of the poet, André), apparently himself a Protestant and an acquaintance of De Rochefort. Chénier was the chancellor to the ambassador of the Two Sicilies and an Austrian agent.

32

supplying the government with a corps of military technicians, and offered to instruct young Turks in modern military methods. De Rochefort pointed out that the best artisans and tradesmen were Protestants and that their skills would be useful in the economic recovery of the country. He argued that the raw materials as well as the wealth of the country were being stolen by Europeans. These Europeans, he claimed, manufactured the raw materials and sold them dearly in the Empire for cash, which was the reason why there was such a dearth of specie in Turkey. He proposed, therefore, that the Huguenot colonies manufacture the raw materials locally and thus increase the wealth of the country. De Rochefort attempted to consolidate his arguments by pointing out that the religion of the Protestants was closely akin to that of the Muslims and by saying that the Huguenots, persecuted by Catholic governments, looked hopefully to the reputedly tolerant Turks for succour and an opportunity to live and worship freely.

Unfortunately, we know almost nothing about the De Rochefort mission, about its composition or its way of approaching the government. We are told, on the one hand, that the Turkish ministers found the military and economic proposals not dissimilar to what had been proposed in the Divan (the supreme council) and that the government considered the plan seriously. The project seems to have failed chiefly through the efforts of the French ambassador, the Marquis de Bonnac, in accordance with his government's policy of preventing the Huguenots from emigrating from France and settling in foreign countries. On the other hand, probably no one at the time dared launch a military reform involving the employment of foreign military experts for fear of precipitating a revolt by the Yeniçeri corps.[13]

It is difficult to believe that there was no connection between De Rochefort's "Projet" and the document in question. Probably the presence of the De Rochefort mission provided an occasion and suggested the conversational device. There was a small group of Huguenots settled in Istanbul; but so far as external stimuli were concerned, there were in Turkey at the time other Europeans possessing a much higher stake in the military adequacy of the Empire. Chief among these were Hungarians who had taken refuge in the course of their struggles with the Habsburg emperors, the leading adversaries of the Turks, for their Catholic persecutions; unlike the other European residents and transients, these

[13] Cevdet Paşa, *Cevdet Tarihi* (Istanbul, 1302), I, 98.

looked to the Turkish armies for offensive power. Among these was a convert to Islam, Ibrahim Müteferrika, who was on the way to becoming the most significant reformist of the period. It seems quite possible that the document was inspired, if not prepared, by Ibrahim, perhaps with encouragement from his former compatriots, for submittal to his patron, the Sadrazam Ibrahim Paşa.[14]

33

Discovery of a New World

Interest in Western civilization began to evince itself from the second decade of the eighteenth century among the educated classes. This interest, which went beyond a mere diplomatic limit, can be illustrated by the writings and behaviour of a prominent father and son. In view of what has been said about the growing relations between Turkey and France, it is not surprising that the first favourable report concerning the West came as a result of a visit to France by this pair.

The Turkish government sent Mehmed Faizi, known as Yirmisekiz Çelebi or Çelebi Mehmed, as a special envoy to the court of Louis XV in 1720. In addition to his diplomatic mission, which was to seek an alliance with France, he was instructed by the Sadrazam Ibrahim Paşa to "visit the fortresses, factories, and the works of French civilization generally and report on those which might be applicable [in Turkey]."[15]

Çelebi Mehmed wrote a small book concerning his visit to the French capital. In the words of a recent historian of nineteenth-century Turkish literature, "No book occupies so important a

---

[14] See Unat, "Ahmet III", 107, n. 3.

[15] Ali Suavi's edition (London, 1872) of *Sefaretname* by Çelebi Mehmed, written in 1720. Other editions are *Paris Sefaretnamesi* (Istanbul, 1888); *Rélation de l'ambassade de Mohammed Efendi* (Paris, 1841). In the Preface of his printing, Ali Suavi (see *infra*, p. 317 makes a comparison between the time required for Çelebi Mehmed to reach Paris and that in his own time. In 1870 the distance was "a matter of a week's time." Another Ottoman ambassador to Paris, Halet Efendi, reached Strasbourg in sixty-six days in 1802. It took five months for Çelebi Mehmed to reach Paris. In the sixteenth century "a year frequently elapsed between sending a message from Turkey to England and receiving a reply." See A. L. Rowland, "England and Turkey: The Rise of Diplomatic and Commercial Relations," *Studies in English Commerce and Exploration in the Reign of Elizabeth* (Philadelphia, 1924), p. 32.

place in the history of the Westernization of Turkey as this little report. . . . Concealed in almost every line of it is an idea of comparison and it contains almost the whole program of subsequent changes."[16] The striking aspect of this simple account is the absence of that sense of superiority, abhorrence, or ridicule which customarily pervaded the writings of earlier times, especially those of the sixteenth century.

Çelebi Mehmed describes his observations as if he had discovered a new world, with its new technical arts, military establishments and methods, with its hospitals, observatories, anatomy halls, ports, quarantine methods, zoological and botanical gardens, parks, operas, and theatres, and, finally, its social habits, especially those regarding the status of women. "In the land of the French," he remarks half in amazement and half in admiration, "the women enjoy higher status than men, and are free to go anywhere they wish. A nobleman of the topmost rank shows the highest consideration and respect for a woman even if she belongs to the lowest class."

It is apparent from Mehmed's memoirs that he was familiar with the printing of books; he shows none of the traditional distaste for the art. The printing press was known and presses existed in the Turkish capital, but the Muslims do not seem to have used them.[17] In view of the new spirit, we can imagine that the ground was ready for planting the idea of printing in Turkish.

Çelebi Mehmed describes his visit to the Paris observatory, in which he had a particular interest, and his meeting there with Jacques Cassini, the son of Dominique Cassini, the famous Italian-French astronomer (both father and son were official directors of the Paris observatory). He tells us that the young Cassini showed him the father's corrections of the zodiacal tables prepared by Uluğ Bey (1395-1449), the prince-astronomer and a grandson of Timur. Çelebi Mehmed brought to Turkey a manuscript of Cassini's tables given him by the son since, as he says, "they were not yet printed" in France.[18]

[16] Ahmet H. Tanpınar, XIX. Asır Türk Edebiyatı Tarihi (2nd ed.; Istanbul, 1956), I, 10.

[17] See Selim Nüzhet Gerçek, Türk Matbaacılığı (Istanbul, 1939), I, 34 ff. Printing in Turkish began in 1587, but was never established among the Turks. See Mustafa Paşa, Netayic-ül Vukuat (Istanbul, 1879), III, 130; O. Ersoy, Türkiye'ye Matbaanın Girişi (Ankara, 1959), pp. 22-23.

[18] See Gerçek, Türk Matbaacılığı, I, 45-46; Adıvar, Osmanlı Türklerinde İlim, p. 179.

Describing Çelebi Mehmed's visit to Paris in his *Mémoires*, St. Simon says:

During the four months of his stay, he observed with taste and discernment all that Paris could offer him in curiosities and royal houses roundabout, where he was magnificently entertained and received. He seemed to understand machines, and manufacturing especially coins and the press. He seemed to know a great deal and have great knowledge of history and good books. He ... intended, on his return to Constantinople to establish there a printing press and a library ... and he succeeded in this.[19]

St. Simon goes on to describe his grand manner, his charm with ladies, and his appearance. According to St. Simon Çelebi performed his devotions strictly, though he did not refuse to decorate his house for a Catholic procession—while he and his suite kept indoors under lock and key. He did not drink in public, but attended banquets and balls.

Çelebi Mehmed was accompanied by his son, Said Mehmed, who was then a mature young man. Said Mehmed's career was short but distinguished. He seems to have been the first statesman to learn and speak French (or indeed any Western language). This and his universally acknowledged learning (he wrote a book on medicine) made him one of the most prominent and progressive men of his time. A French diplomat described him as a man of ideas and an admirer of France and of French liberty.[20] He became Sadrazam in 1755, but was soon deposed and sent into exile, like his father who had been exiled to Cyprus after the 1730 Yeniçeri revolt; and so we shall never know what he might have contributed to the reform policies.

In 1741 Said Mehmed was sent to Paris to negotiate Franco-Turkish policies towards Russia. During his six-months residence in Paris, he met his friends of twenty years earlier, distinguished himself by his mastery of the French language and customs (he did not mind drinking wine at banquets), and by his manners. He is reported to have been a favourite of the ladies abounding then in the court of Louis XV, and he was particularly fond of the operas and the plays of the Comédie Française. (Voltaire post-

---

[19] *Mémoires*, ed. A. de Boislisle (Hachette ed.; Paris, 1887), XVII, 249.

[20] M. de Peyssonnel to Marquis de Caumont (Jan. 14, 1739), quoted by Albert Vandal, *Une Ambassade française en Orient sous Louis XV* (Paris, 1887), p. 208.

poned the staging of his play *Mahomet* during Said Mehmed's
residence in Paris as a gesture of courtesy!) Said Mehmed's visit
to the French capital seems to have augmented the interest of the
higher classes in what were then called *turquérie* fashions and suggested a number of scenes to French painters of the time.

The reports of Çelebi Mehmed and Said Mehmed were undoubtedly received with interest by Ahmed III, and Ibrahim Paşa.
The most immediate and striking result was the decision to sanction the opening of a press. This was founded by Said Mehmed
in partnership with a man who epitomized in his life, personality,
work and ideas, the major features of the period. He is known as
Ibrahim Müteferrika.

The First Innovation

Ibrahim Müteferrika (1670?-1754) was, perhaps, the first of a
series of Europeans who were destined to play a role in the history
of the Westernization of Turkey as carriers of new ideas and as
intermediaries between cultures. Ibrahim made an important contribution to the history of that process in which we are here
interested.

What little we know of his early life appears to be considerably
distorted. According to the story, "a young Hungarian of 18 to
20 years, who was studying to become a Calvinist minister, had
the misfortune of being captured and enslaved by Turks in 1692
or 1693 in [the Magyar prince] Tekely's war [against the Habs-
burgs]. Having fallen into the hands of a cruel master, he suffered
quite a miserable life for a long time. Unable to bear slavery longer,
he finally became a Muslim. Ibrahim was . . . the name he
assumed."[21] He was born in Kolozsvár, Transylvania, between
1672 and 1675. His original name is unknown, but his biographers

---

[21] See Saussure Czezarnák, *Lettres de Turquie (1730-39) et notices
(1740)*, ed. K. Thály (Budapest, 1909), p. 93. Czezarnák was a
Hungarian aristocrat accompanying Prince F. Rákoczy when the
latter came to Turkey from France (where he had taken refuge
having lost his claim to the Transylvanian kingdom) to join the
Turks' war against Austria. Ibrahim was appointed liaison officer
to the Prince and Czezarnák met him then. The later accounts of
Ibrahim's conversion all derive from him. For a bibliography of
these see T. Halasi Kun, "Ibrâhîm Müteferrika," *İslâm Ansiklopedisi* (Istanbul, 1951), V, 900. For a more detailed discussion of
the question of Ibrahim's religious and intellectual identity see
Niyazi Berkes, "İlk Türk Matbaası Kurucusunun Dinî ve Fikrî
Kimliği", *Belleten* (September 1962), XXVI, 104, 715-37.

claim that he was of a poor Calvinist family. After his conversion at an unknown date he appears to have progressed rapidly in his knowledge of the Turkish language and customs. Also at an unknown date he became acquainted with the Sadrazam Ibrahim Paşa and was employed in various governmental and diplomatic capacities. He was promoted to the rank of *müteferrika* (royal quartermaster), probably between 1705 and 1711. He is said to have known French, Italian, German, and Latin in addition to Turkish and Hungarian.[22]

In 1710 Ibrahim wrote a treatise entitled "Risâle-i Islâmiye" which has been described by his biographers as a defence of his new religion. Examined closely, this work, which exists in manuscript only, appears *not* to be a defence of Islam, but rather a polemic telling much about Ibrahim.[23] It forces us to doubt the authenticity of the story about his Calvinism and the conditions under which he was converted.

The work is a polemic against Papism and the doctrine of Trinity. Saying nothing of his supposed Calvinism, Ibrahim introduces his work with a brief summary of his studentship at Kolozsvár, Transylvania. He opens with a statement about his disputations on the Trinity. He says that he studied *secretly* the parts of the Bible which, as he puts it, had been declared abrogated. His major arguments concern what he claims to be the systematic falsification of the Christian scriptures. The only "Islamic" element in the whole is his claim that the coming of Muhammed was prophesied in the New Testament (John 16: 7-15) and that this prophecy was suppressed by the Church; he relates this to the Kur'an (LXI:6), although the idea of the prediction of the coming of a Comforter after Jesus goes as far back as Servetus, the initiator of Unitarianism.

It is obvious that we are confronted, not by a Calvinist, but by a Unitarian. If we go back one century and trace the development of religious and political conditions in Transylvania, we shall not fail to appreciate that neither Transylvanian Unitarianism nor Ibrahim's folk were unfamiliar with or too distant from Islam.

Kolozsvár was the centre of the threefold struggle of Cathol-

---

[22] F. Babinger, *Stambuler Buchwesen im 18. Jahrhundert* (Leipzig, 1919), p. 12.

[23] In Esad Efendi Library, Istanbul, No. 1187. Imre Karacson, "İbrahim Müteferrika," *Tarih-i Osmanî Encümeni Mecmuası*, I, No. 3 (Aug., 1910), 180, gives the date as between 1705 and 1711. See Berkes, *İlk Türk Matbaası*, 731.

icism, Calvinism, and Unitarianism.[24] Unitarian writings and de-
bates influenced by Servetus had begun in Transylvania about 1566.
When Habsburg rule over Hungary was terminated by the Turks
after the battle of Mohacs in 1526, Transylvania, recognized by
the Turks as an independent state in 1543, enjoyed a regime of
religious freedom and secular government. This lasted from 1543
till 1595.

38

After 1571, when Transylvania once again became a vassal of
Austria, the Unitarians began to be persecuted by the Calvinists
and Catholics. In 1579 their leader Francis Dávid denounced the
Christ cultus and was sentenced to life imprisonment. The Unitarians were accused of being Judaizers or Islamizers. Those who
denied the adoration were sentenced to death and their properties
confiscated. The separation of the church and state was terminated.
Many, urban as well as rural, took refuge with the Turks. This is
reflected in a letter of 1631 by a Turkish governor to the Palatine,
Nikolaus Esterházy, in which he said, "You can measure the
degree of your tyranny by the fact that the people, your co-
religionists, flee from you and take refuge with the Turk and seek
his help."[25]

The Prince Tekely (Thököly) uprising in 1679 was one of those
against the Austrian rule and was conducted in alliance with
Turkey. The Turkish retreat from Vienna in 1683 brought the
Catholics and the persecution of Calvinists and Unitarians finally
to Kolozsvár. In 1692 the Reformed Churches in Kolozsvár were
given to Catholics, and in the same or following year Ibrahim
"fell prisoner" to the Turks, ostensibly having been involved in
Tekely's uprising—with Turkish support!

It is absurd to accept the standard biography of Ibrahim, evidently invented by Czezarnák to excuse a compatriot's apostasy.
It is logical to think that Unitarian beliefs persisted in Kolozsvár
and that Ibrahim either was or became a Unitarian while studying
theology at the former Unitarian college, which had become a
Calvinist institution. He was clearly a follower of Dávid. His

[24] Earl M. Wilbur, *A History of Unitarianism* (Cambridge, Mass.,
1952), pp. 34, 41-47, 85; H. J. McLachlan, *Socinianism in Seventeenth Century England* (London, 1951), p. 159; Stanislas Kot, *Le
Mouvement antitrinitaire au xvie et au xviie siècle* (Paris, 1937),
pp. 60-61; Ludwig Fekete, "Osmanlı Türkleri ve Macarlar, 1366-
1699," *Belleten*, XIII (1949), 738-39 (see 740-41 for further details
on Turkish influences in food, fashions, clothing, furniture, etc.).

[25] L. Fekete, *Türkische Schriften aus dem Archive des Palatins Nikolaus Esterházy 1606-1645* (Budapest, 1932), p. 93.

"secret" studies may well have been of Unitarian tracts or, possibly, of either Servetus' version of the Scriptures or its Hungarian paraphrasing.[26]

Ibrahim's Unitarianism explains the ease with which he reconciled himself to Islam. It explains also the ease with which he was received and promoted by Turkish statesmen and his career as a printer, editor, translator, and reformist. As we shall see presently, he was intensely interested in modern scientific progress, and he transmitted to Turkey the new scientific ideas advanced in more than one case in Europe by religious nonconformists.

Although Ibrahim never wrote on religious subjects after his "Risâle", his interest in the Unitarians seems to have continued. This interest was no longer connected with matters of religious controversy, which had ceased to be of dominant concern in Europe where religious freedom was a fact and was already bearing fruit. His interest lay in science. Ibrahim was the man to introduce the idea of change and progress and modern scientific thinking into Turkey.

The first step was to open a printing press for which the ground had already been prepared. There is evidence that Ibrahim had done some printing,[27] but his career as a publisher and editor, with Said Mehmed as a partner, started upon Çelebi Mehmed's return from France. He had already gained the support of the Sadrazam Ibrahim Paşa.

Ibrahim wrote a treatise on "The Means of Printing" (*Wasîlat al-Tıbâ'a*) in 1726 and submitted it to the Sadrazam, the Şeyhul-Islâm, and the Ulema. He explained the importance of printing for

[26] See John F. Fulton, *Michael Servetus, Humanist and Martyr* (New York, 1953), p. 86 on Servetus' *Christianismi Restitutio*'s being known in Kolozsvár. One of the three extant copies of this work is known to have been in Kolozsvár after Ibrahim's flight. It is quite possible that there were more contacts between the anti-Trinitarians and the Turks than has been suspected heretofore and that the contemporary accusations that anti-Trinitarians were "no better than the Turk" or that they were "Mahometans" had more at base than a simple theological prejudice. It is even conceivable that there was some connection between De Rochefort's mission and the Unitarians through the diffusion of anti-Trinitarian views among the French Huguenots around the time of their expulsion from France. See Wilbur, *History of Unitarianism*, pp. 532-34. Ibrahim's biblical quotations in "Risâle-i Islâmiye" suggest that the Servetus Bible had been used. Ibrahim's transliteration of the Latin into Arabic characters is partially undecipherable and he appears to have written from memory.

[27] Since 1719, according to Gerçek, *Türk Matbaacılığı*, I, 55; see also 34 ff.

the Muslims. In the past, he said, Muslims showed more care in preserving their Scriptures than Jews or Christians, but later on, thousands of books were lost forever with the destruction caused by the Mongol invasions and during the expulsion of the Moors from Spain. Then he went on to describe how the art of book-copying declined and how, consequently, copyists distorted the texts. He enumerated the uses of printing: it would help the propagation and the revival of learning among the peoples of Islam; it would facilitate reading and ensure the preservation of a work, since the printed page is legible and durable; it would reduce the cost of new books and thus enable everybody to buy them; it would facilitate the founding of more libraries; it would put an end to the printing of Islamic books by Europeans who fill them with errors and ugly type-face; and finally, it would make the Turks the sole leaders and protectors of learning in the world of Islam.[28]

Receiving the approval and encouragement of the Sadrazam, Ibrahim submitted his formal application in 1727 in which he demanded a *ferman* and a *fetva* authorizing him to print books. He requested that "the act of printing be declared by the Şeyhul-Islâm as commendable and useful for the Muslims and in accord with the glorious Şeriat."[29] It is interesting to note that sixteen leading *ulema* of the time, including the Şeyhul-Islâm Abdullah, wrote favourable comments on the treatise when it was printed.

Calligraphers constituted the main opposition group; they even staged a demonstration against the printing press; they sought to instigate the people against printing in the name of the safety of religion.[30] However, when the *fetva* was issued permitting the printing of books except the Kur'an and books on Prophetic traditions (*hadîth*), theology (*kalâm*), Kur'anic exegesis (*tafsîr*), and law (*fiqh*)—that is, permitting the printing mainly of dictionaries and books on mathematics, medicine, astronomy, physics,

---

[28] This treatise was printed in 1729 together with the first book of the press which was a dictionary called *Vankulu*, a translation of *Sihah Jawharî*. See Ihsan [Sungu], "İlk Türk Matbaasına Dair Yeni Vesikalar," *Hayat*, III, No. 73 (April 19, 1928), 414; Gerçek, *Türk Matbaacılığı*, I, 50-51; Adıvar, *Osmanlı Türklerinde İlim*, p. 147.

[29] The facsimile of this petition is reproduced in Gerçek, *Türk Matbaacılığı*, supplementary plates; and in Ihsan [Sungu], "İlk Türk Matbaasına," 413.

[30] Karacson, "Ibrahim Müteferrika," 183-84; also Gerçek, *Türk Matbaacılığı*, I, 58.

geography, and history—neither the calligraphers nor the *ulema* made further trouble. They probably knew that most of the reading public was interested in the kind of book that would not be printed, and the *ulema* of the time did not care about secular learning. Thus, Ibrahim received permission with surprising facility. He even received the moral support and encouragement of the Şeyhul-Islâm, and was given a small group of traditional scholars as proof-readers.

41

Thus were laid the foundations of the first printing press in any Muslim country in the year 1727, about a year earlier than Benjamin Franklin's press in Philadelphia.[31] The first book from the press appeared on January 31, 1729. The quality and accuracy of the early publications and the beauty of the *naskh* type used were not surpassed till the middle of the nineteenth century. Von Hammer says:

The establishment of a printing house in Constantinople under the direction of the Hungarian renegade, Ibrahim, is one of the characteristic traits of this period, a period distinguished chiefly by a marked impact of Occidental customs upon those of the Orient and by the close ties of Ottoman policy with the policies of Europe. The choice of the first ten works printed in the Empire shows the tendency of the Turkish government to enlighten itself by studying the history of the relations which the Empire had since its origin either with Persia or with the maritime powers of the West.[32]

---

[31] Arnold J. Toynbee, following A. Pichler, *Der Patriarch Cyrillus Lukaris und seine Zeit* (Munich, 1862, pp. 137-38), mistakenly attributes the founding of the first press for printing Turkish to a "Grand Vizir Ibrahim, who was a Hungarian renegade." See his *A Study of History* (London, 1954), VIII, 164, n. 1. Ibrahim Müteferrika has been confused with his patron, the Sadrazam Ibrahim Paşa. Abbé Toderini, *De La Littérature des Turcs* (Paris, 1789), III *passim*, gives an account of the establishment of Ibrahim's press and a list of the books printed with explanatory notes.

[32] Von Hammer, *Histoire de l'Empire ottomane*, XIV, 106.

Observations on European Polities

42

The place of Ibrahim Müteferrika in the history of the Turkish awakening is not only that of a printer. He had already shown, in his tract on printing, his concern for renovation and awakening in Islam, and the importance of introducing new methods and ideas from the West.

Ibrahim Müteferrika's most significant work for our purposes is his book printed in 1731 under the title *'Usûl ul-Hikam fî Nizâm ul-'Umam* (Rational Bases for the Polities of Nations).[33] This book, submitted to the new ruler, Mahmud I, was a logical continuation of the idea that Turkey had to learn and adopt from Europe. The aim of the book was to investigate the reasons for the aberrations in the organization of the Turkish state and for the strength of European states, and those things that the Turks had to learn and take from the latter in order to regain their power. "Why," Ibrahim asked, "do Christian nations, which were so weak in the past compared with Muslim nations, begin to dominate so many lands in modern times and even defeat the once victorious Ottoman armies?"

According to Ibrahim, there are three forms of government: monarchy (under which "the people obey a just and wise sovereign and follow his opinions and measures in all of their affairs"), most governments are of this type; aristocracy (in this form "sovereignty is in the hands of the dignitaries of the state and one among them is elected as head, but he is dependent upon the rest in counsel and decision, lest he tends to deviate from the law of justice"); and democracy (in which "sovereignty belongs to the people"; its aim is to eliminate tyranny). Ibrahim described briefly the method of popular representation, parliaments, and the mechanism whereby the representatives of the people control the government. He mentioned the Netherlands and England as examples of the democratic form of government. Was he aware of the ideas of John Locke, his senior contemporary and a Unitarian like himself?[34] Ibrahim's presentation of the forms of government is the first of its kind in any modern Muslim country, and it certainly

---

[33] Translated into French under the title *Traité de la tactique* by Baron Rewicski and published in 1769 in Vienne, France. See Von Hammer, *Histoire de l'Empire*, XIV, 494; Toderini, *De La Littérature des Turcs*, III, 103-4.

[34] See Maurice Cranston, *John Locke* (New York, 1957), p. 390, and H. J. McLachlan, *The Religious Opinions of Milton, Locke, Newton* (Manchester, 1941), p. 328.

shone with a new vision. Furthermore, he, for the first time, spoke of a democratic form of government in a little more detail than the other forms, and even with a definitely approving tone.

After describing the forms of government, Ibrahim discussed the role of the army in all forms of government, and went on to describe and criticize at length Turkish military organization and methods. His conclusion was that persistence in maintaining antiquated methods inevitably led the Turkish armies into peril.

43

To paraphrase Ibrahim's arguments, the "Christian" world has achieved several great advances. It is now divided into the old and the new worlds. The American continent has been colonized. The Christians have secured access, through navigation, to every corner of the world, and have taken several lands in the Eastern and Western oceans into their possession. They have succeeded in discovering a new route to the Far East. They have gotten hold of the cities of China, India and Sind, conquered many places, discovered several unknown islands in the Eastern Ocean, and brought them into their orbit and, thus, become powerful. The peoples of Islam, on the other hand, have remained in a state of ignorance, heedlessness, stagnation, and utter contempt for the conditions of other peoples. Although, because of the proximity of Europe "to our own country," it is absolutely necessary to study their governments and their rulers, this is neglected through sheer contempt and religious hostility; "pure ignorance is preferred to knowledge," and "ignorance is persistently accepted while it is of the utmost importance to understand the malicious behaviour, the power, the populations, and the general condition of neighbouring states" (here he undoubtedly meant Austria and Russia) which are surely "planning to attack our state at any moment while we remain in a state of utter unpreparedness."

While the Europeans were once "a minority of lesser importance," weak, and confined to a limited region, they began to transform themselves into world powers, to develop "wise methods and ways in their political regimes," to accept political laws and procedures as their new principles in regulating the public weal, public rehabilitation and improvement, and finally, new methods in defending and protecting their lands. Thus, they gradually began to be victorious "over the great Ottoman power."

As neither the statesmen nor the public cared to learn the causes of these events and did not consider them important, it has now become an evident and urgent need to collect information about the details of European affairs in order to repel their harm and to prevent their malice. Let the Muslims cease to be unaware and ignorant of the state of affairs and awaken from the slumber of heedlessness. From now on let them be informed of the condition of their enemies. Let them act with foresight and become intimately acquainted with new European methods, organization, strategy, tactics, and warfare. This will be possible only by ending the state of slumber and indifference, dropping sheer fanaticism with regard to learning of European conditions, stopping tolerance of laziness, indifference and carelessness towards corruption and difficulties in the state and commonweal.

This appeal was followed by a detailed description of the new military methods used in the West.

The second part of the book was devoted to the importance and uses of geography. Sound geographical knowledge, Ibrahim said, is an absolute and indispensable necessity for those who rule a country. After arguing for the use of geographic knowledge by statesmen, he pointed out its importance for traders and, finally, its importance for "the creation of a sentiment of cooperation and unity among the Muslim countries which are scattered over wide areas of the world and remain unaware of each other." Then, speaking of naval charts, he explained that sailing the seas without such charts was nothing but "vagabondage" and that it was a shame for the Turk to need Frenk charts. It was thanks to the knowledge of geography that the Frenks discovered the New World and the route to the East Indies and conquered Muslim lands. It was thanks to geographical knowledge and his understanding of naval charts that Columbus rendered such an unforgettable service to Christendom.

The third part of the book dealt with the new methods and techniques of military science and warfare developed in Christian countries.

One observation is worth noting: "At present," said Ibrahim, "the Christian nations are not ruled in their laws by Divine Prescriptions (*Ahkâm-ı ilâhiye*), that is, commands and prohibitions coming from God, and, having no Şeriat to settle their conflicts, their orders are entirely based on laws and rules invented by reason." It is difficult to ascertain the extent to which this judgment implies approval. More probably it is only a hint. We must not expect Ibrahim to be too radical on this point as we see him proceeding to say, "We have the Şeriat as our law." For him, non-observance of the Şeriat, laxity in the application of justice, the abandonment of affairs of state to incompetent people, disregard

of the counsel of experts, ignorance of modern improvements in
military science and technique, lack of military discipline, lack of
information about the enemy, and, finally, the practice of bribery
which "is the worst of all," were the main causes of Turkish failures.
"Therefore, our failure is not due to the insufficiency of our
traditional laws and rules, of our political laws, and of the Şeriat,
but to our ignorance of the new methods of the Europeans."

The Frenks, he went on to say, are discussing among themselves
whether or not the Turks are capable of adopting their methods.
Some Europeans believe that the Turks are not capable of this
whereas others believe that they would manage within a short
time. Ibrahim approached his conclusion, significantly enough,
with a reference to the Moskofs (Russians), as an example of the
strengthening of nations by the acceptance of Western methods:

During the last twenty or thirty years an intelligent and informed
ruler whom they call "Tsar" has appeared among the Moskofs; he
studied and learned the methods of other nations in the administration
of state and organization of armies, scrutinized their laws and
regulations, and became eager to promote military sciences; for this
purpose, he sought and brought experts skilled in these sciences from
other countries and reformed his armies by heeding their counsels,
recommendations, and assistance. Within a short time, he succeeded
in bringing his plans from the stage of possibility to that of reality.
Not content with the army, he further paid attention to the navy,
brought skilled experts from the Netherlands and England and
other places, and built up his navy in the Baltic and Caspian Seas.

Ibrahim's final remarks are:

All the wise men of the world agree that the people of Turkey
excel all other peoples in their nature of accepting rule and order.
If they learn the new military sciences and are able to apply them,
no enemy can ever withstand this state.

Entry of Modern Science and Military Methods

In addition to his other interests, Ibrahim Müteferrika was also
an editor and writer of books on scientific subjects. His favourite
subjects were geography, physics, and military tactics. He used
to call himself a geographer and carried on Kâtip Çelebi's tradi-

tion.[35] He edited and printed in 1729 the latter's *Tuhfat ul-Kibâr fî Asfâr 'al-Bihâr* (translated into English by James Mitchell as *The History of the Maritime Wars of the Turks;* London 1831) to which he added five maps. In 1733 he printed Çelebi's famous book

46

of geography called *Cihannumâ,* to which he added maps and figures, a description of the geography of Anatolia and Arabia written by Abu Bakr Bahram ad-Dimişqî, and an introductory section describing the ideas of Copernicus and Tycho Brahe, adding, however, that these ideas were not yet accepted by the Muslim *ulema.*

Utilizing a work entitled *Institutiones Philosophicae* (1695) written in Latin by Edmund Pourchot (E. Purchotio, 1651-1734), one of the earliest Cartesian professors in France,[36] Ibrahim also discussed, for the first time in Turkey, Descartes' theory of vortices, Galileo's rejection of Aristotelian physics, and magnetism and the compass. In 1732 he printed a small book on magnetism under the title of *Fuyuzat-ı Miknatisiye* in which he gave further information about the practical importance of magnetism.[37] Numerous observations of the magnetic declination or variation of the compass were made in Europe in the eighteenth century and it was found necessary periodically to revise Halley's variation chart for 1700. Ibrahim seems to have been acquainted with these observations and the use of the compass in ascertaining latitude and longitude. He stated in his conclusion that, by the new methods, he had corrected Kâtib Çelebi's observations on Istanbul's position.

On the order of Ahmed III, Ibrahim made a translation from Andreas Cellarius, a Dutch geographer, astronomer, and mathematician, under the title *Mecmua-i Hey'et-i Kadîme ve Cedide (Harmonia Macrocosmica,* 1661) to which he added several explanatory notes.[38] In short, while he continued and revived Kâtib Çelebi's scientific interests, outside the *medrese,* Ibrahim became one of the

[35] On Kâtip Çelebi or Hajji Khalifa (1608-57), Turkish historian, geographer, and bibliographer see Adıvar, *Osmanlı Türklerinde İlim,* pp. 105-32.

[36] *Ibid.,* p. 148.

[37] Although this book is stated to be based on a work published in 1721 at Leipzig (to which was added a treatise on the varieties of compass), the original work might be *The Longitude and Latitude Found by the Inclinatory or Dipping Needle* (London, 1719-21) by William Whiston, who was expelled from Cambridge in 1711 on account of his anti-Trinitarian views.

[38] Adıvar, *Osmanlı Türklerinde İlim,* p. 151.

early transmitters to Turkey of the new ideas produced by modern European science.

To introduce the military methods of the West involved the introduction of instruction in Western applied sciences, the opening of a school, and the translation of some European works. We must take into account in this connection the role of another European who was also a convert to Islam, nominally at least. He became known as Humbaracı Ahmed Paşa, but his real name was Claude-Alexandre, Comte de Bonneval (1675-1747), born in Limousin, France.[39]

Adventurous and quarrelsome by nature, Bonneval was expelled first from France and then from Austria, and entered the Turkish service in 1729. He was asked to undertake the training in the European manner of the bombardier (*humbaracı*) corps. Actual measures to introduce something new into the military training date from the work of De Bonneval. Some young French officers served under him; later he was joined by the Irishman Macarthy, the Frenchman Mornai, and the Scotsman Ramsay.[40] His report to the Turkish ruler described the recruitment, organization, and tactics of the French and German military forces and advised the organization and use of smaller units and new training and discipline. He also suggested the formation of a special medical corps, including surgeons, and emphasized the necessity for regular troop payments. Courage was not enough, he said, for the successful prosecution of war; methodical training was also needed, "Thus, the only thing to be done is to imitate them [the French and Germans] and adopt their methods."[41]

The ambitious De Bonneval did not remain a mere military adviser and trainer. He had wide interests in international affairs and

[39] For further details of his life see Vandal, *Une Ambassade française*, pp. 117-46, 173-81, and *passim*. Also, Albert Vandal, *Le Pacha Bonneval* (Paris, 1885); Septime Gorceix, *Bonneval Pacha* (Paris, 1953); Mehmed Ârif, "Humbaracı Ahmed Paşa (Bonneval)," *Tarih-i Osmanî* . . . , III, No. 18 (Feb., 1913), 1153-57 and IV, Nos. 19 and 20 (April—June 1913), 1220-24 and 1282-86; Ahmed Refik, *Tesavir-i Ricâl* (İstanbul, 1915), pp. 76-139; M. Cavit Baysun, "Ahmed Paşa (Bonneval, Humbaracı Başı)," *İslâm Ansiklopedisi* (İstanbul, 1950), I, 199; Lady Georgiana Fullerton, *The Countess de Bonneval* trans. and ed. from the French (London, 1880). The *Mémoires* published as those of Bonneval, English trans. (2 vols.; Paris, 1806), are spurious.

[40] Gorceix, *Bonneval Pacha*, p. 161.

[41] Quoted in *ibid.*, p. 167.

an imagination transcending that of many of the statesmen of his time.[42] Like Ibrahim, he anticipated the future expansion of Russia in Europe and Asia, and believed that Russia's aim was to establish her domination over the Ottoman territories so as to open access to the southern seas. He also realized that Turkey was unable to resist the modernized Russian armies without getting help from a European power. This power, for him, would naturally be France because of her traditional and actual interests. The raising up of Turkey would not be limited to the military domain alone; it was necessary also to develop economically. De Bonneval had projects for exploiting the Turkish mines. He revived De Rochefort's plan of twenty-five years previously.[43]

48

The most important development in the introduction of new military techniques was the opening in Üsküdar in 1734 of a school called Hendesehane, or school of military engineering, to train military engineers. No indication has been found that De Bonneval was personally associated with this institution. The historiographer Subhî merely mentions the founding of a Humbarahane, a training school for bombardiers, under De Bonneval's command.[44] Ata speaks of the opening of the Humbarahane without mentioning De Bonneval and goes on to say, "Mahmud I founded also the Hendesehane in order to teach *ilm-i-hendese* [geometry] upon which the training of bombardiers depends."[45] Baron de Tott states clearly, however, that De Bonneval's adopted son Süleyman Ağa, a converted Frenchman originally named Latour [?], was in charge of the Hendesehane at the time of his visit which post-dated De Bonneval's death.[46]

[42] *Ibid.*, p. 169. On the available Turkish translation of his reports written in Latin see Mehmed Ârif, "Humbaracı Ahmed Paşa (Bonneval)," *Tarih-i Osmanî* . . . , IV, No. 20 (June, 1913), 1282 ff.

[43] De Bonneval appears to have been in communication with the cantons of Berne and Zurich in the latter regard. See Von Hammer, *Histoire de l'Empire*, XV, 68.

[44] Mehmed Subhî, *Tarih* (Istanbul, 1783), leaf 58.

[45] Tayyarzade Ata, *Tarih* (Istanbul, 1874), I, 158. Hendesehane might be translated as School of Mathematics, although School of Military Engineering is the more appropriate modern equivalent. On the school see Adıvar, *Osmanlı Türklerinde İlim*, pp. 161-62; also Mehmed Esad, *Mir'at-ı Mühendishane* (Istanbul, 1896); E. Mamboury, *Constantinople: Tourist's Guide* (Constantinople, 1925), p. 361; Osman Ergin, *Türkiye Maarif Tarihi* (Istanbul, 1939), I, 50, n. 1.

[46] *Mémoires* (Amsterdam, 1784), II, 178; *Memoirs of Baron de Tott* . . . , English trans. (London, 1785), II, Part III, 171.

It seems that the contacts with European scientific literature beginning with Kâtip Çelebi and continuing under Ibrahim Müteferrika, were maintained and that there were Turks concerned with modern mathematical and natural sciences. The appearance of two books about the time that the Hendesehane was founded is noteworthy. The first, "Ilm-i Kiyas-ı Müsellesat", existing in manuscript only, deals with trigonometry and appears to have been the first modern work on mathematics adapted from a European language and used for military training. The second was a translation of Raimondo Montecucculi's *Memorie della guerra*.[47] Cevdet Paşa, who frequently quotes Montecucculi's opinions of Turkish military tactics, indicates that, although the translation remained in manuscript, it circulated and was read extensively by Turkish rulers and statesmen. We can assume safely that both books were prepared for military education and, as Adnan-Adıvar says, "there is no doubt that modern mathematics were introduced into Ottoman Turkey through the military channel."[48]

49

The interest in translating European works into Turkish continued. Bernhardus Varenius' *Geographia Generalis* was translated from German into Turkish in 1750 by Osman bin Abdul-Mannan.[49] This was the first book on modern geography translated directly from a European work into Turkish.

The first book on modern medicine was translated into Turkish from Hermann Boerhaave's *Aphorismi* in 1771.[50] Through this translation, Harvey's ideas concerning the circulation of blood were introduced into Turkish medical literature for the first time. William Harvey's *Exercitatio Anatomica de Motu Cordis et Sanguinis* was first published in 1628. Thirty-six years later, in 1664,

---

47 Raimondo Montecucculi (1609?-80) was the Austrian general who from 1661 to 1664 defended Austria against the Turks.

48 Cf. Adıvar, *Osmanlı Türklerinde İlim*, p. 163. It is probable that Montecucculi's book was one of the works in Turkish ordered by Mehmet Ali of Egypt for his new schools; see J. Heyworth-Dunne, *An Introduction to the History of Education in Modern Egypt* (London, 1939), p. 101.

49 Bernhardus Varenius (1622-50), a Dutch physician and Cartesian geographer. His *Geographia Generalis* published in 1650 contained modern knowledge from astronomy to geology and was so much in use in its time that Isaac Newton edited and commentated it at Cambridge in 1691. About the translator see Adıvar, *Osmanlı Türklerinde İlim*, p. 167.

50 Hermann Boerhaave (1668-1738), was a famed Dutch doctor and an innovator in clinical medicine; see *ibid.*, pp. 177-78.

Alexander Mavrogordato, an Ottoman Greek from Chios, wrote his doctoral thesis, *Pneumaticon instrumentum circulandi sanguinis*, on blood circulation, at Harvey's alma mater, Padua University. This thesis is said to have been utilized by later European doctors in the field,[51] but in spite of the fact that Mavrogordato held a high position in the Turkish government, his knowledge of modern medicine does not seem to have exercised any influence in initiating modern experimental medicine.

It was noted earlier that the Sadrazam Ibrahim Paşa had encouraged letters; he appointed a committee of twenty-five persons in 1717 to translate Eastern and Western works into Turkish. One of the members of this group, Esad Efendi, a member of the Ulema and a proof-reader at Müteferrika's printing house, translated Aristotle's *Physics* from Greek into Arabic and mentioned among his annotations the telescope and microscope "for the first time in Turkey and probably in the whole East."[52] Other individuals continued the translation in later years.

Several translations remained in manuscript, probably because Ibrahim's printing press ceased to be operated after his death (1745) and printing virtually stopped until 1783. The lack of printing facilities diminished the effect of the efforts to disseminate modern scientific knowledge. A study of the causes for this interruption will throw much light upon the arrest of the progress initiated during the Tulip Era in which there had been in silhouette so many signs that gave the appearance of a renaissance.

[51] *Ibid.*, pp. 113-14.
[52] *Ibid.*, pp. 139-40.

A SECULAR TREND, which made Turkey seem like a country experiencing a renaissance, was the dominant feature of the Tulip Era. Westernization was not inherent in it, any more than a drive towards the Orient was implied in the interest taken in Muslim civilization by the early secular minds of Europe. The Turkish reformists of the Tulip Era were basically as loyal to their heritage and institutions as the forefathers of European rationalism were to theirs. The reformists were only unfortunate in that their tentative excursions into the unconventional and unfamiliar were followed, in the second part of the eighteenth century, by the rise of a power struggle between Russia and the West, represented by France. When this struggle contributed ironically to the furtherance of Russian expansion, when France obtained more and more commercial, diplomatic, and religious concessions from Ottoman reformist statesmen, and when, as a result, both Russia and France showed aspirations, conflicting but from the Ottoman viewpoint identical, of establishing themselves in the Balkans or the Levant, then conditions were ripe in Turkey for a reactionary movement opposing all West-oriented reforms.

During this struggle, Russia tried to undermine Ottoman power not only by war but also by appealing to the religious sentiments of the Christian, mostly Greek Orthodox, peoples within the Empire. France obtained from Ottoman statesmen the formal recognition of her right to protect all Catholic orders, churches, and missionary efforts to proselytize the Orthodox Christians and to establish Catholic supremacy in the Holy Land and Lebanon.

Meanwhile, although French culture and the French Enlightenment were popular in Russia, and the Russia of Peter the Great and Catherine II enjoyed prestige among the leading minds of France, anti-Turk and anti-Muslim prejudices were expressed by French thinkers such as Voltaire, publicists such as Volney, and even diplomats and mission heads sent to help Turkey, such as the ambassador, Choiseul-Gouffier, and the general, Baron de Tott. For there had arisen in Europe, and particularly in France, an attitude which came to be called anti-Islamic, although it was far from the attitude of the old crusaders. On the contrary, it was the child of the modern rationalist spirit of pre-revolutionary France —the very spirit which the Turkish reformists were prepared to emulate.[1]

Such developments placed the francophile Ottoman reformists in an awkward position and gave a religious colouring to the anti-reform movement. The religious reaction held the reformists responsible for the destruction of both *din* (religion) and *devlet* (state), not only because of their alien innovations which undermined the ancient tradition, but also because of their complicity with those infidels who were now threatening Muslim rule from two sides and from within. Thus a religiously oriented anti-Western movement became the second strand running across the whole history of the Turkish transformation, in contrast to the Westernist strand whose beginnings we traced in the first chapter.

In the following chapters we shall see that the opposition between Westernists and anti-Westernists was not confined to the Tulip Era. In later periods, reforms suffered repeated setbacks from the reactions provoked by international power struggles. The more reforms were attempted, the more the reaction became established as a distinct tradition. The religious iron curtain between Christianity and Islam became a fixed barrier and added to the usual difficulties of introducing changes into a traditional order. This religious reaction not only became a feature of the Turkish transformation, but also spread to all Muslim societies, appearing in the second half of the nineteenth century in the ideology of pan-Islamism. This feature made the Turkish transformation different from the Japanese, or even the Russian, in which Westernization did not seem to meet opposition on religious grounds.

[1] Cf. Norman Daniel, *Islam and the West* (Edinburgh, 1960), pp. 288-94.

Religious resistance to change by these early Ottoman conservatives gave rise in the West to the view—which in time became an established conviction—that East and West were fundamentally dissimilar, that civilization was a purely occidental creation, and that non-European races were incapable of progress because of their superstitious religions. We thus find a strange confluence between the attitude of Europeans and that of their Muslim adversaries, both of which were in opposition to the spirit of the Tulip Era.

53

The Limitations of the Reformists

The reformists of Ibrahim Müteferrika's time were aware of the rise in the West of a new worldly *nizâm* (polity) based on secular and rational principles, but they persisted in believing that the traditional system was basically sound and would eventually prove its superiority once technical ameliorations were made. They were interested in what may be called the externalities of Western civilization, in the material products of the new *nizâm* rather than its foundations. They believed that these aspects were not intrinsic to the institutions within which they were operating, and that they could therefore be appropriated in the same fashion as the empirically useful arts of medieval Christian societies had been appropriated by Muslim civilization.

We may discern in the Tulip Era signs of progress in the reformists' understanding of the problems facing them, but the optimism and exuberance of the earliest reformists were lacking in their immediate successors. Their basic timidity is reflected in the following saying of Rağıb Paşa, the reformist Sadrazam during the waning years of the Tulip Era (1757-63): "I am afraid that we shall be unable to re-establish order [*nizâm*] if we once break the harmony of the existing institutions."[2]

A poetic conversation among the leading representatives of the four most valued institutions of the traditional order will illustrate the pessimism and nostalgia for the past that swept over the reformists even from the middle years of the Tulip Era. The ruler Mustafa III (1717-74) described the conditions of his time in the following lament:

[2] Quoted by Hâmit and Muhsin, *Türkiye Tarihi* (Istanbul, 1930), p. 313.

The world is in decay, Do not think it will right with us;
Base Fate has given the state over to the mean.
Now the men of rank about us are all cowards
Nothing remains for us but immortal compassion.

54

Ismail Âsım, the Şeyhul-Islâm, took up the metre and rhyme to find hope in religion:

Truly the worldly state is grasped by the mean,
Order no more comes to hand by honest thinking;
Even the leaves and rain are the cowards' loot
May the Şeriat's waters right the garden of the state!

Rağıb Paşa, the Sadrazam, followed the pattern with a mystic note:

What are these, your restless world desires?
The wheel turns on in its eternal cycle,
Fear not, O my heart, the coward finds a moment's joy,
The Creator gave a mean world to the mean.

And Rasih Enderunî, the mystic Şeyh, concluded:

If God's judgments would be delved,
Knowing is exhausted without an end attained;
Contrariness avails naught, because
The tent lines of His rule are lashed to an eternal base!
Humility and resignation are wanted, O my soul,
That is the only answer to the affairs of Fate.[3]

The incongruity between the spirit revealed in this passage and the requirements of modern statecraft is reflected in the economic policies of the period. Although in many ways the unfortunate victims of circumstance, the reformists of the eighteenth century themselves helped to create one of the most formidable obstacles to reform throughout the nineteenth and well into the twentieth century: the system of capitulations. They failed to see the implications of a new phase of European economic development. Quite distantly removed from the orders of society adversely affected by Western economic penetration, and indebted by the mediation of France in ending a desperate war (1736-39), they ignored earlier reformist counsel. In the face of efforts to terminate the traditional capitulatory agreements, a reform government con-

---

[3] Quoted by Atâ, *Tarih* (Istanbul, 1876), IV, 67.

cluded a new capitulatory agreement with France in 1740. This extended the traditional, and added new, exterritorial privileges for foreign traders to an increasing number of nations; provided the bases for all their economic treaties and diplomatic relations with the Ottoman Empire until the eve of World War I; stripped the medieval Ottoman economy of various protective measures; and launched a new era of intensified economic penetration.[4] The reformists paid for a cessation of hostilities with one adversary, Russia, by the sale of the economic resources of a disordered Turkey to what the conservatives believed to be an equally obnoxious foe, France.

The disappointments of France in the New World had caused her politicians, merchants, and diplomats to focus upon Ottoman territories as a source of, and highway to, compensations. Greatly alarmed by Russia's success in gaining a foothold on the Black Sea, one section among the makers of French diplomacy supported the view that the Ottoman Empire should be helped to stand as a bulwark against Russian expansion. At the same time, the French turned to projects of expanding their commerce in the Levant, Egypt, and the Black Sea area as compensation for the losses to other Western powers in North America and South Asia. The boom in French trade initiated by the Treaty of 1740 not only widened French commercial interests (*échelles* were established in almost every trade centre in the Levant) but also intensified Catholic propaganda and made French diplomacy dominant in the Porte. Even in the eighteenth century, foreign aid and technical assistance could prove to have strings attached.

The real test of the limited program of the reformists came when Turkey plunged into her biggest, longest, and costliest war against Russia (1768-74). It was encouraged by French diplomacy, and precipitated by the cries for *jihâd* (holy war) of their adversaries—those bellicose Turkish conservatives who believed more in the power of religious zeal than in modern techniques borrowed from the French. The Treaty of Kaynarca, concluded after this war, disappointed the expectations of both groups. Instead of halting Russian power, the French had indirectly helped it to expand and establish itself, upsetting French interests from the Black Sea to the Levant. Instead of proving the superiority of traditional methods inspired by religious zeal, the traditional military forces had failed abysmally.

[4] On the capitulations in general see N. Sousa, *The Capitulary Regime of Turkey* (Baltimore, 1933).

The New Reform Efforts

The war had proved the extent to which the Ottoman system was disorganized and its very foundations shaken. Its spirit could no longer be animated by religious zeal alone. The entire *timar* (benefice) system had already fallen under the impact of those economic factors which had destroyed European feudalism; the army of benefice-holders (*sipahi*) had virtually disappeared as a result of the expropriation of fiefs by derebeys, government, Yeniçeris, and tax-farmers. The system of recruiting, training, and remunerating the Yeniçeris had fallen into disrepair. The organization of the corps had become a machinery by which the impoverished *esnaf* (artisans, petty tradesmen, and men of odd jobs) could live parasitically off the government treasury.

After describing these changes, an anonymous writer of the period said:

At that time, very few liable for service as benefice holders or enrolled members of the Yeniçeri corps would join the war with religious zeal. No real incentive for battle remained because everyone could obtain benefices for money or through nepotism and, therefore, the traditional military order has lost its whole meaning.[5]

He continued by saying that the ʿasabiyya (principle of solidarity) of the Ottoman system had been religious warfare or *ghazâ*. The morale of the political as well as the military organization had been destroyed with the evaluation of everything in pecuniary terms. Considerations entirely devoid of moral values had replaced the raison d'être of the Ottoman system. Defeats were the inevitable result. Rather than recognizing this, the protagonists of war insisted upon waging it behind a religious banner, and further weakened the power of the state.

The writer saw, correctly, the natural consequences of disintegration in a traditional order. He believed that several matters relating to welfare in the worldly estate should be freed from the yoke of tradition, or religious considerations, and subjected to rational criteria. To make such a separation would require a fundamental change in the view of the system of religion-and-state

---

[5] Quoted by Cevdet, *Tarih* (1302), I, 65-66. Ibn Khaldûn's work attracted increasing attention from the Ottoman Turks in this period of decline. His *Muqaddima* (Eng. trans. F. Rosenthal, *The Muquaddimah*, 3 vols.; New York, 1958) was translated into Turkish by the Şeyhul-Islâm Pîrîzade Sâib (d. 1749).

(*din-u-devlet*). It would require a re-evaluation of what was external and what intrinsic to the traditional, and to the necessary, policies.

There are indications that the reformists were aware of these relevant distinctions. The split between the traditional and early reformist outlooks can be seen in the reflections of Ahmed Resmî (1708-83) upon the rejection of the peace policy, and upon the war and its consequences. Resmî was the only responsible critic of the war policy with the courage to sign the Treaty of Kaynarca and he was later a close associate of Halil Hâmid, the first Sadrazam to attempt reform in the sense of institutional innovation. Perhaps in justification of his own position, but yet significantly, Resmî criticized the ignorance and arrogance of the conservatives. He held them responsible for the war and the defeat. For probably the first time, he dismissed as visionary and dangerous the old myth of the Red Apple (Kızıl Elma) according to which the Turks were destined to conquer Christendom, and the idea that the "true Believers" would triumph irrespective of their armaments and military preparations—because of their divine destiny. He wrote, in part:

Men of reason and experience have learned and understood that
prosperity and power in the worldly realm are dependent upon
peace and reconciliation with the enemy when circumstances so
require. Those who follow this rule of wisdom and those who realize
that war is not always the best thing have preferred peace to war
and, thus, have given security and comfort to the State and its people
whom they serve. . . . Those old-timers who, because of their lack
of reason or experience, disregarded this established rule and believed
that it was incumbent upon all Muslims to annihilate those who
belonged to other religions or to keep them always defeated were
responsible for the beginning and the losing of the war.[6]

Resmî set out to prove that the defeat was due, not to the failure of the modern methods recently introduced, but to the blindness of the conservatives. He emphasized that the old Ottoman power was gone. It was not possible to match the Russians, who had enormous material resources at their command in addition to their military improvements, by maintaining the conservative position.

[6] Ahmed Resmî, *Hulâsat-up İtibar* (Ebuzziya ed.; Istanbul, 1889), pp. 2, 75-76. The "red apple" is believed to refer to the apple-shaped pinnacle at the top of the dome of St. Peter's in Rome. About the myth see F. W. Hasluck, *Christianity and Islam Under the Sultans* (Oxford, 1929), II, 736-40.

58

A peaceful and tolerant policy towards the nations of other religions should be pursued. Politics should not be animated by religious fervour, they should be reconciled with the methods of non-Muslim civilization. Politics and administration should be based primarily on considerations of material strength and improvement.

The lesson to be learned from the first ordeal of the reform experiment was that the efficient use of new methods and techniques could not be assured so long as the traditional institutions and ideas prevailed. Mere innovations were fruitless unless the institutions which were to receive them were reshaped or even abolished. Thus the twofold problem of technical improvement and institutional reorganization came to be a little better clarified after the war. Reforms attempted under the Sadrazam Halil Hâmid (1736-85; Sadrazam, 1782-85) illustrate a second stage in the Turkish attitude to reform.[7]

While wiping out the achievements of the Tulip Era and exhausting the moral and economic resources of the people, the war broke down further the hesitation of the reformists to ally themselves with Christians and gave new impetus to reforming efforts. During the war, the ruler Mustafa III invited the French general, Baron de Tott, already in Turkey studying the military situation, to train cannoneers in rapid artillery fire, to modernize the ordinance arsenal, draft plans for the defence of the Straits, introduce modern pontoon elements, and perform other battle-front tasks. This was a continuation of the earlier idea that the Turkish problem was purely technological, but the action was precedent-setting. For the first time a foreigner and a recognized infidel was employed openly as such. Towards the end of the war, the ruler established two other precedents without, apparently, encountering conservative resistance. The Turkish government officially asked the French government for the use of certain specified military technicians. The first military unit independent of the Yeniçeri system and established on European lines was created in 1774 upon the arrival of the first French military mission.

Despite the importance of these developments, they fell within the scope of action recognized by the Ulema as permissible to the ruler on the basis of expediency. The conclusion of the Treaty was seen to end that expediency and, while those innovations made were not then eliminated, further significant use was not made of the French technicians until the coming of Halil Hâmid in 1782.

---

[7] See I. H. Uzunçarşılı, "Sadrazam Halil Hâmid Paşa" *Türkyiat Mecmuası,* V (1935), 213-67.

(In the interim between the war and his employment by the new reform party, De Tott was engaged in the Levant as an agent of the French government gathering information for the possibilities of French expansion.)[8]

The war, its outcome, and especially the participation in the war of volunteer martyrs, gave shocking instruction in the role of training in the modern sciences in the development and application of new military techniques. As a result, the new reformists revived the interest of the Tulip Era in the establishment of non-traditional educational institutions and in the translation into Turkish of European works on science. In the face of conservative opposition, the reformists did not entertain the idea of modernizing the educational program of the Yeniçeri system.

Staffed largely by French officers, a new engineering school was opened in 1776, which was strictly for naval officers and was the forerunner of the present Naval Academy. Among those employed were Campbell Mustafa Ağa, (a converted Scotsman), De Tott, Lafitte-Clavé, and Laurent-Jean Francois Truguet. (The last two mentioned contributed to the Turkish literature on modern military techniques. In 1786 a two-volume treatise on castramentation and temporary fortifications by Lafitte-Clavé was published at a press founded by the French ambassador Choiseul-Gouffier; the same press published the following year a book on naval maneuvers and tactics by Truguet.)[9]

An important addition was the re-establishment in 1769 of the School of Engineering (Mühendishane) of the Tulip Era,

[8] Baron François de Tott (1733-93) was a French general of Hungarian origin. He was appointed by the French government as an inspector of the French *échelles* in the Levant. See H. L. Hoskins, *British Routes to India* (New York, 1928), p. 17.

[9] Jean de Lafitte Clavé, *Usûl-ul-maârif fî tertîb-ul-urdu* (2 vols.; Istanbul, 1786). Laurent-Jean-François Truguet, *Usûl-ul-maârif fî vech-i tasnîf-i sefâin-i donanma* (Istanbul, 1787). See Adnan-Adıvar, *Osmanlı Türklerinde İlim* (Istanbul, 1943), pp. 184-5; S. N. Gerçek, *Türk Matbaacılığı* (Istanbul, 1939), I, 100-102; Uzunçarşılı, "Sadrazam Halil Hâmid Paşa," 235. These were the earliest books on such subjects printed in Turkish. Mehmet Ali of Egypt later seems to have procured them for the library of his military school; see J. Heyworth-Dunne, *An Introduction to the History of Education in Modern Egypt* (London, 1939), p. 110. The French Embassy press also printed a grammar of Turkish in 1790 as *Elements de la langue turque*. (The first grammar for learning Turkish through French was prepared by a dragoman of the French Embassy under the direction of the Jesuit father and orientalist Jean-Baptiste Holdermann, and was printed by Ibrahim Müteferrika in 1730 under the title of *Grammaire turque*).

staffed by Turkish teachers. This institution was the first expression of some realization that a degree of continuity was required between the regular and specialized education of the new military officers, and it became the forerunner of the School of Artillery and Fortifications of the late nineteenth century. Abbé Toderini who was in Turkey between 1781 and 1786 speaks of this institution very favourably, and following his visit he reported that he met teachers who knew English, Italian, and French and that "the best books of Europe and marine instruments" were used. He said that he

> saw different atlases and nautical charts of Europe, the Gian-Numa [*Cihannumâ*], or little atlas of the Turk Hagi Calsah [Hajji Khalifa, that is Kâtip Çelebi], a celestial globe showing the constellations and stars of the first degree by Turkish signs and characters in gold without figures, the work of the professor; an armillary sphere of metal made in Paris, some Arab astrolabs, Turkish and French sun-dials of several kinds, a very beautiful English octant of Jean Hadley, different Turkish compasses, the compass of Galilei, with other marine instruments.

He found among the many European books

> the astronomical tables of M. de Lalande and the translation made from them into Turkish. . . . The professor showed me tables on artillery translated from European books, notebooks on astrolaby, on sun-dials, on the compass and on geometry.[10]

Charles de Peysonnel, the French consul and a correspondent of the French Royal Academy, noted the broadening outlook. He wrote in 1788,

> The most manifest proof of the new disposition was evinced in going to the expense of procuring persons to translate the French *Encyclopédie* into the Turkish language; . . . the utter encouragement possible is held out to learning, arts, sciences, and commerce; and to profit by an intercourse with them. . . . There are at the moment in the Ottoman army a great number of European officers, particularly French. . . . Effects proportionate to such exertions have been already visible in the good order and discipline of their armies and have been extended to their dress. . . .[11]

---

[10] Abbé Toderini, *De la littérature des turcs* (Paris, 1789), I, 161-67.

[11] Charles de Peyssonel, *Examen du livre intitulé Considérations . . . par M. de Volney* (Amsterdam, 1788); Eng. trans. *A Reply to a Pamphlet Entitled Consideration on the War with the Turks by M. de Volney* (London, 1789), p. 55.

While the foundations of a new army were thus being prepared, Halil Hâmid was planning to take a surgical knife to the perennial problem of the *timar* and Yeniçeri organizations. The reformists had come to the decision that corrupted institutions obstructing the new military development had to be eliminated and that the Yeniçeri could not offer resistance to this incisive move. While correct on most points, the reformists were very mistaken in believing that a lion with worn out paws could not scratch; they took one step further towards their Waterloo by showing indications that they intended to make institutional reforms just when the intensification of French activities in the Levant and of Russia in the Crimea gave the conservatives all the ammunition they needed to hang the reform party.

The Power of the Conservatives

The weaknesses of the reformists were the strength of the conservatives. The first conservative revolt against the policy of peace and reform (1730) genuinely reflected the fact that developments within the traditional system had made any anti-reform slogan a powerful appeal to many among the rulers and the ruled.

The two orders designated to uphold the traditional system, the military and the Ulema, were foremost among those who had deviated from the medieval ideal, but were nevertheless the strongholds of conservatism.

Once a well-knit group dedicated to warfare and separated from the peasantry, artisans, and political groups, the Yeniçeris were now engaged in interfering in state affairs or in rebellion and plunder when their demands were not accepted. Many of their rebellions were probably uprisings of the impoverished *esnaf* rather than simple military mutinies. The Ulema had to make common cause with the Yeniçeris because in a similar manner and perhaps in greater degree they could not afford to have their structure altered in terms of either traditional or modern criteria. They too had undergone a change in social composition and role; an increase in quantity and a decrease in quality, stratification into higher and lower ranks, with the lower more and more parasitical, were the features of the transformation. The higher Ulema were engaged in extra-curricular activities such as selling offices, degrees, ranks, and favours, usurous dealings, even in tax-farming and the expropriation of estates (*malikâne*), and, above all, in controlling the pious foundations (*evkaf* properties). At the lower levels too numerous clericals had to maintain existence in the same parasitical relationship to society as the Yeniçeri corps did. A few did not participate in the race after worldly ambitions because of their piety, but, because of their fundamentalist position or unworldly attitude, they became neither the agents nor the supporters of reform. Once a force limiting the real and assumed power of the Ulema, the mystic orders (*tarikats*) ceased to be centres of a more liberal and flexible outlook. Even the most liberal-minded Bektaşi order became a power behind the Yeniçeris because of their connection with the lower classes.

In other words, the impoverished social classes and estates were in common opposition to reform, irrespective of their original differences and antipathies, in order to maintain their parasitical status. Their primary opponents were the men who stood for reform, above all the rulers and secular minded statesmen who aimed at creating an effective, scientifically trained officer corps. Their dread of such a corps was justified repeatedly—even until today—as it was the new class of the military and the intellectuals who invariably saved the cause of progress against conservative reactions. As an antidote the conservatives always took pains to dominate the ruler, and, when this proved impossible, to incite a revolt of accession. They possessed no independent power to enforce their interests. They were always reliant for their effect upon their influence with the ruling powers or the people. Their religiously supported arguments appealed to the corrupted orders such as their own and the military, to the economic orders in decline through the reversals in the Ottoman economic affairs or fearful of decline as a result of possible changes in the military industries, and to those few who still represented the pristine qualities of the Ottoman system. Towards the end of the Tulip Era, it was clear to the leaders of the conservative groups that there would be no end to the reforms once the status quo had been tampered with. Probably the corrupt elements recognized that their time was running out—that the genuine traditionalists would join forces with the reformists, as they did in 1826, once they realized that no hope remained in the traditional symbols, slogans, and institutions. Therefore, the conservatives directed all of their efforts to discrediting reform parties before they could take any action. Because of the intimate connections throughout the body politic, the first steps towards institutional reform in the military institution would reverberate throughout the whole, beginning with the economic bases of the ruling and learned orders. Thus, they rejected reasonably the naive view that "externalities" such as techniques of warfare could be added or subtracted at will without secondary effects.

A second source of strength of the conservatives was that they found support in the wider social bases of the society, whereas the reformists represented no group or class interest, not even their own. One reason for failure in the reform concept was the fact that reformism was initiated by the rulers and ruling class rather than by a new class constituting a pressure group against the ruling principles. The reformists were not reliant upon or indebted to the economic classes in the manner of their European counterparts. They did not encourage the development of a new entrepreneurial class. On the contrary, through their belief that the primary threat to Turkey was military and from Russia, they failed to take a proper account of the menace implicit in the Western economic impact. They facilitated the growth of politically organized anti-reformism by allowing one-sided competition between the new Western and the medieval Ottoman economies in support of their military reforms and ends.

The introduction of Frenk methods was viewed by the great masses of people not as an advantage or as a mere expediency, but as an instrument of destruction turned against the Şeriat, the traditions, and the well-being of themselves. They instinctively recognized that innovations in the military field amounted in the long run to an overthrow of the traditional knowledge and techniques of industry and the artisan crafts ancillary to the prosecution of war and military occupation. The implications put into alliance the reformists and the foreign traders, whose disappearance following the discovery of a new route to India precipitated crises and whose reappearance with goods of the new European economy brought not new prosperity but a still more serious decline. Very little was required to stir up the masses' fear of still worsening conditions and latent hostility for the West into a religiously coloured outburst against reform and the reformists.

France: Image of Western Civilization

64

It was the misfortune of the reformists that they were drawn to the point of striking up a friendship with France at a time when French public opinion and diplomacy were unfriendly to the Ottoman Empire. French interests in the Ottoman territories had become so established and Russian ascendancy so menacing after 1774 that new views and projects began to develop in France concerning the Ottoman Empire and the Islamic world of the Near East.

After the Russo-Turkish War of 1768-74, Russia enjoyed fame and prestige in European public opinion. French men of letters applauded those countries where enlightened despots were expected to achieve progress by the promotion of science. Russia's spectacular appearance on the European scene and her successes under Catherine II appealed greatly to men like Voltaire, Diderot, and D'Alembert. To Voltaire, who had admired the Tulip Era, the war between Catherine II and Mustafa III was a war between reason and fanaticism, civilization and backwardness.[12] Anti-Turkish views were propagated by all the publicists; political pamphleteers speculated wildly about when the Turkish Empire would fall and how it would be partitioned. Volney suggested, in his *Considérations sur la guerre des Russes et des Turcs*,[13] the creation of a Greek Empire as an alternative to the Russian and Austrian partition plans. Volney, of course, wanted the idea, originally Catherine II's, to be carried out by France and with the French in control. The invasion of the Turkish Empire would give new life to Asia. Like Voltaire, he wanted the "barbarians of the Bosphorus," the "enemies of art," the "extinguishers of *la belle Grèce*," booted out of Europe; war rather than aid was the only proper course against that "ignorant and degenerate nation."

One of these admirers of Russia and dreamers of a Greek Empire was a French aristocrat, Choiseul-Gouffier (1752-1817), whose embassy in Turkey caused a great deal of harm to Turkish reforms

---

[12] A. Lotholary, *La Mirage Russe en France aux xviie siècle* (Paris, n.d.), esp. pp. 109-35.

[13] Translated in English as *Consideration on the War with the Turks* (London, 1788). See also L. Pingaud, *Choiseul-Gouffier, La France en Orient sous Louis XVI* (Paris, 1887), p. 208. Volney made in 1783-85 an extensive tour in Syria and Egypt. His *Voyage en Egypte et en Syrie* (2 vols.; Paris, 1786) was translated into English as *Travels Through Syria and Egypt* (2 vols.; London, 1787).

and gave definitive shape to the anti-Westernism of the conservatives.[14] In his youth, in 1776, he had made a "voyage pittoresque" to Greece and recorded his findings in two folio volumes, the first of which appeared in 1782. In 1783 Choiseul-Gouffier wrote a supplementary preface to his book, entitled "Discours préliminaires", in which he expressed his indignation at the servitude of the children of Athens and Sparta to "le stupide Musulman."

65

In 1783, he wrote a memorandum for his government, entitled *Notions sur l'état actuel de l'Empire Ottoman*, in which, anticipating Talleyrand and Napoleon, he urged the establishment of French supremacy in the Mediterranean to compensate the French losses in Canada and India. By dominating Greece, the Aegean, Egypt, and the Red Sea, France would strike a counter-blow to Britain; this, however, would require keeping the Black Sea and Turkish territories out of Russian hands.[15] These suggestions won him membership in the Academy and an ambassadorship to Turkey. After a vain attempt to buy up all the copies of "Discours préliminaires" on the market (he even sent agents to England and Germany) and to disown his remarks about the Turks and the proposed Greek Empire, he left for Turkey in 1784.

With Choiseul-Gouffier came successive waves of French officers, technicians, cartographers, astronomers, geographers, travellers, and even poets and painters.[16] All these found friendly support in the person of Halil Hâmid. The growing suspicions of the conservatives, who had managed to get hold of the "Discours préliminaires," concerning the extracurricular activities of Choiseul-Gouffier's technical assistance staff were confirmed by the arrival in 1784 of Duc Charles de Montmorency, the son and aide-de-camp of Maréchal de Montmorency (Duc de Luxembourg). The Maréchal was proposing a plan to reorganize the Ottoman army and navy. He wanted authorization to establish headquarters on Rhodes or Crete, accompanied by a large retinue—actually an army. When the proposal was discussed in the Divan, the conser-

---

[14] About Choiseul-Gouffier's life and career see Pingaud, *Choiseul-Gouffier*.

[15] *Ibid.*, p. 62.

[16] When the war broke out between Russia and Turkey in 1787, the French government was besieged with plans for the annexation of Cyprus, Crete, and Egypt to France; see Hoskins, *British Routes to India*, p. 49. On the details of the projects for the defence of the Near East against Russia, see Pingaud, *Choiseul-Gouffier*, pp. 95 ff., and Uzunçarşılı, "Sadrazam Halil Hâmid Paşa," 255 ff.

vatives argued that it was indeed strange for such an important lord to seek employment in Turkish service and to require such a large staff on a strategic island beyond the ready control of Turkish forces. They were already familiar with Choiseul-Gouffier's scheme of establishing the first link of the French imperial system in Egypt. Captain Truguet was aboard a French vessel, on his way to negotiate with the Mameluk Beys of Egypt. De Tott, nominally in the Turkish service but actually inspector general of the French Échelles de Levant, was on a cognate mission to negotiate navigation rights in the Red Sea and to survey the possibilities of breaching the land barrier by a canal. Both missions had been undertaken in secrecy but were not unknown to Gazi Hasan Paşa, Admiral of the Ottoman naval forces, arch-enemy of Halil Hâmid, and the most influential leader among the conservatives. As a man of the sea, he was the one who best understood that the Ottoman Empire would become a geopolitical impossibility with Russia in the Crimea and Black Sea and with France dominating the eastern Mediterranean trade, anxious to seize its strategic islands, and preparing to invade Egypt and the Red Sea.

The hostility of the conservatives towards the West increased in the face of such threats. The association between mistrust of the French and hatred of all innovations is well illustrated in the following comment by the contemporary historiographer, Vâsıf (d. 1806). In connection with the Maréchal's project he said:

It is evident that the imperial state would not demean itself and condescend to learn unfamiliar martial sciences from those who belong to the same kind as its enemies [other Christians] because of having been defeated once [by Russia]. . . . Success or failure depend upon the conduct of Almighty God. The beliefs of the Christian nations are contrary to this, as they follow the doctrine of a school of philosophers according to whom the Creator has no role in particular matters (Heaven forefend!). As war is one of such particular matters, they believe that the side superior in material means of warfare becomes victorious over the other. . . . How is it permissible to attribute victory merely to the perfection of the means of warfare and defeat to shortcomings in those means? . . . To accept aid from the French . . . is bound to bring immediate and ultimate damages and fatal consequences, besides the fact that their purpose is not entirely friendly and that trusting the Christian states is utterly impermissible.[17]

[17] Quoted by Cevdet, *Tarih*, III, 7071.

The conservatives had no difficulty in rallying the masses to their viewpoint when they could point to foreign manipulations and emulation of the Frenk as inspiring the proposed reforms. Numerous incidents during Choiseul-Gouffier's incumbency gave substance to the belief that the reformists were traitors in league with the French.[18]

One can easily imagine the difficulties of maintaining a tolerant attitude towards the West in the face of such behaviour by the leading representatives of France. It was hard not to be influenced by the traditionalist argument that so-called modern ideas were simply a new stratagem of Christendom to divide and conquer Islam. The last straw contributing to the downfall of the reformists was Russia's unilateral annexation of the Crimea in 1785, which seemed to confirm the fears that Islam was being threatened from both sides. Hâmid was denounced publicly in 1785 as a traitor to the state and to Islam. He was dismissed, exiled, and murdered; and a number of his followers were assassinated. Significantly, the placard attached to his corpse (a traditional practice in explanation of an execution and in warning to other miscreants) read: "The enemy of the Şeriat and of the State."[19]

In his brief career as Sadrazam, Hâmid encountered those internal and external obstacles to modernization which not only existed in the eighteenth century but survive even today. His tragic end exemplifies the persistent dilemma of all Muslim reformists.

With very few exceptions, European observers attributed the

---

[18] One of these was the secret correspondence of Selim, the heir to the Ottoman throne, with Louis XVI. See Salih Munir, "Louis XVI et le Sultan Selim III," *Revue d'Histoire Diplomatique*, Anné 26 (1912), 516-48; I. H. Uzunçarşılı, "Selim III'ün veliaht iken Fransa kralı Louis XVI ile muhabereleri," *Belleten*, II, nos. 5-6 (1938), 191-246; also Pingaud, *Choiseul-Gouffier*, pp. 82 ff. The conservatives charged that Selim and his followers were dominated by French ideas and were plotting for a coup d'état. The letters, reproduced from the French and Turkish archives in the above sources, contain nothing to suggest that Selim and his men were involved in a conspiracy. The young prince conveyed his wish for an alliance with France upon his accession to the throne. He also expressed his admiration for European civilization, his determination to introduce reforms along European lines, and his hope of receiving aid from France for carrying out his reforms. The charge of conspiracy persisted and, with the succession of the incidents uncovering the French design upon the Ottoman empire and culminating in Bonaparte's invasion of Egypt, gave the conservatives ample evidence to convince the people that Selim's reforms meant the destruction of the Ottoman empire.

[19] Uzunçarşılı, "Sadrazam Halil Hâmid Paşa," 243-44, 246.

failure of the reforms and the conservative hostility to change to some strange characteristic of the Turks, or Muslims—to an inherent incapacity of the Oriental for progress. It was at this time and especially in connection with Franco-Turkish relationships that the idea of an inscrutable "Oriental mind" became a stereotype—even to the extent of creating a specialization called "Orientalism" to plumb its mysteries. Eighteenth-century European rationalism failed to see the conditions with historical or sociological perspective.

There is, perhaps, no better example of the Enlightenment attitude towards the reform problems of Turkey than that expressed in the *Mémoires* of Baron de Tott.[20] Published in 1784, these so touched the heart strings of eighteenth-century Europe that they were translated immediately into several European languages, passed through a number of editions, and, in short, became the standard work for understanding this period of Turkish history. De Tott's descriptions were permeated by delight in the odd, the arrogant assumption that he was the very personification of Pure Reason, and a complete indifference to the very qualities of accuracy, honesty, and integrity upon which De Tott based his differentiation between the West and the Turks.[21] It is not difficult to find between the lines of De Tott's reminiscences that intricate and melodramatic struggle which was to become the touchstone of subsequent Western literature on the Ottoman Empire. The Davids and Goliaths of De Tott's accounts bear but

[20] De Tott's book was translated into English as *Memoirs of Baron de Tott, containing the state of the Turkish Empire and the Crimea . . ., with numerous anecdotes, facts and observations on the manners and customs of the Turks and Tartars* (2 vols.; London, 1785). In addition to his job as an inspector of the Levant *échelles*, he was loaned to the Turkish service as a military expert, was instructed to learn the Turkish language and the institutions, and also to gather information about the Suez and the Dardanelles. He failed only in learning the language and the institutions, judging from the unrecognizable forms of the Turkish words found in his book and the fantastic meanings he attributed to them.

[21] The fact that these memoirs became one of the sources of inspiration in the composition of the mendacious stories known as the *Adventures of Baron Münchhausen* may give an idea about the credibility of De Tott's observations. For a criticism of the *Memoirs* see Charles de Peyssonel, *Lettre . . . contenant quelques observations relatives au Mémoires, qui sont parus sous le nom de Mr. le Baron de Tott* (Amsterdam, 1785). Two English translations of this book appeared: *Strictures and Remarks on the Memoirs of Baron de Tott* (London, 1786), and *An Appendix to the Memoirs of Baron de Tott* (London, 1786).

little resemblance to their prototypes; the "good" men are those whose loyalty to the medieval economic ethics make them fair game for exploitation, or whose admiration for Western achievements make them useful subjects for the abracadabra suggestions of a French spy; the "bad" men are those "ignorant and prejudiced fools" who, for all of their stupidity, managed to catch De Tott virtually in the act of seditious espionage. Even the journalistic passages of De Tott's memoirs lose their analytical value as a result of his ignorance of the Turkish language, his contempt for the people he was supposed to assist, and his tendency to generalize on specific examples relevant less to his role as a technical adviser than to his role as an intriguer against a host state.

What was viewed as strange by foreign observers was neither the product of mere ignorance nor a reflection of an immutable Oriental or Muslim mentality. It was the natural consequence of an antiquated system that was, in its many details, incongruous with the demands of new methods and techniques. Caught between external enmity and internal hostility the Turkish reformists would be repeatedly confronted on the one hand by the necessity of showing to the Western powers that they were not prejudiced against reasonable change or the practice of religious differentiation, and on the other, of satisfying the conservatives of Turkey that they were not lackeys of the infidels, the Frenks, or European imperialism.

In the years from the death of Hâmid to 1826, we shall find that the necessity of some institutional change as an integral part of the successful appropriation of modern techniques was recognized, but that the conservative opposition as well as the external powers proved to be even stronger in bringing about the failure of a comprehensive reform.

The New Order and its Fall | *chapter 3*

THE PERIOD of progressive reforms following the Treaty of Kaynarca was ended by a conservative reaction and another war with Russia in 1787. This war, in which (with the outbreak of the French Revolution) Turkey was entirely isolated, was ended in 1792. It was a major incentive for launching the reforms projected under Selim III, who had come to the throne in 1789. This ruler realized the necessity of making more comprehensive reforms. Modernization, it was felt, would require a thoroughgoing examination of the basic traditional institutions themselves. It came to be realized that a policy of innovation could not be carried out while the traditional system remained entirely intact, and that it would necessitate some alterations in those institutions that were the main obstacles to change.

In addition to external challenges the new phase of reform was stimulated by certain economic and political trends which were products of the silent and indirect impact of the West: (*a*) the increasing impoverishment of the people, especially the peasantry, and the increasing financial difficulties of the government, (*b*) the rise of strong local lords to challenge the central authority, and (*c*) uprisings followed by movements for independence among the non-Muslim peoples.

The disintegration of the two important bases of the traditional political order, the *sipahi* and the Yeniçeri organizations, was closely connected with these trends. The impossibility of preserving these two bases, or of restoring them to their original form under the new conditions, had now become much more apparent.

Their decline would inevitably have repercussions for the future of the traditional system. The ruling institution would have to reorganize itself, partly by rearranging its constituent elements and partly by adding new ones.

72

Proposed Reforms

From his youth Selim III entertained an admiration for French civilization. He was so imbued with the desire to carry out reforms that he embarked upon his New Order (Nizam-ı Cedid) immediately after the conclusion of the peace with Russia.

In spite of stately intentions, however, he was a man lacking in determination and foresight. From this personal weakness emerged something which we might call an innovation: his habit of organizing councils and committees to discuss the affairs of state, in which he invited his advisers to submit projects of reform and insisted on having them express their opinions in absolute freedom.

An advance to be credited to Selim's time, if not to his person, was the widening of scope in the view of what reforms were necessary. This included at least three major points: (*a*) that the problem of rehabilitation was not merely a matter of military reform but also a matter of civil reform; (*b*) that a comprehensive reform plan should be devised by deliberation and universal consent; and (*c*) that economic recovery should occupy a major place in the reforms.

Most of the reports were concerned, above all, with military reforms.[1] On this major topic the opinions fell into three groups: (*a*) that the Yeniçeris and other military orders must be restored to their original forms; (*b*) that modern methods should be introduced under the pretext of restoring them to their original

---

[1] The most important reports are quoted extensively by Cevdet Paşa from a text unifying and summarizing them. See Cevdet Paşa, *Tarih* (Istanbul, 1303), VI, 9. This text was published by E. Z. Karal, "Nizâm-ı cedide dair Lâyihalar," *Tarih Vesikaları*, I, No. 6 (April, 1942), 414-25; II, No. 8 (Aug., 1942), 104-11; II, No. 11 (Feb., 1943), 342-51; and II, No. 12 (April, 1943), 424-32. The two best reports are printed in full in *Tarih-i Osmanî Encümeni Mecmuası*: Şerif Mehmed, "Sultan Selim-i Salis Devrinde Nizam-ı Devlet Hakkında Mutalâat," VII, No. 38 (June, 1916), 74-88; Abdullah Tatarcık, "Selim-i Salis Devrinde Nizam-i Devlet Hakkında Mutalâat," VII, No. 41 (Dec., 1916), 257-84, VII, No. 42 (Feb., 1916), 321-46, and VIII, No. 43 (April, 1917), 15-34.

forms; and (c) that these traditional military institutions and their methods are not capable of reform and therefore must be abolished altogether and modern methods must be introduced.

The old military system was so inextricably connected with several other institutions that a radical change would necessitate far-reaching alterations in the whole body politic. Thus, a majority advised the pursuance of a dichotomous policy, that of continuing the training of new military forces and of gradually converting the entire military organization to the type of these new forces. Nearly all agreed on the absolute necessity of inviting more European military officers as trainers. The majority mentioned Prussians; others, French and English officers. Translations from European works on military science were also mentioned in some of the reports as one of the urgent needs.

Besides these basic points, the reports contained details about the needs of the various branches of the military forces, such as artillery, arms equipment, topography and map-making, shipbuilding and arsenals, etc.

A second major topic handled in many of the reports was the problem of reforming the *timars* and other benefices. However, there were no new and interesting proposals regarding the solution of the difficulties. As many repeated the necessity of enforcing the law (previously passed under Halil Hâmid) to reform the *timar* system, a modified form of the same law was prepared later following the suggestions given in the reports. Many of the reports emphasized the point that the benefices fallen vacant should not be sold or farmed (a practice which had given rise to the *mültezims* and *derebeys*); their revenues should be collected directly by the Imperial Mint.

The third major point discussed was the need for reforming the currency. The idea suggested was that of liquidating the debased currency and restoring the real value of coins. Yet Selim, under the economic pressure of the Russian war, had to resort to the old policy and issue debased money. Although this had secured some additional income to the Treasury, it led ultimately to further economic difficulties.

In spite of the general recognition that a change was absolutely necessary, and that no illusion could be entertained any longer about the soundness and vitality of the traditional institutions, the majority still reasoned in terms of an amelioration within the general framework of the medieval system. Those who could say something radical displayed no new conception of the modern state and society in terms of which such radical change would have significance.

However, we find close agreement in the conviction that the West should be taken as the source and model of anything to be introduced. It can be assumed that these reports remained influential, since many of the proposals contained therein were realized in the succeeding years. The reports were incorporated in a document combining and classifying the various proposals, and it was sent for the approval of the Şeyhul-Islâm.

74

Towards A New Order

The outstanding innovation in the thinking underlying the reports was the major place given to economic measures. Some of the measures considered will illustrate this as well as the inadequacy of the means chosen.

The idea of getting foreign loans as a remedy for the financial crisis was raised for the first time. However, receiving a loan from a European country met with opposition on the ground that it would be degrading for a Muslim government. Some suggested arranging a loan from a Muslim country, but there was found none able to lend. Secret negotiations with the representatives of the Netherlands met with no success. There remained, then, the three traditional fiscal methods: confiscation, compulsory donation, and the debasement of the coinage; however, these did not alter the conditions materially, but only led to inflation and the devaluation of the money paid by the government.[2]

The prohibition of export of precious metals and stones and the exploitation of mines were recommended by the reports in connection with the financial crisis. We find also at this period the rise, in primitive and rudimentary form, of the idea of state industrial enterprise. The founding of powder and paper mills were among the attempts made in this direction.

It was also recognized that the financial well-being of the country depended upon a favourable balance of trade, and, as the main source of the commerce was seaborne, it was believed necessary to create a Turkish merchant marine. One of the major problems occupying the minds of the statesmen was that of bringing Turkish commerce into the hands of the subjects of Turkey. Among the Muslims those who had money should invest in the merchant

[2] Cevdet, *Tarih* (1303), IV, 57-58.

marine; they should buy ships and establish companies.[3] However, as one obstacle to the realization of this idea, naval duty was traditionally the honoured prerogative of the Greek community, and attempts to create a new merchant marine coincided with the rise of a national separatist movement within the community.

None of the measures taken in accordance with the recommendations of the reports produced any tangible economic reform; they only implied the birth of consciousness that the lack of a modern national economy lay at the root of the troubles.

An effective implementation of a comprehensive reform needed, above all, an effective government, and that was believed to be dependent upon a new army. Selim's desire was to be rid of the Yeniçeri forces altogether once a dependable new force had been organized and trained.

The emphasis of the new measures was therefore upon new military and naval schools, the improvement of gun foundries and arsenals, and the establishment of a new army, called the Nizam-ı Cedid (New Order), independent of the Yeniçeri system.

In 1793 the Turkish government sent to Paris a list of the officer and technician positions it wished to fill from France. A similar but longer list was sent in 1795. (One of those who applied for service in Turkey was Napoleon Bonaparte.)

In 1769 the School of Engineering (Mühendishane) was re-established for training engineer-officers. This school expanded in 1792 and in 1795 under Selim III. Most of the teaching in this school was done by Turks. Foreign help was provided chiefly by Frenchmen, but we also find a few English and Swedish names among those listed as teachers and instructors in the military establishments. Two foreign languages, Arabic and French, one representing the traditional Islamic sciences and the other the new European sciences, were compulsory for all students.

The subject-matter of the courses during the four-year program of study was as follows:

First Year: Calligraphy, Dictation, Drawing, Elementary Geometry, Arithmetic, Arabic, French.
Second Year: Arithmetic, Geometry, Geography, Arabic, French.
Third Year: Plane Trigonometry, Algebra, Topography, Geography, Military History.
Fourth Year: Conics, Differential and Integral Calculus, Dynamics, Mines, Ballistics, Fortifications, Astronomy.[4]

---

[3] *Ibid.* (1303), VI, 57-58.
[4] Mehmed Esad, *Mir'at-ı Mühendishane* (Istanbul, 1896), pp. 9-26, 30-31.

Selim III took a direct interest in the books and library. He donated some instruments and a number of books on mathematical sciences. He was particularly interested in artillery and had even written a treatise on the subject while still a prince. He encouraged the translation of books from French; one was a work by Vauban, the French engineer of fortifications that were considered inpenetrable in Louis XIV's time.[5] Selim was a frequent and outspoken admirer of Vauban's book as well as of the new military techniques of the Europeans.[6]

It was at this time that books in Western languages came into use. The engineering school had an attached library. Most of its holdings were in French. Dictionaries and works on mathematics and military sciences predominated. It is reported that there was also a set of the French *Encyclopédie*. While written at a later date, the following foreign account of the engineering school will give some idea of the atmosphere there:

In their school of engineers, we find Turks engaged in mathematical studies; also a library, with all our best treatises on such subjects; instruments of geometry and astronomy, and all the details of fortification, within and without the body of a place. Selim III was its founder. . . . The school of engineers and miners contains forty pupils, who devote a number of years to the acquisition of skill in their occupation. They learn mechanics, elementary mathematics, fortification, the theory of mining, and the drawing of maps, of which they have a collection indifferently well executed. . . . In one of our visits to the school of Solidze [Sütlüce] we met with the head of the establishment. He showed us different works on fortifications, and elementary mathematics, composed by himself, and printed at Scutari. One of the maps which he unrolled before us was that of Europe. . . . He told us, with a smile, that he presented nothing with which we were not fully acquainted. . . . Both he and the other professors seemed overjoyed at meeting persons to converse with on these subjects. The physiognomy of all the individuals in this sanctuary of the sciences denoted the beneficial influence of instruction, in a physical and moral point of view. Religion, here, had not lost its sway over the mind; it had only shaken off its fanaticism. . . . I learned that the . . . ulema . . . are by no means averse to the diffusion of knowledge. . . . Both young and old felt

[5] Sébastien Vauban, *Traité des mines* (Paris, 1740 and 1790), Turkish trans., *Fenn-i Lağımda Risâle* (Istanbul, 1793).

[6] On the state of scientific knowledge see Adnan-Adıvar, *Osmanlı Türklerinde İlim* (Istanbul, 1943), pp. 186-92.

76

the most lively interest in our conversation. . . . The most enlightened, however, as well as the most ignorant, seemed alike insensible to any danger of downfall in their empire.[7]

Among the various reports under discussion, one penned by Raşid advised "sending men to Europe to study and observe European methods." Following this advice, permanent embassies were established in 1793 at the leading European capitals (London, Paris, Vienna, Berlin, and Madrid). This widened the window to the West first opened by Çelebi Mehmed. Henceforth, there were to be found at least a few Turks who had resided for some time in Europe and experienced life there. Ambassadors were instructed to study both the military situation in the countries to which they were assigned and the administration and civil organization. To each were to be assigned a few young men to learn the language of the country and other knowledge useful to the state.

The ambassadors' reports show that they were eager to learn about the countries to which they were assigned and that they were not at all negatively disposed towards European life. On the contrary, the dominant note was that of admiration. It was through these men that an early first-hand knowledge about European affairs began to accumulate. Some wrote detailed reform proposals. One by Ebubekir Ratib was of this order. Having been sent to Vienna in 1791, he submitted information on the military and civil services of the Austrian Empire and characterized the modern state as possessing: (*a*) a disciplined army, (*b*) ordered finances, (*c*) enlightened, honest, and patriotic public officials and (*d*) popular security and prosperity. Selim seems to have been particularly impressed by Ratib's report. He sought to implement it by founding a special council composed of ten young men.[8] About these men and in the new schools was a handful of younger men who, fitted not only with interest, but also through some study and knowledge, were in a position to be the real supporters of reforms in the new period. During the eighteen years of Selim's reign, the European way of life came a little closer to the Turks. Many of the unconscious changes in the Turkish mind, which

[7] Charles Pertusier, *Picturesque Promenades in and near Constantinople and on the Waters of the Bosphorus*, trans. from the French original (London, 1820), pp. 46-49. Pertusier was an artillery officer who had been in Turkey from 1812 to 1815.

[8] E. Z. Karal, "La transformation de la Turquie d'un empire oriental en un état modern et national," *Cahiers d'histoire mondiale*, IV, No. 2 (1958), 431.

were expressed concretely only later, may be said to have their beginnings in this period. The increasing number of foreign residents inevitably led to the infiltration of some European ways of life. Contemporary writers such as Âsım, and later Cevdet, speak of the spread of French "fashions" among the Turkish upper classes, but, strangely enough, their references are far from concrete or tangible.[9] This, however, might possibly be taken as an indication of the unconscious character of the process. These writers stressed that the innovations were openly supported and encouraged by Selim's entourage. Âsım speaks about the increased desire among the youth to learn French.

A tiny group of secular intellectuals was formed under Selim's reign. Some of these new men assumed importance in public affairs with the reforms attempted by Selim III; some survived the latter's downfall and went to Egypt to work under Mehmet Ali. At this stage, however, the intellectuals who had received even a modicum of secular education were insignificant both in quantity and in quality. We need notice only two men who distinguished themselves in the naval engineering school. One was a mathematician Gelenbevî (1730-91); the other was Çelebi Mustafa Reşid (d. 1807) who played an important role in the reforms planned by Selim and was the director of the engineering school.

Meanwhile, some of those educated in the new schools, or in contact with European life through other means, began to write on scientific subjects in French and also in Turkish. Perhaps the most typical case is that of Seid Mustapha (Seyyid Mustafa).[10] In the Preface to his book, he related how he became interested in mathematics, how the perfection of the European works on mathematics led him to study French, how within a short time he acquired enough knowledge of this language to read the works of the French authors, and, how finally these works gave him an intense desire to go to France to study. However, since Selim had founded the School of Engineering, he decided to study at that school. Seyyid Mustafa described the reaction of the people to the teachings of the school. It was then for the first time, he said,

---

[9] Âsım, *Tarih* (Istanbul, 1865), I, 375.

[10] His book was written in French; Seyyid Mustafa, *Diatribe de l'engénieur sur l'état actuel de l'art militaire, du génie et des sciences à Constantinople* (Istanbul, 1803). Reprinted in Paris in 1807 and 1810.

that the ignorant people had heard these public lessons in mathematics and saw the geometricians work in open assembly; the voice of lack of skill and ignorance arose from all sides; we were molested, almost persecuted; people screamed at us saying, 'Why do they draw these lines on the paper? What advantage do they think they are getting from them? War is not waged by compass and ruler', and we were overwhelmed by a thousand other words like these.

In spite of such reactions, he noted, it was possible, thanks to Selim's patronage and active interest, to apply modern mathematics to the arts of war and to develop knowledge and skill in making fortification plans, topographic maps, etc. He believed that the school was a success.

After this Preface, Mustafa made some interesting new comments on the causes of the decline of learning in the East. Once the seat of learning, the East had been surpassed by the scientific and technical advancement of the West, and this technical superiority had given the West military supremacy. Thus, he says, strength and valour were matters of bygone times. According to him, religious fanaticism and superstition were the main bulwarks against progress and innovation. Selim understood this point and his reforms were designed to overcome their inertia. The ruler encountered several difficulties in carrying out his innovations, he resisted these forces and knew how to overcome them; he was compelled to use force to do it. The rest of the book is a description of the military institutions and improvements undertaken by Selim.

We see, as Adıvar says, that "this little book was a good illustration of the enthusiasm felt by the youth of the time which had been created by the introduction of modern science into Turkey at the beginnings of the nineteenth century."[11] L. Langlès, the French orientalist who wrote the Preface to the edition of Seyyid Mustafa's book published in 1807, when Selim was still in power, says:

If we are to judge by the activity and energy that this people has expended to second the prudent and vigorous measures suggested and directed by an ambassador whose military gifts are not inferior to his diplomatic ability, then the brilliant success of these measures, to which the capital of the Ottoman Empire and the Empire itself owe their salvation, suffices to justify our author in the eyes of his

---

[11] Adıvar, *Osmanlı Türklerinde İlim*, p. 187.

compatriots; he proves to them how well founded was his enthusiasm for the arts and sciences of Europe.[12]

80

Another example of the new intellectuals anxious to educate themselves in the institutions of European civilization under the regime of Selim III, and enthusiastic supporters of the reforms, was Mahmoud Rayf (Mahmud Râif).[13] Like Seyyid Mustafa, Râif wrote a book in French to describe the achievements of Turkey in his time. Unlike Seyyid Mustafa, he had been in Europe. He went to London in 1793 as a member of a diplomatic mission. At that time, very few Muslim Turks knew any European language, and, therefore, it was a custom of Turkish diplomacy to attach Greek dragomans to the service of the Turkish representatives abroad. Selim sent young Turks to Europe with his ambassadors, ordering them to learn European languages and get acquainted with European institutions. Mahmud Râif was one of these.

His book—written in French, published in 1797 by the press of the new Mühendishane, and entitled *Tableau des nouveaux règlements de l'empire ottoman*—is interesting for the information it gives about the author, as well as for the information it gives about the Ottoman Empire. Râif's preface tells how he became increasingly interested in European political institutions during his studies in Turkey, how he felt the need to learn a European language in order to widen his knowledge about European affairs, and how he felt frustrated so long as he did not have the chance to visit Europe. It tells how he learned French and studied French books in order to learn about political conditions, financial methods, military institutions, and public law of the European powers.

Mahmud Râif occupied important positions in Selim's administration later on and, like Seyyid Mustafa, was murdered by the Yeniçeris when they rose against Selim's reforms. The Yeniçeris claimed that men like Mahmud Râif intended to dress them like Europeans and to introduce European headgear. In Turkish history he was nicknamed Ingiliz Mahmud (English Mahmud), which shows the attitude of the people towards men who had become somewhat associated with European life.

---

[12] Seyyid Mustafa, *Diatribe de l'engénieur* (Paris, 1807), Preface.

[13] Ihsan Sungu, "Mahmund Râif Efendi ve Eserleri," *Hayat*, I, No. 16 (March 17, 1927), 309-12; also Ahmet H. Tanpınar, *XIX. Asır Türk Edebiyatı Tarihi* (2nd ed.; Istanbul, 1956), I, 22; and Adıvar, *Osmanlı Türklerinde İlim*, pp. 187-88.

The enthusiasm and optimism, but especially the rationalistic attitude towards progress as expressed by Seyyid Mustafa and Mahmud Râif, may explain to us the meaning of the sense of alarm about the spread of French ways of behaviour which had been one of the causes for the reaction against the reforms that Selim had only partially implemented.

Selim seems to have been heedless of the psychological disturbances created among the people by his innovations. There are indications that his ambitions were wider than his achievements. Langlès, writing about 1810, two years after Selim's death, claimed that besides his desire to have a modernized army Selim intended to crush the resistance of the Ulema, and that he wanted to restrict the authority of the Şeyhul-Islâm in order to be an independent enlightened monarch; and finally, that he wished to benefit from the developments which the Europeans had achieved in sciences and arts. In view of the circumstances, it is questionable whether he would have been capable of carrying out these intentions. In spite of the advancement in the views of reform, the traditional state had no established machinery for applying decisions, and little strength to enforce them. The traditional government organization was still intact, and in its corrupt and incompetent version.

But one thing seems to have been certain: the trend which had started from the beginning of the eighteenth century seemed to have reached a turning-point. External conditions were not yet as dangerously complicated as they were going to be very soon. Friends, as well as adversaries, of Turkey were anxiously expecting the launching of genuine reorganization and reforms. The ideas as to what had to be done seemed to have reached a stage of clarity, if not maturity. The existing forces for change and reform were not negligible, as may be seen from the fact that after Selim's downfall, whatever was introduced in the line of reforms, first by Mehmet Ali in Egypt during the first quarter of the nineteenth century and afterwards by Mahmud II in Turkey, was carried through, at least initially, by those men and by the ideas that had been the products of Selim's time and that had been salvaged from the terrific storm of reaction and destruction.

The Fall of the New Order

82

The forces of opposition were enormous; the whole program of reform was swept away in bloodshed and destruction in 1807. A new reaction set in to reign for two decades, not only to banish every element of progress, but also to carry to virtual completion that process of decline brought about by the forces of fanaticism, ignorance and corruption.

Instigated by the Ulema, the Yeniçeris, the *derebeys* and *âyans*, and even by some of Selim's ministers, a mutiny started on May 29, 1807, and led to unprecedented killing, plunder, and devastation. The climax was reached in the accusation that Selim was no longer the defender of Islam, but was under the control of the Frenks.[14]

The despair created by this uprising, is well reflected by Cevdet Paşa's comment:

As it was impossible to administer the state under these conditions, all of those who wanted the well-being of the state, and even those fanatics who thought that the revolution would turn conditions to the better, fell into despair and helplessness.... Several causes, each of which was alone sufficient to destroy a state, then existed in Turkey, and there seemed to be no solution to any of them under normal conditions. It is not unknown to the historian that among the states of the past there have been several that succeeded in surviving great crises, but among them there is none that has ever succeeded in saving itself after having fallen into such fatal and so numerous dangers all existing at the same time.[15]

This judgment does not seem to be groundless in the case of Turkey, as we can safely assume that the end of Selim's reign meant in reality the end of medieval Turkey.

Several factors contributing to the downfall of Selim's reforms have been enumerated by Âsım, the contemporaneous chronicler.[16] Following him, Cevdet Paşa later elaborated on them.[17] Briefly, they were the ruler's personal weakness and lack of determination; the treason of his men; the agitations of the Yeni-

---

[14] For details see Cevdet, *Tarih* (1303), VIII, 129-45.

[15] *Ibid.*, 163, 280.

[16] Âsım, *Tarih*, II, 2-19.

[17] Cevdet, *Tarih* (1303), VIII, 115 ff.

çeris; the distress of the people under the weight of rising prices; the fears and confusion created by the uprisings in both ends of the Empire (in the Balkans, and in Arabia by the Wahhabis), the propaganda created by the French and Russians as well as by Phanariot Greeks; the penetration of French ideas; and the spread of atheism and heresy.

Of these the last two concern us particularly. What was the nature of that French influence—the penetration of French ideas and ways? Did it mean the impact of the ideas of the French Revolution, or, at least, the philosophy of the Enlightenment insofar as that philosophy contributed to the ideas of the French Revolution? And was that philosophy reflected in the atheistic or heretic ideas that Âsım and Cevdet mentioned as being openly expressed, and as being responsible for antireform reaction?

It has been stated that the French Revolution was influential upon the contemporary Muslim peoples in general, and upon those of Turkey in particular, and that the ideas of the Revolution found an echo among the Muslim and Turkish intellectuals.[18] The available documents give no evidence of the penetration of the ideas of the French Revolution. In view of the stage of development of the idea of reform in Turkey towards the end of the eighteenth century, such influence would be almost miraculous.

In their criticism of the French penetration, the appearance of the Frankish manners and ideas, both Âsım and Cevdet spoke rather vaguely.[19] Cevdet, for example, wrote:

In Istanbul appeared many French affairs and several European things which were necessities of civilization. The grandees of the sultanate and too-eager government officials exceeded reasonable limits and initiated French ways in everything. They began to follow European ways, necessarily or unnecessarily.[20]

Neither Âsım nor Cevdet said specifically what they meant by "many" and "several". It seems that they echoed the opinions of those who interpreted all deviations from tradition as denial of

---

[18] Cf. Bernard Lewis, "The Impact of the French Revolution on Turkey," *Cahiers d'histoire mondiale*, I, No. 1 (1953), 106.

[19] Âsım, *Tarih*, I, 62, 374, 375-6.

[20] Cevdet, *Tarih* (1303), VIII, 122-3.

84

the Şeriat. We have no written document showing a favour-able treatment of the ideas of the Revolution by any Turkish or Muslim writer of the time. For this we have to wait until the fourth decade of the nineteenth century. Even then we shall see that these ideas did not seem to have come directly from the ideology of the French Revolution.

It is certain that increasing contacts with Frenchmen did con-tribute to the widening mental outlook, to a better realization that the Western world had superior knowledge, technology, industry and economic power. There was a further relaxation of the hold on traditional beliefs. However, both widening outlook and relaxing traditionalism had started much earlier than the out-break of the French Revolution. The growth of what one might call a materialistic or a deistic spirit was evident from the Tulip Era. Some knowledge of modern European science, mostly as represented by European non-conformists and deists, had come in chiefly through Ibrahim Müteferrika. The difference now was that the change in outlook assumed wider proportions. Now free-thinkers, sceptics, rationalists, men who believed in the supremacy of the modern European sciences, men who were erroneously identified as atheists and followers of Voltaire, presented an additional threat. It would be too much, however, to claim that this implied an ideological impact of the French Revolution.

We find no indication during this period of the existence of the ideas of liberty, equality, fraternity, or of the idea of nationality, represented either by an individual writer, or by an intellectual or political movement, or by any social class. These ideas reached the Christian peoples of the Empire, but even that came at a later time. It is true that the traditional ideas, which were the complete opposites of those principles of the revolutionary ideology, were in the process of breaking down one by one, but new ideas to take their places were far from being accepted.

Before the penetration of revolutionary ideas into the field of the Turkish reformists, further steps were required to prepare a receptive ground for them, and they had to be taken by the very authority against which these ideas were to turn, as will be seen later when we pass over to the following period of reforms.

If the French Revolution had any impact on the reforms of Selim, this was not to their good, but to their detriment. The Revolution was indirectly responsible for the downfall of Selim's reforms by sharpening and accelerating international rivalries between the great powers of Europe and by leading to a policy of invasion, or of partition of the Ottoman territories.[21] The Napoleonic expedition to Egypt had given the chance to the conservatives in Turkey to revive the custom of identifying the reformists with French perfidy. The reform movement came to an impasse and remained in abeyance for about a quarter of a century.

[21] On the details of French-Turkish relations see E. de Marcère, *Une Ambassade à Constantinople, la politique orientale de la révolution française* (2 vols.; Paris, 1927). See T. J. Djuvara, *Cent projets de partage de la Turquie* (Paris, 1914), for a history of France's designs on Ottoman territories.

THE BREAK-THROUGH 1826-78

Foundations of a Secular State | *chapter 4*

AFTER ITS BETRAYAL and downfall in 1807, the New Order was revived by the forces that had brought about its birth, only to suffer a mortal blow in 1809. Reformism then lay dormant until 1826 while Ottoman sovereignty itself lay in the balance. Never during these seventeen years were the reformers to manifest the attitudes of Selim's time—these found expression, received their accolades, and met their test only in Mehmet Ali's Egypt.

The absence of an attitude of reform did not mean that changes having implications for reform did not occur. On the contrary, the events of two decades preceding 1826 evoked and compelled changes having far greater portent for the future than all the previous reform efforts combined.

The changes of this interim period as well as the succeeding era of reform were shaped and directed with reference to four constellations of events: (1) the obviously final, hence, desperate drive of the Yeniçeris to establish themselves as the supreme political power; (2) the intensified drive of the *derebeys* to realize full hereditary independence from the central rule; (3) the rise of national-separatist movements as an indirect result of Western economic penetration; and (4) the internal transformation and realignment of forces in the West as a result of the War of 1812, the defeat of Napoleon, the Industrial Revolution, and, particularly, the development of steam navigation.

Antipathetic as each of these constellations was to Ottoman sovereignty, paradoxically, they did not achieve what had been seen as imminent in Europe since the middle of the eighteenth century, viz, the dissolution of the Empire. On the contrary, they served the creation of a new Ottoman Empire, smaller than the old to be sure, but capable of withstanding increasing adversity for yet another century. When Mahmud II, ruler from 1808-39, raised the standard of reform dramatically in 1826, it bore a new aspect. It displayed that radical design, unmistakably Mahmud's own, that was to distinguish Turkish reformism.

90

The most significant aspect of the innovations initiated by Mahmud II was the emergence of the idea of an Ottoman state, composed of peoples of diverse nationalities and religions, based on secular principles of sovereignty as contrasted with the medieval concept of an Islamic empire. The real beginning of modernization and secularization was in this change. We shall trace from this chapter on the process of gradual separation between state and religion—and the rise of a worldly-religious dichotomy in various institutions.

The Curtain Closes on the Medieval System

The most propitious development within Turkey between 1809 and 1826 was the transformation of the Ottoman ruling institution into something different from anything that had existed before. God-given authority of the Padişah was for the first time subjected to a written document by a pact dictated by the Yeniçeris upon Selim's fall.[1]

The Yeniçeri dictatorship lasted less than a year. Those men of the New Order who had managed to escape massacre enthroned the youthful Mahmud, the only Ottoman heir to survive deaths and depositions. They invited the *derebeys* and other orders to an unprecedented meeting, the Meclis-i Meşveret (Consultative Assembly).[2] After what the chroniclers tell us was a lively discussion, it was decided to draw up an *ittifak* (pact or alliance) between the ruling institution and the *derebeys*.

Although the *ittifak* remained on paper, it represented an important step in legal-political development. It was an attempt

[1] The text of this document, called the *şer'î hüccet,* is given in Âsım, *Tarih* (Istanbul, 1865), II, 46-49; also, Cevdet, *Tarih* (Istanbul, 1292), IX, 332-39.

[2] The names are given by the chroniclers Âsım and Cevdet. See Âsım, *Tarih,* II, 49; Cevdet, *Tarih,* IX, 3-7, 338-39.

to establish in clear terms the respective responsibilities and mutual demands of the estates of the realm.

There was, however, a bewildering lack of uniformity in the terms used for the principals to the pact. Although the chroniclers mention only the ruler and the *derebeys* as being party thereto, the Yeniçeris and the Ulema were made subject to it from the very first article. The pact contained the germ of the idea of separating the government from the ruler. Certainly no one questioned that all owed allegiance to the Padişah, but every precaution was taken to prevent the Sadrazam and the Şeyhul-Islâm from deviating from the kanûn and Şeriat.

The project was placed before the ruler, the *derebeys*, and the Yeniçeris; the commoners were not involved. Only four of the *derebeys* signed. The remainder of those coming to the capital left for the security of their bailiwicks as soon as they saw the way the wind was blowing. Bent initially upon the abolition of the Yeniçeris, they had no intention of surrendering their own prerogatives or of submitting to legal controls their exactions from the people, Muslim as well as non-Muslim. As they represented neither the people nor traditionally legalized seigneurial rights they were more than willing to let matters stand.

The new ruler undertook to create a new type of army, which was nothing but a continuation of Selim's new army. The Yeniçeri corps was to be liquidated peaceably; the treasury would buy up circulating commissions while the Yeniçeris entering the new forces would receive higher pay. This civilized policy detonated a new and mightier rebellion in 1809. For the next seventeen years, the Yeniçeri and the corrupt Ulema reigned supreme once again.

To the intensified feudalization of the medieval Ottoman imperial system were added new movements of religious or national separation. These struck not only on the unintegrated periphery but also at the very birthplace of Islam (Wahhabism) and against the very core of the Ottoman realm. There was also a hiatus in Western support of the Ottoman sovereignty as a bulwark against Russian expansionism. Not only was the house of Osman dismissed as a factor in the future of Europe but also an intense propaganda campaign was carried throughout Europe and America to "be rid of the Turk forever." In 1809, Mahmud II was not even considered when the French and Russian diplomatic advisers speculated on the partition of the Ottoman territories and the creation of empires and states under either French or Russian protection. Mahmud was not only young and inexperienced; he lacked any real might and was surrounded by ignorant and treacherous courtiers.

How then did Mahmud appear upon his death in 1839 as the founder of a new Ottoman state? The plain answer is, Mahmud found a new basis for the Ottoman sovereignty: the people. He threw away his cloak of sacred power with all its trappings and made himself not the defender of the faithful but the enlightener of the Ottoman citizenry. He founded an absolute monarchy supported by a centralized bureaucracy and a state army recruited from among commoners and formed with a new, secular, and progressive orientation.

It was during Mahmud's time of greatest weakness that the idea of an Ottoman nationality composed of all the subjects of the Empire irrespective of their origin, language, and religious affiliation, and the idea of the Padişah as the temporal ruler of the Ottomans began to form. The Yeniçeris had wiped from the minds of the people the last vestiges of awe and respect for their order by failures in wars and by lawlessness. The achievements of Mehmet Ali, the independent governor of Egypt, proved beyond question the potentialities of Selim's projected reforms and convinced everyone that the destruction of the Yeniçeris was a prerequisite of establishing an effective military force. In 1826, two years before steamships appeared in Turkish waters, Mahmud destroyed an institution of five centuries' standing in a few hours of cannonfire.[3] Other changes in the political, administrative, legal, and educational practices followed suit.

Beginnings of a New Era

Mahmud's innovations have yet to be given their due. They were overshadowed in their time by the achievements of Mehmet Ali, which dovetailed with Western observers' preconceived notions of

---

[3] For a brief description see Harold Temperley, *England and the Near East: The Crimea* (London, New York, and Toronto, 1936), pp. 16-20. The original account by Mehmed Esad, *Üss-u Zafer* (Istanbul, 1827); trans. into French by A. P. Caussin de Perceval as *Précis historique de la destruction du corps des Janissaires par le Sultan Mahmoud en 1826* (Paris, 1833). For a detailed account in English see Howard A. Reed, "The Destruction of the Janissaries by Mahmud II in June 1826." (Unpublished doctoral thesis submitted to the Department of Oriental Languages and Literatures, Princeton University, June 1951).

how to reform an unenlightened society. They have been pushed into the background by concentration upon the reforms of the following Tanzimat period. The harvesters of Mahmud's sowings, in the Tanzimat period and even until the present day, have reaped the credit owing to this daring iconoclast. It has been claimed that Mahmud's reforms were devoid of plan. With the striking exception of DeKay, the American observer, foreign observers criticized Mahmud's reforms, especially those which tampered with the quaint and exotic.[4]

Reformers like Mahmud are confronted by the need to make people want to change and to make them believe that change is possible and desirable. This is a task sometimes a thousand times more formidable than that of drafting consistent programs. If we realize this, what must interest us more than the planlessness of Mahmud's innovations is their overall consistency when cast in terms of the analytical view which came into being only decades after Mahmud's death. A thorough examination of his reform period would throw much light on the course of the Turkish transformation and the developments in subsequent periods. We shall survey only those of his acts that indicated a definitive turn in the course towards secularization and Westernization.

It was in Mahmud's time that the idea of a purposeful change for the improvement of society began to form. In initiating this, he opened the window to the West for all to see, and he did not hesitate to challenge tradition openly. Moreover, by the practices which he established, the Padişah became an enlightened monarch whose primary concern was not to maintain the traditional order

---

[4] See James E. DeKay, *Sketches of Turkey in 1831 and 1832* (New York, 1833), pp. 155-56, 232 ff., 241, 433-35, 490-91; Ed. Engelhardt, *La Turquie et le Tanzimat* (Paris, 1882), I, 16-33; Marshal Marmont, *The Present State of the Turkish Empire*, trans. Frederic Smith (London, 1839), pp. 91 ff.; Adolphus Slade, *Records of Travels in Turkey, Greece &c. in the Years 1829, 1830 and 1831* (London, 1833), I, especially pp. 208 ff. Slade, who was a naval officer in the Turkish navy, wrote: "Had Mahmud II entrusted the government of the provinces to the derebeys and strengthened the authority of the ayans, he would have truly reformed his empire, by restoring it to its brightest state, have gained the love of his subjects, and the applauses of humanity. By the contrary proceeding, subverting two bulwarks (though dilapidated) of national prosperity — a provincial nobility and magistracy — he has shown himself a selfish tyrant . . ." (p. 220). For a relatively objective modern account of the reforms initiated by Mahmud see F. E. Bailey, *British Policy and the Turkish Reform Movement* (Cambridge, Mass., 1942), pp. 30 ff.

94

but to ameliorate, while changing, the conditions of his subjects. Mahmud found the support for his sovereignty in none of the traditional orders of the society, but among the people. Mahmud not only appeared before the people but also mixed with them. He became a popular figure and model for emulation. From his dress to his mode of travel and entertainment he ceased to be a symbol of the sacred tradition and became the symbol of the unfamiliar and unaccustomed. His language conveyed the idea that he was restricting his absolute rights and granting rights to the people.[5]

There could not have been any trace of the idea of a democratic regime in Mahmud's mind, but he popularized two ideas that were bound to bring forth the doctrines of government by law and equality before the law irrespective of race, creed, or position. Sometimes typified as the "infidel Padişah" (especially in near contemporary Western writings), Mahmud was accorded the attribute title Adlî which, we believe, epitomizes his role in the Turkish transformation. The title as well as the role can be understood best through a comparison of the three legal concepts of Şeriat, kanûn, and *adâlet* (justice).

The Şeriat was believed to be beyond the power of human enactment or codification and was identified as the basic law of the traditional system of life. While tolerant of the existence of religious communities other than the Muslim, the Şeriat could not admit of their equality in matters over which it ruled. The kanûns were enactments of edicts dealing with matters regarded as being outside the realm of the Şeriat and were promulgated on the theory recognizing as legitimate the exercise of the "will" of the ruled as the Caliph of the Muslims. The concept of kanûn did not imply legal equality among Muslims and non-Muslims.

In the medieval system, justice meant to give each his due in the interests of order and stability; it did not mean equality before a common law. Mahmud brought the concept of *adâlet* to the field of legal enactments where it meant the promulgation and juridical execution of rules outside (and later superseding) the "will" of

---

[5] See Temperley, *The Crimea*, pp. 40-41. For similar statements by Mahmud see Engelhardt, *La Turquie*, I, 33; Mehmed Galip and Ali Rıza, "On Üçüncü Asr-ı Hicrîde Osmanlı Ricâli," *Peyam-ı Sabah* (Nov. 8, 1920), quoted by Reşat Kaynar, *Mustafa Reşit Paşa ve Tanzimat* (Ankara, 1954), p. 100; Charles Pertusier, *Picturesque Promenades in and near Constantinople and on the Waters of the Bosphorus*, English trans. (London, 1820), p. 107.

the ruler, as ruler and as Caliph, and outside the Şeriat. He used the word *adl* in a number of the institutions he established; the most important was the Divân-ı Ahkâm-ı Adliye (Council of Juridical Enactments) whose work will be noted later.

This, then, represented the embryo of a concept of justice different from those in the Şeriat and kanûn, in the sense of implicit (later explicit) recognition of a source of legislation in addition to and different from God and the ruler. Such a concept was incompatible with the fundamentals of the medieval form of political organization. In the popular title Adlî, one senses not only the secularization of the rulership (the subordination of the attribute of caliphate) but also the disallowance of legal and civil divisions among the medieval orders of society, that is, the introduction of a process of democratization.

The attitude implied in the new concepts of justice was bound to effect a series of modifications in the conceptions of the religious and temporal among both the Muslims and non-Muslims and, eventually, the abolition of certain legally established medieval practices. The period of reform opened by Mahmud thus demanded a new conception of society. The subsequent periods reflected misunderstandings of the implications of the new concept and also the difficulties in implementing the necessary changes. Above all, they posed the central question of laying down the base of emerging public law in terms of a modern state founded among men of different creeds as citizens of a common political community.

In the latter part of Mahmud's reign we see only the beginnings of the problems arising from the implementation of the new concept. Two factors, foreign intervention on the one hand, and the emergence of nationalism among the *millet* communities on the other, emerged gradually to limit the implementation of the new concept.

The implications of Mahmud's utterances concerning the equality of Muslims and non-Muslims before the laws of his administration may be illustrated by his administrative measures as well as by the difficulties in harmonizing these measures and their underlying principles with the measures attempted within the field of education, as we shall see later.

We can infer from certain diplomatic events, from Mahmud's particular relations with the non-Muslim communities, and from his favouring of the Greeks, Armenians, and Jews who cooperated with him in the regime he had set out to build, that Mahmud wanted to abolish the *millet* divisions in accordance

96

with his concept of equality.[6] Events showed, however, that the *millet* was no longer a traditional institution which was a combined product of the Islamic and Christian medieval conceptions, nor was it a question of internal policy.[7] Two great contending forces (the Western powers and Russia) had become intensely interested in the question not only in respect to their relations with the Ottoman Empire but also in respect to their relations with each other on every front. Furthermore, both religion (Catholicism and Orthodoxy) and race or nationality (in consequence of the French Revolution and the rise of Russian pan-Slavism) had become complicating factors. And there was a third factor newly entering upon the scene—the emerging British Near Eastern diplomacy with its Protestant colouring as personified in the ambassador Stratford Canning. The *millet* system began to emerge in international diplomacy as an inviolate system that was no longer a unilateral grant of status and privileges to the non-Muslim communities; they were seen as having acquired rights as *nationalities* guaranteed by the protection of the Christian powers of Europe.[8]

All of the difficulties to be encountered by the new conception of justice and equality would stem from the transformation of an originally medieval institution into a question of nationalities that had become a prime stepping stone of modern European diplomacy in the Near East. These powers, although rival to each other, would resist any attempt to deprive them of their assumed "right of protection" over the Orthodox, Catholic, or Protestant *millets*. From Mahmud's time until the end of World War I, reforms had to be forwarded in the knowledge that the *millet* system was an immovable obstacle and a cause of failure to attempts at secular reform.

To Mahmud goes the credit for overcoming the Muslim resistance to new principles and for silencing the Ulema outside of their

---

[6] See Arnold J. Toynbee, *A Study of History* (London, 1954), VIII, 184 ff., for a brief description of the organization, administration, and politics of this regime in the Ottoman state.

[7] John Reid, *Turkey and the Turks: Being the Present State of the Ottoman Empire* (London, 1840), p. 75.

[8] On the problems of the non-Muslim communities in the politics of the Ottoman Empire see Engelhardt, *La Turquie*, I, 53-65, 143-51, 179-86; II, 57-86. The best survey of the *millets* in the nineteenth century is in A. Ubicini, *Lettres sur la Turquie* (2nd ed.; Paris, 1854), II, English trans. Lady Easthope, *Letters on Turkey* (2 vol.; London, 1856), II.

allotted zone. His impress continued well beyond his death until foreign intervention with religious implications forced the Ulema to come out and enter the political arena once again. In contrast with the Ulema, who were barred from politics, we find during Mahmud's reform era, the patriarchs intriguing in politics, and the Catholic and Protestant churches in the very midst of diplomacy.

97

The new form of the *millet* system had a number of consequences for reform, such as those in the field of education and in matters of concern to the Muslims alone. It led Mahmud to make a distinction between worldly and religious affairs. He excluded the latter from the area of reform and established no council to advise him on religious affairs. This contributed to the difficulties when the boundaries between the two areas became obscured by the logic of the reform efforts.

Foundations of a New State

In 1834 Mahmud laid the foundations for a new governmental administration which has become identified with the Tanzimat. He turned away from the previous governmental organization and created the Porte, which became known to European diplomacy as the centre of government and as ascendent over the court in political and administrative affairs.

Mahmud is renowned for abolishing the Yeniçeri military institution. That he also abolished another pillar of the traditional system has been recognized seldom. Two personages stood above all other temporal and religious officeholders in the traditional system: the Sadrazam and the Şeyhul-Islâm. These represented two supreme institutions, one executive (administrative and judicial) and the other consultative or interpretative (in terms of the Şeriat as well as the kanûn; they represented the ruler's dual functions as Sultan-Caliph. Mahmud put an end to this system by first abolishing the office of Sadrazam as the "absolute vicar" of the ruler.[9] In place of the Sadrazam, he appointed a *başvekil* (chief minister) and *vekils* (ministers) to departments of government on the basis of a new division of labour and powers. As many of the Sadrazam's prerogatives were given over to the new ministers, the new chief

---

[9] The term Sadrazam was restored later, but it no longer denoted the old office.

ministry became simply a co-ordinating agency and a link between the government and the ruler.

The ministries or departments became quasi-autonomous offices for internal, external, financial, educational, commercial, agricultural, and industrial affairs. However, the differentiation of functions was not completed in Mahmud's lifetime. The last four services, for example, came within the administration of a consultative council called the Meclis-i Umur-u Nafia (Board of Useful Affairs). The established ministries had advisory councils whose tasks were to draft reports and plans and to write up decisions for promulgation by the ruler.

The status of the Şeyhul-Islâm's office underwent change also. It was pushed outside the realm of temporal government. Equating the office of the Şeyhul-Islâm with the *millet* organizations, Mahmud relegated matters of concern to it to the "religious realm" and, hence, outside the scope of reform activity. Henceforth, we shall watch with interest changes in the functions of this office.

One measure adopted under Mahmud decided for some time to come the shape of a number of problems. When the office of Sadrazam was abolished, those courts (later designated as *şeriat* courts) that had been under the jurisdiction of the Sadrazam through two chief justices (called Kadıasker) represented in the traditional Divan, the Supreme Council of the Vizirs, were given over to the jurisdiction of the Şeyhul-Islâm (1837). Thus, the latter's office, which was originally only for interpretation and consultation on religious-legal matters concerning temporal affairs, became the highest office of the judiciary regarded as "religious" and having jurisdiction only over Muslims, and believed to remain beyond the scope of reform.

On the other hand, Mahmud established a council to consider legal and judicial matters specifically outside of the realm of the Şeriat. The one achievement of this body in Mahmud's time marked an important step in Turkish legal thought. Mahmud promulgated in 1838 what are known erroneously as the first Turkish penal codes.[10] In fact, these represented the first attempt to establish a public law outside the Şeriat. These codes defined the responsibilities of government officials and judges and the proceedings to be taken against men of state shown by investigation to be in dereliction of their duties. Heavy penalties were prescribed for

98

[10] Hıfzı Veldet, "Kanunlaştırma Hareketleri ve Tanzimat," *Tanzimat* (Instanbul, 1940), I, 170. See also Kaynar, *Mustafa Reşit Paşa*, pp. 295-301, for the text.

cases of bribery and other forms of corruption. The code concerning judges marked the first step in limiting the realm of the Şeriat.

The very idea that men of state were in some way publicly responsible and, therefore, subject to the provisions of law rather than to the arbitrary will of the ruler was so novel as not to appeal to the very public that the code sought to safeguard. It was, however, a direct precursor of Mahmud's later attempts to change the concept of administration from that of government to that of public service.

We must not pass over these earliest instances of codification without noting a point that we shall encounter again in the era of codification, the Tanzimat. Customary concepts and procedures persisted. Thus, these codes manifested certain formal and substantive aspects of the Şeriat and kanûn. For example, punishments remained undetermined; that is, great scope was left to the discretion of the judge, who acted according to an interpretation of the Şeriat or as the delegate of the ruler. Sentence was passed by the judge according to the status of the culprit and in terms of the gravity of his offense. A practice that worked in the medieval system would begin to give way henceforth to another; there would be increasing emphasis on the individual's criminal responsibility, further determination of punishment, greater and greater clarification of the lines of demarcation between criminal and civil, secular and religious, and private and public law.

A New Concept of Education

The innovations discussed above provided an institutional basis for the emerging view that reform and progress were continuing processes to be directed through the exercise of specialized competencies. Governmental and administrative changes pointed up the role of education in reform and the need for a new concept of education. The traditional concepts of knowledge and learning and of the institutions of education were approached in a new way only in Mahmud's time. The idea of *maârif*, that is, the process of becoming acquainted with things unknown, sprang up to challenge the traditional lore (*'ilm*) of the Ulema.

The learning acquired in the *medreses* had long since ceased to have any relevance for industrial and technological life. It consisted of *'ilm*, that is, the acquiring of knowledge pertaining to God, to man's duties to Him, and to the relationships among men in terms of those duties. Therefore, when the new learning came in the eighteenth century, it had not been called *'ilm*. It was called *fen*, which meant "art" or "practical skill"; and the scientist was never called an *âlim* or "learned man," but a *mütefennin*, a "jack-of-all-trades." Traditionally, *'ilm* was the monopoly of a class of people who constituted an order. It was not open to all. So long as the Ulema held a monopoly on the interpretation of matters pertaining to life-and-afterlife, the people could remain ignorant and without need of literacy.

We can imagine how discouraging widespread illiteracy was in an age of innovation accompanied by the sudden disappearance of certain fundamental institutions. The great danger of having masses of people dependent upon the spoken word seems to have come to the fore suddenly when things had to be done, not according to routine tradition, but according to unfamiliar and foreign rules.

The novelty in educational thinking may be illustrated better by contrasting it with the situation in the eighteenth century and with a document dating from the period of Mahmud's reign preceding the destruction of the Yeniçeris. Education had not become a part of the reform projects when the earliest new schools of higher learning were opened. These schools were founded with the view that they had nothing to do with the educational system as a whole. Education in the sense of schooling was a "religious" matter; the new schools were thought of only as a means of teaching certain skills, primarily for military purposes. Consequently, no institutions were founded in which to prepare students in the alphabet of modern science; there arose the strange situation of teaching engineering students such elementary subjects as writing, composition, Arabic, French, elementary arithmetic, etc.

Modern Turkish educational historians like to point out that Mahmud issued a decree making primary education compulsory in 1824. Leaving aside among other things the question of the impossibility of implementing such a decree under existing conditions, one may see very readily the unworldly and unpragmatic concepts underlying this seemingly modern attempt. One slightly abbreviated passage of the decree reads:

While, according to Muslims, learning the requisites of religion comes first and above everything else and while these requisites take precedence over all worldly considerations, the majority of people lately avoid sending their children to school and prefer to give them to a trade as novices to artisans when they reach the age of five or six because of their ambition to earn money immediately. This condition is the cause not only of widespread illiteracy but also of ignorance of religion and, hence, has been a primary cause of our misfortune. As it is necessary to deliver the Muslims from these worldly and other-worldly misfortunes, and as it is a religious obligation for the entire *ümmet* of Muhammed, irrespective of trade or occupation, to learn the affairs of religion and the faith of Islam, no man henceforth shall prevent his children from attending school until they have reached the age of adulthood.[11]

101

"As for the schoolmasters," the decree continued, "they shall instruct their pupils carefully and, following the teaching of the Glorious Kur'an they shall educate them in the faith and obligations of Islam. . . ."

This idea of popular education was not very different from that in contemporary Europe. It was deemed adequate for children to read by rote, to ape the teacher's recital of the Kur'an in Arabic, to know the beliefs and ritual obligations of Islam, and to write a bare smattering of Turkish. The view was in complete contradiction with the idea of education as a means of progress.

The traditional view of primary education persisted even when a new concept began to emerge and certain objective conditions led the reformers to approach in a roundabout way the problem of creating a new educational base to society, through the military channel. Before discussing this as a very significant offshoot of a contemporary development in the West, let us look closely at the major factor causing a split or bifurcation of the new educational outlook from its very inception.

When Mahmud excluded the office of the Şeyhul-Islâm from his projected reforms and gave the administration of the Şeriat to this functionary, he was also forced to exclude Muslim primary education from the "temporal" realm. In doing so, he was merely reaffirming the idea that primary education was a communal and religious matter of no concern to the state. However, under the pressure of new needs, he undertook two measures that were consistent with the new view of education. One was aimed at the enlightenment of the adult public for the purpose of leading it to accept change. We shall return to examples later. The second, the

[11] The full text of the decree is given by Cevdet, *Tarih* (1302), XII, 277-79.

most arresting though least known educational development in nineteenth-century Turkey, was directly related to the building up of the new army.

The destruction of the Yeniçeris was followed by the idea of opening a school for the training of officers. However, this was not done immediately. Instead of recruiting traditionally educated boys as officer candidates (as Mehmet Ali did in Egypt), Mahmud established training units within the military corps. Mature soldiers, corporals and sergeants with some prior schooling or proof of a special aptitude, were assigned to teaching companies (*mektep bölü-kleri*).[12] Most of the outstanding officers of the next generation received their first formal instruction in these special training units. While this form of officer training was the only kind in existence, a noisy controversy among the Christians of Istanbul drew the attention of the Turkish military authorities to an educational innovation ideally suited to their situation.

In 1831, Turkey was touched by the first intercontinental movement of popular education in modern history. At the turn of the nineteenth century, not only the indigent but even the lower middle class children in England could obtain formal primary education only in the church schools or schools for the poor. The educational principle underlying both of these was not different from that in the traditional schools of Turkey. While nonconformists opposed the catechetical emphasis of the free schools, they too, in the main, held the teaching of religion as the primary justification for popular education. The fear that too much learning would breed radicalism and social discontent was far from conquered in spite of the active reformers of the time. Except for Robert Owen, the first person to give concrete educational expression to the secular and democratic tendencies of the time was Joseph Lancaster (1778-1838), a Quaker of modest origins.[13] It was he who solved the problem of teaching the masses the rudiments of modern primary education and utilized the school as a training ground for responsible citizenship, the exercise of democratic liberties, mass enlightenment and cultivation, and popular secondary education. Although challenged at home by the upholders of tradition, Lancaster's monitorial system attracted attention wherever secular democratic movements were strong.

---

[12] Mehmed Esad, *Mir'at-ı Mekteb-i Harbiye* (Istanbul, 1894), pp. 8 ff.

[13] J. G. Fitch, "Joseph Lancaster," *Dictionary of National Biography*, (1892), XXXII, 39-42 and the articles referred to therein.

Curiously, the monitorial system attracted particular attention
in the Near East.[14] It was carried from the United States and Malta
to the Ionian Islands by the American missionaries during the
Greek War for Independence. The Greek nationalists were attracted by its potentialities for popularizing education at low cost
with the limited number of teachers available.[15] By 1831, Lancasterian schools were popular among the Greeks of Istanbul and had
begun to attract the attention of Armenians, who had also begun
to imbibe of the fountain of nationalism. As did the Church of
England and the Church of Rome, so the Greek and Armenian
patriarchs looked disapprovingly upon primary schools that did
not inculcate dogma or religious discipline, but the matter took
quite a sharp turn with the arrival in 1831 of the first American
Protestant missionary in Istanbul, William Goodell. He opened
a Lancasterian school for Greek boys; the next year he opened
what appears to have been the first such school for Greek girls.[16]
It was this which precipitated the controversy referred to above.

Opposition to the new schools and, more particularly, to the
Protestant threat spread rapidly among both Greek and Armenian
clergymen. The Greek synod threatened in 1832 to anathematize
all who supported the school for girls, and in 1834 the priests
demanded the complete abolition of the Lancasterian schools.

The monitorial system made its impact upon the Turkish
authorities from quite a different direction.

---

[14] DeKay, *Sketches of Turkey*, p. 489, says that Osman ('Uthman Ef.
Nur-addin) opened Lancasterian schools in Egypt under Mehmet
Ali on his return from Europe in 1817. Heyworth-Dunne, on the
other hand, found no such evidence. Mehmet Ali did receive literature from the half-missionary, half-liberal society which took up
the Lancasterian cause and employed a monitorial system in his
military school for the lack of qualified teachers, but he never became interested in a general educational revival and prohibited
private efforts to open non-sectarian Lancasterian schools. See
J. Heyworth-Dunne, *An Introduction to the History of Education
in Modern Egypt* (London, 1939), pp. 113 n. 3, 117, 152 ff., 234-35,
281-82, and 413. William Allen, the disaffected partner of Owen,
patron of Lancaster, and missionary of non-sectarian religious education, reports that he told several people about the Lancastrian
schools during his visits to Istanbul and Izmir in 1819. See W.
Allen, *Life of William Allen with Selections from his Correspondence* (London, 1847), II, 98-102.

[15] DeKay, *Sketches of Turkey*, pp. 287-88.

[16] William Goodell, *Memoirs, or Forty Years in the Turkish Empire*,
ed. E. D. G. Prime (New York, 1876), pp. 143, 165.

104

> Amidst the . . . controversy among the Greeks and the Armenians [August 1832], almost unexpectedly there sprang up a desire on the part of the Turks to have schools for the benefit of their own children, a few enlightened men taking the lead, and taking also the responsibility, which was not light. At an examination of the [Greek] school at Arnaut Keuy . . . several Mussulmans were present, among whom was a bin-bashy [major] and an on-bin-bashy [colonel]. . . . They are determined to have a school among the Mussulmans, and have already selected a house . . . and prepared seats, with the knowledge of the Sultan. . . . This project was fully carried out. One school for Turkish children was established at Beshik-Tash and another at Scutari. . . .[17]

It was Mahmud's men who hit upon the conversion of the Lancasterian system to an entirely new purpose: adult education within a professional organization for the furtherance of that organization. This idea was neither inherent in, nor did it ever appear significantly in, the main channel of the Lancasterian movement. Goodell, who played a role in the implementation of the idea, never seems to have noted its existence or significance for he makes no distinction between the schools for children opened through the initiative of military men and the barracks schools for soldiers and officer candidates. As the first-hand accounts of Goodell and Marshal Marmont show, the new project was pushed with energy between 1832 and 1834.[18] The content of the Lancasterian program was expanded to meet the needs not only of primary education among the soldiers but also of preparatory and professional education among the officer candidates.

This development shows that the heads of the *millets* were no less opposed to secularizing influences than the most conservative Ulema, that dissatisfaction with the traditional Muslim primary education was expressed openly in action supported by the ruler, and that it resulted in the establishment of Muslim primary schools divorced from the *medrese*, that is, outside the sphere of "religious" affairs. The entire experiment was proof for the Muslims that literacy training had "worldly" implications; it showed the benefits of educational continuity from the pre-literate level through professional education. It marked the rise of a non-traditional group capable of examining the content, aims, and methodology of Muslim primary education critically.

---

[17] *Ibid.*, p. 143.

[18] Marmont, *State of the Turkish Empire*, pp. 78-79. See also Esad, *Mir'at-ı Mekteb-i Harbiye*, pp. 8-12.

We shall return later to the manifold implications of the experiment for the future of Turkey. Here we must note the impact of military developments upon civilian affairs and the dissipation of that impact before the persistence of the *millet* system.

These developments provided a milieu congenial at last to a new decree concerning primary education. We find what may well have been the substance of the view of the new era of education in a report prepared by the Board of Useful Affairs in 1838. In resumé, the report stated:

All arts and trades are products of science. Religious knowledge serve salvation in the world to come, but science serves perfection of man in this world. Astronomy, for example, serves the progress of navigation and the development of commerce. The mathematical sciences lead to the orderly conduct of warfare as well as military administration. Innumerable new and useful inventions, like the use of steam, came into existence in this manner. Several new facilities exist in the arts and trades thanks to the growth and spread of the known sciences and the rise of several new sciences. Through science one man can now do the work of a hundred. Trade and profit have become difficult in countries where the people are ignorant of these sciences. Without science, the people cannot know the meaning of love for the state and fatherland (*vatan*). It is evident that the acquisition of science and skill comes above all other aims and aspirations of a state. The Ottoman commonwealth had schools and scholars, but they disappeared. Later, military, naval, engineering, and medical schools were opened with great effort, but the students entering these schools lacked even ordinary knowledge for the proper reading of Turkish books. This was because of the defectiveness of the primary schools. In discussing every project for the recovery of agriculture, commerce, and industry, the Board has found that nothing can be done without the acquisition of science and that the means of acquiring science and remedying education lie in giving a new order to the schools.[19]

This document was anti-traditional to a degree almost beyond belief. Not until the twentieth century were such ideas to be expressed again.

Having come to the conclusion that primary education was a "worldly" affair, the Board of Useful Affairs could see itself competent to make recommendations for reforms. Having submitted

---

[19] The full text in *Takvim-i Vekayi* (Dhu'l-Qa'da 21, 1254 H./A.D. 1839); reprinted in Mahmud Cevad, *Maarif-i Umumiye Nezareti Tarihçe-i Teşkilât ve İcraatı* (Istanbul, 1922), pp 6-10.

its report, however, this body discovered that it lacked the authority to prepare a decree for the establishment of a secular-national primary education. The report shuttled back and forth and was sent to the Şeyhul-Islâm for suggestions. All idea of reforming primary education was killed in the process; the discussions bogged down on the ways and means of teaching the Kur'an and the other traditional subjects. In the long run, while the Turkish military pursued an independent, autonomous, and progressive course, civilian primary education continued to be a communal and religious affair until the downfall of the Ottoman Empire.

Bifurcation in Education

The only decision emerging from the discussions on primary education was to appoint one of the Ulema as the director of primary and secondary education. The persistent confusion, or lack of orientation, over the boundaries of the "worldly realm" is shown by the fact that Mahmud passed the recommendation for appointment along to the Şeyhul-Islâm, the matter being considered a "religious" one.

By 1838 the Board of Useful Affairs realized the futility of trying to do anything about primary education and decided on the basis of its original report to open *ruşdiye* schools (for adolescents). Apparently these were conceived of as providing a link between the "religious education" of the primary schools and the "worldly education" of the schools of higher learning.

Actually, no *ruşdiye* schools were opened in Mahmud's time (the first was opened in 1840 and although it is not certain that they were begun on a non-sectarian basis, there were non-sectarian *ruşdiye* schools in later years). Instead, a special school was opened in 1838 or 1839 to educate a limited number of promising boys who had completed primary school for future employment as government functionaries. This was called the Mekteb-i Maarif (School for Secular Learning). Some of the prominent figures of the late Tanzimat era graduated from it. Parallel to this was the Mekteb-i Ulûm-u Edebiye (School of Literary Sciences), principally to train government translators. The students of both schools first studied Arabic grammar, then French; they also studied geography, geometry, history, and political science, but the teach-

ing of these subjects does not appear to have assumed importance
for several years.[20]

The significance of the first school was that it removed yet
another segment of governmental affairs from the monopoly of
the *medrese*. It provided, indirectly, the means for a clearer distinction between the temporal administration and the Şeriat. The
significance of the Mekteb-i Ulûm-u Edebiye was that it made
possible the elimination of the special prerogatives of the traditional dragoman families and thus blocked the channels which
made the private affairs of the Turkish government public knowledge in every European capital. Perhaps another reason for opening
this school was to facilitate the translation of European scientific
works into Turkish; in any case, it had this as its most noteworthy
effect.

In later years, the Board of Useful Affairs confined itself to
matters of commerce and agriculture. In the meantime it made one
last effort to give shape to primary education and to establish a
link between the primary and other levels of education. But the
appointment of one of the Ulema as the director of secondary as
well as primary education threw the linking secondary education
over the wall from the "worldly" to the "religious" realm and may
well account for the delay in opening any *ruşdiye* schools.

The report of Mehmed Esad, the man appointed as director, is
indicative of the lonely path Mahmud was forced to tread in
bringing new aims and conceptions to bear on society. Esad
(1785-1847) was the first editor of the first Turkish newspaper
and one of the most progressive among the Ulema. The report he
submitted on assuming office did not deviate one iota from the
traditional view of primary education: children should be sent to
school around the age of five or six; they should be taught in the
letters of the Arabic alphabet; they should be taught verses and
the short chapters from the Kur'an and certain prayers, all by
heart of course, as they were in Arabic; those children who finish-
ed reading the entire course (*khatm*) should be taught to recite the
Kur'an according to the rules of correct pronunciation (*tajwîd*)
during the second course of reading, and they should memorize
the chapters following the ninety-third chapter of the Kur'an;
children of eight to ten years should be taught the rules of ablution,
prayers, and other religious obligations and rituals; those with
good voice and natural gifts should become *hâfiz*; from among the

107

---

[20] See Ihsan Sungu, "Mekteb-i Maarif-i Adliyyenin Tesisi," *Tarih
Vesikaları*, I, No. 3 (Oct., 1941), 212-25.

108

graduates of the primary schools, those who showed a special aptitude for further education should be accepted in the *ruşdiye* schools to be established. To prepare and pass students on to the *ruşdiye* for later training in the institutions of higher learning remained a subsidiary objective.[21]

Unless Mahmud was prepared to nullify the traditionally sanctioned prerogatives of the Grand Rabbi, the Greek Orthodox patriarch, and the heads of the other recognized *millets* and to withstand the external and internal cries that he was usurping "rights" rather than granting "equality," he could do nothing more than order the non-Muslim religious authorities to take the necessary measures to ensure that all children within the community receive adequate primary education. Failing to abolish the prerogatives of the *millets*, that is, failing to secularize the state entirely, Mahmud could not do more than pass an identical order on to the Şeyhul-Islâm who, unlike his counterparts, possessed no independent power of sanction and no administrative or supervisory machinery for primary education; otherwise Mahmud would have been liable to the charge that he was contravening the Şeriat and depriving Muslims of rights guaranteed to the non-Muslims—that the "infidel Padişah" had made the Muslims inferior to the Rayahs!

One need not speculate upon the effect of any such order. The *millet* heads opposed the liberalization of the school program; the teaching in the schools under their control was at least as dogmatic and obscurantist as that in the Muslim primary schools. Although the Turkish government sought to remain aloof from affairs of a religious nature, it found itself pressed by the *millets* and their foreign protectors to suppress educational and other institutions opened privately by the more enlightened members of the various communities.

Meanwhile, those who ran the *medreses* had long since washed their hands of the worldly new schools. If they heard about the controversies of 1831-32, they concurred with the priests. If they failed to raise an outcry against the primary schools opened by the army men, it was because they were hoarding their small influence with Mahmud to defeat the really "dangerous" reforms, such as the attempt to put sun visors on the soldiers' caps. So firm were they in their control of primary education and, thereby, in the maintenance of the division of worldly and religious realms,

---

[21] The text of Esad's report will be found in Cevad, *Maarif-i Umumiye*, pp. 10 ff.

that they could afford to ignore the deviations of the Christianized army men. We shall see that for almost a full century their complacency was not misplaced.

However, from Mahmud's time onward, the word "religious" acquired a new meaning and connotation. We should not confuse it with either "spiritual" or "ecclesiastical" in the Christian sense, as the point of differentiation rested neither upon the spiritual nor upon the temporal. Theretofore, nothing had been designated as "non-religious"; every department of life contained a mixture of temporal and religious elements and injunctions. But now, the "religious" began to be identified unconsciously with that which is unchanging and, hence, separate from or opposed to that which is changing. The static or traditional was perceived as being "religious", irrespective of its sources of inspiration, while the "changing" and the "new" were understood to be "worldly" or "non-religious" even though the sources may have been partially or wholly religious in nature.

This meant, in terms of education, that many individuals were going to develop a culturally split personality or a personality with a dual culture. The educated man would be a product, on the one hand, of a primary education that remained as the matrix which cast the mold of tradition upon the growing child and, on the other, of an educational system which recognized virtually none of the premises of that tradition. While some became representative of the second to the exclusion of the first, others remained torn between the two, and both were opposed to those who continued upon the course of primary education into the *medreses*, which experienced further loss through the competition of the new schools. The implications of this duality or cultural bifurcation which began in this period will be seen later. Under the Tanzimat, bifurcation as the form of secularism extended to increasing areas of life and created new conflicts of a more intense nature. Furthermore, the old or "religious" appeared incompatible with the new in a number of areas of life; clashes between the two ensued, sometimes on the objective level, sometimes in the inner experiences of men, and sometimes perhaps at the level of the unconscious.

Within the field of education, the rift between the secular and the religious deepened in proportion to the firm establishment of the new education and the degree to which that education proved to be useful. Usefulness remained the chief criterion of the necessity for secular education for a long time, as did the view that modern institutions should be allowed only insofar as they transmitted the techniques and sciences of the West.

Despite the broadening in concept, new education at this stage meant only the acquisition of useful knowledge; a little later it would mean to be "enlightened", and the "educated" as well as the "intellectual" would be designated as the "enlightened" (*münevver*). The part of the culture covered by primary education remained untouched by the forces of social change. Until the rise of a secular approach to primary education following 1908, primary education continued to represent the traditional basis of the culture while higher education represented the new, changing culture as exemplified by the West. Neither fowl nor good red herring, secondary education remained an unstable mixture of the two educational approaches. We can not forget that its beginnings were laid during the reign of Mahmud. On the other hand, the novel forms of public education also inaugurated by Mahmud were to supersede in importance all manner of formal education except, perhaps, that provided in the institutions of higher learning.

Higher Learning for Secularization

In contrast with the persistence of traditionalism in primary education, the steps taken in the field of higher education were radical. The differences between the developments at this time and those in the previous century have been pointed out already. It was in this period that the earlier School of Engineering (the Mühendishane), as well as the other new schools, became firmly and permanently established.

From this time onwards no rival traditional institution possessed enough power to close down the new schools, or even to compete with them. On the contrary, the engineering school, the medical school, and the military academy constantly drained off the potential students of the *medrese*; the *medreses* were finally brought to a position where they had to close their own doors. This was a conspicuous aspect of the secularization trend in Turkey. It can be contrasted with the situation in other Muslim countries. An institution such as, for example, al-Azhar in Egypt is still a powerful institution of traditional learning. In Turkey, on the other hand, even when schools were opened to teach religious subjects after the closing down of the *medreses*, they never became seats of traditional learning. They were auxiliary rather than essential,

experimental rather than traditional in the general framework of
higher education.

The School of Engineering received greater attention after the
disappearance of the traditional military institution. It was the
only existing institution that could be converted readily into one
of higher learning and modern education. A naval engineering
school was separated from the Mühendishane in 1827; it became a
naval academy that has survived until the present day. The number
of students in the main engineering school, which combined civil
and military engineering, increased. Because of the great demand,
even the upper class students were recruited as technical officers
in Mahmud's new army. There were students of forty—even sixty—
years of age in attendance. The teaching was done in Turkish, but
the text books were in French.[22]

It was in 1834 that Mahmud finally opened the Military Academy. The Turkish military now had an entirely new tradition.
Not only had the ties with the Yeniçeri tradition been severed
completely, but the traditional links between the military and the
religious institutions had been broken decisively. In addition to
having a wholly secular base, the new army tradition had evolved
from within; it had not been superimposed by European officers.
Therefore, the Turkish military had roots in the society. From
Mahmud's time until our own, Turkish officers have been in the
vanguard of social, political, intellectual, and educational progress.
Failing to be satisfied with the civilian preparatory schools and
unable to reform them, the military developed an autonomous
system. The military pioneered the simplification of the Turkish
script which led to the adoption of the Latin alphabet, exceeded
all other bodies in mass educational activities, and contributed
some of the outstanding educationalists. One will not fail to note
Mahmud's stamp upon the Turkish officers even after the downfall
of the Empire despite the later association of the military with the
European officer traditions.

Mahmud did send some military students to England, France,
Prussia, and Austria in 1835.[23] It was not until after his death,

---

[22] Mehmed Esad, *Mir'at-ı Mühendishane* (Istanbul, 1896), pp. 46-47.
The school of engineering became entirely civil later on and a
number of military schools, such as the schools of artillery and of
fortification, later branched out from the military engineering
school.

[23] See Cevad, *Maarif-i Umumiye*, p. 4; Esad, *Mir'at-ı Mekteb-i
Harbiye*, p. 19.

however, that French and Prussian teachers were employed in the Military Academy (beginning in 1840).

112

Mahmud acted most radically in founding the modern School of Medicine, which became the institution of higher learning to play the most important role in Turkish intellectual and political life. We can not fail to appreciate the significance of Mahmud's measures if we note the persistence of the practice and belief in the medieval medicine (called *Yunanî*) in some Muslim countries.

Mahmud first attempted to modernize the traditional medical institutions and established a State Medical School, Tıbhane-i Âmire as early as 1827.[24] Either the same year or, more probably, in 1828 or 1829 he founded the Cerrahhane (school of surgery) for the training of surgeons. These institutions were both reorganized in 1831. Younger men with some training in the modern medical sciences and some European physicians were appointed as teachers. Sade de Gallière, a French professor who appears to have been known in Europe for his work as a surgeon in Berlin and St. Petersburg, was employed to reorganize the Cerrahhane. Several general preparatory courses were given as well as courses in anatomy, pathology, surgery, surgical chemistry, and military surgery. Some of the graduates were sent to Europe for study, and some of these became prominent physicians.

Mahmud decided later to follow the European practice of combining the schools of medicine and surgery. Abdül-Hak Molla, a Turkish physician, was directed to reorganize the medical school which was reopened in 1838 under the title Dar-ul Ulûm-u Hikemiye ve Mekteb-i Tibbiye-i Şahane (Imperial School of Physical and Medical Sciences).[25] A young Viennese professor named Karl Ambroso Bernard (1808-44) was given charge of the academic program; he was allowed freedom in organizing the teaching and supervision.[26] He also taught internal medicine and allied subjects and wrote medical works that were translated into Turkish.

[24] On the traditional medical teaching of the *medreses* see S. Ünver, "Osmanlı Tababeti ve Tanzimat Hakkında Yeni Notlar," *Tanzimat* (Istanbul, 1940), I, 944. On *Tıbhane* see Rıza Tahsin, *Mir'at-ı Mekteb-i Tıbbiye* (Istanbul, 1906), I, 4.

[25] For details, see *ibid.*, 13 ff.

[26] Semavi Eyice, "Mekteb-i Tıbbiyenin İlk Müdürü Dr. Bernard'ın Mezarı," *Istanbul Üniversitesi Edebiyat Fakültesi Tarih Dergisi,* II, Nos. 3-4 (1952), 89-96. See also S. Ünver and M. Belger, "Tam bir Asır Evel Istanbul Tıbbiye Mektebinde Avusturyalı bir Muallim-i Evel: Dr. C. A. Bernard," *Tıp Fakültesi Mecmuası*, III (1940), 1420 ff.; N. Uzluk, "Istanbul Tıbbiyesi için Avusturyadan Getirtilen Ilk Hekim," *Dirim* (1937), pp. 203-8.

Mahmud gave a speech at the opening ceremony. It is a fine example of the spirit of his reforms. He said, in part:

I have given precedence to this school because it will be dedicated to a sacred duty—the preservation of human health. . . . The instruction in medicine will be in French. You may ask why this should be in a foreign language. Let me explain the difficulties which enforce this now. . . . It is true that many books were written among us [Muslims] on medical sciences and that the Europeans even learned many things by translating these books into their own languages. The books were written in Arabic however, and, as they ceased to be objects of interest and care in the Muslim schools for many years and as the number of men who knew them decreased, they became obsolete. To go back to these works now and plunge into their study in order to translate the science of medicine into our own language, Turkish, would be a painstaking job actually requiring many years. Having appropriated these works into their own languages, the Europeans have been busy improving upon them for more than a hundred years. In addition, they have facilitated the methods of teaching these subjects greatly and have added their new discoveries. Therefore, the Arabic works seem to me somewhat defective in comparison with these European works on medicine. Even if we claim that these defects can be overcome by borrowing from the new works, still they can not be translated into Turkish quickly because it takes at least ten years to master the Arabic language in addition to five or six years for the study of medicine. And what we need is well-trained doctors for our troops and for our people, on the one hand, and to have the medical sciences incorporated into our own language and our own medical literature codified, on the other. Therefore, my purpose in having you study the French language is not to teach you French as such but that you may learn medicine—and in order to incorporate that science step by step into our own language. Medicine will be taught in Turkish in our land only when this has been done.[27]

113

These words show how far in advance of the eighteenth century Mahmud was. If we remember that men regarded as enlightened even a decade earlier could raise a howl against the attempt of a handful of young men to learn French in order to study modern sciences, we can understand the magnitude of Mahmud's courage. While he was radical enough to insist on the necessity of learning a branch of modern sciences through a European language and from European books and European professors, he had the far-sighted sense of national consciousness to predict that the scientific

[27] The full text is in Tahsin, *Mir'at-ı Mekteb-i Tıbbiye*, I, 18-21.

114

language of the future would not be Arabic—as it was during the pre-modern period—but Turkish, and that carrying on the teaching in French would be only a temporary expedient. His words signalled the ending of the medieval tradition of the *medrese* teaching, carried on mainly in Arabic, and the beginning of efforts towards the creation of scientific Turkish. Although never noticed by any Turkish scholar of the nationalist movement in Turkey, Mahmud's remarks make him a prophet insofar as the importance of language in national revivals is concerned. His wish for the creation of a Turkish medical language and literature proved to be realistic. In less than thirty years (in 1866) Turkish replaced French as the instructional language of the School of Medicine. As the event coincided with the earliest expression of a nationalist movement on the part of the students of the school, we shall return to it later.

Following the opening of the school, Mahmud decreed that all Ottoman subjects, irrespective of religion, could gain admittance.[28] Turkish sources made no mention of non-Muslim students in the early years, but three of the four graduates sent to Vienna in 1846 for further study were non-Muslims—one Armenian and two Catholic Greeks.[29] In 1847, the government was subsidizing completely the education of 314 Muslims and 95 non-Muslims; Charles MacFarlane, who seems to have made quite a careful survey, notes that there were in attendance in that year approximately 300 Turkish, 40 Greek, 29 Armenian, and not more than 15 Jewish students.[30] John Mason, a Protestant medical missionary to the Jews of the Empire, accepts as correct the following explanation for the absence of Jewish students prior to 1847:

> Religious difficulties have, till the present day, prevented the Jewish children from participating in the benefits of the School. . . . The Government, who, from the first, had not excluded them, waited, to no purpose, for five years. At last it took the initiative, in ordering the Jewish community to send thirty-eight children to the college. His Excellency the Hekim-Bashy [Chief Physician] had had several conferences with the Grand Rabbi and the heads of this community; all difficulties have been removed, and the Government has not demurred at any sacrifice, in order to exercise its civilizing influence upon this portion of the subjects of the

[28] *Ibid.*, 22.

[29] Ünver, "Osmanlı Tababeti," 943.

[30] Charles MacFarlane, *Turkey and its Destiny* (Philadelphia, 1850), II, 163, 165.

empire. The Jewish pupils will occupy a separate domicile, under the superintendence of one of their rabbis, whose care will be to see that their religious duties are regularly performed. They will also have a separate refectory. Their food will be prepared by an Israelite, and the necessary flesh will be supplied by a . . . butcher, of their own community. . . . Israelitish physicians issuing from the college will enjoy the same advantages guaranteed to the Mussulman and Christian pupils. They will serve as physicians in the army, or in their own communities, and will receive rank according to their merit.[31]

According to the regulations of the school, the Muslims were to perform prayers in the mosque constructed at the school; the non-Muslims were specifically exempted from this duty.[32] MacFarlane notes that the coexistence of Muslim, Jewish, and Christian students enforced a three-day weekend which disrupted the teaching program, and one may infer from his anecdotes and commentary upon the relations between the Jewish and other students in his time that the introduction of communal differentiation in the school was viewed oddly by the Muslim and Christian students alike.

As Mahmud's anti-traditionalistic spirit was particularly apparent and persistent in the School of Medicine, we may well project our present discussion of it beyond his time. One event of interest is the breaking of a tradition that also existed in the West until the medieval traditions were in the process of breaking down. Believing that dissection and autopsy were against Islam, the Ulema had opposed their introduction into the school with the result that the students were taught from wax models. In 1841 Professor Bernard

---

[31] John Mason, *Three Years in Turkey: The Journal of a Medical Mission to the Jews* (London, 1860), p. 178, quotes the 1847 Commencement report of the School's director, Dr. Spitzer, "an Israelite by birth . . . fallen into scepticism" (*ibid.*, p. 235). In view of the contemporary evidence, Avram Galante, *Küçük Türk Tetebbular* (Istanbul, 1925), I, 163, is clearly wrong when he says that there were no Jewish students in the School until about 1863. Mason notes the arrival in Turkey in 1847-48 of a number of liberal Jewish professionals, especially from Germany. Despite this, the Jewish community appears to have reacted conservatively at each educational juncture, for example with respect to the specialized training of midwives and, as will be seen in the following chapter, in the establishment of the Lycée of Galatasaray; see Galante, *Küçük Türk Tetebbular*, I, 162. (Representatives of the Alliance Israélite noted this conservatism later in the century and instituted corrective measures.)

[32] Tahsin, *Mir'at Mekteb-i Tıbbiye*, I, 24.

116

came to the conclusion that the students could not learn anatomy properly in this way and demanded formal permission to use human corpses. This was given by an imperial decree.[33] In 1847 MacFarlane saw a "good anatomical theatre" and the Muslim students making autopsies without supervision and in a manner suggesting that the experience was no novelty. He asked one of them if this was not contrary to his religion and was taken aback by the response. "He laughed in my face," he writes, "and said, '*Eh! Monsieur ce n'est pas au Galata Sérai*[34] *qu'il faut venir chercher la religion!*'" The corpses were almost all those of Nubian slaves bought upon delivery for 20-25 piastres; the authorities feared that the soldiers would revolt if the bodies of their comrades who had died of cholera were given to the school; Muslims, Christians, Jews—none would offer bodies.[35]

At first, that is before the reorganization under Dr. Bernard, the students were subjected to preparatory general training. In this preparatory period, they were taught Arabic, French, and religious knowledge in addition to Turkish grammar and Persian literature. Arabic continued to be taught during the period of actual medical training. With the reorganization of the school and the decision to carry out teaching in French, the courses in Arabic and religious knowledge were dropped entirely. The students were separated into two groups, those who knew French and those who did not. The latter were given an intensive course in French while the former studied French literature and European history.[36] Thus, French literature took the place of Persian literature, which ceased to be taught. Thus also, it was in the School of Medicine that European history and literature were taught to the Muslims for the first time. MacFarlane's observations in 1847 are a good index of the scientific, cultural, and intellectual role that this was to play.

All the last improved implements of Paris, London, and Vienna, were to be found in the Galata Sérai. There was a small but not bad botanical garden. There was a Natural History museum, with a

---

[33] *Ibid.*, 9; the date of the decree is given as 1838 by Ünver, "Osmanlı Tababeti," p. 941, n. 2, and as 1841 by Osman Şevki Uludağ, "Tanzimat ve Hekimlik," *Tanzimat* (Istanbul, 1940), I, 969.

[34] Or Galatasaray, the name of the building and of the district where the medical school was situated. The school was called this among the people.

[35] MacFarlane, *Turkey and its Destiny*, II, 163, 165.

[36] For details see Tahsin, *Mir'at-ı Mekteb-i Tıbbiye*, I, 7-18.

collection of geological specimens . . . there was a very sufficient
medical library *the books being nearly every one French*. There
was . . . an excellent "Cabinetto Fisico", stocked with electric-
machines, galvanic batteries, hydraulic presses, and nearly every
machine and adjunct necessary to teach, or to experimentalize in
the physical sciences. . . . In a long, airy gallery we found a pretty
good collection of botanical engravings, coloured, and very neatly
executed at Paris and Vienna. . . . There was also a tolerable
chemical laboratory. . . . Among the books in this medical library
there were but too many of *that* period [French Revolutionary], or
of the *philosophismizing* period which immediately preceded it. . . . It
was long since I had seen such a collection of downright materialism.
A young Turk . . . was sitting . . . reading that manual of atheism,
[Baron d'Holbach's] *Système de la Nature*! Another showed his
proficiency . . . by quoting from Diderot's *Jacques le Fataliste*,
and . . . *Le Compère Mathieu*. . . . I saw a few works in German,
and there appeared to be a few translations of English medical
books. . . . *Rapport[s] du Physique et du Morale* [Moral] *de l'Homme*
of Cabaneis [Cabanis] occupied a conspicuous place on the shelves.[37]

Visiting the hospital attached to the military barracks and headed
by a member of an Italian family from Pera who had studied at
Pisa and Florence, MacFarlane found,

His assistants were all young Mussulmans who had studied in the
Galata Sérai. . . . One of them spoke French very well, and had a
decided turn for translation and composition. He had put into choice
Turkish some of the most spicy passages of Voltaire's *Dictionnaire
Philosophique*. A friend . . . asked him what he was doing now.
He was translating Voltaire's "romans", he had already done *Candide*,
which he found very amusing and delightful.

MacFarlane, who seems to have had a particular dislike for the

---

[37] MacFarlane, *Turkey and its Destiny*, II, 163, 167. Baron d'Holbach
(1723-89), one of the Encyclopédistes, defended a secular morality
and education on the basis of a materialistic philosophy expounded
in his major work *Le Système de la nature* (2 vols.; London,
1770), edited by D. Diderot, (Paris, 1821). Pièrre Cabanis (1757-
1808), a professor of medicine at Paris, belonged to the group of
idéologues which included Helvétius, Condorcet, and Mirabeau.
He wrote on education, and anticipated the science of sociology
by his view that moral and social facts should be studied in accordance with the methods of natural science. In his *Rapports du
physique et du moral de l'homme* (2 vols.; Paris, 1802) he discussed the effects of age, sex, and climate upon social institutions.
Both Holbach and Cabanis deviated from Rousseau in their educational views.

French philosophers of the Enlightenment had still another shocking encounter with the Turkish doctors:

118

> I had, at last in this military hospital at Scutari, found something in Turkey upon which I could bestow an almost unqualified praise. Yet I could not leave even this establishment without meeting with evidence of the rapid progress of Gallic philosophism.
>
> We were invited into an elegant saloon, set apart for the use of the doctors and the young Turks their assistants. A book was lying open on the divan. I took it up. It was a copy of a recent Paris edition of the Atheist's manual, *"Système de la Nature"*, with the name of the Baron d'Holbach on the title-page as the author. The volume had evidently been much used; many of the striking passages had been marked, and especially those which mathematically demonstrated the absurdity of believing in the existence of a God and the impossibility of believing in the immortality of the soul. As I laid down the volume one of the Turks said to me, *"C'est un grand ouvrage! C'est un grand philosophe! Il a toujours raison."*[38]

Teaching new scientific subjects in the new schools led in time to the appearance of books written on these subjects, in the form of handbooks and treatises. It seems that the earliest, perhaps best, of the handbooks for students was written by Ishak, a teacher in the Mühendishane. Ishak (d. 1834), known in Turkish sources as the son of a Jewish convert to Islam and described by DeKay as "a worthy Hebrew who had renounced the faith of his fore-fathers,"[39] was in 1823 the second Muslim appointed to the trans-lation office (Tercüme Odası) at the Porte and, in addition to his work as chief translator, was supposed to teach European langu-ages to the young Muslims desirous of such learning. He is be-lieved to have known Arabic, Persian, Greek, Latin, French, and Italian, in addition to Turkish. His work entitled *Mecuma-i Ulûm-u Riyaziye* (Book of Mathematical Sciences) was published in 1831 in four volumes. It was significant not only because it was the first presentation of contemporary mathematical and physical sciences in Turkish but also because of its codification of the new scientific terms in Turkish. Ishak used the holy language of the *medrese*, Arabic, as the basis of his neologisms; this made necessary the studying of Arabic for secular learning. Most of his neologisms,

---

[38] MacFarlane, *Turkey and its Destiny*, II, 181, 184.

[39] DeKay met him when he visited the Mühendishane in 1832; cf. *Sketches of Turkey*, p. 138. Chemistry occupied a limited space in Ishak's work. More advanced and comprehensive books on chemis-try were written after the foundation of the medical school.

coined from Arabic roots, became established in teaching and writing. However, Ishak also introduced some European terms into Turkish, such as *elektrik* (electricity).

Şanizade Ata'ullah locked the door on *Yunanî* medicine and opened the way for works on modern medicine in 1819 with the publication of his *Mi'yar-ul atibba*.[40] Ata'ullah studied in the Suleymaniye medical *medrese* and then in the Mühendishane; he associated himself with Christian physicians who had studied medicine at Padua. Dr. Adnan-Adıvar rates him as the first modern Turkish physician. According to Karl Süssheim, the main portion of *Mi'yar-ul attiba* was translated from a book written by the Viennese professor Baron von Stoerk (published in 1776, 1786, and 1789); Ata'ullah added a section on vaccination on the basis of other European works. He seems to have been an encyclopedic man as he wrote on mathematics, natural sciences, and was the author of a well known *tarih* (history).

Ata'ullah's rival and the first director of the medical school in 1827, Mustafa Behçet, was another pioneer of modern medical writing in Turkish.[41] He is reported to have visited Italy in his youth and to have recognized the importance of modern medicine then. In addition to a treatise on cholera to be mentioned again, he is said to have translated part of Buffon's *Natural History* (completed and published by his nephew, Hayrullah), a book on physiology (*Vazaif-ul Âzâ*) from Italian, a book on vaccination (unpublished) from an Italian translation of Jenner's book in Latin, and a book on syphilis from the Italian translation of a German work. Despite these, Dr. Adıvar believes Behçet did not represent a real transition from medieval to modern medicine.

Another translator was Seyid Osman Saip, who was also a teacher and onetime director of the medical school. Like the previous two, he was a *medrese* graduate and a member of the Ulema order. In 1835 he published a work on pathology trans-

---

[40] See Adnan-Adıvar, *Osmanlı Türklerinde İlim* (Istanbul, 1943), pp. 193-94 and Karl Süssheim, *Eski Viyana tıb talimi ve onum Adlî Sultan Mahmud zamanında İstanbula yayılması* (Istanbul, 1937). Şanizade was accused of materialism and atheism. See Cevdet, *Tarih* (1301), XII, 212.

[41] His brother, Abdulhak Molla (1786-1853), a physician graduated from the medical *medrese*, became an organizer of the new school of medicine. On Behçet see Ünver, "Osmanlı Tababeti," 936-37; DeKay, *Sketches of Turkey*, pp. 153, 518 ff.; and Adıvar, *Osmanlı Türklerinde İlim*, pp. 195-96.

lated from the French entitled *Mebahis-i Emraz*, and in 1852 he published another book on the same subject entitled *Ahkâm-ul Emraz.*[42]

Another teacher in the medical school, Hafız Mehmed, wrote a book on syphilis.[43] Works written by the European professors invited to teach in the school were also translated and published.[44]

By 1831, Mahmud had had a number of medical treatises written and published at his greatly expanded press. The value of these books was not in any quality of originality but in their effect upon the mentality of the people.

One of these was a treatise on cholera drawn up by a committee of physicians headed by Mustafa Behçet and published over his signature in 1831. DeKay, himself a physician, gives the following significant information about this treatise,

> On our way down . . . we suddenly came upon an old Turk who was occupied in rather an unusual manner. He was . . . poring over the pages of a book with so much intentness that our presence was unheeded until we were close by his side. . . . He turned the conversation to the book which occupied his meditations. He informed us that it was a treatise on cholera . . . distributed gratuitously throughout the empire. The doctrines of fatalism are generally represented to be carried so far among the Turks that it is thought unpious to endeavor, by human means, to avert any impending danger. . . . To counteract this self-abandonment is one of the objects of the treatise, and it is shown that this pernicious belief is in no way connected with, or dependent upon, their religion. . . . When it is recollected that only a few years ago such a measure would have endangered the throne, and the life of its author, the enlightened views and singular firmness of the present Sultan may be justly appreciated.[45]

There seem to have been three controversies rife among the *ulema* at the time. The first was the disturbing claim that the earth was round; the second concerned the permissibility of taking quarantine measures against epidemics; the third concerned vaccination. Having exhausted their resources of interpretation and

---

[42] See Tahsin, *Mir'at-ı Mekteb-i Tıbbiye*, I, 6; Ünver, "Osmanlı Tababeti," 937.

[43] *Mecmua-i Da-ul Zühreviye* seems to have been translated from a European language. See *ibid.*, 938.

[44] See Tahsin, *Mir'at-ı Mekteb-i Tıbbiye*, I, 35; Ünver, "Osmanlı Tababeti," 938, n. 3.

[45] DeKay, *Sketches of Turkey*, pp. 153-54.

exegesis of religious texts, the *ulema* were perturbed by the strange ideas on these subjects creeping into the minds of some Muslims from afar. Those who were modern enough to approve of the two preventive health measures did not differ one bit from their adversaries in their reasoning; their total armoury consisted of scholastic logic and medieval texts. We are told of a duel between a Tunisian Mâlikî *allâma* and a Hanafî *muftî* in which the first rejected and the latter accepted the imposition of quarantines; the former emerged victorious with the proposition that interfering with epidemics would mean opposition to God's absolute will by the recognition of man's free will![46]

Quarantines were established probably shortly after DeKay's departure in 1832. An Algerian, Hamdullah bin Osman, who was employed as a translator in the medical school, was ordered to write a treatise showing that quarantine measures were not contrary to the Şeriat.[47] This was to counteract the dissatisfaction among the people and it can be presumed that this work was distributed in the same manner as the treatise on cholera. A new government service, a port health authority, was established. In 1836 a series of articles explaining the use of the new measures and the means of preventing epidemics was published in the paper *Takvim-i Vekayi*.[48]

The objections to vaccination or variolation also had to be overcome. Şanizade Ata'ullah introduced ideas about vaccination twenty years after the publication of Jenner's *Inquiry* (1798). The first practice of variolation seems to have been in 1839, but the *fetva* legitimizing it religiously was given only in 1845 or a little later; it appeared in a treatise on vaccination.[49]

---

[46] Rifâ'a, *Takhlîs al-îbriz fi Talkhîs ilâ-Bârîz* (Cairo, 1834); Turkish trans., *Seyahatname* (Cairo, 1839), pp. 36 ff. Rifâ'a was an Egyptian sent to France by Mehmet Ali. His book on his observations on European life was translated into Turkish because Mehmet Ali could not read Arabic. *Seyahatname* was widely read among the Turks. The book reveals its author as an open-minded observer.

[47] This treatise was entitled *Ithaf al-Atıbba*. See Ünver, "Osmanlı Tababeti," 947. The *fetva* in favour of quarantine was promulgated in 1837.

[48] For the subsequent measures taken for the prevention of contagious diseases and for various sanitary measures, as well as hospitals, see *ibid.*, 948 ff.

[49] Entitled *Talkih-i Cüderi Hakkında Risâle*, printed by the school of medicine in 1845. For further details see *ibid.*, 953, Rıza Tahsin, *Mir'at-ı Mekteb-i Tıbbiye*, I, 37-38, Adıvar, *Osmanlı Türklerinde İlim*, p. 194.

Westernizing Reforms

122

The foregoing has been an account of the secular side of the reforms. There was another feature to Mahmud's innovations that had portent for Westernization. To this category fall those innovations that evoked much criticism within and without the country.

One important underlying belief can be discerned easily throughout Mahmud's reform efforts. Aside from the acceptance of the superiority of the material features of the modern civilization, there was also the recognition of the need to replace certain traditional habits and customs by others in greater harmony with the new conditions. The notable element in this insight, giving to it the colour of Westernization, was the belief that the modern West was worthy of being taken as a model in the efforts to establish new ways. Mahmud's explanation of why modern Western medicine should be taken over, learned, and practised in place of the old Greco-Arabian medicine was a succinct formulation of this outlook.

Mahmud initiated the acceptance of Western attire, and certain social practices relating to etiquette, taste, and the like. He became an enemy of long beards; he declared war against the traditional Turkish saddles and style of riding; he appeared before the people and became a public orator and ribbon cutter; he caused his ministers to sit in his presence; he went on steamer trips; he began to learn French; he imported European musicians and concert masters; he is reported to have ordered samples of European headgear with a view toward recapping his troops or, perhaps, even popularizing these among his people. His own example was followed by some. The turbans, ample trousers, old-fashioned shoes, and decorative paraphernalia were dropped, beards were shortened or shaven completely, European pants were adopted.

It was against this type of change that foreign observers, with the exception of DeKay, directed their greatest criticism. They bemoaned the disappearance of what they believed to be peculiarly oriental. The great champions of equality between the Rayahs and the Turks complained of their new-found difficulty in distinguishing one from the other.[50]

The traditional costumes of a changing society were bound to disappear under the force of actual conditions. DeKay character-

[50] Marmont, *State of the Turkish Empire*, p. 42; MacFarlane, *Turkey and its Destiny*, I, 41.

istically tries to understand why a ruler would care what the people wore; in doing so, he shows us that in many respects Mahmud merely legitimized what had been occurring in contravention of the tradition, and he gives clues to the need for conscious changes in people's attire. He writes of the military:

The dress of the modern Turkish soldier has *partaken of the general change which has occurred within the last ten years* [from about 1820], and whatever it may have lost in picturesque effect, it has certainly gained in effectiveness for military duty. Instead of loose, slipshod slippers, he now wears stout serviceable shoes securely fastened by leather strings. The huge baloon chaksheers [trousers], which impeded his every movement have given place to woollen trowsers, still rather ample about the nether man, but not so large as to prevent him from making a rapid charge upon the enemy, or from running away. The glittering and flowing jubbee [gown] and bayneesh [robe] are well exchanged for a smart tight-bodied blue jacket, closely hooded in front, and allowing perfect freedom to the limbs; while the turban, infinitely varied in shape and colour, often ragged, and frequently dirty, suggesting the idea of walking toadstools, has forever disappeared. In its place the soldier sports a tidy red cap, with a blue tassel gracefully depending from its crown. With the exception of the cap, and the still lingering amplitude of the trowsers, the Turkish soldiers could scarcely be distinguished from the regulars of any European nation.[51]

What the Europeans mourned had had social significance in the traditional system. Headgear was a mark of religious, vocational, and national identity as well as an insignia of one's rank and status. The differentiations within women's attire had particular significance—as they have to a degree today. The disappearance of the old orders, or the changes in their status, and the rise of new classes necessitated the adoption of new dress. The appearance of the horse-drawn carriage, the decline in certain trades, changes in the structure and in functions within the government, business, industry, and even education, and the appropriation of certain new amenities in home furnishings imposed upon the people the search for a new appearance.

Confusion and even anarchy threatened when the elaborate traditional system of attire became severely damaged. People did not know what to put on; the streets assumed a carnival appearance, as is the case in Karachi today, in the absence of a new

---

[51] DeKay, *Sketches of Turkey*, p. 225 (italics added).

124

Clothing

uniformity. People appeared incognito in apparel of their own invention. Mahmud determined to give some order and eclat to the dress of the people. Significantly, he chose for himself, his ministers, and the people, designs of the utmost simplicity. His efforts represented an attempt to solve the problems of the identity of the people, insofar as external appearances went, in their new phase of historical existence. There is evidence that he was ready to accept the existing European costumes rather than invent new ones.

Historical forces, however, led to deviations and exceptions from the general rule. The resultant picture may be taken as a fairly accurate photographic index of Turkish society in the second part of the nineteenth century. First of all, the changes were confined largely to the urban population. They reached their maximum only in the army and among the officials and intellectuals in that order. They remained at a minimum among the Ulema. (Among the Rayahs the businessmen underwent change most and the clergy least). Despite the absence of a clergy in Islam, the differential rate of change in apparel created the appearance of one, at least in externals. The Ulema, which had until that time been only one among several medieval orders, became singled out as a class of clergyman distinguishable from laymen through their conservatism and insistence upon retaining their medieval attire. Furthermore, through this conservatism the distinctiveness of the various ranks of the order of Ulema disappeared because, under the impact of change, the garb underwent a process of simplification; the nuances distinguishing the Ulema from ordinary "clergymen" were lost. Only the turban, ample trousers and gown were retained; thus, all those connected with religious affairs were reduced to a more or less uniform attire distinguishable only from the lay dress.

Shoes, pants, coats, shirts did not encounter resistance. The real difficulty arose over the question of headgear. It is difficult to explain why, after so many changes along European lines, this became such a bugbear. The only clear explanation appears to be religious, although the transitional state of European men's headgear (between the wig and the equally odd and impractical top hat) may have contributed to the difficulty. According to DeKay, "it was the wish of the sultan to have furnished the cylindrical cap, fez, he introduced into the military . . . with a small rim in front, to protect the eye from the glare of the sun," But, he continues,

This daring innovation was opposed, and successfully too, by the ulemah. . . . It was argued that no true Mussulman could perform his devotions without touching his forehead to the ground, and the proposed leather projection would render this impracticable. As no one happened to hit upon the idea that the cap might be turned around while at prayers [as many Turks do today], the sultan was compelled to give up the point.[52]

This consideration may explain the rejection of European head-gear or, more correctly, those forms of European headgear with a brim or visor. However, religious considerations can not explain adequately why the fez was chosen, especially in view of the fact that the fez was originally European and had nothing to do with any historical Muslim headgear. The fez adopted by Mahmud was quite different from the one popularized later in Turkey, Egypt, and India and taken over by the Shriners; it was a red or mauve beret, easy to maintain and comfortable. It was probably easier to manufacture and less expensive than the other headgear of the time. It was already in use among North African Muslims. These factors probably made the fez more readily acceptable and, accordingly, the fez was adopted formally in 1829.

Attributing allegedly religious value to the fez and rejecting the use of the hat came much later. It came to be seen, especially during the Hamidian Islamism, as a mark of religious nationalism among the Muslims (even outside of Turkey and, especially, in India), and as a sign of loyalty to the Khalifa. Consequently, the fez fell by the way in Turkey at the time of the fall of religious nationalism and the Caliphate.

The elimination of differential dress among the Muslims, Christians, and Jews within the Empire marked an important step in the direction of secular liberalism. On his second visit to Turkey in 1846, MacFarlane was put into a dilemma that he never resolved satisfactorily. "In many cases," he said, "it cost me thought and trouble to distinguish between Mussulmans and Rayahs. Twenty years ago, there was no possibility of confounding them. . . ."[53] Significantly, the Jews and Armenians of the commercial centres adopted the new official dress with alacrity; the former even wore the fez while reading the Scriptures. The notables among the Rayahs not only aspired to appear like their Muslim countrymen but also sought to enter into private competition with the highest

[52] *Ibid.*, p. 226.

[53] MacFarlane, *Turkey and its Destiny*, I, 41.

government officials in differentiating themselves from the ordinary people of all faiths.

In addition to these changes, a wide variety of practices became established through Mahmud's encouragement or tolerance. DeKay describes sympathetically the changing manners and customs of the government officials as indices of the extent and nature of the anti-traditionalism of the period.[54] Adolphus Slade, the British naval officer employed as an admiral in the Turkish navy, believed that the chief feature of Mahmud's reforms was "contempt of their prophet's wisest law" which justified the people in "considering the sultan and his ministers as little removed from infidels."[55] Writing some seventeen years later, MacFarlane complained, in effect, that the Turks had become too knowledgeable of the West and too modern either to be awed by his superior attitude or to be irritated by his offensive and presumptuous conduct.[56]

An innovation of the greatest importance in Mahmud's policy of Westernization was the establishment of the first newspaper in Turkish. Newspapers had been published previously in Turkey in French by the French; newspapers in languages other than Turkish began appearing towards the end of the first quarter of the nineteenth century.[57] To Mehmet Ali goes the credit for establishing the first newspaper in the Islamic world; his *Waqâ'i' al-Misrîya* founded in 1828 was published in Turkish and Arabic; it encouraged Mahmud to undertake a similar project.

Mahmud founded a newspaper press in 1831. He chose the title *Takvim-i Vekayi* (Calendar of Events) for the Turkish edition edited by the historiographer Esad. He employed Alexandre Blaque, a Frenchman who had published a paper in French in Izmir, as the editor of a French edition entitled *Moniteur Ottoman*. Upon beginning publication, Mahmud declared, "The newspaper, being not inadmissible from the point of view of the Şeriat and the *kanûn*, is an institution of great benefit to my dominions." He is said to have written unsigned articles for the paper in which he styled himself as an innovator and Europeanizer.[58]

126

---

[54] DeKay, *Sketches of Turkey*, pp. 333 ff.

[55] Slade, *Record of Travels*, p. 254

[56] MacFarlane, *Turkey and its Destiny*, II, 93 ff.

[57] Selim Nüzhet Gerçek, *Türk Gazeteciliği, 1831-1931* (Istanbul, 1931), pp. 10, 15-21.

[58] Quoted in Temperley, *Crimea*, p. 403, n. 33.

DeKay provides a truly "front page" account of the founding of the newspaper, its reception among the various communities, and its implications for the development of public opinion internally and externally.[59] We need add to his description only that Esad seems to have been the first writer to feel the need for simplification of written Turkish;[60] as we shall see more fully below, the foundation of a periodical press played a significant role in language, and later alphabet, reform efforts.

Despite its many defects, the *Vekayi* was both a mirror of Mahmud's era and a forecast of the direction in which the people were to be led.[61] The absence of news related to Eastern countries was conspicuous. The Turkish edition brought to the reading public not only news of the reform activities but also information and concepts theretofore unrepresented in Turkish.

We learn of a number of unnoticed changes through the early issues of *Vekayi*. Among the advertisements in 1832 were some for the sale of printed books on religious subjects. These, it will be recalled, were specifically excluded from the *fetva* authorizing printing a century earlier. The change seems to have come about gradually without fuss or a new authorization. From the very first issue we begin to find mention of institutions unknown in Turkey, such as the British House of Commons (translated as Meşveretgâh-ı vükelâ) and the House of Lords (translated as Meşveretgâh-ı hânedân). In other words, it was through the mouthpiece of the absolute monarch that the people were exhorted to read of their faith and that ideas of constitutionalism began to filter down to the reading public!

Mahmud decided to send to Europe a group of 150 students from the schools of medicine, engineering, and military science. The first group of students and graduates from the military and

---

59 DeKay, *Sketches of Turkey*, pp. 373-74, 401-2, 405-6.

60 Fuad Köprülü, *Millî Edebiyat Cerayanının İlk Mübeşşirleri* (Istanbul, 1928), p. 31. On Esad's life and works, see M. Münir Aktepe, "Es'ad Efendi," *İslâm Ansiklopedisi* (Istanbul, 1948), IV, 363-65.

61 *Vekayi* was not a paper that could be read and understood by the man in the street. The language was still medieval Ottoman and the sentences long and involved. There were no paragraphs and no punctuation. The print was like that of Müteferrika's first publications, showing that there had been no improvement in the techniques of printing since that time. The paper was not a daily and was not sold on the streets; one had to subscribe. It was actually not published in other languages until 1839; then Armenian and Arabic editions appeared irregularly.

engineering institutions was dispatched to England, France, Prussia, and Austria in 1835. It seems that no medical graduates were sent abroad until after 1840.[62]

128

Mahmud's diverse educational endeavours bore fruit later. The number of the enlightened multiplied out of proportion to those of Mahmud's time. The Tercüme Odası (translation bureau) established by Mahmud played a role different from that originally intended. It was established to take over the translation work of the Porte in its external and intercommunal relations. The first translator, who was appointed in 1821, was Yahya, a Turkish Greek convert to Islam. Yahya was a teacher in the Mühendishane and had translated (probably from French or Italian) works for the use of the teachers. The second chief of the bureau, appointed in 1823, was Ishak who was also a convert. In time, the office became a college of foreign languages; it was there that the future Turkish intellectuals got their start.[63] The most eminent men of Turkey not only in the field of diplomacy but also in the various branches of administration and intellectual life have been "graduates" of the translation bureau. It was through this institution that the traditional Turkish literature advanced beyond the stage of the Tulip Era.

Appraisal of European Civilization

The Westernizing reforms initiated under Mahmud II were not merely the product of a ruler's whim, but inevitable consequences of the breakdown of traditional institutions, and the emergence of a degree of liberation and secularization.

The way in which reformers of non-Western societies understand Western civilization is influenced by the degree to which minds have been liberated from the traditional institutions. Western civilization, yet maturing while establishing its mastery over the world, was a product of complex factors not understood at that time even in the West with its own inherent problems. Facing such a civilization with the firm determination to emulate it was a hazardous job. Turkey was the first country outside the Western

[62] See Cevad, *Maarif-i Umumiye*, p. 4; Ünver, "Osmanlı Tababeti," 943-44; Esad, *Mir'at-ı Mekteb-i Harbiye*, p. 19.

[63] Esad, *Mir'at-ı Mühendishane*, p. 34; Ubicini, *Letters on Turkey*, I, 43; Cevdet, *Tarih* (1301), XI, 166; Tayyarzade Ata, *Tarih* (Istanbul, 1876), III, 122.

world (if we exclude Russia which had begun its Westernization one century earlier) to undertake the task. Japan followed suit very shortly. The later development of the two cases is one of the most instructive lessons for the student of Westernization.

Westernizing reforms in the Turkey of this era had their own merits and faults, which we can grasp best if we understand the concept of the West which existed in the minds of the Turks. We shall take the observations of two men as illustrative of the prevailing view of the "enlightened." These manifested a greater degree of understanding of the problem of Westernization than had existed previously.

The first was Mustafa Sâmi (d. 1855) who visited Rome, Florence, other Italian cities, Vienna, Prague, Berlin, Frankfurt, Brussels, Antwerp, London, and, finally, Paris, to which he went as a member of the Turkish legation, in 1838. Upon his return he wrote a little book, *Avrupa Risâlesi*. In spite of its brevity and its great resemblance to its one-hundred-year-old predecessor, Çelebi Mehmed's account, this book contains a few points that serve as indices of what the Turkish intellectuals had learned in the intervening century. We find in Sâmi's book the earliest attempt to explain the causes of things to be admired in the civilization of Europe.

One of the features he noticed was the role of science in European progress. Religious freedom he found to be another. A third was the continuity maintained in European civilization between the new acquisitions and the achievements of the past, by which Europe enabled itself to make marvellous mechanical inventions. Explaining his visits to museums, for example, he says,

What is the utility of these? The inventions of the Europeans (so many discoveries—which are being improved every day to make everything convenient—those superhuman achievements such as steam navigation, those industries which Muslim countries need so badly for the everyday necessities such as paper, textile, glass and watch-making, and finally those wonderful attempts to fly in the air, and to communicate with distant places through wires laid underground) were all made possible by preserving the works of the ancients and predecessors, and by adding to them their own inventiveness. If we realize this we then understand why the products which we call antiques attract so much attention and care in such an age of invention. . . . From all this it is clear that such a degree of orderliness reached by the Europeans in every work and action, and the indispensability of skill and knowledge in them, are due solely to the diffusion of the sciences and the arts.

130

This became possible through the diffusion of school education. "Men and women alike," he says with the exaggeration of enthusiasm, "everyone reads and writes in Europe. Especially in France, every person, even an ordinary porter or a shepherd, is capable at least of reading a letter sent to him." Exaggerating again, "Nobody in Europe is constrained for matters of religion or sect. Whatever religion a man may have—even the Jew—he is employed by the governments as long as he deserves." "All this is due to the progress of science (*fen*)." Thus, he concluded, once knowledge of the modern sciences was implemented in Turkey through education, the country would cease to be dependent upon European goods, and its wealth would be saved for further progress.[64]

Sâmi later became a supporter of the Tanzimat and created much opposition by his unrestrained criticism of the traditional customs and unreserved praise of European life and manners.[65] He was attacked as *kâfir* (denier) and *mulhid* (unbeliever). He was an editor-in-chief of *Takvim-i Vekayi* and wrote the earliest articles in simple language for the people. Sâmi was not only the first predecessor of the Westernist school of writers but also the writer who introduced the conception of patriotism (*hubb-i memleket ve millet*, love for fatherland and people) which was elaborated later by Şinasi and Namık Kemal.

The second writer, Sadık Rifat (1807-56), was another predecessor of Westernism, a supporter of reform, and, perhaps, the one who formulated the basic ideas of the Tanzimat before its formal promulgation. He went to Vienna in 1837 as ambassador. Among his voluminous writings, two lengthy essays, "Essay concerning European Affairs" and "On the Reform of Conditions in the Ottoman State," will interest us here.[66]

Like other visitors to Europe, Sadık Rifat portrays European life in favourable colours. He too speaks of the reign of religious

---

[64] Mustafa Sâmi, *Avrupa Risâlesi* (Takvim-i Vekayi Press, 1840); the long quotation is from pp. 12-13, the others from pp. 26, 35, 36-38.

[65] Ahmet Lûfti, *Tarih* (Istanbul, (1873), I, 8, quoted by I. Mahmud Kemal Inal, *Son Asır Türk Şairleri* (Istanbul, 1940), IX, 1646-47; see also Ahmet H. Tanpınar, *XIX. Asır Türk Edebiyatı Tarihi* (2nd ed. Istanbul, 1956), I, 93-96.

[66] "Avrupa Ahvaline Dair Risale" (1837) and "Devlet-i Aliyenin Islah-ı Ahvali," in his *Müntehabat-ı Âsâr* (Istanbul, 1844). See also Abdurrahman Şeref, *Tarih Musahabeleri* (Istanbul, 1924), pp. 125 ff.; Tanpınar, *XIX. Asır*, I, 88-93. Sadık Rifat wrote his essays from Vienna where he went first in 1837 as minister and then in 1839 as ambassador.

freedom, the stability in government administration and the honesty of functionaries, the universality of education and literacy, the importance of books and the press in the education of the people, the exhibitions, the incentives for investors, steam-power, railroads, banks, postal services, the cleanliness of hotels and restaurants, entertainments, music, institutions for the poor and sick, etc. But, he was basically interested in telling his people something else and that was something new. Sadık Rifat was probably the first Turkish statesman able to see not only the mere externals of European civilization but also its fundamental distinctiveness from non-European civilizations. As A. H. Tanpınar says,

> The most important aspect of the *Essay* is its conception of the problem of reform as a problem of a "way of thinking." In contrast to a system in which custom and tradition . . . reigned—and to a great extent ruled arbitrarily—it portrays a realistic and rational state and administration which is based on man's nature, rights, and needs.[67]

Sadık Rifat spoke of the *civilization* of Europe, even introducing this word untranslated and in its French form, and pointed out that European civilization was based on the fullest realization of human rights, the freedom and security of life, property, and honour. He wrote,

> There the governments are for the welfare of the citizens—and not the citizens for the sake of the governments. It is because of this that the governments are run according to the rights of the people (*millet*) and according to law.

Western civilization, freedom, people, and the rights of man! All were new concepts, used and explained probably for the first time. It is likely that he could not realize that what he was calling for was a total transformation from one system of civilization to another. However, the credit for first talking of these concepts and introducing them into Turkish usage belongs to him.

Sadık Rifat's second essay contained the fundamentals of the whole Tanzimat philosophy of reform. These were the abolition of arbitrary rule, the codification of judicial and administrative laws, and the establishment of principles for regulating people's obligations, such as the paying of taxes and the performing of

132

military service. He stressed the importance of education, the organization of the army and navy, the pursuance of a consistent peace policy, the training of honest government functionaries and the guaranteeing to them of security and stability, and above all, the protection and encouragement of industry. As a historian of the Tanzimat period stated, he was one of the few who "wholeheartedly believed in the Tanzimat reforms," and who "perceived the necessity for modern banking and credit institutions for the revival of Turkish economy."[68] Interpreting this to convey that Sadık Rifat could see and adapt to his own thinking what Mahmud had done, we can agree very well with T. H. Tanpınar who believed that this essay "laid the foundations for the Gülhane charter and that he [Sadık] sowed the seeds of the Tanzimat reforms."[69]

The understanding of Western civilization exemplified by the two observers can explain a few features of the reformism pioneered by Mahmud and followed to a greater degree during the Tanzimat. Western civilization has a superior technology; it is the product of modern sciences; it can be implemented by education; the instrument for carrying it out is government. When carried to their logical consequences, these were in sharp contrast with the medieval view and practices.

The State as the Agency of Transformation

While lawmaking was to become the distinguishing feature of the Tanzimat, it was Mahmud who opened the way for this. In accordance with his distinction between secular and religious affairs, he followed the policy of the old Turkish rulers of enacting kanûn with the addition of a new element. Enacting temporal kanûn was becoming gradually a more or less systematized process towards the creation of a body of public law separate and even contradistinct from the şeriat law. So far there had been no distinction between public and private law. Mahmud's administrative, military, and "penal" enactments laid the foundations for a future body of public law. Furthermore, by the increasing impli-

---

[68] Şeref, *Tarih Musahabeleri*, p. 118. During the Tanzimat period, Sadık Rifat was the president of the Supreme Council of Tanzimat, a member of the Council of Education and of the Encümen-i Daniş, founded in 1850.

[69] Tanpınar, *XIX Asır*, I, 92-93.

cations of public law for the private sector, they tended to alter the more important position of the Islamic private law, as will be seen more clearly when we discuss the consequences of the Tanzimat codification. With Mahmud's initiative, furthermore, the medieval conception of the temporal law as an expression of the "will" of the ruler, or as an affirmation of local customs and usages or of Islamic practices, tended to give way to a new conception in which an impersonal legislative agency in law-making was recognized by enacting regulations not according to religion or tradition, but according to the requirements of "reason." The following period simply carried this process further, ultimately as far as to the drawing up of a constitution.

Another manifestation of the new concept was an unconscious reformulation of the governmental function. Mahmud's reformism needed a government that would abandon medieval practices and concern itself with those things which medieval governments had neglected. The chief concern of the medieval government was to maintain the general order while keeping each "order" within its traditional boundaries both spatially and socially. The economic and administrative roles of the medieval government were secondary, largely prohibitive, and subordinated throughout to religious or military objectives. There was no concern or instrumentality for changing or improving the society on the basis of a dynamic conception of welfare and progress. The welfare of society was seen to lie in status and tradition. Thus, not the government but the Şeriat, custom, and tradition were the fountainheads of social and individual welfare.

The government emerged in Mahmud's time as the supreme functionary, the prime mover, and the agency of change and progress. The novelty in the advance Mahmud represented lay in his perception that a government viewed in a new light would be the agent to introduce a new economic system. To that extent Mahmud became the founder of a new government and law. The weakest point in the Turkish political transformation lay in the fact that the new conception of government was not the product of the aspirations of a rising middle class but rather the creation of the traditional political authority in its struggle to maintain its existence. This led to increasingly clear contradictions in subsequent periods, but the implications of the new conception for economic policy can be seen even at this stage.

The inevitable realization that the state had to lead in the implementation of a modern society, in which industry and education appeared to be the major differentials, was bound to lead to some modernization in the conception and organization of the government. This can be seen best in connection with Mahmud's economic attempts.

134

Turkish views of European civilization show the continuing lack of a clear understanding of the existence of a new economic system and doctrine behind the observed scientific and technological advancement of the West. On the other hand, it is clear from Mahmud's innovations, even from his economic enterprises, that he had faced up to the question of the economic function of the state under modern, or nineteenth-century, conditions. This was a question that no nation outside the European community, excepting Russia which was partly European, had tackled; Japan was still out of the picture. Although the days of mercantilism by absolutist monarchies had long since passed and pressure was being exerted for the acceptance of laissez-faire policies, Mahmud instinctively found the path followed in the previous two centuries by the absolutist monarchs of Europe.

But, Mahmud had little chance to develop a new economic policy as the major instrument of modernization. There were several factors unfavourable to the formation of such a policy. Among them were the absence of peace and internal security, the capitulations, the non-existence of an enterprising middle class and the existence of foreign merchants gaining increasing diplomatic and even military support, and the concentration of potential investment capital among non-Turkish middlemen, bankers, and usurers, many of whom claimed dual or even multiple citizenship and had no interest in building a national economy. There was also the pressure of the uneconomic and unhistorical thinking of those whom Mahmud had sent for training to Europe that they might advise him well. This last factor played a significant role in his initiation of a laissez-faire regime just before his death. Still, he deserves credit for initiating steps towards an etatistic view of economic modernization. Most of his innovations were preliminaries towards the launching of new economic policies, but we can guess the direction they would have taken under more favourable conditions from his governmental reforms and partially from his unco-ordinated economic ventures.

Noteworthy less for their economic achievements than for the germinal idea they represented are his refusal to accept the loans pressed upon him by the agents of the Rothschilds, his close interest in the United States, his employment of American shipbuilders, and his abortive attempt to contract a comprehensive alliance with the New World (revived in the abortive attempt by his protégé Reşid Paşa to establish a technical assistance program through diplomatic negotiations), his direct investment in naval reconstruction and the founding of a press, his efforts to cut down on the extravagant expenditures of government and the Turkish notables, and the interests of his government in leather, paper, textile, and ammunition manufactories. Noteworthy also is the "discovery" by the Board of Useful Affairs of the need to co-ordinate educational and industrial efforts administratively as well as in terms of their objectives.

135

Tanzimat: the Economic and Political Impact of the West

THE DOORS TO THE WEST were thrown wide open in 1839. A new regime called the Tanzimat was proclaimed. The Turkish economic, political, legal, and educational institutions began to change in a way which involved basic social values for the first time.

The promoters of reform in this period of about twenty years had, above all, to meet the economic challenge of the West in such a way as to insure progress. They had to build up a legal system to guarantee the freedom and equality of the people, to create a modern state machinery, and to facilitate economic progress. Finally, they had to encourage the development of modern cultural institutions.

We shall see how the difficulties encountered in the experiment produced a reaction, on the one hand, and further criticism of the traditional institutions, on the other. This bifurcation in the response to the Tanzimat served to clarify the problem of the adaptation of Islam to modern civilization—the principal element in the problem of secularization.

Forcing the Doors Wide Open

Commenting upon the appearance of the steamship in Turkish waters two years after the destruction of the Yeniçeris, an English observer wrote,

138

Lately things have changed; the universal peace in Europe and the introduction of steam-boats into the Mediterranean have brought the Europeans and the Turks comparatively close together. It seems to me that the effect of the steam-boats here has already begun to be felt. . . . I have no doubt that in two or three years you will be able to go from Paris to Constantinople in fifteen or twenty days; and when the time comes it will throw vast numbers of Europeans into the East which will have a sensible effect upon the manners and customs of the people. These Eastern countries will be invaded by all classes of people. . . .[1]

It did not take long for the prophecy to be realized. A couple of years later an American bishop travelling in Turkey remarked:

The destruction of the Janissaries overthrew the great barrier to the influence of foreigners upon Turkey. . . . The doors to a free intercourse have been thrown wide open. . . . Europe, finding the flood-gates lifted up, has poured into the Empire the scum and off-scouring of her population . . . Turkey has asked of Europe the blessings of civilization; Europe has sent her her civilized vices.[2]

The years 1840-70 were indeed revolutionary in bringing Turkey and Europe into close contact and in furnishing conditions under which Europe began to exert its influence directly. The impact made itself felt most in the field in which the West wielded its most decisive superiority over the rest of the world—the field of economy.

Previously, Western Europe had not been able to exert such a force. There were a number of practices that were impediments to free trade with the Empire, especially for foreigners. Among the worn and decrepit yet protective barriers were the tolls, octrois, price controls, prohibitions against exports and, above all, trade monopolies granted to individuals and also exercised by the government.[3] As the foreign traders and statesmen complained, these virtually negated the concessions under the capitulations and kept

---

[1] John G. Stephens, *Incidents of Travel in Greece, Turkey, Russia and Poland* (Dublin, 1839), pp. 176-77.

[2] Horatio Southgate, *Narrative of a Tour through Armenia, Kurdistan, Persia, and Mesopotamia* (London, 1840), II, 328-29.

[3] Harold Temperley, *England and the Near East: The Crimea* (London, New York, and Toronto, 1936), p. 32, and Vernon J. Puryear, *International Economics and Diplomacy in the Near East: A Study of British Commercial Policy in the Levant 1834-1853* (Stanford, 1935), p. 118.

the overhead costs of trading within the Empire high.[4] Enterprising foreigners could undertake the rational exploitation of Turkish resources only by becoming Ottoman subjects and, thereby, renouncing their exterritorial privileges and advantages under the capitulations. Otherwise, the fruits of their privileged position would be shared by the non-Muslim traders who were in the process of becoming the sole monopolists in several branches of internal and external trade.

The British, French, Dutch, and other merchants and governments needed a general revision of the whole system in its financial, economic, and commercial aspects.[5] In persuading the Turkish government to abolish the existing restrictions, the European powers would both get rid of the incubus of their own protégés and obviate the likelihood of the Turks' doing what the Americans and Russians had done and the Japanese were soon to do—closing the doors to protect the national economy.

Following the end of the Napoleonic Wars and with the changes in the political and commercial relations between Great Britain and Russia and the formation of a new British Near Eastern policy, Britain assumed France's eighteenth-century role in Turkish affairs.[6] This reversal of the British policy towards Turkey led to negotiations in 1838 for a new commercial treaty. It was based on the assumption that the abolition of all restrictive practices and the establishment of a free-trade policy would not only benefit the British traders but also bring growth to the Turkish trade and prosperity to the Turkish people.[7]

The Turkish government undertook to fulfil certain promises compromising its sovereignty over its own economic policies. Even the national interests of the country under abnormal con-

---

[4] *Ibid.*, pp. 121-22.

[5] Temperley, *The Crimea*, pp. 33-34.

[6] See F. E. Bailey, *British Policy and the Turkish Reform Movement* (Cambridge, Mass., 1942), pp. 63-178, on the growth of British commercial and political interests in Turkey.

[7] The Turkish text of the Convention, in *Muahedat Mecmuası* (Istanbul, 1891), I, 272 ff. See also G. E. Noradounghian, *Recueil d'actes internationaux de l'Empire Ottoman* (Paris, 1900), II, 249-53; Lewis Hertslet, *A Complete Collection of the Treaties and Conventions and Reciprocal Regulations . . . between Great Britain and Foreign Powers . . . So Far as they Relate to Commerce and Navigation . . .* (London, 1840-1924), V, 506-14; J. C. Hurewitz, *Diplomacy in the Near and Middle East: A Documentary Record* (Princeton, 1956), I, 110-11. See Puryear, *International Economics*, pp. 124-25 on the implications of the treaty.

140

ditions would not constitute a barrier to its zeal for the free-trade doctrine; for example, the government would not have the right to pre-empt the national produce in the face of famine and, ultimately, would be forced to contract new foreign loans to wage defensive war while financing through her creditors wars among other powers. All the fetters on the foreign merchants were removed. The import-export tariffs were fixed and, indirectly, this prepared the ground for future foreign intervention in tariff policies. The earlier privileges were reaffirmed and even declared to be unalterable while the right of other nations to duplicate the provisions of the treaty was recognized. Effects of the new economic liberalism became manifest within two decades and produced a number of changes in the economic, demographic, and occupational conditions of the people.

Trade increased greatly. Modern means of communication with European countries were established. The first telegraphic lines between Europe and Turkey were opened during the Crimean War, in which front line journalism was born. Telegraphic communications were established with London in 1861; the same decade saw the opening of many other lines, largely for commercial purposes. That decade also witnessed the beginning of road, railroad, and harbour construction by foreign investment companies.

Industry as well as agriculture was brought into direct relationship with the capitalistic market mechanism. The Ottoman territories acquired increasing importance for European economy both as a market for industrial produce and as a source of raw and agricultural materials. The persons, the methods, and the institutions of modern economy began to enter in and become established. Commercial companies, banks, insurance companies, stock exchanges, etc. were founded.

The new activities were concentrated in the coastal areas, or in new urban centres, or in areas to which modern means of transportation penetrated. Two related effects of the modern economy began to operate in opposite directions in proportion to the degree of penetration. Progress was made in certain agricultural areas not only in the extension of agriculture and the increase of productivity but also in the amount of specialization or diversification. This progress did not, however, contribute to the formation of a modern national economy through a new integration with commerce and industry. On the contrary, the new agricultural branches became severed from the national economy and, in time, dependent on the European national economies. Several agricultural areas came to be integrated with one or another European national economy. The developments prepared the pattern upon which the Ottoman Empire would disintegrate and be partitioned in the future.

The new economic factors worked against the Ottoman economy in another line as well. The new trade hit the medieval towns and their industries most severely. It altered the old relationships between the towns and their dependent villages. The traditional village economy sank and the village communities remained inaccessible to any development. Whole villages became desolated as mass migrations increased. Peasants swarmed into the new towns where there were no modern industries to absorb or transform them. They remained unassimilated, without either urban or rural roots.

In general, the urban population increased. There are no census figures from which to determine the growth of the major cities between 1838 and 1880. The estimates suggest that the major cities tripled or even quadrupled in size and that the rates of increase became greater with the passing years.[8] These cities attracted a cosmopolitan population. The number of Europeans, Levantines, and, especially, European colonial subjects increased, as did the Muslim and non-Muslim Ottomans.

The urban Muslim Turkish population became increasingly differentiated from the rural Turkish population and from that of unaffected interior towns. One could speak of a Turkish middle class only with reference to the Turks in the new urban centres

---

[8] The population of Istanbul in 1815 was estimated as 700,000 and the city proper 250,000. See J. E. DeKay, *Sketches of Turkey in 1831 and 1832* (New York, 1833), p. 172. (The population of New York at the same date is given as 213,000 in J. R. McCulloch, *A Dictionary, Practical, Theoretical, and Historical of Commerce and Commercial Navigation* (London, 1834), p. 834; Berlin, Vienna, and Petersburg had 436,000, 486,000, and 492,000 inhabitants respectively. Only London and Paris had more than 1½ million, the first being close to 2 million. Rome had a population of 180,359, and Cairo about 200,000, which rose to 240,000 in 1834. See Edward W. Lane, *Manners and Customs of the Modern Egyptians* (Everyman's ed.; London and New York, 1936), p. 24. In 1844 Istanbul's population is estimated as 891,000 in A. Ubicini, *Letters on Turkey*, English trans. Lady Easthope (London, 1856), I, 24. Izmir had a population of 120,000 around 1830, 162,000 in 1847, and 300,000 in 1891. See McCulloch *Dictionary of Commerce*, p. 1064; and Charles MacFarlane, *Turkey and its Destiny* (Philadelphia, 1850), I, 25. Salonika is estimated as 100,000 in 1832; see DeKay, *Sketches of Turkey*, p. 521. About the commercial growth of the coastal cities see Bailey, *British Policy*, pp. 95-114.

142

after the middle of the nineteenth century. One cannot speak of a rising Turkish bourgeoisie. The artisan classes of the medieval guilds (predominantly Turkish while the Rayahs were predominantly agrarian) were on the verge of extinction. They as well as the Turkish business classes were now underprivileged by comparison with both the Europeans and the non-Muslim traders; none from among them occupied any government posts or were engaged in the government-sponsored economic enterprises. The descendents of the guild artisans competed with the displaced peasants as petty peddlers, small shopkeepers, labourers, servants, or porters.

During this period, the *medreses,* ignored from the beginning of Mahmud II's reform period, were given an elixir. They became the refuge of the impoverished peasantry. They housed, thanks to their endowments, a reserve army for a reaction against the Tanzimat or, more correctly, against its failures.

Not from an economic but from the political and intellectual point of view, the most important category within the Turkish urban population consisted of the products of the new secular schools (the *münevver*). Under the circumstances, these constituted the "middle class." They were the upper echelons of the administrative, military, legal, and financial bureaucracy. (The lower echelons and a few who achieved prominence were still recruited from among the *medrese* graduates.) The numbers possessing at least some education outside of the traditional educational complex increased out of proportion to those of the previous periods. There was some added differentiation in their training and they began to assume much wider intellectual functions, but, for example, the majority of the Tanzimat finance ministers had a *medrese* education or were *littérateurs* of the old school.[9]

The development of trade under the impact of the European economic penetration created further economic differentiation between Muslims and non-Muslims in the predominantly Turkish parts of the Empire. Nineteenth-century European visitors portrayed the Turks as a people who did not engage in industry or trade and were peasants, administrators, or soldiers by nature. The striking differentiation they saw was the creation of the developments under discussion. Historical circumstances placed the non-Muslims in a position to benefit from the European economic penetration. However, the economic prosperity of the urban non-

---

[9] Cf. M. Z. Pakalın, *Tanzimat Maliye Nazırları* (2 vols.; Istanbul, 1939-40).

Muslims, especially of the middle classes, was far from heralding a genuine or independent capitalist class. Before the new era, the Greeks especially had benefited from foreign trade and had competed dangerously with the foreign traders, as MacFarlane remarked upon most ruefully.[10] Many non-Muslims, especially the Armenians, accumulated great but precarious wealth as the capitalist underwriters of the tax-farmers and as usurers. By the beginning of the new era, there was a money-owning class only among the non-Muslims, and it even constituted a bankers' colony at Galata and loaned money to the government from time to time. With the elimination of the restrictions that had made "men of straw" necessary and with the ascendance of European capital, they lost their former power. They possessed no experience in legitimate business and management under the conditions of a capitalist economy. Their attempts at investing in industry brought them to bankruptcy, or they were driven out by the European giants (for example, the indigenous Bank of Constantinople was supplanted by the Ottoman Bank which was an Anglo-French concern), or they became parasitical appendages to European capitalist enterprises.

This very brief description of the changes produced by the penetration of European economy suggests how the fall of the traditional system after long resistance opened the way for still broader changes and, thus, how very complicated the questions of the Tanzimat were.

Until 1838, Turkey had not been involved in the economic and political network of European civilization. The West was no more than a source of inspiration for ideas and methods. The reform policies were framed basically by the leaders of Turkey.

The political impact of the West upon the policies of reform began during the Tanzimat in the form of diplomatic intervention by the European powers.[11] Throughout the conflicts over the so-called Eastern Question, religion was used as a cover for power politics. Russia, France, and Great Britain pursued their policies on the basis of claims to the right of protection over the Orthodox, Catholic, and Protestant communities of the Ottoman Empire. Russia as a foe, and England and France as friends, demanded re-

143

---

[10] MacFarlane, *Turkey and its Destiny, passim.*

[11] The classic study of the Tanzimat in its connections with European diplomacy is Ed. Engelhardt, *La Turquie et le Tanzimat* (2 vols.; Paris, 1882-84).

forms with respect to the conditions of these communities. The demands inevitably had implications for reform policies, led to diverse interpretations of the reforms, and, finally, caused further complications of the principles enunciated in a charter known as the Gülhane or Tanzimat Charter.

144

The Tanzimat Charter

The fundamentals of a new regime were proclaimed in the Charter on November 3, 1839, about five months after Mahmud was succeeded by his son, the young Abdül-Mecid. We do not have to look at the English or French political impact in order to discover the origins of the ideas contained in the Tanzimat Charter and we shall not find them in the Muslim political thinking of the past. The ideas embodied in the Charter were simply a formulation of those that had become more or less crystallized during the latter part of Mahmud's reign. In fact, the contents of the Charter were under discussion before Mahmud's death.[12]

The word *tanzimat* is the plural of *tanzim* which means ordering. Hence, *tanzimat* meant a series of acts that would give a new

[12] See Abdurrahman Şeref, *Tarih Musahabeleri* (Istanbul, 1924), p. 48. In Western writings the document is known as Hatti Shérif or Khatti Chérif, which was the heading on the official French translation. The original Turkish text was published in *Takvim-i Vekayi*, No. 187 (15 Ramadan, 1255 H./A.D. 1839). Facsimiles of the two are in *Tanzimat* (Istanbul, 1940), I, following page 48. A French translation is in A. Ubicini, *Lettres sur la Turquie* (2nd ed.; Paris, 1853) I, 527-30; also A. Ubicini and Pavet de Courteille, *État present de l'Empire Ottoman* (Paris, 1876), pp. 231-34; and Engelhardt, *La Turquie*, I, 257-61. English translations are in Edward Hertslet, *The Map of Europe by Treaty* (London, 1875), II, 1002-5; Bailey, *British Policy*, pp. 277-79; William Goodell, *Memoirs, or Forty Years in the Turkish Empire*, ed. E. D. G. Prime (New York, 1876), pp. 480-82; Hurewitz, *Diplomacy in the East*, I, 113-16. For a résumé of the content of the Charter, see Temperley, *The Crimea*, pp. 160-61. On the Tanzimat in general see the collective work published by the Turkish Ministry of Education on the centenary of the proclamation of the Tanzimat Charter entitled *Tanzimat* (Istanbul, 1940), I. This volume (only the one having appeared) contains thirty-three contributions by Turkish scholars, some of which contain original material on various aspects of the Tanzimat reforms. For information on the organization of the state and the life and institutions of the peoples of the Ottoman Empire see the two volumes of A. Ubicini, *Letters on Turkey*. On the statesmen of the Tanzimat see Ali Fuad, *Ricâl-ı Mühimme-i Siyasiye* (Istanbul, 1928), p. 11; I. M. K. Inal, *Son Sadrazamlar* (10 vols. Istanbul, 1940-49), and Pakalın, *Tanzimat*.

order to the organization of the state. Perhaps the closest equivalent in English would be the Reforms; however, we shall use the word Tanzimat as the name of the regime that took definitive shape between 1839 and 1860 (the approximate date of the rise of a constitutional movement as a reaction).

145

The written instrument, often called the Gülhane Charter, proclaimed the principles of the Tanzimat. It granted and guaranteed certain rights that were said to be the fundamentals (Mevadd-ı Esasiye). A Protocol prepared by a Consultative Council (Meclis-i Şura) stated that: (*a*) the old disordered system had to be replaced by one based upon new laws (*kavanîn-i cedide*), (*b*) these laws would be in accordance with the Şeriat, (*c*) they would be based upon the inviolability of life, property, and honour as legal fundamentals, and (*d*) they would be equally applicable to all Muslims and to the peoples of the *millets*.[13] The Protocol emphasized that nothing would result in the desired reordering of the state unless the fundamentals of the laws (*nizamat*) were laid down in advance. As time would be required to realize the new order completely and as the non-observance of the new laws in the meantime would produce a state far worse than that which already existed, it was essential to maintain sharp vigilance over legal behaviour and to punish all violators of the laws whether they were persons of rank or common people.

The ruler added in his own handwriting his statement of oath. He pledged himself to execute faithfully the Şeriat laws embodied in the Charter as fundamentals, to observe the decisions by majority vote of the Council concerning the details of the fundamentals, to issue no decree or judgment concerning any person which was not in accordance with the laws instituted, and to refrain from abrogating the laws laid down on the basis of the Charter.

It is obvious that this is the earliest constitutional document in any Islamic country. While the Protocol and Charter did not form a constitution, there is no doubt that they contained the organic law by virtue of which a new political organization would exist. They designated the fundamentals to be incorporated in the organization of the state and its legal structure.

The Charter had two aspects of major importance to our subject—political and religious. In both respects, the ambiguity or,

---

[13] The complete text is printed in Reşat Kaynar, *Mustafa Reşit Paşa ve Tanzimat* (Ankara, 1954), pp. 172-73. The facsimile of the document will be found in *Tanzimat* (Istanbul, 1940), I, 709.

more correctly, equivocation in terms would create problems for the entire Tanzimat period.

The Charter contained the idea of limiting the arbitrary executive powers of the Padişah. It did not contain the slightest hint of popular sovereignty, but it expressly declared the abolition (or renunciation) of the central concept of the medieval doctrine of sovereignty, that is the prerogative of the ruler to exercise will (*irade*) for the enactment of kanûn within the areas left free by the Şeriat. The Charter made the sovereign an executive bound to the laws made by others.

However, as the Charter did not provide for any popular representation, the source of legislation would be the councils of deliberation (*meşveret*). The members of these were all appointed by the ruler for the duration of his will. The novelty was that in the past such bodies had been called or instituted only for the purpose of deliberation; they were advisory bodies with no law-making powers. Now they were invested with such powers, but the laws accepted by them through free discussion and majority decision acquired legal sanction only through ratification by the ruler.

In other words, the laws that the ruler solemnly declared he would execute and observe owed their formulation and sanctioning power, in the long run, to his will. This was certainly not a foolproof system, and its defects when there was a weak or irresolute ruler were to become apparent quickly. The understanding of constitutionalism or parliamentarianism did not go beyond the idea of *meşveret*, but one hesitates to be critical of the shortcomings of the Charter promulgated sixscore years ago in view of the existence even today of those believing that this old institution can suffice to make any regime a constitutional one.

The Charter was also equivocal respecting the judiciary. It contained no hint of the independence of the judicial function or its separation from the executive and legislative. The old concept that the judge (*qâdî*) was a delegate of the ruler persisted. This was to create difficulties when the reforms were extended to the judicial organization and, especially, during the establishment of procedural laws and regulations.

The second facet of the Charter was even more pregnant with problems. This was the acceptance in one breath of both the Şeriat and Fundamentals as the basis for the future statute laws. On the one hand, a return to the reign of the Şeriat was implied. On the other, the need was declared to institute new laws based on non-customary rights conferred by the temporal ruler. What then was the relation between the divinely given Şeriat and the temporally established laws? It is significant that a traditional practice was forgotten or ignored when the Charter was proclaimed; although it obviously concerned the Şeriat it was not accompanied by a *fetva* that would bring about its legitimization by the Şeyhul-İslâm. Thus, the Charter opened the first formal breach between the "temporal" and the "religious." The separationism characteristic of the Tanzimat secularism was thus formalized with the Charter.

The formalization of Mahmud's concept of *adalet* (the administration of justice in terms of equality before the law) as the basis for the Charter's Fundamentals was bound to create the difficulty of reconciling statute laws with a number of practices derived from the Şeriat and perpetuated through the *millet* system. Complete legal equality is a modern concept arising out of the needs of a modern political and economic system. During its beginnings and under Mahmud's strong personal rule, the anomalies in the execution of a new legal conception did not create marked crises. The situation changed with the promulgation of the Charter, with the attempts to regularize the principle, and with the intervention of the powers on behalf of the *millets* as a whole and without distinction for the inequalities cutting across religious boundaries. The difficulties were magnified with the promulgation of the Edict of 1856, which will be discussed later. The vexing task of eliminating the distinctions between the medieval communities of society while separating the "temporal" and "religious" was complicated by the opening, with the Tanzimat, of the most unfortunate period in Turkey's relations with Europe. The economic interests of the European powers pressed for secularization while the political-cum-religious interests of the same powers demanded the perpetuation of communal differentiations ranging from the legal and political to the educational field. The two interests were so contradictory and impelling that the application of the Tanzimat ideas became a matter, not simply of governmental administration or of politics, but of a religious-cultural nature transcending the political, administrative, and even economic problems.

Conflicting Views on the Tanzimat

148

"Probably few nineteenth century documents," commented an historian of the Tanzimat period, "have been more misunderstood or misinterpreted than the Tanzimat Charter."[14] For some it meant the preservation of the traditional order and implied neither constitutionalism, nor the adoption of the European political systems. Tanzimat meant to Palmerston "progressive improvement and development of the old Institutions . . . and in truth bringing them back to their ancient purity."[15] Metternich expressed a similar understanding much more articulately.[16] He too rejected the idea that the Tanzimat implied the introduction of a constitutional regime, which he believed was a peculiarity of the Christian countries. The Ottoman Empire, he wrote, was facing the danger of confusing that which was useful with that which was harmful, and that which was possible with that which was impossible. The only criterion not to be forgotten by any society facing such a situation was its own basic structure, because anything incompatible with the basic structure of a society was bound to fail. True reformers would not introduce those elements of European civilization that suited the peculiar needs of the French, English, Russian, or Austrian nations. They would give them, rather, a national character. One of the sources of the troubles of the Ottoman Empire was the attempt to bring about reforms in a European way. Metternich expressed himself officially saying,

> We recommend to the Porte the following policy—Build your government upon the basis of adherence to the religious institutions which are the essentials of your very existence. . . . Do not destroy

---

[14] Bailey, *British Policy*, p. 193.

[15] Palmerston to Ponsonby, No. 18, Feb. 4, 1840, quoted in *ibid.*, pp. 199-200. Ubicini wrote in 1851: "The . . . Tanzimat . . . does not denote, as has been erroneously supposed, a new order of things but, on the contrary, a regeneration or return to the ancient system, into which abuses had crept owing to lapse of time . . ." *Letters on Turkey*, I, 27. The French press viewed the Tanzimat as a revolutionary change and a sign of Westernization. For a review of the opinions of the French press concerning the Tanzimat Charter, see Sabri Esat Siyavuşgil, "Tanzimat'ın Fransız Efkâr-ı Umumiyesinde Uyandırdığı Akisler," *Tanzimat* (Istanbul, 1940), I, 747-56.

[16] See his *Mémoires*, ed. Richard de Metternich (Paris, 1883), VI, 378-86; in Turkish, *Muharrerat-ı Nadire* (Istanbul, 1873), XVII, 697-707; and Hıfzı Timur, "Türkiyede Abdülmecid'in Islahatı Hakkinda," *Tanzimat* (Istanbul, 1940), I, 703-8.

your ancient system in order to build a regime that would not
fit your customs and way of life. . . . Do not borrow from European
civilization institutions that do not agree with your institutions,
because Western institutions are based on principles that are different
from those forming the bases of your Empire. The bases of the
West are Christian laws. *Restez turcs: mais alors consultez la loi
musulmane. . . .*[17]

149

The opposite view was held by a statesman who represented
Great Britain several times and for many years in Turkey and
who played an important role in Near Eastern diplomacy. He was
Stratford Canning (Lord Stratford de Redcliffe after 1852). As
his views and activities led to incidents of diplomatic interference
having direct concern for our central problem, we shall dwell
upon his missionary rather than his strictly diplomatic behaviour.

Canning was a zealous Protestant and believed firmly that civilization and humanity would come to the East only with the
spread there of his faith. In addition to having a faith approximat-
ing fanaticism, Canning possessed an arrogant and tactless personality which caused a great deal of embarrassment, displeasure,
and dislike for him not only among the Turkish ministers but also
among his European colleagues.[18]

[17] Quoted by Engelhardt, *La Turquie*, I, 48.

[18] Stanley Lane-Poole, *The Life of Lord Stratford de Redcliffe*
(Popular ed.; London, 1890) portrays him as the architect of the
Tanzimat. However, "Canning had no original liking for the
Turks. He was the first to express an ardent hope that they would
be expelled from Europe with 'bag and baggage' ", *Encyclopedia
Britannica* (1957), XI, 461. Sir Henry Layard, who was close to
him and later became the British ambassador to Turkey, describes
him as follows: "It was not easy to satisfy Sir Stratford Canning.
. . . I was always of the opinion that the manner in which [he]
was in the habit of treating Turkish statesmen . . . did more harm
than good. . . . If some demand which he had made was not
acceded to, he would rise to his feet, knit his brows, and would
pour . . . a torrent of invective, accompanied by menacing ges-
tures. . . . The habit of . . . browbeating and domineering over
the Turkish Ministers and the Porte was . . . productive of very
evil consequences. . . . Moreover, the success which was supposed
to have attended his method of treating the Turkish Ministers
. . . induced other foreign Representatives to have recourse to the
same means to obtain their ends. . . . He set that fashion of using
threatening language in order to obtain concessions. . . . The
system he adopted was calculated to destroy the little prestige and
authority which remained to the Porte, and it gradually undermined its independence. . . ." Henry Layard, *Autobiography
and Letters* (London, 1903), II, 83-85. On Canning's diplomatic
career in Turkey see Harold Temperley, "The Last Phase of
Stratford de Redcliffe, 1855-58," *English Historical Review*, XLVII
(1932), 259.

150

One of Canning's ambitions was to obtain recognition of the Protestants (mostly Armenians proselytized from the Armenian Church) as a *millet* in order to have a religious stepping stone to diplomatic rights comparable to those claimed on an historical basis by Austria, Russia, and France. To the displeasure of the Austrian, Russian, and French governments, Canning succeeded in obtaining recognition of a Protestant church at Jerusalem. In 1850 he obtained full recognition for the Protestants of the Empire with the status of a new *millet*.[19]

The second objective of Canning's personal diplomacy was to extend the principle of *laissez-passer* underlying the Commercial Convention of 1838 to the field of religion and, by using the principle of freedom of conscience, to abolish the prohibition on apostasy. This prohibition was upheld by the Ulema and was enacted upon the demand of the Greek Church in 1834 by Mahmud II. It was upheld also by the Armenian Church following the influx of Protestant missionary groups after 1831 and the making of large-scale conversions. The real reason for the prohibition was to curtail the increasing schisms and religious animosities introduced for political ends.

Canning's religious liberalism, however, assumed the appearance of a campaign. He was convinced that Islam was responsible for the lack of religious freedom. Exploiting a complicated and not entirely religious case of double apostasy, he launched a religious offensive against the Turkish government in 1844. In fact, his real target was the Şeyhul-Islâm and his real aim was to obtain a pronouncement from *both* the government and the Şeyhul-Islâm, to be confirmed and proclaimed by the Padişah, recognizing unlimited freedom for the missionaries to proselytize among both Muslims and Christians.

Canning's demand was refused by both the government and the Şeyhul-Islâm. The latter declared that the Şeriat did not condone the proposed freedom and that he was not in the position to declare to the Muslims their freedom to change their religion, but, he added, the government would provide the competent judgment where a state of necessity existed.[20] The government, on the other

---

[19] See H. G. O. Dwight, *Christianity in Turkey: A Narrative of the Protestant Reformation in the Armenian Church* (London, 1854), 340-41.

[20] The Kur'an threatened the apostate with punishment in the next world only. The death penalty appeared later in *hadîth* literature. In *fiqh* literature the male apostate was to be put to death, but only if he had reached the age of adulthood, was sane, and had not

hand, replied that neither it nor the Padişah as Caliph (that is the executive of administration and justice according to the Şeriat but not as its interpreter; or, in Ottoman terminology, as one having the right of *taʿzîr* but not *iftâ*) could enforce a religious decision upon the Şeriat, but that it was within the power of the government to refrain from enforcing the prohibition of apostasy. The head of government and Abdül-Mecid assured Canning that apostates would not be punished. This, however, could not satisfy the zealot in Canning and he pressed for a formal declaration by the Şeyhul-Islâm.

151

Such undiplomatic behaviour would be answered almost universally by a request for the withdrawal of the ambassador, but Canning had so successfully inculcated the Tanzimat ministers with the belief in his right to interfere that they accepted the humiliation. Only the unbending Şeyhul-Islâm gained honour from the affair; but his standing up to the unreasonable European facilitated the return of the Ulema to the political arena.

The news of Canning's crusade for freedom spread throughout Europe and America. Hardly anyone knew the real nature of the matter. The impression given was that the Christians were being martyred through "Mohammedan fanaticism" as in the arenas of Rome, and a new revulsion for the Turk coursed through the Christian feelings. In fact, as Engelhardt noted, the tempest was aroused at a time when complete freedom of conscience had yet to be established in Catholic, Protestant, and Orthodox countries. Jews, Catholics, and nonconformists were struggling against several disabilities in Canning's own Great Britain. The Constitution of Greece prohibited Greek citizens from becoming converts to any but the Greek Orthodox faith. In the United States, the Mormons were enduring great trials and the constitutional principle of religious freedom had yet to be clarified. But all of the evidences of intolerance close to home paled before the vision of a Turkish blood bath. And, more importantly, these seemingly religious incidents were used to justify intervention or for diplomatic blackmail. Canning established this technique, together with bristling aggressiveness, as features of nineteenth-century European diplomacy in Turkey.

---

acted under compulsion. Females, on the other hand, were only to be imprisoned. For further details see W. Heffening, "Murtadd," *Encyclopaedia of Islam* (Leiden, 1936), III, 736-38 and the works cited there. On Canning's behaviour over the question of proselytization, see Engelhardt, *La Turquie*, I, 130-32.

Despite the formal repeal of the decree on apostasy in 1847 (the same year slavery was declared illegal), Canning persisted in his religious intervention. Before the convention in Paris, he proposed that Turkey declare of her own accord the further extension of the privileges of the Christians and the acceptance of international control over the implementation of these privileges.[21]

152

The Reform Edict and After

The result of the discussions was the proclamation of the Reform Edict (Islahat Fermanı) on February 18, 1856.[22] The Edict included: (a) a reaffirmation of the rights granted by the Charter and the need to take efficacious measures for their fullest implementation, (b) a reaffirmation and renovation of all ancient privileges and spiritual immunities granted to the non-Muslim religious communities (millets), (c) a guarantee of complete freedom in the exercise of all religious beliefs and rites, (d) the prohibition of all defamatory designations for any class of people on account of religion, language, or race, (e) a guarantee of equal treatment of the adherents of all creeds in matters of education, appointment to government posts, administration of justice, taxation, and military service, (f) a promise of reform of judicial tribunals and the creation of mixed tribunals, the reform of penal and commercial codes to be administered on a uniform basis and the reform of prisons, (g) a guarantee of the right of foreigners to own real property, (h) the representation of religious communities in the deliberations of the Supreme Council, and (i) a proposal for the devising of necessary measures for the commercial and agricultural improvement of the provinces with help to be forthcoming

---

[21] Quoted by Temperley, "The Last Phase of Stratford de Redcliffe," 230; see also Engelhardt, La Turquie, I, 133. On the demand for the abolition of the capitulations see Ali Fuad, Ricâl-ı Mühimme, p. 70.

[22] This is also referred to as the Hatti Humayun. See Thomas X. Bianchi, Khaththy Humaioun ou Charte Impériale Ottomane du Février 1856 (Paris, 1856); Engelhardt, La Turquie, I, 139 ff.; Ahmed Refik, "Türkiyede Islahat Fermanı," Türk Tarih Encümeni Mecmuası, XIV, No. 4 (81) (July, 1924), 193-215; E. Z. Karal, Osmanlı Tarihi (Ankara, 1947), V, 256-60; (1954) VI, 1-28; the Turkish text of the edict is in ibid., V, 266-72; the French version in Engelhardt, La Turquie, I, 263-70; the English version in Bailey, British Policy, pp. 287-91, and Hurewitz, Diplomacy in the East, I, 149-53.

from education, the sciences, and European funds. In other words, the Edict implied political, legal, religious, educational, economic, and moral reforms in which equality, freedom, material progress, and rational enlightment would be keynoted.

The central theme in the rivalries of the European powers over the Eastern Question was the position of the non-Muslim *millets* and their relationship with the reforms. The Russian thesis, stated clearly in 1867, was the extension of the privileges of the *millets* to the point of autonomy or independence.[23] While Great Britain opposed this view, Canning's policy made little difference in the long run because, for him, equality meant the equality of the *millets* as corporate communities and not the equality of Christians and Muslims as individual subjects of the state, as the Turkish government claimed. For him, the Ottoman state would have no social or national basis; it would establish peace and security while its existence would have no support other than an international guarantee.

The Tanzimat view on the *millet* question became clarified following the Crimean War, and its concept of secularism was given its best expression when the government felt constrained to enter into a British family affair. When in 1864 Canning's successor, Sir Henry Bulwer, refused to uphold unconditionally his predecessor's interventionist diplomacy, the British members of the Bible Society appealed to Lord Russell for support, claiming that the "sacred freedom of conscience" was "being violated with impunity in a country where the indignant remonstrations of the English nation should certainly be listened to and respected."[24] In the course of the dispute between Bulwer, the Foreign Office, and the missionaries in Turkey, Âli Paşa, the Ottoman prime minister, wrote for transmission to the British government:

The government of the Sultan has consecrated [by the Reform Edict] the free exercise of all rites professed within the Empire. It has always observed this promise scrupulously. . . . We can assert that the Christians of all rites enjoy in Turkey rights that they would be happy to possess in the majority of Christian countries in Europe. It would be useless to enumerate the restrictions imposed

153

[23] Engelhardt, *La Turquie*, I, 220-21.

[24] This and the following are quoted in *ibid.*, II, 83, 84. For a general discussion of the question of equality and toleration in nineteenth-century Turkey see Roderic H. Davison, "Turkish Attitudes concerning Christian-Muslim Equality in the Nineteenth Century," *American Historical Review*, LIX (1954), 844-64.

154

upon the liberty of conscience in other states, not excepting
Britain. . . . The imperial Ottoman government which has not
allowed free proselytization on behalf of the religion of the state can
not allow the contrary. The principle of religious tolerance can
not be, in our eyes, reconciled with open aggression against any
religion. . . .

We see here that Âli Paşa still regarded Islam as the official rite
of the Ottoman state, but pledged to keep the affairs of state
separate from Islam's provisions. Spanning the entire period, the
letters home of the Reverend Goodell show in exemplary fashion
how faithfully the government sought to separate "worldly" and
"religious" affairs and how persistently the nineteenth-century
Western impact upon the non-Muslim Ottomans confounded the
government's "separationist" secularism.

According to the Tanzimat statesmen, the *millet* privileges that
were of a purely religious nature would be preserved as they
concerned the freedom of conscience, but those relating to civil
and judicial affairs ought to be eliminated as incompatible with
the uniform execution of the reforms. The Ottoman state could
be secularized only when the *millets* became religious congregations (*cemaat*) and each Ottoman subject was individually responsible and equal before the laws. Then the Şeriat would cease
to be the basic law. It would remain only as the private law of
the Muslims while the state would be administered according to
newly enacted administrative, procedural, criminal, civil, and
commercial codes. There would be a rule of tolerance in the
sense understood by Âli Paşa. Education would foster tolerance, equality, and common Ottoman citizenship. Finally, an end
would be put to the political activities of the Ulema, the churches,
and the missionaries brought into the lists by Canning's religious
agitations.

The Secularism of the Tanzimat | *chapter 6*

THE EXPERIMENTS of the Tanzimat reformers gave shape, under the impact of the conditions surveyed in the previous chapter, to a policy of secularism in the sense of bringing forth a differentiation between the "temporal" and "religious" in the Turkish-Islamic context. The developments in administration, law, education, and literature will illustrate the creation of a dual system, or a series of dichotomies that would eventually plunge the separationist or dualist secularism of the Tanzimat into the insoluble dilemma of the Constitution of 1876.

The Problem of Government

The diverse problems of government were bound to become intensified during the Tanzimat. In view of its dedication to reform, to the realization of several non-customary rights, and to the establishment of new laws, the government itself should have been reformed. Certain of its traditional prerogatives ought to have been abrogated; government as well as its reformation should have been carried out by new, non-traditional social classes. The very core of innovation, particularly in the economic field, should have been political reform. But, the Tanzimat did not bring about any substantial change in the highest institution of the state and this was one reason why it failed to bring about economic Westernization.

156

The Tanzimat provided no constitutional framework for regulating relations between the governing and governed, between the sovereign and his administration, or between the legislative and administrative on the one hand, and the judiciary on the other. Although the inferior quality of the Tanzimat rulers enhanced the importance of the prime ministers, Mahmud II's innovation was not developed into a cabinet system. The system was maintained of having a prime minister (the title Sadrazam was restored in place of *başvekil*) together with individually appointed and individually responsible ministers. In consequence, the Tanzimat governments lacked stability and homogeneity—although the ministers were all conspicuously secular in outlook.

The governmental advances were in essence no more than the development of two of Mahmud's innovations. One was the accentuation of the Ottoman monarch's attribute of enlightened, or benevolent absolute rule at the expense of his caliphal attribute. The other was the transformation, noted above, of the Council of Judicial Enactments into a judiciary body, the *adliye* court system, unconcerned with both the Şeriat and kanûn, but based upon the principle of *adalet*.

Under the Tanzimat, each of the ministerial departments, except for foreign affairs, came to have a permanent council for the preparation of projects and regulations.[1] These organs became increasingly divorced from the Şeriat and kanûn as their *ulema* constituents began to be replaced by a new type of educated man—the product of the secular schools of higher learning. The councils constituted the legislative organs of the Tanzimat.

Mahmud's Council of Judicial Enactments continued to function as the supreme body, or Supreme Council. The Supreme Council assumed a more parliamentary character with the passage of time. Its rules of procedure were the rudimentary rules of parliamentary discussion.[2] Abdül-Mecid introduced the custom of addressing the Council annually and the Council adopted the custom of discussing and answering the speech from the throne. This was the first step towards treating the ruler as though he were a constitutional monarch. However, the members of the Council all came from among the highest civil office holders, the highest ranks

[1] For details see A. Ubicini, *Letters on Turkey*, English trans. Lady Easthope (London, 1856), I, 41-42.

[2] See Ahmed Rasim, *İstibdattan Hâkimiyet-i Milliyeye* (Istanbul, 1923), I, 239-44.

of the Ulema, and the dignitaries of the *millet* organizations. The masses of people had no role to play as citizens in the government.

Unrepresentative as the Council was, there began to emerge some recognition of the right of the people to watch over the execution of laws. The Criminal Law of 1840 expressed this right clearly.[3] Need was felt after 1845 to establish greater articulation in the relations between government and people. Two experiments were undertaken with this in mind. One was to invite delegates from the provincial councils (founded by Mahmud) to attend the meetings of the Council. The delegates were representative of the religious communities and were appointed for one year only. They were not recognized as constituting a separate or permanent body. Their only prerogative was to explain the needs of the people and the provinces upon request by the Council. The other experiment operated in the opposite direction. The provincial councils were made semi-representational bodies following the re-organization of the provincial administrations in 1864. Whereas all of the council members had hitherto been appointed, half of them came to be elected by the local people.[4] These councils did excellent work despite the contentions of the British ambassador to the contrary.[5]

A further step was taken in 1868. The Council was separated into two bodies, the Divan-ı Ahkâm-ı Adliye (Board of Judicial Enactments) and the Şura-yı Devlet (Council of State). The former became the highest judicial organ and evolved into the Ministry of Justice with jurisdiction over the secular (*adliye*) courts; it was presided over by the conservative jurist Cevdet Paşa. The Şura-yı Devlet was presided over by the liberal administrator Midhat Paşa and became the source of the constitutional movement culminating in the drafting of a Constitution in 1876. The following remark of the ruler, Abdül-Aziz, in his opening address to the new Council, shows the emergence of a conception of differentiation in function: "The new organization is based upon the separation of the executive power from the judicial, religious, and civil powers."[6]

---

[3] See Hıfzı Veldet, "Kanunlaştırma Hareketleri ve Tanzimat," *Tanzimat* (Istanbul, 1940), I, 177.

[4] See Ed. Engelhardt, *La Turquie et le Tanzimat* (Paris, 1882), I, 75-76; Rasim, *İstibdattan*, I, 256-58.

[5] See Harold Temperley, "British Policy towards Parliamentary Rule and Constitutionalism in Turkey (1830-1914)," *Cambridge Historical Journal*, IV, No. 2 (1933), 162-63.

[6] Engelhardt, *La Turquie*, II, 20.

158

These were gradual and tantalizing movements towards a constitutional system whose nature and feasibility in terms of the Şeriat had yet to be discussed seriously by anyone. To arrive at such a stage, sought by no statesman either Turkish or European, the Tanzimat had to traverse a course of further secularization within the field of law, and this characterized its reform experiment.

Among the significant developments of the time that will not be discussed in detail was the silent transformation within the *millets* or, as the Tanzimat saw them, within the ecclesiastical communities (*cemaat*) of the non-Muslims. Traditionally and until the Tanzimat, the Armenian, Greek, Jewish, and other recognized communities had been little theocracies within an empire. The spiritual head of each community had had civil, fiscal, educational, and even penal jurisdiction over his flock. The Greek patriarch, for example, possessed the apparatus for sending Ottoman subjects of his religious community into exile; he was within his rights in demanding that the government recognize his absolute jurisdiction over the education of the children of reformist Greek Ottomans.

Millet

Following the Reform Edict, these communities underwent secularizing constitutional changes. Lay bodies acquired certain rights in the conduct of ecclesiastical affairs; they and the ecclesiastics combined with freely elected representatives of the people to legislate, execute, and judge all the religious, administrative, financial, educational, and civil affairs of the community. With these changes giving scope for new political experiences the *millets* became little non-territorial republics and incipient "nations." The Armenian community, for example, had a national assembly whose composition and mode of election resembled those of a parliament, as Engelhardt observed. The following short description of the Armenian case will illustrate the development generally:

> This practical self-government . . . encouraged the growth of a community life which eventually gave birth to a longing for national life. . . . The constitution approved by the Sultan in 1863 gave the Armenians in Turkey the status of a self-governing nation in a political sense under the sovereignty of Turkey. . . . The more the reforming movement progressed in Turkey the more the Armenians benefited by it.[7]

---

[7] A. Safrastian, "Armenia," *Encyclopaedia Britannica* (1957), II, 379. On the organization of the non-Muslim communities see Ubicini, *Letters on Turkey*, II; A. Ubicini and Pavet de Courteille, *État présent de l'Empire Ottoman* (Paris, 1876), pp. 191-212; Engelhardt, *La Turquie*, I, 150-51.

By contrast, the Muslims, especially the Turks, did not benefit constitutionally from the Tanzimat secularism or Reform Edict. There was no communal organization of the Muslims outside the state apparatus. Neither the medieval Islamic conception of *umma* nor the Tanzimat conception of the limits of reform were conducive to the development by the Muslims of a *millet* organization in the new understanding of the term. The lack of national homogeneity among the Muslims was a further deterrent to such a development. Therefore, while Muslims in other parts of the world, for example in Russia, India, and Indonesia, developed community organizations closely resembling those of the *millets* in the Ottoman Empire, the Ottoman Turks continued to place themselves directly under the state which was no longer an Islamic state.

Most of the problems to be found in the secular and religious institutions emanated from the threefold consequences of this situation: (*a*) there was no autonomous development in the religious institution, (*b*) the secularization of the state took place in the form of a duality, or dichotomy, within the cultural institutions, not in the form of a state and church duality, and (*c*) the state became increasingly devoid of a national substratum, hence, of a popular basis. Removed from its traditional foundations, the state remained baseless in a constitutional sense and rootless in a national sense. Before the new and enormous problems incurred by the sudden change in Turkey's economic and political relations with the West, the Tanzimat state became a political machine whose function began to be conceived as that of maintaining order (*nizâm*) for the promotion of interests which eventually became definitely non-Turkish. *i.e. European*

The end of the political Tanzimat came when the Turkish element showed signs of revolt against its economic and political nonentity. Despite its national basis, the reaction was still far from being nationalistic. The anti-Tanzimat movement took the form of an amalgam of constitutionalism and religious nationalism as was represented by the Young Ottoman movement. It was more progressive than the Tanzimat while it retrogressed from the Tanzimat secularism. As we shall see, the duality within the anti-Tanzimat movement was converted easily by Abdül-Hamid towards the formation of an Islamic State.

Codification and Judicial Innovations

Our second topical consideration will be the development of Tanzimat secularism within the field of law. The problems of differentiation between the legislative-executive, legislative-judicial, and judicial-executive arose there within the limits set by the lack of a Turkish *millet*. The need for codification arises when there is a multiplicity of traditions that do not meet new requirements. Law codification was a natural consequence of Mahmud's introduction of the concept of *adalet* as distinct from that of the Şeriat and kanûn. Just as the innovations under Mahmud introduced the concept of *maârif*, or the learning of unfamiliar things, as a vehicle of modernization, so they brought *adliye* not only in the sense of the administration of justice, but also in the sense of laying down new rules to establish a new order.

The changes in the economic and political conditions pointed up the inadequacy of the traditional laws and procedures under modern conditions. The new economic and political forces necessitated the replacement of a non-formal, moral-religious legal system by one based upon formal and positive statutes. The Tanzimat brought law codification rather than parliamentary legislation as its distinctive feature. Its attempts at codification constituted the first such experiment in a Muslim country in the modern era.

The term codification is used generally in the sense of putting laws into writing with some degree of systematization in form and substance. The Tanzimat codification, however, involved reducing to written form by making a selection among diverse rules, by unifying or reconciling contradictory rules, and by introducing new rules. The supreme body of law-making formed by Mahmud became under the Tanzimat the organ that would undertake the job of codification according to the *adalet*, which had become expressed in the Charter as the Tanzimat's organic law.

The Tanzimat Charter had declared loyalty to the Şeriat. At the same time, it had declared with greater emphasis the necessity of framing *new* laws. It stated that the major cause of misrule, injustice, and disorder was the lack of laws as written instruments, declared and accessible to the public. Neither the Şeriat nor the kanûns fulfilled these conditions. The Şeriat was not a codified or written law comprising civil, commercial, and penal provisions. The kanûns were written and promulgated, but they were not accessible; neither were they juridical in a real sense because, by definition, they were subject to the separate will of each ruler.

For the first time it appeared that laws should be framed on the basis of a superior law. Codification was, therefore, the first attempt to differentiate between law and religion and to legislate, after deliberation and selection, from among the available sources and upon certain rational or secular criteria. A number of problems implied in each proposition constituted the major issues of the Tanzimat secularism within the legal field.

161

Codification is itself an unmistakable sign of secularization in a Muslim society as it is a planned, concerted human effort to formulate the Şeriat as a positive law. Even though the result may be based upon the Şeriat, the process makes it a code distinguishable easily from religion and relating only to legal action. Whether codification is realized through the acts of a legislature representing the will of the people, or by a competent person or body, it is nevertheless another feature of secularization since it involves selection and deviation from tradition, as set either by religion, or by state, or by both. Selection means screening the provisions of the schools of *fiqh*, or choosing between the Şeriat provisions and the Western codes, or making eclectic combinations of the two. And, finally, doing all this implies the existence of absolute criteria that have to be different in nature from those of the Şeriat and tradition and, as such, secular *par excellence*.

The appearance of a separation between the "world" and "religion" in the form of a law codification rather than in the form of a separation between state and church was the result of a difference between Christianity and Islam referred to earlier. The secularization of law began in an area that was traditionally outside the scope of the Şeriat with the formation of the first completely secular code. This code was the result of commercial relations with outsiders. The expansion of these relations following the Commercial Treaty of 1838 led to the codification of a commercial law and to the organization of the first tribunal independent of the *şeriat* courts or Christian ecclesiastical courts.

From the early part of the nineteenth century, Turkish and foreign traders began to form Mixed Traders' Councils to adjudicate cases between them. European customs and practices were applied in the settlement of disputes in these Councils which were recognized formally after 1840, under the title Ticaret Meclisi (Commercial Board). Negotiations between the government and the European powers holding capitulatory privileges resulted in 1847 in the formal recognition of mixed tribunals composed of ten foreign, ten Muslim Ottoman, and ten non-Muslim Ottoman

162

citizens.[8] The recognition of these bodies and their manner of procedure was with the implicit sanction of the Şeriat as it recognized the right of disputants to choose their own arbiters. These "courts" did not utilize any formally codified law or procedure and their members were not judges in the real sense. They enacted entirely upon the basis of established commercial precedent.

The establishment of these purely secular courts led to the enactment of the first secular code in 1850. This was the Commercial Code taken from the French Code of 1807.[9] A second, again borrowed from French commercial law, was enacted as an addition to the first in 1860. By it, the commercial courts were made responsible to the Ministry of Commerce. Thus, they became the first secular courts outside the jurisdiction of the Şeyhul-Islâm.[10] Codification of commercial law was completed by the Code of Procedure of the Commercial Courts in 1861 and the Code of Maritime Commerce in 1863.

Deviations from the *şeriat* procedure were made first in these courts, with the acceptance of non-Muslim witnesses against Muslims.[11] When this practice was extended to the *adlî* or *nizamî* (secular statutory) courts on their foundation, it did not arouse any opposition.

The first act of codification had three major effects: (1) the secular courts began to expand their jurisdiction at the expense of the *şeriat* courts, (2) a need began to be felt to organize the whole judicial system so as to separate the functions of the secular

---

[8] See Ubicini, *Letters on Turkey*, I, 171-74; Harold Temperley, *England and the Near East: The Crimea* (London, New York, and Toronto, 1936), pp. 233-34.

[9] See Ubicini, *Letters on Turkey*, I, 166; Veldet, "Kanunlaştırma, Hareketleri," pp. 196-97.

[10] For further information concerning the evolution of these commercial courts, see Şevket Mehmet Ali Bilgişin, *Türk Ticaret Hukuku Prensipleri* (Ankara, 1936), pp. 33 ff.; Hazım Atıf Kuyucak, *Ticaret Hukuku* (Istanbul, 1939), pp. 8 ff.; Vasfi Raşit Sevig, *Ticaret Kanunu Şerhi* (Istanbul, 1935), I, xli ff.

[11] See Ubicini, *Letters on Turkey*, I, 179. The English translation of Ubicini's letters omitted the following comment by Ubicini on the acceptance of the non-Muslim witness: "this great and liberal measure of admitting all the subjects to take oath according to the rite to which they belong is a considerable achievement and contrasts with the civil and political incapacity of Jews in England — a country which marches at the head of civilization — even today [1853]." A. Ubicini, *Lettres sur La Turquie* (2nd ed.; Paris, 1853), I, 195.

and religious courts while demarcating their areas of jurisdiction, and (3) efforts began towards the codification of legal areas previously covered entirely by the Şeriat.

The first test in modernizing the Şeriat came in the attempt to draw up a penal code. It was inevitable that the first step would be in that direction for the very essence of the Tanzimat Charter was to ensure "life, property, and honour." Penal law was a field of legislation which had been subject traditionally to the kanûn enactments of the rulers. While the kanûns on penal offences had not abrogated the penal provisions of the Şeriat, they had made obsolete such provisions as those relating to *qisâs* (retaliation) and *diya* (blood-wite).

163

The Supreme Council prepared a penal code for promulgation in 1840. It was a marked improvement over the one drawn up in Mahmud's time. It was both the first legal expression of the Charter and the first expression of the duality of the Tanzimat. It contained provisions emanating from modern secular criminal codes side by side with others taken from the Şeriat. It confirmed the principle of equality and followed the principle that no one would be punished without a trial and court sentence; it ruled that trials would be public and that the impartiality of the judges was essential. On the other hand, it revived Şeriat provisions such as *qisâs* and *diya* (Chap. I, Art. 1; Chap. IX, Art. 3; Chap. X, Art. 2; and Chap. XL, Art. 3). The code was also defective in nomenclature and in the definition and classification of criminal acts. Several offences were omitted. Above all, it maintained the character of the medieval law books; it was a collection of precepts rather than a precise digest of acts, punishments, and procedures.[12]

The shortcomings of the Code of 1840 led to another in 1851.[13] This was not substantially different from the first. The two were attempts to "modernize" the penal provisions of the Şeriat and the kanûns by producing a sort of *digest* rather than a *code*.

The situation changed radically following the promulgation of the Reform Edict. An entirely new Penal Code was enacted in 1858. This was an adaptation of the French Penal Code of 1810

---

[12] See Veldet, "Kanunlaştırma Hareketleri," pp. 176-79; Tahir Taner, "Tanzimat Devrinde Ceza Hukuku," *Tanzimat* (Istanbul, 1940), I, 226-28; Ubicini, *Letters on Turkey*, I, 164-65; for the text of the code see Kaynar, *Mustafa Reşit Paşa ve Tanzimat* (Ankara, 1954), pp. 303-12.

[13] The Penal Code of 1851 re-affirmed the Şeriat provisions to an even greater extent, Taner, "Tanzimat," I, 229.

164

and was, thus, the first introduction of a Western legal formulation in the field of public law. It remained in force longer than any other (from 1858 until 1918) with marked revisions in 1911 and 1914.[14] With this code, the Tanzimat introduced the new legal principles declared in the Charter of 1839 and in the Edict of 1856: the principle of equality in the application of punitive provisions, the principle that no one was punishable for an unspecified act, and the principle of individual responsibility.

The Penal Code of 1858 was incomparably modern in form and substance. Its provisions were predominantly secular. However, it was not entirely free from certain Şeriat provisions in its original form. Article 1 stated that the Code did not abrogate the *uqûbât* (penal) provisions of the Şeriat, that it was enacted merely to codify within the limits of the rights of *ta'zîr* of the *ûlu'l-amr*, (the chief executive, that is, the ruler) and that it would not infringe upon claims for *qisâs*, *diya*, or personal rights determined by the Şeriat; the code contained specific articles to these effects (Arts. 171, 172, 177, and 180).

We see here an example of the efforts to draw up a secular code in the belief that it could be modern in form and content although based upon the Şeriat. In fact, the co-existence of the two within the code gave rise to several unexpected clashes in the field of legal administration. One example will illustrate the gap between the legal provisions applying in the two realms and the extent of the difficulties to which these differences could lead.

A statutory court handling a case of homicide acquitted the defendant on the basis of the discretionary powers which the Penal Code accorded to the judge in the absence of direct evidence. On the basis of Article 171 of the Penal Code, the heirs were still entitled to file a suit in the *şeriat* court, which recognized only legal proof (principally direct and oral). The *şeriat* court judge sentenced the defendant to death on the basis of *qisâs*. Death sentences could be executed only following their ratification by the ruler according to both laws, but, according to the Penal Code (Article 172), the penalty for commuted death sentences was fifteen years to life imprisonment. Thus, internal contradictions made a mockery of the Penal Code and of the courts established on the basis of its underlying secularist principles.[15]

---

[14] For an analysis of this code, see *ibid.*, 230-31.

[15] *Ibid.*, 231. For more details concerning the conflict of laws, see the articles by Veldet, M. R. Belgesay, and Taner in *Tanzimat* (Istanbul, 1940), I, 202 ff., 214, 231.

The new codes were applied to the secular courts called *nizamiye* (statutory) or *adliye*, which were under the jurisdiction of the Ministry of Justice. As a result of the policy of separating the secular from the religious, these operated side by side with the *şeriat* courts which were left to the jurisdiction of the Şeyhul-Islâm.

Attempts to remove the conflicts between the two systems of law and courts continued throughout the Tanzimat and the succeeding periods. Stage by stage, increasing areas of life had to undergo legal redefinition and even reorientation; bit by bit, areas had to be removed from the sphere designated as "religious." Once the two areas were set free from tradition, a process of transvaluation from one to the other began. The more the areas of private and civil law became involved in the transvaluation, the more a battle impended between the Şeriat and the new codes.

The process of legal secularization encountered difficulties in defining the boundaries between the secular and religious when it reached the stage of codifying civil law. This was because of the interconnections between areas of law. Even strictly commercial cases had criminal or civil implications. It became increasingly untenable to confine the jurisdiction of the secular courts, but for a long time no one dared promote the idea of establishing secular courts that would be outside the jurisdiction of the Şeyhul-Islâm and competent to handle civil law cases. The decision to do this was reached finally in 1868 with the establishment of the Divan-ı Ahkâm-ı Adliye.

The task called for a man who was one of the *ulema* and yet was progressive enough to undertake the establishment of secular civil courts. This man was Cevdet Paşa (1822-95) who had renounced his status as a member of the Ulema in 1866 to become a secular minister.[16] With diplomatic aplomb, Cevdet legitimized the establishment of secular courts upon the authority of Jalâl al-Dîn Dawwânî's tract (*Dîwân-i Dafʻi Mazâlim*, written originally in Persian) showing that secular courts were not only compatible with Islam but also were necessary to it. The Divan-ı Ahkâm-ı Adliye, divided into civil and penal departments, became

---

[16] On his life and work see Fatma Aliye, *Ahmed Cevdet Paşa ve Zamanı* (Istanbul, 1916), and Ebül'ulâ Mardin, *Ahmet Cevdet Paşa 1822-1895* (Istanbul, 1946).

under Cevdet the highest court of the new statutory (*nizamî*) court system.[17]

Once the new organization reunited the hearing of civil, criminal, and commercial cases under one roof, the questions of codifying the civil law and unifying judicial practices were bound to become intensified. All sorts of strange situations arose, sometimes in the final disposition of a single case. For example, an institution unheard of in the *şeriat* court tradition had come into existence in 1852 when it was discovered that certain criminal cases could not be handled by the courts for the lack of a plaintiff; this was the office of Prosecutor General whose function was such a novelty that it caused much confusion and many amusing courtroom scenes. As in some comic opera, the judge and court changed their appearances to suit the nature of the cases on the docket; commercial and criminal cases were heard according to the new procedural codes and judged in terms of the new statutory laws, but civil suits were heard and judged according to the Şeriat and its procedures. The only innovation was that the court was under the jurisdiction of the secular or temporal authority at all times.

The most interesting and difficult phase of codification began with attempts to resolve the anomalies of the new court system through codification of the civil law. This concerned the area in which the Şeriat was particularly sensitive and also especially well equipped. Thus, when the idea of codifying arose, it met with opposition.

It seems that the idea of adopting the French Civil Code had existed from the beginning of the Tanzimat. About 1840 the preparation of a civil code seems to have been "confided to a French man of letters," but the attempt was abandoned.[18] However, the idea appears to have been revived in 1855 because Cevdet Paşa writes:

With the increase in the number of Europeans coming to Turkey, and with the increase of contacts with them because of the Crimean War, the scope of trade widened. The commercial courts became unable to deal with the commercial lawsuits arising every day.

[17] These courts were at first called new courts (*mahakim-i cedide*), or *tribuneaux régulièrs*, and later *tribuneaux règlementaires*, in French. The latter corresponds to the term *nizamî* — that is, operating on regulations or sets of laws and distinguished from the traditional courts.

[18] Engelhardt, *La Turquie*, I, 41.

166

The foreigners did not like to go to the *şeriat* courts. The inacceptability of the testimony of non-Muslims against Muslims and of Musta'man [non-Muslim foreigners] against *dhimmî* [non-Muslim Ottoman subjects] in the *şeriat* courts became very annoying to the Europeans and they objected to the trial of the Christians in the *şeriat* courts. Thus, certain persons took up the idea of translating French [civil] codes into Turkish for judgment in the *nizamî* courts. This idea was not acceptable because changing the basic laws of a nation would entail its destruction. The *ulema* believed that those who had gone astray to hold such Frankish ideas were unbelievers. The Franks, on the other hand, used to say "bring forth your code; let us see it and make it known to our subjects."[19]

After a long battle between those who desired the adoption of the French Civil Code and those who wanted to codify a law from Islamic jurisprudence, the government decided upon "drawing up a book in Turkish to be called *Metn-i Metîn* (Basic Text) and to cover the part on transactions (*mu'âmalât*) of the *fiqh* and to be written in language comprehensible to every man."[20] Cevdet was made a member of the committee formed for this purpose. However, the idea of adopting the French code persisted and we find the Sadrazam Âli Paşa mentioning the adoption of the French Civil Code as an urgently needed reform in his memorandum of 1867.[21] Apparently a committee was working on an adaptation of the French code when the decision was taken to open secular courts in which civil cases would be heard. In letters dated July 10, 1867 and March 10, 1868, the French chargé d'affaires and the French Ambassador reported that Âli Paşa had

---

[19] Cevdet Paşa, *Tezâkir 1-12*, ed. Cavid Baysun (Ankara, 1953), pp. 62-63. Those who favoured the adoption of the French Civil Code of 1804 were trying to persuade the government to adopt the translation they had prepared. Leading those who wanted the French Civil Code translated and adopted was Mehmed Kabulî Paşa, who became Minister of Commerce in 1867. Sir Henry Layard says of him: "the third rising Turkish statesman with whom I was intimate, was perhaps the most truly liberal in his convictions. . . . He was . . . well acquainted with the French language, and with the literature of Europe. He gave proof of his liberal opinions, and of his desire to introduce social as well as political reforms amongst his Mussulman fellow-countrymen, by having his wife taught French and the piano." Henry Layard, *Autobiography and Letters* (London, 1903), II, 94.

[20] Cevdet, *Tezâkir*, pp. 62-63.

[21] The text of the memorandum is in Ali Fuad, *Ricâl-ı Mühimme-i Siyasiye* (Istanbul, 1928), pp. 118-27.

formed such a committee and that fifteen to sixteen hundred articles of the French Civil Code had been translated into Turkish by a committee.[22] Cevdet records his objections:

168

> The basis of laws and by-laws in every state is the civil code. As our state was based upon the Şeriat, it should, therefore, be the basis for our laws and by-laws. . . . The opinions of the ministers were divided on this point. One group [headed by Cevdet] was in favour of the composition of a book of the Şeriat compiled according to the needs of the time from the *fiqh* literature on *mu'âmalât*. This would be a book of the laws of the Şeriat for the Muslims and would be applied as *kanûn* among the non-Muslims. . . . The other group [of which the Minister of Commerce was a prominent member] favoured the translation of the French code which would be applied in the [new] statutory (*nizamî*) courts. The French Ambassador M. Bourée, being the most influential foreign representative, wished to see the French codes applied in Turkey and all those who supported the pro-French policy favoured this unsound view. The Minister of Commerce, Kabulî Paşa, insisted upon this view and even tried to pass the code which he had had translated into Turkish, but he was defeated by our opposition in the Council.[23]

Dawwânî's tract came to Cevdet's rescue once again. He found in it grounds for the application of a statutory code derived from the *fiqh*. Dawwânî's thesis that the testimony of every man irrespective of his religion was permissible seems to have overcome a major cause of the deadlock.[24] Convinced by his arguments, the government appointed Cevdet to head a committee for the compilation of a book of law, the Mecelle (Arabic, *Majalla*).

The provisions of the Mecelle would be derived exclusively from the Hanafî school of law; and where the Hanafî jurists disagreed, the opinion closest to the *nass* (revealed injunctions given in sacred texts) and most suitable to expediency would be preferred.

The Mecelle actually codified a part of what in the *fiqh* literature was known as *mu'âmalât*. The compilation of its sixteen

[22] Cf. Ihsan Sungu, "Galatasaray Lisesinin Kuruluşu," *Belleten*, VII, No. 28 (1943), 323, and Baron de Testa, *Recueil des traités de la Porte Ottomane* (Paris, 1866), VII, 469. It had been realized that owing to the extension of the jurisdiction of the commercial courts to civil cases and the inadequacy of the Commercial Code of 1850, the latter should be supplemented by the adoption of the provisions of the French Civil Code on contracts and obligations.

[23] Quoted by Mardin, *Cevdet Paşa*, pp. 63-64.

[24] *Ibid.*, p. 61.

books continued from 1869 until 1876 with interruptions. The committee was dissolved in 1888, having been inactive following the establishment of Abdül-Hamid's reign.[25]

The ascendancy of Cevdet's thesis pleased neither the Westernists, or Frankists as Cevdet called them, nor the *ulema*.[26] The newly appointed Şeyhul-Islâm, Hasan Fehmi, argued that any such compilation fell within the jurisdiction of his office rather than that of the Ministry of Justice (the new name for the Divan-ı Ahkâm-ı Adliye). Although there was no precedent, he interpreted the matter of codification as an act of *iftâ* (interpreting the provisions of the Şeriat on a particular matter) which was the real function of his office. His opposition, which caused an interruption in the work of the Committee in 1870, illustrates what was regarded as the specific prerogatives of the religious institution as opposed to the secular prerogatives. The "religious" opposition continued until the Committee was dissolved without having codified the family, marriage, and inheritance laws which were the core of the Şeriat. The stronghold of the Şeriat thus remained intact.

169

Encroachment Upon the Şeriat

With the extension of the statutory courts (penal, commercial, and civil), the scope of the functions and jurisdiction of the *şeriat* courts was severely contracted. The jurisdiction of the office of the Şeyhul-Islâm was curtailed in favour of the new Ministry of Justice. On the other hand, the statutory courts did not have jurisdiction over cases to be judged according to the uncodified Şeriat, or according to the ecclesiastical laws of the *millets* which were administered in their courts.

It proved difficult to demarcate the scope of the jurisdiction of the *şeriat* courts. At the outset even the statutory law of commerce recognized the jurisdiction of the *şeriat* courts on commercial lawsuits provided the parties concerned preferred it that way and

---

[25] For an analysis of the content of the sixteen Books of the Mecelle, see Sıddık Sami Onar, "Majalla," *Law in the Middle East*, ed. Majid Khadduri and H. J. Liebesny (Washington, 1955), I, 292-308; on the members of the Mecelle Committee, see Mardin, *Cevdet Paşa*, pp. 160-66; on the sources of the Mecelle, *ibid.*, pp. 167-69; on the successive stages of its preparation, *ibid.*, pp. 66-139.

[26] *Ibid.*, pp. 91 ff.

170

the question of Christian witnesses was not involved. The administration of the statutory and *şeriat* courts was separated in 1869 and, much more clearly, in 1878. In spite of the differentiation of the two types of courts, they continued to overlap and contradict each other. The two types of laws and courts had different legal conceptions concerning procedure. Furthermore, the statutory laws were neither entirely secularized nor entirely based on the Şeriat.

The statutory laws covered cases with certain implications that still fell under the jurisdiction of the Şeriat. But, as we have illustrated in the instance of homicide, when the provisions of the Şeriat were applied to a case already settled by the statutory court, the settlement of the *şeriat* court was incompatible with that of the statutory.

The continuation of the conflict between the two legal systems and the increase in the difficulty of separating the respective areas of the two were admitted as late as 1886 in a statement issued by the Ministry of Justice. This statement attempted to bring about a new solution. It enumerated specifically the matters that would come under the *şeriat* court jurisdiction (such as marriage, divorce, alimony, retaliation, blood-wite, wills, and inheritance); it also enumerated those commercial and criminal matters over which the statutory courts had exclusive jurisdiction. The remainder was left subject to the *şeriat* courts if the parties agreed, and to the statutory courts if they did not. That this failed to resolve the difficulties is shown by another attempt made as late as 1914. This time, only the cases for the *şeriat* court were specified; the remainder were to be assigned to the statutory courts.

The difficulties arising from the conflict of laws would probably have been diminished if the *mu'âmalât* had been completed as a statutory law. Since this was not allowed, the whole legal system of Turkey was split into three parts—one being borrowed from the French codes, another being the traditional Şeriat, and the third being the codified portion of the second. In spite of all the efforts to establish harmony and consistency, the Tanzimat experiment showed that the failure was due not to the legal difficulties involved, but rather to the impossibility of such a reconciliation. As the Turkish jurists recognized and declared following the dissolution of the Ottoman Empire, the difficulty was due to the fact that the bases of the two legal systems were different and irreconcilable, as they were the legal foundations of two different civilizations—medieval and modern.

The situation was a reflection of the state of transformation in which Turkish society found itself at the time; it was due mainly to the persistence of the most legalized aspect of medieval society. The Şeriat was incapable of accepting any revision in its entire outlook. It did not raise its voice during the first part of the Tanzimat because there was not yet any infringement upon its own sphere to cause worry about the need for any reform on the part of the Ulema. The Şeriat was not upset by the introduction of the new penal and commercial laws because these legal aspects were regarded as being outside its own jurisdiction; it even accepted them as products of the right of the ruler to enact kanûns.

Confronted by the expansion of the secularized law, the Şeriat could either renounce all of its provisions covering worldly affairs and retire into a purely religious area, or continue its claims within those aspects of private law that were necessarily religiously defined—in other words, renounce all of its provisions with regard to constitutional, criminal, and commercial law and codify its remainder in a way not inconsistent with the principles of the new laws, the principles of the Tanzimat regime. The Westernists demanded the first alternative; reformists like Cevdet Paşa the second. The Şeriat ignored the Westernist demand, but it reacted violently when the second demand came from among the ranks of the Ulema.

Although by no means a legislative act of parliament, the enactment of the Mecelle was the first instance of legislation within the field of the Şeriat exclusively by the sovereign and his government in their temporal capacity. Although no one could find any religiously legitimate grounds for declaring the Mecelle unacceptable from the viewpoint of the Şeriat, there was no precedent for it in the tradition. As the matter involved a new encroachment upon the religious or traditional realm and, ultimately, the jurisdiction of the Şeyhul-Islâm, the latter consistently strove to reassert the right of his office to promulgate the provisions of the Şeriat and to interpret the disputed issues submitted for ratification by the ruler.

An acceptance of the new procedure would amount, in the long run, to the complete secularization of the Şeriat. The Şeriat would subject itself to the enactments of the temporal power as the statutory laws of the state; it would be forced to open the long sealed gates of free opinion (*ijtihâd*) and consider the changing world, if not above, at least on a par with the unchanging traditional

principles; once this was done, who could foresee the consequences
—religious as well as legal?

172

The Şeriat would then be forced to confine its autonomous
authority to purely spiritual matters. This the religious institution
could not accept for three reasons: it would relegate its autonomy
to a position similar to that of the churches of the *millets*; it would
be forced to renounce its claim to mold the whole society for its
believers; and, finally, it would be forced to retire into an area in
which its predominantly legal character would have no function—
an area to which it paid the least attention and in which it was the
least well organized and powerful. Retrenchment would upset its
whole tradition—its only support for existence—and destroy the
organization through which its tradition could be maintained and
transmitted. It would deprive itself of its hold over the state and
society; it would be forced to tolerate the establishment and evolution of a constitutional political regime in which not the traditional principles of divine law but the principles of the doctrine of
natural rights would reign freely.

Throughout, one cannot fail to see the unbending consistency
of the upholders of the Şeriat, in their opposition to the Mecelle.
In the same way they tirelessly fought the secular university which
would usurp their prerogatives over the teaching of the traditional
or religious sciences. In the end, they triumphed, and effected a
return to the Şeriat to rule over the lives of the Muslims for about
a third of a century under the reign of Abdül-Hamid. They
brought about the dismissal of the Mecelle committee and pre-
vented further codification of the *mu'âmalât*. The codification of
the *munakahât* (marriage law) remained entirely out of sight. A
secularized civil code did not come into existence for another half
century.

The reformers did not take the opportunity to go to the bases
of the Şeriat jurisprudence in order to make a critical evaluation
of these vis-à-vis those of the modern codes borrowed from the
West. The judicial institutions of the Şeriat played no role in the
movement of codification. The Tanzimat codification secularized
the externals of social life by legalizing innovations. By codifying
the most secular parts of the Şeriat, it put a new border line
between secular life and the Şeriat. But it left the core of social
relationships on the Şeriat side of the fence. This was in accordance with the Tanzimat principles, but it left unanswered the
ultimate question: Would religion be the basis of polity?

Progress and Pitfalls in Education

As in every other field, the Tanzimat's measures in education were expansions upon the developments of the preceding period. As everywhere else, the Tanzimat's view of education was circumscribed by external factors and by its conception of secularism.

173

Addressing the Supreme Council in 1845 while it was discussing the formation of a Council of Education, Abdül-Mecid defined the aims of education: "To disseminate religious knowledge and useful sciences, which are necessities for religion and the world, so as to abolish the ignorance of the people." The report drafted by the Council expressed the same view in another way: "It is a necessity for every human being to learn first his own religion and that education which will enable him to be independent of the help of others and, then, to acquire *useful* sciences and arts."[27] These contained the gist of the Tanzimat view of education.

If we compare the Council's report with that prepared by the Board of Useful Affairs in 1838, we shall have little difficulty in discerning that the Tanzimat restored religious teaching. Despite the enhanced importance given to the dissemination of secular learning, there was definite retrogression in the degree of secularity with which the government viewed the function of religious instruction. This reflected resignation to the implications of the *millet* system insofar as primary education, the main target of the 1838 report, was concerned.

In the early years particularly, the chief educational problems were seen to be: (*a*) the expansion and improvement of primary educational facilities, (*b*) the multiplication of the bridges between the religious education of the primary schools and the secular learning of the higher institutions, (*c*) the extension to the female population of secondary and, to a lesser degree, professional educational facilities, and (*d*) the foundation of a university that would incorporate the humanities and general sciences taught hitherto only as cultural embellishments, or ancillaries, in the medical and engineering schools. Theoretically, the realization of a university would be the least problematic because the foundations of secular higher education were already well-established and, generally, unopposed. Paradoxically, one of the major conflicts of the entire period centred around the attempts to form a

---

[27] Both statements are quoted in Mahmud Cevad, *Maarif-i Umumiye Nezareti Tarihçe-i Teşkilât ve Icraatı* (Istanbul, 1922), p. 27.

174

comprehensive institution of general higher learning; this delayed the establishment of the first Turkish university until the Meşruti-yet (the Constitutional Era). The organized undertaking of female schooling was original to the Tanzimat. The Tanzimat reformers manifested boldness in this field once they worked up courage to make a beginning. In terms of future developments, the Tanzimat can be said to have made its greatest, if not its solitary, contribu-tion in the area of secondary education. But here again, the inno-vators followed the middle course, broadening the gulf between different segments of society and creating a split within the minds of individuals.

Despite its repeated efforts, the Tanzimat achieved almost noth-ing in the field of primary education. In this area, competition from, rather than the opposition of, the traditional institutions proved to be too great. No new attempts were made to secularize primary education until the 1870's, that is, until the Tanzimat had exhausted its force. Following a course quite like that of the British in India, the Tanzimat sought merely to reform the externals of primary education. Having relegated to others the content of primary education, the Board of Useful Affairs advocated and undertook in a limited way the construction of new and more commodious school buildings. The Evkaf administration and the secular Ministry of Education gradually took up this work, but dark, crowded, and unhealthy conditions continued to be the norm in the neighbourhood and mosque primary schools.

Responding to the widespread criticism of the dry and oppres-sive teaching in both the neighborhood fee schools and in the public schools of the Evkaf, men of state like Cevdet and Sadık Rifat began to write small, friendly books for children. Sadık Rifat's *Ahlâk* became the first school book to teach religion as a spiritual, as well as a worldly, morality; with time, it replaced the old standard works which conceived moral education in the light of hell-fire.[28] The title of Cevdet's little book *Malûmat-ı Nafia* (Useful Knowledge) would seem to put the work alongside the simplified discussions of geography and science that were beginning to appear in the West; and yet it contained stories of the prophets and exemplary Muslims and information about differ-ent religions.

[28] *Risâle-i Ahlâk* (Istanbul, 1847; and an earlier undated edition) was taught in primary schools for many years.

Mahmud's reign had brought in the idea of governmental supervision over the public educators. Still, there was no idea of training teachers for a specialized and secular vocation. While those having a *medrese* education were looked upon as qualified to instruct children, those with greater training at home or abroad in the secular sciences were understood to be suitable teachers in the institutions of higher learning—as they were also in Europe. The need to train teachers began to be felt when the Tanzimat reiterated the idea of founding *ruşdiye* (adolescent) schools. Just as the foundation in the West of non-traditional public primary schools had given stimulus to the creation of a modern teaching profession, so the foundation of a non-traditional and also indigenous type of education gave rise to the need for teachers with formal training. The conditions described above led to the creation of a teaching profession at the secondary rather than primary level, and contributed to the points of differentiation which can be observed still.

Partially because a secular primary education upon which to construct modern teacher-training facilities did not exist, the training of teachers, when it came, again had a connection with the *medrese*. The first schools for preparing secondary, later primary, school teachers were organized by the *medrese* graduate Cevdet Paşa. Recruited from among the *medrese* students, the first generation of professional teachers in Turkey was trained to inculcate Cevdet's approach to reform.

The so-called Normal School for Boys (Dar-ul-muallimin) was established in 1848. This was followed in 1870 by a Normal School for Girls (Dar-ul-muallimat). The titles are deceptive. There was hardly anything about these institutions even until 1908 suggestive of their professional intentions. Like the *ruşdiye* schools, these were intended to be merely a bridge between religious and secular learning. The only substantial differences between them and the *medreses* were: (1) that courses in the humanities and general sciences were introduced, (2) that the more arduous studies of the *medreses* (such as *tafsîr* and *hadîth*) were watered down to the level required by teachers of children, and (3) that students and graduates were attached to the secular Ministry of Education in the same way as *medrese* students and graduates were attached to the office of the Şeyhul-Islâm.

The results of the Tanzimat's efforts in teacher training were manifest in the *ruşdiye* schools. Despite the fact that these were entirely secularized and the only link between the existing primary schools and the schools of higher learning, the teaching of medieval books, such as the *Ahlâk* of the ultra-reactionary sixteenth-century fundamentalist Birgevî, continued in these schools alongside subjects intended to inculcate boys and girls with worldly interests.[29] Nonetheless, these schools did eventually perform an important secularizing function. They brought to a higher level of sophistication the work of the periodical press among the literate middle classes.

After wasting a number of years through fear of breaking with tradition, the government began to support and encourage secular education for girls around 1862. Although coeducation was traditionally accepted in the Kur'an schools, the thought of its extension to the *ruşdiye* schools was far more than the Tanzimat Westernists—and even most Western countries themselves—could envisage.

The beginning of secondary and trade schools for girls (dealing mainly with home crafts such as sewing, cooking, and fancy work) soon necessitated the opening of the Normal School for Girls. This seemingly very progressive step was, in part, a reaction against the idea of schools for adolescent girls run by men. Yet, it opened the modern era of official employment of Muslim women. This led to a chain of consequences that was not severed entirely even during the subsequent period of reaction. The first women secondary school teachers were employed in 1873; a woman teacher gave a public graduation address for the first time in 1881; after 1883, women began to become educational administrators, that is, government officials; female education began to extend to the provinces.

The absence of any attempt to reform the *medrese* shows that the religious institution preferred to remain intact within its traditional domain.[30] Increasing defections among the *medrese* students to institutions on the secular side of the fence do not appear to have bothered the *ulema* yet. The increasing influx of uprooted peasants

---

[29] Mehmet Birgevî (1522-73) described love for the world (*hubb-u dünya*) as an enemy of religion: "deadlier in its harm than that which a pack of hungry wolves can bring to a flock of sheep." Playing, talkativeness, laughing, singing or listening to music were the highest sins. See *Vasiyetname*, ed. E. M. Ozak (Istanbul, n.d., [1958]).

[30] See M. Serefeddin Yaltkaya, "Tanzimattan Evvel ve Sonra Medreseler," *Tanzimat* (Istanbul, 1940), I, 463-67.

and impoverished townsmen kept the *medreses* going in their hibernation.

In contrast with the absence of any sign of change in the *medreses* and the slow and confounded developments in primary and secondary education, the institutions of higher learning became more firmly established and enjoyed expansion. The two secular institutions of the previous periods experienced significant development during the Tanzimat. The Mühendishane underwent reorganization and was expanded in 1846-47. Several of its graduates were sent to France, England, Austria, and Germany for study in 1846, 1850, 1854, and 1855.[31]

The School of Medicine continued to be the favourite institution of higher learning. In 1843 it produced its first graduates. The number of years needed to complete the study of medicine was increased to nine—four of which were preparatory. In the preparatory phase, students were taught general courses, among which French literature, geometry, algebra, history and geography were taught in French. The majority of the teaching staff was composed of Europeans, converts, and non-Muslim natives.[32] In 1840 a Board of Medical Affairs was founded within the school to survey, control, and supervise the practitioners of medicine, pharmacy, and surgery, and midwives and vaccinators. Those who carried a certificate or diploma, or proved their qualifications by examination, were allowed to practice—others were forbidden. In time, this Board also acted as a court for professional cases involving pharmacists, and as a council of legal medicine.

The bifurcation in the total educational system deepened during the Tanzimat. Two mentalities arose and began to diverge from one another. They became not only increasingly estranged but also mutually hostile. The products of one educational path were incapable of understanding those of the other. Remembering the type of mentality among medical graduates, too radical even for a European like MacFarlane, we can visualize the implications of the split between the world-outlooks reigning in the "religious" and in the "secular" areas of intellectual and educational life.

The Tanzimat does not seem to have been entirely oblivious to this disparateness. An institution, called Encümen-i Daniş (Society of the Learned), was established in 1851 seemingly with the object of working out an integration, within the educational field, be-

---

[31] Mehmed Esad, *Mir'at-ı Mühendishane* (Istanbul, 1896), pp. 94-122.

[32] Rıza Tahsin, *Mir'at-ı Mekteb-i Tıbbıye* (Istanbul, 1906), I, 26-29.

tween the "secular" and "religious," or between the "new" and the "traditional." Cevdet (at that time still a member of the Ulema) was assigned the task of formulating the function of this institution. According to him, the Encümen-i Daniş was founded to provide the ultimate aims for discussions, scholarly studies, and recommendations directed towards eradicating ignorance and promoting sciences.[33]

178

The only major achievement of the Encümen illustrates the outlook that this institution meant to represent. This was a history of the Turkish reform movement commissioned to Cevdet. Cevdet wrote his twelve-volume history of events taking place between 1774 and 1826 with astounding speed and competence—to tell the men of the Tanzimat that all the past reform efforts had been defeated by the ignorance, superstition, and corruption of the *ulema* and the men of government, on the one side, and by the blind imitativeness of the admirers of the West on the other. It is clear from Cevdet's account of several dramatic debacles that he meant to say that success in renovating Turkey lay neither in stubborn resistance to change, nor in automatic imitation of the West, but in the intelligent revival of the traditional institutions by the infusion of Western scientific and technological inventions.

Carrying this view into the field of higher education, the Encümen decided to establish an institution of higher learning in which the natural and moral sciences, or more correctly the traditional sciences ('ilm) and modern sciences (fen) would be assembled. This never materialized during the lifetime of the Encümen.

Another institution which succeeded the Encümen, called the Cemiyet-i Ilmiye-i Osmaniye (Ottoman Scientific Society), represented a severance between modern learning and the entire medieval education. This is clear from the activities of the society and from its journal *Mecmua-i Funûn* (Journal of Sciences, 1862) around which were collected those readers of Voltaire, Diderot and d'Holbach who loomed before MacFarlane wherever he went. From this society emerged the idea of establishing a House of Sciences (Dar-ul-funûn) to replace the projected institution of the Encümen-i Daniş. The first experiment in a Muslim country to establish a modern university over against the traditional medieval ones constitutes an interesting case which is epitomized in the Dar-ul-funûn incident of 1870.

---

[33] The full text of Cevdet's statement is in Aliye, *Ahmed Cevdet*, pp. 60-68.

The courses begun in 1863 were simply general public lectures. The aim was "the promotion of interest in the progress of industries and the enlightenment of minds."[34] The idea seems to have been inspired by the *conférences publiques* initiated in France by Jean Victor Duruy, the French educational reformer and Minister of Education who played the role of the first foreign educational adviser to the Turkish Government. The Dar-ul-funûn remained in an amorphous state from 1863 until 1868 while the temper of Tanzimat educational thinking underwent some change.

A new interest in modern general education led to a few measures which brought the reformers back again to the question of the university in 1869. A High Council for general education was formed in the Ministry in 1864 to which representatives of all the *millets* (Greek, Armenian, Catholic, Protestant, and Jewish) were appointed.[35] This was the first step towards founding a secular education through which the secular concept of "Ottoman nationality" would be formed and propagated. The next year, a Board of Translation, under Münif, was added to the Ministry of Education; this Board played a role in education similar to that played generally by the translation office of the Porte in that it fathered the dissemination of Western educational views. A comprehensive organization of the educational system upon a secular basis was under discussion as an adjunct to the struggles over the introduction of a secular civil code. The French government suggested in 1867 a program of concrete reforms that was headed by Duruy's project concerning Turkish education.[36] Duruy's proposals dealt with the establishment of interconfessional secondary schools, the foundation of a university for the teaching of sciences, history, administration, and law, the establishment of new professional schools of higher learning, and the opening of public libraries. The project was accepted by the Turkish Government. By a statute of general education (Maarif-i Umumiye Nizamnamesi) passed in 1869, the foundations of the Ottoman educational system

---

[34] *Mecmua-i Funûn*, No. 6 (1863).

[35] For details see Cevad, *Maarif-i Umumiye*, pp. 83-86.

[36] Victor Duruy became Minister of Education in France in 1863. He reorganized French higher education, introduced secondary education for girls by lay teachers, and also introduced courses in modern history and modern languages into the curriculum of the French lycées. In primary education he achieved improvements, but his proposals for making it compulsory and gratuitous were rejected by Napoleon III.

were established[37] A year earlier, primary education was declared gratuitous and compulsory, several provincial secondary schools were opened, and a *lycée* was founded on the French model.

180

The new law of education made provision for the permanent establishment of the Dar-ul-funûn.[38] It was to consist of three faculties: Philosophy and Letters; Law; and Mathematical and Physical Sciences. Courses were to be given in Turkish, or in French when a competent lecturer was not available and a foreign professor was employed instead. Among the courses enumerated were some which gave the *ulema* a jolt: *kalâm* and *ahlâk* in the Faculty of Letters and *fiqh* and *usûl al-fiqh* in the Faculty of Law.

The date for the opening was set in 1870. The numbers seeking enrolment were encouraging. Of more than a thousand applicants, over 450, most of them *medrese* students, were accepted following an entrance examination. The opening ceremony took place on February 20, 1870. Speeches were given in Turkish by Saffet Paşa (Minister of Education), by Münif (President of the Council of Education), and by Tahsin (director of the Dar-ul-funûn); in French by Jean Aristocles (an Ottoman Greek member of the Council of Education, professor in the Greek gymnasium, and, later, professor of ethnography and history of art in the Turkish Academy of Fine Arts). The final speech was in Arabic and by one Jamal al-Dîn [al-Afghanî], "a man of excellence and perfection from Afghanistan, who has recently been in Istanbul by way of travelling," as the official communiqué put it.[39]

Tahsin, the director of the university, was one of the most remarkable figures of the Tanzimat and deserves some mention

---

[37] *Maarif-i Umumiye Nizamnamesi* (Istanbul, 1286 H.). The text is also in Cevad, *Maarif-i Umumiye*, pp. 469-509.

[38] Cf. Cemil Bilsel, *Istanbul Üniversitesi Tarihi* (Istanbul, 1943); M. A. Aynî, *Darülfunûn Tarihi* (Istanbul, 1927).

[39] Quoted in Cevad, *Maarif-i Umumiye*, p. 113. It is generally believed that Afghanî was previously appointed as a member of the Encümen-i Daniş; see E. G. Browne, *The Persian Revolution of 1905-1909* (Cambridge, 1910), p. 6. This is incorrect; the body to which he was appointed was the Council of Education (Meclis-i Maarif). His name does not appear among the members in the Yearbook (*Salname*) of the Hijrî years 1286 and 1287 (A.D. 1869-71); see Ali Canip, "Cemaleddin Afganî," *Hayat*, III, No. 77, (May, 1928), 492. However, the 26 Jumada I., 1287 H./July 13, A.D. 1870 issue of the *Takvim-i Vekayi* reported the appointment of "Jamal Efendi" to the membership of the Council. The official communiqué referred to above mentioned him as a traveller, not as a member of the Council of Education because the appointment took place about five months after the opening of the university.

here. Born in 1812, Tahsin was sent to Paris by the government in 1857 when he was a *medrese* teacher. During the twelve years he spent there he became a zealous disciple of modern science, a free-thinker, and a believer in progress.[40] His new creed was the kind of materialism that raged in Europe after the publication in 1855 of Ludwig Büchner's *Fraft und Stoff* (in its French translation, this book continued to be the favourite of the Turkish doctors despite its suppression during the reign of Abdül-Hamid II).

181

Although a member of the Young Ottomans and interested in the revival of the Muslim nations, Tahsin believed that the road to progress lay in the repudiation of religious dogmas and in enlightenment by science and education. He and his close friend Tahir Münif, who had gone to Europe about the same time as Tahsin, had also studied science in Germany, and in addition to French and German learned English, were perhaps the first to represent this view. This was also the view behind the projected House of Sciences.

Tahsin did not get involved in politics. His absorption in a number of other things (such as performing physics experiments, making astronomical instruments, devising an alphabet written from left to right to replace Arabic script, experimenting on children with his alphabet, writing on child education, on astronomy, biology, and psychology, translating Volney's *La loi naturelle* or Swift's *Gulliver's Travels*) looked odd and eccentric to others. Under the existing circumstances his entrepreneurial talents were bound to remain amateurish. They won for him nothing but the derogatory nickname Monsieur Tahsin, and the suspicion of the *ulema*. After the coming of the era of reaction he was haunted by hostility till his death, in poverty, in 1880. But, scarcely any of his preoccupations failed to be taken up by the reformers of the later generations.

Tahsin and Münif seem to have found a new recruit to their idea of the House of Sciences with the arrival of Jamal al-Dîn. We can doubt that this young *mullah*, who had never been in Europe,

---

[40] See I. M. K. Inal, *Son Asır Türk Şairleri* (Istanbul, 1940), X, 1871-82; Şemseddin Sâmi, *Hafta Mecmuası*, No. 6 (1882), 75 ff.; Necip Âsım, "Hoca Tahsin," *Türk Tarih Encümeni Mecmuası*, XVII, No. 19 (96) (June, 1928), 57-63; Abdurrahman Şeref, *Tarih Musahabeleri* (Istanbul, 1924), pp. 183-86; Bereketzade Ismail Hakkı, *Yâd-ı Mazi* (Istanbul, 1916), pp. 38-39. His pupil Abdül-Hak Hâmid, the poet, wrote a beautiful eulogy in memoriam; see *İçtihat*, No. 153 (May 1, 1923).

182

knew no European language, and had never seen a laboratory or natural science museum, understood all this talk of modern sciences, called *fen* as against *'ilm*, the traditional religious sciences of the *ulema*. Probably he thought that they were the same as those forgotten "Arab sciences" of medieval Islam. (Years later he proved that he did not know a thing about the most talked-of scientific topic of the time, the theory of evolution.) Although we can see the reflections of Tahsin's influence on Jamal al-Dîn's later career, the latter seems to have held an idea that neither Tahsin nor those secularist representatives of the Tanzimat seem ever to have entertained—the belief that the science which was thought in Turkey to be new and European and something to be used to revolutionize the Muslim mind, was nothing but what Islam itself had originally meant. The so-called Dar-ul-funûn incident was created by the reaction of the *ulema* to this idea.

As a continuation of the practice begun during the previous Ramadan (before the opening of the university), a series of public lectures was announced by the university for December, 1870 (Ramadan of 1278 A.H.). The tenth topic, announced for the tenth of Ramadan, was "The Progress of Sciences and Arts." Tahsin suggested that Jamal al-Dîn give this lecture.[41]

It is generally believed that in his lecture Jamal compared the body politic to a living organism, each of whose parts had functions analogous to those of the human body—a favourite analogy of medieval Muslim writers on politics. He went on to say, according to this story, "Thus is the body of human society compounded. But a body cannot live without a soul, and the soul of this body is either the prophetic or the philosophic faculty, though these two are distinguished by the fact that the former is a divine gift, not to be attained by endeavour, but vouchsafed by God to such of His servants as He pleases . . . , while the latter is attainable by thought and study. They are also distinguished by this, that the prophet is immaculate and faultless, while the philosopher may go astray and fall in error."[42]

---

[41] It is generally believed that Afghanî wrote his lecture in Turkish, and it was read and approved by Tahsin, Münif, and Saffet, the Minister of Education. It seems, however, that he wrote it in Persian, after which it was probably translated into Turkish by Tahsin and read by Afghanî from the Turkish version. (See below p. 185 n. 48).

[42] Quoted by E. G. Browne, *The Persian Revolution*, p. 7, without reference to a source.

It is believed that Jamal al-Dîn's lecture created such a furor that eventually it led to the closing down of the university. Muslim and Western biographers of Jamal, usually repeating one another, believe that certain of his words "on the role of prophets in the organization of societies" were "twisted to look like rationalism."[43] Consequently, he was accused of heresy and, fearing the outbreak of trouble, the government was forced to ask Jamal to leave the country. This was done at the instigation of Hasan Fehmi (1795-1880), the Şeyhul-Islâm, who was alarmed at the growing popularity of the young Afghânî because his too radical ideas on education were threatening the income of the Şeyhul-Islâm.[44]

Like many assertions about al-Afghânî, this account is not convincing—nor does it accord with the information available in contemporary sources. The writers on his life and career present the case as a matter of personal jealousy on the part of the Şeyhul-Islâm.

The story of the Şeyhul-Islâm's jealousy probably originated with Jamal. His belief that Fehmi feared him as a possible successor may merely reflect a far-fetched ambition. In the history of the Ottoman Empire there had been only one case of a non-Ottoman Persian appointed to this office; this was an exception which had occurred four centuries earlier. Until the twentieth century the Şeyhul-Islâms were chosen from among the members of the Ulema corps who had attained the highest rank (frequently in the judiciary). Jamal was a foreigner, a young man of about thirty-three, who had not yet achieved prominence, and did not belong to the Ulema corps in Turkey or elsewhere. The very fact that he was considered for an appointment to the High Council of Education (Meclis-i Kebir-i Maarif), one of the new, eminently secular institutions, and not to a body traditionally representing the religious institution, indicates that he was not regarded as belonging to the Ulema category.

That Afghânî invited protest because of his proposals to make education more general is also highly unlikely. The members of the High Council of Education were far ahead of him in their

---

43 See I. Goldziher—J. Jomier, "Djamâl al-Dîn al-Afghânî," *The Encyclopedia of Islam* (new ed., Leiden and London, 1962) II, 417a. The article gives a good summary of the conventional biography of al-Afghânî and a bibliography.

44 Charles C. Adams, *Islam and Modernism in Egypt* (London, 1933) p. 6, relying upon J. Zaidan, *Mashâhîr al-Sharq* (Cairo, 1907) II, 55.

184

liberal views. It does not seem that he had yet been made a permanent member of the Council or had had time to acquire an intimate knowledge of educational problems. As the opening address of the Minister of Education shows, the founders of the university were far more radical than Jamal al-Dîn gave any suggestion of being. After speaking of the great developments in astronomy, geology, physics, and chemistry which had uncovered truths about the nature of the universe previously beyond the comprehension of the human mind, the Minister said:

In view of the progress of science, the discoveries and inventions that seem so marvellous to us today will, in the future, become mere commonplace, and innumerable speculations will materialize. The further great achievements of which the human mind is capable are amply proven to us by these preliminaries. . . . If the encouragement, respect, and protection bestowed upon the men of sciences and arts in the first two centuries of Ottoman history had continued for another two hundred years—if contact with the civilized nations of Europe had been established and maintained, and the pace of progress had been kept alongside those nations— the Turkey of today would be in a different state.

The chief reason for the failure, he went on, lay "in the maintenance of a state of isolation" from the civilized nations; "progress in the rational science depends only upon the exchange of ideas and upon discussion among those who are engaged in these sciences. The civilized nations of Europe have been able to achieve such a degree of progress only by this." He finally stated that the Dar-ul-funûn had been established with these things in mind and added:

The facilities available in communications, transportation, and travelling, which have come into existence through continuous inventions in the progress of science and art, are progressively creating changes in the conditions and customs of nations and giving rise to new needs. It is therefore necessary for all classes of the Empire to adapt themselves to the requirements of the time and to enter upon the road of progress in all branches of the sciences and arts.

The Dar-ul-funûn would be the temple of the modern sciences and arts.[45]

[45] The speech appeared in *Takvim-i Vekayi,* and was reprinted in an anthology edited by A. Constantinides, a member of the Council of Education, entitled *Müntahabat-i Âsar-ı Osmaniye* (Istanbul, 1871). The above quotations are on pp. 116, 117, and 118.

His argument was further elucidated in a statement he made in 1879 when he was no longer Minister of Education and Abdül-Hamid II was in the saddle. He said,

The truth of the matter is that unless Turkey ... does from now on enter seriously and truthfully into the road of reform and accept the *civilization* of Europe *in its entirety*—in short, proves herself to be a reformed and civilized state—she will never free herself from the European intervention and tutelage and will lose her prestige, her rights, and even her independence.[46]

The belief that the Dar-ul-funûn was closed down because of the commotion created by Jamal's lecture is also unfounded.[47] The Dar-ul-funûn was closed either at the end of 1871 or at the beginning of 1872 for reasons unconnected with any recorded incident. The fact that the exact date of the closing is not known indicates that it simply died in the experimental stage before becoming a firmly established institution.

That Jamal's words were twisted and his thesis distorted does not seem to be true either. In the light of clues provided by a book specifically written to discuss and refute Jamal's utterances,[48] we can reconstruct the controversy and not only clarify the nature of the alleged distortion but also see the differences in outlook between the orthodox, traditional Ulema and the modernists of Jamal's ilk. This book by Halil Fevzi shows us an aspect of the lecture which is not recorded or noticed by those who maintain that Jamal's ideas were twisted—an aspect familiar to those ac-

---

[46] In a letter written in 1879 from Paris and published by I. H. Uzunçarşılı in *Belleten*, XV, No. 58 (1951), 289-90. In another letter Saffet referred to the closing of the Dar-ul-funûn, and regretted that "an Afghanî of dubious background" was allowed to make "that stupid claim that prophecy was an art" and thereby cause an unnecessary provocation. Saffet's much more radical views did not provoke the *ulema* because, unlike Afghanî, he did not use their reasoning and terminology.

[47] The lectures were suspended and Tahsin was dismissed, according to an announcement which appeared in *Takvim-i Vekayi*, 17 Ramadan, 1288.

[48] Halil Fevzi, *Suyuf al-Qawâti'* (Arabic and Turkish editions, Istanbul, 1872). The quotations from Jamal al-Dîn's lecture are given in this book in Persian. This suggests the existence of a text written in Persian which Fevzi believed to be the original, and which he preferred to the Turkish translation from which Jamal al-Dîn probably lectured. The original text may have been obtained by the Şeyhul-Islâm's department where several of the listeners were invited and interrogated.

quainted with the opposition of the orthodox sunnî *kalâm* to the Muslim philosophers' approach to religion.

Jamal al-Dîn Afghanî discussed the sciences and arts and their role in the development of human societies and in the progress of man. Translated into modern phraseology, his main thesis seems to amount to this: the existence, the survival, and the progress of man are based upon the artefacts of civilization, particularly upon technology, science, and philosophy. Halil Fevzi analyzed the logical premises upon which this thesis was constructed and showed its implications for orthodox religion. It meant that neither man's existence nor his survival depended on God's will, creation, or law. In the past such an assumption had been held only by naturalists, materialists (called *dahriyyûn*), and philosophers in general. Islamic theologians maintained that man is capable of knowing through reason only those things whose existence is known by evidence (as the creation of the universe is evidence of the existence of God); but that reason is incapable of explaining matters of belief or the rules of obligation and prohibition, which are revealed by God through His prophets. The assumptions of the philosophers, however, negate the creation of the universe and the day of judgement, and thus deny the universal and immutable validity of the *shari'a* as eternal law. Although Jamal had indicated three differences between prophethood and philosophy, these distinctions were inconsistent with his view of prophecy as an art like philosophy or science. By his own definition, every art is acquired by experience, and the revealed truths of religion are not in contradiction to those of reason but are merely expressed by different methods or in different terms. Therefore his thesis amounted to the old view of the philosophers that, because the common people were incapable of reason, the prophetic art is needed to convey truths through irrational symbolism. In other words, the prophet interprets the Book and its laws in terms of his own time, by means of an art acquired through experience and not through the open or hidden inspiration of God. According to such a view, the prophet Muhammad's *shari'a* was neither God-given nor immutable since, as the lecturer said, "there is no need for law-giving prophets in every age because God's *shari'a* is sufficient for several ages; but men need rational regulators of life in every age." Since he also asserted that man's survival was possible by means of technology and the arts and sciences of civilization, there seemed to be no need for prophets.

That philosophy and religion conveyed the same truths, that

man's existence and happiness required reason but not necessarily the revelations to Muhammad—these were contentions which could be found nowhere in the Kur'an or the *hadith*. Neither *ijmâ'* nor *kalâm* of orthodoxy (ahl al-sunna) substantiated them; they merely represented a belief entertained by the philosophers and were nothing but *kufr* (denial of Islam). Halil Fevzi then drew on sources in the Kur'an, the *hadith*, the *fiqh*, and the *fetvas* of past Şeyhul-Islâms to condemn the holders of such views. As might be expected, his conclusion was that Afghanî was a *kâfir*, a denier of the God of Islam, and that his punishment should be execution.

Jamal al-Dîn, of course, was neither executed nor even brought to trial. Not even in the past had Şeyhul-Islâms had the power to prosecute, let alone execute, heretics without support, or more correctly, direction from the temporal authority. During the Tanzimat, as we have seen, the Şeyhul-Islâm refrained from applying the provisions of the *fiqh* against the apostates simply because the temporal authorities did not act. The refutation of Afghanî's lecture remained a private disputation; there is no evidence to show that the Şeyhul-Islâm took any action that was not within his power. The incident served, in reality, as a denunciation by the Ulema of the attempt to establish a university which would be the secular duplicate of the *medrese*. Afghanî was an incidental figure in the conflict. By discussing the problem of modernization in the familiar language of scholastic philosophy and theology, he gave the Ulema a chance to state their position in their own terms. The incident did not occur simply through the jealousy of the Şeyhul-Islâm but concerned an issue identical with that which arose in the field of law over the Mecelle.

As we have already seen, the custodians of tradition did not object when the school of medicine and other secular schools of higher learning were established; they ignored them as being outside their own realm and, perhaps, as ephemeral, worldly institutions expedient to the needs of secular life. This was because the *medrese* had already banished the secular branches of learning; there was no overlapping between the areas of higher learning over which the *medrese* claimed a monopoly and the sciences which the early secular schools had brought in. But from the early years of the Tanzimat, the *medrese* lost ground inch by inch in the field of education. Still the *medrese* was not overly alarmed, just uneasy. It would not wage a battle over the "frivolities" introduced into the education of children. Occasionally, someone from its ranks would penetrate into the administration of secular education, stage a raid, create terror among the teachers, and cause them to stuff the children's drawings down the toilet drains—but that was all. The *medrese* did not care to wage a struggle over the minds of children so long as it maintained its hold over the minds of adults. For that it was enough to train in its own image the thousands of lads coming from the impoverished towns and villages in search of a means of life,

ulema not worried not primarily re but re educ - re higher

But when the *monsieurs* of science began to talk of teaching humanistic studies such as history, philosophy, economics, law, and even Roman law, that was too much! To the men of the *medrese*, the Dar-ul-funûn showed its real intentions by daring to include even *fiqh* and *kalâm* among its godless and blasphemous arts. If once established, the university would be the *medrese's* real rival—in subject matter, in its human material, in intellectual function—in everything. Here, not in the imaginary fame of the "man of unknown parts" from Afghanistan, lay the source of the Şeyhul-Islâm's crusade. If there was any reason why a particular issue was made of Jamal al-Dîn's lecture, it was because he presented a thesis which had been well refuted since the time when *kalâm* triumphed over philosophy. By using this age-old controversy and its terminology, he unknowingly served the purposes of the Şeyhul-Islâm, who welcomed a pretext to attack the new institution.

The Babel Universitaire

In contrast to the failure of the Dar-ul-funûn, the success of an institution similar in conception but foreign in inception deserves our attention. Its story shows the Tanzimat's secularist concept of nationalities. It also illustrates the *medrese's* lack of a national consciousness and its indifference to the existence of foreign cultural transplants on its own soil. It was also unmindful of the fact that such foreign-inspired institutions would be breeding-grounds for more *dehrîs* (secularists) and future Westernists. The institution in question is what is still known as the Lycée of Galatasaray.

The complete application of the Reform Edict had been confounded by the opposition of the *ulema* and the non-Muslim churches, and the resultant confusion and hesitation among the Tanzimat statesmen. Of all those concerned, the religious leaders of the *millets* were the most strongly opposed to the secularizing provisions of the Reform Edict.[49] As the representatives of the

[49] See Engelhardt, *La Turquie*, I, 139-51.

Western powers failed to appreciate fully, the abolition of the *millet* system would have been only slightly more distasteful to the ecclesiastics than the idea of sharing their reconfirmed powers with lay bodies and the common people. In fact, from the rise of a secular—later nationalistic—spirit among the Greeks in the eighteenth century, the major issue of the *millet* system had been the inability of the Turkish government to satisfy the conflicting demands of the churches and their secularized members. As we have seen, one important bone of contention was the matter of secularization in primary education.

Mahmud, as we have seen, had inaugurated the attempt to bring about some fusion among the members of the various religious communities by making it possible for all, and inviting all, to study under one roof in his institutions of higher learning. In the new phase of the struggle over the Eastern Question, after 1867, the Tanzimat statesmen undertook educational measures with the idea of creating understanding and political fusion between Muslims and non-Muslims. They inaugurated the policy of pan-Ottomanism. This found its best expression in a new sort of educational institution, the Lycée of Galatasaray.

The Lycée was opened in 1868 as a result of the recommendations of Duruy.[50] French was accepted as the language of instruction. In addition to French language and literature, the curriculum was to contain Turkish, Latin, Greek, history, and sciences. The teaching was to be entirely *laïque*. Muslims would attend the little mosque attached to the school while the Christian and Jewish students would go to their own places of worship located near by. While the institution would be open to all on the payment of a tuition fee, the Turkish government would support fully 150 Muslims and 150 non-Muslims. Among the teachers there were Muslim Turks, Armenians, Greeks, Frenchmen, Englishmen, and Italians. The first director was a Frenchman, succeeded by an Armenian; the third and fourth were Greek. The fifth director, appointed in 1876, was a Turk and from then on—apart from one Greek director who served in 1895-96—the directors were all Turks.

The earliest reaction against the institution came from the Vatican. Before the opening of the school, "the Pope prohibited,

[50] *Ibid.*, II, 12-13. For further information about the school, see *ibid.*, II, 14-16; also Ihsan Sungu, "Galatasaray," 315-457; De Salve, "L'Enseignement en Turquie: le Lycée Impérial de Galata-Séraï," *Revue des deux mondes* (oct. 15, 1874), pp. 836-41.

by two successive briefs, the attendance at the Lycée of his believers in the Orient."[51] The French newspaper *Monde*, commenting upon this action, said:

190

The Şeyhul-Islâm approved the Pope's brief strongly . . . and had
the head of the Ulema still enjoyed in Constantinople his old
influence, the Ottoman ministers would surely not have dared to
agree to the creation of this little *Babel universitaire*.[52]

The Russian legation instigated the Greeks not to allow their
children to attend the school. The Jewish community too did not
approve of sending their children to "an institution owned by
Muslims and directed by Christians" but some Jewish families
overcame their prejudices and agreed to enroll their boys on condition that the Hebrew prescriptions concerning food were observed.[53] There does not appear to have been organized reaction
from the *ulema* although there was undoubtedly hesitation among
individual Muslims. The Turkish press assured its readers that this
school would produce the engineers, teachers, and economists of
the future; that it would prevent the youth of the country from
going abroad to study; and that the contacts with non-Muslim
students would not harm the religious beliefs of the Turkish
students.[54]

In spite of the international character of the school and in spite
of difficulties in arranging a number of details caused by the co-
existence of the Muslim, Christian, and Jewish students, no major
issue seems to have arisen among the teachers and students of different religions. "On the contrary," says M. de Salve, the director,

The sentiment of respecting the religious beliefs of others had
become so predominant in the traditions of the institution that one
could see every day students of different religions performing their

---

[51] Engelhardt, *La Turquie*, II, 14.

[52] Quoted in *ibid.*, II, 14. The open hostility of the Vatican invited
some comments from the Turkish press. The newspaper *İstanbul*
(Aug. 24, 1868) remarked: "Here is the spiritual head of the two
major churches [the Roman Catholic and the Armenian Catholic]
of the Christian nations that pretend to be the leaders of civilization obstructing the opening of a school which is established for
the sole purpose of propagating the arts and sciences. On whose
side is fanaticism—the Muslims or the Christians? Let conscientious
men provide the answer!"

[53] Engelhardt, *La Turquie*, II, 13.

[54] For quotations from the press, see Sungu, "Galatasaray," pp. 328-29.

rites among their colleagues in perfect freedom—and that constituted the most impressive spectacle for us. We saw in this the surest sign of the possibility for a unity in the future among the peoples of the East.[55]

In spite of the existence of a marked feeling of resentment against the French character of the school—especially against the use of French as a medium of instruction—the Lycée of Galatasaray flourished, and in a few years, with the addition of law, economics, and engineering, became almost a university. (It was the first secular institution in which law was taught, from 1874.)

The success of the Lycée and, at the same time, the failure of the Dar-ul-funûn present a paradox. Our surprise increases when we learn that, at the first graduation ceremony held at the Lycée in 1875, Hasan Fehmi, the same Şeyhul-Islâm who, contrary to the common belief, had been absent from the opening of the Dar-ul-funûn, was among the attending dignitaries (secular and religious, Muslim and non-Muslim). He heard the director of the Lycée, Savas Paşa, a Greek Ottoman, say in the convocation speech, "To-day I announced to the public that two departments of the long-desired Dar-ul-funûn, Law and Civil Engineering, have been added to the Lycée and, thus, our institution has been raised virtually to the level of a university."[56]

What was the meaning of this paradox? The religious institution had succeeded in closing the doors of a modern institution of sciences and humanities that was entirely a Turkish product. What had been banished from a truly national institution had returned through the back door in the hands and language of the Frenk and with European support. Probably the Şeyhul-Islâm was reconciled and took the whole affair as one of political *maslahat* and of no concern to his realm. The religious institution was devoid of a sense of national culture. Through its opposition, the initiative for promoting modern education was wrested from the hands of the Turks and delivered into those of foreigners.

The lost initiative did not return to the Turks for a half century. While not the product of foreign diplomatic initiative, the Protestant counterpart of the Lycée, Robert College, appeared almost simultaneously. French-Catholic, Austrian-Catholic, English, American missionary, German, and Italian lycées, colleges, and high schools not only for boys but also for girls crowded one after the

---

[55] De Salve, "L'Enseignement en Turquie," p. 839.

[56] Cevad, *Maarif-ı Umumiye*, p. 155.

192

other. While many of these were concentrated in the cosmopolitan commercial centres, the missionary schools in particular penetrated far beyond the foreign economic enterprises. A few of these were secular institutions, all were cosmopolitan, and while many expanded their curricula to cater to the national cultures of their polyglot student bodies, the absence of Ottoman, let alone Turkish, cultural influences was conspicuous. When the foreign schools began to transcend their own national educational outlooks, they turned, not to the culture of their predominantly affluent and sophisticated student bodies, which was essentially Ottoman, but rather to the folk arts and cultures of the constituent groups. As is illustrated best in the case of the Bulgarian students attending the Galatasaray as well as the American colleges of Istanbul, they helped to stimulate national revivals and national separatist movements.

Seeds of Nationalism and Liberalism

The last phase of the Tanzimat witnessed the first signs of innovations in language and script, journalism and literature. The latter two became the vehicles of the earliest liberal ideas and of nebulous nationalist concepts.

The governmental and literary language inherited by the Tanzimat period was called not Turkish but Ottoman. Just as the pre-Tanzimat Turkish Empire had been a composite of races, nations, cultures, and religions, so it had a composite linguistic tradition. There was not an official national language called Turkish. Arabic was the language of the *medrese* learning. Schools taught Arabic and Persian, but not Turkish. Turkish was the language only of the *raâya*, in many places even of the non-Muslims.

For the *medrese*, the Turkish language had a place only in the vulgar sectors of life. The *ulema*, whose professional language was classical Arabic, were unable to think about or teach any serious subject in Turkish, although most of them used Turkish vocabulary and the rudiments of a Turkish grammar for household and mundane purposes. Not only did the *medrese* oppose the translation of the Kur'an into Turkish, but it also opposed writing in a language comprehensible to the people. When those educated in the *medrese* tried to write religious tracts for the common people, they produced masterpieces of gibberish; the only attraction of these strange mixtures of classical Arabic and plain Turkish was their sounding like magical incantations.[57]

The disparity between the language of religion and that of the people alienated the *medrese* from the national language and ossified its reasoning with the consequence that it ceased to play any role in the worldly life of the people. The *medrese* was not interested in understanding even the Kur'an. To its way of thinking, the holy book was not intended to be understood; it was the highest symbol of the divine mystery which could be interpreted only by the religious institution. The *medrese* was also opposed to the Kur'an's dissemination through printing. The belief that the Kur'an in its Arabic form was the very word of God was so deeply ingrained that nobody dared to translate it. When recited with correct diction and intonation, it only produced a magical effect upon its Turkish listeners.

For the educated non-religious classes, Turkish was merely the natural linguistic substratum for a vocabulary of Arabic and Persian acquired through literary training. During the Tulip Era, this literary amalgam had reached its height of artificiality and sophistication. The process ended with the creation of an élite language, called during the Tanzimat the Ottoman language.

When the secularizing reforms of the Tanzimat discouraged the continuation of Arabic as the language of new learning in the new schools, the avenue was opened for the cultivation of Ottoman as a modern literary dialect of Turkish. With the accumulation of the scientific neologisms initiated by Ishak through the use of Arabic roots, the Ottoman language emerged as the language of secular learning, of modern government, and of modern education. With its non-national and composite character it also seemed to fit the international character of the Tanzimat Ottomanism.

To the extent that the educational traditions of the *medrese* and the modern secular schools diverged, all but the most versatile of the secularly educated lost access to the writings of the *ulema*. In addition to the isolation of the *medrese* from the national language, its isolation from modern thinking became a factor contri-

---

[57] An English translation of a tract of this kind, dated 1820, is given in R. Walsh, *A Residence at Constantinople* (London, 1836), II, 494-97. Walsh was unaware of the nature of his material as he presented it as a *fetva* and made several omissions from the repetitive incantations.

buting to the dissociation of Islam from the political developments of the Tanzimat.

194

The movement for the further cultivation of Ottoman through government and education as a secular linguistic vehicle was also a reaction against the impact of French upon the educated élite. The possible invasion of French as a medium of teaching, and as a vehicle of expressing new ideas and ideals provided the stimulus for an awakened interest in a modern Ottoman and for identifying it with the Turkish language itself. The difference between the two was believed to be a difference between literacy and illiteracy. The reaction against the inroads of French opened the eyes of the reformists to the Turkish language, and led once more to a middle road—development of a modernized Ottoman capable of expressing new concepts but still based upon traditional foundations.

The codification of the Ottoman language appears to have been one of the major concerns of the Encümen-i Daniş. It was decided to establish a special committee for the preparation of a standard dictionary. There were even indications of the consciousness of the independence of the Turkish language from Arabic and Persian and of the need for Turkish as a means of disseminating learning among the people. That such a codification of the Turkish vocabulary did not take place should not surprise us. Actually what the Tanzimat was doing was cultivating Ottoman as a new literary and scientific instrument. The cultivation of Turkish came only half a century later.

The most significant achievement in the drive to improve the Ottoman variety of Turkish so that it could stand against Arabic, on the one side, and French, on the other, took place within the field of medicine—as Mahmud had predicted. A movement started in 1861 to have medicine taught in Ottoman Turkish rather than French, to codify medical terms, and to translate medical books. The Ottoman Medical Society was formed in 1866 and it published the first medical review, *Vekayi-i Tıbbiye*. Following three years of work, the Society published a dictionary of medical terms. This drive for the naturalization of the medical science and teaching led to the replacement of French by Ottoman Turkish between 1867 and 1870 as the language of instruction in the Medical School.[58] The School of Medicine became not only a secular scientific institution, but also the most effective channel through which liberal and national ideas fomented and disseminated.

[58] For details, see Osman Şevki Uludağ, "Tanzimat ve Hekimlik," *Tanzimat* (Istanbul, 1940), I, 971-73.

The language developments of the Tanzimat were tried out in school-teaching, in literature, and in the press. In the first we again find Cevdet Paşa a prominent figure. He wrote the first Ottoman Turkish grammar in 1850 in collaboration with Fuad (later the Sadrazam). Cevdet used the new Ottoman Turkish as the medium for teaching the religion of Islam in a way different from that of the *medrese*. In his *Kısas-ı Enbiya ve Tarih-i Hulefa*, he used Turkish to make religion understandable to the common literate people. To him also goes the credit for obtaining permission to print the Kur'an. In 1874 he obtained permission from the government, ignoring the Şeyhul-Islâm.[59] The date, the reader will remember, was one and a half centuries, less four years, after the introduction of printing in the Turkish language! The question of translating the Kur'an into Ottoman Turkish also seems to have been raised at this time, and Cevdet seems to have made some experiments himself. However, the language problem as an important object of reform in the drive for modernization and secularization did not seem solved as long as it was taken merely as a matter of cultivating Ottoman. The experiences of the new school teaching and of the press demonstrated the negative effects of the enormous gap existing between the literate language of the élite and the Turkish language of the common people. As the difference between the two was believed to be only a difference between literacy and illiteracy, the necessity of facilitating the dissemination of the Ottoman through literacy began to appear the real crux of the language problem. Thus interest shifted from language to script—to the means of its dissemination through reading and writing. The first to discuss this problem was Tahir Münif (1830-1910), the founder of the Ottoman Scientific Society (Cemiyet-i İlmiye-i Osmaniye, 1860) and the Journal of Sciences (*Mecmua-i Funûn*), and perhaps the most enlightened among the Tanzimat statesmen.[60] In 1862 he forwarded the idea that the use of the Arabic script was an obstacle to teaching and a factor in the prevalence of illiteracy, and that a reform was needed for educa-

195

[59] On the printing of the Kur'an, see Cevdet Paşa, "Vakanüvis Cevdet Paşanın Evrakı," *Tarih-i Osmanî Encümeni Mecmuası*, VIII, No. 46 (Oct., 1917), 228; Mardin, *Cevdet Paşa*, pp. 126-27.

[60] On his life and works see I. M. K. Inal, *Son Asır Türk Şairleri* (Istanbul, 1938), VI, 997-1013.

tional purposes.[61] Two years later, an Azerbaijani writer and innovator, Fath Ali Akhund-zade or Akhundov (1811-78), who had already taken an interest in the matter in his own country, came to Turkey to seek the government's support in devising a reform.[62] He submitted a project which was sent to the Ottoman Scientific Society and discussed there in his presence.

Akhund-zade's thesis contained the following points: (*a*) the existing Arabic script caused illiteracy; (*b*) the script problem was not a religious one, hence, there could be no religious objection to the adoption of a new script; (*c*) during the period of transition, his script could be used alongside the existing one. The discussion revolved around the feasibility of devising, promoting, and disseminating a reformed alphabet. In Akhund-zade's projected alphabet, the dots of the Arabic letters would be replaced by invented signs set between the related letters, rather than above or below them, and joined to them. New vowels were invented to replace the Arabic diacritical marks and to facilitate the rendering of the phonetics of Turkish. These vowels would be placed beside the consonants as in Roman script.

The report of the Society on the discussions stated that the need for a reform was recognized unanimously; and that the fact that this need had been felt in another Muslim country showed it to be genuine and an expression of real existing difficulties. However, to abolish a script that had been in use for so many centuries was a most formidable matter; to introduce a reformed script would create serious typographical problems.

Münif and Akhund-zade would, probably, have favoured a still more radical solution—the adoption of the Roman script. But, as usual, the Tanzimat tried a middle course. Even then, no decision was reached and no program of reform was instituted. While accepting the difficulties involved, Münif urged that experiments be begun and that books be printed in an improved script (his preference, given the circumstances, was for the use of newly in-

---

61 "Islah-ı Resm-i Hatta dair bazı Tasavvurat," *Mecmua-i Funûn*, II, No. 13 (1863), 69-77. See F. A. Tansel, "Arap Harflerinin Islahı ve Değiştirilmesi Hakkında İlk Teşebbüsler ve Neticeleri (1862-1884)," *Belleten*, XVII, No. 66 (April, 1953), 223-49; and A. S. Levend, *Türk Dilinde Gelişme ve Sadeleşme Safhaları* (Ankara, 1949) on the discussions and experiments on script reform.

62 Akhundov was educated in Russian schools and had become a colonel in the Russian army. He is said to have been influenced by Molière, Pushkin, and Gogol, and wrote plays in which he satirized the alchemists, misers, and the exploiters of the people. See *Türk Yurdu*, No. 5 (Istanbul, 1912), 127-31.

vented vowels placed between unjoined letters); these books should be used in the schools so that their use would be extended gradually.

While nothing was done formally, subsequent years witnessed several private attempts at reform. The most notable was one by the leading printer and editor, Ebüzziya. The discussion of script reform continued throughout successive periods.

If one factor impelling interest in reforming the Turkish language was the expansion of secondary and higher education, another was the growth of the press.[63] The second newspaper in Turkish was founded in 1840 by an English merchant named William Churchill and was called *Ceride-i Havadis. Tercüman-ı Ahval*, founded in 1860 as a rival, was the first newspaper of opinion in the real sense. Its leading writer was Ibrahim Şinasi. A year later, in 1861, Şinasi founded his own *Tasvir-i Efkâr* which became the most long-lived and influential Turkish newspaper. In 1863 a military, and in 1865 a commercial paper appeared.

One of the significant developments of the Tanzimat after 1860 was the rise of a secular intellectual life. It is from this period that the intellectual expression of Turkey's cultural problems began to appear and contribute to the formation of schools of thought. Şinasi played a prominent role in this development.

Ibrahim Şinasi (1824-71) was the first modern Turkish writer and enlightener.[64] He pioneered many fields and, although he left no work of first-rate value in any one of them, he took the first steps in such a way as to put his stamp on the development of each field so long as it contained unsolved problems.

Şinasi's journalistic contribution did not stop with creating a public taste for reading. He also opened a new phase in the history of Turkish prose. He advocated and himself used short sentences and simple Turkish. He not only established a new style of prose that was grammatically revolutionary, but also a new mode of thinking, and new words to express it, such as *citizens' rights, freedom of expression, public opinion, liberal ideas, national consciousness, constitutional government, liberty, natural rights of*

[63] On the rise and the development of the Turkish press see S. N. Gerçek, *Türk Gazeteciliği, 1831-1931* (Istanbul, 1931); S. Iskit, *Hususî İlk Türkçe Gazetemiz* (Ankara, 1937).

[64] See E. J. W. Gibb, *A History of Ottoman Poetry* (London, 1907), V, 40-44; Ahmet H. Tanpınar, *XIX. Asır Türk Edebiyatı Tarihi* (2nd ed.; Istanbul, 1956), I, 155-79; Ahmed Rasim, *Şinasi* (Istanbul, 1927).

the people, etc. The Turkish language owes to him the first use of the word *millet* in the sense of "nation".

198

Şinasi was a literary pioneer in every sense. He deliberately ignored the elaborate and ossified rules of medieval literature. He made the first edition of collected folk sayings—ignored and despised by classical literature—and pointed out their literary value. He tried what was an unknown literary form: the play. His short play was the second written in Turkish; Fath Ali Akhund-zade's, in Azerbaijan, preceded it by a few years. In his play, Şinasi deliberately distorted the traditional, unphonetic Ottoman spelling in order to reproduce what the people actually said and in order to give life to staged dialogue—something practically unknown before. He initiated the anarchy of subsequent periods in the use of Arabic letters, an anarchy which finally ended in the downfall of Arabic script. Not limited to this, Şinasi introduced with his play another facet to Turkish literature: social criticism. His play was a satire on marriages arranged without the knowledge or mutual consent of the bridal couples.

Şinasi made some translations from French poetry and, thus, enabled it to cast its first spell over the Turkish lovers of poetry; but his importance in this field lay elsewhere. He drew attention to European literature, expressed the need to make translations from it, and disseminated his belief—which became a correct prophecy—that a modern Turkish literature would be born on the models of Western literature.

Şinasi's short life did not permit him to bring to fruition two ambitions which were only realized long after his death. His dictionary of Turkish was never completed, and seems to have been lost or destroyed. Yet, it was the first attempt, carried on over many years, to revise the Turkish vocabulary, not on the basis of Arabic and Persian, but on the basis of the current vocabulary of the people. His strenuous efforts to simplify the printed Arabic letters, by making a merger between the *nashk* and *kûfî* calligraphies, only succeeded in reducing the more than five hundred signs used since Müteferrika first cut his type to 112 (still an unwieldy number).

Şinasi was the father of the early constitutionalist movement, but he soon came to the conclusion that revolutionaries were bound to fail because they could not give voice to the uneducated and unenlightened masses of people. He devoted the remainder of his life to the pursuit of his belief that the first task of the Turkish intellectual was to educate the people.

Contemporaneously, the effects of the translation bureau founded by Mahmud II began to become manifest. From the time of Müteferrika to that of Mahmud, the translations from European languages had been largely confined to the scientific and technical fields. Interest turned to literary works during the Tanzimat. This new trend reflected the search for new modes of thinking having a bearing upon cultural values. The earliest objects of interest show this well. Translations were made from almost all of the French literature which provided the intellectual background for the French Revolution.[65] The works of Voltaire, Montesquieu, Rousseau, Fénélon, Fontenelle, and Volney enjoyed particular attention. There are several indications that these were the favourite Western writers of the Tanzimat intellectuals. The degree of their popularity and influence can not be measured by the number of translations made and, especially, by the numbers published. A number of the translations reported were never published and are not even extant. One reason, perhaps, was the difficulty in translating these revolutionary works and concepts into the existing Turkish. Another, of course, was the obstacles against their publication—economic as well as political.

The first known published translation was by Münif in 1859 (an earlier translation, in 1857 by Ziya Paşa of Molière's *Tartuffe*, was never published). This was an anthology of writings by Voltaire, Fénélon, and Fontenelle entitled *Muhaverat-ı Hikemiye* ("Philosophical Dialogues"). The quality of Münif's translation surpassed not only that of his contemporaries, excepting Şinasi, but also that of subsequent generations. His selections also had a bearing upon Turkey's current intellectual interest—the supremacy of reason over superstition and the importance of enlightenment and education.

Judging from its numerous translations over the years, Fénélon's *Télémaque* (1699) appears to have been popular in Turkey and also the favourite in other Muslim countries. The original seems even to have been read in the French literature courses at the medical school in Mahmud's time. A Turkish translation appeared in 1862, followed by another in simpler Turkish by Vefik Paşa. Its popularity seems to have been due to the fact that the political theme of this famous utopian-political novel was the maxim, "Kings exist for the sake of their subjects and not subjects for the sake of kings"—the eighteenth-century belief in paternal

---

[65] See C. Perin, *Tanzimat Edebiyatında Fransız Tesiri* (Istanbul, 1946), pp. 209-32.

government. *Télémaque's* dictum for kings was, "Change the state and habits of the whole people and rebuild anew from the very foundations."

The importance of these early movements in language, script, literature, and translation can hardly be exaggerated. Their sequels will be found in the subsequent periods. If one were to select the most important contribution of the Tanzimat, it would be found in this area of culture.

The Constitutional Movement | *chapter 7*

TO THE EXTENT that it failed in its economic Westernization, the Tanzimat regime showed to the Turkish people its lack of a genuine social substratum. Even its successes had increasingly deprived the Tanzimat of any of its possible supports. Ottoman sovereignty was no longer based upon Islam. It no longer meant rule over a number of subordinate theocracies called *millets*. It was not even a sovereignty sustained by a Turkish "nation," as that did not exist either in the modern sense of nationality, or in the sense of religious community. And it was not based upon the interests of an economic class, because its usurer-capitalists and adventurous speculators did not constitute a rising class capable of creating a modern nation.

The demand for constitutional reform came when the desire to base the institution of sovereignty upon a concrete social foundation arose. The earliest expressions of the constitutional movement were clear in their criticisms of the absolute prerogatives of the rulers and in their recognition that the Tanzimat regime lacked both the traditional pillars of Ottoman sovereignty and a constitutional doctrine which would base legislation and government upon the will of the people. The movement was unclear from the beginning concerning the substratum desired as a source for Ottoman sovereignty. It was, therefore, destined to become lost in confusion when faced simultaneously by this question and by opposition to itself.

The constitutional movement was complicated at the time of its rise by the relations among the three partial supports of Ottoman

202

sovereignty: the Turkish people, the Islamic tradition, and the Western powers. Constitutional ideas were to become confused by the admixture of the doctrines of Islamism, nationalism, and Western parliamentarianism. To solve the constitutional problem solely from any one point of view meant to unbalance the tripod upon which sovereignty rested as a figurehead. It meant to bring an end to the Ottoman Empire and to the political and cultural doctrine of Ottomanism.

The Origins of the Constitutional Movement

It is not possible to attribute the emergence of constitutional ideas in Turkey to any single source or factor. Neither in its first stage (1859), nor in its second (1865), does the constitutional movement appear to have arisen as a result of a direct Western impact.[1] Rather, it originated indigenously under the pressure of economic, political, and cultural crises created by the Tanzimat.

In the latter half of the nineteenth century, the religious basis of Ottoman sovereignty was becoming increasingly unstable. The Western powers had turned against the Ottoman sovereignty, especially after 1870. The Turkish basis had yet to be discovered as a fulcrum for political and cultural reconstruction. Under pressure of the impoverishment of the people and the developing bankruptcy of the state, some began to ask whether the whole idea of Westernizing did not mean the extinction of the Turkish people. In the face of the material and communal successes of the non-Muslim *millets*, some asked also if the Turks, too, did not have an existence outside the state which had ceased to look like their state. At this stage, the questioners found in their Islamic heritage the only basis for unity. The Ottoman state would have to be an Islamic state in order to represent that unity.

It was because of this logic that the earliest manifestations of the constitutional movement had religious, anti-Western, and anti-Tanzimat colourings, in addition to ambiguity in basis and aims. Nobody really knew what the movement opposed until the conflicting ideologies underlying it began to be clarified.

[1] Harold Temperley, "British Policy towards Parliamentary Rule and Constitutionalism in Turkey (1830-1914)," *Cambridge Historical Journal*, IV, No. 2 (1933), 166-67, shows that British policy did not favour the introduction of a constitutional regime in Turkey.

Like the movement, the dominant ideology, which we shall analyze, was indigenous in origin. It maintained its non-Western element even after Western ideological elements entered into it.

The first manifestation of a constitutionalist movement appeared in 1859 when a secret political organization was formed. It was so ephemeral that knowledgeable sources do not agree even upon its name. It was either the Society for the Preservation of the Şeriat (Muhafaza-i Şeriat) or the Society of the Self-Sacrificers (Fedâ îs). The group, soon exposed, became known by the name of the place where its members were tried (Kuleli, a military barracks on the Bosphorus); and their plot was erroneously called the Kuleli Incident.

The paucity of information about the members of the group and the contradictory reports about its aims tell us much. Among those arrested and tried were army officers, intellectuals, *ulema*, *şeyhs*, *medrese* students, and a few others. They were charged with an attempt to assassinate the ruler and to destroy the Tanzimat reforms. All were convicted by trial; five were sentenced to death, but their sentences were commuted to life imprisonment. The whole incident had no important issue and would not even deserve mention here were it not that it represented in embryo the pattern of its successors.

Information as well as opinions about the case come largely from contemporary sources. Both are undocumented and vague in detail, but strong in sentiment. According to one side, the event was the first instance of a secret revolutionary movement aiming at the establishment of a constitutional regime.[2] According to the other, it expressed a reactionary movement against the Tanzimat

---

[2] Ed. Engelhardt, *La Turquie et le Tanzimat* (Paris, 1882), I, 158-59. Wanda, the Polish-French observer, presents the case as an indication of a liberal movement inspired by the contacts with British and French officers during the Crimean War, *Souvenirs anecdotiques sur la Turquie, 1820-1870* (Paris, 1884), p. 75 f. Arminius Vámbéry also presents the incident as a revolutionary movement aiming at a constitutional regime, *The Story of My Struggles* (London, 1904), I, 123-24. According to him, Hüseyin Daim Paşa, one of the leaders of the group, was influenced by the Hungarian revolutionaries who were refugees in Turkey, and the aim of the Kuleli conspirators was to force the Padişah to grant a constitution because they believed that absolutism was incompatible with the teachings of the Kur'an; Arminius Vámbéry, "The Future of Constitutionalism in Turkey," *Nineteenth Century*, LXV (1909), 361-62.

reforms.[3] There are grains of truth in both representations, but neither is adequate, since both were formed in terms of ideological views not held by members of the movement.

According to the understanding of the group, a genuine application of the Şeriat would entail the formation of an assembly representative of the people, and a government directly responsible to the *ümmet*. Thus, its advocacy of applying the Şeriat was the first expression of the liberal constitutional movement. At the same time, its formation was a reaction against both misgovernment and, perhaps to an even greater degree, the economic plight of the Muslim masses as a result of foreign intervention and foreign economic penetration—for which the Tanzimat government was held responsible. Originating as a reaction to this aspect of the Tanzimat reforms, the movement only later acquired nationalistic and anti-Western attributes.

A second secret society, which called itself Ittifak-ı Hamiyet (Patriotic Alliance), was formed six years later, in 1865.[4] It was similar to the first and, like it, soon uncovered. Later it became known in Turkey as the Society of Young Ottomans, and in Europe as the *Jeunes Turcs*.

According to Ebüzziya, the chief but not always reliable source of information, the Society was originally formed by five persons as a "revolutionary society" that would take measures "to change

[3] Ahmed Midhat, *Üss-ü İnkilâp* (Istanbul, 1878), II, 74-75; Mehmed Gâlib and Ali Rıza, "On Üçüncü Asr-ı Hicrîde Osmanlı Ricâli," *Peyam-ı Sabah*, Nov. 15, 1920; and Uluğ Iğdemir, *Kuleli Vak'ası Hakkında Bir Araştırma* (Istanbul, 1937). The latter is a monographic study based upon the records of the "court." The descriptions in these records of the accused are not reliable since they are contradicted by other contemporary observations. See also Roderic H. Davison, "European Archives as a Source for Later Ottoman History," *Report on Current Research, 1958* (Washington, 1959), pp. 38-41.

[4] See Ebüzziya Tevfik, "Yeni Osmanlıların Sebeb-i Zuhuru," *Yeni Tasvir-i Efkâr*, Nos. 1-270 (May 31, 1909–Feb. 29, 1910), in instalments 1-154; Ihsan Sungu, "Tanzimat ve Yeni Osmanlılar," *Tanzimat* (Istanbul, 1940), I, 777-857; Mehmed Kaplan, *Namık Kemal Hayatı ve Eserleri* (Istanbul, 1948), pp. 54-70; Abdurrahman, Şeref, *Tarih Musahabeleri* (Istanbul, 1924), pp. 172-83; Tarik Z. Tunaya, *Türkiyede Siyasî Partiler* (Istanbul, 1952), pp. 91-96, and the sources given. Also see Ahmet H. Tanpınar, *XIX. Asır Türk Edebiyatı Tarihi* (2nd ed.; Istanbul, 1956), I, 204-23; "Turquie," in Ernest Lavisse and Alfred Rambaud, *Histoire générale* (3rd ed.; Paris, 1925), XII, 482-86; Arminius Vámbéry, "Freiheitliche Bestrebungen im moslemischen Asien," *Deutsche Rundschau*, LXXVII (Oct.-Dec., 1893), 64-65; and Arminius Vámbéry, *Western Culture in Eastern Lands* (London, 1906), pp. 324-25.

the absolutistic regime to a constitutional regime." Other sources give quite different stories, and it seems that there was more than one nucleus. Whether or not there was a real or regular connection among these cannot be determined because of the confusion created by the various accounts—all of which were written much later.

If the movement failed to bring about a coup d'état, it succeeded in becoming an intellectual crusade against the Padişah and his government by Young Ottomans who had fled to Europe and assembled in Paris and London. The man who set off the first verbal blast and financed the organization was Mustafa Fazıl Paşa, a grandson of Mehmet Ali of Egypt and a one-time Minister of Finance in Turkey. It seems that the Young Ottomans took their signal from a lengthy letter of 1867, written, or underwritten, by Mustafa Fazıl and addressed to the ruler, Abdül-Aziz. We learn from this letter that Fazıl had already established in Paris a group of Young Ottomans calling themselves Jeunes Turcs; according to Engelhardt, the constitution of this society was published on April 30, 1867.

Nine of the Young Ottomans within Turkey succeeded in escaping to Paris during April and May 1867. Befriended by the European liberals, their closest associates seem to have been men such as Léon Cahun and Arminius Vámbéry, both of whom were interested in Turkey or in the Turks. They found in addition other Muslim and non-Muslim Ottoman subjects already in France and connected with the Young Ottomans.

Under pressure from both the French and Ottoman governments, the Young Ottomans, or Jeunes Turcs, were forced to move to London where they established their headquarters and papers. They quickly split into rival groups and then into rival individuals. No party remained after about two years. This dissolution *as a group* was due partly to the difficulties arising from Mustafa Fazıl's reconciliation with the Turkish government and hence his withdrawal of financial support, and partly to the differences in the views of the members.

The Young Ottomans were in full agreement in demanding a "constitutional " government. They wanted to put an end to the absolutism of the Padişah since they believed that it was not possible to retain the absolute rights of the ruler while reforming the laws of the state.

They discussed repeatedly in their principal organs, *Hürriyet* (Liberty) and *Muhbir* (Messenger), the need for a *nizam-ı serbe-*

stane (liberal regime), for the establishment of a *kanûn-u esasî* (fundamental law), and for a *meclis-i meb'usan* or *şura-yi ümmet* (assembly of representatives or national assembly). They pressed strongly on three points: (*a*) the economic plight of the masses of Muslims (and the financial condition of the government which, in fact, declared bankruptcy in 1875), (*b*) the increasing dependence of Turkey upon the rivalries of the great powers and the increasing interference of these powers in the internal affairs of Turkey, which intensified the bitterness between the Muslim and Christian subjects of the Empire, and (*c*) the irresponsible policies of the government and the financial follies of the ruler. The dangers implicit in these conditions made the institution of a government controlled by the people and of a monarchy subjected to law more urgent than ever.

Despite their agreement on these points, the Young Ottomans were confused and in disagreement over the matter of achieving their aims. Their intellectual confusion revolved around the question of how the desired constitutional regime, implying the sovereignty of the people, could be reconciled with the historic tradition of the Ottoman political system. The latter they always identified as Islamic, and based upon the Şeriat.

The Young Ottomans rejected one possible solution—that Turkey should be forced by the European powers to undertake a constitutional reform whose continuance would be placed under their guarantee. They accused the Tanzimatists of causing the degeneration of the reforms by resorting to them only as measures to appease the European powers. They also charged that the Tanzimatists had opened the gates to European economic penetration and political intervention by failing to introduce genuine measures, on their own initiative. They believed that the powers were not seriously interested in the recovery of the Muslim nation and did not envisage a real program of reform—let alone a constitutional reform. Furthermore, the Young Ottomans were deeply irritated by the anti-Muslim prejudices growing in the West and held the Tanzimat policies largely responsible. According to them, the statesmen of the Tanzimat proved to Europeans that Muslims were incapable of reform and that Islam was an obstacle to progress. Also, if the Europeans meant what they were saying, their idea of a constitutional reform would be to dissolve the Empire and subjugate the Muslims to their own rule.

If the imposition of a constitutional reform from the outside was undesirable, the logical thing was to expect it to come from within the "nation" itself—particularly as, in this case, it was the sovereignty of the people that was involved. Should, therefore, the Turkish "nation" rise and establish its sovereignty by a revolution?

The Young Ottomans were not unaware of the revolutionary implications of their liberalism and anti-interventionism. There were among them a few who not only saw the logical consequences of their promises but also were convinced that a constitutional regime should and could be established by the action of the masses of the people; but these few were the exceptions.

By and large, the Young Ottomans were neither revolutionaries nor revolutionists. Perhaps this was because they did not belong to any class possessing real or potential power. Their education separated them from the impoverished peasants and artisans, and there was as yet no middle or professional class in Turkey. The intellectuals (*münevver*) could not live except as servants of the government or with the financial support of relatives. It was only much later, during the Young Turk movement, that the revolutionary intellectual independent of the government appeared on the scene.

The following quotation from one of the members of the group, Nuri, shows the ideological confusion as well as the desperation among the Young Ottomans about the feasibility of a constitutional revolution emanating from the people:

I had fallen into much doubt as to the possibility of realizing the aims for which we were working when I began to ponder the fact that a country would not easily change on the wishes of a few men. Realizing that without education the finding of truth would be impossible, I began to consider myself a student who should take this opportunity of going to Paris to study. Mehmed believed that the true establishment of the liberal regime in our country would only be possible with the support of a national movement. Ziya, on the other hand, believed that the realization of our aims would depend upon gaining power by reconciliation with the Sultan. Agâh thought that in order to arrive at key positions in the furtherance of our aims, we should try to reach reconciliation with the government. As for [Namık] Kemal, he was convinced that "the Ottoman nation was loyal to its Ottoman rulers; with us nothing was done unless the Padişah really wanted it" . . . and therefore he was of the opinion that there was no means other than . . . bringing to the throne a Padişah determined to enforce the desired reforms. Rifat . . . insisted that any attempt should be carried out according to law: Reşad . . . was conscious of the fact that we were in an insolable dilemma, and, without making any recommendation,

found the most useful course of action in the enrichment of his
knowledge through as much study as possible. [Ali] Suavi's craziness,
his moral faults, and his selfish aims, were known to all of us, and
one of our concerns was to treat him tactfully to prevent him
from any kind of action that would create bad impressions against
all of us.[5]

208

The practical impasse to which the members of the Society of
the Young Ottomans were led was perhaps the primary cause of
disunity in the group and the ultimate reason for the dissolution
of the Society in exile. This, however, did not mean the end of the
constitutional movement. On the contrary, it grew stronger against
increased opposition and within six years its efforts led to the
promulgation of the first constitution. The intellectual and political obstacles that it faced were, on the other hand, so real that
the constitution was born the child of confusions and dilemmas.

The Young Ottoman Ideology

Mustafa Fazıl's open letter to Abdül-Aziz was the first manifesto
of the liberals. Freedom, it stressed, was the essential prerequisite
of progress. The decadence of the nation and intervention of the
Western powers were due to misrule which, in turn, resulted from
the absence of liberty. It was not sufficient to make reforms; what
was needed was a liberal regime whose continuance was guaranteed. This, though, did not mean robbing the Padişah of his independence, neither did it mean robbing the people of their religion
and customs. A liberal regime would ameliorate the internal maladies, would bring about normal relations with the European
powers, and would be equally good for the Muslims because
justice was of only one kind. The letter said:

Religion . . . rules over the spirit, and promises other worldly
benefits to us. But that which determines and delimits the laws of
the nation is not religion. If religion does not remain in the position
of eternal truths, in other words, if it descends into interference

[5] Quoted by Ismail Hikmet [Ertaylan], *Turk Edebiyatı Tarihi* (Baku,
1926), I, 217-20, and by Kaplan, *Namık Kemal*, pp. 67-68. See M. C.
Kuntay, *Namık Kemal* (Istanbul, 1948), pp. 357-60, on the hetero-
geneity of the Young Ottomans. On Ali Sauvi see below, p. 317.

with worldly affairs, it becomes a destroyer of all as well as of its own self.[6]

This letter contained two ideas which gave subsequent writers much trouble: that constitutional regime was the only legitimate form of government for Turkey; and that it was universally valid and, therefore, had nothing to do with religion, or tradition. The inevitable implication was the recognition of the separation of the state from religion. It was this implication that led the liberals of this period into confusion both in their intellectual attitudes and in the field of political action.

The best intellectual exposition of the problem of Turkish liberalism was made by Namık Kemal (1840-88).[7] He was the first thinker to discuss the problems faced by the Muslims according to a coherent intellectual system, and in him we find a good example of the confusion just mentioned.

Namık Kemal developed his ideas about the causes for decline in Turkey, the means of reversing the process, and the immediate steps to be taken, in the Young Ottoman publications. The causes were economic and political; the means were to be found in education; and the first step would be the institution of a constitutional regime. The Tanzimat Charter was not, according to him, a con-

---

[6] This letter, written in French, was published in Paris and probably also in Istanbul in about January, 1867, as a pamphlet entitled *Lettre adressé à Sa Majesté le Sultan.* Several printings were made in February of the same year of a Turkish translation by Sadullah (later, Paşa). The version used here is entitled *Paristen Bir Mektup* (Istanbul, 1910).

[7] See Kuntay, *Namık Kemal* (Istanbul, 1944), I; (Istanbul, 1949), II, Part I; (Istanbul, 1956), II, Part II. This work is based on hitherto unknown original material and is the best written on N. Kemal. Its completion has been interrupted by the author's death. See also Kaplan, *Namık Kemal.* A collective work entitled *Namık Kemal Hakkında* (Publications of the University of Ankara; Istanbul, 1942) contains nine essays on the various aspects of Kemal's intellectual career, and an annotated and lengthy bibliography which is the most exhaustive so far published. On his social and political ideas see Niyazi Berkes, "Namık Kemal'in Fikrî Tekâmülü," *ibid.,* pp. 221-47, and B. S. Boran, "Namık Kemal'in Sosyal Fikirleri," *ibid.,* pp. 251-77. The originals of all the quotations from Kemal's political writings given in this work will be found in these two essays. There is no edition of Kemal's complete works. A number of essays were published under the title *Makalât-ı Siyasiye ve Edebiye* (Istanbul, 1911) and another collection of some of Kemal's articles is in M. N. Özön, *Namık Kemal ve İbret Gazetesi* (Istanbul, 1938). A very useful collection of excerpts from the writings of Kemal will be found in Sungu, "Tanzimat ve Yeni Osmanlılar," and *Türk Ziraat Tarihine Bir Bakış* (Istanbul, 1938), Chap. 5.

210

Namık
Kemal

stitution and the Tanzimat had not introduced a political regime based upon the right of the people to control the government. Legislation, administration, and the execution of justice were all unified in the government. This was the source of failure. The resulting regime was inferior even to the old Ottoman political system. It failed to solve Turkey's economic problems. It invited the political intervention of the European powers. The weight of blame for all of this rested upon the unrepresentative government. Had a real government reform, based on constitutional principles, materialized, economic relations with the European countries would have resulted in progress rather than in decline.

This analysis led Kemal to discuss the nature of the political system required. It was here that he made the first attempt to expound liberal doctrine on the basis of the theory of natural rights.

Since the time of Selim III, many, realizing the impossibility of revitalizing the original Ottoman institutions, believed that the decline and dissolution of the Ottoman state was inevitable. Over against this idea based upon Ibn Khaldun's philosophy of history, which had then become fashionable, Kemal believed that a declining state could regain health and strength if it was conducted according to the requirements of nature.

In Kemal's analysis, the normal condition of a state was to be based upon the consent of its citizens, who were endowed by nature with certain rights. The function of the state was to provide the authority necessary to the preservation of these rights. The right of sovereignty naturally belonged to all. There could be no will or sovereignty outside, or above the will of the people. Although sovereignty lay with the people, it was impracticable for them to exercise it and, therefore, a group from among them was invested with the duty of exercising sovereignty. The people delegated their sovereignty in different ways, but the best form of government was the one that least threatened the liberties of the individuals.

Namık Kemal explained these ideas in a series of articles entitled "Letters on Constitutional Regime."[8] So far as we know, these were the first attempts to explain to Turkish readers the theory underlying liberalism and constitutionalism. No effort is required to appreciate the importance of Kemal's doctrine of natural rights and the sovereignty of the people. It was a milestone in the struggles of the Turkish intellectuals to strike a new course in that

[8] Namık Kemal, "Usul-u Meşveret Hakkinda Mektuplar," *Makalât-ı Siyasiye ve Edebiye* (Istanbul, 1911), pp. 176-231.

maze leading from the medieval to the modern world. It was also the first tangible evidence of the impact of the Western mind. The doctrine of natural rights had never had a place in the philosophical and legal thinking of Islam and, if we are not mistaken, Namık Kemal was the first Muslim to understand the real essence of liberalism and the meaning of the sovereignty of the people.

There were, however, three serious objections to Kemal's reasoning: Was a constitutional regime based on the principle of the sovereignty of the people in accordance with the Şeriat? Would what he proposed not mean the abolition of the right of sovereignty of the Ottoman rulers who were the symbol of the Turkish national sovereign rights? Would the constitutional regime imply the restoration or revivification of the old Islamic forms of government, or would it necessitate institutions borrowed from the Western nations? The entire history of the first constitutional experiment in Turkey was nothing but a complicated battle over these questions.

Kemal's answers determined the subsequent line of development in his reasoning. This deviated successively from the doctrine of natural rights, in order to reconcile the conflicting demands of Islam, nationalism, and the West.

In order to claim that the constitutional regime was in accordance with the Şeriat, Kemal was forced to revise his understanding of the doctrine of natural rights. To be legitimate, he said, political sovereignty had not only to be based upon the sovereignty of the people but also to fulfil right and justice. If government originated from the need to limit the rights of individuals in order to safeguard the rights of other individuals, then the question arose as to how the limits of individual rights should be determined. They could not be determined, or decided upon by the individuals themselves. Individuals having absolute natural rights would not recognize these limits. Anarchy, or the imposition of the claim of the majority over the minority would result if the law determining the limitation of rights was left to individual decision. Therefore, there should be a source outside the popular sovereignty determining this. That source was the good (*husn*) created by God in nature. Right was determined according to the degree to which human beings conformed to the abstract good. The government could limit individual rights and liberties only by laws conforming to the abstract good. Otherwise, it would not create or determine the right; it could merely maintain it. "In other words, justice is only protected by the power of the majority.

212

Namık Kemal

This does not mean that justice exists in what the majority prefers, or in what it regards as useful."[9] "An unjust act is unjust and unlawful even if it were sanctioned and carried out by the whole population; still it would be tyranny."

By what criteria, then, would the laws and acts of government be judged as to their harmony with the abstract good or right? Laws change in space and time and they seem to be relative, but was there not a uniformity and order or a principle underlying them, a principle that was the work of a transcendental power? The origin of right and justice could not be the wills of men, but a principle for which we search the universe. Laws were necessary relations originating in human nature—but according to and in conformity with the abstract good. The duty of the legislator was to uncover these relations in terms of the abstract good. Thus, a political sovereignty had to fulfill two conditions for legitimacy: (a) it should be based on the consent of the people, and (b) it should act according to the law derived from the abstract good. "In Islam the good and bad are determined by the Şeriat which is the expression of the abstract good and the ultimate criterion of the truth."

Could an essentially medieval concept of justice as the basis of the Sultanate be reconciled with a naturalistic conception of law and sovereignty as a basis for democracy?[10] It is obvious that in Kemal's reasoning there was no proof that the will of the people would necessarily be identical with the rule of the Şeriat, or that the gap between the two was removable.

The second objection to Kemal's theory of natural rights was this: If sovereignty belongs to the people, would not the acceptance of a republican form of government be the most logical consequence?

[9] This and the following short quotations are from Namık Kemal, *Makalât-ı Siyasiye ve Edebiye.*

[10] During his "revolutionary" period Kemal took for granted the compatibility of the doctrine of natural rights with the Şeriat. Upon his realization of the revolutionary implications of the first he seems to have devoted more thought to this question of compatibility. In an article written in 1872 and entitled "Hukuk" he made a major deviation from his early belief in the doctrine of natural rights. The above description is derived from this article. It is reprinted in Özön, *Namık Kemal,* pp. 46-51. See also Kemal's "Bazı Mülâhazat-i Devlet ve Millet," reprinted in Özön, *Namık Kemal,* pp. 130-35. His new view was further elaborated in an essay entitled "Hukuk-u Umumiye" and published in 1875-76 in *Muharrir* edited by Ebüzziya [Tevfik], Nos. 2-3. See also Kuntay, *Namık Kemal,* II, Part I, 483-94.

Kemal asserted that Islam was not incompatible with the re-publican form of government and that, in terms of the Şeriat, "the right of government was transferred to the House of Osman by the act of legitimate *bîat*." Constitutional government was not, therefore, a *bid'at* for Muslims. It was implemented by the consensus (*icma*) of the community (*ümmet*). The decisions of the community were not innovations, but parts of the Şeriat.

213

Kemal's answer to the third question on the restoration of Islamic forms of government and possible Western influences was that the provisions (*ahkâm*) of the Şeriat were capable of alteration in accordance with the requirements of the time. "As we are commanded to receive all products of progress from any part of the world, there is no need to return to the past, or to come to a halt in the present." It was not possible to go back to the traditional Ottoman practices such as supervision (*nazaret*) and counselling (*meşveret*). Since constitutional systems had already been developed and tried in the West, there was no need to waste time inventing a new one.

Upon comparing the British, French, and American systems, Kemal found the second to be the most adaptable to the needs of Turkey. He proposed the following assemblies: a council of state (Şura-yı Devlet), composed of forty or fifty members, to draft bills and regulations and to decide upon the execution of the administrative laws; a national assembly (Şura-yı Ümmet) to legislate the bills prepared by the first body and to control the budget; a senate (Meclis-i Âyan) to act as a moderating power between the legislative body and the executive power by keeping alive the maintenance of the basic laws and the liberties of the people, and to ratify for promulgation all laws in these terms.

Thus, Kemal laid down the outlines of a constitution and the institutions needed to implement it. His project became the basis for framing Turkey's first constitution. Two ideas he brought forth, that a legitimate government had to be based upon the consent and control of the people and that legislation had to be separated from the executive power, put Namık Kemal far in advance of the Tanzimat's conception of constitutionalism. He became the central figure and the victim of the struggles arising from the incompatibility of these two ideas and those believed by all, including himself, to be inherent in the Şeriat.

The same three questions and the difficulties to which they led were the main cause for the disappearance of the Young Ottomans as a group, but that did not put an end to speculations on constitutionalism. Belief in the possibility of erecting a modern constitutional system based upon the traditions of Islam continued for a long time. A good illustration of that mode of thinking is to be found in a book written by a Tunisian pasha named Hayreddin (Khayr al-Dîn) who claimed:

214

> The causes preventing thus far the introduction of reforms and [the Muslims'] gradual development, and, finally, the establishment of complete political and administrative freedom in the Muslim countries are . . . neither the precepts of the Coran, which, on the contrary, favours freedom and progress, nor the incapacity and alleged ignorance of the masses. . . .[11]

Hayreddin drew his proof from the early Muslim jurists (*faqîhs*) who, he claimed, agreed that the powers of the councils or individuals exercising certain sovereign prerogatives were not limited simply because they were delegated by the sovereign. Administration, for example, in Ottoman polity was delegated to the Ulema and the ministers; they were empowered to warn the ruler whenever he deviated from the law and to dethrone him if he persisted in violating the law, also to elect his successor. According to Heyredden, the political function of the ministers and Ulema was the same as, or more important than, that of the parliaments in the constitutional states of Europe. What was needed, then, was the revival of the constitutionalism of the past.

Namık Kemal could not accept such reasoning, but the ideological turn in his thinking led him to drop revolutionary ideas and to discuss instead the problems of reform generally. He developed certain ideas of progress and of the nature and limits of Westernization, and, finally, the idea of Islamic nationalism. Kemal exerted his greatest influence over succeeding generations through his writings on these subjects; they constituted the first analytical account of the various facets of the Turkish transformation.

---

[11] Hayreddin's book, entitled *Aqwam al-masâlik fî ma'rifat ahwâl al-mamâlik* (Tunis, 1867), was written in Arabic and printed in Istanbul in 1876. Part of it was published in French as Khérédine, *Réformes nécessaires aux états musulmans* (Paris, 1868); a second edition appeared in 1875. See Kuntay, *Namık Kemal*, I, 202, on Kemal's opinion about the work. Hayreddin later became Sadrazam under Abdül-Hamid. The quotation is from *Réformes nécessaires*, pp. 53-64.

Progress and Westernization

Upon returning from exile in Europe in 1870, Kemal turned to discussion of the problems of progress and Westernization. He stressed the importance of modern technological advances in creating a new civilization in Europe. His descriptions were instrumental in imbedding in the hearts of the Turkish intellectuals the notion of the superiority of the civilization achieved in the West.

Kemal's conclusions were: (*a*) that the West's achievements were possible only through the victory of the ideas of liberty and progress over those of fatalism and resignation which characterized the East; and (*b*) that, for Turkey and Islam to survive, the people had to take liberty and progress as their articles of faith. The superiority of modern Western civilization could be doubted no longer. There could be no hesitation about following in its wake. That was the only means of survival. Furthermore, the awakening and progress of the nations of Asia and Africa would be served by their entering upon the road of progress—eventually creating a commonwealth of Muslim nations as a force to counteract the European political weight and to realize anew the power which in the past the Muslims had attained by mastering the civilization of their time.[12]

It would be incorrect to portray Kemal as an unconditional Westernist. He warned against the dangers arising from the widening gulf between the traditionalist conservatives and the imitative Westernists. This led him to search both for those elements of the culture that were obstacles to progress and for those aspects of Western civilization that should not be taken over. He began by demolishing to his satisfaction a belief that he regarded as a myth in the minds of both the Turks and their critics, namely, that the major obstacles to the progress of the Turks was their religion. He then found that all obstacles to progress were due to the failure of the Tanzimat reforms vis-à-vis European economic and political penetration. Kemal was the first Turkish writer to see clearly the importance of the economic penetration of the West and his descriptions of the evils of the existing economic, financial, administrative, and educational conditions were accurate and pioneering.

215

---

[12] See his three famous articles, "Terakki" (Progress), 1872, reprinted in Özön, *Namık Kemal*, pp. 187 ff.; "Istikal" (Future), 1872, reprinted *ibid.*, pp. 31 ff.; "Medeniyet" (Civilization), 1873, reprinted *ibid.*, pp. 215 ff.

216

Kemal was a pioneer too in discussing the limits within which change was imperative. For him, Turkey should acquire without hesitation everything that was superior and useful in Western civilization, but whenever Kemal used the term "civilization" (*medeniyet*), he referred only to industry, technology, economy, the press, and education. He did not seem to realize when he insisted upon differentiating between the "good" and "bad" aspects of Western civilization that those rational, technical, scientific, material, or utilitarian aspects of the West which he admired did not come into existence, or continue to exist in a cultural vacuum. Kemal's approach indirectly fostered the obscurantism of the Hamidian era because, in terms of Kemal's reasoning, how could one prove that democracy and parliamentarianism were not "bad" aspects of Western civilization?

The crucial test of this method of demarcation came when Kemal discussed the problems of legal reforms. For him, the legal reforms of the Tanzimat were not only inconsistent but also harmful, first in damaging the legal foundations of the Islamic state and, second, in opening the legal and the intellectual gates for the West to undermine the historical existence of the Muslim community. The Tanzimat introduced codes from sources alien to the Islamic legal traditions and thus undermined the integrity of the *fiqh* system, which was the legal foundation of the Şeriat. The *fiqh* was, in his words, the "greatest monument of the Islamic civilization," and "a product of several centuries" and of the painstaking labours of Muslim jurists and judges. It was possible to derive the most modern codes to suit the most modern needs from this "great ocean."

Kemal went even further and asserted that the fundamental principles (that is, the natural law), which the Western philosophers discovered only "through philosophical deductions" from certain human premises "because they did not have a Şeriat," were given to the Muslims once and for all in the injunctions of God and the *hadîths* of the Prophet; therefore, there was no need to produce or discover them by philosophical reasoning. That these principles were instituted by God, with the foundations of the Islamic law as the first data, gave that law the greatest authority because, obviously, man-made laws could not have the same universality or powers of endurance as divinely inspired ones. Kemal even made the following statements, which were enough to cut the ground out from under his own arguments about constitutionalism.

Considering its greater power to impose universal obedience by
material and spiritual means, the Islamic provision for politics is
many times superior to the European method of legislation.

Being the product of a thousand-years' historical development, the
fiqh had reached the level of technical perfection; therefore, it
was incomparably superior to those laws stolen hastily from the
French codes. The provisions of the *fiqh* were better suited to the
interests not only of the Muslims but even of the Christian subjects
of the Empire than those of the French laws. The matter did
not stop even here. Being the product of centuries, the provisions of
fiqh had become the property of the whole Muslim *ümmet* and
part and parcel of the mores, customs, and traditions of the people.
Therefore, they were not mere legal norms.

Is there any other religion in the world which has succeeded in
associating justice with moral virtue (*ihsan*) and thereby transforming
moral obligations into *legal* obligations?[13]

As we have seen previously, Kemal's thesis was originally Cevdet
Paşa's. It was an irony of history that when Kemal drafted the
constitution in a special committee, Cevdet Paşa emerged as its
strongest adversary by arguing on the basis of the *fiqh* that in
Islam there could not be a constitution; and still later, he became
Abdül-Hamid's chief instrument for persecuting the constitutionalists, including Kemal himself. Cevdet knew that there were
two systems, two forms of civilization incompatible at their bases
although capable of co-existing *à la Tanzimat*. He did not attempt
to prove that the basic doctrine of liberalism—that of natural
rights and a social contract—was rooted in the Şeriat because he
did not believe that there was any need to borrow a European
doctrine to justify Abdül-Hamid as the Khalifa of the Muslims
and as the Padişah of the Ottomans.

Kemal turned his severest criticism against the dualism of the
Tanzimat secularism. According to him, the Tanzimat committed
its gravest error by copying the Western concept of the separation of state from religion. This not only damaged the religious
foundation of the state but also cleared the way for European
interference. It gave grounds for the European belief that the
Muslims were incapable of reform, encouraged the separation of
the non-Muslim *millets* as independent nations, and, by substitut-

---

[13] On Kemal's statements on this subject, including those quoted here,
see Sungu, "Tanzimat ve Yeni Osmanlılar," 800-16.

218

ing the spurious aspects of Western civilization for genuine historical traditions, created an unbridgeable gulf between the part of the culture that had become pseudo-Islamic and the part that had become merely pseudo-Western. Kemal was not unaware of the importance of the secularization of the state in the West, but he did not believe that a similar revolution was necessary in the case of the Islamic state.

Can anyone show anything in the provisions of *uqûbât* and *mu'âmalât* that is basically in conflict with the Greco-Roman and European laws? Is it reasonable to regard the provisions of the *fiqh* as chains of slavery simply because they were based on religious provisions? Does discarding them because of their religious basis not imply a preference for injustice rather than the justice based on religion?

The *fiqh* had the advantage of being religiously sanctioned. Why divest the state of its religious support just for the sake of borrowing legal provisions from Western codes? Did everything have to come indiscriminantly from the West? The Muslims did not need to borrow the moral (*manevî*) civilization of the West. "The standards of our own morality are amply sufficient to meet all the requirements of modern civilization."

Kemal's romantic ideology of patriotism was born of his fight against Tanzimat secularism in favour of Islamist constitutionalism and was conveyed through his poetry, romantic historic novels, and plays. The one-time disciple of Locke, Rousseau, and Montesquieu became, in time, a thoroughgoing romantic. We shall review this phase of his career before coming to the story of the making of the constitution in 1876 as it throws additional light upon the confusing complex of conditions awaiting the first experiment of the Turkish constitutionalists.

Reaction of Islamic Nationalism

The Tanzimat trend in favour of Westernism was turning rapidly towards a reaction against the West. There were growing internal factors to bring the anti-Turkish, anti-Muslim feeling in the West and the anti-Western, anti-Christian sentiment in Turkey to a climax. The climax was reached between the fall of the Tanzimat in 1871 and the proclamation of the Constitution in 1876.

A most unfortunate set of events forced the Turkish liberal reformers to join battle when there was no support in the West for such reformers and no desire to see either a constitutional reform instituted, or its fruits harvested. The liberals found themselves in the anomalous position of promoting Westernization by constitutional reforms while supporting and encouraging reactions against the hostile manifestations of the West. In the long run, this benefited not the cause of liberalism, but the coming of the Hamidian absolutism. Namık Kemal's ideology of patriotism, meant originally as a way of arousing the masses against the unconstitutional regime, slipped from his control and was utilized by the obscurantists to kill the constitutional movement.

The liberal patriots' task in facing European prejudices against Muslims was more difficult and exasperating than that confronting the Muslim apologists of, for example, India or Egypt. The latter were concerned only with defending Islam while the first had, simultaneously, to defend the Turk who had, once again, suddenly become the bugbear of European publicists. The misfortune of the Turkish liberals was that they came to the political scene when the barometer of the Turks in European affairs was at a new record low and the Ottoman Empire was the centre of the most violent hurricane of the time. Not unexpectedly, the tempest was blown up by economic conditions.

Toward 1876, Turkey approached the brink of total financial bankruptcy through the complementary ministrations of the Tanzimat rulers and European finance. Furthermore, the influential segment of British statesmen who had been demanding an end to the cold war with Russia, reigning since the 1830's, was gaining serious attention. The real trigger for the widespread anti-Turk campaign was, however, a decree of 1876 suspending the debt service on the foreign loans. "Inasmuch as the majority of the bondholders of the Ottoman loans were located in France and England, it was in these two countries that the greatest outcry was heard against the action. . . ."[14] This move precipitated Gladstone's fierce campaign to wipe the Turks off the face of the earth. The publications associated with this campaign would fill volumes, but their tenor can be judged from the reactions of two authors of presumably sober outlook. Wrote the British historian Edward A. Freeman in 1877:

---

[14] Donald C. Blaisdell, *European Financial Control in the Ottoman Empire* (New York, 1929), p. 81.

220

The presence of the Turk and the "eternal Eastern Question" which his presence causes, is really only an "incident" though it is an incident which has gone on for five hundred years. The Turk's presence in Europe is incidental. It is something strange, abnormal, contrary to the general system of Europe, something which keeps that system always out of gear, something which supplies a never-failing stock of difficulties and complications. The Turk in Europe, in short, answers to Lord Palmerston's definition of dirt. He is "matter in the wrong place." The sooner the "incident" of his presence is "terminated," by the help of whatever "inspiration," the better.[15]

Another eminent historian, Heinrich von Treitschke of Germany, wrote at the same time:

The conscience of the European world has never recognized the existence of the Turkish realm as a morally justified necessity. The conscience of nations knows of no superannuation of what is wrong. War and conquest are only means towards the right; they can only prove that the victor possesses the moral superiority whereon the right to rule is based, but they alone cannot base a right to rule on physical domination. . . . Sooner or later . . . the historical law shall be fulfilled, which enjoins on our toiling century that there is no longer a place in Europe for a race of horsemen and consumers of income. . . . He who . . . surveys the concatenation of centuries, cannot but admit that even there in the East, as everywhere else, Christian civilization disposes of an endless power of rejuvenation and self-renewal, whilst all the peoples of Islam infallibly reach a point at least at which the word of the Koran is fulfilled: "Change is innovation, innovation is the path to hell."[16]

In Turkey, on the other hand, there was the growing belief that the Tanzimat had gone too far in carrying out pro-Western reforms, in giving too many concessions to the non-Muslim "nations," and, thus, in preparing the ground for the non-Muslim nationalisms which jeopardized the traditional existence of the Muslim "nation." The prevailing sentiment was that the supremacy, the laws, the sentiments, and the ideals of the Muslim "nation" should be maintained. By this, the Padişah, Abdül-Aziz was relieved of his fears of a constitutional revolution. He even began talking in a way anticipatory of Abdül-Hamid II. He warned his government that

---

[15] Edward A. Freeman, *The Ottoman Power in Europe: Its Nature, Its Growth, and Its Decline* (London 1877), pp. xvii-xx.

[16] Heinrich von Treitschke, *Germany, France, Russia, & Islam* (London, 1915), pp. 29-30, 32, 33.

the reforms thenceforth should be carried out only in terms of the "ancient customs and traditions" and, as the Khalîfa, he reminded them of the inviolability of the laws of the Şeriat.[17]

It was under the pressure of this situation that the discussions of the ideological basis of constitutionalism gave way to an exposition of the utopian bases of a feeling of patriotism. The most influential exponent of this patriotism was Namık Kemal.

Kemal's ideology of patriotism was pan-Ottomanism with Islamist "nationalism" at its base.[18] The national and religious differences among the ethnic groups composing the Ottoman Empire were not, according to Kemal, obstacles to an Ottoman patriotism. Except in Arabia, the various nationalities were so intermingled that all were bound by common interests to the common fatherland. As for the Arabs, their religious ties and allegiance to the caliphate were such that Arab separatism was inconceivable. Far from being an obstacle, the multi-national character of the Ottoman commonwealth was to its credit. "Every people (*kavm*) maintains its religion (*milliyet*) and its language" in this commonwealth. If a correct policy were pursued, that is, if all peoples enjoyed rights and liberties, if common education inculcated all with the worth of the fatherland, if it were shown that those who pursued separation would fall victims to the exploitation of the European powers, then all would subordinate their religious or national sentiments to a higher sentiment of patriotism.[19]

How great would be the strength of such a commonwealth once it was armed with modern civilization? The realization and continuation of the Ottoman inter-nationality depended upon the utilization of the new means of progress, modern education and the modern sciences. The realization of three objectives—the unification of the Muslims (*ittihad-ı Islâm*), the fusion of the *millets* (*imtizac-ı akvam*), and modernization—would create Ottoman unity, a power that would be the answer to the challenge of the European political and economic supremacy.[20]

---

[17] Engelhardt, *La Turquie*, II, 100-101, 112.

[18] It is interesting to note that in an English translation of a song from Kemal's play *Vatan* the original word Osmanlı (Ottoman) was translated as "Turk" throughout; see Charles Wells, *The Literature of the Turks* (London, 1891), p. 189.

[19] "Vatan," reprinted in Özön, *Namık Kemal*, pp. 263-71. There were not yet words for "nation" and "nationalism".

[20] "Imtizac-ı Akvam" (The Coexistence of Nationalities), 1872, reprinted in *ibid.*, pp. 81-85; compare with "Ittihad-ı Islâm" (The Union of Islam), 1872, reprinted in *ibid.*, 74-78.

222

Islam was the only religion in the world which recognized the religious autonomy of other religious communities. The Ottoman system was the only one in history that had recognized the cultural autonomy of these communities; it had also recognized recently their political equality. What else, then, did the Muslims and non-Muslims need to love the Ottoman Fatherland? Were not the struggles for a constitutional regime being waged for the welfare of the non-Muslim compatriots? The latter should not be deluded into thinking that their welfare was safeguarded by Russia and the European powers, because these nations were interested in them only to manipulate their own interests. Therefore, commanded Namık Kemal, "Unite and Progress!"

Namık Kemal's ideas, developed before 1872, on the decline of the Muslims and the ascendancy of the West, on Muslims' need for change and development of a new sense of solidarity or patriotism; his belief that Islam should be the basis of this patriotism; his idea that reforms could succeed only if they were carried on in accordance with Islam rather than by imitating European institutions; and, finally, his belief that Islam essentially is compatible with modern civilization and with a constitutional form of government appear to anticipate similar ideas in almost all Muslim countries during the last quarter of the nineteenth century. These were repeated by many, but perhaps the best international representative of them was Jamal al-Dîn Afghanî. It may be said that in some places the outlook has not even today gone beyond that stage in certain schools of thought. The Tanzimat experiment served as a testing ground for the problems of modernization of all Muslim societies. Kemal's ideas were evolved as reactions, on the one hand, to the problems of adaptation which this experiment raised before the Muslims and forced them to ask where were the bases or leverages for change, and, on the other hand, to the Western assertion which grew after 1870 that the Muslims were doomed because their religion or civilization was essentially incapable of reform and incompatible with modern progress.

THE YOUNG OTTOMANS' constitutional ideas were brought to the test by the events leading to the promulgation of the Constitution of 1876. As the leading exponent of constitutionalism, Namık Kemal played an important role in the making of the Constitution. But the man who led the movement to the stage of implementation was an extraordinarily successful governor of non-Muslim and non-Turkish provinces, Midhat Paşa (1822-84). On 30 May 1876 Midhat succeeded in having Abdül-Aziz deposed and, as President of the Council of State under the new ruler Murad V, initiated the formal discussion for a constitutional regime.

The seven months from early June to late December 1876 witnessed many events all of which are relevant to an understanding of the first constitutional experiment in Islamic history. We must dwell at some length on the developments in this brief span because they reveal what was understood by "constitutional regime" and implicitly foretell the outcome of the experiment. It will be well to remember three points while reviewing the rapid succession of events and the last-minute confusion and haste in the preparation of the constitution.

First, there were no precedents in any Muslim country for the preparation of a written constitutional instrument. Secondly, there did not exist even in Europe, where the states possessing constitutions were still new, much experience or any established traditions concerning the drafting of constitutions. In some European countries constitutions were yet far from being really democratic; the great rival of the Ottoman Empire, Czarist Russia, had neither a

224

constitution nor a parliament. Thirdly, the first Turkish constitutional experiment was carried out under the pressures of international politics, which reached their height in 1876-78, the crisis years of the so-called Eastern Question. As so often happened both before and after this period, the power struggle between the West and Russia became an important factor in determining the failure of Turkish reforms.

In the second part of the nineteenth century, diplomacy concerning the Eastern Question dealt for the most part with the Balkan provinces of the Ottoman Empire. While in the past France and Great Britain had been the champions of the Christian *millets*, in the second part of the century Russia emerged as their rival, with a double advantage. As the majority of the Christian nationalities under the Turkish rule were Slavs or Eastern Orthodox Christians or both, Russia was in a position to utilize religious as well as nationalistic pretexts in her propaganda and diplomacy. On the eve of the constitutional negotiations in Turkey, an additional factor served to strengthen further the Russian position. While Western diplomacy supported Turkey against Russia before and after the Crimean War, an anti-Turkish campaign swept across Western Europe after Turkey's moratorium in 1875 on the payment of the debt services of the foreign loans drawn from Paris and London. The Gladstonian crusade against the Conservative government in Great Britain[1] made this hostility a powerful factor in forcing the British cabinet to waver and modify its diplomacy to Russia and Turkey.[2] The confusion and opportunism of the British cabinet assured the effectiveness of the Russian campaign begun in 1870, whose real aim was repudiation of the terms of the 1856 Paris Treaty, concluded after the Crimean War and restricting Russia's power over the Black Sea and the Straits.[3]

By the summer of 1876 it was becoming clear that the British government would yield to the Russian offensive. The Western governments accepted the convention of an international conference in the Turkish capital in order to formulate a program of reforms to be carried out under European supervision and partial occupation of the Balkan provinces.

[1] See Henry A. Elliot, *Some Revolutions and Other Diplomatic Experiences* (New York, 1922), pp. 255-57.

[2] R. W. Seton-Watson, *Britain in Europe* (Cambridge, 1955), pp. 521-23.

[3] Edouard Driault, *Le Question d'Orient* (6th ed.; Paris, 1914), p. 204. See also B. H. Sumner, "Ignatyev at Constantinople, 1864-74, Part I," *The Slavonic and East European Review*, XI (Jan., 1933), 32.

On the other hand, liberal and constitutional ideas had originated in Turkey from opposite considerations, as we have seen in Chapter 6. They came as a response, not to the question of a European guarantee of the integrity of the Ottoman Empire, but to the question of the economic and political independence of Turkey from European domination and interference. Although the Young Ottomans, in their revolt against the Tanzimat, often confused these national and international sides of the problems of Turkey, they believed that neither economic progress nor political independence could be achieved under the rule of arbitrary and irresponsible governments; Turkey would always be a pawn in the hands of the diplomats in their game over the Eastern Question. They found the solution in the introduction of a constitutional regime by which the ruler and the government would be brought under the control of the representatives of the people. And once the peoples of the Christian provinces were represented in the legislative assembly, no foreign power could legitimize the promotion of her national interests by the pretexts of representing the rights of these peoples on the bases of religious or ethnic bonds.[4]

There was thus a variance between Turkish and foreign understandings of the aim of constitutional reform in Turkey—an important difference, but one that could easily be overlooked. Under pressure of the Russian offensive, Western diplomats (particularly Henry Elliot, the British ambassador in Turkey) and some of the Turkish politicians (particularly Midhat Paşa) began to regard the introduction of the constitutional regime as a device against the liberating pretension of absolutist Russia. Implementation of such a regime, if successful, would rob Russia of her claims; it would even have repercussions, as it did, within the Russian Empire. The promoters of constitutionalism in Turkey came to realize also that the forthcoming international conference could be utilized to prove the necessity of the reform and overcome opposition at home. The international and national developments were thus associated in such a way that the two culminated symbolically and dramatically in the same place and on the same day. On the day that the Turkish constitution was promulgated,

---

[4] Against the argument that the constitutional movement in Turkey was invented only to defeat the Istanbul conference of 1876, Sir Henry Elliot recalls that he knew of the existence of the movement as early as 1875, long before the conference was conceived. See Henry A. Elliot, "The Death of Abdul-Aziz and the Turkish Reform," *Nineteenth Century* (Feb., 1888), p. 279.

226

the conference was formally opened in Istanbul. Did this promulgation succeed in averting the Russian offensive and in gaining the support of the West? Did it convince the Turkish conservatives of the usefulness of a constitutional regime in which all subjects, irrespective of their religion and nationality, would be represented on equal bases? The results of the coincidence upon the fate of the constitution will be seen later. First let us turn to the story of the constitution itself.

Preliminary Discussions

Midhat Paşa succeeded in calling a meeting within a week of Murad V's accession to discuss "whether the introduction of a constitutional regime would be preferable or not." The meeting was the first occasion on which the subject was discussed formally. Again for the first time, the advocates of constitutionalism argued their position face to face with their opponents—after twenty years of offside skirmishing. Significantly, the meeting took place in the office of the Şeyhul Islâm. It was attended by religious, administrative, and military dignitaries.

It was made apparent from the beginning that, despite all that had happened in the previous dangerous and tumultuous three years, the government and the meeting were in the hands of men who did not believe in the necessity of a constitution. Three groups were represented: those who wanted measures taken immediately for the promulgation of a constitutional regime; those who were outspoken in their opposition to the first group; and those who shared the views of the second group, but remained silent. Cevdet Paşa and the Şeyhul-Islâm were among those few constituting the third party. There were only six persons in the first, but among them were Midhat and Süleyman Paşa, the chief of the armed forces. The second party held a majority; its chief spokesmen were the Sadrazam, Rüstü Paşa, and the juristconsult (Fetva Emini) of the Şeyhul-Islâm.

Midhat had brought to the meeting a draft constitution which was probably based upon Kemal's project, or prepared in conjunction with that project. But, as he could not convince the assembly of the need for a new type of regime, he failed even to have the draft raised for discussion. The Sadrazam captured the meeting from the beginning and it ended in disagreement over the basic issue.

The Sadrazam's argument centred on the view which was current among contemporary European opponents of popular democracy, or universal adult franchise. The Sadrazam claimed that the nation was not suited to a constitutional system and gave as his chief arguments that the people were ignorant and that they would therefore misuse any liberties given to them. The result, he said, would be anarchy. The Fetva Emini spoke in the following significant way:

227

> The State has been entrusted to you. . . . How can you assemble those ignorant Turks of Anatolia and Rumelia and consult with them on the affairs of state? It is necessary to run the affairs of state according to the Şeriat. Have recourse to the holy *fetva* whenever you are in doubt.[5]

He went on to say that a board composed of members of the Ulema should be instituted within the office of the Şeyhul-Islâm to solve the problems of the state according to the holy Şeriat.

Other anti-constitutional speakers used the argument that, as non-Muslim subjects would be represented in the legislature of a constitutional regime, laws might be passed that would be contrary to the Şeriat; therefore, such a regime was not religiously permissible. Agreeing in part, one of the pro-constitutionalists demanded a constitution according to which the parliament would be composed solely of Muslims.

This meeting indicated that the Sadrazam and the Ulema were far from accepting the need for important reform in the institution of sovereignty itself. Their understanding of this sovereignty, based upon Islamic theories and Turkish practices, would not allow them to make such a radical reform. The Sadrazam even accused the constitutionalists of imitating European radicalism. He called them "reds" (repeated in French as *les rouges*, meaning the followers of the 1871 Communards).[6] For him, the needed reforms could very well be implemented, *à la Tanzimat*, without constitution or parliament.

Against this solid opposition, help was not forthcoming from the new ruler, Murad V, who had been brought to the throne

---

[5] Süleyman Paşa, *Hiss-i Inkilâp* (Istanbul, 1910), pp. 60-64; Mahmud Celâleddin, *Mir'at-i Hakikat* (Istanbul, 1910), I, 125-26.

[6] Süleyman, *Hiss-i Inkilâp*, p. 63.

228

only because he was believed to be pro-constitutionalist. His Sad-razam at first declared that Murad regarded the preparation and promulgation of the constitution as untimely; later it was announced that Murad was suffering from a mental disturbance. The conflicting diagnoses of the attending doctors and the rumours emanating from the heir presumptive, Abdül-Hamid, led the constitutionalists, particularly Midhat, to believe that whether the ruler was incurable or suffering from a temporary disturbance they had to look somewhere else for support if they wanted to push ahead.

On July 15 the government convened a Grand Council to discuss the necessary measures of administrative, legal, and financial reforms in accordance with the Sadrazam's views. Midhat, however, repeated his plea that more basic reform was necessary. Surprisingly, he won support this time from a member of the Ulema corps represented in the Council. Seyfeddin, of the rank of Chief Justice (*Kadıasker*), cited the Kur'an and the *hadîths* to show that Islam was not incompatible with constitutional rule; in fact, it had even enjoined it. The rest of the Ulema, however, found the inclusion of nonbelievers inadmissible in the legislature of a Muslim state. The meeting once more ended in an impasse though the Council decided to convene again to discuss matters further. Instead, on August 17, the government announced the appointment of a special committee composed of five Muslims and three Christians to draft a program in which the questions of constitutional reform would be totally ignored.

It seems that at this juncture Midhat began to point to the impending international pressure and to use it as a weapon for overcoming the opposition. In the meantime he had been attracted by the pro-constitutional propaganda originating from Abdül-Hamid, who had mobilized all those talents which were soon to make him internationally famous. Hamid's aim was to convince the liberals that their cause was hopeless as long as an incurably ill ruler remained on the throne and in the hands of anti-constitutionalists. If brought to the throne with dispatch, Hamid would come to it as a constitutional monarch. A meeting with Midhat was secretly arranged, in which, according to the scanty information available, agreement was reached between the two on the following points: the constitution would be drafted and promulgated immediately after Hamid came to the throne; the cabinet system would be introduced; the ministers would be responsible as a whole through the prime minister; the ruler would not appoint ministers individually; and he and his court would not interfere with the departments of the ministers.[7]

Following this agreement, Murad V was deposed on September 1, 1876, by a *fetva* on the ground of insanity, established, it was believed, by a medical report signed by both Turkish and European doctors. The coming to the throne of Abdül-Hamid, who had unequivocally accepted the idea of a constitution, appeared to be an important victory for Midhat and his followers. They did not realize that from now on the struggle would no longer be between constitutionalists and anti-constitutionalists, but between opposing views of the type of constitution desired. It moved to more slippery ground, becoming a struggle between Abdül-Hamid and Midhat, with their respective followers.

229

Contrary to the universal belief, Abdül-Hamid did not oppose the drafting and promulgation of the constitution; nor does it seem that he lied to Midhat when he said that he wanted a constitution. To understand the battle on the basis of this premise, propagated much later by the followers of Midhat, is misleading. Abdül-Hamid had enough intelligence and shrewdness to see the insoluble dilemmas confronting the constitutionalists, and he did not seem to share Midhat's naïve conviction that British conservatives would stake their power against the liberal onslaught at home in order to support Turkish liberals abroad. Furthermore, he foresaw that he could establish his sovereign powers best on religious, caliphal grounds by such a constitution as was conceived by the

---

[7] No reliable information is available on this meeting, on the decisions or points of agreement. The following sources may be consulted with caution and scepticism: Celâleddin, *Mir'at-i Hakikat*, I, 168 (perhaps the most reliable); *Tabsıra-i İbret*, ed. Ali Haydar Midhat (Istanbul, 1909), p. 394; Ahmed Saib, *Tarih-i Sultan Murad* (Cairo, n.d.), p. 302. A number of allegations were made, such as that a written document was signed by Abdül-Hamid and kept by Midhat and that Hamid's efforts to regain this document were the cause of his later persecution of Midhat. There is no evidence to support such tales; they seem to have been invented to explain Hamid's fear or hatred of Midhat. The real nature of Murad's illness is also shrouded in mystery and has been the subject of much contradictory speculation. It is said that Murad was not insane but lived in a special prison for many years, that there were attempts to deliver him from the palace where he was imprisoned, that he had secret contacts with the plotters, but that all efforts failed. In this mass of speculations, the only certainty seems to be that Midhat was easily and quickly persuaded that Murad was incurable. Probably he underestimated Abdül-Hamid's talents or overestimated his own ability to dominate him. He may have believed that once the constitution and the parliament were established the ruler's powers would be crippled.

Abdul Hamid

230

Young Ottomans. He certainly wanted a constitution, but one that would suit his own needs. And when he got it, he seemed to abide by it; and we know that he never abrogated it.

Abdül-Hamid's irreconcilable differences with Midhat stemmed from their totally opposite views on two major matters: the general question of the respective prerogatives of the ruler, the government, and the parliament on executive, legislative, and religious affairs; and the particular issue of centralized versus decentralized government. Midhat's program had called for: the institution of a parliament to which alone the government should be responsible; the composition of parliament on a national basis, representative of the people irrespective of religious and ethnic affiliations; and the delegation of varying degrees of administrative autonomy to certain provinces where the majority of the population was non-Muslim or non-Turkish. There seems to have been little difference between the two men on the first two points although, as we shall see, the basic terms proved full of semantic ambiguities especially when Islamic interpretations unfolded during the controversial drafting of the constitution. Any disagreement concerning the powers and composition of the proposed parliament was over details and was the result of a more fundamental disagreement on the third point—the question of granting a certain degree of autonomy to non-Muslim, non-Turkish provinces. On this point Abdül-Hamid was able to win important concessions thanks to inconsistencies in the ideological position of the constitutionalists on the relationship between religion and state, between Muslims and non-Muslims, and between Turks and non-Turks.

Not only Abdül-Hamid but also many others saw little potential difference between Midhat's views and the external demands which had inspired the approaching international conference, and which the promulgation of a constitutional regime was supposed to avert. Young Ottomans like Namık Kemal did not favour Midhat's view of decentralization—a view which seems to have been inspired by Henry Elliot. They compared it to the proposals of Russia and the Western powers to divide the Empire into zones of influence along economic, religious, or ethnic boundaries. Midhat's plan also seemed tantamount to satisfying old, and encouraging new, national separatist demands. And Abdül-Hamid did not intend to come to the throne in order to liquidate the Ottoman Empire. Midhat, like Namık Kemal, believed that Muslim and Christian, Turk and Arab would all fuse to form an Ottoman nation within a constitutional and democratic regime; but Kemal conceived an Islamic rather than a secular state, one in which the sovereign rights of the padişah and khalîfa would prevail through the central government. Both Midhat and Kemal saw Ottoman unity as a mighty bulwark against Russian expansion, and Midhat hoped that the Western powers would welcome such a protection. Abdül-Hamid, however, rather than seeking to hold the Empire together by a policy of appeasement, projected a counterattack as the best line of defence. He consistently strove for the maximum degree of centralized power and for a minimum curtailment of the powers of the sovereign as padişah and khalîfa.

231

Needless to say, in a period of Islamic nationalism, the Hamidian view had a greater appeal to the majority of the Turkish and Muslim people. The same mood could be found all over the Islamic world. That is why the best spokesman of this world, Jamal al-Dîn Afghanî, denounced the constitutionalists and sided with Abdül-Hamid.[8] Many Turks and Muslims felt, as Abdül-Hamid did, that under the veneer of Western liberalism, so much admired by Turkish liberals, there was something anti-Turkish and anti-Islamic, which had nothing to do with whether or not Turkey had a constitution.

Not only internal but also international developments were to Abdül-Hamid's advantage and Midhat's disadvantage. Hamid rode the tide of events, but always steered the vessel a little closer to his own goals. During the preliminary discussions, he succeeded in trapping the constitutionalists with their own inconsistencies and goaded the Muslim conservatives into vigorous opposition to them. The opportunism of Western, particularly British, diplomacy forced the constitutionalists into one compromise after another. Withholding his trump card until they had thoroughly committed themselves, Abdül-Hamid achieved at the zero hour the sort of constitution to which he could happily put his signature. The ideological confusion and compromising haste of the constitutionalists produced a document whose dominant note was not the safeguarding of the rights of the people, but the safeguarding of the rights of the sovereign and the sacredness of the khalîfa. It was this document which was to serve as the legal basis of the long era of Hamidianism.

[8] See below, p. 267.

Portraits of Constitutionalism

232

How did men who rejected an absolute view of government come to give precedence to the sovereign's rights and even add the attribute of sacredness as khalîfa, which had never been accorded to the old Ottoman-Turkish rulers? How did the desire to curtail the arbitrary use of power produce not only the affirmation but also the legalization of this power? Where and why did the makers of the constitution lose sight of the main objectives?

Before seeking to analyze the course of the constitutional movement, we must consider the meanings of three key terms used throughout the struggle. The first of these is *meşveret*. This has been translated heretofore in this chapter as "constitutionalism," or "constitutional regime." However, the proper equivalent for "constitutional" is *meşrutiyet*, which means "conditional" or "limited" monarchy. The term *meşrutiyet* was known but used rarely during the period in question, and came into general use only much later, as a result of the confusion created by the varying usages of *meşveret*. In most cases, *meşveret* was understood and used in the sense of obtaining the opinions of others in deciding the affairs of the community, or of relegating the process of policy-making to specially constituted councils. In both these senses *meşveret* was acceptable to the anti-constitutionalists. Still a third meaning of the word emerged when it was used by the Young Ottomans—at least by Namık Kemal. In his "Letters," Kemal used the combined term *usul-u meşveret* to mean "constitutional regime," or that form of government in which the government was subject to a fundamental organic law embodied in a written document. Kemal took *usul-u meşveret* as a necessary corollary to his idea that sovereignty lay with the people. In fact, Kemal used the terms *meşveret* and *meşrutiyet* interchangeably.

Similar confusion existed with regard to an expression for "constitution." When, probably for the first time, the term was used by Mustafa Fazıl, it was translated from the French as *nizâmat-ı esasiye*. This meant, literally, "fundamental regulations." The term *Kanûn-u esasî* (fundamental law) for "constitution" appears to have emerged in the discussions of the committee drafting the constitution.

Even more trouble was created by the attempt to express "parliament," or "national assembly." Several terms were used, for example, *şura-yi ümmet* (council of the *umma*, used by Kemal), *meclis-i umumî* (general assembly), *millet meclisi* (national assembly), and, finally, *meclis-i meb'usan* (assembly of deputies). Each of the terms had a different connotation, but unless specifically indicated otherwise, as in Kemal's case, all were used generally to denote consultative rather than legislative assemblies.

233

The hidden misunderstandings between Hamid, Midhat, and their respective followers persisted, with increasing obliteration of the original meanings of these already unclarified terms. Thus, for example, when Midhat submitted to Hamid his draft for the traditional decree from the throne (*hatt-ı humayun*), delivered eleven days after Hamid's accession on September 12, 1876, the latter struck out virtually everything relating to reform except the promise to institute a general assembly (*meclis-i umumî*). In place of the promises for a constitution (*kavanin-i esasiye*, fundamental laws), Hamid defined the purposes of the general assembly vaguely as follows:

To guarantee the complete enforcement of the laws needed; to make them in accordance with the Şeriat and the real and legitimate needs of the country and the people; to supervise the balance of revenues and expenditures of the state.[9]

Furthermore, he stipulated that the establishment of the assembly would be discussed and arranged only by his ministers.

In the following days, the matter was brought to the council of ministers and, then, to a larger convention held on September 26 and attended by about two hundred persons including the ministers and dignitaries of the civil, military, and Ulema grades. Despite opposition from among every group, Midhat succeeded in winning over the Ulema. Seyfeddin again explained at length, "by *aklî* [rational] as well as *naklî* [traditional] evidences," that *meşveret* was "perfectly in accordance with Islam." To the delight of the constitutionalists who interpreted *meşveret* in their own way, Seyfeddin supported Midhat with a number of *hadîths* and the Kur'anic injunctions such as *washâwir hum fi'l'amri* and *wa'tamirû baynakum bi-ma'rûfin* ("and consult with them upon the [conduct of] affairs," Surah III, verse 159; "and consult together in kindness,"

---

[9] The text of the two versions of the decree are in Ahmed Midhat, *Üss-ü Inkilâp* (Istanbul, 1878), II, 281-91. For Ahmed Midhat's comparison of the two see *ibid.*, 171-76. (The author of this book is not to be confused with Midhat Paşa. About Ahmed Midhat see below, pp. 281 ff.

234

Surah LXV, verse 6). On the other hand, the juristconsult Kara
Halil repeated his opposition to a "constitutional regime." He
objected to Seyfeddin's use of the Kur'an and asked vainly, "To
whom does *hum* [them] in the verse refer." Seyfeddin won the
day for the principle, but the meaning of the principle remained
obscure.[10]

It is evident that the anti-constitutionalists understood the real
intentions of the constitutionalists far more clearly than did the
constitutionalists themselves; Kara Halil, for example, pointed out
that the Kur'anic verses quoted by the secularly educated constitutionalists and their supporters among the *ulema* did not imply
constitutionalism. But, the constitutionalists were so gleeful at defeating the Şeriatists by the authority of the Kur'an that they did
not mind compromising their own rationalism, and they forgot
the real implications of their own doctrine.

The two Kur'anic quotations above illustrate the fatal trap into
which men such as Kemal and Midhat walked. If the reader
finds the passages in question, he will note that both are parts of
longer verses neither of which has any direct relevance to the
constitutional form of government—or even to government in
general. The first occurs in a verse dealing with God's approval of
the Prophet's leniency towards deserters from the Battle of 'Uhud.
The second is even further afield. It appears in a verse dealing with
the just treatment of divorced women; the ex-husband is enjoined
to consult with the divorced wife with respect to the suckling of
their child. The method of deriving justification for a constitutional government from the Kur'an (to re-emerge after the 1908
Revolution) was nothing but a continuation of the medieval practice of dissecting the Kur'an, abstracting verses, sentences, or even
phrases from their context, and applying these to the solution of
problems in terms of the lexicographical meaning of the selected
phrases. For example, Surah IV, verse 59, had been utilized to
legitimize the sultanates and a raft of passages were found to uphold the sort of regime which that of Abdül-Hamid later became.

Following the decision of September 26, Abdül-Hamid decreed
on October 7 the appointment of a committee

composed of the *ulema* competent to reconcile the new laws with
the sacred provisions of the Şeriat and of the civil officials capable
of distinguishing and determining which of the methods used

---

[10] Celâleddin, *Mir'at-i Hakikat,* I, 189.

by other civilized states in their general administration are useful and suitable to the morals and customs of our country, and whether their selection and adoption according to the Şeriat would be free from all harm and danger.

This committee was to

draw a fundamental law for the formation of a general assembly, and to lay down the rules for the internal functions of this assembly, as well as the regulations for the general administration of the state, particularly the principle of responsibility to be maintained for the ministers and state officials.[11]

The last sentence in its original Turkish was intentionally written to confuse, or was a reflection of the confusion in the mind of its author concerning what was to be done. However, it may give us some clue that Hamid was concerned chiefly with restricting the functions of the assembly and the prerogatives of the ministers, rather than those of the ruler. He aimed at creating not a constitutional monarchy but, as it was aptly called by a contemporary writer, a "constitutional absolutism," in which every organ of the state would be conditional, but the supreme head of the state absolute. We shall see that he succeeded, with the help of the constitutionalists, in reducing the General Assembly to a body virtually ineffective in legislative function and making the body of ministers simply a tool in the hands of the ruler. It sounds ridiculous, perhaps, that an absolutist system based upon a constitution could be devised. But such was the child of the marriage between two antithetical political outlooks. This will become clearer as we study the contents of the Constitution.

The committee consisted of twenty-four (later twenty-eight) members. It was presided over by Midhat Paşa. All the members held official positions. They represented state and municipal government, the military, the judicial, public works, foreign affairs, education, and commercial and fiscal departments. Four of the members were Ulema (among them Halil and Seyfeddin). All six of the non-Muslims (three Greeks and three Armenians) were secular officers (one, Savas Paşa, was the director of the Lycée of

---

[11] The last quotation is given in slightly different wording by B. S. Baykal, who refers to an unpublished document in "93 Meşrutiyeti," *Belleten*, VI, Nos. 21-22 (1942), 55, n. 24; also by Ahmed Midhat, *Üss-ü İnkilâp*, II, 196; he begins the sentence with a quotation mark but does not have one at the end. Both quotations are ambiguous and grammatically inadequate.

Galatasaray). Ziya, Kemal (who had been appointed a member of the Council of State on October 20, 1876), and a few other well-known liberals were included.[12]

236

As the committee got down to work, matters relating to a constitutional regime began to be discussed in the press and among the people, by ministers and dignitaries, as well as by the ruler and his advisers. Such discussions penetrated the walls of the consultative chambers and were disseminated among the common people for the first time. Above all, the ruler himself was busy listening to the views of prominent men, including Kemal and Ziya, on how to compile the best possible constitution. It is said that nearly twenty projects reflecting these opinions were submitted to him.

These projects and the publications of the press did not help to clarify the situation. Rather they further confused the public. "Nobody really knew what he was talking about."[13] However, the noise created numerous incidents. The Ulema instigated *medrese* students as well as the public against those "infidels," such as Midhat Paşa, who were going to introduce the practices of infidels and bring the Christians to the Assembly to pass laws contrary to the Şeriat, such as the abolition of the veil for women. A defamatory pamphlet claimed to have been signed on behalf of the "Entire Believers" and printed after the meeting of the first convention, circulated "secretly" and extensively.[14] The agitators held meetings and widened their agitation, especially among the *medrese* students.

Abdül-Hamid was delighted, no doubt, to see that there were so many divergent points of view and that none of them was really against his authority. He patiently learned lessons from the orgy of political freedom which day by day was making ideas more and more confused. He even made his own contribution to the confusion by encouraging the voicing of divergent views. By so doing, he also appeared as a tolerant and liberal-minded ruler.

---

[12] For the number of the members and their names see M. C. Kuntay, *Namık Kemal* (Istanbul, 1956), II, Part II, 75-79, see also 106. The sub-committee which actually wrote the draft seems to have been composed — according to a statement made by Kemal — of Kemal, Ziya, Abidin, Sava Paşa, Ohanes, and Odyan; in other words, three Muslims and three Christians.

[13] Celâleddin, *Mir'at-ı Hakikat*, I, 190; see also Ahmed Midhat, *Üss-ü İnkilâp*, II, 178-79.

[14] Reprinted in *ibid.*, 316-21; quoted by Namık Kemal in his articles reprinted in Kuntay, *Namık Kemal*, II, Part II, 125 ff.

First and foremost was the opinion of most, but not all, of the *ulema,* who were against the reform in principle.[15] Two basic views were voiced. According to some, the Padişah is the *khalîfa* of Allah and the *imâm* of the Muslims; his *shar'* (law) and *amr* (command) are incumbent upon everybody; nothing but these are to be obeyed. The other group emphasized the claim that a constitutional regime would impair the rights of the Muslims. A constitution and an assembly would entail the acceptance of non-Muslims as law-makers; this would mean subjecting the rule of the Muslims' state to non-Muslim opinions, votes, and policies, and might imply the application of laws contrary to the Şeriat.

The most radical view opposing a constitutional system in Islam may be illustrated from the editorial introduction to the Turkish translation of an old Arabic treatise on statecraft.[16] The two forms of government prevalent in the Christian West, aristocracy and democracy, were incompatible, said the writer, with Islam. Democracy was the result of the rise in the

supposedly civilized European countries of certain beliefs and ideas which have changed the methods of ruling the societies in various ways. . . . Looking at them, certain [among us] who believe in and clamour for progress would like to bring about the same changes. In the name of progress and reform, they are doing their best to change our conditions and our morals. . . .
The entire force of European men of philosophy and literature have, almost unanimously, confessed that nothing but secularism (*dehrîlik*) and denial of God could be found concealed behind the term democracy under the guise of the fabricated terms such as freedom of speech. . . .

The basis of the Islamic state, on the other hand, is neither aristocracy nor democracy, despite the suppositions of the Europeans and of [our] light-minded, new-fashioned intellectuals, who accept secularism (*dehrîlik*) as a virtue, and who claim that the Islamic state is democratic both in morals and in religion.

The writer went on to explain that the Islamic state was based upon absolute *tawhîd* (belief in the Oneness of God), and *Kitâb*

---

[15] Cf. Celâleddin, *Mir'at-ı Hakikat,* I, 188-89; Ahmed Midhat, *Üss-ü İnkilâp,* II, 177-203.

[16] *Kitâb Sulûk al-Mâlik fî Tadbîr al-Mamâlik* by Shihâb ad-Dîn Ahmad bin Muhammad bin abi'r-Rabî', translated by Mehmed Nusret Paşa and presented to Abdül-Hamid; later printed in lithography (Istanbul, 1878) from where the following quotations are taken.

238

(the Kur'an) and Sunna (the tradition of the Prophet), and no form of democracy had any connection with it whatsoever. The absolute obedience to the *amîr al-mu'minîn*, who ruled according to justice and according to the dictum of "commanding that which is permitted and prohibiting that which is rejected," was incumbent upon every Muslim. Conditioning the prerogatives of the sovereign—or, as in democracy, abolishing them altogether—would mean the abrogation of the provisions as well as the penalties (*hadds*) of Islamic law. In the Islamic state, all Muslims being the children of Muhammad and hence brothers, the foundations of government were personal equity (*hakkaniyet-i şahsiye*) and common justice, in which everybody would naturally and evidently be content with his position, as to each one a duty was appropriated.

Every person knew his position and rank (*makam* and *mertebe*) and would not transgress the limits assigned to him. He would obey those above him, and would not attempt to compete in station, value, administration, or government with those above him. In this way, the affairs of the world and of human beings would reach the hierarchies of aims delimited by divine wisdom, by prophetic Şeriat and by rational [?] traditions, and attain the peace and prosperity of the realm. In it, all headships would be subjugated to the supreme rulership of the single head. The supreme head remained the highest in rank of all stations attainable by all men. The man in the highest rank was the one possessing the required virtues, and as long as he ruled in justice, the graces of God continued to favour him.

How, therefore, could the Islamic state be democratic?

A restatement of the medieval concept of polity in its distinction from the concept of the sovereignty of the people could not be made in any better way than this at the threshold of the twentieth century. This writer did not mince the verses of the Kur'an, or produce scraps of sentences to prove that Islam enjoined constitutionalism and democracy, or a republican form of government. Neither was it unknown to him, or to those who reasoned like him, that the practice of *meşveret* (council) was anything but novel or that it ever entailed parliamentarianism. The idea of *meşveret* was known, at least, by the seventeenth-century Turkish writers on statecraft; it had never implied the sovereignty of the people.

We do not discover any writings from this brief period of anti-constitutionalism in Turkey presenting verse 59 of Surah IV—

the verse that was used in medieval times to legitimize obedience to sultans—as evidence in refutation of democracy. We find this being done frequently during Hamid's reign in defence of his absolutism. But at this stage, no consistent Şeriatist would use the Kur'an to defend absolutism. As a matter of fact, nobody did defend absolutism; everyone was for the reign of *meşveret.* The Kur'an was used now not to reject the constitutional regime, but to reject the kind of constitutional regime that the constitutionalists claimed to have discovered existing in the Kur'an.

Thus, we find the author of a manifesto of the anti-constitutionalists laying the blame for the constitutionalist trend on a wrong interpretations of quotations from the Kur'an through their extraction from their respective contexts.[17] He claimed that references to the Arabic pronoun *hum* were missed, or intentionally concealed. The people with whom consultation was enjoined were solely Muslims. Besides, he said, the opposition quoted from the Kur'an whatever suited it, while ignoring explicit statements in the Kur'an that did not fit in with its aims. In proof, he quoted verse 1, Surah LX; verse 51, Surah V; and verse 120, Surah II—all of which, according to him, clearly stated the exclusion of the non-Muslims from the *meşveret.* The non-Muslims were subject to the rule of the Muslims. "Has there ever been any nation (*millet*)," he asked, "which subjugated a group to itself as a partner in its rule?"

There are millions of Muslims under the rule of the Russian state. Does this state ever make them participate in the rule of the state? . . . The British—who have a constitutional state—have under their rule more than one hundred and fifty million people in India. Has there ever been a representative of the people of India in the British parliament?

And then he concluded:

That which is incumbent upon government is to treat its subjects with justice and to protect their security—but not to give the reins of the government into the hands of the peoples of different races [religions]. . . . If those who claim equality mean that the Muslims are prosperous and rich while the others [non-Muslims] are miserable and poor, everyone knows that the truth of the matter is just the opposite.

---

[17] Reprinted in Ahmed Midhat, *Üss-ü İnkilâp,* II, 316-21; quoted by Namık Kemal in his article reprinted in Kuntay, *Namık Kemal,* II, Part II, 125 ff.

We see, therefore, that one group rejected a constitutional regime on the grounds that it implied democracy, or the participation of the people—Muslim and non-Muslim—in the sovereignty of the Padişah. The second group rejected it because it implied a secular regime and meant the participation of non-Muslims in the government of the Islamic state.

A third view opposed the constitutional reform from the standpoint of Tanzimat ideology. The constitution, according to this view, implied recognition on the part of the sovereign of the right of subjects to make his rights subordinate to their approval. The sovereigns had already granted rights and freedoms to their subjects, but by their own will and not because the subjects possessed these rights inherently. Specifying the rights of the ruler in a constitution, even if it did not restrict them, would be an infringement of them. These rights were necessary corollaries of the Islamic view of the ruler, though the ruler might grant certain rights to his people, according to the exigencies of the times. But the two represented different categories, and, as always conveyed by the Tanzimat, should be kept apart. This was the view defended by the surviving representatives of the Tanzimat regime, such as Rüstü Paşa, the Sadrazam, and Cevdet Paşa, the Minister of Justice.

By way of contrast, the view of the constitutionalists on the eve of drafting the constitution may be summarized from a book written to explain the matter to the common people: a constitutional government meant a government run according to a fundamental law.[18] The Ottoman state was an Islamic state, that is, its government was based on and regulated by the Şeriat. As such, it was basically constitutional; but, because of the non-observance of the Şeriat, it had turned into an absolutism. The *ümmet* should restore the government and its rulers to a constitutional condition. This could be done only by making the *ümmet* the supreme controller of the government, that is, by instituting an assembly representing the people. The duties of this assembly were: (*a*) to supervise the revenues and the expenditures of the state; (*b*) to see to the full execution of the Şeriat and the laws; and (*c*) to demand the modification of laws harmful to the interests of the country. The assembly, therefore, was not a body to make laws, or to execute them. Its members were rather "the defence lawyers of the people, so to speak." The duty of the assembly was only to watch, check, and defend the interests of the people against the

---

[18] *Usul-u Meşruta* by Es'at (Istanbul, Nov. 5, 1876); reprinted in *Süleyman Paşa Muhakemesi,* ed. Sâmi (Istanbul, 1912), I, 79-88.

improper execution of the laws. It was a body to enlighten the
ruler against the tyranny of the government, and the only means
through which to voice the needs of the people and to check the
government. This function of the assembly did not curtail the
sovereign rights of the ruler. The enforcement of the Şeriat, and
the approval and execution of the laws were within the authority
of the ruler. The institution of this assembly with non-Muslim
members was also not contrary to the Şeriat, because the Assembly
was not constituted to discuss or decide upon religious affairs. The
protection and enforcement of the Şeriat were the duties of the
sovereign as the Khalîfa of the Muslims. But the Şeriat did not enjoin the exclusion of the non-Muslims from the right of representing themselves against the government. Muslims and non-Muslims
were equal in terms of law. An assembly defending the rights of
the people was needed more by the Muslims than by the non-
Muslims, because the non-Muslim people of the country were already defended by the foreign powers while no one defended the
rights of Muslims. There had been hundreds of cases of interference with the government on behalf of the non-Muslim peoples of
the country, but there was not a single case of interference in
defence of the Muslims. In introducing the constitutional regime,
there was no need to imitate the systems of European countries,
because the Muslim Şeriat provided all the necessary principles
amply and comprehensively. It was enough to apply them to contemporary needs. Those who were against the formulation of a
constitution, chiefly the *ulema* and some within the government,
held opposite views for fear that their illegitimately acquired privileges would be abolished under the rule of the Şeriat.

Framing the Constitution

The committee appointed to draft the Constitution worked under Midhat's presidency and independently of the government.
Although the committee included a few members of the government, among them opponents of the constitutional regime, the
sub-committee members, appointed to edit the preliminary draft,
seem to have been ascendant and to have regarded themselves as
representing the people. They, among them Namık Kemal, believed that once the assembly came into existence as an organ of
the state, it would be able to assert the sovereignty of the people

and improve upon the constitution. It was this belief that made the formulators of the constitution less obstinate, or determined in appearance, then they were in their individual struggles against absolutism and Hamid.

242

It seems that Midhat believed initially in the possibility of convoking a general assembly before the proclamation of the constitution. It was probably because of this that the committee busied itself at first with provisional laws concerning the election of representatives and the internal regulations of the assembly. Hamid personally threw a wrench into this manner of procedure, because Midhat had succeeded in carrying the committee's proposals through the Council of Ministers. Hamid insisted upon having the constitution completed before the calling of elections. By doing so, he left the sub-committee members no means of escape from their own inconsistencies and lack of any popular mandate.

It seems that the committee agreed to take as its preliminary draft the document Midhat vainly brought to the first constitutional discussion group.[19] It appointed a sub-committee to modify and rearrange the draft, but, according to Kemal, the result, prepared by the sub-committee and accepted by the committee, was not merely a refinement upon the original.

Although neither the draft of the committee nor the version submitted to Hamid are available—both differed from the promulgated text—the latter was based essentially upon Midhat's draft, believed to be based upon the Belgian constitution of 1831 and was influenced by the French Constitutional Charter of 1814 and, on minor points, by the 1871 Constitution of the German Reich. It will be remembered that both these provided for a semi-autocratic state ruled by the King and government. For example, Article 13 of the French Charter read, "The person of the King is sacred and inviolable." Article 14, which closely resembled Article 7 of the Turkish Constitution, began, "The King is the supreme head of the State." And Article 15 read, "Legislative power is exercised jointly by the King, the Chamber of Peers, and the Chamber of Deputies of the Departments." The Constitution of the German

---

[19] Reprinted in Ahmed Midhat, *Üss-ü İnkilâp*, II, 321-33. Namık Kemal rejected the claim that it was Midhat's project, but did not state who had written it. See his letter to Ahmed Midhat, and his articles in *Ittihat*, reprinted in Kuntay, *Namık Kemal*, II, Part II, 90-91 and 119, respectively. There were other projects, in particular those drawn up by Süleyman Paşa, and Said (Paşa). For comparison, see *Süleyman Paşa Muhakemesi*, I, 63-66, and Ahmed Midhat, *Üss-ü İnkilâp*, II, 332-55, respectively.

Reich made in did not provide a cabinet system and subjugated the legislative capacity of the parliament to the king. The 1875 Constitution of the French Republic, which was translated, was inacceptable as a model because it did not fit into a monarchical regime.

243

The first section of the sub-committee's final draft contained five articles which enumerated and described the rights of the Padişah. The next section dealt with the common rights of the Ottoman subjects. Another section covered the responsibilities of the ministers, abolished the Sadrazam, and replaced this office with a prime minister as the head of the cabinet. The prime minister was appointed by the ruler, and he and his ministers were responsible to the ruler and the assembly. Yet another section dealt with the functions of the general assembly, which would comprise a house of representatives and a senate.

When the committee submitted the draft to the ruler on November 13, 1876, it was rejected obstreperously by his ministers. They objected to the statement of the sovereign rights of the ruler and, perhaps especially, to the abolition of the office of Sadrazam. The Padişah was above such a law, they said, in a manner reminiscent of the youthful Mahmud II's corrupt courtiers. His sacred rights required no affirmation. Furthermore, the ministers had to be appointed directly and separately by the Padişah. They should be responsible to him alone.

Needless to say, Hamid's courtiers feared the day when they might have to deal with numerous elected representatives rather than the more predictable Hamid. They abhorred the thought that one day the assembly rather than the court, or the Porte might dominate the conduct of government. After about two weeks of consultation, Hamid gave the committee, on November 25, one of his characteristically vague answers. He said, in part:

The draft contained in its comprehensive clauses [?] certain provisions that were not compatible with the established practices and inclinations of the country. . . . Our best intention is to reconcile the needs of our subjects with the right of sovereignty [?] Therefore, it is my wish that the draft be discussed by the Council of my ministers and modified accordingly.[20]

The draft was predestined to be murdered in the Council on which sat Cevdet Paşa and the Sadrazam. The entire section on the

---

[20] Abdül-Hamid to Midhat Paşa in *Tabsıra-i İbret*, p. 328.

244

sovereign rights of the ruler was thrown out. The cabinet system was rejected. An article stating, "The religion of the Ottoman state is Islam," was inserted into the section on the common rights of Ottoman subjects as a replacement for the more circumspect, "The regime of the Ottoman state is fundamentally based upon and tied to the holy Şeriat." Also, a preamble in the form of the Tanzimat charters was added. In other words, the constitution was given essentially the shape of the earlier absolutist reform pledges.

Kemal barraged Hamid with memoranda in which he attacked the alterations being made by the ministers in the draft.[21] He begged Hamid to realize that the inclusion of clauses concerning the sovereign rights of the ruler was in complete accord with the "founding of a regime of *meşveret* based on the authority of the Khalîfa"; it did not in any way impair the ruler's sovereign powers. Probably more influentially, Süleyman Paşa defended the same ideas. It appears that he threatened Hamid, who was ever hypersensitive to the possibility of his deposition, with the consequences of altering the draft.

Through these efforts, the draft was rescued from the hands of the ministers, but, in the furor of restoring the text, a few of the changes remained awhile unnoticed. One of these was the clause

[21] Kemal's memoranda were later exploited by Hamid, through his mouthpiece Ahmed Midhat, to accuse him of being against the Constitution. See Ahmed Midhat, *Üss-ü Inkilâp*, II, 200. Kemal answered this accusation in a long letter from exile in 1877, but as his writings were at that time banned the letter was published only thirty-three years later when he was long since dead. It was published as a pamphlet entitled *Ahmed Midhat' a Cevap* (Izmir, 1911), and printed in *Mecmua-i Ebüzziya*, XV, Nos. 153-57 (1914). These memoranda were never published, although a few fragments were printed in I. M. K. Inal, *Osmanlı Devrinde Son Sadrazamlar* (Istanbul, 1942), III, 344, 347. From these fragments and his explanations in the letter mentioned above, it is easy to understand that Kemal's main target was the distortion made by the Council of Ministers to convert the Constitution into a Tanzimat charter. However, he seems to have been overwhelmed by his distrust of the ministers, so much so that he appeared to be defending the sovereign rights of the ruler; thus, he gave the chance to Hamid to point to him as the defender of the rights of the Padişah. See *Süleyman Paşa Muhakemesi*, I, 59-62. Süleyman Paşa also drafted a memorandum to explain the damage caused by the alterations to the draft. The text of this memorandum is printed in the *Memoirs* of Said Paşa; see "Eginli Sait Paşa Hâtıratı," *Türklük*, II, No. 9 (Istanbul, 1939), 186-88; also in Kuntay, *Namık Kemal*, II, Part II, pages following p. 67. The ideas in this memorandum seem to be in accordance with Kemal's. Süleyman Paşa played a decisive role in forcing Hamid to give his final consent.

declaring Islam in effect as the religion of the state. When noticed, this invited more ridicule than criticism—it was said that individuals, but not legal entities such as states could have a religion and, therefore, the clause was meaningless, or at most awkward —and the clause remained in the promulgated text. Far more important was the failure to observe that the ministers had modified Articles 31, 32, and 34—all designed to curb the ministers and make them subject to closer control by the Assembly—in such a way that the Assembly could do absolutely nothing about a minister whom the Padişah wished to keep in office, or uphold. Thus the only really constitutional part of the promulgated Constitution was negated.

All other matters remained in the shadows because full attention was drawn to a wedge introduced by one of the ministers who was Hamid's closest intimate, in fact, his brother-in-law. This was the famous Article 113. This article provided the ruler with the right to banish from the country, without court trial, or decision, any person of whom he had doubts. In a memorandum submitted to Hamid, Kemal explained that Article 113 would suffice to destroy not only a constitutional regime, but even the whole of the Tanzimat reforms. At the time when, he considered, Turkish history was about to open into a new era of freedom and liberty, he warned that even those freedoms granted by the Tanzimat charters were at stake. He warned the Padişah that the use of such arbitrary rights caused revolutions, and that the ruler would gain nothing but "an army of spies and an army of exiles turned into revolutionaries" if he used the right given to him by Article 113.

Kemal and Ziya insisted that Article 113 should be rejected categorically. Midhat also believed that a bomb had been placed under the foundations of the Constitution and the detonator given into the hands of the not yet fully established ruler, Hamid. But, alas, only ten days remained until the date set for the promulgation of the new regime and the formal opening of the International Conference; there were ten days and then either the representatives of the powers would confirm Ottoman constitutionalism by dissolving their convention or, as an alternative which had not yet appeared real to the constitutionalists, succumb to the Russian design to partition the Ottoman Empire.

The time had now come for Hamid to play his trumps one by one. He appointed Midhat as his Prime Minister on December 19 and ordered a last meeting of the Council to end the deadlock. At the opening of the meeting on December 22, Cevdet Paşa tabled the proposition that all of the talks about establishing a constitutional regime derived from the nation's experience with tyrants and mad rulers. "Now that a wise and sane ruler has come to the throne," he said, "there is no need for a Constitution in the terms of the Şeriat.

246

Midhat exploded. After a bitter and personal exchange with Cevdet, he threatened to resign if the aim was to obstruct the promulgation of the Constitution.[22] He walked out of the meeting, leaving the impression that he could be badgered into accepting Article 113 only if there were no alternative; he thus gave Hamid's camp a double tactical advantage. After midnight, Hamid put the finishing touches to Article 113. He made the supreme sacrifice of allowing his right to banish those he found engaged in subversive activities to be subject to the reports of the police! Early in the morning of December 23, 1876, he signed the Constitution.

The Major Provisions of the Constitution

The first thing to be said about the Constitution is that it was not framed by representatives of the people, but granted by the ruler. The Constitution acquired its legal and binding character only by the ratification and promulgation of the sovereign, after it had been given shape by bodies none of which could claim to represent the people. The ruler was not bound by the Constitution; the Constitution was bound by his will. The admirers of Abdül-Hamid usually boasted that he did nothing to violate it. Any fair observer must admit that the claim is true. Hamid jealously preserved the Constitution while he prorogued the assembly for more than thirty years. He introduced his absolutism upon the basis of that Constitution. The political doctrine upon which it was made was not the idea that sovereignty lay in the people, but the idea that sovereignty still belonged to God and to His earthly vice-regent, the Padişah; His law was the Şeriat of which the Constitution was only a part.

The Padişah had the last word in several provisions of the Constitution. The Constitution itself gave the ruler the right to dismiss the National Assembly and prorogue the Constitution. The sections dealing with the sovereign rights of the ruler were full of far-reaching implications for the life of the individual as well as

[22] *Tabsıra-i İbret*, p. 188.

for the whole of society. On the other hand, the section dealing with the "common rights of the subjects" contained about twenty provisions (given in Articles 8 to 26) declaring rights (such as the inviolability of personal freedom, of property, of speech, of forming associations, of education, of domicile, of fair trial, etc.), all of which were devoid of sanction, or of any implication for the conduct of the ruler.

247

Not only did the Constitution not represent progress in the Tanzimat's secularism, it became the legal document for the rejection of the idea of a secular state and the legal affirmation of the Islamic aspect of the Turkish state. Articles 3, 4, 5 and 13 placed the ruler's temporal powers (which were not restricted by the Constitution) on the basis of a religious legitimacy.

Because of its fundamental principles, the Constitution was devoid of the provisions which, in the modern state, are necessary to ensure constitutional rule. The most fundamental of them—the separation of the legislative, executive, and judicial powers—was conspicuously absent. The National Assembly was not an independent legislative organ. Even in those fields regarded as the specific prerogatives of the Assembly, it could not make any decision that did not require either the permission or the approval of the ruler (Article 54). Even the meeting or the adjourning of the Assembly was subject to the ruler's discretion (Article 43). The members had to take an oath of loyalty to the ruler (Article 46), but the ruler did not have to take an oath of loyalty to the Constitution, because "the person of His Majesty the Padişah is sacred" (Article 5). In the event of a disagreement between the Assembly and the government, the Padişah had the right to dismiss either the government or the Assembly, according to his wish (Article 35).

The government also rested entirely upon the will of the ruler. The appointment and dismissal of its members was his responsibility. The Assembly could not vote down a government. The principle of the responsibility of the cabinet was not accepted; each minister was separately responsible to the ruler. The ruler could maintain indefinitely ministers who did not win the confidence of the Assembly, whereas ministers who did win the confidence of the Assembly could be dismissed by the ruler at any time (Articles 7, 27-29, and 36). The ministers could not enjoy any protection from the legislature.

The legislative power was, in fact, in the hands of the ruler, despite outward appearances. The Assembly could act as a legislature only according to the directives of the ruler and with regard

248

to the matters willed by the ruler. No liberty or initiative was given to the Assembly to introduce or pass a new bill, or to introduce a bill amending or changing a law (Article 53 reserved the last right to the ministers). Although Article 54 recognized the right of the members to introduce bills to the Assembly, this right was conditioned by the vague proviso that "they should concern the matters which fall under the specified functions of the Assembly." In short, by several circumscriptions, the function of the Assembly was reduced to that of a consultative body whose nature hardly fitted any organ within the terms of modern constitutional law. The members of the Assembly were recognized to have the right to demand interpellation from the government, according to Article 38. But even this was a limited right, because a clause recognized that the ministers could postpone their responses indefinitely.

What was more, the Constitution recognized a kind of independent legislative authority of the ruler. Article 36 recognized the authority of the ruler to issue decrees which had the power of temporary laws. Article 7 recognized the right of dissolving the Assembly as one of the "sacred rights" of the ruler. Although Article 7 added, "provided the Assembly will be elected again," it did not specify any time limit. Finally, Article 113 extended the limits of the rights of the sovereign over the borders into absolutism.

The kind of constitutional ideology, represented best by Namık Kemal and shared by others at that time, was ultimately the foundation for the Hamidian regime. No more telling example can be found in history of the inevitable consequences of ideologies that are inherently inconsistent and contradictory.

The Fate of the Constitutional Movement

While the cannons declared the promulgation of the Constitution on the morning of 23 February 1876, the Istanbul conference was just beginning its proceedings. The reaction of the delegates would seal the fate of Midhat, who had hoped that the conference would give international recognition to the new regime. All members, except those of Turkey, had already had unofficial meetings at the residence of the Russian ambassador and no doubt had agreed to ignore the promulgation. Lord Salisbury, the chief

British delegate, to the great surprise of the ambassador, Henry Elliot, sided with the Russian representatives.[23]

The conference settled down to its work as though the Constitution did not exist. On January 15, it handed down a list of demands much in line with what Russia hoped to get. The proposals were unanimously voted for rejection at a special congress to which the lay and ecclesiastical representatives of all religions and churches had been invited by the Turkish government. The rejection was followed by a declaration of war by Russia, and declarations of neutrality by Great Britain and the other European powers.

Midhat and the cause of constitutionalism were thus cruelly betrayed. Abdül-Hamid's judgment of the West proved to be correct. Midhat's policy of circumventing European consent to Russia's attack collapsed; his scheme of implementing reforms by subjugating the ruler to the will of parliament failed miserably; war and consequent defeat and the following Berlin conference, which imposed upon Turkey terms harsher than those of the Istanbul conference and than those dictated by the Russian armistice, gave ample reasons to Abdül-Hamid to take the reins into his own hands and not to relinquish them for thirty years. Before parliament convened, he gave orders for Midhat's arrest. On the basis of Article 113, the latter was deported on 5 February 1877 by special yacht and landed in a European port—a slap in the face of European civilization.

Parliament was opened on 19 March 1877 and from its first day to its last proved to be a success. Christians, Jews, Turks, and Arabs were represented, not on the basis of religion or nationality, but according to the proportion of these within a constituency. In the words of Harold Temperley, "Midhat's ideal of reconciling Turks and Christians was to a certain extent realised. The cleavage in Parliament was not on religious or racial lines. Indeed, it was the success of the parliamentary experiment which caused its failure."

Abdül-Hamid prorogued parliament by a decree of 14 February 1878, again in accordance with the Constitution and on the grounds that an extraordinary condition of crisis impelled him to do so. Military, diplomatic, and financial troubles created by this crisis made parliament, constitution, and liberalism forgotten affairs. He

---

[23] Elliot, *Revolutions*, pp. 276-77, 287-88. Salisbury was convinced that Russo-British co-operation was a practicable and safe solution for the Eastern Question (Seton-Watson, *Britain in Europe*, p. 522).

250

did not bother to call parliament again until 1908. The leading liberal constitutionalists were persecuted step by step. Midhat was at first allowed to return from exile; then in 1881 he was put on trial and sentenced to death; the sentence was commuted to life imprisonment in the ancient fortress of Taif in Arabia, but he was murdered there in 1884. Namık Kemal was tried and banished to an Aegean island, and although he was later made a local administrator, he was not allowed to return to Turkey; his works were censored or confiscated, and he died in exile in 1888. Süleyman Paşa was put on trial in 1878, was sentenced to banishment, and died in exile in Baghdad in 1892. Other liberals who did not retire from political activity or compromise with the Hamidian regime received similar treatment. Turkey lapsed into a long period of reaction and isolation. Disappointed and betrayed by the West, many intellectuals rallied around Abdül-Hamid. From 1878 to 1908, Abdül-Hamid ruled the Ottoman Empire singlehanded on the basis of the Constitution of 1876![24]

Yet, as early as 1879, the opening signal was given for the struggle between Abdül-Hamid and a new generation whom Europeans were to call Young Turks; the first of them made their escape to Europe, to be followed by many others during the next decade. The struggle, predicted by Namık Kemal, began between the "army of spies" and the "army of exiles turned into revolutionaries."

[24] Celâleddin, *Mir'at-i Hakikat*, I, 222, aptly called this rule a "constitutional absolutism."

THE REACTION 1878-1908

EXTERNAL AND INTERNAL PRESSURES had produced the compromise of a constitutional experiment in which one of two conflicting elements in the Young Ottoman ideology emerged triumphant. The "constitutional absolutism" of Abdül-Hamid was the result of the constitutionalists' attempt to solve inconsistencies created by the duality of state and religion in the Tanzimat regime; it was not a system imposed by a single man against the will of the people. Only after the Ottoman Empire had shown unmistakable signs of dissolution was Abdül-Hamid singled out as the man responsible for its collapse. Then different men representing irreconcilable interests—the spokesmen of European imperialism, the Young Turks who remained loyal to the Young Ottoman heritage of Union and Progress, those who aspired to Armenian or Arab nationalism, and those who, after serving the Hamidian regime, outdid all others in their denunciation of it—spoke out in the name of liberty and portrayed Abdül-Hamid as a tyrant.

In reality, the Hamidian regime took shape under conditions crying for its establishment. Several factors made the regime not an anomaly but a true reflection of conditions prevailing not only in Turkey, but throughout the Islamic world.

The Muslim World at its Thirteenth Centennial

The first feature of the Islamic world, at the approach of its thirteenth centennial, was the establishment of European rule by

254

Great Britain, France, and Russia (with Germany and Italy clamouring behind) over vast areas of Muslim territory in Central Asia, India, Egypt, and North Africa. From 1830, when the French penetrated North Africa, the Muslims of Morocco, Algeria, Tunisia, and Tripolitania had turned their eyes toward Turkey.[1] One of the Western-educated statesmen of Tunisia, Hayreddin Paşa, even became Sadrazam to Abdül-Hamid; and Abdül-Hamid established good relations with the Tripolitanian people and was friendly with the Sanusis. Egypt had become virtually independent of Turkey in 1873, but soon fell under British occupation and began to develop an anti-Western Muslim nationalism. In the northeast sector of the Islamic world, the conquest of the Turkish-Muslim states was being consummated by Russia. By the 1850's and 1860's, the khans of these states had begun sending emissaries to the caliph in search of interest and help. Several educated men from the Turkish-speaking territories that had fallen under Russian rule—such as the Caucasus, Azerbaijan, Crimea, Kazan, and Turkestan—took refuge in Turkey and helped to arouse concern for the condition of Muslim countries. In the south east,

a sentimental attachment to an idealized conception of the Ottoman Empire began to appear . . . among the [Indian] Muslim diaspora—Shii as well as Sunni . . . as a psychological compensation for the loss of their former imperial dominion . . . to the British.
The Ottoman Empire was, indeed, the only political rallying point on which the Muslim victims of Western and Russian imperialism could fall back—not so much in virtue of her dubious and long-neglected title to the inheritance of the Caliphate as because, even in her nineteenth-century infirmity, she was by far and away the most powerful, efficient, and enlightened Muslim state in existence.[2]

When, at the beginning of the fourteenth Islamic century, in 1882, Abdül-Hamid was hailed with congratulations from Muslim lands outside Turkey and Persia, these lands were all under foreign domination. We can imagine the degree to which they attached importance to the caliphate after the loss of political independence to millions of Muslims.

The second major feature of the Islamic world at this time was the cessation of political rapprochement between Turkey and the

[1] See Arnold J. Toynbee, *A Study of History* (London, 1945), VIII, 692-95.

[2] *Ibid.*, 693.

West. Following the gradual reversal of British policy, beginning with the betrayal of the constitutionalists in the crisis of 1876 and the acquisition of British control over the Suez Canal, the Ottoman state found herself in a political vacuum. Great Britain could afford to leave her to her own destiny or even to try to isolate her from her Islamic parts, which were wide open to direct British penetration. But Turkey's isolation was understood by many Turks and Muslims to mean that the Padişah and Khalîfa had become independent of Europe. Abdül-Hamid appeared to them as the capable Muslim ruler who played the Powers off against each other. In fact, when Abdül-Hamid turned to, and sought support from, the Muslim world beyond the Ottoman territories, even Western statesmen imagined great powers in his caliphate.

The economic condition of the country also led the people of Turkey to rally around the throne of Abdül-Hamid. The failure of the constitutional experiment coincided with the collapse of all the measures of economic development undertaken by the Tanzimat through foreign aid. The agricultural, industrial, and educational efforts of the Tanzimat ended in the financial bankruptcy of 1875, and made the people feel that modernization meant bondage to European capital, decline of domestic economy under the domination of European industry, and further pauperization of the masses.

All these conditions explain why the Hamidian regime appealed to the people. The people believed it to be their own. It did not appear to be sustained by external support and imported Western institutions; it appeared to be indigenous, tradition-loving, Islamic, and free from the worries and discomforts of change. Abdül-Hamid's personal austerity, sobriety, and piety were very appealing to the masses who had had their fill of spendthrift Tanzimat rulers and their emulators. The characteristic that most impressed them was the Caliph's appearance as a self-confident Muslim ruler, independent of all foreign influences and interventions and capable of striking back. In addition, he fostered everything that preserved, glorified, and justified tradition. The man in the street could feel comfort in the security of this tradition. The Hamidian regime built up for him a dream world in which his illusions appeared to be coming true. The period was one of escape from actual conditions, and a time of reaction against the efforts as well as the frustrations of the Tanzimat.

The unconditional and willing acceptance of the absolute authority of the Padişah, who was also revered as the Shadow of

God on Earth, was so contagious that for many years virtually no one who might be called intelligent remained immune to the spell.[3] Even a number of Young Turks could not free themselves from the spirit of submissiveness. At the onset of the 1908 revolt, the revolutionaries never considered deposing Abdül-Hamid. He was not deposed until about a year later, when the turbulent months following the revolt had liberated the people from the magic spell of his regime. Whatever the legitimate charges against its administration, that regime did not alone create such a spirit in its subjects, although it sedulously cultivated and maintained the allegiance which it discovered.

256

Portrait of the Hamidian Regime

The administration of the Hamidian regime, which was considered the constitutional model of the Islamic state, deserves examination. Once it had won universal allegiance, neither constitution nor parliament counted for much, although they remained in theory. But a parliament could have no reality unless it had legislative powers and represented the will of the people; and certain provisions of the Constitution negated both these conditions. All power was concentrated in the hands of the ruler, whose religious and temporal prerogatives remained above those of parliament. Thus the ruler could surround himself with a number of special committees which served him as organs of *meşveret* (counselling) on political, religious, and military affairs. (Among these there might even be foreign advisers such as the German general, Von der Goltz.) Abdül-Hamid, perhaps more honestly, founded a system closer to what the Islamist Young Ottomans conceived as *meşveret*, the essence of Islamic constitutionalism.

One of the products of this concentration of power was a vast bureaucratic organization. This became the weakest and most oppressive part of the system because of the absence of the means, the methods, and the personnel of a rational administration. The only modern device readily accepted as useful for such a centralized bureaucracy was telegraphy. The telegraphic machine be-

Abdul Hamid's reign

---

[3] The writer happened to see, in 1959, how a piece of cloth, once sent as a gift by Abdül-Hamid, was revered as a sacred object in a spontaneous ceremony at the foremost Islamic institution in India. This may give some idea of the breadth and length of the spell!

came the most popular gadget to be borrowed from Western civilization. The devising of codes for countless secret communications between the capital and the provinces constituted an important technique in the running of the government, and it contrasted sharply with the clumsiness of official Turkish for written correspondence. The first telegraphic line was built in 1855 during the Crimean War; but under Abdül-Hamid more than thirty thousand kilometres of lines were constructed, extending even to remote corners of the Hejaz and Yemen. The capital was connected by underwater cables to islands such as Crete and Cyprus. The Morse code was quickly adapted to Turkish, up-to-date telegraphic machines were imported, students of telegraphy were sent to France, and many practical courses were started for the training of operators. A French telegraphic engineer, employed in the Turkish service, commented that "Turkey was the first country to introduce telegraphic lines into places where roads and railways were as yet unknown."[4]

This type of administrative bureaucracy necessitated the development of another organization, composed of informers and spies, to insure the loyalty of the administrators. This second organization was secret, amorphous, and informal, but it possessed unlimited freedom in gathering and reporting information. Its best-known legacy to the Turkish vocabulary testifies to its bureaucratic origin. The *jurnals* of the informers (from French *journal*) were daily reports submitted to heads of departments. While this organization of spies seems to have had a central ministerial office with an official head and large financial resources at its disposal, a great many of its agents were volunteers bent upon protecting the ruler and themselves from everything unusual. It does not appear, however, that this organization served the ruler as well as did his official bureaucracy. Even its victims do not seem to have been as numerous as was believed. But it served to create, maintain, and legitimize the psychological atmosphere of the time.

In the absence of a well-developed and modern rational administration, the status of the bureaucrat gained new value and prestige. The ideal man of the time was the government servant. The greatest desire of the educated youth was not to become a businessman or engineer, but to enrol in the Imperial School of Civil Servants (Mekteb-i Mülkiye-i Şâhâne), which became the best school of higher learning in default of a university. The corps of civil serv-

---

[4] Emile Lacoine, "Elektriğin Memleketimizdeki Tatbikatı," *Tercü-man-ı Hakikat ve Servet-i Funûn* (special issue, 1895), 38-40.

258

ants—their outlook, practices, etiquette, and hierarchy of values—personified the spirit of the regime. Obedience and servitude were the highest virtues, and any suspicion of disloyalty implied the gravest offence against religion and state.

The Hamidian administration got most of its support, however, from outside the government apparatus. The foundation of Hamidian rule was the great mass of the people—with all their beliefs and superstitions, and also their sense of honour and decency. In addition, Abdül-Hamid had the support not only of the Ulema, the ministers, and the intellectuals, but also of a type of religious professional which gained new status in the regime and thrived all over the Islamic world during the period of its economic decline. There were two classes, the aristocracy and the poletariat of the religious trade. The Caliph was surrounded by the first, society as a whole by the second. In place of the traditional Ulema, there was a mushroom growth of "men of religion"—*şerifs, seyyids, nakîbs,* and *amîrs*—genuine or spurious, representing either traditionalism or obscurantism. The term *şerif* originally meant a descendant of the Prophet through his grandson Hasan, *seyyid* a descendant through his other grandson Husayn; in time these descendants came to constitute an officially recognized religious aristocracy, whose leaders were called *nakîbs.* The *amîrs* were chieftains or tribal princes; they no longer represented any genuine descent or relationship. Arab *shaikhs* also occupied a special place with Hamid. The shaikhs or patriarchs of the orthodox religious orders came mostly from Syria, Arabia, and North Africa. Some had great reputations as astrologers, necromancers, and sorcerers. Abdül-Hamid's chief secretary records in his reminiscences that, for this type of religious aristocracy, coming from distant lands,

the ruler kept special quarters in his Palace, called the Imperial Guest House. For the higher celebrities he maintained special mansions given over for their use. Shaikh Jamal al-Dîn al-Afghanî, Shaikh Jawâd, Seyyid Fadl of Hadramut, the Amîr of Masqat, and the like belonged to this category.[5]

The most important of the Arab shaikhs, who outdid all others in influence, was the notorious Abu'l-Hudâ al-Sayyâdî of Aleppo, whose alleged supernatural powers gave him a position in the imperial court which was sometimes likened to that of his contemporary Rasputin. The presence of these men served to symbolize the link between the Caliph and the Muslim *umma.*

[5] Tahsin Paşa, *Abdülhamid ve Yıldız Hatıraları* (Istanbul, 1931).

The second class consisted of men who crowded the mystic orders and the scholastic *medreses*. Those in orders, called the *tarîqas*, enjoyed a veritable boom; it was a time for them to multiply. The convents spread profusely. The Rifâî, Şâdhilî and Nakşibandî orders were especially in favour. Even certain groups, such as the Tijaniyya, unheard-of until then among the Turks, came from North Africa and established themselves as popular orders. From the Maghreb (North West Africa) there was a great traffic of healers, quack medicine men, breath-curers, and diviners. People enjoyed colourful superstitions, incantations, amulets, and visits to the tombs of saints. Half-beggar dervishes and *medrese* students journeyed freely from village to village in all parts of the Empire. It was their heyday.

Parallel with this increasing religious professionalism were the measures taken to enforce publicly the traditional Muslim puritanism. The police were given new powers to force the people to observe the Şeriat. The trends, initiated by the Tanzimat, towards greater individual freedom for both men and women and towards the cultivation of entertainment were not only halted but even reversed.

The most conspicuous feature of the period, when compared with that of the Tanzimat, was the prevalence of outward religiosity. Perhaps in no other period of Turkish history was there so much talk of *din*, or so frequent use of the word *şeriat*. Many dignitaries of the time were ideal specimens of religious hypocrisy. As Musa Kâzım (1858-1919), a Şeyhul-Islâm of the post-Hamidian era, commented,

The celebrities of corruption used to indulge in worshipping in order to cover up their sins, and used to have their prayer rugs follow them wherever they went, even to their offices. . . . In order to become a favourite of the Palace and Government, one had to enrol in the flocks of the religious orders.[6]

According to Musa Kâzım, "the khalîfa was elevated to the rank of deity" in this rage of religious hypocrisy.

The regime of reaction succeeded not only in keeping the masses happy in their ignorance and stupor, but also in providing an ideal hatchery for professional obscurantists. In its endeavour to control the minds of the people, the regime established the principle of censorship. All publications, including daily papers, were

[6] Musa Kâzım, *Devr-i İstibdat Ahvali ve Müsebbipleri* (Istanbul, 1911), p. 29.

subject to inspection before printing. Censorship existed not only to prevent the publication of dangerous thoughts, but also to "educate" writers to write in the proper way. The censors had to carry their imaginations to the borders of nonsense. Once a writer prepared an article for *Servet-i Funûn* under the title "Literature and Law," in which some references were made to the French Revolution. The article passed the censor. But after its publication, an informer sent a clipping of the article to the Padişah. He stated in his *jurnal* that the

260

purpose of the article in presenting the case of the French Revolution to the public was sedition of the people to rise against our Khalîfa of the Earth, and that the punishment for this kind of action was lynching in America and very heavy also in Europe, etc.[7]

Anything could be interpreted in any way by the peculiar logic of the time. There was unlimited freedom of thinking in this field.

The whole design of the regime was to obscure reason and curtail free thinking, which was branded as *dehrîlik*. Musa Kazım said in his reminiscences:

Even the styles of writing and talking were stereotyped to the extent that all thought was suppressed. Those who expressed their thoughts outside of the prescribed official style were regarded with suspicion and contempt. To write clearly, to talk plainly—even to explain something—was branded as pedantic and impudent. Official writings appeared as puzzles; it was difficult to obtain a clear and sound understanding from their long sentences. Neither was it possible to make any inference from their short sentences, as they were cleverly and enigmatically arranged cryptic sentences.[8]

In this way, the system which Islamic constitutionalism and the liberalism of Young Ottomans had aspired to establish developed under the disfiguring forces we have surveyed. Yet only infidels, predatory European governments, atheist Young Turks, and certain Arab and Armenian nationalists were against it. When all such opponents, representing divergent and even irreconcilable interests, were lumped together, it was easy for the regime to

[7] Ahmed İhsan, *Matbuat Hatıraları* (Istanbul, 1930), I, 109. This work contains abundant information concerning the state of the press and literature of the time.

[8] Kâzım, *Devr-i İstibdat*, p. 34.

represent each one as a traitor or enemy of Islam. The group which suffered most from this unwelcome classification were the Young Turks, whose story we shall turn to in the next chapter.

Official Trends of Thought

The dominant trends of thought in the Hamidian regime were naturally opposed to those of the Tanzimat. Although traditionalism, apologetics, anti-Westernism, and pan-Islamism had appeared just before the coming of Abdül-Hamid, we find them being elevated to a higher plane under him.

Anti-Westernism became the major plank of every policy. It ceased to be an ideological standpoint; it was necessary for isolation. The dominant desire was to turn all eyes away from the West. This was achieved by pointing out the unbridgeable gulf between the two worlds. Information concerning the current political affairs and ideas of the West was ignored. Newspapers refrained from printing news about such European "vices" as parliamentary discussion, party struggles, changes of government, and labour strikes—and especially anything to do with a coup d'état, bomb attempt, assassination, anarchism, or nihilism.

The supplement to anti-Westernism was the cultivation of an attachment to the past and to the old. For the first time since the beginning of the eighteenth century, the Orient and the medieval Islamic past replaced the modern West as models for reform. The period witnessed the rise of modern Muslim apologetics among the Turks and opened a new era of refutation literature.

A comparison will show the change. No matter how feverishly the Young Ottomans had deduced liberal ideas and institutions from Islamic traditions, they had still drawn their basic inspiration from the West. Under their camouflage was a persistent groping for Western institutions. They used the language of the past, but for them *ümmet* meant nation, *icma* mean social contract, *bîat* meant the relegation of sovereignty to the ruler by the people, *içtihâd* meant parliamentary legislation, *meşveret* meant democracy, and *'ilm* meant science. By equating certain Islamic categories with certain Western categories, the liberals had thought that they could bridge the gap between old and new in the transition from a medieval to a modern civilization. In their eyes, this was not borrowing foreign ideas. Hamidianism abandoned the

262

self-deceiving semantics of the liberals. Just as it deflected the reformism of the Young Ottomans, so it repudiated their tendency to twist Islamic institutions to make them appear different from what they traditionally were. It saw no reason to vindicate Islam in this fashion because it did not doubt the superiority and correctness of the institutions and vocabulary it understood so well.

To the mentality of the Hamidian period, that for which the regime stood was visible only in the past. Thus, instead of reading John Locke and then searching the Kur'an to unearth the principles of representative government, Abdül-Hamid's men resorted to medieval treatises on statecraft. Books were written to compile, translate, and interpret conveniently the ancient *hadîths* on the prerogatives of the Padişah. The impossibility of a Muslim state being other than what it was under the auspicious rule of the Shadow of God was the subject of numerous works written for both foreign and domestic consumption.

Even Namık Kemal and his followers helped form the Hamidian atmosphere. Like many other Muslim thinkers in Turkey, Egypt, and Russia, Kemal reacted promptly upon receiving in exile in 1883 the text of Ernest Renan's lecture on Science and Islam. In this lecture, Renan asserted that orthodox Islam, as the creation of the Arab mind, was the enemy of science and philosophy. In Islamic history, science and philosophy flourished only when orthodoxy was softened or weakened. But even then, they were not truly Arab in concept. Both had been taken over from the Greeks and the Sassanids; or their creators were not Arabs in race or mentality; or they were fashioned by men who had revolted against their faith, and were regarded as heretics. Islam—as an amalgam of the spiritual and the temporal, as a state basing itself upon revelation, as a society regulated by religion—was averse to progress; that was why Muslims were incapable of progress.

Kemal was aware when he wrote his Refutation (*Renan Müdafaanamesi*)[9] that these statements were made by a freethinker and liberal who was only saying about Islam what he would have said about the Christian theocracy. Yet he was deeply angered by Renan's thesis, which struck at some of his own basic convictions. As a result, he set out to expose a number of errors in details, but failed to cope seriously with Renan's basic point. Instead of demonstrating that most of these errors stemmed from Renan's

---

[9] *Renan Müdafaanamesi*, published by Ali Ekrem, Kemal's son, in his edition of Kemal's collected works (incomplete) *Külliyat-ı Kemal* (Istanbul, 1908).

racialism, Kemal undertook to defend the idea that the great men of Islamic science and philosophy were Arabs. By converting the opportunity to discuss problems of religion and state in the struggle for modernization into an occasion for passionate apologetics, Kemal showed that, despite their fiasco of 1876, the constitution-alists were far from realizing the inconsistencies in their own ideo-logy. His Refutation set an example for the kind of apologetics and for the glorification of "Arab science" which became the favourite themes of the era of reaction.

263

A characteristic of the Hamidian period was finding roundabout ways to explain continued borrowings from Europe. This was accomplished by replacing the symbol of Western civilization by that of Arab civilization. It had never occurred to the Young Ottomans to claim that the constitutional system they found in the West had been taken over from the Arabs. They simply be-lieved that in the past Islam, too, had had its constitutionalism. The Hamidian period was far bolder. Not only was the whole of Western science and technology originally a Muslim (Arab) possession, but Europeans owed their constitutional system also to the Muslims (Arabs). The history of Arab civilization contained everything that was good about the West—algebra, chemistry, physics, gunpowder, the compass. Therefore, the Muslims did not need anything from Europe, except those incidentals upon which Europeans had made useful improvements.

In 1886 there appeared in *Tarik* a series of articles under the general heading "The Islamic Civilization." The main purpose of the articles was, first, to show the achievements of the Arabs (rather than Muslims) in science,[10] technology (*fen*), literature and historiography; and, second, to prove that all of these were taken over by the Europeans.

This idea was repeated in a book written by an author named Akyiğitzade Musa, a teacher of economics who had migrated to Turkey from Russia. This work was written with the specific purpose of appraising Western civilization. Its title was *Avrupa Medeniyetine Bir Nazar* (Looking at the European Civilization).[11] The opening sentence of the book gives an idea of the standpoint of the author: "The bases of contemporary civilization are nothing but the actions and traditions of Muhammad." The thesis may be

[10] See especially *Tarik*, No. 789 (Istanbul, June 5, 1886).

[11] Akyiğitzade Musa, *Avrupa Medeniyetine Bir Nazar* (Istanbul, 1897).

264

further explained by another quotation from the book: "The Muslim civilization which was derived from the Kur'an and the *hadîths* of the Prophet delivered Europe from medieval barbarism and ignorance." The author enumerates the contributions of the Arabs to European civilization in mathematics, astronomy, navigation, gunpowder, tannery, agriculture, animal husbandry, gardening, postal service, numerals, grammar, and university teaching in general.

The point which was unconsciously missed or simply ignored by those who made these assertions was one which explains a recurring contradiction in the thinking of this period. Unlike the men of the Tanzimat, the men of the period of reaction turned to the proud contributions of a secular Islamic civilization as the epitome of Islam whenever they felt challenged by the material civilization of the West. They were not aware of the unorthodox quality of these contributions. They did not realize that the triumph of orthodoxy coincided with the decline of the spirit in which science and philosophy had flourished. And when they reacted against modern ideas based on the science and technology of the nineteenth century, or against the effects of these ideas on traditional values which they unhesitatingly identified with Islam, they took refuge in the tenets of orthodoxy which they also identified with Islam. In other words, their reasoning operated on two different planes in the face of two challenges—the material superiority of Western civilization and its impact upon traditional Islamic values. This was the source of that duality, found in all prominent men of the era from Namık Kemal to al-Afghanî, which looks to us like contradiction. Whether the shift from one plane to another was made consciously or instinctively, or how far it was due to ignorance, it is difficult to say.

We find the same seeming inconsistency in another characteristic feature of the period—the popularity of literature refuting the materialists (*maddiyyun*) or, as they were sometimes called, naturalists (*tabiiyyun*), and denouncing them as *dehriyyun* (from the Arabic *dahr*, age; the term became linguistically and semantically equivalent to the Western "secularists").

In the history of Islamic thought, the first two terms had been used by orthodox theologians against the philosophers; the third was used to denote the irreconcilability of philosophy and faith, since the attempt to reconcile the two inevitably led to the denial of God. In time, all those who deviated from the tenets of orthodoxy came to be labelled *dahrî*, whether they were philosophers or not, and were condemned as unbelievers. Since the triumph of *kalâm* over all other varieties of thought, classical Muslim philosophy had died out. In the nineteenth century the terms *maddiyyun* and *tabiiyyun* were used to describe the new generations who had become familiar with the ideas of the European philosophers of Enlightenment or those of nineteenth-century materialism, evolutionism, and Darwinism. The practice of labelling as *dahrî* all those who reflected Western ideas in their thinking or behaviour became widespread, as the secularizing effects of these ideas were recognized. Thus even liberals or modernists, themselves denounced by the orthodox *ulema* for their attempt to reconcile the old Muslim philosophy with faith, began in their turn to denounce as *dahrîs* the men of new ideas. These new men thought of Islam in terms of time and change, and no longer in terms of absolute, eternal principles. Since very few could adapt themselves to the medieval thinking of the *ulema*, almost anyone could be branded with the epithet *dahrî*. Invoking the highest religious values in order to denounce the views of an adversary became the deadliest instrument in the hands of the obscurantists.

The prototype of this refutation of "materialist" literature was provided by a man who had himself been charged with heresy by the *ulema* not long before. This was Jamal al-Dîn al-Afghanî, whom we met for the first time in the Turkey of 1870.[12] The same al-Afghanî reappeared on the Turkish scene in 1892, this time not as a visitor to Tanzimat secularists but as the invited guest of Abdül-Hamid. He came as the author of a book written in India in 1878 and already published in its original Persian and in an Arabic translation.[13] It was written against a movement called in Urdu *nachariyya*, from the English word "nature", and meant naturalism. The Arab translator turned the word into *dahriyya*, and from this it was translated back into English as "materialism." *Nachariyya* was believed to have disseminated in India from the ideas of Sir Sayyid Ahmad Khan, whom Afghanî later attacked openly as a British collaborationist. Afghanî's book, however, did

---

[12] See Chap. 6.

[13] *Radd-i Nechariyyah* (Bombay, 1298 H.); Arabic translation by Muhammad Abduh, *Al-Radd'ala al-Dahriyyîn* (Beirut, 1885; Cairo, 1894, 1935, etc.); French trans. A. M. Goichon, *Réfutation des Matérialistes* (Paris, 1942); Turkish trans. Yakub Efendi-zade Muhammad Munir, MS at the Library of the University of Istanbul, Yildiz Collection; Aziz Akpınarlı, *Tabiatçılığı Red* (Ankara, 1956).

266

not directly and specifically deal with materialism as a philosophical approach. In the book, the picture of the *nacharî* encompasses men of every variety of thought from the Greek atomists to Charles Darwin, from Mazdak to Rousseau; every group or movement from Jews to freemasons, from Ismailîs to Mormons, from liberals to socialists or communists. Everywhere, whether in ancient Greece or Iran, Christendom or Islam, India or Turkey, these wretched *nacharîs* were traitors to religion and society, deniers of God, destroyers of law and morality. Behind the different shadowy figures hastily and inaccurately paraded, and attacked with the boldness of rhetoric, emerged Afghanî's real bogy. He was almost exactly the same figure as the one whom Halil Fevzi had attacked anonymously only seven years before in his *Suyûf al Qawâti'* and whom every reader had recognized to be none other than Afghanî himself.

The topsy-turvy picture of Afghanî provided by his Western and Muslim admirers, who tend to lose all sense of proportion when they speak of him, shows him as an orthodox believer at his first Turkish appearance and a liberal revolutionary at his second.[14] If this were true it would be impossible for Afghanî rather than his accuser Halil Fevzi to have written this book or to have presented the authorized Turkish translation to Abdül-Hamid. But if we see Afghanî in terms of the contradictions of his time, we shall understand why he was first denounced as a heretic and later himself denounced as heretics the men of modern ideas, or the readers of L. Büchner. We shall also understand why Abdül-

----

[14] The beliefs that Afghanî was in opposition to Abdül-Hamid and that he inspired the revolutionary movement of Young Turks are the inventions of writers to find an excuse for the presence of Afghanî in Abdül-Hamid's entourage. If Afghanî's opposition to the Persian shah's autocracy and policy of granting tobacco monopoly to foreign investors (see E. G. Browne, *The Persian Revolution of 1905-1908*, Cambridge, 1910, pp. 403-4) was what had made him a revolutionary, one may ask why he did not oppose the Hamidian autocracy and the policy of granting monopolies and railway concessions. C. C. Adams (a writer so unacquainted with facts as to say that Abdül-Hamid was the ruler who received Afghanî in his first visit to Turkey) asserted that "the successful Young Turk movement of 1908 was prepared by [Afghanî's] agitation during the years he spent in Constantinople;" *Islam and Modernism in Egypt* (London, 1933), p. 12. The first Young Turk organization was founded in 1889, three years before Afghanî's coming to Turkey. If Afghanî had ever known Young Turks such as Abdullah Cevdet and Ahmed Rıza (see Chaps. 10 and 11) he would certainly have denounced them as the most abominable *nacharîs* and *dehrîs*.

Hamid invited him and how wise the Caliph was in his generosity. No books gives a more authentic picture than does this *Refutation* of Afghanî of the confused, obscurantist climate of the era. The contradiction between the Afghanî of 1870 and that of 1892 reveals the dual planes of thinking whose semantics can be understood not in terms of the logical construction of the arguments, but in terms of the confusion and complexity of concrete social problems to which the thinker was exposed.

Abdül-Hamid must have been delighted to see that the book confirmed the wisdom of his persecution of the constitutionalists, and to learn that the same *nacharîs* and *dehrîs* who destroyed law and order in the world at large were also responsible for the calamities of Turkey. He must have rejoiced to see the author refer, as usual anonymously, to Midhat Paşa and Süleyman Paşa as men who, like all *nacharîs*, had sold their country to its enemies for petty gains. He had just court-martialled both, and had sentenced one to death and the other to permanent exile; but even he had not gone to the extent of accusing them of treason. Afghanî's boldness must have made him feel almost a coward! Although Afghanî gave no proof to substantiate his accusation, his authority must have helped to relieve the Caliph's conscience. The Turkish version of the *Refutation* contained the following clause, which does not appear in the original: "And these traitors met their deserved punishment by the justice-enforcing hand." In this fashion Afghanî earned the favours of the Caliph. It was a strange way of paying his debt to the "men of modern ideas" to whom he owed his life under the Tanzimat, when the Şeyhul-Islâm would gladly have signed a *fetva* for his execution.

Afghanî served the Hamidian regime not only by contributing a "philosophy" but also by sharing an equally confused element of its ideology—pan-Islamism. Here again, we find a contradiction in Afghanî's career which has given his biographers some trouble to explain. We must be chary of appearances and try to ascertain Afghanî's true position in terms of pan-Islam.

Pan-Islamic ideas were the culmination in Turkey of a reaction against the Tanzimat doctrine of fusing Muslims and non-Muslims into an Ottoman nation. Only Muslims, according to the pan-Islamists, should unite to form the national basis of the Ottoman Empire under the caliph who was also head of that Empire. Even Muslims outside the Empire should rally round the caliph in their struggle for independence from European domination. Talks and writings on *ittihad-ı Islâm* (the unity of the Muslims) and *ihya-i*

268

İslâm (the regeneration of the Muslims) began as early as 1872.[15] Articles and books appeared, a society was formed. In these, the nature of the unit was clear only with regard to those Muslims under the rule of the caliph; it meant political unity. Opinions varied on the nature of the unity which was to embrace all Muslims. On the whole, however, the caliph began to appear as the actual or potential ruler of Muslims everywhere. The caliphate was not merely a spiritual power; it was a state. Islam was not merely a religion; it was a nationality, a political community, a civilization. The cause of decline was not only the loss of unity but also the penetration of secular ideas from the outside world.

Hamidian pan-Islamism was the child of this trend and not the invention of the monarch. The constitution had already given legal recognition to the caliphate as sole prerogative of the ruler, and to Islam as the state religion. What Abdül-Hamid added to the pan-Islamic trend was simply its application internally and externally.

As part of a policy of gaining the support or association of influential Muslims, the presence of Afghanî in Abdül-Hamid's stable of dignitaries would give international prestige to the regime. But there was another reason why Abdül-Hamid wanted Afghanî on his side. A variant idea of pan-Islam was taking shape outside Turkey, with a different form from the Turkish; and Afghanî had connections with it.

The birthplace of the idea was Cairo, and its messenger was not a Muslim but an English poet—Wilfrid Scawen Blunt. Blunt envisaged himself as the deliverer of the Arabs and the reformer of Islam. During his travels in Syria, Egypt, and Najd, and through his contacts with Bedouin chiefs, Egyptian liberals, and Azhar *ulema*, he discovered a new form of pan-Islam. The difference between this and the Hamidian form lay in the question of the legitimacy of the caliphate. The caliphate properly belonged to the Arabs, or rather to the tribe of Quraysh of Mecca. It was not a political, but a religious or spiritual authority. The pontifical authority of the caliph could extend over all Muslims whether they were living under an indigenous ruler or a European government. This was the clue to Islamic reformation. If a spiritual unity were achieved under the caliph's pontificate, Islam would flourish as a religion, and Muslims would be freed from the burden of desire

---

[15] See "İttihad-ı İslâm," *İbret* (1872), reprinted in M. N. Özön, *Namık Kemal ve İbret Gazetesi* (Istanbul, 1938), pp. 74-78.

for a state. They would also be freed from Abdül-Hamid's rule; and since Blunt believed that the British, unlike the Muslim-hating Europeans, were the Muslims' only friends, Great Britain would become the protector of the caliphate.[16] He aspired to be the mediator between the British government and the liberal Arab nationalists in the project of pan-Islam.

The prophetic vision of Blunt was destined to be fulfilled three decades later, but in the eighteen-eighties his scheme was not taken seriously by any British statesman. In 1883, Blunt finally met Afghanî of whom he had heard much from his friend Muhammad Abduh. Despite his recent denunciation of Sayyid Ahmad Khan's collaborationism, Afghanî seemed to be attracted by Blunt's ideas, and Blunt arranged a conference with the top men of the British foreign office in London. It would appear that, as a first step to an understanding between Great Britain and the Muslim national leaders, Afghanî even accepted a proposal to go with a mission on behalf of the foreign office to win the rebellious Mahdi in Sudan. But the British proved to be veritable *nacharîs*; they rejected Afghanî's mediation. An earlier attempt by Blunt to bring about an understanding with the liberal national leader, 'Urabi, had failed because the British favoured neither a constitutional regime nor independence for the Egyptian Arabs. With disgust, Jamal al-Din wandered in different countries and finally accepted Abdül-Hamid's invitation.

Afghanî was not the originator of pan-Islamism in Turkey, and he had no chance to play a part in the pan-Islamic policies of Abdül-Hamid.[17] As usual, he discovered men who were jealous of him; and indeed he probably remained under suspicion of having a connection with Blunt's scheme, which had attracted men

---

[16] See Wilfrid Scawen Blunt, *The Future of Islam* (London, 1882), Chaps. 2, 4, and 5. The chapters of the book had appeared as essays in *Fortnightly Review* in 1881. For Blunt's own narrative of the events leading him to the ideas expounded in the *Future of Islam* see his *Secret History of the English Occupation of Egypt* (New York, 1922).

[17] The belief that Afghanî directed Abdül-Hamid's pan-Islamic policy is common among Western writers on Afghanî's life. Some have noted the difficulty of reconciling this with Afghanî's as-summed revolutionism; others extrapolated even further from the myth. Thus, Lothrop Stoddard gave free rein to his imagination and said: "Naturally the Sultan was enchanted with Djamal, and promptly made him head of his Pan-Islamic propaganda bureau," *The New World of Islam* (New York, 1921), p. 64. Needless to say, there was no such bureau—much less would Afghanî have been the head of it.

270

like Muhammad Abduh, Abbas Hilmi, and the latter's protegé, al-Kâwakibî, who was the first to formulate Arab nationalism in terms of Blunt's ideas of caliphate and pan-Islam.[18] Afghanî did not survive to see the real launching of Abdül-Hamid's pan-Islamic drive, which was provoked and facilitated by British policy in the Near East. This policy, in the eighteen-nineties, had as its aim the domination of territories adjacent to the Suez Canal and Red Sea, but did not include Blunt's ideal of Arab independence and liberal caliphate. Such a policy helped to turn the tide in Abdül-Hamid's favour even in Egypt, where Blunt's ideas came to be regarded as part of a British plot.

Pan-Islamism tended to overshadow two movements which will prove to be more important in coming generations—nationalism and constitutionalism. Pan-Islamists mixed a good measure of wishful thinking with their accounts of such activities as sending emissaries or preachers to far-distant Muslim countries, disseminating religious literature, distributing printed Kur'ans, encouraging pilgrimages to Mecca and Medina, organizing colourful caravans to carry the *surra* (annual funds sent from Istanbul and Cairo for distribution at the Holy Cities), and granting money for mosques and shrines of saints. Such uneconomic expenditures and rituals seemed to accord well with Afghanî's insistence that religion would guarantee independence to all Muslims. But these expressions of religious zeal were ineffective against the material power of European states seeking to dominate both the Near and the Far East. What appeared on the surface as a drive for Muslim unification was in reality a drive for freedom and independence in almost every Muslim country, and it was defeated in a struggle between European powers for the spoils and natural resources of these countries. In this struggle both Turks and Arabs were destined to be losers, and at the same time to turn against each other. The pan-Islamic hallucination found its reward not in a unification of believers around the caliph but in Western-supported nationalist movements. Arnold J. Toynbee's judgment that pan-Islamism served to create parochial nationalisms rather than a universal unity of the Muslims[19] would be closer to the truth if he had granted this achievement to the British rather than to the visionary and contradictory Afghanî.

---

[18] See Sylvia G. Haim, "Blunt and al-Kawâkibî," *Oriento Moderno*, XXXV, (1955), 132-143.

[19] Toynbee, *A Study of History*, VIII, 694.

Realities Behind the Illusions

Having considered some of the illusions of the Hamidian period, we must now turn to its realities. Two important developments took place in the economic penetration by the West. Both were sufficient to make futile all efforts to remain hostile to change. One was the establishment in 1882 of the international financial corporation known as the Administration of the Ottoman Public Debt; the other was the resumption of a flow of European capital into the Ottoman territories for the construction of public works, particularly railroads, and especially the Istanbul-Baghdad railway. These developments represented the cruel light of day in contrast with the moonlit dream of pan-Islamism.

While the men of Abdül-Hamid's reign were boasting of the superiority of the Arab civilization over that of Europe, the economy of Turkey was settling more firmly into the hands of the European bankers. The ruler secured his auspicious absolute rule by allowing the more rational exploitation of the resources of the country—at the cost of relinquishing the full proceeds to the foreign capital owners. There was, apparently, no need for the Muslims to bother themselves with such mundane affairs as those which preoccupied the Europeans! Everything of economic importance (banking, large-scale trade, the construction of railways, harbours, irrigation works, bridges, mines, etc.) was financed and carried on by foreigners. From the date of Abdül-Hamid's famous Muharrem Decree, 1882, the finances of the Ottoman Empire were handed over to European investors by the establishment of the Administration of the Ottoman Public Debt. The revenues of the Empire increased annually following the establishment of the Public Debt, which meant an annual increase in the percentage of the wealth of the country flowing silently abroad. The Public Debt made important advances in the exploitation of the natural resources of the Empire. It began to encourage a further influx of foreign investment capital especially for the construction of railways. This, however, led to rivalries and to a variety of projects designed to concentrate the interests of each power in territorial "zones of penetration."[20]

[20] See Donald C. Blaisdell, *European Financial Control in the Ottoman Empire* (New York, 1929); Parvus [Alexander Helphand], *Türkiyenin Can Damarı* (Istanbul, 1914). For the investment of European capital in the Ottoman Empire generally see Herbert Feis, *Europe, the World's Banker, 1870-1914* (New Haven, 1930).

272

The most important of the developments was the opening of a railroad age in Turkey. It is true that railroad construction had begun during the middle part of the Tanzimat period, but little had been undertaken between 1856 and 1886 when the universal race for railway construction finally reached the Near East.[21] The real impetus came from the Board of the Public Debt. This body obtained concessions to construct railways that were completed in 1888, 1892, 1894, 1897, and 1903. On August 12, 1888 (1300 *Hijrî*) the first train of the Paris-Vienna-Istanbul Simplon Express arrived at Istanbul with great fanfare, and to the displeasure of Abdül-Hamid. Other new lines penetrated only the hinterlands of such centres as Salonica, Izmir, Istanbul, Mersin, and Damascus; while they were largely responsible for the evolution and development of the rural economies of these areas, nonetheless, they remained on the periphery. The most ambitious project of all was that for the construction of the Berlin-Baghdad line.[22] The actual effect of this line on Turkey would be to open up the interior rural districts, those that had always remained outside the range of modernizing change, to the outside world. The project would realize the first modern transportation transversing the Empire and connecting its heart with Central Europe at the one end and the Indian Ocean at the other.

The overall result of the developments was to expose Turkish society increasingly to European influence. Contrary to all the intentions of the Hamidian regime, the exposure, though varying from place to place and in the various strata of the society, was greater in magnitude than had been the case under the more liberal Tanzimat reign. Now even the remote villages of Anatolia began to feel the repercussions of the new conditions. Increasingly, the peasants migrated to the cities to join the crowds of peddlers, watchmen, servants, porters, and beggars. The Turkish peasants, however, remained with no means, no power, no representation in national affairs; they were forgotten or ignored between the European anti-Turk campaign and the Hamidian pan-Islamism.

The small towns were, of course, in a better position. In a town

---

[21] See G. W. von Pressel, *Les Chemins de fer en Turquie d'Asie* (Zurich, 1902). Pressel was a German engineer employed by the Turkish government from 1871. He acted as Abdül-Hamid's agent in dealing with the German bankers in 1888 regarding railway concessions.

[22] For a detailed study of the Baghdad Railway, see E. M. Earle, *Turkey, the Great Powers and the Baghdad Railway* (New York, 1923); also Blaisdell, *European Financial Control*, p. 154.

like Diyarbekir, the father and the relatives of the young boy Ziya (Gökalp) were discussing, before 1900, whether he should be given a European education or not. And the boy himself was already experiencing in his inner depths the clashes of two civilizations. These small towns like Samsun, Zonguldak, Adana, and Eskişehir, which were close to the railways, European commerce, and the seats of banks, became new and larger urban centres with a more cosmopolitan and less traditional population. These new towns were different, even physically, from the old medieval towns.

A new class of people—the industrial workers—began to appear in the new towns, in Zonguldak and Eskişehir for example, as well as in the large cities of the Empire like Istanbul, Salonika, Izmir, Bursa, and Halep (Aleppo). French capital exploited the Zonguldak coal mines; the Public Debt revived the silk industry of Bursa; the tobacco industry thrived in Salonika, Istanbul, Izmir, and Samsun. Several minor and subsidiary branches of industry began to appear. Municipal public utilities, public works construction, and enterprises like the railways, street cars, telephone centrals, gas and electric plants, harbour installations, warehouses, salt refineries, fisheries, ferry and steamship companies began to employ three classes of people who had hardly existed previously. One of these was the half-worker, half-peasant; the second was the skilled technician; and the third was the white-collar worker. Most of these new employees were Muslim Turks. (The Public Debt alone employed nearly nine thousand workers; however, most of its employees were Greeks and Armenians.) These workers, technicians, and clerks were all employees of official agencies and were much like civil servants; they were far from constituting a working class. The first manifestations of a working-class movement, as well as the appearance of women in industrial and business life, was, however, just around the corner. Both appeared approximately together following the 1908 Revolution.

In spite of the fact that these new classes had no political and cultural role, their emergence nonetheless signified the <u>disappearance of the medieval structure of social stratification.</u> It meant also the breakdown in several traditions, habits, tastes, and attitudes. Even the most important traditional class, the *esnaf*, began to change. The guilds continued to exist nominally, but had entirely lost their functions and, together with the other categories mentioned, the *esnaf* constituted the masses for whom the revolutionary Young Turks aspired to initiate their new regime.

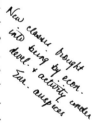

We have reserved until last mentioning three other classes among the Muslim Turks. They differed sharply from those already discussed. These were the government officials (*memur*), the military officers, and the intellectuals (*münevver*). The vast majority of the intellectuals were government officials. During the Tanzimat they were few and inclined to be encyclopedic pedants. The intellectuals of the Hamidian period were far more numerous. Whereas the Tanzimat intellectual was both valued by others and satisfied with his life, the Hamidian intellectual was frightened, oppressed, feared, and suspected. He was skeptical, pessimistic, and rebellious—not in action but in thought and sentiment. The Tanzimat intellectual had no revolutionary tradition. The intellectual of the Hamidian period, on the other hand, had a revolutionary past as a model. Namık Kemal's life and works alone were enough to fire his imagination. Many attended secret night-long gatherings where Kemal's works were read aloud and memorized. The more Kemal's works were suppressed, the more appealing they became.

Withal, the Hamidian intellectual was far inferior in revolutionary courage and active patriotism to Namık Kemal and his contemporaries. These great admirers of Kemal all wrote their revolutionary poems in secrecy and made them known to only one or two trusted friends. Kemal's type of man was so rare or so cowed by the real and imaginary dread of the efficiency of the Hamidian secret service that nearly every intellectual looked upon every other as an informer. Hence, the revolutionary writings of this period remained so carefully guarded that the most skilled detectives of Abdül-Hamid could not discover their existence! Numerous anecdotes are given in the reminiscences of this period to describe the dreadfulness of the Hamidian regime, but they illustrate the political inactivity of the intellectuals. Some of the best minds of the time maintained complete silence. Abdülhak Hâmid, a disciple of Namık Kemal and hailed as the greatest Turkish poet, wrote nothing even when he was in London and Paris and, furthermore, told the Young Turks that all their agitation and publications were useless. To be sure, he wrote a famous revolutionary play *Liberty* but not until after 1908 when there was plenty of liberty!

Most of the Hamidian intellectuals, politically inhibited, saw their surroundings darkly and the future as hopeless. They believed that there was nothing upon which to rely. Some turned to God as a final refuge. Others became sodden with melancholy, pessimism, and the denial of social values. Some committed suicide while some committed moral suicide in opportunism.

There were three professions excepted from the above patterns. One was that of the school teacher, a rarity in the Tanzimat era. The great contribution of this humble group to the modernization of the country has never been assessed properly. The second was that of the army officers, some of whom were by now products of the German military trainers headed by the Prussian general Von der Goltz. At least half of the prominent men of later times came from this group. The third group, also a product of the period and contributing the other half of the prominent men of the future, came from the medical school or, to a lesser extent, from other schools of professional learning such as the schools of engineering, veterinary medicine, law, civil service, and commerce.

In order to see where and how the "mutation of sports" peculiar to the Hamidian system came about, let us turn to the conditions in education. The elementary schools were still the most neglected part of the educational organization. Compared with the developments in other parts of life, primary education was so neglected and so mishandled that most criticism and effort after 1908 had to be directed toward this area. It is sufficient to give the now famous comment of Haşim Paşa, Abdül-Hamid's Minister of Education, to indicate the conditions in primary education. The Paşa won a place in Turkish memory by saying that his ministry would operate wonderfully if only there were no schools!

The secondary schools, however, were incomparably better than those few in existence during the Tanzimat. The schools called *ruşdiye, idadiye,* and *sultaniye,* and corresponding to three stages of intermediary education between primary schools and schools of higher learning, all recorded good progress. Their significance lay in the fact that they brought the Turkish youth face to face with something new after the abundant teaching of the Kur'an and *tajwîd* (the rules of correct pronunciation of Arabic) in the primary schools. They had better science teachers than had other schools. Furthermore, they were not amorphous institutions in form and content like the primary schools. It was here that the minds of the young began to open to the existence of a world beyond immediate experience, that is, beyond the physical and social environment of the Turkey described thus far. Their curiosity was aroused and their traditional beliefs shaken.

More important than these institutions, however, were the schools of higher learning, particularly those giving professional training. Among these the School of Medicine was by far the most important. The first revolutionary organization of the Young

276

Turks was formed there, and the majority of the active Young Turks were doctors. There were also, in addition to the ordinary trade schools, a number of specialized schools such as those training telegraphic operators and mechanics for steamboats.

Quite understandably, the schools of the Hamidian era were intended, and often designed, to educate for servility to the state. All were gratuitous. The ruler lavishly tipped the students, sometimes for servile acts and sometimes in anticipation thereof. Nonetheless, the students proved ungrateful and traitorous. The schools became centres of dissatisfaction and enlightenment. The fault (from the Hamidian point of view) in the Hamidian institutions of learning, including the Harbiye (the Cadet School), was not in their failure to inculcate the virtues of Hamidian servility, but rather in the inclusion within their curricula of innocent subjects such as mathematics, physics, biology, political economy, even history, and above all, French. Each of these opened new vistas for the younger generation and, indirectly, led them to see the contrast between the old and the new. As Abdül-Hamid's financial and foreign policies prepared the conditions for his downfall, the schools were destroying the foundations of his ideology.

One cannot leave the topic without mentioning the foreign schools. These had increased both in number and in affluence. They were American, French, English, German, Austrian, and Italian in support and orientation. Scores of Catholic and Protestant schools for boys and girls spread throughout the Ottoman territories. Although they were attended by only a few Muslims, they had an important educational effect on the Turkish students and, more particularly, the Armenian, Jewish, and Arab youth.

The Undercurrents

The above outline is sufficient to suggest the role of the reactionary period in stimulating clandestine developments in intellectual life. It is an irony that a system designed to isolate the mind from change and innovation coincided with the most devastating infiltration of the prohibited ideas.

We see the paradox best in the case of the press, which expanded in spite of all the restrictions. Namık Kemal noted the expansion as early as 1882 in a letter analyzing the inevitability of Westernization; he showed it as proof of progress in literature "since the rise of the idea of progress among us."[23] Compared with the Tanzimat period, he said, not only the number of papers but also the number of their readers had increased. In a decade even the number of women reading newspapers "increased a hundred times."

Even the shopkeepers and servants are reading papers or listening to those who can read them nowadays. They acquire, even if in summary, a knowledge of matters relating to the affairs of state, to patriotism, to civic virtues, to military achievements, and to the events of war.

Generally correct, Kemal was mistaken on one point. What the public was reading and learning from the press was neither the affairs of state nor patriotism. They were learning something far more humble, but perhaps indirectly producing more significant effects. The press had dropped its interest in lofty matters. As writing on political, social, and cultural subjects became susceptible to unexpected interpretation and, therefore, hazardous, the serious periodicals (even daily papers) began to stuff their pages with news, articles, and pictures that had nothing to do with such matters. It was less possible to read hidden meanings into the types of material which were unpolitical. Thus, a race to publish articles and pictures on semi-scientific subjects began. A few article headings are illustrative: "A Biography of Professor Helmholtz," "Origins of the Species of Vertebrates," "How to Keep Feet Warm," "Coloured Photography," "The Contribution of Arabs to Science," "Travel in Air or Under Sea" (Jules Verne's novels were popular, and the publisher of his translated books made a fortune out of them), "Imam Fakhr ad-Din al-Razi," "The Intelligence of Cats," "Myopia Among Students in Germany," "The Relation between a Man's Height and Weight," "How Much Weight a Horse Can Carry," and endless articles on the life of the Lapps and Eskimos, the voyages of Christopher Columbus, the strange foods of the Chinese, the explorations of Livingstone.

The press of this period, daily newspapers as well as weeklies and monthlies, tell us nothing about the political events of the time. Neither do they echo patriotic themes. They are misleading sources for the times because of the distortions through censorship. On the other hand, in no other period have Turkish publications been so loaded with non-political and non-religious material.

---

[23] Letter printed in *Şark*, (Istanbul, 1882), No. 1; reprinted in *Mukaddime-i Celâl*, Ebüzziya ed. (Istanbul, 1891).

In contrast to the seemingly prevailing religiosity and puritanism, a number of features that were unconventional and even believed to be incompatible with Muslim beliefs surreptitiously crept into the mental make-up of the people through publications.

278

Above all there was a revolutionary change in the reading habits of the public. Reading for entertainment and leisure appeared. In medieval times, reading was regarded as a serious, holy and monopolized craft. The public was expected only to listen to the *âlim*, the *vâiz* (preacher), the *hâfiz* (memorizer and reciter of the Kur'an), and officials in general. Now, not only did reading habits begin to enter the ranks of the *avâm*, but also the material read was vulgar and non-religious, if not irreligious.

It is perhaps difficult in our day when reading is a commonplace to understand what it meant to get people to read. It may be noted that four years of reading practice under supervision is the test of literacy in America where the alphabet can be learned within a matter of weeks or months. What then would be required to understand the substance of writing in an almost foreign langauage when it took two years simply to master the alphabet in its many script forms? Imagine the years of schooling of the ordinary reader, let alone the educated elite! Quite naturally, the very thought of picking up a book had induced sobriety, if not fear, in the past. Now, a reading public was coming into existence through the appearance of mundane "trash" at which the ancients would have been horrified. The literate began to enjoy reading, hence, they read more and bought more books. Thus more books were published, authorship was encouraged, and the impetus to become literate increased.

Slowly, translators and authors began to be known. For the first time, publishers (mostly non-Muslim) were established. One of the innovations made by these enterprising publishers was the method of printing popular novels as weekly serials to be sold through some form of subscription. The most popular series were, for example, Jules Verne's novels, Dumas' *The Three Musketeers*, and *The Count of Monte Cristo*. This method proved so successful that the publishers and, to a lesser degree, the booksellers, began to commission translations and series likely to become best sellers.

There was an unprecedented drive to make translations from popular French literature. The works translated during the Tanzimat were of a high calibre, but were published in limited numbers, and were read by even fewer persons. The works translated in the

Hamidian period were of the popular variety and were read by
many people. There was particular interest in crime, mystery, adventure, and science-fiction publications.[24] These, introduced as a
way to avoid political subjects, eventually had undesired and un-
predicted intellectual effects. Their most significant effect was
their secularizing influence. The cheap press brought to the people
the romance of invention and exploration. It gave stimulation to
imaginations that had been nourished previously only on hair-
raising stories of Hell, or the deeds and misdeeds of the djinns.
The adventure, crime, and mystery books left the most unorthodox precipitations in the subconscious of the readers: every
mystery had its causation and its solution; there was no mystery
on earth that was not caused by natural forces and that could not
be explained in terms of reason!

We may illustrate other secularizing effects of the new publications upon the traditional institutions by mentioning what had
happened in the written language. In contrast with the studied obscurantism of the official writings of the period, the unofficial
written language came increasingly closer to earth under the influence of the popular literature. The language now reaching the
tongues of the people was, so to say, freed from religious association. Many of those who gained literary fame, Ahmed Midhat,
Şemseddin Sâmi, Ahmed Rasim, Hüseyin Rahmi, and Hüseyin
Cahit, to mention some, served their literary apprenticeship translating popular books and articles from the French. It appears that
while doing this they acquired the habits of freeing the language
from religious and ceremonial colouration. Thus, despite the stern
warnings of the special dictionaries showing the correct Arabic
words, the writers increasingly used the *ghalatât*, Turkicized
Arabic words, in order to make themselves more comprehensible
and less pedantic.

Another effect was the introduction into written Turkish of
words and figures of speech that would have caused the Tanzimatist highbrows to scowl and would have evoked the most scorn-
ful and depreciatory epithets from the somewhat earlier writers.
Exclamatory forms and descriptive phrases, which were essentially French, and broken sentences deeply affected the general
style of writing. They brought an element of dynamism into the
language. It became permissible to avoid the old symbolic allusions, which were meaningful only to those with literary training.

---

[24] See Hüseyin Cahit Yalçın, *Edebî Hatıralar* (Istanbul, 1935), for
personal recollections of the literary conditions of the period.

280

The trend introduced the technique of dialogue into written Turkish. Previously, conversations between the characters of an event had to be related indirectly, that is, by the author himself. What the characters said and how they said it in ordinary speech was not thought to have literary value; it was necessary for the author of the work to polish and correct the words of his conversants. When the writers of the Tanzimat introduced some sort of conversational technique, in journalistic as well as literary works, they went only to the extent of putting sentences exchanged in conversation one after another in the most mechanical fashion. It was only with the drive to translate vulgar French novels that the writers brought movement in dialogue into the language.

Another feature of the impact of the European literature was the introduction of new dimensions of literature: modes of psychological states, feelings of conflict, doubt, anxiety, and, above all, the practice of philosophizing and moralizing, both of which were the signs of secularization in mind and morality. These traits will be illustrated later by the works of the chief figures of the period and in the major literary school.

The appearance of pictures and illustrations in printed materials enhanced these effects. It was during the Hamidian period that pictures were printed for the first time in newspapers and, especially, in weeklies of the illustrated-magazine variety. If one remembers that the reproduction of pictures was not approved in the Islamic tradition and that reproductions were popularly believed to be religiously prohibited, it is easy to visualize the secularizing effect of the innovation.

Further, the illustrated magazine brought to the attention of Turkish readers new vistas of European civilization. Previously, it had been only the favoured few who had an opportunity to see Paris or London. Now, the monopoly of those few over the image of what was called "civilization" was broken. Since Islam disapproved the depiction of animate objects, timid printers and editors began to stuff their illustrated magazines, of which *Servet-i Funûn* was the most famous, with pictures of factories, banks, machines, cities, apartments, harbours, bridges, etc. Through pictures, the readers were carried not only to European civilization but even to America! Hardly an issue of *Servet-i Funûn* passed without some gem from the Western hemisphere. Turning the pages, one would think that America was a continent of locomotives and banks. Next to locomotive engines, electric machines were favourite objects of curiosity. While electricity was accepted as one of the wonders of the world, sometimes interest in it could inspire dangerous interpretations; so even here the editors had to anticipate the interpretations of Hamid's *jurnal*-writing informers. Skyscrapers and dreadnoughts were often pictured. There was little chance for parliament buildings, mob scenes, or revolutionary crowds to appear. The great European leaders were not in prominence, except for scientists and inventors like Pasteur, Helmholtz, and Röntgen. This writer does not recall seeing the pictures of Darwin or Marx in the files of magazines dating from the period. On the other hand, there was another and unprecedented feature to these illustrations. In trying to be attractive, the illustrated magazines contained reproductions of European works of art. At least, they embellished their captions or headings with copies of art-work from European magazines. Emphasis was upon imaginary idyllic scenes by the lesser commercial artists.

It is not an exaggeration to say that the secularizing effects of these publications were greater than those of all the Tanzimat publications together. The newspaper, the illustrated weekly, the novel became means of entertainment, means of arousing and satisfying curiosity, means of shattering the traditional view that learning and literacy were matters of embellishment, exclusive literary refinement, didactic teaching, or religious instruction.

From this brief survey we can see how a gulf was growing between the illusions and the realities of the time and that the two contradicted each other. We can see the contradiction reflected even better in the intellectual career of the most representative figure of the time.

Two Sides of Western Civilization Distinguished

The man who best represented the two sides of the Hamidian period was Ahmed Midhat (1844-1912), who took his second name from Midhat Paşa, his early patron and the one who had dragged him into association with the constitutionalists.[25] After a period in exile with Namık Kemal, Ahmed Midhat turned against his associates and became the mouthpiece of the Hamidian regime and a successful publisher, editor, and writer.

[25] See A. H. Tanpınar, *XIX. Asır Türk Edebiyatı Tarihi* (2nd ed.; Istanbul, 1956), I, 433-66 for a good summary of Midhat's life and work.

In spite of his opportunism and conservatism, Midhat made important contributions to Turkish progress. He became the teacher of the ordinary people—those people for whom Kemal sacrificed his life, but whom he never understood and never succeeded in enlightening. Midhat was from the people, he knew the people, and he knew how to reach them. He was like a schoolmaster, teaching the people innumerable subjects through his innumerable publications. His fame and influence became a reality; Kemal remained a myth. Kemal had confused the minds of the people, despite his intentions, while Midhat enlightened them beyond his intentions.

Midhat's review, *Kırkanbar* (Warehouse), shows his ware to have ranged from Schopenhauer's philosophy to the rules of Parisian etiquette, and from Max Müller's linguistic studies to bird calls. Midhat was certainly not a charlatan, as Kemal believed, but rather the First Teacher, as he was known by the people. He was more precise, more correct, more careful and, at times, more subtle in his writing than Kemal. His language and style were incomparably superior to Kemal's insofar as lucidity, clarity, and modernity were concerned. His Turkish is comprehensible to a high school boy even today whereas Kemal's writings are almost Chinese to many adult Turks.

Midhat's way differed from that of Kemal's followers in its insistent conservatism. He believed in the futility of revolution or political reform, and preached a gradual reshaping of the minds as well as of non-political institutions. He was progressive where Kemal was revolutionary. Midhat became the Benjamin Franklin of the Turks in several respects. Like Franklin he was a self-made man, an industrious and practical man, thrifty, enterprising, and enlightening. (The comparison is not entirely original, as it was in Ahmed Midhat's time that the Turks heard tell of Franklin. Franklin's *Poor Richard* suddenly came into vogue in Turkey after 1870; there were at least three translations made of these homilies). As a writer, journalist, printer, editor, and translator—in his personal life, in business, as well as in the morality he represented and preached—Ahmed Midhat was always successful.

Above all, in an age when there was no university, when the press was politically controlled, Midhat succeeded in finding topics in which the people should be taught, in teaching the people, and in teaching them while entertaining them—in short, in capturing their minds and their hearts. His chief gift was his mastery over the popular language. His main achievement was that he managed to build the first successful bridge between the old Turkish folk literature and Western art literature.

To Midhat goes the credit for originating the Turkish novel. The novel as a literary form was unknown in traditional Ottoman literature. With the exception of Fénélon's *Télémaque*, only two European novels were translated into Turkish up to 1870. Victor Hugo's *Les Misérables* was translated in 1862, Daniel Defoe's *Robinson Crusoe* in 1864. From 1870 until 1890, Midhat's novels were the bridge between the folk romances and Western novels. He utilized the narrative technique of the *meddah* (story teller) in the modern novel form. Some of his plots were even taken over from *meddah* stories. Like the ancient story tellers, he conversed with his readers, asked their opinions about the behaviour of the characters, and answered the questions that they were likely to ask. He kept in constant contact with his readers and, by doing so, encouraged them to read.

Midhat's technique of intimacy gave him two great opportunities—to teach, to convey information; and to moralize. Each of Midhat's novels was written to teach a lesson. His heroes were a far cry from Kemal's men of absolute virtues and idealistic self-sacrifice. They were small, average men, shrewd, calculating, successful, even opportunistic.

It would be erroneous to agree with his critics that Midhat taught nothing new. On the contrary, he was, perhaps, a more effective and successful innovator than his many adversaries. He was not only a gradualist and a realist but also a critic. His novels were his instruments to show the readers the wrong and weak sides of their culture without frightening or antagonizing them. There was a social thesis in all his novels. "Thus a brand new element, which is not found in the old folk narration, emerged in his novels—the critique of the social environment."[26]

One of Midhat's targets was slavery and the slave trade. Another was the status and rights of women. In a novel having the main theme of the equality of women in education, Midhat's imagination transcends the boldest speculations permissible in his time and predicts that the day will come when women will enter into every profession. Questions relating to the low status of women, their misfortunes and sufferings as a result of their not having rights equal to those of men, are recurrent themes. Midhat went so far as to defend the rights of women who were forced by circumstances

---

[26] For further details see Pertev N. Boratav, "Ilk Romanlarımız," *Folklor ve Edebiyat* (Ankara, 1942), II, 143.

284

into prostitution; he severely criticized the belief in their sinfulness and the severity of their punishments. Our duty, he said, is to try and save these women from degradation; this will be possible only if we cease treating women as commodities, or as slaves, and they become free to decide their own destinies; therefore, we must go to the help of the fallen and extend a hand to raise them up, rather than stigmatize them forever.

Midhat dealt with the subject of womanhood in a number of his novels. The question of the emancipation of women was one of the theses that occupied him most. He criticized for the first time an aspect of the Muslim marriage which, under modern conditions, came to be regarded as one of the most unfortunate issues of family life—the custom of marrying persons who not only had not cultivated love for each other, but also had never seen each other. He condemned that tradition which led parents to arrange the marriage of their children in terms of their own values and even interests.

Midhat's novels (we must not forget that he was not only a novelist) brought to the attention of a large reading public for the first time the need to reform the basic social institutions and mores. If his novels were devoured by his readers, as they obviously were, we can safely conclude that these ideas left their impress on their minds, the more so as Midhat succeeded in making his readers laugh at themselves.

We find another novelty in Midhat's novels. This became one of the important factors in the Turkish awakening. This was the emergence in print of the half-Westernized or pseudo-Western Turk, and the critique of him and his character. The conduct of this type of person has been called from Midhat's day, *alafranga* (from the Italian *alla franga*). It was contrasted with the behavior of what the European writers called the Old Turk, the *alaturka* (*alla turca*). At least seven of Midhat's dozens of novels treated the life and behaviour of such characters. Their imitativeness and superficiality were criticized and Midhat used these opportunities to discuss with his readers the true meaning of Westernization.

It was not only in his novels that Midhat dealt with this last point. He discussed the question of progress and Westernization in a series of articles written in 1898.[27] He likened the stages of historical progress to a spiral stairway. The more a society ascends the steps and spirals of this stairway, he said boldly, the more it

[27] In *Tarik* (Istanbul, Nov. 7-11, 1898), Nos. 4614-4617, from where the following quotations are taken.

approaches contemporary civilization. We must go up and up, but we must take our steps with care "because we have seen that what we call European civilization has bad sides as well as good sides." To be of the European civilization is not merely a geographical matter. To be European is not only a matter of living in Europe, or belonging to the Latin, German, or Slavic nations. "Our understanding of being a European is to have appropriated the modern sciences and industries as the means of economic and utilitarian pursuits." But, we must be careful not to take the "bad sides" of European civilization. Today this civilization itself has become aware of its shortcomings. It is impossible to believe that the Turks who have been observers over the last forty years have not now understood this. We must have come by now to the stage at which we can set limits upon Europeanization. European civilization is expanding, but in imposing itself upon non-European nations, it is tending to destroy the religions and languages of these nations.

If we try to Europeanize only for the sake of becoming European, we shall lose our own character. If we, on the other hand, add the European civilization to our own character, we shall not only preserve, perpetuate, and maintain our character but also fortify and refine it.

The type of thinking represented by Midhat was decidedly anti-revolutionary. He would tolerate and even encourage the youth to be modern, but he would not tolerate their passing certain boundaries. He was an untiring adversary of those whom he called the *décadents*—the materialists, naturalists (admirers of Emile Zola), atheists, and socialists—all of whom began to appear in this period.

A controversy over a practice connected with a basic institution gives us another illustration of how the question of modernization began to be taken up before the end of the nineteenth century.

In 1896, Mahmud Es'ad, one of the *ulema*, wrote a series of articles showing that the matter of polygamy had become a subject of unusual discussion. He began,

Among ourselves are young men who know European science and culture and the political and social conditions of Europe, but are ignorant of Europe's religious affairs. These men, imitating the Europeans, believe that polygamy is the weak side of Islam.

They are convinced that it is responsible for the disorders in the public morality and a factor of social degeneration.[28]

Es'ad's rebuttal, interesting as representing the latest version of the *ulema* point of view, began with the assertion that the practice of polygamy was not enjoined. It was not, he said, a practice that originated with Islam, but rather in human nature. As a "natural law, it has only been recognized and legitimized by God's law." "No positive law can deny this right given to the male by nature and confirmed by the Şeriat." Following this naturalist, or materialist introduction (quite incongruous especially for a "man of religion" in an age of anti-naturalism and anti-materialism), Mahmud Es'ad proceeded to show that socially beneficial results accrued whenever this natural polygamous instinct was allowed expression in polygamous marriage and that social ills had followed wherever the reverse was true. In proof of his refutation of criticism, he pointed to the contemporary European scene—taking European self-criticism and the image of Parisian vices as exemplary.

Several criticisms of Mahmud Es'ad's articles appeared immediately. One of these was by Fatma Aliye, a well known author and daughter of Cevdet Paşa whom Midhat took as exemplifying his aims for the education of womanhood.[29] We are told by Midhat that when she was ten, Fatma began to study French secretly, "as it was not a custom to teach foreign languages to Muslim girls" and her mother believed that "learning French would mean the changing of her religion." Discovered and encouraged by her Islamic reformist father, Fatma had acquired a fair knowledge of French literature by the time she was fourteen and veiled according to custom. (She reports feeling very unhappy over the event.) She could later speak directly with the European visitors to her household, held long conversations with them concerning Muslim

[28] These articles appeared in 1896 in *Malûmat* and were published in book form in 1898 together with Fatma Aliye's letter and Mahmud Es'ad's rejoinder to her and to Ismail Gasprinsky. The title of the book is *Taaddüd-ü Zevcat* (Istanbul, 1898). Mahmud Es'ad's ideas concerning polygamy were criticized by Ismail Gasprinski in his paper *Tercüman* published in the Crimea. Gasprinski was a prominent leader of the modernizing movement among the Turkish-speaking peoples of Russia.

[29] Ahmed Midhat, *Fatma Aliye Hanım, Yahut Bir Muharrire-i Osmaniyenin Neş'eti* (Istanbul, 1893); from where the following quotations are taken.

and European customs and institutions, and reflected her experiences in her writings.[30]

Fatma Aliye's answer to the learned defender of polygamy was expressed boldly. She said that the practice of polygamy could no longer be defended. In addition, it was impossible to ignore the criticisms of the institution. Biological or physiological justifications had nothing to do with the issue. Taking Mahmud Es'ad's arguments one by one, she concluded,

If we believe that Islam has universally valid principles, we ought
to declare that the monogamous marriage is the one enjoined
by Islam and that the verse of the Kur'an enjoining men to remain
with one wife is in accordance with civilization. It is only then
that we can justify our position.

Mahmud Es'ad's rejoinder did not illuminate his position further, but it illustrated how the ideas of critics and defenders alike were conditioned by the pressures of the Western impact. After admitting that polygamous marriage was not enjoined in Islam and was only a permission under certain conditions, Mahmud Es'ad formulated the conception of Westernization of the era which the following quotation will summarize sufficiently:

A civilization has a spiritual and a material side, the first consists
of its moral acquisitions. The material aspect of the civilization
includes those things ranging from sewing machines to railroads and
battleships; in short, all the industrial inventions, etc., which
we see today. Which is that aspect of [Western] civilization that we
want to take over? If it is the first, we do not need it because
we are not devoid of civilization in that particular sense. We do not
need that aspect of the European civilization which is already
laden with innumerable shortcomings. Our own moral civilization
is ample enough for our needs, let alone that it is far superior to
that of the European moral civilization. Our national [religious]
pride would not allow us to imitate this aspect of civilization.

The distinction made between the material and the non-material or moral aspects of Western civilization and the admission of the desirability of borrowing the former by the traditionalists were

---

[30] See her *Nisvan-ı Islâm* (Istanbul, 1891), from where the following quotations are taken. The discussions on the condition of womanhood began about this date and were continued by Şemseddin Sâmi, *Kadınlarımız* (Istanbul, 1893).

turning points in the development of the attitude towards the West. From this time onward controversies concentrated on the question of the relationship and the boundaries between the two aspects, as well as the question of how, and by which criteria, the two could be kept apart, if indeed they could be kept apart at all.

THE HAMIDIAN PERIOD in its great days looked still on the surface, but its depths were boiling with the signs of a coming revolt. Between the conflicting pressures of conservatism and the Western penetration, the lines of thinking on cultural matters began to clarify and differentiate.

When the intellectuals of the post-Tanzimat era had reflected upon the problems of cultural change after 1870, their opinions were confused by questions of political reform. Cultural issues had been viewed in terms of an amalgam of the traditionalist, reformist, and Western outlooks. The intellectuals had been able to see that there were aspects of Turkish cultural life that were incompatible with modern civilization and, hence, needed to be reformed; yet, when the struggles for political reform began, they had forgotten this and begun to think instead that a constitutional reform would be the panacea. Matters of economic behaviour and mentality, aspects of education, etc., had all been subordinated to the problem of political reform. Many of the existing institutions had begun to be defended while the model (the West) had begun to be attacked.

One of the consequences of Hamid's suppression of political preoccupations was to force the intellectuals to focus upon non-political, cultural questions that had been lost sight of during the constitutional controversies. By severing the cultural questions from the political-religious questions, the Hamidian regime unknowingly encouraged focusing upon cultural matters as such. This focusing was sharpened by factors stemming from the Western impact that the Hamidian suppression failed to prevent.

The Revolt Against Religion

290

The Hamidian regime did not foresee that a policy of political suppression would breed a generation manifesting intellectual characteristics antithetical to the dominant features of the regime's ideology. Under the noses of the zealous "men of religion," a whole generation of "materialists" sprang up. Their view of life contrasted strangely with the most characteristic feature of the mentality of the time—superstition.

By establishing the omnipotence of his *devlet* (state), Abdül-Hamid imperiled the *din* (religion). There came into existence a cleavage in the minds of the intellectuals between the two. Thenceforth, the Hamidian *din-u-devlet* seemed a nightmare to the sincere intellectual. He was cut off irrevocably from trust in the possibility of a marriage between the two. That is why the intellectual today cannot understand how the idea of an Islamic State could be an attractive ideal to many Muslims. He has an ineradicable antipathy for such an ideal as the legacy of the Hamidian period.

Once discussion of political questions was prohibited and minds were freed of political entanglements, three intellectual attitudes began to present themselves more clearly and with finer lines of demarcation. Of these, the Westernist attitude began to emerge as the strongest, as Western influence flooded all those areas of the mind emptied by the Hamidian suppression.

The custom houses of the Hamidian regime were wide open to the material civilization of Europe; even the *ulema* accommodated themselves to this and issued *fetvas* for *laissez-passer*! On the other hand, the *ulema* were unreservedly protectionist with regard to "the non-material" civilization of the West. They placed a high premium on the homemade "non-material" civilization; and, some, such as Mahmud Es'ad, went to the extent of claiming that this could be exported profitably as a drug for the ills of European civilization.

But, in reality, a dramatic smuggling operation was taking place on the borders of the East and West in spite of all the embargos on dangerous thoughts. Abdül-Hamid's secret service was powerless against the contraband trade carried through the foreign post offices, which the Great Powers had managed to establish as one of their exterritorial rights. One gets the impression from published reminiscences that the youth obtaining such contraband did not have to work too hard to get it. They obtained French papers and magazines regularly from one another, papers whose origin they did not even bother to question.[1]

The leading writers after 1908 all recall how they were attracted to the French literature and how little by the homemade "non-material" commodities. Hüseyin Cahit (Yalçın) relates in his "Literary Reminiscences" that he did his utmost to read his father's favourite book, the *Fusûs* of Ibn al-'Arabî. But alas, in vain! This book conveyed simply nothing to him.[2] Furthermore, he says, "None of us bothered any longer to improve our knowledge of Arabic and Persian. We simply did not read the books written in these languages." This was not because learning French was easier and a matter of course. The same writer, and Fatma Aliye, describe how passionately and eagerly, yet with the pain of looking up each word in the dictionary, they laboured to master French. Still, as Fatma Aliye says, "After some time, it became easier to read and understand the French books than the Ottoman-Turkish books because the latter required, if anything, more recourse to the dictionary than the French."[3] Hüseyin Cahit says,

What were the forces that had delivered my mind from the swamps of scholasticism, the forces that opened new horizons before my eyes, the forces that freed my soul from bondage? I find today that it was the French language and culture above all things which was responsible for my awakening.[4]

Another prominent writer of the following decades, Hüseyin Rahmi, speaks even more passionately of the role of European literature in the intellectual awakening of his generation.

Western civilization has been a torch light for our awakening. . . . The Hamidian tyranny . . . suppressed all the publications that are the moral food of a nation. . . . One thing, however, could not be eliminated. Despite the severe inspections of the customs and educational officers, foreign books could reach the shelves of the intellectuals. . . . I used to notice one thing: while the stores selling the Turkish works censored and approved by the government were without customers, despite their colourful window displays, the stores selling foreign books thrived. The vacuum created by the

---

[1] Hüseyin Cahit Yalçın, *Edebî Hatıralar* (Istanbul, 1935), p. 51.

[2] *Ibid.*, pp. 7-8.

[3] Ahmed Midhat, *Fatma Aliye Hanım, Yahut Bir Muharrire-i Osmani-yenin Neş'eti* (Istanbul, 1893), p. 88.

[4] Yalçın, *Edebî Hatıralar*, p. 26.

292

bankruptcy of the traditional culture was filled by the foreign culture. . . . European thinkers, historians, poets, and writers became known as if they were our own. The good effects of foreign literature, however, were felt only by a small élite among the youth . . . as the lights of our minds were on the verge of being extinguished entirely, the sparks flying here from European culture rekindled them. If there are today [1908] men who can think, can write, and can defend freedom, they are those whose minds were enlightened by these sparks. In those dark and melancholy days, our friends, our guides were those intellectual treasures of the West. We learned the love for thinking, the love for freedom, from those treasures. All of the recent developments in our ways of thinking, as well as in our poetry and verse, are the products of the winds blowing from the West.[5]

At no time has the West been so idealized as by the inhibited minds of the Hamidian period. In the eyes of the intellectuals, the West was the world of freedom, comfort, individual dignity, of reason, of decency, and of beauty and art. There was absolutely nothing in the old dissipated, rotten home environment and past to be liked, from which to derive inspiration, to love, with which to identify. The young generation felt disgust for its environment and past; youth felt the existence of its Utopia in the "lands of lights"—Europe.

Turkish writings of the period contain references to an impressive array of nineteenth-century European celebrities. A sampling of the names mentioned in the writings of the period shows who had replaced the French classicists, and Rousseau, or Montesquieu: Schopenhauer, Haeckel, Büchner, Darwin, Draper, Renan, Taine, Herbert Spencer, Gustav Le Bon, Poincaré, Th. Ribot, Charles Richet, Flamarion, John Stuart Mill, Flaubert, Balzac, Zola, and scores of less important personages. This list, it should be noted, does not include the names of European writers who appeared in Turkish writings immediately after the 1908 Revolution. These would lengthen the list several times. The suppressed generation read European literature indiscriminately, like hungry children. No doubt, there were many upset stomachs, but at the same time the ground was being prepared for rebellion.

The rebelliousness of the new generation had no political implications. The intellectuals were not constitutionalists or liberals, socialists or anarchists. Yet, they had the taint of all these. Just as

[5] From the Preface written in 1908, to Hüseyin Rahmi's novel Şıp-sevdi, which was denied publication by the Hamidian censor and appeared for the first time in 1912.

the Czarist autocracy had created its unique type of revolutionary, the Hamidian autocracy created the type of intellectuals for whom I find no better term than the word *dehrî*, the word that had come to be used as a label for those who were believed to be materialists or atheists, but that, in reality, meant nothing but the Western word secularist. They were denounced because of the common thread running through them all—the denial of tradition. They wove from rationalism, materialism, evolutionism and naturalism an attitude rejecting beliefs and practices as absurd, superstitious, and contrary to reason. Everything that was seen to be an enforced belief was rejected as irrational.

In spite of all the approved refutation-of-the-materialists literature, materialism, in the above sense, settled as a philosophical conviction. The best representative of this viewpoint was Beşir Fuad (1852?-87), a young friend of Ahmed Midhat.[6] Beşir was, like his predecessor Hoca Tahsin, one of the radical Turkish intellectuals who was unlucky in life and quickly forgotten in death. He was an archetype of Afghanî's demon though he was destructive only to himself. According to Midhat, Beşir was amazingly encyclopedic, had sound scientific knowledge, knew the major European languages and their literatures, was very patriotic, and a good friend. But he was, Midhat grieved, a convinced materialist and although he was "against those wretched characters who were disturbing the peace of the world in Europe," i.e. the socialists, he was a hopeless atheist. Midhat attributed Beşir's faults to his ignorance of Arabic and Persian; he could read the Kur'an only in its French translation; his knowledge of *hadîth*, *tafsîr*, *kalâm*, and *tasawwuf* was non-existent. "One can imagine the grave consequences of such deficiencies in a Muslim and Ottoman," Midhat deplored. Beşir's life and suicide, so ran Midhat's thesis, was a good lesson in the fate of materialists.

Beşir Fuad was essentially a literary critic.[7] His criticism was

---

[6] On Beşir Fuad see Ahmed Midhat, *Beşir Fuad* (Istanbul, 1886).

[7] Beşir Fuad's published works include *Victor Hugo* (Istanbul, 1884), *Voltaire* (Istanbul, 1886), literary letters, *Mektubat* (Istanbul, 1887), books for the teaching of French, German, and English, a translation of one of Zola's novels, and a number of other novels translated from French, English, and German, all but the first two of which were unavailable to this writer. Yalçın, *Edebî Hatıralar*, p. 36, mentions Beşir Fuad's translation of Büchner's *Matter and Energy*, but I have been unable to find this. For an analysis of Beşir Fuad's intellectual contribution see Güzin Dino in her *Tanzimattan Sonra Edebiyatta Gerçekçiliğe Doğru* (Ankara, 1954).

294

directed against the idealism and romanticism of Namık Kemal. While Namık Kemal took inspiration from Rousseau, Beşir Fuad got his from Diderot, D'Holbach, and D'Alembert as the founders of modern realism and naturalism based on science (physiology and psychology), and given literary expression in the works of Balzac, Stendhal, and Zola. He was the first Turkish intellectual able to perceive scientific realism as the essential difference between Western philosophical thinking and the medieval and Oriental philosophies.

In the past, Turkish intellectuals had been one and sometimes two centuries behind the developments in European thought. On the eve of the French Revolution, and after it, the Turkish intellect was practically untouched by classicism and romanticism. With Şinasi and Namık Kemal the influence of both of these literary movements was manifest. When European thought was under the sway of scientific realism, roughly after 1860 (Darwin's *Origin of Species* appeared in 1859), the Turkish intellectuals were still reading Fénélon's *Télémaque* or, at best, the works of Molière and Racine. Namık Kemal's literary understanding was, in terms of Turkish intellectual standards, a great effort to encompass European classicism and romanticism in one stride. However, with the advent of the Hamidian regime, all literary and quasi-philosophical developments toward understanding European thought were stopped.

It was Beşir who brought a fresh breeze from the contemporary West. We find a new understanding of contemporary European scientific and literary thought in his writings. At a time when even utopian socialism was largely unheard of and ridiculed by the influential writers such as Ahmed Midhat, Beşir Fuad was the only man who knew of the birth of a science called sociology in the West. He was aware of the new experimental approach in scientific thinking. His main interest within the literary field was Zola and the naturalists, and he regarded the modern novel as a branch of sociology.

Beşir Fuad was not an artist. His influence as a literary critic and translator was limited. The new drive to understand contemporary European thought ended with his suicide in 1887. Yet, he exercised a refreshing influence upon the younger generation. Hüseyin Cahit speaks of him as "liberating the youth from the shackles of the *kalâm* and leading the minds to wider horizons."[8]

---

[8] Yalçın, *Edebî Hatiralar*, p. 36.

Turkish readers were not yet ready to comprehend the late nineteenth-century European movements of thought such as realism, naturalism, utopian socialism, evolutionism, or scientific socialism. Under the overpowering authority of Ahmed Midhat, all these were anathematized. To speak of naturalism, especially as represented by Zola, meant in those days arriving at an intellectual position equal to anarchism or nihilism. The Turkish intellectuals produced neither a genuine materialism in philosophy, realism or naturalism in literature, nor socialism in politics. When these nineteenth-century European rays of thoughts passed through the mental prism cut by Abdül-Hamid, they produced an ideology for which the term utopian individualism is the most appropriate.

Utopian individualism was the ideology of the emergent literary school that came to be known as Edebiyat-ı Cedide (the New Literature) and was formed by the literary critics, poets, and novelists who, in 1896, gathered around the literary review *Servet-i Funûn.* It was the ideology of the *décadents* against whom Ahmed Midhat fought to the end.

It is quite understandable why the aesthetes of the New Literature could not identify their literary mission with European naturalism, realism, or socialism. The works of the French realists or naturalists would dispel the utopian picture of European society that had become exalted and beautified in the minds of the new littérateurs. They aspired for the life of the European *individual* in which material comfort, scientific progress, and individual liberty reigned—not for a society criticized for its class inequalities, its crimes and prostitution, its greedy money-makers and exploited proletariat. Hence, they dropped their earlier interest in the *madiy-yûn* (materialists) and the *tabiiyyûn* (naturalists) and turned to the inferior French novelists whose works are almost forgotten beside those of Stendhal, Flaubert, Balzac, and Zola.

None of the outstanding figures of the school, Tevfik Fikret, Halit Ziya, and Hüseyin Cahit, were realists in the European sense, because their own conditions made them utopian individualists. As such, they could neither understand Western realism nor apply the techniques of the realists to the study of their own environment. And yet, their literary products remain as revealing documents of reality as seen through the eyes of utopian individualists and of their ideals and aspirations as reflected in their rejection of reality. Foremost among their ideas was new understanding of the question of Westernization—which constituted a turning point in the attitude toward the West.

Turning to the West

According to the previously prevailing view of Westernization the Turks should continue to belong to the Islamic, or Oriental civilization. The taking over of things from Western civilization would be confined to the material or utilitarian elements. Many of these, the Hamidian view added, were originally the property of the Muslims. In this understanding of Westernization the problem appeared to be quite simple. However, some began to perceive that the material inroads of the Western civilization were being followed or accompanied by certain moral elements as the controversy over polygamy illustrated.

The question of East versus West began to be discussed in the fields of language and literature by the contemporaries of Ahmed Midhat. One of them, Şemseddin Sâmi, put forth an idea that signalled an entirely new point of view. He said:

> So far those who did not know the language and the culture
> of the European nations admitted the superiority of the Western
> nations in their material civilization but were firmly convinced
> that in culture, especially in literature and in poetry, in history, and
> in the philological sciences they were far below us. It should be
> realized that all parts of culture are closely interrelated. A
> civilization cannot exist with only some branches of knowledge.
> If the West were deficient in culture it could not develop its material
> civilization. . . . Those who know European languages and
> literatures will realize that our own language and literature are
> deficient and underdeveloped. A Turkish poet acquainted with the
> European literature cannot sing any longer of those *mugh-beche's,*
> *pîr-i mughâns, kharâbât's,* etc. . . . We too ought to have in our
> literature the verse, the story, the drama, and the novel of the
> type of Western literature. . . . The literary generation previous to
> ours put the West in an oriental garb. The present-day generation
> has approached the West more closely and by doing so has come
> closer to contemporary civilization.[9]

A new conception of civilization thus emerged. According to it, Western civilization was a whole, including within itself the good as well as the bad. The good could not be separated easily from the

[9] Şemseddin Sâmi, "Lisan ve Edebiyatımız," *Tercuman-ı Hakikat ve Musavver Funûn* (special issue, Istanbul, 1897), 89-90.

bad. As the proverb goes, "One who loved the rose would also tolerate the thorn." The new Westernists found this so self-evident that they rarely bothered to see or to trouble themselves with the bad.

The more the suppression and obscurantism of the Hamidian period intensified, and the more its degenerating influences permeated society and its morals, the more European civilization was seen as a bed of thornless roses. Why fuss about the bad aspects of European civilization? Was Islamic, or, as the new Westernists preferred to call it, Oriental civilization any better? How could one be so stupid as to despise a civilization of enlightenment and prosperity amidst so much ignorance, so much ugliness, so much hypocrisy, so much misrule, injustice, and resultant misery? How could one be so choosy as to disdain something out of the wonders of the Western civilization when his own beggarly existence was nothing but a shadow soon to perish anyhow?

The Westernists saw Oriental civilization sinking, sinking not because of the predatory, or immoral, or hostile nature of European civilization, but because Oriental civilization itself was inherently bad and backward; and they saw Western civilization as inherently good and superior, not a civilization taken over from the Arabs, but one based upon entirely new foundations, which were neither Christian nor Muslim. The foundations? That wasn't quite clear yet—the majority of these new Westernists were aesthetes and literary men who knew little history, no economics, and a bare smattering of science. The Westernists' admiration for the Western civilization was similar to the love of a sensitive youth for a beautiful, unknown woman. They did not cry for the preservation of the past; there was nothing worthwhile in it; they longed only for life filled with beauty.

The first announcement of the new Westernism, it is interesting to note, was made as a declaration of war against the fashionable Arabism. The man who fired the first cannon was, as his subsequent political career showed, an unruly young man named Hüseyin Cahit [Yalçın] (1875-1957).

Cahit opened a new era in Turkish thought ten years before the restoration of the Constitutional regime with an article that appeared only after having been emasculated by the censor. He tells us in his "Literary Reminiscences" how the censor hacked away at his text and relates his own amazement that it was passed even in crippled form. The article was written to attack the series of articles referred to above which was intended to prove that the

European sciences and civilization were taken over from the Arabs. Let us see in Cahit's own words how he came to write it:

298

> Was it because of the composition of the Ottoman Empire, or was it the result of the sincere conviction of the writers of those days? I do not know, but there was then in our publications a powerful fashion of Arabism. An Arabism in everything. Were you supposed to write Turkish? You had to know Arabic. Were you supposed to study your religion? You had to study in Arabic books and learn from the Arabs. These notions created feelings of revolt in me. There was, yonder, a world of Western civilization representing all of civilization. Life, freedom, liberty, culture, art, prosperity were all there. The world meant nothing but that world of the West. Over here we were living in stagnation and under humiliation and the yoke, closing our eyes, our ears, our souls to the lights, to the sounds, and to the movements of civilization as if imprisoned within Chinese walls. And, despite that, we were making boastful demagoguery without reckoning ourselves and our limitations. Civilization? The Arabs made it! Science? In the libraries of the Arabs! Life? Ours! Morality, virtue? We're loaded with them! Could there be more happiness, more progress than under his Imperial Majesty's shadow? But, I thought, what could be the use of that Arab civilization and science, even if all this were really true? . . . This talk of Oriental culture, Islamic civilization, the sciences of the Arabs was repeated constantly in every writing, and on all occasions in order to anaesthetize the nation, in order to prevent it from joining the stream of life of the West passing us near by. In addition to the thick and black shroud of ignorance laid upon the nation, we had the twofold ignorance to boast of our condition and to despise Europe. It was impossible for anyone who could more or less sense the situation and who loved his country not to be tormented by such a spectacle.[10]

In the Turkey of 1935, when the above lines were penned, Hüseyin Cahit found his article commonplace and begged his readers to remember the conditions of 1898. This warning should be kept in mind in reading the quotations from that article made here:

We are bound, whether we like it or not, to Europeanize. Just as the pantaloons we wear came from Europe, our literature too . . . ought to come from there. . . . We are bound to turn to Europe even if all the history books of the Arabs were translated; still we have to learn antiquity and pre-history from European science. Ibn

[10] Yalçın, *Edebî Hatıralar,* pp. 85-87.

Khaldûn's philosophy of history belongs to the infantile age of the
science of history. Since then, the child has grown; he became
a boy in Germany; he even grew to old age; nay, the poor fellow
is dead! The modern science of history is to come from Europe,
not from the Arabs. The histories of the Arabs may teach us one
thing today—the then-existing state of historical knowledge.
Articles about the teachings of Arab science have taught me only one
thing: I finally learned that we have been liberated from Arab
civilization forever! If our gratitude to Arab civilization is due to
those Arab sciences, we can declare our good riddance of it without
hesitation. Compared with the modern astronomical devices, the
machines, military methods and techniques, geographical discoveries,
and developments in the medical sciences, those pitiable sciences . . .
of the Arabs are nothing but childsplay. . . . If we want to be
worthy of the fourteenth century of Islam, let us leave those Arab
books and embrace passionately the modern books which can fill
our brains with the sciences and techniques of our time. Surely,
we shall find these not among the Arabs, but in the West.[11]

This article and the discussions on the questions it raised, caused
the Islamists to rally around the battle standard as the opponents of
the Westernists. Mustafa Sabri (who came to be, several years
later, Şeyhul-Islâm) warned the *décadents* to beware lest they lose
their heads! He was particularly indignant over the assertion that
"we" were liberated from Arab civilization. "Who is this 'we'?"
he asked.

What do we count compared to the Arabs? Islam, which enjoins
respect and attachment to the Arabs, is not a matter of utilitarian
ties like Ottoman unity. Islam is so deep in our souls that we
cannot conceive our religion without the Arab sciences. The Arab
sciences, those sciences of *kalâm*, *usûl*, literature, and, above all,
that beloved science of *fiqh* have never been ridiculed by anyone
so boldly.[12]

Among the new Westernists we also find a new understanding
of the nature of the Turkish transformation. We find this stated
by the same Hüseyin Cahit.[13] According to him, the Tanzimat

---

[11] The article entitled "Arab'dan Istifade Edeceğimiz Ulum," appeared in *Tarik*, No. 4630 (1898); reprinted in Hûseyin Cahit
[Yalçın], *Kavgalarım* (Istanbul, 1910).

[12] Mustafa Sabri, "Cür'etli Bir Dekadan," *Malûmat* (Istanbul, 1898).

[13] Hüseyin Cahit [Yalçın], "Edebiyat-ı Cedide—Menşe ve Esasları,"
Kavgalarım (Istanbul, 1910), pp. 96-108, from where the following
résumé and quotation have been taken; the article was partly reprinted in *Hüseyin Cahit Yalçın*, ed. Suat Hizarcı (Istanbul, 1957),
pp. 50-52.

300

signified a fundamental change, and prepared the foundations for the rise of a new form of society. A nation that belonged to an Asiatic civilization had begun to Europeanize. Minds had begun to realize that the new world was not the kind of world known previously, and that they ought to form their own type of society fitting the contemporary world by taking over *ideas* from Europe if they wanted to survive. Then came a reaction; wrapped in a thick cover of bigotry, it aimed at inculcating hatred for the West. Outwardly, it continued to accept the necessity of borrowing from the West, but it constantly emphasized that only the good sides of Western civilization should be borrowed. This was nothing but a disguised form of anti-Westernism. Then in 1896 came the movement of turning to the West (the school of New Literature). But Cahit pointed out that this never meant direct imitation of European institutions.

We should borrow from the West those principles that apply to
all humanity and that would be used as our guiding principles
for the creation of our own national achievements in accordance
with our own place, time, and capacities.

The new Westernist point of view was carried further and to a more comprehensive level by another man, the leader of the new literary movement and almost the ideal type of new Westernist, Tevfik Fikret (1867-1915).

Tevfik Fikret's literary career began under the Hamidian reign but did not end with its downfall. It continued after the 1908 Revolution until his death. The ideological impact of his personality will, therefore, be brought up again in a later chapter. His most striking trait, apparent to some degree in all the Westernists, was something that will appear quite paradoxical. This trait was a preoccupation with moral questions.

From Afghanî to Ahmed Midhat, the *dehrî* (and Fikret was an extreme example) was portrayed as a man devoid of any morality, or as a man who was the enemy of morality as well as religion. Ironically, the leading Westernists were all ideally moral as well as moralists. This was particularly true of Fikret. He sought to teach a new morality, but not in the fashion of the religious moralists. The morality he sought to teach was a secular morality in which unlimited freedom would be recognized to the individual for the interpretation of religious beliefs.

Fikret's masterful combination of the techniques of traditional prosody and free verse was, in itself, revolutionary. But, his inno-

vations did not rest there. In his hands, Turkish poetry was completely secularized both in form and in content, even when the
poem was a hymn (*dua*). Most of his poems written before 1908
were denunciations of tradition and obscurantism. One of his long
poems, *Sis* ("The Fog", symbolizing the Hamidian regime) was
the boldest in condemning the traditional morality. A still longer
poem, *Tarih-i Kadim* ("Old History"), written in 1905, has not
been surpassed by anything in Turkish in the severity of its moral
condemnation of all the institutions of the past, chief among them
being Religion. There has never been a poem that has so influenced
Turkey, or has been so attacked.

"Old History" is a description of the degradation of human
beings through tyranny, injustice, hypocrisy, and slavery. Despite
his anguish over the past, the poet believes that the long night will
end with a bright new day. But who is going to bring about the
Revolution? Most people expected this as a miracle from God. But
is it not in His name that all these sufferings have been perpetrated?
Is it not those little gods, those shadows of Him on earth, who are
His instruments? Could the deliverer be that God who is the prototype of the tyrants—those tyrants who have in their earthly
kingdoms their own prophets and messengers, their own hells and
paradises, their own creatures and torturers? Nay, that God does
not seem to have a reality. A tyrant God can not exist; only the
God who loves and gives mercy to mankind can exist. That other
God, the one described and preached by the fathers of religion, is
a fabrication to enslave the people and enchain their minds. Doubt
is now challenging Him. It is Reason that is in pursuit of Light
(truth or *Hak*.) With all His majesty and grandeur, He is conquered by Reason. No one except the hypocrite and ignoramus
mourns for Him, for that which was nothing but a lie!

Fikret set his new ideals against belief in such a deity in a poem
written as his son's "Credo" (Âmentu). They were: belief in man's
dignity, the brotherhood of men, man's capacity for perfection,
love and peace, individual liberty, and the infinite capacity of
Reason to transform the world.

The youth no longer resorted to the verses of the Kur'an in
their moral thinking. Verses from Fikret's poetry, especially from
"Credo," began to appear as the slogans of new ideals. The verses
were shocking, yet, before 1908 and in the early post-1908 period,
the youth read them subversively as sacred truths.

In an age when everything sang the glories of the past and the
wonders of the auspicious reign of the Shadow of God, in an age

301

302

when apologetics denunciatory of the West were in full bloom, Fikret's poetry was both revolutionary and constructive. Its constructive aspect lay in its artistic expression of new values; these were given to the youth neither in the spirit of the traditional catechists, nor as foreign importations. Whereas the poems and plays through which Namık Kemal introduced a new concept of civic morality, in the form of patriotic virtues, appealed to the ears, Fikret's humanistic morality drove directly to the heart. Kemal's ideals were verisimilitudes; they were all transcendental. Fikret's ideas were not inapproachable clouds, because their centre was man himself, that thing so far denied, despised, and deemed too unworthy even to be considered. Without making the youth feel that what he was preaching smacked of anything foreign, Fikret brought to them the secular morality of individualism and liberalism.[14]

We find in Fikret's morality a new understanding of the West that is connected with the utopian individualism of the Westernists. Probably because of Abdül-Hamid's anti-British policies, the younger generation began to idealize the Anglo-Saxons instead of the French, who had previously provided the image of European civilization. Tevfik Fikret aspired to "the humanist excellence and nobility in the Anglo-Saxon culture based on the spirit of individual liberty, of enterprise, on the sense of individual authority and responsibility, on the individual's dignity and integrity."[15] He was one of the leading proponents of the new conception of the West whose foundation was Anglo-American education and whose values were those of individualism, liberalism, pragmatism, and puritanism. Tevfik Fikret's poetry before as well as after 1908 was the bible of this ethic.

We may turn to another writer of the time for another manifestation of the emergence of the new understanding of Westernization. This writer was the novelist Hüseyin Rahmi (1864-1944).

There are no better examples of the role of the newborn Turkish novel as a mirror of the various aspects of the Turkish transformation than the novels of Hüseyin Rahmi. This prolific writer was a realist novelist. He did not aim at inculcating a moral system. Yet,

---

[14] See Hasan Âli [Yücel] "Fikret'in Fikir Hayatımızdaki Tesiri," *Hayat*, VI, No. 137 (Ankara, Aug. 15, 1929), 13; and Fuad Köprülü, *Tevfik Fikret ve Ahlâkı* (Istanbul, 1918), pp. 36-40; for a list of the printed editions of his poems, see Kenan Akyüz *Tevfik Fikret* (Ankara, 1947), pp. 319-21.

[15] S. N. Keramet, *Fikret'in Hayat ve Eseri* (Istanbul, 1926), p. 80.

all his works shout his awareness of the pre-eminence of the moral question underlying the social problems he described.

Rahmi's novels offer a panorama of Turkish urban society in a state of acute moral crisis.[16] They give a spectacle of a people whose traditional values had been challenged, or who had been torn loose from the traditional values without having found a foothold in new moral values. There were two types of men and two value systems in every instance. The old and the new repeatedly clashed against each other. Hüseyin Rahmi photographed, so to say, the state we may call social *anomie* in the process of transformation from one form of civilization to another. By his constant preoccupation with the disintegration of the old institutions and values and with the comical and tragical acts of individuals caught within the contradictions of a fallen system, Rahmi was able to see that the process taking place in Turkey was not merely one in which new methods, techniques, and objects were taken over from the West and assimilated in terms of an integrated system of values. It was a process in which not only the traditional order crumbled but also every innovation had repercussions accelerating the disintegration of the traditional institutions. Moreover, his were descriptions of a process in which the men within the lopsided framework of the traditional order, and the men lacking a framework within which to operate, constantly confronted each other in ways that made both appear ridiculous and maladjusted. More important still was Rahmi's understanding of the men who thought themselves to be modern, or Europeanized.

Hüseyin Rahmi's contribution to Turkish literature was his portrayal not only of the *alaturka* whom he characterized superbly but also of the *alafranga* whom he was the first to dissect. Just as Cervantes' hero was a visionary who made himself absurd by behaving in terms of the values of a bygone and unreal society, so Rahmi's *alafranga* Don Quixotes did the most ridiculous things imaginable through thinking that they were in a Europeanized Turkish society which did not really exist. But while his predecessors, such as Ahmed Midhat, had criticized only the *alafranga* in order to moralize in favour of the traditional culture, Rahmi left no doubt that the traditional order, mentality, and morality were also in ruins and were bound to disappear. Both the *alaturka* and

---

[16] For a fuller discussion of Hüseyin Rahmi's novels as sociological documents, see Niyazi Berkes, "Hüseyin Rahmi'nin Sosyal Görüşleri," *Ankara Üniversitesi Dil ve Tarih-Coğrafya Fakültesi Dergisi*, III, No. 3 (1945), 3-17.

the emancipated *alafranga,* man or woman, were living in a moral vacuum. Hence, their behaviour lacked rationality and they engaged in all sorts of eccentric, dishonest, degenerate, or other anti-social behaviour.

304

Rahmi's observations of the *alafranga* led him to discuss the nature of Westernization and to distinguish between the spurious and the genuine Westernization. He was under the influence of the ideology of utopian individualism when he made this distinction and, like the new Westernists of that persuasion, believed that true Westernization would involve the development of a secular morality in which individual freedom, rationalism in science, and humanistic ideals would be the basic ingredients. Hüseyin Rahmi's search for a new secular morality after his disillusionment with the Young Turk Revolution led him to further awareness of the deepening moral crisis. Following World War I, he arrived at the brink of nihilism. Altogether his works served to stimulate the awareness that what was going on in society was a transformation made inevitable by the clash between the traditional order and the impact of Western civilization and that that clash implied, above all, a crisis in values.

The Young Turk Movement

Leaving the non-political trends representing the psychological and intellectual reactions against traditionalism, we turn to consider the men who opened a political struggle against Abdül-Hamid, the so-called Young Turks.[17] Their aim was the restoration of constitutional rule and of the Parliament which had been suspended and prorogued since 1878.

[17] The story of the Young Turks has been told and retold in Turkish and other languages, and a great deal of personal involvement and journalistic licence has entered into the accounts. The most recent account in English is E. E. Ramsaur, *The Young Turks* (Princeton, 1957); in Turkish, Dr. Ibrahim Temo, *Ittihat ve Terakki Cemiyetinin Teşekkülü* (Mecidiye, Rumania, 1939); A. B. Kuran, *Inkilâp Tarihimiz ve Ittihad ve Terakki* (Istanbul, 1948); A. B. Kuran, *Inkılâp Tarihimiz ve "Jön Türkler"* (Istanbul, 1945); A. B. Kuran, *Inkılâp Hareketleri ve Millî Mücadele* (Istanbul, 1956); Y. H. Bayur, *Türk Inkılâbı Tarihi* (Ankara, 1952), II, Part 4, especially pp. 5-18, 19-43, 91-97, 124-42; T. Z. Tunaya, *Türkiyede Siyasî Partiler* (Istanbul, 1952), pp. 102-60.

The use of the name Young Turks (or Jeunes Turcs, in French) confused them with the Young Ottomans who were also called by that name in Europe. They are also conceived as constituting a single party or group. This European name is totally misleading for several reasons. It lumps together persons, associations, and parties which actually used other and different names in Turkish, and which represented often opposite views. Whenever the term was used by the Turks, it was in imitation of the European terminology and usually in the French spelling, or rather in the corrupted form of the latter used by the common people. The popular pronunciation may best be reproduced in English as John, and probably many people believed that it really meant John the Englishman—in other words, the foreigner, and the most disliked European in the Hamidian period. Once the name Jeune Turc became John Turk, it gradually came to mean an atheist, a freemason, a radical or, at least, a dangerous and immoral rebel. As it had a derogatory meaning, no Turk, young or old, would style himself by such a name. The most misleading aspect of this European name, however, was its inclusion of the word "Turk", and its conveyance of the impression that it was a Turkish nationalist party. None of the factions grouped under the name ever used that word. All styled themselves Ottomans and this was an important point for them.

Three types of organization had come into existence as reactions against the Hamidian regime: the secret societies that originated in the institutions of higher learning (but included non-students); the factional cliques formed by those who escaped to centres such as Paris, Geneva, and Cairo; and, perhaps the least known but most important in influencing the coming events, the secret committees resembling masonic lodges, made up largely of army officers. The most important of the last was the Ottoman Society of Union and Progress.

We shall use the term Young Turks only to denote those who opposed the Hamidian regime *politically*, often with opposed ideologies, as this opposition was the only element common to them. We can best discuss the ideological and political problems reflected in the struggles of the Young Turks, with the outside and among themselves, by considering three persons, Ahmed Rıza, Mehmed Murad, and Prince Sabahaddin.

Ahmed Rıza (1859-1930) was struck by the plight of the Turkish peasantry during a trip to the country while he was a student. "Since I failed to understand the causes of this impoverishment,"

306

he says, "I thought I had found the remedy in reforming the agricultural methods."[18] Hence, he decided to go to France to study agriculture. On his return as a graduate of the agricultural school, the government appointed him to the Ministry of Agriculture, one of those Hamidian ministries which, like the Ministry of Education, would have felt the greatest pleasure were there no farmers in Turkey at all. During his service, Rıza realized that his department was only a feeding station for bureaucrats and that it had nothing whatsoever to do with Turkish rural improvement.

Upon arriving at the conclusion that "the ignorance of the peasantry was an obstacle to their understanding the need for the application of modern agricultural methods," he shifted to the Ministry of Education because, "education was the best way to enlighten people's minds." It was while he was a director of education that Rıza resigned in disgust and went to Paris (on the pretext of visiting the Paris Exhibition of 1889) where he stayed for six years before entering into political activities.

As he later informed Abdül-Hamid, Rıza spent his time studying the causes of the progress of nations, especially of "those which were, like us, in dangerous conditions." He came to "the conviction that there is no means of saving the country and the nation from the danger other than education and the positive sciences"! Rıza did not tell Abdül-Hamid, but he had also become a convinced Positivist.

In seven memoranda, which he finally published in London in 1894, Ahmed Rıza invited Abdül-Hamid to change his policies and sought to direct him in the way of reason in order to obviate revolution. The people, he said, wanted neither constitution, nor republic, nor the right to strike. What they needed was nothing but an administration that would "not sacrifice their public rights on matters of life and death to greed, and would not waste their existence according to arbitrary whim." The restoration of the constitutional regime would assure such an administration and provide the basis for an educational program "ranging from

---

[18] Ahmed Rıza became the leader of the *Ittihad ve Terakki* (Union and Progress) faction of the Young Turks. Like others he did not play an important role in the political and intellectual currents after the 1908 Revolution, which was achieved, not by the Young Turks, but by revolutionary secret societies. The following quotations are from his memoranda, *Lâyıhalarım*, lithographed in London (1896) and Geneva (1897), addressed and sent to Abdül-Hamid.

primary education to the university," which Rıza submitted to the ruler in elaborate detail.

In trying to explain that there was nothing bad about a constitutional regime, Ahmed Rıza used the old technique of the Young Ottomans, showing that the Şeriat enjoined *meşveret*. He supported his thesis with examples from Muhammad, from Abu Bakr and Omar, and also from the Ottoman Padişahs.

The second prominent figure among the Young Turks was Mehmed Murad (1853-1912), born in Tarhu, Daghistan, Caucasia. After the suppression of the revolts led by the famous Shaikh Shamil after the Crimean War, Daghistan had been reconciled to Russian rule, and Murad was educated in a Russian gymnasium at Stavropole. There he read books such as Rousseau's *Social Contract*, Montesquieu's *Spirit of Laws*, and the historical works of Guizot and Draper. When he was sent in 1873 to Moscow to attend the university, he escaped to Turkey. It was only a few years after his arrival in Turkey that he witnessed the constitutional struggles and their end in the establishment of Abdül-Hamid's rule. Murad became a prominent writer and professor of history in his adopted country. He tried to instil a liberal spirit into his students while emphasizing the sacredness and universality of the institution of the *khilâfat*. He maintained that the awakening of the Muslims could be realized by rallying around the Khalîfa, and through the application of the Şeriat in a constitutional regime.[19]

Gradually, the Hamidian rule shattered Mehmed Murad's pan-Islamic ideals. He approached the Padişah to advise him on necessary reform and, like Rıza, submitted memoranda to that effect. Realizing the futility of his attempts he escaped to Europe in 1895.

Murad outlined his aims in exile thus: to defend Turkey before European public opinion; to explain that it was the Padişah and not the people who was responsible for misgovernment; to force the Padişah (by propaganda) to change his policies; to advise the

[19] Mehmed Murad was the author of two works in several volumes on general and Turkish history and a number of polemical works in defence of his ideas. His most interesting work, however, was a novel, *Turfanda mı Yoksa Turfa mı?* (Istanbul, 1890) which might be freely translated as Pioneers or Degenerates? The ideals and struggles of a new generation, whom Murad describes as Islamist idealists, were presented against the Tanzimat Ottomanism and secularism. Murad was one of the victims of the party struggles following the Revolution of 1908 and died in exile. See F. A. Tansel, "Mizancı Murad Bey," *Tarih Dergisi*, II, Nos. 3-4 (Istanbul, 1950-51), 67-88.

308

Young Turks to avoid revolutionary methods. Murad was disappointed in all his contacts with European statesmen and publicists. Furthermore, he came into fierce conflict with Ahmed Rıza and his followers. It is true that Murad opened the most fierce campaign against Abdül-Hamid in his paper *Mizan*. But, certain of his own ideas together with European hostility for the Muslims and the Turks carried him to a dilemma. They led him eventually to attack simultaneously the Khalîfa, his European enemies and the Young Turks.

For Murad the question of reform rested on two measures: limiting the ruler's absolute authority by the Şeriat's provisions on *meşveret,* and restoring mutual trust among the "nationalities." Failure in the first had been the fault of the Young Ottoman constitutionalists. Midhat Paşa's constitution had failed to provide a guarantee for the enforcement of the constitution. Midhat had depended upon European, and especially British, support for the Turkish liberals, but he had been betrayed by the British, first in the face of the Russian pressure and, then, at the time when Abdül-Hamid was persecuting him. At the dawn of the twentieth century, to demand the restoration of the Constitution of 1876 would appeal neither to European statesmen nor to public opinion. It was necessary to have a new and positive program.

The failure to achieve the second reform was due to the European powers, especially to Russia. The Armenian Question was the latest example of the Western-Russian conspiracy. Murad suspended his campaign against Hamid while he attacked the European politics in defence of Islam. This aim gradually came to overshadow Murad's other objectives. He wrote a little book addressed to European readers in which he emphasized the thesis that Islam was not the cause of misrule; Islam did not constitute an obstacle to progress; the Muslims should not be held responsible for the follies of their ruler because he was their Khalîfa, and they were bound to obey him.[20]

---

[20] "L'Islam," he says, "est libéral au fond; le fanatisme n'est pas une conséquence naturelle de l'Islam," Mourad-Bey, *La force et la faiblesse de la Turquie* (2nd ed.; Paris, 1897), p. 6. Commenting upon Rıza's statement to *La Patrie* (July 4, 1897), "Religion is not a matter of concern to the state but is merely a matter of private concern," Murad said: "In Islam religion is a fundamental and official concern of the state. To think otherwise means ignorance of the most elementary truths about Islam. Furthermore, the [1876] Constitution specifically declared that Islam is the official religion of the state"; *Mizan*, I, No. 27 (July 5, 1897), 3.

In his opposition to the Young Turks of Rıza's persuasion Murad's talk of a new program, which he claimed would be taken seriously by European statesmen, played the decisive role. What was this new program that he said he had explained to Abdül-Hamid? We know only its general outlines, as Murad never elaborated upon it in his writings. The central point was,

to institute a Board of Supervisors that would have the power to repel the encroachment of the government over the existing laws, to compel the government to enforce the obligations undertaken by the Tanzimat Charter and the Reform Edict . . . and, thus, to ensure equality and fraternity between the nationalities.[21]

This Board, the composition of which is given as from thirty to forty in Murad's various writings, was to be accompanied by a still more controversial body—a Supreme Body of Şeriat, composed of spiritual representatives from the Muslim countries of Asia and Africa, under the presidency of the Şeyhul-Islâm, for the enforcement of the constitution according to the Şeriat and the execution of the spiritual leadership of the *khilâfat* over the Muslims of the world.[22]

No agreement was reached between the Rıza and Murad factions of the Young Turks. The first ridiculed Murad's pan-Islamism and khilâfatism, while Murad accused Rıza of atheism and a lack of religious attachment to Islam.

The third figure, Prince Sabahaddin (1877-1948), appeared among the Young Turks in 1899. He was one of two sons of Abdül-Hamid's sister. His flight to France encouraged the Young Turks, but his entry into the movement brought new schisms. As happened earlier with Murad, Sabahaddin carried the majority against Rıza and, yet, his program failed both before and after the

---

[21] Mehmed Murad, *Mücahade-i Milliye* (Istanbul, 1908), p. 207.

[22] Mehmed Murad, *Tatlı Emeller Acı Hakikatler* (Istanbul, 1914), p. 19. Great Britain, France, and Holland would nominate to the Board members from their colonies. This would be the highest spiritual organ of Islam, somewhat analogous to the College of Cardinals of the Vatican. A similar international supreme council of *Khilâfat* (*Şura-yı Hilâfet*) seems to have been under consideration in 1920 during the Allied occupation of Istanbul; see Mustafa Kemal [Atatürk], *Nutuk* (Ankara, 1927), p. 24; English trans. *Speech* (Leipzig, 1929), p. 339.

1908 Revolution. Like Murad, he barely saved his life in the fierce political struggle following 1908.[23]

310

While Ahmed Rıza became the follower of Auguste Comte, Sabahaddin became the disciple of a rival school of sociology in France composed of the followers of Frédéric Le Play. He was influenced by one of Le Play's disciples, Edmond Demolins (1852-1907), whom he knew personally. Following Le Play's admiration for the English administrative system based upon local self-government Demolins had published a provocative book entitled *A quoi tient la superiorité des anglo-saxons?* According to Demolins, societies belonged to one of two major social types—one based on *formation communautaire,* the other on *formation particulariste.* The first is the type of society

characterized by a tendency to rely, not on self, but on the community, on the group, family, tribe, clan, public powers, etc. The populations of the East are the most striking representatives of this type. Societies of a particularistic formation are characterized by a tendency to rely, not on the community, not on the group, but on self. . . . Anglo-Saxons are the most striking representatives of this type.[24]

Sabahaddin used some of his own concepts in deriving from this thesis certain formulae for Turkey. Following his split with Ahmed Rıza, he founded a society called *Teşebbüs-ü Şahsî ve Adem-i Merkeziyet Cemiyeti* in Turkish and *Ligue de décentralisation administrative et d'initiative privée* in French. He founded a paper *Terakki* (Progress) as its organ and expounded in it between 1902 and 1906 a program of action for Turkish reforms.

Sabahaddin's program contained a view that was new to the Turkish scene. His was the first attempt to make a social diagnosis of the troubles lying behind the façade that had theretofore been the main target of the reformers. He also offered a social reform program, again for the first time.

[23] He escaped to Europe and, after an abortive attempt to re-appear in Turkish politics in 1918, he retired to Switzerland where he died thirty years later. About his writings as well as studies of his life and ideas, see C. O. Tütengil, *Prens Sabahattin* (Istanbul, 1954).

[24] Edmond Demolins, *Anglo-Saxon Superiority: To What It is Due,* trans. L. B. Lavigne (London, 1898), p. 50. Sabahaddin applied the same approach to his discussion of the problems of the Westernization in *Osmanlı* which he published from 1897 in Paris and Cairo. See particularly Nos. 130-32 (Cairo, Jan. 20–Feb. 2, 1904).

According to Sabahaddin, the Hamidian tyranny was not the cause of Turkish grievances, but the product of certain features in the society. The real need was not to change the ruler but to change society itself. The real problem of Turkey was to transform society from a collectivistic formation to an individualistic order. It was no longer possible to find panaceas for the ills of a country by arbitrary convictions which were not based on sociological laws derived from the scientific observation of social facts.

311

The institutions of the Ottoman Empire, its administration, its system of property ownership, its intellectual culture, etc., all conformed to the collectivistic type of society. All historical and sociological data showed that the peoples having the collectivistic form of social organization were not capable of progress. These societies, whether headed by a monarch or by an oligarchy, were bound to be ruled by tyranny. The history of reform efforts showed constant failure because every effort was designed to perpetuate this collectivistic aspect of the society.

Abdül-Hamid's tyranny was nothing but a natural product of that history. We are repeating the same mistake, Sabahaddin said, in our attempt at Westernization. The Tanzimat reforms did not aim at introducing the institutions of the individualistic society. Even though the Tanzimat achieved progress in the general conditions of society, it failed to produce a social organization capable of steady, natural, and genuine progress and development. This would be possible only by educating individuals to rely upon themselves. These should have initiative and enterprise and should not use society as a crutch. Failing to create individuals capable of standing alone, the nation has been doomed to remain under tyranny and arbitrary rule whether under absolutism, or a constitutional monarchy.

What, then, should be done? Sabahaddin proposed a public or political program and a private or educational program. A new form of government and a new education—these were the keys to progress. The most important reform in his political program was to be the institution of a decentralized pattern of government and administration. It is necessary, he said, to extend the local government administration as far as the villages. The various parts of the Empire should have their own local governments in administrative, municipal and judicial affairs. Finance and public works should also be handled locally. Englishmen experienced in the administration of India and Egypt should be employed as experts in supervising the boards and the policies in general.

312

Sabahaddin outlined his proposed reforms for what he called private life as the second part of his program. It was first of all necessary to create and multiply the groups based on the principle of individualistic formation, especially entrepreneurial professional groups. A transformation from collectivistic property ownership to private ownership was required. But the most important medium of transformation would be provided by an entirely new system of education. Education would be based on the Anglo-Saxon system. This, Sabahaddin said following Demolins, was based on the idea of training youth with the spirit of initiative and enterprise. The entire problem was to exploit the country's resources and improve it by the enterprise of individuals on the bases of private ownership and initiative.

These were the leading ideas of the three major factions of the Young Turks in exile. As the three exponents exemplified, they differed not only in their views but also in their immediate program of action. By which means would freedom and a constitution be restored? No one believed that the people were conscious of their rights or had the means to assert them. Neither Rıza nor any other Young Turk possessed the power to enforce the traditional Islamic method of deposing a Khalîfa; that was the prerogative of the *ulema* who would not side with the *debrîs* to depose the Khalîfa of the Islamic State. Two possibilities remained: to convince Abdül-Hamid that he should restore the constitution, or to launch a propaganda campaign with the purpose of enlightening the people as to the great calamity approaching.

All the Young Turks rejected a proposed third means: the use of revolutionary, conspiratorial methods as well as pressure from the European powers. It is not difficult to see the reasons for the Young Turks' rejection of revolutionary aims and methods. To accept these would mean to accept Russian allegations about Turkish rule, to accept the European belief that the Muslims and the Turks were not worthy of existence among the civilized nations, and, finally, to endorse Armenian nationalist aims and anarchist tactics. Doing these things would be tantamount to becoming labelled the greatest of traitors in the eyes of the people who were more influenced by the Hamidian than by the Young Turk ideology.

The ineffectiveness of their propaganda devices, the rising tide in Europe of religious and political animosities against the Turks, Old or Young, inevitably caused frustration, arguments and animosities among the Young Turk leaders, especially when they were confronted with the proposals of the non-Turkish revolutionary parties. Two conventions were arranged, one in 1902 and the other in 1907. Delegates of the Rıza and Sabahaddin factions, and Arabs, Albanians, Kurds, Circassians, Greeks, Armenians, and Jews attended both. There was unanimity for the deposition of Abdül-Hamid and the restoration of the Constitution. But, there was no agreement over the questions of the unity or confederation of the Ottoman *millets,* over their respective degrees of autonomy, and over the question of the acceptance of a sort of trusteeship by the European powers for the preservation of the Empire. The conferences served only to clarify the future battle lines, because the delegates had no power to enforce any resolutions. Also, without a settlement of the question of nationalities, no settlement of the questions of government and religion, of education and economy could be worked out.

Within the country, the secret societies, or "committees" were developing. It was one of these revolutionary groups, known as the Society of Union and Progress, that not only forced Abdül-Hamid to capitulate on July 21, 1908, but also emerged as the most important political power thereafter.

Glimmerings of Turkish Nationalism

The challenge of the non-Turkish nationalist movements during the Young Turk congresses did not move the Young Turks in a nationalistic direction but did cause a few of them to think of the possibility for the first time. It is often assumed that movements like nationalism result from ideas imported from Western countries. The Turkish case is a good example of the fact that ideas themselves are not sufficient to arouse a nationalist movement, even when they have been imported, and that the ideas begin to mean something only when certain sociological conditions come into existence; even then, the imported ideas serve only as raw material for a nationalistic doctrine.

Before the events which brought about the awakening of a Turkish nationalism, there were certain developments outside of Turkey which might have stimulated nationalistic ideas. Among these were the rise of political interest in the Turkish-speaking peoples outside of the Ottoman Empire and the beginnings of scientific researches into the history and philology of the Turks in pre-Islamic times. Numerous works in these fields were published by European publicists, travellers, historians, and philologists of the nineteenth century.

314

Indeed, the works of three men (all of whom happened to be Europeans of Jewish origin) were quite influential in the formation of Turkish nationalism, but not during the Tanzimat, or during the Constitutionalist years, or even during the Hamidian era —despite the fact that the three authors were closely connected in one way or another with Turkish life and two of them were known in all three periods.

The first of these was Arthur Lumley Davids (1811-32) whose *Grammar of the Turkish Language*[25] contained a lengthy "Preliminary Discourse" in which the history of the Turkish language and of the Turks from ancient times to the reign of Mahmud II were outlined for the first time. Davids criticized the European writers (and the Turks) for their use of the term "Tartar" to cover the peoples speaking the Turkish language; the correct term, he said, would be "Turk." (He likened the erroneous use of Tartar to the Turks' use of Frenk to cover all European nations.) He portrayed the Turks as a part of the Caucasian race, distinguished from the Mongols, and as constituting one great racial family that had performed great works at various periods, and in various places, and under various names.

Davids' book was undoubtedly known to men such as Şinasi, Ahmed Vefik (Paşa), Ali Suavi, Süleyman (Paşa), and Ziya (Paşa), who became interested during the Tanzimat in the non-Ottoman Turkish language and history. It was translated into French by Davids' mother, after the young author's death, and was dedicated and presented to Mahmud II.

The second person was Arminius Vámbéry (1832-1913)[26] who had travelled to Turkey from Hungary as a young man, become tutor or secretary in the homes of various Tanzimat statesmen (one of whom was involved in the Kuleli incident), travelled as far as Khiva, Bukhara, and Samarkand, and published works on his Central Asian travels and studies of the Turkish language and history. Vámbéry was also interested in the constitutional movement in Turkey and knew the Young Ottomans in exile. His

[25] London, 1832; its French translation *Grammaire Turque* (London, 1836) includes a short account of the life of the author.

[26] About his life and works, see Franz Babinger, "Armin Vámbéry" *Encyclopedia of the Social Sciences* (New York, 1935), XV, 225.

writings about the Turkish-speaking peoples outside of the Ottoman Empire evoked interest not only in Europe but also in Turkey.

The third was Léon Cahun (1841-1900).[27] He wrote novels, *La
Bannière bleue* (1876), *Hasan le Janissaire* (1893), and *La Tueuse*
(about the Mongol invasion of Hungary; 1893), and published in
1896 his *Introduction à l'histoire de l'Asie* in which he dealt with
the historical role of the Turks in a much more colourful fashion
than Davids. He portrayed the Turk as a world conqueror and
Jengiz Khan as a Turk (to the shock of many Young Ottomans
including Namık Kemal) and the greatest empire builder in all
history. In his lesser known writings, Cahun forwarded a theory
according to which a Turanian, or what he called "Finno-Japone"
race inhabited Europe and brought civilization to it before the
Celts, Germans, and Latins. Like Vámbéry, Cahun was a passionate
liberal. He was interested in the Young Ottomans and had close
relations with Namık Kemal.

315

Interest in the Turkish-speaking peoples of Asia was also stimulated by Anglo-Russian rivalry following the Russian advance into
Central Asia after 1860. During these years, some Turkish intellectuals showed interest in similar topics.

Ahmed Vefik Paşa (1823-91), the grandson of a Greek convert to Islam and the holder of several of the highest positions, was
one of those interested in Turkish studies. He was educated in
France and knew French and English literature well. He became
a champion of the old Turkish customs and mode of life. He
opposed Westernization and the constitutional regime, ushered in
the use of plain, current Turkish (he adapted practically all of
Molière's plays to simple Turkish), and wrote the *Lehce-i Osmanî*
which was the first Turkish-Ottoman dictionary.[28] In the introduction to the second edition of this dictionary, he stressed the
idea that the Turkish language was one containing several dialects
(of which Ottoman Turkish was only one) spoken over an area
extending far beyond the regions of the Ottoman Turks and that
all those speaking the same language comprised one and the same
people. He also translated the *Evşal-i Şecere-i Türkî* of Abulgazi
Bahadur Khan from the Çağatay dialect. This book dealt with the
genealogical history of the Turks, and its translation became the
first of its kind in Ottoman Turkish.

[27] See Zadoc Kahn, "David Léon Cahun," *Jewish Encyclopedia* (New
York and London, 1901-1910), III, 492.

[28] *Lehce-i Osmanî* (2 vols.; Istanbul, 1876). Introduction to the
second edition (Istanbul, 1888).

316

Another exponent of a novel view of the Turks during the Tanzimat was Mustafa Celâleddin Paşa, a Polish convert to Islam (1826-76).[29] Mustafa Celâleddin wrote a book in French in 1869 entitled *Les Turcs, anciens et modernes*.[30] There he discussed a number of things relating to the modern and ancient Turks. In the first chapter, entitled "Les anciens Turcs," and in the supplements, entitled "L'Europe et le Touro-Aryanisme" and "Grècs et Romains," Celâleddin forwarded a theory, quite similar to that of Cahun, about the origins and the racial affinities of the Turks. Utilizing French, German, Polish, and Russian sources, he advanced the thesis that the Turks belonged to a proto-race, which he called *la race Touro-Aryenne*, that was the original race of the European nations. He also claimed that, contrary to the universal European belief, the Turks had played an important and civilizing role in world history. Having established his Touro-Aryan doctrine, he found the Westernization of Turkey a natural consequence—since Western civilization was a product of the Touro-Aryans. According to him, a part of the proto-race, the Turanians, separated themselves from the main stock by joining the civilization of the Semites, and by becoming Muslims. The turn of the Turks towards the West, he concluded, was nothing but a turning away from Semitic civilization to join the civilization of their co-racials. Celâleddin's theory was thus not nationalistic but rather international in motivation as well as in orientation.

Three men among the Young Ottomans seem to have had nationalistic ideas. One was Namık Kemal's closest associate, Ziya Paşa (1825-80).[31] In his famous essay, written in 1870 as an introduction to his translation of Rousseau's *Emile*, Ziya discussed the evolution of Ottoman poetry and said,

---

[29] Mustafa Celâleddin or Konstanty Borzecki was born in Poland, received a classical and religious education there, and joined the 1848 Revolution. Upon the failure of the Revolution, he took refuge in Turkey in 1849 together with other Polish and Hungarian refugees. He entered the Turkish army, and became a staff officer and general. He became a Muslim upon Russian pressure for the expatriation of the refugees. Celâleddin wrote to *Courrier d'Orient* and *Basiret*; see Ali, *Istanbulda Yarım Asırlık Vekayi-i Mühimme* (Istanbul, 1908), pp. 4-5. He was killed in action in Montenegro. See Adam Lewak, *Dzieje emigracji polskiej w Turcji* (Warsaw, 1935); and Adam Lewak, "Konstanty Borzecki," in *Polski Słownik Biograficzny* (Polish Academy of Sciences, Cracow, 1936), III.

[30] Paris, 1870. See especially pp. 229-99, 319-62 for the following discussion.

[31] On his life and work see E. J. W. Gibb, *A History of Ottoman Poetry* (London, 1907), V, 40-111.

None of these represent the true Ottoman [meaning Turkish] poetry. . . . Is there not a language and a poetry of the nation to which we belong; and is it not possible to rehabilitate it?

He concluded,

Our genuine language and poetry are the ones living among the people. Our natural poetry and verse are still alive among the common folk.

The second was Ali Suavi (1838-78)[32] who became, in his writings published in Paris, the only apologist among the Young Ottomans to use nationalistic arguments. Contrary to Namık Kemal, he stressed the unrecognized part played by the Turks in Islamic civilization. His views, however, were attributed by his associates to his eccentricity, or pedantry.

The third of these writers was the Süleyman Paşa (1838-92) of the constitutionalist movement.[33] He was the first Turkish writer of the modern period to include the Turks in a history of the world (the first volume of which was published in 1876). There the Turks were conceived as the pre-Islamic forefathers of the Ottomans, inhabiting and ruling vast areas in Asia. However, Süleyman appears, from an ideological point of view, as nothing but an Islamist constitutionalist, despite Afghanî's allusion to him as a *dehrî*.

None of the exiled Young Ottomans, with the exception of Ali Suavi, seems to have entertained any interest in the turkological writings of Vámbéry or Cahun. Cahun exercised an influence over Namık Kemal, not by his turkological ideas, but by his liberalism. In reality, Kemal held historical views completely opposite to those advocated by Cahun. To accept Cahun's views would make a Turk ridiculous in those days. Young Ottoman patriotism was Islamic, or pan-Ottomanist; an ideology based on the Turk—who was believed to be either a peasant, or a *Kızılbaş* (heretic), or a heathen Mongol, or a despised Tartar—would create not even a ripple among the intelligentsia. To Namık Kemal, the most influential mind of the period, what the Europeans called Turks were

---

[32] As a Young Ottoman Ali Suavi's career and ideas caused controversy and conflicting opinions. Perhaps the most balanced evaluation is made by A. H. Tanpınar, *XIX. Asır Türk Edebiyatı Tarihi* (2nd ed.; Istanbul, 1956), I, 204-23.

[33] See above, Chap. 8.

nothing but the "Osmaniyân." Even that was a political concept; in a cultural sense, there were only Muslims, or, more correctly, the "Sunni Hanefi Muslims speaking the Ottoman language."

318

During the later part of the Hamidian reign came a number of manifestations that were closer to a Turkish nationalism. Then some of the European works mentioned above began to find ears.

The rise of a Turkish nationalism was contingent upon two conditions: the disintegration of the Ottoman *millet* system, and the decline of the idea of *ümmet* and of the Islamic *din-u-devlet.* The beginnings and development of nationalism were conditioned by the degree to which the concepts of *millet* and *ümmet* were secularized.

The transformation of the Greek, Serbian, Bulgarian, and Roumanian nationalities into separate and independent nation-states signified the secularization of the *millets*. We find from this time onwards the appearance of the term *millet* as a designation for the Muslims in parallel with the non-Muslim *millets*. The term only later began to mean nation, however. During the Hamidian era, the Turk was not yet differentiated from the Muslim. The *millet* of Muslims, now believed to be the sovereign *millet* of the Ottoman Empire, still meant a religious community, which is the correct meaning of the term.

The Balkan nationalisms did not originally have the effect of stirring up Turkish nationalism. The situation changed when national movements appeared among the non-Muslims in territories that could not be ceded from the Emipre without injury to the Turkish population. Most influential was the rise of an Armenian nationalism. In the Ottoman system, the Armenians constituted a *millet* that did not have a territorial basis and was, therefore, incapable of being transformed into a nation-state. In addition, the schismatic struggles since 1847 among the Gregorian, Catholic, and Protestant churches not only shattered the Armenian *millet*, but also severed it from its traditional status in the Ottoman system. The desire of the Armenian nationalists to establish an independent Armenia was frustrated hopelessly by the conflicts among the churches, the geographical and occupational distribution of the Armenians within the Ottoman Empire, and also the rivalries between Russia and Great Britain, who alternately supported and dropped the Armenian nationalist aspirations.

The terrorist and subversive activities of the Armenian nationalist societies, formed in 1885 and 1890 in Europe and backed and encouraged by a wide variety of political and religious circles in

Europe and America, helped Abdül-Hamid to divert the revolutionary activities of the Young Turks. The terrorist tactics of some factions among the Armenian nationalists,[34] on the one hand, and the anti-Turk crusade enflamed by Abdül-Hamid's response to these, on the other, dealt severe blows to the Young Turk movement while providing Abdül-Hamid with a fine opportunity to retaliate against Western insolence and to show the people the menace of revolution, the need to stick to the traditional institutions, and the importance of uniting as a *millet* around the Khalîfa.

All this helped the coming of a second stage in the development of a nationalistic consciousness among the Turks. This was simultaneous with a focusing of the religious and political animosity in the West against the Turks. At this stage, however, Turkish nationalism was not yet a secular one; like the crusade invoking it, it had a religious colouring.

The decisive factor in converting this religious nationalism into a secular form was the rise of nationalist movements among the non-Turkish Muslim peoples. The Arab and, to a lesser extent, Albanian, and Kurdish, political movements were not yet genuinely nationalistic; they entailed only demands for autonomy, or political separation. Their ideologies were still in infancy and confused. However, the process of transformation in the traditional self-concept of the Arabs and Albanians in particular played a significant, if indirect, role in the secularization of the Turkish nationalism.

Unlike the Turks who, like the present-day Muslims of India and Pakistan, were devoid of a racial, ethnic, and genealogical sense, the Arabs and Albanians retained their racial *'asabiyya* to some extent. Arabs always distinguished themselves from the Turks whereas the Turks, especially the common people, identified themselves only as Muslims. In the past, all Muslims recognized the Arabs as a Chosen People, but in the late nineteenth century, a few Turks began to question the religious validity of this recognition. They began to see that through their renunciation of national ties upon becoming members of the universal brotherhood of Islam, they had become a people without a sense of nationality. The Turks' gradual sense of differentiation from their co-religionists may be illustrated in connection with the language question which became a much discussed topic around 1896-98.

[34] See William Langer, *The Diplomacy of Imperialism 1890-1902* (New York and London, 1935), p. 148-61 for details on the formation and activities of the Armenian secret societies.

320

So many changes had taken place in Ottoman Turkish from about 1860 that even a conservative like Ahmed Midhat was constrained to say, "The Ottoman language is such a rotten structure that whichever part is touched falls down. . . . We have to give up making repairs. It is better to pull it down and build upon new foundations."[35] Following this trend of thought, the language question began to assume an anti-traditional nature. It blossomed as a revolt against Arabic, which had come to be viewed as synonymous with scholasticism and obscurantism. The revolt, in reality, was not against Arabs, but against the *medrese* system.

The first instructive analysis of the language question was made by Şemseddin Sâmi (1850-1904) who was an Ottoman writer (the author of a number of Turkish dictionaries) and an Albanian nationalist. In addition to achieving fame for his knowledge of Turkish dialects, he is known as the founder of the modern Albanian alphabet derived from the Latin script. In spite of his service to the rise of a modern Albanian nationalism, he is counted by Turkish nationalists as one who performed a great service to the revival of Turkish as a national language. During a controversy in 1896-98 over the simplification of Ottoman Turkish, Sâmi explained that the disruption of traditional Ottoman was all to the good. From the disintegration of the Ottoman language would arise a modern Turkish; the process of change would continue until written Turkish was freed from the yoke of unassimilated Arabic and Persian rules.

The nature of the trend dating from Şinasi's time was explained coherently for the first time by Sâmi. Sâmi pointed out in addition that the transformation in the Turkish language was a reflection of the transformation occurring in the vocabulary and mentality of the people and in literature. The simplification of Turkish was inevitable because, above all, the traditional Ottoman literature was dead and a new literature, inspired by the West, was in the process of becoming. New ways of thinking could be expressed no longer within the framework of Ottoman. The new Turkish nation was arising and it needed its own national language.[36]

The secularization of Turkish thinking on nationality was reflected thus, not in the political field, but rather in the literary and educational fields. The language question arose, not as a nation-

---

[35] Ahmed Midhat, "Münakaşa-i Lisaniye," *Tarik*, No. 4624 (Nov. 18, 1898).

[36] Şemseddin Sâmi, "Şiir ve Ebebiyattaki Teceddüd-ü Ahirimiz," *Sabah* (Istanbul, Nov. 29, 1898).

alistic question, but as an aspect of the trend of enlightenment. In this way, it was not by accident concommitant with the revolt against Arabism exemplified by Hüseyin Cahit. That is why secular Turkish nationalism came by way of a literary drive rather than as a political movement. Such manifestations as the translation of Cahun's works into Turkish, the use of the Turkish syllabic poetry as against the Arab prosody, etc. were of this nature.

While the imperialistic rivalries as well as the sociological impact of the Western penetration were gradually transforming the Ottoman territories into an amphitheatre for a struggle between nationalities, the ideas of a Turkish nationalism did not invite the interest of the Turkish intellectuals. Neither did such ideas stimulate the Young Turks. The three factions of the Young Turks all advocated Ottomanism, opposed the nationalisms of the non-Muslim and non-Turkish groups, and entertained no ideology of a Turkish nationalism. If Ahmed Rıza appeared to be concerned with the defence of the Turkish element, it was not because of any belief in Turkish nationalism; he was a firm believer in the assimilation of the nationalities within the framework of the Ottoman citizenry.

There was, however, a young man among the Young Turks watching their factional struggles with critical eyes. He agreed with no faction, but did not dare say outright that they were wasting their time. What he had in mind for the Turks' future would be incomprehensible and ridiculous to Rıza, Murad, and Sabahaddin and many of their followers alike.

This man was Yusuf Akçura (1876-1933).[37] With his blonde goatee, he looked like a Russian revolutionary. He was, in fact, from Russia, born in the same town as Lenin six years later (Simbirsk, now Ulyanovsk, on the Volga). Akçura (in its Russified form, Akçurin) came to Turkey as a boy with his mother when his father, a manufacturer, died. Before he graduated as a staff officer he was banished by Abdül-Hamid's court to Fezzan. He escaped to France and studied political science and history under such men as Albert Sorel and Émile Boutmy. Like Sabahaddin he came to the belief that the real problem was the need for a social transformation. But for him the trouble lay in the morbid nature of the Ottoman Empire as a conglomeration of nationalities. The Young Turks were under a delusion. What was imminent was not a union of the nationalities, but a fierce struggle among them.

---

[37] About his life see Y. Akçura, ed., *Türk Yılı 1928* (Istanbul, 1928), pp. 396-412; M. F. Togay, *Yusuf Akçura* (Istanbul, 1944).

322

In a lengthy article entitled "Three Policies"[38] and published in 1904 in Cairo, Akçura surveyed the ideologies of Ottomanism and Islamism and the policies of pan-Ottomanism and pan-Islamism. Comparing the Islamic, Ottoman, and Turkish components of the problems facing the Young Turks, he asked "Are the interests of these three components common and identical?" The interests of the three major elements in the Ottoman Empire—the Turks, non-Turkish Muslims, and non-Muslims—did not altogether coincide. It was inevitable to recognize the national aspirations of the non-Turks and non-Muslims. Hence, there was only one thing left for the Turks: to recognize their own national aspirations, to forget about being Ottomans, and to be content with being Turks.[39]

Would this mean the pursuance of a policy of pan-Turkism (*tevhid-i etrâk*) as there were more Turkish-speaking peoples outside the Ottoman Empire than inside it? Akçura found pan-Turkism as fraught with difficulties as the other two policies. There was yet no national consciousness among the Turks. He concluded his article with a question: was it not likely to appeal to the Turkish people when the other two policies collapsed?

Before the 1908 Revolution and even for a few years thereafter, no Turk, Young or Old, took Akçura's question seriously. Turkish nationalism was to be enflamed only by further shocks from the West, by nationalisms within the Empire, and by Turkist nationalist developments in Russia.

---

[38] Reprinted as *Üç Tarz-ı Siyaset* (Istanbul, 1912).

[39] Akçura believed that it was inevitable that these nationalities would attain national independence unless they were given autonomy and the Ottoman Empire constituted as a federative union.

SEARCH FOR A FULCRUM 1908-19

The Meşrutiyet | *chapter 11*

THE MAJOR POLITICAL and social issues of the new constitutional era called the Meşrutiyet and opened by the Revolution of 1908 were predictable from the differences among the Young Turk factions and the three schools of thought that were crystallizing in the years before 1908. In preparation for the discussion of the controversies and secular achievements of the Meşrutiyet (1908-18), we shall consider here the conditions affecting the reform policies, together with the identities of the three Turkish schools of thought.

Union and Progress

The Young Turk movement, together with the disputations of the new Westernists, had boiled down to two aspirations. These had been introduced first by Namık Kemal and were encompassed by the two words: *union* and *progress*. Union meant the co-operation of all nationalities within the Ottoman unity. Progress implied the bringing about of a social revolution through educational and economic measures.

For union to be translated into action a number of prior conditions were needed: (*a*) the factors encouraging nationalistic separation within the Empire should cease to operate, (*b*) the international status and unity of the Ottoman Empire should be recognized, and (*c*) the relationships between religious-national and political affairs should be clarified and amicably settled. The last

325

326

condition implied that each religious community (*millet*) should be recognized as a cultural, and not as a political, entity, each should disaccociate itself from political loyalty to the church, that is, secularize itself fully, and the Muslim Turks should develop themselves as a secular nationality and cultural community disentangled from the state religion. In other words, the state should cease to be Islamic through the separation from it of the caliphate and the further secularization of its foundations and organs.

Progress required the existence of a number of favourable conditions in addition to the genuine appropriation of the contemporary civilization through educational and economic measures. These conditions would be different from those that had created the spurious Westernization of the Tanzimatists and Hamidian Islamists. In order to achieve progress it was necessary (*a*) to be able to mobilize and develop the educational institutions in such a way as to produce men who could and would be the carriers of Ottoman national progress, and (*b*) to regain scope for the utilization of the existing and new economic forces as levers of social uplift. Since none of these prerequisites was realized, or could be realized, the ideological ship of 1908 was bound to have a rough voyage.

Political Awakening of the Turkish Element

The Revolution of 1908, or the restoration of the Meşrutiyet (constitutional regime), will appear as less than even an ordinary coup d'état unless the psychological, later organizational, transformation it brought is recognized.

With the coming of the 1908 Revolution something made itself felt for the first time: the Turkish masses reacted politically rather than religiously. Unnoticed, the Hamidian regime had served to split the *din* from the *devlet* in the minds not only of the educated but also of the masses. At last, the masses had entered into a stage where there could be a political association existing apart from the state and continuing when government collapsed.

In contrast with the non-Muslim *millets*, as we have observed, the Muslim Turks did not constitute a religious community in the Ottoman system. With the exception of the mystical orders and those guilds that were neither political nor ecclesiastical associations, they knew no form of association outside of the Ottoman state. They lacked both the freedom and apparatus to perpetuate their own religious and cultural institutions and constituted an amorphous entity politically, religiously, and culturally. Their cohesion and existence depended entirely upon their association with the state.

Under medieval conditions the ties of natural community (tribe, village, town, and family) and professional and religious voluntary associations played their respective sociological functions in the lives of individuals outside of the political field. The more the medieval system disintegrated and modern conditions developed, the less the individual was able to identify himself with traditional social groups. There came into being a growing mass of Turks who felt the state to be their strongest and most natural unit of self-identification. This trend progressed furthest in the new urban centres and, especially, among the people uprooted from their traditional places through wars, the loss of lands, and the search for new means of livelihood.

The Turks did not reorganize themselves in the face of these new conditions as did the *millets*, or the Muslims who experienced the development of modern conditions under a political rule imposed from the outside—as, for example, the Muslims of Russia, India, and Indonesia, among whom one finds striking parallels with the transformation of the Ottoman *millets* and the development of associations and movements of a religious or economic nature, or both. In the final analysis, the Turk felt himself to be nothing but a Muslim and a member of a Muslim state. But the more the state lost its traditional features, that is, the more the state's religious and political features became separated and the more the state was portrayed as a political association of *millets*, the more the members of the *ümmet* of the Turks found themselves in a vacuum. The *ümmet* ceased to exist in a real sense; the term became an empty word while the Turks were an aggregate which did not even have a name for national and cultural self-identification.

It is because of this situation that the Young Ottomans and Young Turks soon fell into despair and blind man's buff. While the non-Muslim pan-Ottomanist liberals were fighting for the rights of their respective *millets*, their Turkish colleagues had neither support nor response from a *millet*. Consequently, it soon became clear to both the Young Ottomans and the Young Turks that their revolutionary activities did not have any effect upon the Turkish masses.

328

What the revolutionaries in exile failed to accomplish for over a quarter of a century the Revolution of 1908 achieved in just a few months. This bringing of a sense of community to the Turkish masses was not one of its direct aims. In fact the Revolution of 1908 did not even aim at the deposition of Abdül-Hamid and hardly affected the composition or policies of the government until the new political movement reached maturity. The coup had its effects by bringing an interruption to the Hamidian government and by giving scope for the effects of the Hamidian policy of *din-u-devlet* to express themselves.

The telegraphic lines, so essential to the Hamidian regime, became the means of its real downfall. In 1908 for the first time, a nationwide political change made itself felt through the telegraph network. There was no awareness among the people that the event was a national one, but the uniform spread of the news and its vagueness precipitated a like-mindedness that became the foundation for a nationalism. Mass psychology and crowd demonstrations could now be exploited by any leader or demagogue. Through their control of the one universal mass medium, the telegraph system, the organizers of the Society of Union and Progress quickly channelled events to their advantage and against the conservatives among the Young Turk exiles who had just returned.

This first process was facilitated by a second that took place at another social-psychological level. When the telegraph office at Yıldız went off the air, the governmental apparatus and functionaries became virtually paralyzed. Then young men who were either secretly Young Turks or Young Turk sympathizers came forward to organize a sort of people's councils for the purpose less of politics or government than of organizing celebrations, council elections, etc. They spontaneously formed hundreds of branches of the Society of Union and Progress, one in almost every town. Thus, like wildfire, there came into being nuclei for the provincial political organization of the Turks. The product was not yet a political party in the usual sense of the term. In the course of the Society's transformation into a political party, these nuclei would later become expanded and differentiated, sometimes into rival party branches and sometimes into groups dominated by tenuous eclecticism.

The Society of Union and Progress thus established itself spontaneously as a national organization. It became the basis of the emergent Turkish nation. Its genesis, however, does not tell us everything about the nature and orientation of the movement represented by the Society, nor does it tell much about the Society's social basis, or the composition of its leadership.

The Society became the expression of the changing part of the Turkish social organization; it did not encompass the peasantry, which was not yet enveloped in the changes; it did not gain the allegiance of the conservative generations and classes which have remained even until our day Hamidian in spirit. The mass basis of the Society was amorphous and evolving; this was reflected in the shapelessness of its ideology. Its class basis gradually shifted from that of the unrooted masses to the *esnaf* (artisans) and the *tüccar* (merchants) of the towns—the classes out of which the Party of Union and Progress later sought to forge a Turkish bourgeoisie.

The most important element of the Society, especially at the beginning, was its leadership. Most of the leaders, or at least the most influential ones, were from Rumeli (the Balkan Provinces of the Ottoman Empire) rather than from Anatolia, and were up-rooted Turks, or Turks who had broken with tradition through education, or non-Turkish Muslims who had been Turkified by modern education. Army officers, doctors, and teachers were prominent among them. By Hamidian standards, they were all *dehrîs* in their politico-religious views; they were firm believers in progress. Their mental make-up contrasted sharply with those of the Anatolian traditionalists and the political élite of some other Muslim countries.

Different Meanings of Union

The Society of Union and Progress championed the Tanzimat and Young Ottoman conceptions of fusion. It encountered opposition on the questions of the nature and status of the *millets*, the nature of the union or fusion among them, and the concept of Ottoman citizenship from three forces: the liberal faction of the Young Turks (represented earlier by Sabahaddin), the political and semi-political organs of the non-Turkish nationalities, and the conservative Muslim group (represented earlier by Murad). Through their opposition, as well as through its own changing role, the Society became the Party of Union and Progress in 1913. When, later, rival parties became harbingers of anti-Ottoman nationalisms, Turkish nationalism gained some influence in the Society, but never replaced Ottomanism.

330

In the years following the Revolution two political parties came into existence in opposition to the Union Party.[1] One was called Liberal (Ahrar), or, as it re-emerged later, the Party of Liberty and Conciliation (Hüriyet ve Itilâf), known to the European press as the Liberal Entente. The other was a political formation calling itself the Muhammedan Union (Ittihad-ı Muhammedî), which wanted Islamic unity as the basis of the Ottoman state. The nationalists (Armenian, Greek, Arab and Turkish) joined these parties only to influence them or to cover their own secret or suppressed organizations. The Arab and Armenian secret organizations were the most active.

The political struggles between the parties centred about two seemingly separate issues: the relationship between state and religions, and the relationships between the *millets* and Muslim nationalities. While the two issues had, in fact, mutual dependencies, the conditions of the time were such that taking a given side on one issue said nothing of one's attitudes regarding the other. The interests of rival parties and nationalities were not only opposed but also self-contradictory.

The question of state and religion provided the major contest. The Liberals were separationists, that is, secularists *à la Tanzimat*. They supported the non-Turkish *millets* without, demanding in return the renunciation of political prerogatives as religious communities. The Liberals tended to interpret secularism as meaning an ultra-liberal government amounting to a nonentity as a central political authority. By supporting liberal economic policies and demanding the freedom of private enterprise, the Liberals in effect were supporting the nationalism of the non-Muslims. They were providing greater scope for national separatisms by their advocacy of decentralization in administration.

The Unionist understanding of secularism was directly opposed. It meant a religiously ineffectual but educationally and economically strong central government. This was seen as indispensable to the interests of Ottoman unity, which was for them the goal above all national aims. Their Ottomanism has been erroneously identified ever since with Turkish nationalism, especially by the Arab nationalists. The Unionists' understanding of union, however,

---

[1] For further details about the political parties of the period 1908-18, see T. Z. Tunaya, *Türkiyede Siyasî Partiler* (Istanbul, 1952), 174-368.

was equal citizenship for all Ottoman subjects irrespective of religion or race. There would be no nationalism, not even a Turkish nationalism. The central government would be made strong enough to enforce this concept of union, and the state would carry out the necessary policies for economic recovery and educational assimilation and advance.

331

The Unionists believed that the communalism of the *millets* was incompatible with the political sovereignty of a state. While the nationalities demanded further religious, educational, and political concessions as nationalities, the Unionists sought to restrain even those that had existed traditionally. The right of maintaining autonomy, cultural and political, which meant union to the separatists, meant dissolution to the Unionists. All individuals, irrespective of the *millets* to which they belonged, would be regarded as equal insofar as political rights and duties were concerned and would, therefore, be represented in parties, elections, government, military service, and, finally, parliament, as individual Ottoman citizens not as members of corporate bodies, religious or political.

What would be the nature of the association of the *millets* as nationalities? The Unionists denied the existence of such collectivities as legitimate political elements constituting a political association called the Ottoman Empire. The term *millet* had already undergone a secularizing transformation. The Unionists reserved it for the Ottoman *millet*, comprising individuals who temporally belonged to the same state but religiously belonged to different faiths. In place of the term *millet* for a religious community they used the two new terms, *cemaat* (religious congregation) or the still more colourless *unsur* (pl. *anâsır*, elements, connoting the ethnic differentiation among the Ottoman citizenry).

The nature of the association among the congregations and elements was understood variously. In contrast to the Unionist tendency to ignore the *millets* as collectivities having political and national significance and to view them as spiritual bodies, the non-Muslim *millets* were by then political nationalities aspiring to independent nationhood in which religion would be an instrument of politics. Those non-Muslims who regarded themselves as Ottoman subjects indirectly and through their membership in a *millet* tended to regard association within the state not as a matter of nationalism, but as a partnership based upon a voluntary, contractual, or co-operative relationship. The Armenian nationalist intellectuals seem to have been most outspoken on this matter. One

332

writer likened the union at the basis of the Ottoman state to a *şirket*, a company or association.[2]

Unprepared and unable to adopt an outright nationalistic ideology, the Unionists were caught in a dilemma. For them the basis of association could not be nationalism of any of the elements constituting the Ottoman community because there was not one but several nationalities with clashing aspirations. It could not be Islam because of the non-Muslims. Islam as represented by the institution of *khilâfat* and the Şeriat could not be renounced because of the Muslims, especially the non-Turkish ones.

While the Tanzimatists relied largely upon education to realize the fusion of nationalities the Unionists seem to have favoured government and economic policy as the means. However, their efforts were taken by both non-Muslims and non-Turks as a policy of Turkification, even though everyone knew that the Ottoman state was not a Turkish state in terms of composition, constitution, legal structure, or even official language. The only element of Turkishness lay in the rulership of the Ottoman dynasty, which had neither political nor spiritual power left. (The cabinet, government, administration, foreign service and secular courts were manned more by non-Turks proportionately.) What was left was the conception of unity in which being an Arab, a Kurd, a Circassian or an Albanian, as well as a Jew or an Armenian or a Greek Christian, resembled being English, Irish, French or Scandinavian and being of the Protestant, Catholic or Jewish faith within the American nationality.

No less a man than Ziya Gökalp, who became a prominent Unionist after 1911 and the most influential nationalist, thought and wrote in 1909 along this Ottomanist line.[3] He spoke of the fusion and amalgamation of races in the creation of Ottoman nationality. "The Ottoman lands," he said, "will be the free and progressive America of the East." Turks, Arabs, Greeks will first call themselves Ottoman, he said, and then Turk, or Arab, or Greek.

The greatest stumbling block for the Unionists was in the secularization of the state, the first prerequisite for the creation of the type of nationality to which they aspired. There were signs, after

[2] *Içtihad*, No. 2 (Geneva, Jan., 1904), 15-16, and *Içtihad*, No. 64 (Istanbul, May, 1913).

[3] Essays reprinted in S. Beysanoğlu, *Ziya Gökalp'in Ilk Yazı Hayatı, 1894-1909* (Istanbul, 1956); see pp. 94-95, 99-101, 105-6, 109-10.

the restoration of the constitutional regime, of the Sultanate's losing its attribute of Caliphate and of a new impetus toward secularization in legislation, in education, and in other fields. The first was opposed by Muslim, the second by non-Muslim nationalities. Ironically the greatest opposition to Unionist Ottomanism came, not from non-Muslim nationalisms, but from the nationalisms of Muslim (especially Arab) nationalities.

Two consequences of the Muslim nationalist movements were of decisive importance for Turkish Ottomanism. Firstly, they shattered belief in the unity of the Muslim nation. Secondly, they separated Turkish nationalism from religion. The years 1911-13 were decisive in forcing the Union to support Turkish nationalism over against non-Muslim nationalisms. From 1914 on the same thing happened with respect to the non-Turkish Muslim nationalisms. Thus the final attempt to maintain the multi-national unity of the Ottoman Empire failed, and a fierce struggle ensued between the Turks and the non-Turks over the liquidation of the Empire.

Europe for Disunion

There were still other forces running counter to the ideals of union and progress. These came from the relations with the European powers.

All factions of the Young Turks had believed that the loss of financial and political independence was the result of the Hamidian autocracy, and they had entertained hopes of Western support for a fresh start towards economic recovery. There had been the growing realization that the key to progress was economic development and that this was not a matter of learning certain skills from the West, or of inviting, or allowing Europeans to run the country's economy, but rather of revolutionizing the economic system. This had led to the question of achieving an economic transformation.

The predominant view, especially as expressed in the Private Enterprise Program of Sabahaddin, was that the foundation of Western civilization was liberal capitalism. On this there was not substantial disagreement between the rival political parties. Economic liberalism was the magic formula. A liberal economy was the natural order of things and, hence, a liberal policy was the policy best suited to the interests of Turkey. The doctrine of economic liberalism would bring Turkey into the order of the world of capitalistic economy.

The Turkish supporters of economic liberalism opposed the capitulations not from interest in the requisites of a national economy, but because the capitulations were contrary to laissez-faire liberal capitalism and, therefore, potentially inimical to the liberal development of the Turkish economy. In terms of this view, the Western powers would naturally and voluntarily renounce their capitulatory privileges in return for Turkey's borrowing more money and encouraging greater foreign capital investment. Here the Young Turks, especially the liberals, showed their economic and diplomatic naïveté.

Once in power, the Young Turks learned very soon that the European statesmen and bankers were far from being the true disciples of Adam Smith and J. B. Say. None would give a quarter of an inch on the capitulations; they refused to loan a penny unless Turkey gave new concessions and ceded further privileges. Just as the *millets* demanded privileges in addition to the traditionally existing ones as a condition of their participation in the Ottoman partnership, so the powers, especially France, demanded concessions in addition to the traditionally existing capitulations before extending economic assistance. It had become axiomatic in economic as well as other circles that the Turks were incapable of progress. Leaving aside the fact that it would be miraculous if an economically arrested country were able to compete with industrially advanced countries on an equal footing, the powers had not the slightest intention of letting off the hook a country subjected to the capitulations, mortgaged to European capital, and already divided into economic spheres of influence. No Asiatic nation, excepting Japan, had dared claim the right to economic independence of Europe; and such an ambition, especially the desire to industrialize, was regarded as antithetical to the economic interests of the advanced countries. Already, the European powers were discussing the necessity of rationalizing further their investments in the Ottoman Empire. Even as the Young Turks assumed power, the partition of the Ottoman Empire had become a normal theme in European diplomatic negotiations. In short, there was no interest whatsoever in seeing the integrity of the Empire preserved.

The schemes and intentions of the European powers were not unknown in Turkey. There was widespread belief after 1911 that the Ottoman Empire was facing the most critical moment in its history. A delegate to the 1911 Union party convention said,

334

Under the circumstances, it is evident that Ottoman society
stands . . . as a freak of nature. What will be the fate of the Turk in
this monstrous situation? What will be his lot if the Ottoman state
loses its independence? . . . What will happen to him at the
hands of the imperialistic hectors?[4]

335

The Birth of Economic Nationalism

It was these conditions that brought the Union to power in 1913
and caused change in the meaning of the name. It no longer meant
the union of various ethnic elements, but the unification of the
Turks. This unification had to take place in the face of challenges
from the other ethnic elements, on the one hand, and from European imperialism, on the other. The aim would be to make the
Turks economically independent of internal and external rivals.

Two ideas began to emerge from the press and party conventions held in 1911, 1912, and 1913: that economic independence
was the basis of national independence, and that economic independence could be achieved only through developing a national
economy backed by the government. The first meant a shift from
the view that Turkey's independence could be guaranteed by her
incorporation into the European economy to the view that Turkey's independence was inimical to European political interests,
just as her economic interests were incompatible with the economic interests of Europe.

The new economic view supporting the emerging policies was
supplied by a man known as "Parvus," one of the leading Marxian
socialists of the era. He was Alexander Helphand, who lived in
Turkey during the years 1910-14.[5] It was with Parvus that anti-
liberal and anti-imperialistic economic ideas along Marxian lines

[4] Celâl Nuri, *Ittihat ve Terakki Kongresine Muhtıra* (Istanbul, 1911),
pp. 20-21, 23.

[5] Born in Beresina, Russia, in 1867, Helphand (or Helfant) joined the
Russian revolutionary movement early and escaped to Switzerland.
He hurried to Petersburg from Germany at the outbreak of the
1905 Revolution and was elected to the Petersburg Soviet together
with Trotsky, over whom he exerted considerable influence. He
was arrested and exiled to Siberia the same year. Escaping in 1906,
he returned to Germany and socialistic journalism. "Though im-
pecunious, he managed to travel to Constantinople, where he ultimately got in touch with the Young Turks. They were not slow
in discovering and using his great financial knowledge, and made

336

began to appear in the Turkish press. Parvus' concern for the Turkish case was associated with his theory of socialist revolution. According to his view, capitalism would destroy itself only if the socialists could abolish imperialism; therefore, Turkey should have, not a socialist regime, but rather a bourgeois democratic regime. This was to be realized by breaking the shackles of imperialism.

Parvus emphasized in his Turkish writings: (1) that the Turkish economy was enslaved to European capitalism; (2) that European capitalism had established imperialistic control over Turkish agriculture, natural resources, railways and public utilities, customs, taxation, trade, and finance through the capitulatory privileges and, especially, the establishment of the Administration of the Ottoman Public Debt; (3) that given such control, the Turkish agricultural economy was incapable of advancing beyond its primitive condition, native industries were doomed to decline or extinction, and no government could pursue a national economic policy, or even alleviate the financial distress except through further borrowing of European capital which would lead to still further economic impoverishment; and (4) that the realization of financial independence and economic recovery would require, under prevailing conditions, the repayment of so great a sum that Turkey could not hope to buy even the conditions for economic progress. By a detailed analysis of the history of the Turkish loans, Parvus showed the Turkish case to be the most extreme example of imperialistic swindling. He showed that the country had repaid the foreign loans several times over, argued that the introduction of further foreign capital would not only fail to initiate economic developments but would also cause still further decline, and mocked the idea that the imperialistic governments would abolish

---

him their adviser," M. Beer, *Fifty Years of International Socialism* (London, 1935), p. 195. He became a regular contributor to Akçura's *Türk Yurdu*. He published also in *Bilgi Mecmuası, Tanin, Jeune Turc*, and *Tasvir-i Efkâr*. His major work in Turkish, *Türkiyenin Can Damarı*, was published under the pseudonym "Parvus" in 1914. On his socialist ideas see G. H. D. Cole, *The Second International, 1889-1914: A History of Socialist Thought* (London, 1956), III, Part I, 489, 492, 501, and 956-958; on his role in the Russian Revolution, Z. A. B. Zeman, ed., *Germany and the Revolution in Russia 1915-1918: Documents from the Archives of the German Foreign Ministry* (London, 1958). Helphand seems to have played an important role in arranging with the Germans the passage of Lenin through Germany to Russia, but was rejected by Lenin when he showed a desire to join the Bolsheviks. He remained in Germany as a supporter of the Social Democrats, and died in 1924.

the capitulations, restrain the Public Debt, or recognize Turkey's sovereign rights over her natural resources, customs, and taxation.

Parvus' direct advice was that the Turks had to abolish the capitulations as a pre-condition to the struggle for economic and financial recovery, but his writings served much broader ends and influenced the nationalist intellectuals considerably. Parvus shattered the illusions of liberal Westernism and pointed up a paradox in the Turkish situation. With the desire to join the West being felt most optimistically, it began to appear that Turkey would have to fight the West in order to be able to join the orbit of Western civilization. An étatiste view of the economic policy needed for national reconstruction began to oppose, even to supplant, policies of economic liberalism.

Within three or four years, the significance of the Revolution of 1908 began to be viewed in a new way. It was seen to signify the real end to the Ottoman Empire. The developments scanned above were seen by many as heading towards an internal struggle between the nationalities of the Empire and imperialistic warfare over the particles of the Empire between the two Western power blocks.

Three Schools of Thought

The political turmoil of the years surveyed above brought into the open the differentiation that had taken place since the Tanzimat between three schools of thought which did not correspond to the new party divisions. These became known as the Westernist, Islamist, and Turkist schools during the years from 1908 to 1918. The controversies of these years, to be surveyed in the following chapters, will be understood best as three varieties of an attempt to find a new foundation for the political existence and cultural reconstruction of the Turks, whose peril was perceived to have extended to their entire traditional existence. The different views expressed in the ten-year battle between the schools of thought represented a comprehensive accounting of the accumulated problems of the Turkish transformation. Allowing for the differences of time and place, several of the questions raised, together with the attitude taken, are still current in our time in Turkey and in other Muslim countries.

It is interesting to note that the names for the three schools of thought—Westernists, Islamists, and Turkists—were not established until after the emergence of the Turkist group, who, under the influence of the Russian use of such labels as Westernists, or Westernizers, and Russophiles, called their adversaries Westernists and Islamists. The latter group retaliated by coining the word Turkist, which they used in a derogatory sense. In time, however, the labels were accepted by the public, and they are used today even by the groups in speaking of themselves.

THE WESTERNISTS

The Westernists came out as the most vigorous group following the Revolution. However, certain conditions operated to their disadvantage. Except for the followers of Sabahaddin, they did not have the sectlike cohesion of the Islamists and Turkists. They were highly vulnerable to attack as the champions of unconditional Westernization when the West appeared as the avowed enemy of the Turks, or Muslims.

The Westernists' ideas deviated radically from the prevalent view of Westernization, best formulated by Ahmed Midhat. The essence of Westernization in their eyes would be a radical moral and mental transformation. The greatest problem was to cast aside the old system of values in order to develop a new morality based upon the Western system of values. In other words, modernization was to the new Westernists a cultural and moral issue far more than a material one. *as was to earlier westernizers*

For all their boldness, the Westernists were pitifully ill-equipped when it came to a sustaining ideology which would take into account Turkish and Islamic factors in explaining the ways and means of such a fundamental transformation. Their economic, educational, and historical views were too remote from realities.

Despite their weaknesses, the Westernists were the thesis against which the Islamists constituted the always violent antithesis, and the clash of the two helped the development of the Turkist position as an alternative. This role of the Westernists as the initiators of reaction can be seen best in the cases of the two prominent figures of the Westernist school, Tevfik Fikret[6] and Abdullah Cevdet.

Fikret's poem, "Old History", which was known to many, although not published, under the Hamidian regime, was an attack upon the doctrine of the Islamic State, not upon religion itself. In the new era the Islamists, who did not alter their traditional point of view with regard to the question of religion and state,

[6] See above, pp. 300-2.

quickly beclouded Fikret's real target; divesting the attack of its anti-Hamidian allusions, they presented "Old History" as an attack upon religion and God. In 1912, the Islamists launched against Fikret a crusade which is still going on.

The Islamist campaign incited Fikret to write his even more inflamatory *Zeyl*, (Appendix to "Old History"). This caused all of the stocks-in-trade of the Islamists against expressions of a new morality to be employed against Fikret. Since then, every resurgence of the Islamist reaction in Turkey begins, significantly, with a violent barrage against Tevfik Fikret.

The other Westernist representative was not, like Fikret, a man of solitude. He was as aggressive as the Islamists and as brash as the Unionist politicians. Dr. Abdullah Cevdet (1869-1932) survived Fikret by many years and served for years as a scourge of bigots, obscurantists, and men attached to the past in general. Throughout, he possessed a strange boldness in the face of the most severe attacks, which he did everything to invite.

Although never prominent as a leader among the Young Turks in exile, Cevdet had been in reality one of the founders of the Society of Union and Progress. After escaping to Europe, together with others from the Medical School, he began publishing a review in Geneva called *İçtihad*, which became the chief organ of the Westernist ideas and crusades.[7]

During his exile, Cevdet, like Sabahaddin, believed that the cause of the troubles in Turkey was not the ruler, but rather the nation that put up with such a ruler; what had to be changed was not the ruler, but society. Unless the masses were enlightened, the Young Turks would always fail; even if Hamid died or was deposed, there would be others as bad or worse to take his place. Cevdet attacked the Young Turks in exile, both for their inability to carry on revolutionary action and for their failure to perceive the position of Turkey vis-à-vis the West.

Back in Turkey, Cevdet mobilized all his powers to expose every manner of obscurantism—religious, political, and national. For him, the trouble with the people of Turkey, in fact with Muslims throughout the world, was self-evident; indolence, ignorance, subservience to superstitions erroneously identified with the religion of Islam, self-subordination to degenerate and stupid clericals,

---

[7] *İçtihad* began to appear in Geneva in 1904; it was moved to Cairo the next year. From 1911 until Cevdet's death in 1932, it was published in Istanbul. It was closed a number of times by various governments and Cevdet himself had to stand trial.

340

and the consequences of these—technological, scientific, economic, and even biological degeneracy. The remedies were equally obvious and simple: to push, pull, if necessary lash the people into moving, working, earning, seeing, and thinking like the infidels of the West. Quite naturally, Cevdet made his arch-enemies among the Islamists, who more than once succeeded in having him dragged before the courts of law.

An impartial survey of the files of *Içtihad* will show that Cevdet was an enemy neither of Islam nor of religion in general. There was not even a general condemnation of religions, such as was expressed in Tevfik Fikret's "Old History." One even finds expressed there frequent interest in Islamic reformers. For example, *Içtihad* gave space to Muhammed Abduh long before the Islamists said anything about him. Constant interest was shown in the movements of religious awakening in Turkestan, Egypt, and India. Furthermore, Cevdet knew the Arabic and Persian languages and literatures to perfection, and his knowledge of the Islamic religious sciences does not seem to have been inferior to that of the most competent Islamists.

THE ISLAMISTS

The Islamist position will be illustrated best by a short description of the exponents of the three Islamist groups. The first was a small and short-lived group made up of the leftovers of the Hamidian period. In time, they became organized in a society called Cemiyet-i Ilmiye-i Islâmiye (Islamic Society of Men of Learning) and had *Beyân al-Hak* as their organ. Mustafa Sabri, their most prominent figure, became famous during the Allied occupation of Istanbul (December 1918 to August 1923) as the collaborationist Şeyhul-Islâm.[8]

Beyân al-Hak began publication in September 1908. The motto of the review was declared to be "*amr b'il-ma'rûf wa nahy 'an'il-munkar*" (command that which is approved and prohibit that which is rejected). Its early issues applauded the constitutional regime. "Today," the lead article of the first issue began, "thanks be to God, no obstacle to our progress and development remains" —Abdül-Hamid had been the obstacle! The review pledged itself to fight against the belief that Islam was the obstacle to progress. News and special articles about the world of Islam would consti-

---

[8] See above, p. 299. He held office during the years 1919 and 1920; he died in 1944 in exile in Egypt.

tute the major portion of the review. Pan-Islamism would receive special attention.

When the Westernists raised their voices louder and louder in the freedom of the new regime, *Beyân al-Hak* began to change its colour. In a series of articles entitled "The Controversial Questions of the Religion of Islam," Mustafa Sabri discussed matters ranging from polygamy and divorce to the permissibility of being photographed. Giving an initial appearance that these questions would be dealt with in a manner worthy of modern times, he came eventually to the point of declaring that photography was nothing but *kufr*.

The second group consisted basically of the Muhammedan Union mentioned above. The leader of this group, Vahdetî, published several papers, instigated the so-called March 31 Mutiny of the Soldiers, and was hanged together with others of the group following a court martial. The only long-time survivor of the group was Said Nursî (1867-1960), known as Bedi-uz-Zaman (the Wonder of the Times); even at his death, he was the leader of a political-religious order called the Followers of *Nûr* (light).

The publications, speeches, and sermons of the Muhammedan Union may be summarized thus: in accordance with the constitution, the religion of the state is Islam. The constitutional regime is bound to enforce this article, that is, to enforce the Şeriat. The Şeriat consists of two types of provisions. First, there are the duties incumbent upon the individual, such as prayers and fasting. The performance of these does not mean that the Şeriat is in force. It is equally incumbent upon Muslims to enforce the second type of provisions. The state must be Islamic and its laws the law of the Şeriat. So long as the provisions on transactions (*mu'amalât*) and on punishments (*uqûbât*) of the Şeriat are not enforced, there can be no talk of Islamic state and of the application of the Şeriat. The new regime is not Islamic; it is a state of *dehrîs* (secularists). Under the pretext of the existence of non-Muslim nations and the pressure of the European powers, the promoters of this regime do not apply the Şeriat. This is contrary to constitutional government and democracy. In a democracy it is necessary to follow the will of the people. The majority of the people of the country are Muslim, therefore the law of the land should be the Şeriat.

The third and the most influential group of the Islamist school gathered around *Sırat-ı Müstakim*. This review which survives even today under its later title *Sebil-ur Reşad*, began publication with applause for the new regime and condemnation of the

342

Hamidian regime, both on the basis of Islam. Its early articles contained profuse quotations from ancient literature concerning the constitutionalism of Abu Bakr and Umar. Islam was in perfect accord with the Meşrutiyet or, more precisely, the Meşrutiyet was nothing but the true application of the true Islam. In all cases, constitutional regime meant government by *şura* or *meşveret* (consultation).

Shortly, *Sırat-ı Müstakim's* writers showed their intolerance of the new views on womanhood, education, religious institutions, language, and the alphabet. Their first bogies were the Westernists, but later they found themselves in the gunsights of both the Westernists and the Turkists.

The outstanding figure among the Islamists was the poet Mehmed Âkif (1870-1936).[9] No one has given better expression than he to the feelings of a man throbbing with Islamist sentiments. His long poem "Sermon from the Süleymaniye Pulpit" (1912) deserves summarization as a survey of the problems of the Islamic world. It is told as from the mouth of Âkif's friend Abdurreşid Ibrahim (1853-1943), the pan-Islamic traveller from Turkestan.[10]

The "Sermon" begins with a description of Islam in Turkey and Asia during the Hamidian period. Everywhere Islam was followed blindly by its adherents. The traveller found only the Muslims of India deserving his praise. He was greatly impressed by the Islamic zeal and idealism he met there. India's youth, though educated in England, did not, like Turkish youth, ape the West. Surely such a nation would win independence one day! However, throughout the East, he found his ideal only in Japan. He tried to explain why the Japanese advanced so successfully: the Japanese had appropriated all the good aspects of Islam in the form of Buddhism! How did Western civilization fail to corrupt this essentially Islamic ethic of the Japanese? The answer was self-evident: the Japanese took only the science and techniques of the West; they rejected the superficialities imitated by the Muslims. Upon the proclamation of the Meşrutiyet in Turkey, the traveller had interrupted his visit to Hyderabad and returned to Turkey believing that the day of

---

[9] The best study of Âkif is by F. A. Tansel, *Mehmed Âkif* (Istanbul, 1945); Eşref Edib, ed., *Mehmed Âkif* (Istanbul, 1938), is a collection of writings by his admirers. Emin Erişirgil, *Mehmet Âkif: Islâmcı Bir Şairin Romanı* (Ankara, 1956), suffers from an effort to make Âkif a hero, but otherwise provides valuable observations.

[10] In his *Âsım*, vol. IV of his collected poems *Safahat*, written in 1919 (Istanbul, n.d.).

awakening, of true restoration of Islam had come. He returned to find the politicians fighting each other like bandits. Some attacked religion because they were atheists, others because they believed in freedom of conscience. In Âkif's view the two positions were identical. His dreams shattered, he rushed to the pulpit of the Suleymaniye Mosque to deliver a sermon, crying: Awake! This nation cannot endure another struggle; the Muslims cannot survive with nationalistic divisions. Look at what has happened to the others;

Look at Morocco, Tunisia, Algeria—
They are all gone!
Iran—they are dividing it too!
This is most natural, the field is the runner's
The right to live was given to the strong by God.
Muslims! a nation afflicted with factional dissent,
Will civilized Europe not eat them in three bites?
O community, if only for God's sake, awake!

The chief cause of the ills, the preacher explained, was the existence of a gap between the intellectuals and the masses. While the intellectuals found the remedy in imitating the West, the common people found the introduction of European methods the cause of their decline. Could there be genuine progress in a country where such a rift existed? The intellectuals believed that all nations follow the same road to progress. They believed the religion of the people to be an obstacle to progress. They should look for the progressive spirit of Islam in the past, in the early days of Islam—the mere contemplation of which carried the preacher into a near trance. There was one final error: failure to see that progress is attainable only through evolution! Look to Japan for proof of this! A nation is a tree with roots in the past. Don't let the woodsmen cut the tree to cure the blight!

In the following chapter we will repeatedly encounter Mehmed Âkif's views on the controversial issues as typifying the Islamist outlook.

THE TURKISTS

The third group, the Turkists, the first exponents of Turkish nationalism, appeared later than the other two groups, yet grew rapidly in spite of the resistance they encountered and the heterogenity of their sources. Turkism originated as a movement of thought concerned primarily with the problems of reform in

344

Ottoman Turkey and as a response to the Westernist and Islamist lines of thinking on the same problems. As the term Turkism was later used indiscriminately and in confusion with pan-Turkism and even pan-Turanism, we must bear in mind that there were differences while, however, remembering that the terms overlapped at points.

The Turkist school of thought originated in Turkey and, following a weak appearance during the last two decades of the Hamidian rule, came forward first in Salonika with the movement called the New Life. The term Turkism began to be used by a group which came out of the New Life movement and was influenced by the pan-Turkists coming from Russia.[11] The change began to take shape during the discussions among a number of intellectuals who gathered around two reviews published simultaneously in Salonika. One was a literary review called *Genç Kalemler* (Young Pens), the other was a sociological-philosophical review called *Yeni Felsefe Mecmuasi* (New Philosophical Review).

The original group held regular meetings where the reform problems of Turkey were discussed. The participants showed two separate tendencies. There were those who took a critical, rationalistic, radical approach with marked (utopian) socialist tendencies. Those in this group wrote their articles around the ideas of the European, mostly utopian, socialists. Then there were those

[11] In terms of origin, aim, and duration, there were differences between Turkism, pan-Turkism, and pan-Turanism. The last two had their origins outside Turkey—one in Russia, the other in Hungary; one was aimed against Czarist rule, the other against pan-Slavism. During World War I, both, together with pan-Islamism, were sponsored by Germany as a propaganda device against Russia and Great Britain for reasons best explained in a series of articles to *The Times* (Jan. 3, 5, and 7, 1918) believed to have been written by A. J. Toynbee.

Turkism was presented to the Western readers as identical with pan-Turkism by a Tekin Alp, the alias of Moses Cohen, in *Türkismus und Pantürkismus* (Weimar, 1915). The second part of this propaganda tract appeared first in Turkish as M. Cohen, *Türkler Bu Muharebede Ne Kazanabilirler?* (Istanbul, 1914). Tekin Alp seems to have been presented as "a profoundly informed Turk" by Mr. Churchill and as the originator of pan-Turkism by others; see C. W. Hostler, *Turkism and the Soviets* (London, 1957), p. 115. His German book was translated into English as *The Turkish and Pan-Turkish Ideal* (March, 1917) by the Admiralty War Staff Intelligence Division and labelled *Secret*. He has occasionally been taken for Gökalp and vice versa by persons unaccustomed to the Turkish names; however, Mr. Cohen is a businessman of Istanbul who played no part in any of the major intellectual currents.

who manifested a romantic, idealist, and nationalist tendency; they were likewise preoccupied in their articles with European idealistic philosophies.

Turkism was the further development of this second tendency within the New Life movement. The Turkist approach differed from both the Westernist and Islamist approaches although it borrowed many elements from both. In a sense it was a synthesis of the two, although none of the original basic tenets remained unchanged.

The man who turned the New Life movement into Turkism was Ziya Gökalp.[12] His approach to the problems of his times was already established before he moved from Salonika to Istanbul in 1912 and came into contact with the pan-Turkist nationalists.

The pan-Turkists had emigrated mostly from Russia. They had already established nationalist organs and organizations, and were collaborating with the Islamists. The most prominent among them were Yusuf Akçura, Ahmed Agayev (later Ağaoğlu), and Halim Sabit. The pan-Turkists were not necessarily Turkists on the questions of reform; they could be Westernists or even Islamists. On the understanding of nationality particularly, there was a substantial difference between the pan-Turkists and Gökalp's Turkism. For the first, nationality meant race; for the second, it meant culture.

For Gökalp, the Turkish nation would come into existence as a result of the breakdown of the Islamic *ümmet* under the impact of the modern technology of Western civilization, whose constituent elements were democratic, secular nationalities. There were Turks but not as yet a Turkish nation. Although he reiterated this view later, Gökalp and his reviews were influenced considerably by the pan-Turkists, especially when the latter were at their peak during World War I.

Gökalp observed that just as the Westernists were bent on imitating the West and the Islamists on reviving ancient Islam, so the pan-Turkists sought to revive the dead ethnic customs of the pre-Islamic Turks. For him, a nation was neither a collection of individuals united by the common ties of modern economy and technology, nor an *ümmet*, a religious community united in the faith of Islam, nor a race or ethnic family united by archaic, tribal

---

12 About his life and work see Uriel Heyd, *Foundations of Turkish Nationalism* (London, 1950); Ziya Gökalp, *Turkish Nationalism and Western Civilization*, ed. and trans. Niyazi Berkes (London and New York, 1959), Introduction.

346

customs. Nationality was different from all three in such a way that it could neither be reduced to any one nor compounded from all of them. As a whole it transcended all three by certain attributes that could be found in none of the constituent elements. These attributes were to be discovered in what Gökalp called national ideals, the ultimate objectives toward which the nation aspired.

Turkism was merged with pan-Turkism through the nationalist society called the Turkish Hearth (*Türk Ocağı*), founded in 1912, and the review called *Türk Yurdu* (The Turkish Homeland), established in 1911.

Three Proposed Roads to Reconstruction | *chapter 12*

THE CONTROVERSIES of the Westernists, Islamists, and Turkists may be reviewed best in terms of a list of problems drawn from the literature of 1908-18. The predominant issues were: (1) the quest for a revolutionary change; (2) the causes of the Turkish, or Muslim decline; (3) Western civilization and the scope for Westernization in the reforms; and (4) the reform of the institutions of state, religion, family, economy, education, and the complex of language, script, literature, and art. The first three issues will be discussed in the present chapter; the balance in Chapter 13.

Quest for a Revolutionary Change

Even before 1908 there were those who felt that a change of government would be only the prelude to social reform. The Westernists spearheaded the common quest for a social transformation (*içtimaî inkilâp*), by which they meant the reforms to be made in the major social institutions as well as in the moral values and attitudes of mind so as to produce a total transformation. The pan-Turkist Yusuf Akçura repeated that the real aim of the 1908 Revolution should be a social revolution rather than the mere restoration of the constitutional regime,[1] while his colleague, Ahmed Agayev, said, "the Revolution has been . . . only military

---

[1] Yusuf Akçura, *Içtihad* (Cairo, 1909), p. 9.

347

and political and confined to the educated classes. The people of different social classes are still living and thinking in their old ways."[2] The intellectuals around Ziya Gökalp in Salonika were also busy searching for the New Life to be built upon scientific bases. Even the Islamists expressed the view that what had been done was only to remove the stumbling block to progress: Turkish society would be reformed thoroughly—according to the principles of Islam that had been forgotten under un-Islamic tyrannies.

Although they agreed that the restoration of the constitutional regime was only a beginning, the three schools differed with regard to the direction and nature of the social revolution.

Causes of Decline

The first question on which the groups disagreed was one that would determine all of their subsequent views. That was the question of the cause, or causes, of the decline. Why did the Turks, or Muslims, remain stagnant and lag behind the European nations?[3]

Içtihad's answer to the question was simple:

It is nothing other than our own Asiatic minds . . . our own degenerate traditions and institutions. . . . The power that is defeating us is none other than our own eyes which do not want to see, our brains which do not know how to think. . . . These are the forces that have defeated us, that are defeating us, and that will always defeat us.[4]

The Westernists, thus, found the explanation in the intellectual barrier keeping the Muslims from understanding both their own ills and Western civilization. This mental barrier, according to them, was created by Islam; the domination of the Şeriat over all departments of life was at the base of all the backwardness.

The Islamists of the post-1908 generation took a diametrically opposite view although, unlike their immediate predecessors, they

[2] Ahmed Agayev [Ağaoğlu], *Sırat-ı Müstakim*, No. 113 (Istanbul, 1910).

[3] What were the causes of the decline of the Muslims? What are the most efficient means of delivering the Muslims from the state of decline? These were questions asked by *Içtihad* in a questionnaire to which a number of European and Muslin writers responded. See *Içtihad*, No. 1 and the subsequent issues (Geneva, 1904).

[4] *Iştihad* (the successor of *Içtihad*, which had been suppressed by the government), No. 114 (1914).

agreed that the Muslims were far behind the West not only in their material civilization, but also in their non-material civilization including religion and religious institutions. The decline, they said, was due not to Islam, or to the influence of the Şeriat, but rather to the fact that the Şeriat was not applied and had not been made to cover every department and detail of life. Declared one of their secularly educated spokesmen, Said Halim Paşa (1863-1921):

> No religion has ever been an obstacle to progress. Christianity did not prevent the Europeans from achieving progress; neither was Buddhism an obstacle to the Japanese. This is even more true of Islam. Because Islam is a rational religion. The best proof is the heights reached by the Islamic civilization in the past.[5]

Said Halim went on to deny that fanaticism was the cause of decline and to assert, "The term 'Muslim fanaticism' implies, in reality, not the Muslims' enmity towards Christians, but the West's inherent enmity towards the East."[6]

The new Islamists borrowed their diagnoses basically from the Egyptian Modernists, although there were Turkish Muslim models available. In one of his writings, Said Halim declared,

> Between the influences of pre-Islamic institutions and of Islam itself there came into being such an unchanging equilibrium as to be a constant fetter to progress. To ensure the progress of Muslim nations, it is necessary to upset that equilibrium by increasing the influence of Islam at the expense of the other.[7]

By this he meant that national traditions had remained alive among the non-Arab Muslims and, consequently, their Islamization (or Arabization) had remained incomplete. Unable to realize the

---

[5] Muḥammad [Said Halim], *Inḥitat-ı Islâm Hakkında Bir Tecrübe-i Kalemiye* (Istanbul, 1918), p. 10. Said Halim was the grandson of Mehmet Ali of Egypt. In 1913 he became the Sadrazam, to serve until 1916. He was imprisoned by the British at Malta after the termination of World War I, and was shot by the Armenian nationalists in Rome after his release from Malta. His writings, which were published when he was in office, appeared under his first and little-known name, Muhammed. They were probably translated into Turkish from French by Mehmed Âkif, as the Sadrazam could not write in Turkish. At a time when the Turkish Government was accused of pursuing a policy of Turkification, its Sadrazam was an ardent Islamist who wrote only in French and Arabic.

[6] Muḥammad [Said Halim], *Taassub* (Istanbul, 1917), p. 13.

[7] This and the following quotations are from *Inḥitat-ı Islâm*, pp. 6-18.

danger of these survivals, they had distorted Islam itself. On the track of this, the incessant enmity of Christianity had curtailed Muslim progress, led to the subjugation of the Islamic world, and produced the contemporary lack of unity among Muslims—following the initial blow of the Mongol (implicitly Turkish) invasions. When the Muslims had been plunged into endless metaphysical disputation following their contact with Christianity (implicitly philosophy), the Christians had benefited and developed the experimental sciences. The crisis in Islam had been noted first when Muslims began to fall under the Western yoke; the appearance of a universal decline gave the Christians the impression that Islam was the source of the Muslims' backwardness. Such a generalization befitted the age-old Christian enmity, obscured the real fault, and gave religious colouring to the matter among Muslims as well. Influenced by Christian antipathy, some attributed the decline to tyranny, some to the ignorance of the *ulema,* some to the neglect of religion, and some to religious fanaticism. "The innumerable varieties and conflicts among these opinions should teach us that the confusion reigning in our minds has curtailed our capacity to distinguish and discover the causes of our decline."

Contemporary Muslims, Said Halim wrote, could not progress under Western domination. The West had succeeded in imposing the view that the Muslims could progress only by becoming like itself. From this arose the gap between the "Westernists who aspire to establish new principles based exclusively upon Western theories and convictions" and the "religious nationalists [Islamists] who pursue the policy of Islamization in Persia, India, Egypt, and Turkey." "These extreme worshippers of the West mistake borrowing from the West for Westernization" and appeal only to the intellectuals while the Islamists enjoy the support of the common Muslims. The gap between the two attitudes is itself an impediment to progress. The failure of present-day Muslims to see what should and should not be taken from the West is the same as the failure of Muslims in the past to understand what of their pre-Islamic heritages ought to have been eliminated.

Said Halim couched his answer to the Westernists in terms of comparison between Christianity and Islam. He found Islam superior in political, moral, and social matters. The remedy, therefore, lay not in Westernizing, but in Islamizing—in more complete Islamization than ever before. This was neither fanaticism, nor ignorance. "It is a logical consequence of Islam."

Ziya Gökalp's criticism of Said Halim's thesis illustrates the Turkist etiology of the decline:

If ethnic traditions and survivals were the cause of the decline of Islam, they would have evinced their effect from the beginning. . . . One should seek the causes of decline, not in ethnic traditions whose most powerful influences existed coincidentally with the Islamization of these nations, but in the events occurring immediately before the appearance of the signs of decline.

351

A nation may be destroyed by an external power, but may not be caused to decline by it. The existence of the challenge of a mortal enemy is, to the contrary, one of the stimuli to the revival and progress of a nation. It is, therefore, again wrong to point to the Crusades as the cause of the decline of Islam. The Crusades caused the revival and progress of Christian Europe. Why, then, does one and the same event cause decline in one and progress in the other? Especially if we remember that the world of Islam was then in the prime of its civilization? . . . The West . . . did not show fanaticism in imitating and borrowing the achievements of the Muslims of the time. . . . Why, then, did we show fanaticism when their civilization has excelled ours?[8]

The causes of decline, therefore, lay neither in the impact of external forces (Mongol, Crusade, and modern European domination), nor in the survival of the pre-Islamic institutions. The Muslims declined, explained Gökalp, first because of their disregard for the changes in their conditions of life and their refusal to recognize that religion had to be interpreted in terms of the new conditions in order to maintain a living significance. The reason for the fanaticism shown toward the Western civilization when it appeared as a superior civilization again lay here. A second cause was the loss of the national culture through Islam's tendency to superimpose itself as a civilization at the expense of the national cultures.

[8] *Yeni Mecmua*, II, No. 40 (1918), 275. This article does not carry Gökalp's signature; it should be remembered that Said Halim was the Sadrazam of the government of the party of Union and Progress and that Gökalp was a member of the central committee of the same party!

Western Civilization and Westernization

352

As all three schools proceeded on the assumption that all the problems of social change were occasioned by the impact of Western civilization, it was inevitable that, in the discussions concerning the modernization of Turkish society, views concerning that civilization would figure prominently. Needless to say, each group attributed to the West what it liked or disliked; what each group was analyzing was, in reality, not the West itself (which was only an image, an abstract, that was never studied objectively), but its own social condition as seen through its ideological judgments.

The Westernists regarded the West as the best of all possible worlds. Western civilization meant not only unprecedented material achievements but also a completely different mode of thinking. The material achievements of Western civilization were only manifestations of Western ideas and values. Without adopting the cultural and intellectual foundations of the West, neither social reform nor Westernization could occur. The imported elements would be distorted and would not fit in with the old values and ideas.

Thus, the Westernists were, surprisingly, more concerned with the appropriation of the non-material aspects of Western civilization than with acquiring its material aspects. Individual freedom as against suppression of the individual by the state or religion, reason as against the domination of custom and superstition, the application of the scientific mind as against ignorance—these were the basic differentials, and the powers enabling the West to make an impact on the East.

The West meant Christianity to the Islamists more than anything else. As such, the West was not only different from Islam but also incompatible with it. As Halil Halit wrote: "The West and the Islamic East have been diametrically opposed to one another on almost every point of life, sentiment, and morality since the beginnings of the Crusades."[9] Hence, talk of Westernization for the Muslim nations in the sense in which the Westernists understood the term could only mean the renunciation of the very principles of Islam.

[9] Halil Halit, "Avrupaya Talebe Izami Hakkında," *Sırat-ı Müstakim,* No. 89 (1910).

The Islamists of this period admitted unhesitatingly the superiority of Western sciences and techniques. Not once after the fall of the Hamidian regime did an Islamist claim that the Islamic or Arab sciences were superior to those of the West. No Islamist, not even an ordinary citizen, paused before going to a physician trained in Western medicine, but such was the only concession made by the Islamists. The material civilization of the West was still secondary in their discussions; borrowing it continued to be viewed by them as a simple matter that did not involve cultural, social, or religious reforms. The modern sciences were viewed as only quantitatively different from the so-called Arab sciences. When not ignored, the philosophical and religious battles, the political and economic revolutions that had accompanied the birth and progress of modern science and technology were seen as proofs of the Islamist belief that modern science was not a product of the Christian civilization of the West, but the product of a struggle against it, that is, a further proof of the superiority of the "rational religion of Islam."

Despite having said initially that no religion was an obstacle to progress, Said Halim took quite a different tack as he warmed to his subject. Religion had been an obstacle to the progress of science in the West because of an inherent contradiction between Christianity and modern science. The situation was different in Islam because, being a "rational" religion, Islam enjoined science; it did not regard science as inimical to faith. Furthermore, the very nature of the problems of the Western and Islamic civilizations were basically different. The quest for democracy, for example, had been a great social problem and struggle in the West because, according to Said Halim,

Western society was based on inequality and class difference. . . . Secondly, Western society was ruled basically by feudal lords, kings, and emperors or oligarchs, hence, the prevalence of fanaticism and absolutism against which the struggle for freedom had to be waged. That is why Western society was torn with social questions. Islam, on the other hand, was egalitarian and based on individual freedom. Hence, there was no question of democracy and no want of freedom in Islam.[10]

Imagining the existence of such social questions in Islam was simply blind imitation. Attempting to transplant the West's remedies to its own ills, such as constitutional systems, legislative bodies, parlia-

[10] Said Halim, *Buhranlarımız* (2nd ed.; Istanbul, 1919), pp. 18-19.

354

mentarianism, was not only meaningless, but would even be harm-ful to the full self-realization of Islam. Islam, this prince and Paşa believed, did not need such institutions, symptoms of inherent Western weakness. The same was true, chimed Mihriddin Arusî, of the other ills of Western civilization such as communism and socialism.[11] Such movements existed in the West because Western society was inherently afflicted with social ills from which Islam was free.

One of the relatively enlightened members of the group, Salâ-haddin Âsım, believed that the West was morally degenerate and wrote:

> European behaviour is utterly contrary not only to Islam, but also
> to the principles of any social life. . . . What painful wounds
> the European civil laws have opened on social life in terms of morals
> and ethics is obvious. . . . It is true that we have . . . to benefit from
> European civilization, industry, and knowledge; and yet it is
> absolutely imperative for us . . . not to allow their customs, morals,
> and conduct to enter into our countries.

> To reform society into a state in which all humanity would benefit
> and happiness would be attained will be possible only by applying
> the sacred provisions of the Şeriat. If we ever run our affairs
> according to European principles, the moral degeneration which
> has fallen upon them will be inevitable for us.[12]

Some Islamist writers sensed that there was a view of religion in the West different from that of medieval Christianity. Wrote one, for example, "The Europeans understand by religion merely certain morals and ethical rules and reduce religion to them." But, in the Islamists' view, this was wrong

> because ethical rules never had the capacity to regulate a civil
> society. . . . The decline of Christianity in proportion to the progress
> of the material civilization is due to this concept of religion. . . .
> Those who always seek truth only in the writings of Europeans
> have begun to believe that, like Christianity, Islam consists of a code
> of morality. Thus, they think that the more the people are enlightened
> by education, the more Islam will weaken and decline. . . . The
> truth is to the contrary. The more education and enlightenment
> spread among the Muslims, the more their faith will become

[11] Mihriddin Arusî (pseud.?), *Yirminci Asırda Âlem-i İslâm ve Avrupa* (Istanbul, 1911), pp. 86-87.

[12] *Sırat-ı Müstakim*, No. 28 (1908) and No. 32 (1909).

strong, and the niceties of the Islamic provisions as well as the sublimity of Islam will unfold to them proportionately.[13]

The idea that science and religion were incompatible in the West, that the first grew at the expense of the second, and that this led to the reduction of religion to certain moral precepts which were insufficient to maintain society, gave way to one of the favourite beliefs of the Islamists: the West is dominating the world not because of the superiority of its religion, not even because of the superiority of its sciences, but because of the secular morality that has taken the place of religion and sanctioned the unscrupulous desire to exploit and enslave other nations. Hence came the Islamist conception of the West as a bestial civilization.

In short, what the Westernists believed to be the distinguishing mark of Western civilization and the aspect most worthy of emulation—the separation of life from the domination of religion—was the very aspect for which the West should be rejected according to the Islamists.

The Turkist attitude to the West, or rather to the Western Question, was different from the rationalist and intellectualist approach of the Westernists, and from the religious approach of the Islamists. Consequently the Turkists were neither anti-West nor pro-West or, to put it another way, they were as pro-Western as any Westernist and as anti-Western as any Islamist. They accepted both attitudes, but only partially.

The Turkists agreed with what the Westernists said about the role of the mind and reason. The West had produced a type of society and civic morality that was essentially different from those of both medieval Christendom and the Islamic *ümmet*. However, the Westernists failed to identify the true nature of the West. European civilization was an international community of modern nations which were distinguished from each other by their national cultures. The basic reality of the modern Western civilization was not reason or humanity, but nationalism in which even religion played a part. This was because in the present world only nations were cultural realities. To join modern civilization, as the Western nations had, was, therefore, a matter of appropriating the international civilization, but not the national cultures of the Western nations. The Westernist view was not only deceptive but also dangerous for the development of Turkish nationhood.

[13] Fehmi, *Hikmet-i Hukuk-u Islâmiye* (Istanbul, 1913).

The Turkists found the Islamist view equally untenable unless it was seen in terms of nationalist categories. The West certainly was not, but might truly become, humanitarian and international. This would be possible only when non-Western and non-Christian nations were accepted into its fold after they had reached the stage of joining Western civilization by becoming true nations. Nationalism meant Westernism only in this sense.[14]

356

Balkan Wars Spur More Controversies

The reactions invoked by the Balkan Wars illustrated concretely the three attitudes towards the West. While the Westernists were singing the praises of European civilization, the attitudes and machinations of the European powers gave confirmation to the beliefs of the Islamists and Turkists.

The Islamist press raised its pitch an octave at each martial gesture of the West against the Ottoman Empire. By the eve of World War I, it had top score for condemning European civilization, abusing the Westernists, and bewailing the fate of Islam. It announced assuredly that the Christian West was launching a global assault against the world of Islam.[15]

The Westernists interpreted the reverses suffered by the Empire as the fulfilment of their own earlier claims. Abdullah Cevdet wrote on the occasion of the Tripolitanian War,

The calamity was due to our ignorance, slumber, unpreparedness, and backwardness, and worse events are awaiting us if we do not come to our senses. The war with Italy is only the outward, tangible aspect of another and real war. We are, in reality, waging the most merciless warfare with other enemies, and are being defeated in it incessantly, with greater defeats every minute. To understand this it is sufficient to look at the customs statistics, to study the financial and educational establishments of the [European] Powers in Turkey.[16]

---

[14] See Ziya Gökalp, *Turkish Nationalism and Western Civilization*, ed. and trans. Niyazi Berkes (London and New York, 1959), Chaps. 3 and 5.

[15] Mehmed Âkif, "Vaaz" (Sermon), *Sebil-ür Reşat*, IX, No. 232 (1912).

[16] *İçtihad*, No. 32 (1911).

The Balkan Wars aroused a more forceful expression from the same writer. When he learned that the Şeyhul-Islâm had issued a circular to all the Turkish schools ordering each child to repeat an Arabic prayer 4,444 times that God might help the Turkish soldiers, he exploded:

Have we gone mad? The Bulgarians have made the best of prayers; they have worked day and night for thirty-one years. They have prepared the means of their victory and they deserved it.[17]

Not many Westernists were as steadfast as Abdullah Cevdet. The shock of the Balkan defeat was so intense that even Cevdet's close colleague Celâl Nuri revolted: "I am incapable," he wrote,

of explaining our plight further. The whole world is our enemy. . . . The whole world of infidels! Friendship for the West is the vilest of all crimes I can imagine. A nation incapable of hating the West is doomed to extinction.[18]

Abdullah Cevdet wrote, perhaps, his bitterest article in reply. He said, in part:

This tragedy like all our tragedies, all those colossal and successive tragedies of the world of Islam, is due to that cult of hatred. . . . This religious hatred diffused into all of our affairs. . . . We deemed every good thing coming from them bad. *We* are the culprits of all our plights. *We* are to be accused. . . . The relation between Europe and us is the relation between strength and weakness, between science and ignorance. . . . A nation that has borne the whims of a tyrant like Abdül-Hamid II for thirty years . . . must first and foremost declare hatred for its own ignorance and weakness. Yes, Europe means supremacy; let hatred for it be far from me. My hatred is turned against those things that are the obstacles to our attaining power equal to that of Europe. . . . Our plight is not due to our lack of hatred of foreigners. . . . Our mortal enemy is our own inertia, ignorance, fanaticism, and our own blind following of tradition. . . . The West is our teacher; to love it is to love science, progress, material and moral advancement. . . . To be an industrious and thankful disciple of the West—that is our lot! . . . To believe that the entire world is our enemy and that the world of Christianity is working against us is a symptom of a persecution mania. The West slapped Japan only once; it awakened. We have been slapped a thousand times; if we are still not awake, is it the

[17] *Ibid.*, No. 54 (1912).

[18] Celâl Nuri, "Şime-i Husumet," *İçtihad*, No. 88 (1913).

West's fault? . . . We have been so accustomed to despising the non-Muslim nations, that we do not take seriously the most brilliant victories scored against us. . . . Let us face the mirror and look at ourselves courageously. Let us look and take countenance if we have the heart. And let us put the mirror before the noses of those who do not want to look at it. Enough of seeing ourselves in convex mirrors. . . . We have to understand one thing—there are not two civilizations, there is only one to which to turn, and that is Western civilization, which we must take into our hands whether it be rosy or thorny. . . .[19]

358

The Balkan Wars brought about a rapprochement between the pan-Turkists and the Turkists. They also furnished Gökalp and his disciple Fuat Köprülü with an opportunity to point out that Turkism did not mean breaking away from the Islamic international community. More people began to understand what nationalism meant and more people began to look around for co-religionists or co-racials. As M. Cohen, alias Tekin Alp, said, "With the loss of Salonika and Rumelia, the Turks turned their faces to Turan."[20]

The Balkan defeat was received by the Turkists not with a religious outcry, but as a spur to national regeneration. Kâzım Nami, one of the early Turkists, wrote:

We understand the scope of our backwardness better. We must begin all over again, starting with criticizing ourselves. The greatest service we can render to our country is to scrutinize our faults in minute detail and to see how to correct them.[21]

Akçura declared,

We have been defeated. The Bulgar, the Serb, the Greek—our subjects of five centuries, whom we have despised, have defeated us. This reality, which we could not conjure up even in our imaginations, will open our eyes, will serve as a terrific slap in our faces to turn our heads in sane directions—if we are not yet entirely dead.[22]

---

[19] Abdullah Cevdet, "Şime-i Muhabbet," İçtihad, No. 89 (1913).

[20] Tekin Alp [Moses Cohen] Türkismus und Pantürkismus (Weimar, 1915), p. 15; English trans., The Turkish and Pan-Turkish Ideal (London, 1917), p. 13.

[21] Kâzım Nami [Duru], "Yeni Hayata Doğru," Türk Yurdu, III, No. 2 (1912), 45.

[22] Ibid., III, No. 2 (1912), 62.

Islamization, Turkification, and Westernization

The Balkan Wars brought again into consciousness the urgency
of the major task—the launching of radical social reforms. This
inevitably roused and intensified the controversy over the relative
proportions of Western, Islamic, and nationalistic elements to be
fused into the new measures.

Controversy was revived when the Islamists admitted that the
"good and useful" aspects of the West should be adopted with all
haste and asked, "But is there not the danger that the 'bad' might
slip in while one is trying to take the 'good'? Worse yet, might
not one mistake the 'bad' for the 'good'? What would be the effects
of the intruding 'bad' upon the Islamic [in reality, traditional]
institutions?"

Musa Kâzım explained what was "good" in the West thus: "We
have to adopt only the sciences (*ilim*) and the industries (*fen*) of
Europe, in the manner of the Japanese."[23] But, as the Islamists had
no conception of science other than the so-called traditional
sciences, and naturally did not appreciate in what way and in
which contexts the modern experimental sciences differed from
the medieval sciences (Eastern or Western), they tended to think
that taking over the European sciences and techniques was a
mechanical matter something like acquiring knowledge at the feet
of a master, as a *mullah* did. "Seek knowledge, even if it is in
Europe!" became a current Islamist aphorism.

However, the Islamists, especially Said Halim, stressed the need
to be very careful in borrowing so as to avoid confusing good and
bad. The Islamists sensed that even the good aspects of the West
held certain intrinsic dangers for religion, hence, they pondered
deeply over this problem. A writer for *Sırat* expressed the common
view saying:

This dictum must be kept in view at all times: to preserve our
oriental and Islamic civilization! . . . European civilization is of no
use to us. It is true that Europe has reached perfection today
from the standpoint of science. No one can deny that. But, that
civilization does no good for mankind from a moral standpoint. Thus,
one must pick the rose, and beware the thorns! Unfortunately,
we are taking up their moral vices before getting their sciences. . . .

[23] *Sırat-ı Müstakim*, No. 7 (1908).

If we must send our youth to Europe, we should send them only after having taught them our own customs and morality. . . . We are orientals and we shall always remain so.[24]

360

The possible dangers of sending students to the West for study were a peculiar concern of the Islamists. Halil Halit wrote amusingly from his alma mater Cambridge, where he was employed:

The new regime has dispatched new groups of students to Europe. Who will take care of the influences exerted upon their morals? During the Hamidian regime students were not sent to Europe because it was believed that it would create spiritual anarchy among the youth. Now it is very likely that the students sent abroad will become the means of disseminating ideas likely to shake our religious-national morality to its foundations and will disseminate irreligiosity or hatred for Islam.[25]

In illustration of careless appropriations from the West, correspondents of *Sırat* reported actually seeing *photographs* of Muslim students in Europe wearing *hats*! This, they said, was behaviour contrary to the Şeriat and Islamic morality.[26] Halil Halit reported that a government supervisor of students abroad had openly discussed "the fantastic idea of adopting the Latin alphabet when talking to Professor E. G. Browne." Musa Kâzım warned once more:

Imitating a country's sciences and techniques does not . . . necessarily imply imitating its morals, customs, and mode of living, as there is no conceivable relationship between the two. Every country has its own peculiar mode of living and customs. But no country and no nation has its own industry, techniques, and sciences. These are common everywhere and to all men. . . . What we need is, by taking the Japanese as our model, to acquire these from Europe with the utmost speed while avoiding imitation of European customs, morals, and mode of living. . . .[27]

Mehmed Âkif thus stated the same idea:

Those who want to introduce change must know that in matters susceptible to imitation there must be a social affinity between the imitated society and its imitators. If there is not, the second

[24] Piriştineli Kadri, "Dinsizlik," *Sırat-ı Müstakim*, No. 95 (1911).
[25] Halil Halit, "Avrupaya Talebe Izamı Hakkında."
[26] *Sırat-ı Müstakim*, No. 57 (1909); also No. 94 (1910).
[27] *Ibid.*, No. 7 (1908).

dissolves and is absorbed by the first. There is no such social affinity between our society and that which we want to imitate. But that is not the case as regards matters of techniques, because such matters are transmitted by imitation.[28]

The Japanese case of borrowing European sciences and techniques was the Islamists' favourite example. "Why did Japan benefit more from sending students abroad than Turkey?" asked Halil Halit. "Because we have failed to determine the safe path in borrowing knowledge and skill form the West." All believed that the Japanese knew what to imitate and borrow and what to reject and retain. The view that Japanese Buddhism was almost identical with the "real" Islam was even echoed in a myth current among the people.

What, then, would be the area of life in Islam that would be safeguarded against the intrusion of foreign elements? Since Islam was the core that distinguished the life of Muslims from that of Europeans, the logical answer would be, "Anything that has not been covered by the Şeriat of Islam is open to change and replacement from any culture that is found superior in that respect." In spite of the docility and progressiveness of the Islamists at this period, we find them unable to give a simple answer. On the contrary, they persistently sought arguments for enlarging the scope of the Şeriat to cover areas of life that were traditionally regarded as outside the Şeriat.

Though never expressed openly or clearly, it was the area of Turkish life lying outside the Şeriat that was actually being affected by the so-called material civilization of the West. The Islamists did not concede that this area was really of indifference to the Şeriat and therefore subject to change. They knew that what they were protecting under the cover of the Şeriat was, in fact, a far larger area of life than was covered by the Şeriat. The real Şeriat, they knew, was shielded by a thick cultural crust containing elements ranging from the form of government to the mode of cleaning one's teeth. This crust was nothing but what we may call custom, usage, and taste that had taken variant shapes in different Muslim countries. The Islamists were aware that this "cake of custom" must be kept intact because if it were once cut into, the Şeriat's turn would soon come.

This apprehension was the real motive underlying the Islamists' fast surrender on the question of a quick imitation of the European

[28] *Ibid.*, No. 3 (1908).

sciences and techniques. Again, this was at the base of their admiration for the Japanese; Japan was an excellent example of the preservation of traditional customs that had, by Islamic standards, not the slightest religious sanctioning.

362

The first clue to an Islamic formula was given by Musa Kâzım. He proposed a rule for demarcating between the areas of life within which Westernization was and was not permissible. According to him, *'urf* (mores) would have the force of *nass* (injunctions given in sacred texts) on matters concerning which there was no *nass*; as *'urf* is related not only to the *mu'âmalât* (matters of civil law), but also to all parts of living, the *mu'âmalât* would also be encompassed by the Şeriat. Ergo, Westernization was impermissible, even in matters of custom that were thought to be outside the Şeriat. Thus, the wearing of European hats by students sent abroad was impermissible, although the Seriat said nothing for or against the practice. Wearing the fez was, in reality, also outside the concerns of the Şeriat, but wearing the fez had become customary while wearing the hat meant to take a new bite out of the "cake of custom"; the customs, in the absence of *nass* concerning that to which they referred, were equal to *nass*, hence, the Şeriat would not allow wearing the hat and would enjoin the wearing of the fez.

It was this line of thinking that made some of the Islamists cautious about opening the doors to the European sciences and techniques. Their hesitation and emphasis on discrimination concerned the contamination of faith by the Western science. Western sciences tended to make people deny religion. In other words, according to their logic, the progress of science in the West did not follow the decline of religion but rather the reverse. This condition was tolerable in Christianity, because Christianity had divided the world and religion into separate departments. Christianity would see no harm in science's spreading irreligiosity. In Islam, on the other hand, irreligiosity carried an entirely different meaning. Doubt, if it was the beginning of philosophy and science, was the deadliest enemy of faith. As faith encompassed all of life as well as afterlife, breaking down one corner of this system would bring the whole to ruin.

The acquisition of Western sciences, therefore, always presented a thorny dilemma to the Islamists. They wrote a great deal of confused literature on the subject. A writer for *Sebil* stated:

> The progress of science in Europe damaged religion. . . . The decline in religion is no longer confined to Europe because of the

advancement of civilization. Through the various means of civilization, such as telegraph, post, railways, and steamships, it is contaminating every corner of the world. The Ottoman lands, being geographically closer to Europe and becoming even closer as a result of the new means of communication and transportation, are not left untouched by the spread of atheism brought by science. However, unlike other religions, the religion of Islam, which God bestowed upon us, is immune from melting under the bright sun of science. . . . What we need is to prove, by comparing the shining truths of our religion with the lights of science, that these lights were born of these truths.[29]

363

One way of saving oneself from the dangers of Western science was to believe that the Kant-Laplace or Darwinian theories were contained in the Kur'an. Lesser Islamist lights went even further and derived the atom, electricity, microbiology, etc., from the Kur'an and the traditions relating to the Prophet (*hadîth*).

The Islamists' tendency to throw the protective cloak of the Şeriat over the entire complex of custom was in accordance with their program of Islamization. Social reform would be achieved by rescuing custom from deterioration, by putting even its details under the sacred sanction of religion. Social behaviour and relationships would, thus, be thoroughly Islamized.

We shall see later that Islamization was proposed during the Meşrutiyet in a way not attempted even under the Hamidian regime. There lay the reason, it may be noted in passing, why the Westernists viewed the Islamists as arch-reactionaries, despite the fact that the Islamists' counterparts in Egypt and other Muslim countries were considered "modernists" by European orientalists. Still, the Islamists performed a service by pointing up a matter overlooked by the Westernists. In their zeal for Westernization, the Westernists overlooked the role of certain traditional elements of culture, and consequently, reached the limits of absurdity in their demands for borrowing.[30] By bringing the heart of the

---

[29] Babanzade Mustafa, "Müslümanlık Ilmî ve Fennî Bir Dindir," *Sebil-ür Reşad*, No. 207 (1912).

[30] Many Westernists were convinced that the Turks were incapable of modernizing themselves; and believed that they should, therefore, allow or invite Europeans to draw up plans for Turkey's Westernization on the basis of experiences obtained in the colonies under their rule. For an angry review of a proposal to invite Lords Cromer and Minto, Jomard (French governor of Algeria), and Lord Bryce (a famous anti-Turk) to reform Turkey, see *Sebil-ür Reşad*, No. 228 (1912).

reform question to the contrariety of tradition and change, the Islamists paved the way for the Turkists' approach to the subject.

The Turkists began with the Islamists, but quickly veered in an opposing direction. The New Life group similarly rejected the wholesale imitation of the West, but since it accepted the view that the challenge of the West was what had initiated change and controversies over change, it focused, not upon the defects in Western civilization, but rather upon the faults in Turkish society that had carried it to the position where its two schools of thought took such different stands.

The question the New Life group posed itself was: Which of the traditional institutions are in a state of decline, are thus factors of cultural maladjustment, and therefore are to be eliminated as a pre-condition of reforming those parts of life related to them? This was a new formulation and probably the most crucial enquiry to be surveyed here.

Since the group saw no basic argument over the adoption of the material civilization of the West, it sought to come between the Westernists and Islamists on the matter of the Muslim-Turkish culture. It first noted that there were institutions within the recognized province of the Şeriat which had to be held responsible for the failure to borrow or assimilate useful things successfully. At this point Gökalp began to assume leadership of the group. The whole problem, according to him, was to decide what was pathological and what was normal in the society. Once that had been determined, all that remained was to take appropriate measures for the elimination of the former and the fostering of the latter.

Like the dichotomy of good and bad, this one begged the question of the criteria of pathological and normal. Gökalp made a detour in order to answer the question. First of all, reason or utility could not be criteria, as the Westernists and Islamists thought. Social life was not oriented by rational, or utilitarian standards. The orientation toward which a society bent its course was determined by values and ideals. Ideals referred to the gropings of the society. The major problem facing the Turkish reforms, therefore, was not the imposition of programs based upon utility or reason. The task was to analyze the self or the consciousness of the society and to discover the new orientations towards which its aspirations were turned. The leaders, thinkers, reformers, and artists could do only one thing in this matter: turn the unconscious gropings into conscious, cultivated, systematized, co-ordinated ideals.

What, then, were the ideals of the Turkish society? This,

364

Gökalp answered by a process of elimination. The ideals represented by the Islamists were no longer moving forces but fetters to society. The society that had created those ideals was an *ümmet* in which the source of the supreme values was religion. Turkish society was on the way to transforming itself from an *ümmet* into a *millet*. The controversy between the Westernists and the Islamists was one of the symptoms of this transformation. Not only in Turkey but almost everywhere, the religious ideals were weakening because the predominant contemporary type of society was the nation, not the religious community. All modern societies were ruled and motivated by national ideals.

365

Before deciding what should be taken over from the West, it was necessary to clear away those institutions that had been taken into the Şeriat and made identical with Islam. The civilizational elements carried through the Şeriat (now conceived to be identical with religion) would be eliminated, as they were incompatible with modern civilization, and a society could not have two civilizations if it wanted to be free of conflicts. These elements had already lost their function with the decay of the civilization to which they belonged. The Islamists' efforts to revive fossils were in vain. Islam would survive insofar as it became a living part of the national culture. Western civilization, or what the Islamists called its material elements, would be borrowed unreservedly, but the cultural elements of the West would be appropriated only as models for the cultivation of a *modern* national culture. The final aim would be to cultivate a national culture that was neither the Şeriat nor the pre-Islamic ethnic culture, nor the culture of the Western nations. Without the cultivation of Turkish culture, there could be no genuine reform and modernization.[31]

Had the Islamists been able to predict the outcome of their questioning the relationship between techniques, national culture, and religion, they would have bitten their tongues. By their slip, they invited the Turkists to look more closely at what constituted the complex of values and institutions believed to be under attack by the West. The Turkists emerged from their analysis with conclusions contrary to those of the Islamists; and they proved to be far more effective adversaries of the Islamists than the Westernists. By a process of reasoning contrary to that of the Islamists, the Turkists, instead of loading up the Şeriat with national customs, scooped out the content of the Şeriat itself.

[31] Gökalp, *Turkish Nationalism, passim.*

Turkist Their reform program would consist, not of secularization via Westernization, but of secularization via Turkification.

366

With the emergence of this approach, the problem of social reform took a direction entirely different from those of the Westernists and the Islamists. In fact, from this phase on, the initiative for positive action on the questions of social reform was held by the Turkists. Only they produced concrete and conscious policies to guide social reform over against the uncreativeness of imitation or conservatism.

WESTERNIZATION, Islamization, and Turkification were, as we have seen, the competing bases for the reformation of the major social institutions—state, religion, family, education, and economy. The present chapter will survey the way in which the upholders of these three policies viewed the reforms needed in the several institutions.

The State

The Turkish state appeared to all three schools of thought devoid of a sound basis and in need of a real fulcrum. While the political regime of the new era was not considered secular by the Westernists or national by the Turkists, so also it was not felt to be Islamic by the Islamists.

The Westernists demanded liberalism in government and education, and a return to the laissez-faire economic and religious policies of the Tanzimat. They demanded, in general, the secularization of society. They could not, however, demand that the state renounce its connection with religion. The Islamic character of the Ottoman state was no longer a matter of Tanzimat separationism. The Young Ottomans had made it an article of the Constitution in 1876—that Constitution which it was the purpose of the 1908 Revolution to reactivate. The Hamidian regime had made this constitutional article a universally recognized and accepted attribute to the Ottoman state. So intimate had become the connection that it did not occur to even the boldest Westernist to demand a thorough constitutional reform based upon the separation of the state from religion.

The Young Ottomans' *bid'a* had atrophied Turkish political thinking and it would require another sixteen years to be repudiated; this was the chief cause of the 1908 Revolution's failure in secularism. Because of an accepted impasse with respect to the secularization of the state, the Turkists turned their energies toward the secularization of religion. We shall discuss these efforts under the heading of religious reforms, although they implied also the reformation of state.

Quite naturally, the Islamists countered the idea of a secular state and a secularized religion with the idea of the Islamic State. At the proclamation of the Meşrutiyet, the Islamists, who had once been busy proving that the Hamidian regime was in perfect accord with the Şeriat, outdid all others to prove that the constitutional regime, or more correctly the *meşveret*, was the only political system taught by the Şeriat. Autocracy, on the other hand, was now seen as absolutely incompatible with Islam.

The most daring exposition of the thesis that the constitutional regime was in accordance with the Şeriat was written by Ömer Ziyaeddin in a book entitled *Mir'at-ı Kanun-u Esasî*.[1] The title page presented the book as "showing the conformity of the Constitution clause by clause, and sentence by sentence, with the provisions of the Şeriat together with substantiating quotations from the accepted traditions." The author quite seriously and diligently took each clause of the Constitution, found a verse or a *hadîth* substantiating its legitimacy, and put the two together with assurance. For example, with respect to Article 65, which provided that one deputy should be elected for each fifty thousand males, he quoted a verse in which the number one hundred thousand was mentioned and commented "Here the significance of the number one hundred thousand is evident. It means fifty thousand men and fifty thousand women." Ergo, Article 65 was in accordance with the Kur'an![2] The author even found sacred substantiation for the article of the Constitution declaring Istanbul the capital of government in the *hadîth* recorded by Bukhari and predicting the conquest of that city by Muslims.

368

---

[1] Published in Istanbul, 1908.

[2] Ömer Ziyaeddin, *Mir'at-ı Kanun-u Esasî*, pp. 71-72.

Another author, al-Hâjj Ahmed Hamdi, explained in a book entitled *Hikmet-i Siyasiye*:

> The Prophet founded the Islamic polity on the eternal divine law. So long as the pure Şeriat is followed there will be no place for arbitrary governments. . . . The glorious Kur'an laid down, not only Man's duties to God, but also his political, civic, civil, and domestic duties.[3]

In discussing the various forms of government, al-Hâjj said, "Liberty does not mean, contrary to what some narrow-minded men of our time believe, to dare to do certain unbecoming acts not conforming to the Şeriat."[4] The constitutional regime which "the Europeans believe to be their own invention is nothing but the totality of the sacred Şeriat."[5]

> A republican form of government, however, is impermissible: because in Islam the *imam* for religious and worldly affairs is necessary, and the *imam* should be elected and appointed by a superior group from among the dignitaries of the *ümmet* and the *ulema*. As this is a conditional *farz*, all of the people do not have to take part in the election.[6]

Underneath al-Hâjj's constitutionalism lay nothing but the medieval political mentality. For instance, his discussions of the imamate, or caliphate, and the prerequisites of a legitimate caliph were completely traditional. On the basis of a *hadîth* the *imam* or the Padişah was likened to a shepherd. "The nation," he said,

> is like milk sheep to the Padişah. Just as a shepherd obtains benefits from his sheep to the extent of the care he shows them, so the Padişah serves the increase of his treasury and, hence, the elevation of his fame and majesty to the extent he cares for the welfare of his people.[7]

The above quotations exemplify the outlook of the elder Islamists. Quotations from *Sırat-ı Müstakim* will show what the new generation had to say. The first article of the second issue of *Sırat* was entitled "Liberty and Equality" and was written by Musa Kâzım, who later became a Şeyhul-İslâm. It declared:

[3] *Hikmet-i Siyasiye* (Istanbul, 1912), pp. 16-17.

[4] *Ibid.*, p. 28.

[5] *Ibid.*, p. 29.

[6] *Ibid.*, p. 38.

[7] *Ibid.*, p. 73.

370

The Constitution is nothing but the embodiment of some parts of the fundamental provisions of the Kur'an relating to worldly affairs. . . . As our Şeriat . . . comprises provisions relating both to the world and to the afterworld, and as most of our instituted laws . . . are derived from the provisions of the Şeriat, we are bound to be circumscribed by the *ahkâm* of the religious laws. . . .[8]

What the Islamist writers understood as constitutional reform was to put the state into the service of religion, that is to use the government as a power to force the people to abide by the Şeriat. The state was conceived simply as the means of promoting the Şeriat.[9] Not only was there no place for the conception of a secular state in the thinking of the Islamists, but the very idea of democracy was rejected by their best minds. The prince Said Halim Paşa stated this clearly when he wrote:

In addition to the Westernists' mistaking the effect for the cause, there is the other, equally erroneous and, yet, very widespread belief among them that democracy is a necessity for every nation that wants modernization and progress. There is no need for democracy in Islam. The West needed it because there was no equality there. The West seeks justice through laws whereas Islam finds it in faith.

The prince also ridiculed the restoration of the Constitution and criticized the modifications designed to limit the powers of the ruler. By these modifications, he said,

The Sultanate has been divested of its most fundamental and absolutely undeniable rights and prerogatives. The executive power has become responsible to parliament. In fact, it is now understood that parliament is the source of all ills. . . . The cause of all these failures is the idiotic innovations (*bid'a*) introduced incessantly under the name of reform. The Constitution is a blunder. It is absolutely incompatible with the social and political conditions of the country as well as with the psychology and beliefs of the people. It is even a real danger for the existence of the Ottoman nation.[10]

---

[8] *Sırat-ı Müstakim*, No. 2 (1908). The complete article is reprinted in the collected works of the author, *Kulliyat-ı Şeyhul-Islâm Musa Kâzım* (Istanbul, 1920), pp. 243-53.

[9] *Sırat-ı Müstakim*, No. 2 (1908).

[10] Muhammad [Said Halim], *Inhitat-ı Islâm Hakkında Bir Tecrübe-ı Kalemiye* (Istanbul, 1918, pp. 23-24, and Said Halim, *Buhranlarımız* (2nd ed.; Istanbul, 1919), pp. 7-12.

Shortly after the re-opening of parliament in 1908 the Islamists forwarded their idea of the Islamic State so successfully as to instigate steps to make the legislative powers of parliament sterile in a way not even attempted by Abdül-Hamid. Commenting upon the use in a parliamentary speech of the word *teşri'* (in Turkish usage, legislating), *Beyân-al-Hak* declared,

The use there of the word *teşri'* is an error and a good example of the disregard for religion. *Teşri'* properly means enjoining the *şer'* of God. To claim for His slaves the [legislative] right belonging only to God is something that not even the Europeans have done.[11]

According to the review, hundreds of citizens submitted petitions to parliament demanding the "application of the Şeriat." It reported one month before the Islamist-led attempt to restore Abdül-Hamid to full power, the March 31 Mutiny, that a number of members of parliament had made a motion for the *fiqh* to be accepted as the source of projected legislation. It quoted a report of the judicial committee as follows:

Upon scrutiny of the attached proposals, our committee has agreed upon reviving the Mecelle committee to improve and expand the Mecelle in accordance with the demands of the time. It has been found necessary, however, that there be competent *faqîhs* of the four *fiqh* schools on the revived committee and that provisions be borrowed from the Shâfiî, Mâlikî, and Hanbalî codes if necessary.[12]

Although given a sharp setback by the mutiny and its aftermath, insistence continued that parliament was not entitled by Islam to legislate and that a Mecelle committee should be reinstated. The Şeyhul-Islâm even signed a decision, without the knowledge of the cabinet or parliament, to form a new Mecelle committee.[13] Legislation, which is the most natural function of a parliament, was nothing but blasphemy according to the modernist Islamists. Their "modernism" went to the extent of allowing the use of the once rejected non-Hanafî opinions lest the parliament make borrowings from Europe to legislate a civil code.

[11] *Beyan al-Hak*, No. 15 (1908).

[12] *Ibid.*, No. 22 (1908).

[13] The Şeyhul-Islâm even took autonomous (*re'sen*) decisions on matters of personal law and submitted them to the ruler as caliph for ratification, ignoring parliament and the cabinet. For details, see Ebul'ulâ Mardin, *Ahmet Cevdet Paşa* (Istanbul, 1946), pp. 106-11, 153.

Commenting upon the idea of separating the state from religion, *Sırat* editorialized:

> What will happen if religion and state are separated? First, the *khilâfat* will be demeaned to the position of a papacy. Then, there will be a sultanate separated from the first. In other words, there will be two sovereigns in one country![14]

The Islamists held tenaciously to the article of the Constitution stating, "The religion of the state is Islam," as a support for their polemics against the legislative power of parliament. Said Halim said:

> Constitutionalism is one of the results of the erroneous idea of achieving reform by making laws drawn from Europe. European constitutionalism will not work here. . . . In Islamic society, the personal or functional prerogatives of a ruler do not mean absolutism, though they may mean it in the West. The tyrannies of the West were made in the name of religion and church. This is not so with us. The internal class struggles of Western society do not exist in Islam. Islamic society progressed so long as the principles of Islam were applied. Democracy, which has been found as a remedy to the inequalities inherent in Western society, therefore, is entirely irrelevant to us. . . . Ottoman political unity is not based on nationality as it is in the West, but rather on Islamic unity and brotherhood.[15]

The Islamists did not recognize the right of the new weak Padişah to legislate, any more than they did that of the blasphemous parliament. They aspired to a state more Islamic than even Abdül-Hamid would allow. As the Şeriat was the constitution of the Islamic polity and the *ulema* its proclaimers, protectors, and interpreters, the implementation of the Islamists' reform policy implied the legitimate rule by the *ulema* for the first time in Ottoman, even Islamic, history. The so-called legislators would be allowed only to give codified shape to the Şeriat, or merely to formalize the codified editions of the Şeriat and regulations prepared by the expert committees of *ulema*. The Islamists demanded "legislation" only for the enforcement of the provisions of the Şeriat. Parliament would be expected, for example, to pass laws for the enforcement of a feminine costume approved or designed by the *ulema*; it would institute approved modern sanctions against gambling, drinking, breaking the fast, etc.

[14] *Sırat-ı Müstakim*, No. 170 (1911).
[15] Said Halim, *Buhranlarımız*, pp. 14-22.

The aspiration of the Westernists to a liberal democratic state recognized as a legislative, judicial, and executive power independent of religion, therefore looked unattainable before the constitutional arguments of the modernists. The progress of secularism was, however, destined to become a possibility, but only after the Turkists had worn down the Islamist conception of state. In order to bring the problem of the nature of the state into clearer focus, we must revert to the opening of a Turkist-Islamist battle over a seemingly irrelevant issue.

373

There appeared to be neither the desire nor the opportunity to introduce any secularizing political reforms in the climate of the Balkan Wars. With the spread of anti-Westernism, all looked to Islam for support. The Islamists virtually held the field. Unnoticed at first, Turkists swept Islamists aside on the issue of religion versus nationality. Even to raise this issue was the deadliest of blasphemies to the Islamists. The matter resulted, therefore, in probably the noisiest controversy of the entire period.

It is probably difficult for many readers, especially today, to understand why the Turkish Islamists should have been so perturbed by the rising tide of Turkish nationalism. The simple answer is that the Islamists recognized themselves to be in entirely new and untested waters. They had had no opportunity to work out safely their position with respect to nationality, as they had done with respect to the relationship between religion and state, or even the national expressions of the non-Turkish Muslim Ottomans. They appear to have sensed from the beginning that the Turkists would do from the flanks what the Westernists had failed to do by a frontal attack.

Although Islamist opposition to nationalism broke out only in 1913, even in 1912, during the Balkan Wars, the Islamist organs showed their dislike for the appearance among the Turks of words such as "Turk."[16] It sounds strange, of course, but it was only at about this time that those who were called Turk by everyone except themselves began to use this name, and then not universally or officially. Islamists scolded such innovations, and denounced *kavmiyet* (nationalism) as blasphemy.

An anonymous writer to *Sebil-ür Reşad* reminded his readers that the use of the terms "Turkish government," "Turkish army," "Turkish territories," and the "Turkish *hakan*" (monarch) were

---

[16] A. Süleyman, "Islâmiyet ve Türklük," *Sebil-ür Reşad*, No. 191 (1912) and Tahir al-Mevlevî, "Türk Hakanının Tahta Çıktığı Gün," *Sebil-ür Reşad*, No. 192 (1912).

374

rousing indignation among the Ottoman elements and explained that such usage was nothing but sacrilege. "What is a Turk?" he asked. "He is nothing but one member of the political association (*şirket*) constituted under the name of the Ottoman Sultanate and the Islamic Caliphate."[17]

Süleyman Nazif, a famed man of letters, declared that the devastations made by the Turkists in the previous two or three years were greater than those made by the Balkan Wars.[18] He said:

In our veins, there is only Ottoman blood. Like our language, our blood has deviated from its original through contacts and mixtures. And, especially, our affinity with the Tartars and Mongols is nothing but sheer myth.[19]

The former Young Ottoman Ebüzziya scoffed at being told he was akin to the Tartars "whose blood flowed in Russian veins, making the latter a nation always prone to blood-thirstiness no matter how Westernized they might look outwardly." "Our Turkishness," he said, "is nothing but a symbolism. We are all assimilated in Islam, and we are only Muslims." "Even the Khans of Bukhara," he growled, "cannot regard themselves as belonging to the Turks, or Tartars, or Mongols, because their ancestors were nothing but Arabs who had conquered Turkestan."[20]

But, it was too late for the Islamists to brake the influence of the Turkists. The more the voices of nationalism were raised among the non-Turkish nationalities, the more the sound began to appeal to the Turkish people.

The most violent attack against Turkish nationalism was made by Ahmed Naim, later a professor of philosophy at the University of Istanbul. In his *Islâmda Dava-yi Kavmiyet* (Nationalism in Islam) he called the Islamists to a Holy War against the Turkists.[21] Nationalism, he wrote, was one of those evils taken over from Europe. It was a "foreign innovation as deadly to the body of

---

[17] *Sebil-ür Reşad,* No. 232 (1912).

[18] *İçtihad,* No. 74 (1913).

[19] *Ibid.,* No. 72 (1913).

[20] Ebüzziya [Tevfik], "Türklük ve Tatarlık Bahsi," *Mecmua-i Ebüzziya,* No. 94 (1913), 483-92.

[21] *Islâmda Dava-yi Kavmiyet* (Istanbul, 1913). Naim (1872-1934) belonged to the Kurdish Baban family and was made a member of the *Âyan Meclisi* (the Senate) during the reactionary reign of Mehmed VI. He had no *medrese* education, but was a graduate of the Lycée of Galatasaray, and the Mülkiye.

Islam as cancer is to man." With the aid of scores of *âya* and *hadîth* he argued that nationalism was condemned and prohibited by the Şeriat. It was the severest blow yet directed against the unity of Islam.[22] "At a time when the enemy has set foot on our breasts," he said, "it is madness to divide Islam into nationalities."

According to Naim, Turkishness was nothing but an artificial invention of the Turkists. There was no Turkish history "apart from that of Islam." "The Turkists have made a people in whose veins not a single drop of Turkish blood remains believe themselves to be Turks." "They have introduced those strange Turkish names in place of those beautiful Muslim names." "They have invented strange national days. They would almost revive the ancient Shamanistic cults." "They have found Islam responsible for the calamities falling upon the Turks." "To know and to learn the Turk's past is not needed." "To know the *shar'* of Muhammad, the land of Islam, the heroes of Islam—these are what we need." "The Arab nationalists have not extended the praise of their national greatness beyond Islam." "The Turkists have unreasonably bemoaned the sufferings of the Turks in view of what Islam is suffering." "How many Turks have there been in the past who have done any service to Islam?" "Boasting of a Turkishness that has no place in the Şeriat is ridiculous." Islam forbids the exaltation of nationality. "Even the Arab race, which every Muslim is under obligation to love—even that race is forbidden this." The Turkists should not attempt to derive meanings from the *hadîths* praising the Arabs in favour of their thesis because

the Arab race has to be praised by everyone, above any race, even above our own race, for their Islamic zeal, for their racial affinity to Muhammad, for their language being the language of the Kur'an, and for the sake of our gratitude to them for having brought Islam.

Utilizing several quotations, Naim showed three reasons why the Turks were under an obligation to love the Arabs; a saying of the

[22] Commenting on the claims that a Turkish nationalism would incite the non-Muslims as well as Arabs and Albanians to separatist nationalism, Ismail Gasprinsky wrote: "The nationalisms of these peoples are already facts. Kurdish nationalism is fifteen years old. Arab nationalism is now past twenty. The Albanian is more than thirty years old. Armenian nationalism goes back at least forty years, Bulgarian sixty, and Greek more than eighty." Quoted in *Türk Yurdu*, No. 69 (1914), 2291-3. The first Kurdish nationalist organ began publication in 1892; see C. J. Edmonds, *Kurds, Turks and Arabs* (London, 1957), p. 58.

Prophet stated: "I am an Arab, the Kur'an is in Arabic, and the language of the people of Paradise is Arabic." Another *hadîth* said, "To love the Arab is to be of the Faith, to dislike him is dissent"; still another, "Whoever curses the Arab, he is a heathen."[23]

376

Ahmed Naim's provocative language caused the rallying of the Turkists and a greater rapprochement between the Turkists and pan-Turkists. In a long serial article published in *Türk Yurdu*, Agayev claimed that the *hadîths* used by Naim condemned tribalism (*'asabiyya*) and not nationalism.[24] The Prophet promoted the development of an Arab consciousness of national unity over against Arab tribalism. The Kur'an, not only with its religious teachings, but also in its language, played a miraculous role in promoting the development of Arab national unity.

Even today is it not this factor which is making the peoples from Marakesh to Iraq feel themselves members of the same nationality, despite so many differences among them in mentality, mode of living, and culture?

To confuse tribal allegiance with national unity, to seek to make this primary enemy of Islam the basis of Islam, is nothing but a gross error from an Islamic point of view.

Neither in the *hadîths*, nor in the Şeriat in general was there anything rejecting nationalism. In order to prove that the divisions in Islam were due to nationalism, one had to prove that until the rise of nationalisms among Muslim nations all Muslims lived in perfect harmony and unity. From the time of the early khalîfas to the present, the Muslim nations and states had fought each other incessantly. There was not a single Muslim state in history that did not make war against another Muslim state. The Turk had carried the burden of Islam upon his shoulders for a thousand years and was still carrying the heaviest burden. Islam had become his national religion and would remain so, but the Turk had done more than his duty to Islam. For the sake of Islam he had forsaken everything—his nationality, his language, his past—while the Arab

---

[23] Naim, *Islâmda Dava-yi Kavmiyet*, pp. 51-52.

[24] *Türk Yurdu*, No. 70 (1914); see also the subsequent issues. In an earlier article, quoted in *Türk Yurdu*, No. 65 (1914), Agayev emphasized that a Turkish nationalist would entertain a particular respect for Arab nationalism and that Turkish nationalism would not imply the negation of the nationalism of any other Muslim nation. He, then, added: "What the Turkists demand is nothing but the recognition of the Turk's right to have what all other Ottoman Muslim nationalities regard as natural to themselves."

remained an Arab. Things had come to such a point that even the Turk's existence in the past and in the present had begun to be denied—even by the Turks themselves.

Naim's Arabism also gave Gökalp the chance to clarify the points differentiating the nationalism of the Turkists from that of the pan-Turkists. His analysis aimed at the rejection of the three existing understandings of nationality: pan-Islamic, pan-Ottoman, and pan-Turkist. The first, he wrote, confused nationality with *ümmet*, or an international religious community. The second confused nationality with the association of several nationalities, religious or non-religious, in a political unity. The third erroneously based nationality upon race, or ethnic unity. While rejecting all three concepts, Gökalp took elements from all three in proposing a new understanding of nationality. For him, Turkish nationality was the modern product of the disintegration of the Islamic *ümmet* and of the Ottoman Empire, just as all nations were born out of the dissolution of a Universal Church and Empire.[25]

Religion

The Islamists' insistence upon making the state an Islamic state and the Westernists' struggle to deliver the state from religion led inevitably to a discussion of the relations between religion and state. The Turkists raised the question of secularization in such a way as to catch the Islamists by surprise; they turned the discussions from rehashing the controversy over the secularization of the state to the novel subject of the secularization of religion.

Beginning with the 1908 Revolution, recognition of the need to reform the religious institutions became universal. The Westernists, who had not believed these institutions capable of any reform, and even the Islamists, who had never before conceded that any alterations were required, took serious and hopeful interest in religious reorganization.

[25] See also Köprülüzade Mehmed Fuad, "Türklük, Islâmlık, Osmanlılık," *Türk Yurdu*, IV (Istanbul, 1913), 692-702. Another writer, Cami [Baykut], expressed the view that the Ottoman state should rest upon the Turkish and Arab nationalities, *Osmanlılığın Âtisi* (Istanbul, 1915). In 1918 Gökalp wrote again on the recognition of Arab independence and proposed a federation of independent Turkish and Arab states; "Milliyetçilik ve Beynel-mileliyetçilik," *Yeni Mecmua*, No. 35 (1918), 163.

378

The Westernists' understanding of the religious reforms was similar to the Islamists' in some respects. They shared a pet belief of the Islamists, namely, that Islam was a rational, even a natural, religion. The writers in *İçtihad* consistently differentiated between an "original" and a "corrupted" Islam; they believed implicitly in the possibility of developing a religious reform by purging the familiar Islam of superstitions and the rapacious hands of the clericals. A frequent writer on the subject and known contributor to *İçtihad*, Kılıczade Hakkı, retorted to the criticism of a member of the Office of the Şeyhul-Islâm saying:

> *İçtihad* is warring not against Islam, but against fanatics of your kind. . . . The enemies of Islam are not in the Balkans or in Europe, but right here—in the *medreses*, and in the Şeyhul-Islâm's office. . . . We have never thought of abolishing religion . . . because we know that, aside from their sublime spiritual values, religions are the most effective forces to keep men and, especially, the debauched clericals under control. . . . One thing ought to be learned categorically: reform in Islam can be realized only through the aid of Western learning. . . . Islam owns nothing today; it has exhausted everything. It is dependent upon the West to regain its life. It is dependent upon the West even to learn its own principles. . . . How can we restore the vitality of this great religion with these Şeyhul-Islâms, with these snuff-addicted preachers, with this army of vagabond *softas* whose ideas of faith do not go beyond voluptuous desires to own beautiful girls (*hûris*) and boys (*gilmâns*) in Paradise? . . . Islam is a religion that has prohibited such actions practised by these men as telling lies, committing adultery, homosexuality, drinking. . . . It is to bring happiness and success, not misery and failure. Talk about the after-life, which has continued for fourteen centuries, has gone on long enough. Let me talk of this world from now on. What the Muslims need are not illusions, but realities.[26]

According to Kılıczade, there were 178 *medreses* in Istanbul attended by 7,000 students. According to information given in *İçtihad*, there were, in 1914, 348 students in the Faculty of Religious and Literary Sciences, 200 in Mathematical Sciences, and 2,119 in the School of Law of the University of Istanbul. The majority of the *medrese* students were aged thirty-five and a great many were between forty and fifty years of age. The *medreses* were the refuge of the lazy and an escape from military service. Kılıczade called for a radical reform in these institutions and added,

[26] Kılıçzade Hakkı, *Son Cevap* (Istanbul, 1915), pp. 51-64.

"If we go on with such institutions, we shall not only be thrown out of Europe, we shall be wiped off the face of the earth."[27]

Kılıczade wrote a great deal on the religious reforms of the Russian Turks and praised the ideas of their contemporary reformer Musa Cârullah (Musa Bigiev) who claimed that many of the beliefs of the Orthodox *ulema* since the rejection of the Mutazila were simply the result of ignorance.[28] According to Kılıczade, science should be brought into the *medreses* and a new generation of *ulema* with earthly views should be raised; the *meşihat* should mobilize itself "to preach to the people the religious teachings of Islam that encourage industry, commerce, in short, worldly gains."

Another writer, Hüseyin Kâzım, made concrete proposals for religious reforms. The *sûfî* (mystic) orders should be abolished altogether. Translating the Kur'an into Turkish was a religious duty and a moral obligation. The understanding of Islam as a religion concerned mainly with worldly morality rather than with the world to come had to be propagated.[29]

Abdullah Cevdet stressed the importance of translating Western works on Islam as a means of enlightening the *ulema*. Having himself translated Dozy's *History of Islam* (which had created a great furore among the Islamists), he recommended that the Şeyhul-Islâm have Leone Caetani's *Annali del' Islam* translated![30]

In 1913, three teachers at the Lycée in Kastamonu were arrested by the police, the first, a teacher of natural science, for having

---

27 *İçtihad*, No. 60 (1913).

28 Musa Cârullah was born in Rostov in 1875, travelled and studied in Russia, Turkestan, Turkey, Egypt, (where he became a disciple to Abduh), and India. See *Türk Yurdu*, No. 89 (1915), 2696-703. Among his books the most interesting ones were *Halk Nazarında Bir Niçe Mesele* (Kazan, 1912) and *Rahmet-i İlâhiye Burhanları* (Orenburg, 1911). The second invited an angry reaction from Mustafa Sabri in *Yeni İslâm Müçtehitlerinin Kıymet-i İlmiyesi* (Istanbul, 1919). Musa's books, published in Russia, were popular among the Turkists. After the Russian Revolution he left Russia and spent the rest of his life in Finland, Egypt, and Japan. See Abdullah Battal, *Musa Cârullah Bigî* (Istanbul, 1958).

29 Şeyh Muhsin Fani [Hüseyin Kâzım] *Istikbale Doğru* (Istanbul, 1915).

30 Related later in *İçtihad*, No. 150 (1922) and No. 156 (1923), 3211. Caetani's work was translated later by Hüseyin Cahit [Yalçın], *İslâm Tarihi* (10 vols.; Istanbul, 1924-27). This history was believed to be intensely anti-Islamic and sacriligious; its translation invited angry refutations from the pen of Ahmed Naim.

380

expounded the Darwinian theory of evolution, the others, teachers of mathematics and French, for supporting the first when the teacher of Arabic accused him of committing *kufr* and incited the students and other teachers to create protest disorders. The incident gave Cevdet another occasion to lash out:

> A country in which the teaching of the Darwinian theory is still believed to be blasphemy has not yet come out of the Middle Ages. And a country still in those ages has no right to a place in the twentieth century. This has got to be understood by every head, with or without a turban—every head that does not want to be smashed.[31]

While the Westernists were blaming the Meşihat and the government for backing fanaticism by not fighting it,[32] the Islamists were alarmed by the increasing incapacity or unwillingness of the government to defend and enforce the Şeriat. *Sırat* often reported violations of fasting in government office, instances of drinking at school picnics, the "unbecoming" costumes of women government employees when among men and at picnics, etc. *Sırat* demanded that the Meşihat fix a religiously approved costume for women and that the government enforce its universal adoption.[33] According to it, the government was aiding and abetting the spread of disbelief by sending students to Europe, especially to France. All of these were seen as symptoms of "irreligion" (*dinsizlik*).[34]

A very frequent issue for the Islamists was the inherent and fundamental differences between the West and Muslim countries with respect to irreligion. Comparing the "insensitivity of Christianity" on the matter with the position of Islam, Said Halim, remarked,

> In Islamic society, irreligion implies the rejection and negation of all moral and social values. It leads to moral disintegration of the individual and, hence, to the dissolution of society. . . . Irreligion is the gravest calamity to befall Muslims and Islamic society.[35]

---

[31] *İçtihad*, No. 58 (1913).

[32] The Şeyhul-Islâm gave orders to chiefs of police "to prosecute those who dared violate the rules of fasting during *Ramadan* and to administer severe punishment"; reported in *Sırat-ı Müstakim*, No. 105 (1910).

[33] *Ibid.*, No. 89 (1910).

[34] See *Sebil-ür Reşad*, No. 195 (1912) and *Sırat-ı Müstakim*, No. 102 (1910).

[35] Muhammad, *Inhitat-ı Islâm*, p. 21.

Ahmed Naim wrote in 1917, with disparaging allusions to Gökalp's trust in the power of sociology,

> Imagine the . . . consequences of habituating the people . . . to an
> irreligious government! . . . An Ottoman state divested of religion
> cannot survive. . . . Separating the state from religion has another
> great social danger. Our people who view the state as under the
> obligation . . . to implement religion will begin to neglect their
> religious duties as well as their moral and social obligations as soon
> as they become accommodated to a secular state. The injunctions
> of the Şeriat are an indivisible whole. Once you molest one part,
> you destroy the whole. And once the whole is destroyed, it will
> be of no use even if you call on all the sociologists of the world to
> save our social order from its doom.[36]

381

It can be surmised from the above that the Islamists did not mean a reorientation of religious thinking when they demanded reform. Their sources of inspiration were the Egyptian al-Azhar reforms and the Salafiya movement. According to Musa Kâzım, what was required was: (*a*) to reform the methods of teaching religion; (*b*) to adapt the books on *kalâm* to the requirements of the age; and (*c*) to unify the Muslim *medhabs* (schools of legal doctrine). The extent of the Islamists' intentions on the first point may be judged from the fact that the Meşihat continued to demand by rote marathon prayers in Arabic from Turkish primary school children. Rashîd Ridâ of Egypt represented the ultimate of modernity for the Turkish Islamists on the subject of the unification of the *medhabs*; his book was translated with supplements by the Islamist Hamdi Aksekili.[37] An important innovation was implied in the second reform recommendation, but nothing tangible was done during this period in terms of the envisioned approach.

Despite their sincere desire to promote religious reform, the Westernists had no constructive plan for the separation of state and religion. And, there was no indication that the state desired or had the power to free itself from its obdurate companion. It devolved, therefore, on the Turkists to find a new solution, and they perceived that if the state could not be wrested from religion, perhaps religion could be wrested from the state. Gökalp initiated

---

[36] Quoted in Osman Nuri [Ergin], *Mecelle-i Umûr-u Belediye* (Istanbul, 1922), I, 299.

[37] *Mezahibin Telfiki ve Islâmın Bir Noktaya Cem'i* (Istanbul, 1916). See also Musa Kâzım's articles on the same subject, *Sırat-ı Müstakim*, No. 52 (1909) and subsequent issues.

from this premise a secularizing drive that will appear to be upside-down to those familiar with the Kemalist secularism.

382

The Islamist effort to bring all areas of life, except those designated as concerning modern science and technology, under the fold of the Şeriat had led the Turkists to analyze the areas of religion, culture, and civilization and to ask what were the fields of action: (*a*) genuinely defined by *nass* (revealed injunctions); (*b*) codified by the Şeriat as taken over from the *'urf* (the practices of the Islamic community); (*c*) viewed by the Islamists as *bid'a* (innovations); and (*d*) subjected to the provisions of the Şeriat on the grounds that the gate of *ijtihâd* (free opinion) was closed. In other words, they attempted to ascertain the spheres of the sacred and the secular in the Islamic system of ethical-legal-religious values.

The Westernist charges of ignorance and fanaticism in the religious institutions and the Islamist complaint of religious laxity among the people were for Gökalp nothing but the two sides of the same coin: the failure of religion to fulfil its social function. Like other institutions of Muslim-Turkish society, the religious institution was not in a normal state because of the incongruence with the requirements of modern society of the amalgamation of religious, legal, and ethical values into a single formal system called Şeriat. This system comprised, not only matters of belief (*itikadât*) and ritual (*ibâdât*), but also details on social relationships (*mu'â-melât*) ranging from economic to domestic life. Most of the religious norms brought under the sway of the Şeriat were of the last type. The origins of the provisions of this nature were social practices, the *'urf*, of the Muslim community given *nass* (sacred text) sanctioning. The divine law was believed to be immutable and absolute, but very few such injunctions came from the revealed law given by *nass*. In the majority of cases, the *nusûs* (plural of *nass*) referred to specifics; they reinforced, modified, or abrogated the *'urf*. The *'urf* maintained its existence under religious sanctioning so long as the type of society to which it pertained operated. With the change in social life, however, the *'urf* changed and so did the relation of the *nass* to the *'urf*. Every age understood and interpreted the *nass* in terms of the *'urf*. It was the *'urf* which predominated; it even overrode the *nass*. There were, for example, a number of *nusûs* that remained obsolete because of the disappearance of the *'urf* to which they referred; for example, those relating to *qisâs* (retaliation). It was, therefore, the dynamism of the social customs that determined the evolution of the Şeriat which had come to be viewed as an immutable law. In the evolution of the Şeriat, however, something difficult to explain had happened. While religious provisions concerning faith and moral conduct (*diyanet*) had tended to be legalized as articles of faith and rules of action in the Şeriat through the inclusion of their details in the *fiqh* literature, the legal aspects of the Şeriat had not developed into legislated codes (of civil, penal, constitutional, and commercial laws) and thus had remained mixed with religious-ethical provisions. In this way, matters of religious belief and action had ceased to be matters of conscience, and the legal matters had ceased to be concerns of constitutionally enacted legislation.

Gökalp did not see this state as inherent in Islam. It was rather the product of certain worldly conditions found in the origin and evolution of Islam. The trend of contemporary Muslim society was incompatible with this state. If Islam was to have the capacity to survive and play a role in the lives of the believers, not as a stumbling block but as a facilitating power, morality and law, religion and state, had to be separated from one another. The entire question of religious reform, therefore, consisted of taking measures to make religion a matter of conscience while subjecting the legal aspects of Islam to secular legislation. The first was the concern of the men of religion and the religious institutions, while the latter was a job for the state. It was only then that the religious leaders would be in their natural area where their cultivation of religious life would gain a new and creative meaning.[38]

Gökalp's associates (especially Halim Sabit and Mansurizade Said) elaborated on this thesis during their polemics with the Islamist writers.[39] We shall return to the matter in connection with the question of polygamy and the prohibition of interest. Here we can only point out the implication of Gökalp's approach for the problem of secularism.

The Turkists felt it was not the *ulema's* ignorance of modern knowledge, but their errors in *ijtihâd* which led them to a systematic misrepresentation of the questions pertaining to the religious and legal matters under the cover of Şeriat. Mansurizade rejected the right of these custodians of the Şeriat to assume a negative and censoring attitude toward all changes even in the field of permissibles. He said:

[38] See Ziya Gökalp, *Turkish Nationalism and Western Civilization*, ed. Niyazi Berkes (London and New York, 1959), pp. 199-214.

[39] Halim Sabit, *Islâm Mecmuası*, Nos. 5, 10, 11, 12, 14, 18, 19, 21, 22, 24, 25, 26 and 27.

384

> The Islamists explain simple matters of common sense by quotations from the books of *hadîths*. What a pity it is for men to believe themselves devoid of reason and dependent upon books of tradition on matters which are nothing but simple matters of logic. . . .[40]

Since the *ulema* left aside the use of simple logic and used tradition in its stead in every matter, a series of what he called errors in *ijtihâd* became the basis of a false understanding of the Şeriat and *fiqh*. The trouble was not that the gate of *ijtihâd* had been closed, but that *ijtihâd* had become based on tradition and its practice monopolized by one class of people. It was imperative to liberate and cleanse the legal principles and provisions from the influence of errors in thinking of the *ulema*. To handle matters concerning worldly life, such as law and politics, was not their job. It was time to demarcate the area of *diyanet* and *iftâ* and differentiate them from law, whether that law was based on *fiqh* or innovations, and to make matters pertaining to *diyanet* the legitimate territory of religion.[41]

According to the discussions of the Turkists on religious reform, not only were the matters of national mores no concern of the Şeriat but also many matters traditionally believed to be the concern of the Şeriat were, in fact, outside it. Matters of political constitution, economic and family life were not legislated, nor could they be legislated, by the Şeriat.

Gökalp's approach to the idea of a secular state was bound to remain inconsistent with his views on religious reform, because he attempted to prove that the Islamic state was a secular state. Under the pressure of circumstances maintaining the existence of the Caliphate and Sultanate, his attempts to prove the compatibility of these two institutions with a modern secular state were pure fantasies. From an historical point of view, however, the reforms carried out in accordance with Gökalp's ideas prepared the downfall of both institutions by removing from under them those pillars that had been left by the Tanzimat reforms.

[40] *Islâm Mecmuası*, No. 24 (1915), 583.

[41] *Ibid.*, No. 23 (1915), 564-65.

The Family

Every aspect of family existence was of special concern following 1908. The Westernists, in a very liberal spirit, discussed the
veil, details of marriage, women's education and participation in
public affairs, and family life generally; their opponents replied
with great freedom and lack of inhibition.

The subject mushroomed to such a degree that we can not
reflect even the scope of the discussions here.[42] For example, one
writer declared, "The chief cause of Turkey's decline was the
abominable status of womanhood"; "this was due to religion";
"the chief instruments for the perpetuation of this state were the
clericals"; and "the latter were responsible for the degradation of
the Turkish nation." While publishing *İçtihad* at Geneva, Abdullah
Cevdet had sent a questionnaire concerning the required means of
reform in the life of the Muslims to a number of Muslims and
Europeans. A witty French man of letters replied tersely: "Fermer
le Coran, ouvrir les femmes." Cevdet turned this to: "Both open
the Kur'an and unveil the women" and made it his motto of
reform.[43] After 1908 he opened a campaign against the veil and
seclusion. He followed this with one for the prohibition of the
Şeriat's permission of polygamy.

Such criticisms and demands for reforms of traditional practices
concerning womanhood and marriage had never been made before.
Furthermore, the question was not taken up only by men. Women
writers raised their voices even more radically in the defence of
the rights of women. All such developments were indicative that
social change had passed into family life. "In order to commence
our social reforms in a radical manner" said one writer, "we must,
above all, re-establish our family life around a new axis." Various
writers demanded equality between men and women as the prerequisite for modern family life. This equality could be obtained
by educating the two equally.

Westernist Cevdet

---

[42] Among the materials on the subject the following titles offer a
selection: Celâl Derviş, "Hayat-ı İçtimaiyemiz ve Kadınlar," *Zaman*
(Salonika, March 8, 1908); Ali Kemal, "Aile Hayatı," *Mahasin*,
(Istanbul, 1908), p. 105; Hakki Behiç, "Hukuk ve Vazaif-i Nisvan,"
ibid., pp. 406-10; Süleyman Nesip, "Konferans" (a lecture given
to a group of women), *ibid.*, pp. 382-7; Evliyazade Makbule, "İsmet
Hakkı Hanımefendiye," *ibid.*, pp. 344-45; Binturreşit Ubeyde,
"Amerikada Nisvan," *ibid.*, 355-56.

[43] *İçtihad*, No. 4 (Geneva, 1907); *ibid.*, No. 29 (1911).

386

The sudden discharge of suppressed opinions on womanhood and the demand for radical changes made the conservatives sure that the Muslim family was falling to perdition, and they began to exploit certain incidents as the manifestations of a universal loss of morality. One of these was the appearance after 1908 of women unveiled and in mixed company. In contrast to the Westernist complaint of the backwardness of the state of womanhood, the Islamists raised a howl over feminine degradation resulting from the non-observance of the Şeriat.[44]

One must not be deluded into thinking from the outcry of the Islamist press that all Turkish women were unveiled or could sport about in cars with whom they liked. The Islamist writers embellished the facts and generalized exceptions to show that a moral calamity was not only imminent, but had arrived.

The incidents reported were merely manifestations of a process that accelerated gradually under the new regime; they referred only to the cities and to certain groups within these. Women in the towns were still entirely behind the veil while the majority of Turkish women, the peasants, had never been veiled or secluded. During the Hamidian reign women were not only behind the veil, but were liable to be picked up by the police if they ventured out of their houses without a male guard (husband, father, brother, or servant). With the coming of the new regime, violations appeared. Even men felt freer and there was some measure of night life outside of that of the month of Ramadan. The advertisements in the new illustrated papers and magazines show the influx of new fashions for men and women. (Illustrated women's magazines, such as *Kadınlar Dünyası*, *Mahasin*, *Kadın*, and *Demet*, began appearing at the beginning of the new regime. They were devoted to literary writings and topics related to women, including fashions. Women were numbered among the contributors.) Urban women began to develop an outdoor dress that was a mixture of Muslim, Russian, and European forms. Their hair was concealed under a blue or black net wrapped like a turban or drawn back to drop in folds. The veils followed the current fashions in Europe and were more decorative than concealing. By a two-stage development, the enveloping *çarşaf* was transformed into a short cape clipped across the chest and a long overskirt. Underneath this was worn an open-necked blouse and the then-current long European skirts; heavy black stockings and modish petticoats were worn beneath

[44] *Beyân al-Hak*, No. 24 (1908); *Sırat-ı Müstakim*, No. 106 (1910); see also Nos. 94, 95, 105, 106 (1910) and No. 156 (1911).

these and some women adopted the European high-heeled button boots. Middle- and lower-class women wore light mohair or damascene *çarşafs* with no veil, especially when many of them had to work during World War I.

The changes in dress were only one of the changes frightening and repugnant to the Islamists. The Government, except when frightened by anguished outcries, was increasingly reluctant to interfere in the activities of women, except to foster their freedom. There was a marked drive to increase the number of schools for girls. Trade schools for girls were increased and reformed. Several day and evening courses in cooking, sewing, and child care were opened. The first girls' lycée was opened in 1911. Courses for nurses were started in 1913 and the number of scientifically trained nurses and midwives increased. Girls were admitted to secretarial and commercial courses. Women began to be active in exhibitions, ceremonies, and philanthropic societies, especially in the Red Crescent Society founded in 1907. They began to appear here and there, working in family stores and other small businesses. Thousands of women were employed in industry during World War I; these were mainly in the textile factories, and in the tobacco processing plants from which most of the men had been taken into military service. There was a purposeful drive to increase the number of women primary school teachers; special training courses were opened for them. From among the women emerged some who gained prominence in national affairs, such as Halide Edip.[45] Women's associations were founded in Salonika and Istanbul: Tefeyyüz (Exuberance) and Cemiyet-i Hayriye-i Nisvaniye (Women's Charity Society) in the first, and Nisvan-ı Osmaniye (Ottoman Womenhood), Müdufaa-i Hukuk-u Nisvan (The Defence of the Rights of Women) in the latter. The last mentioned, with its paper *Kadınlar Dünyası*, led the feminist movement.

Women did not yet go to restaurants, even with their husbands. Street cars and ferry boats continued to have partitioned sections for women. Men were not supposed to salute a woman acquaintance on the street. Sea bathing and swimming were not yet open to them; gymnastics were done in private places; lectures, concerts, and plays were repeated for female audiences. Girls entered the University and the higher schools of learning during World War I, but sat behind a curtain drawn across each class room or attended

387

---

[45] See her *Memoirs* (New York and London, 1926). For a good contemporary survey of the condition of womanhood, see Yusuf Akçura, *Türk Yurdu*, VI, No. 64 (1914), 2135-41.

388

separate sessions. Thus, the contention that catastrophic changes had taken place was misleading. Also, proportionately more non-Muslim and foreign women took advantage of the new freedom. Nevertheless, the changes among Muslim women were bound to make the controversy over womanhood more heated than any other, particularly when the initial ideas in favour of feminine freedom began to open avenues for questioning traditions most revered by the Islamists, namely, issues relating to marriage, divorce, and polygamy.

Once, after explaining that Meşrutiyet meant Şeriat and that everybody would have to live according to the laws of the Şeriat under the new regime, Musa Kâzım stated that one of the laws to be enacted would concern the observance of veiling (*tesettür*). He said:

Unfortunately, following the restoration of the Constitution many people did not observe it; God forfend, it is likely to give rise to great trouble very soon if it goes on like this. . . . The fourth and seventh clauses of the Constitution state that the religion of the state is Islam. . . . Every citizen of the Ottoman state is under legal obligation to observe all the rules of this sublime religion. The government is under the obligation of taking punitive measures against the violators. . . . One of the obligations is the covering of women, including their hair, with cloths devoid of luxury and in a way not to arouse voluptuousness in others.[46]

Musa Kâzım was liberal enough, however, to grant to women the right of arranging entertainments, concerts, and lectures among themselves. Education should not be denied them, but higher education was not necessary. After enjoying so many privileges given to them by the Şeriat, the women had no need to enter into commercial pursuits like the women of other nations.

So much liberality was too much for other Islamists such as Muhammad Abduş. Yes, there ought to be schools for girls, he admitted, but not ones teaching French, piano, and singing; girls should be given a thoroughly Muslim education. Mustafa Sabri also took a stiff attitude on the question of womanhood. While discussing the government's employment of women, he emphatically rejected women's equality with men.[47] He exploded with righteous indignation on the employment for the first time of a

[46] *Sırat-ı Müstakim*, No. 2 (1908), 21-22.

[47] *Beyân al-Hak*, No. 26 (1909).

female (a gypsy girl) as a model "in her natural form" by the School of Fine Arts.

Since the increase of our contacts with the Europeans, one of the hundreds of evils we have taken from them for the sake of a few good things has been this outrageous photographing and painting the figures of human bodies. It started with picture-taking, and now see how it has gone as far as painting the entirely naked bodies of women.[48]

389

Still angry, Sabri attacked an Islamic apologist who had claimed in *Ikdam* that the belief that women hold an inferior status in Islam was a wrong idea, saying:

The religion of Islam does not need such lying and ignorant defenders. . . . What that writer said did not exist, does exist, and what he said to be wrong, is correct. . . . Certain men, who dare to defend Islam without competence, are attempting to deny the existence of such great rules in Islam. . . . To distort the truth and to attempt to reconcile the views of the adversary, and, by this, to approve of the views of the adversary, is not a service to Islam, but treason.[49]

He went on to say that women *are* inferior in Islam and that this is one of the great truths of Islam. He also rejected the apologist's view that Muslim women had the right to divorce in Islam saying, "This is a lie."

Mehmed Âkif joined the fray by translating the Egyptian Farid Wajdi's *Refutation* of Qasim Amin's liberal book *Tahrîr al-Marra'*.[50] Âkif wrote disparagingly in his preface,

The Europeans have long since capitalized on the seclusion of women in Islam. In recent years, this custom began to be disliked by the Orientals too. . . . Those who now want change in the status of women want them to become like European women.

Said Halim had this to say on the subject:

The men who have become enslaved by this idea believe that Western civilization is the product of absolute freedom, thanks to women's

---

[48] *Ibid.*, No. 26 (1909) and No. 19 (1908).

[49] *Ibid.*, No. 27 (1909).

[50] Amin's book was translated into Turkish as *Hüriyet-i Nisvan* (Istanbul, 1915). Wajdi's book was serialized in translation in *Sırat-ı Müstakim*, No. 3 (Aug. 28, 1908) *et seq.* and was later published in book form. The views in Wajdi's book were the same as those of the Turkish Islamists.

superior status in Western society. . . . In fact, it is one of the confirmed truths of history that civilizations have been sunk more than once by the absolute freedom and sovereignty of women. . . . The desire for freedom and liberty is unfortunately misleading many of us.[51]

390

As on the question of seclusion, so it was on the question of polygamy. Here even the most open-minded Islamist did not concede an inch. Musa Kâzım wrote:

Conditions such as pregnancy and menstruation entitle men to polygamy. . . . Just as marriage is a requirement of natural drives, so the tendency to variety and multiplicity is a natural instinct. . . . However, the Şeriat does not command polygamy. It only allows it, if equality obtains between the wives. Thus, there is nothing incompatible with freedom in this. In like manner, men's superior position in divorce is necessary.

He replied to the idea that women had, or should have, the right to go to court for divorce: "As women are temperamental, everyone will go to the court and, thus, no family intimacy will remain."[52]

Emphatic as the Islamists' refutations of the Westernists appeared to be, the controversy over womanhood took on serious proportions only when the Turkists led by Gökalp entered the scene. Gökalp dealt with three aspects of the emancipation of women: (*a*) women's participation in social life, especially in economic life, and entrance into professions, (*b*) equalization of the educational opportunities for men and women, and (*c*) legal reforms to ensure equality to women in marriage, divorce, and inheritance. On the bases of these, Gökalp urged reforms to be carried out, with all their economic, educational, and legal ramifications.

The writings of Gökalp and his associates raised such a tempest among the Islamists that their opposition to the Westernists assumed the appearance of a summer breeze. One example will illustrate the Islamist opposition to the Turkist position.

The champion of the Turkist thesis on the subject of polygamy was the professor of *fiqh*, Mansurizade Said. Proceeding from

---

[51] Said Halim, *Buhran-ı İçtimaimiz* (Istanbul, 1916), chapter on "Freedom of Women," pp. 23-24.

[52] *Sırat-ı Müstakim*, No. 6 (1908). Musa Kâzım claimed that divorce, the use of the veil, and polygamy were matters of human nature and of social life, and should be of no concern to the constitution of a government.

Gökalp's views about *fiqh*, he brought the controversy to that point which we can say without hesitation was the real beginning of the end for the Şeriat in Turkey.

After reviewing the Western criticisms of polygamy and the Islamists' counter-arguments, Mansurizade said,

> In defence against these criticisms the *ulema* have raced each other to prove the virtues and the reasonableness of polygamy; none of them has said that there is nothing legitimizing polygamy in Islam, that it is entirely a matter to be left to the legislator's permission or prohibition, or that Islam absolutely allows the prohibition of polygamy.

One of the points upon which there had been complete agreement in *fiqh* was the dictum that the laws of the legislator were as binding as the law of the Şeriat in matters on which the Divine Law enjoined neither command (*amr*) nor prohibition (*nahy*). The practice of polygamy (like the practices of marriage and divorce) was one such matter. The legislator was, therefore, entitled by *fiqh* to legislate regarding the practice in whichever way he deemed necessary. And, thus, there was no need to legislate in a way to limit or circumscribe the practice of polygamy by utilizing, for example, the condition of maintaining justice and equality among the wives; polygamy could just be prohibited outright by law.[53]

This thesis detonated a mighty blast from the Islamists. *Sebil-ür-Reşad* published an angry answer in which the mistake was made of claiming that "polygamy was not a matter of *ijtihâd*, but a matter of *ijmâ*." This was followed by a lengthy argument between Mansurizade and the writers mobilized by *Sebil* on the technical question of whether permissibility is a matter of Şeriat provision and whether what was permitted could be prohibited. Excerpts from Mansurizade's argument follow:

> I ask the *ulema* of *fiqh*: Has there ever been a single *imâm* of any school who said that if the legislator prohibited something permissible, this prohibition was contrary to the Şeriat and, hence, not binding? If there has not been any, is it not a matter of simple logic (it is not even a matter of *ijtihâd*) to conclude that whatever "permissible" the legislator prohibits, this prohibition is binding? In spite of the fact that this is the plain truth, the *ulema* want to prevent men from reasoning in terms of the simplest rules of

[53] Mansurizade Said, "Taaddüd-ü Zevcat İslâmiyette Menolunabilir," *İslâm Mecmuası*, No. 8, (1914) 233-38.

deductive logic under the claim that "the gate of *ijtihâd* is closed."
What they really want is to close, not the gate of *ijtihâd*, but the
gates of the mind. They are ignorant even of the meaning of *ijtihâd*.
A matter like the permissibility of polygamy, concerning which
there is absolute *nass*, they claim to be a matter of *ijmâ*. This is
similar to claiming that the obligatoriness of prayers is based
on *ijmâ*. The *ulema* are not entitled to issue commands on matters
of the Şeriat; the application of their opinions is only dependent
upon those who have sovereignty—a prerogative that the *ulema* lack.[54]
The *ulema* want to bring all actions of men under the scope of the
Şeriat by the claim that permissibility is subject to the Şeriat.
In this way, the permissibility of many acts is lost and men are
bound hand and foot. The Şeriat's judgment upon every innovation
becomes nothing but non-permissibility. Similar to the prohibited
matters, the "permissibles" are made subject to *iftâ* and *fetvas*
are passed on them. As there is no clear statement in the Şeriat on
innovations their permissibility remains unknown. In this way the
Şeriat has come to an impasse and become impracticable. The *ulema*
have paralyzed the whole Şeriat on the basis of a mistake in logic.

Permissibility is not a matter of Şeriat provisions. The law is to
regulate human actions. Permissibility does not imply regulation,
but implies freedom of action. Anything believed to be permissible
in a law is outside of the provisions of that law. Otherwise, it
would be necessary to bring even the matters of eating or drinking
or walking into the jurisdiction of law by providing verses expressing
their permissibility. Nothing could be more ridiculous than this.
If all verses and *hadîths* concerning "permissibles" were examined, it
would be found that each came, not to express the permissibility,
but for other purposes. Permissibility is neither God's legislation, nor
the product of His legislation; it is merely an indication of the
non-existence of such legislation. Just as the telegraphs and telephones
neither need a *fetva*, nor are subject to any Şeriat provision, so
the Şeriat could not include the matters of permissibility in marriage,
divorce, and polygamy. The legislator can very well enact laws
on them in accordance with the desires of the nation and of the age.[55]

While the Islamists were loading even the matters of custom
into the Şeriat, Mansurizade was tossing out even the traditionally
accepted contents of the Şeriat! Would this not, in the long run,
amount to reducing to nothing the content of the Şeriat, especially
on many matters of worldly affairs and of social relations? Şere-
feddin (the head of the Department of Religious Affairs under the

[54] *Ibid.*, No. 9 (1914), 280-84.

[55] *Ibid.*, No. 10 (1914), 295-303.

Republican regime) joined the controversy and drew conclusions quite close to this. Once matters accepted as permissible were proven not to be covered by the provisions of the Şeriat, then there would be no more need for issuing *fetva* on these matters, according to him. Those which had been declared prohibited by *fetvas* in the past should be liberated from the jurisdiction of the Şeriat, and subjected to the enactments of the legislator.[56] In this way, many areas of life would be freed from the restrictions exercised by the *ulema,* the *muftîs,* and Şeyhul-Islâm.

393

The Economy

The need to release the mind from tradition became impelling in another area also. This was the field of economic behavior. All realized that without economic progress Turkish society was doomed, and that economic and technological backwardness lay at the base of all the ills. The Islamist's acquiescence in admitting European sciences and techniques was based upon this realization.

The Westernists did not blame Western imperialism for the economic difficulties of the country. They held the nation squarely responsible for turning the opportunity of benefiting from modern civilization into a calamity by remaining slaves to tradition. To hold Western imperialism responsible would blind the eyes to their failures for which no one but themselves was responsible. It would enhance obscurantism by spreading hate-the-West demagogy.

Clarifying this most touchy side of the matter was so important for the Westernists (and its importance and appropriateness at the time cannot be denied) that they failed to go on to a deeper diagnosis, as well as to a more realistic and practical policy of economic progress. They viewed past and future economic relations between the arrested countries and the advanced economy of the West in terms of competition and laissez-faire. This did not mean that they wanted their country to remain economically and politically subjugated to the West or that they wanted the capitulations and other economic disabilities incurred by opening the doors to Western economic and financial penetration to remain as they were. The Westernists were not so naive or blind as to

[56] *Ibid.,* No. 12 (1914), 367-71 and No. 13 (1914), 397-403.

invite their countrymen to compete under such conditions. Their concentration was simply upon another aspect of economic life.

As in government, administration, religion, education, family, mores and customs, and script, unconditional Westernization in economic life was to the Westernists the antidote for the poisons which had made the nation the "sick man of Europe." A nation that was not sovereign, a people that was illiterate and ignorant enough to accept tyranny, individuals who believed superstitions taught them by their religious guides, would be incapable of maintaining an existence even if all the European nations renounced their rights of exploitation. If the Turks broke the chain enslaving their minds to a system of beliefs no longer adequate, if they liberated themselves from the institutions no longer fitting the demands of the times, they would be strong enough to compete and defeat the external impediments hobbling their feet. Only then they would have the right and the might to demand justice and to impose the requirements of their own interests. The model throughout was the West—its capitalistic economy, freedom of individual enterprise, working for the accumulation of wealth, rational and liberated minds, material power, and technological advancement.

It is easy to see that the Westernists' approach was inadequate. However, they did a service by bringing to the country's attention the problem of economic ethics and mentality. With their untiring hammering upon the traits of and the contrasts between the "Oriental" and the "Western" mentality, that did not serve the solution of Turkey's economic problems, but they did serve to make recognized the fact that economic change required changes in the mental attitude to the world. To quote extensively from the Westernist writings characterizing and contrasting the two types of mentalities would be tedious. The reaction to one incident may illustrate how preoccupied they were with the question of mentality even in an irrelevent situation.

Turkey had her first airplane crash in February 1914. Two Turkish aviators had left Istanbul to cross the Taurus mountains and land in Egypt. The two succeeded in reaching their destination. On the way back, however, they crashed into the sea near Beirut. This caused countrywide grief. In commenting upon the event, Abdullah Cevdet said,

When the European explorers went to the Arctic and their aviators flew in the skies, we used to laugh at them and say, "Look how these stupid Europeans get themselves eaten by polar bears and blown to pieces in plane crashes." We did not realize that by these "stupid" acts they realized their domination over the world. Now our men too have begun to crash. This is not something to grieve over. We must rejoice! For me, it is the sign that we are regenerating and that we shall not die![57]

395

Scorn for other nations, apathy, fatalism, dislike of change, etc., were all, according to the Westernists, the attributes of the Oriental mentality inculcated, primarily, by men who claimed to be the guardians of religion. The major task was to liberate the people from these influences and to educate them in institutions that would consciously inculcate the modern mentality.

As we might expect, the Islamists attempted to show, over against the Westernists, that the economic ethics of Islam were not what their detractors claimed them to be. They were tireless in proving that Islam preached the economic ethics most conducive to worldly gain.

Articles were written from the beginning of the period about how Islam encouraged work, gain, and the accumulation of wealth. One of the senior writers for *Sırat*, a famous preacher, wrote about "the encouragement given to acquisition, trade, and industry in Islam," and listed numerous verses and *hadîths* in proof thereof. Using a similar title, another writer proved that Islam encouraged progressive work and labour. Islam appeared to the latter so capitalistically oriented that he claimed, "The day will come when Islam will shine as brightly in Europe as it shone in *Asr-ı Saadet* [the Prophet's age]."[58]

Perhaps the best example of the collection and interpretation of the *hadîths* concerning Islamic economic ethics was given in a book entitled "The Position of Wealth in Islam," by Ahmet Nazmi.[59] It contained forty-seven *hadîths*. The author made his compilation to prove that, contrary to the beliefs of the modern Turks and Europeans, Islam encouraged work and gain. As these *hadîths* showed, work was conceived as the source of all material and moral capital. Nazmi, however, believed that the Muslims:

ought to know the principles and the laws of modern economy. Without such knowledge, no use may be made of wealth. . . . All of

[57] *İçtihad*, No. 95 (1913).

[58] Sadi, "Sai ve Amelin Nazar-ı Islâmdaki Mevkii," *Sırat-ı Müstakim*, No. 77 (1908).

[59] *Nazar-ı Islâmda Zenginliğin Mevkii* (Istanbul, 1921).

the modern inventions . . . as well as the growth and the domination of European civilization were the products of knowledge and research. . . . Borrowing from and imitating European civilization consists of learning its sciences, techniques, industries and economy, and applying these accordingly. The duty of the Muslim is to attain worldly happiness as well as other-worldly salvation. He should work for this world without sacrificing the other world, and for the other world without neglecting this world.

Laziness and wasting time in unproductive indulgences such as drinking and gambling were reprehensible. Islamic economic doctrine favoured neither the rich nor the poor. Socialism and communism resulted in Europe because of the primacy given to capitalism there.

[There is] neither capital, nor labour in Islam, because each strives to dominate the other. Both are indispensable to the world; let each class only treat the other with equity and justice. . . . Each individual's interests should be maintained in a social hierarchy guaranteeing the prosperity of all. . . . For this reason, the untoward desire for wealth must be discouraged. Through his misuse of liberty man has become tired of the world. What the men of today need is less freedom and more order, discipline, and hierarchy. Seeking after individual interests is nothing but selfishness. . . .

The struggles between labour and capital and movements like socialism and communism were of much interest to the Islamists. None of them defended capitalism, or socialism and communism. They treated all as the necessary evils of European civilization which, despite its superior technology, was based on wrong moral principles.

One of the enlightened members of the last generation of the Turkish *ulema*, Eşrefzade Şevketî, summarized the Islamic view of the class struggle in answer to a questionnaire eliciting "the attitude of Muhammedanism" on capitalism and addressed to the Şeyhul-Islâm on behalf of the Anglican Church. Şevketî who was assigned to prepare an answer as a member of the Dar-ul-Hikmat-ul Islâmiye (School of Islamic Philosophy), first contrasted "two ways of life." Western civilization had chosen the way that gave unrestricted freedom to the pursuit of strict economic interests. Present-day class struggles were the result of choosing the capitalistic system. The solution, however, was neither in socialism, nor in communism. Neither did it lie in Christianity, which had failed to check the growth of capitalism. The only solution would be found in turning to "the other way of life," to Muhammad's teachings. Şevketî conceded that the Christian world would be unlikely to follow this way.[60]

These examples show sufficiently that the Islamist economic views, even on contemporary economic problems, were determined by a basically medieval economic theory and ethic. Both were based on a predominantly moral view of economic behaviour, equity, a just price and the rejection of interest—all viewed in terms of a pre-capitalistic economy. It is interesting to note the absence of the terms *fard*, *sunna* and permissibility (*ja'iz*) in the eulogies of Islamic economic virtues although the Islamists were very careful in resorting to such technical terms when discussing matters of government and family. Work, business, wealth, equity, etc., were neither *fard* (obligatory) nor even *sunna* (a recommended duty), but simply things approved or encouraged for which the word *merğûb* (desired) was used. This was not a technical term of the Şeriat.

What was the economic system the Islamists preached as encouraged by Islam? This can be seen by learning first the social class in which the Islamists were most interested and then by observing some aspects of the economic ethics they preached. The Islamist reviews, books, and pamphlets on the Muslim *esnaf* (artisan) and *tacir* (trader) reveal the social class to which the Islamists appealed and from which they gained support. One piece of economic advice, sometimes given as an economic policy, was that Muslims should trade with Muslims. Pamphlets including the names and addresses of the Muslim manufacturers, wholesalers and retailers, importers and exporters, practisers of traditionally Muslim crafts, artisans such as tailors, shoe-makers, down to the small shopkeepers, grocers, and barbers were distributed free of charge. The boycotting of Austrian and Italian goods during two political crises of the period provided occasions for encouraging the establishment of the first Muslim woollen goods factories and macaroni factories. The economic class to which the Islamist ideology appealed most, therefore, was not the peasantry, or the working class, or the intellectuals who would promote state enterprise, but rather the Muslim businessmen and traders, and secondarily, the *esnaf*, all of whom aspired to prosper in a system of private competition and enterprise along the lines of traditional practices and standards.

[60] Eşrefzade Şevketî, *Sai ve Sermaye Mücadelâtının Dinen Suret-i Halli* (Istanbul, 1923).

In attempting to promote the interests of this type of middle class while showing that Islam favoured progress, the Islamists were confronted by a few thorny questions on which they never dared to deviate from the traditional economic ethics of the Şeriat. One of these was the question of interest. The second was the question of insurance.

The practice of interest was never accepted or legitimized in Islamic literature and the silence of the Islamists on the subject did not signify a change of mind. One of the "modern" *tefsîrs* (commentaries on the Kur'an), written as late as 1935 by a member of the last generation of the *ulema* contained the following:

> Interest [*fâiz*] transactions practised all over the present-day world are in essence nothing but the usury practised in the Age of Ignorance before Islam. Periodic decreases and increases in the rates of interest in no wise change the nature of the transaction. What in the Arab *'urf* was called *ribâ* [usury] was nothing but what is called today the increment or surplus from the use of money. . . . In any society where the belief that interest is indispensable grows and where the means to legitimize it are searched for, there decline and decay begin. . . . The salvation of present-day society from the practice of *ribâ* depends upon the realization of a serious social reform which would abolish poverty. The more poverty is decreased, the more interest is likely to be abolished. The more interest-taking is practised, the more wealth is accumulated and monopolized. The abolition of interest began to be an ideal, although the present-day tendencies are to envisage only its restriction and not its abolition. Such an ideal, which the modern world is far from entertaining, was once made a fact by God in Islamic society. Thus, the Kur'an is still a book of Divine Law to inspire the highest stage of evolution among present-day humanity.[61]

There was no provision in the Şeriat for insurance. To many it looked like another form of *ribâ* and an expression of distrust in the power of God. However, we find a slight softening of attitude, especially under the influence of the new and attractive descriptions supplied by the Russian Turkists about the wonders obtained in Russia by Muslim oil millionaires, manufacturers, and traders.

One of the Turkestani émigrés and a regular contributor to *Sırat*, Abdurreşid Ibrahim, dealt somewhat open-mindedly, yet very timidly with the topic of insurance. Ibrahim approved only of fire insurance. He avoided discussing its permissibility. In a

---

[61] Hamdi Yazır, *Hak Dini, Kur'an Dili — Yeni Mealli Türkçe Tefsir* (Istanbul, 1935), I, 952 ff.

roundabout way, however, he pointed out its inevitability. He went on to claim that the Muslims were not pleased by the practices of existing insurance companies and, finally, he proposed an insurance scheme to be carried out by municipalities on the basis of taxation for "mutual guarantee." "Only in this way," he said, "will insurance be an enterprise for public benefit, and then an insurance practice compatible with the Şeriat will have been found."[62]

The scantiness of Islamist literature on insurance is not an indication that the Islamists had given up the traditional view or accommodated themselves to hard realities. In a book written to refute materialism, insurance was shown as one of the most absurd manifestations of the modern materialistic mentality. Insurance meant disbelief in God's will. If property was lost or burned it was God's will, hence what was the use of insuring? Also, insurance was an invalid and void transaction according to the Şeriat because what was bought and sold did not exist (*ma'dûm*); the commodity was only the "probability."[63]

Despite the typical "modernity" of the Islamists on economic questions and their thesis that the Islamic economic ethics were worldly-oriented, they failed, like the Westernists, to identify the nature of modern economic civilization. The economic ethics depicted by the Islamists, who thought themselves modern by holding these views, were nothing but the ethics known and practised by the medieval mercantile and artisan classes. The Islamists had neither an understanding of the economic implications of those European sciences and industries toward which they thought themselves to be so liberal and modern, nor the slightest knowledge of the economic system that was upsetting so deeply all medieval systems of economy and society. This showed itself especially in their refusal to find legitimacy for interest in the Şeriat.

It was the Turkists who led an advance toward the understanding of the economic problems facing Turkey—even though they saw the problems in non-economic terms. Mansurizade Said tackled the question of interest in his "Errors in Ijtihâd". His attack was so devastating on this matter that the Islamists did not dare to retaliate. He accused the *faqîhs* of prohibiting interest on the basis of a wrong application of the definition given to *ijâra* (rent). It

---

[62] *Sırat-ı Müstakim*, No. 160 (1911).

[63] Hacı Mustafa, *Redd-ü Isbat* (Istanbul, 1914), pp. 203-6. The book was a refutation of Ludwig Büchner's *Kraft und Stoff* (Tübingen, 1855).

400

came to be believed, he said, that the Şeriat regarded money transactions with increments accruing from such transactions as *ribâ*,
which was definitely condemned in the Kur'an. This inference
was entirely incorrect: "What the *nass* prohibited was the sale of
money for more money and not the rent of money." The verses
and *hadîths* concerning *ribâ* clearly referred to the *ribâ* which is
of the nature of sale. In fact, the early *faqîhs* regarded *ribâ* as one
of the *fâsid* (invalid) sales and treated the renting of money not
under the section on *ribâ* but under the section on *ijâra*. They
dealt with it, not as *ribâ*, but as a prohibited transaction, as in
"*ijâra* concluded on the basis of the consumption of kind." Thus,
money could not be sold for more money but could be rented or
loaned in the Şeriat. Renting money was perfectly permissible in
the Şeriat; there was nothing prohibiting it. Hence, what the Şeriat
prohibited was usury not interest. The interest allowed by law
was perfectly in accordance with the Şeriat because it was determined according to the amount of money and according to the
duration of time. Being so, interest is nothing but the rent of the
money loaned.[64]

The absence of controversy over the question of interest is
significant. The Islamists would have been embarrassed by a new
discussion of the matter. They all knew that the Şeriat had developed its famous "fictions" by which the practice of usury was
made possible without giving the slightest twinge to the consciences
of the believers. Even the children knew that something unlawful
was being practised in a lawful way. This, however, did not imply
the legitimization of interest by the Şeriat; it only concerned the
practice of the pre-capitalistic usury. As interest-taking was a
hundred times more innocent than the practices of the blood-
sucking usurers, it would not bother minds that had already adapted themselves to usury.

Education

The controversies of the period were not limited to economic,
legal, and religious affairs. They extended to wider areas of customs and mores, and increased the interest in education. Once
again education enjoyed the importance it had under Mahmud II.

[64] Mansurizade Said, "İçtihad Hataları," *İslâm Mecmuası*, No. 28
(1915), 649-50.

The liberal school, in particular, put unlimited faith in education as the elixir for all maladies. Education, based on principles contrary to those prevailing in the social environment outside the school, would be a means of working against presently-constituted society. It would build up individuals who would be the very opposite of the types in the existing society.

A new type of reformer arose immediately following the Revolution to criticize the traditional institutions and their educational effects. We may call these men mass educators. They are worthy of description because they arose in a manner unheard of in other countries and shook the Turkish mores sorely. One of their common characteristics was that they made their influence felt, not by writing or discussion, but rather by demonstrating their views, creating a mass psychology, and converting it into small social movements and a number of fashionable myths. These mass educators emerged from among the previously obscure army officers, doctors, poets, teachers, and civil servants. Each was the popularizer of one or two novel ideas. All skyrocketed to fame and were as popular as the top politicians. Most of them were colourful personalities and a type of public figure never before known in Turkey. Under normal conditions, all of them would have been called eccentrics, if not lunatics. But at no other time in Turkish history has the educator been so popular, possessing such magical powers over the crowds.

The most famous of these educators were Rıza Tevfik (1868-1949), Selim Sırrı (1874-1957), and Ismail Hakkı (1889-). No one has surpassed the theatrical skill with which these men combined radical ideas with plain common sense. In fact, when the politicians were hopelessly confusing the entire Young Turk ideology, it was to these men only that the people listened with interest. They were the forerunners of the professional public lecturer who appeared later in other parts of Turkey to promote new educational views on womanhood, art, hygiene, etc. They developed a novel and effectual style of spoken Turkish.

The first thing that these men introduced was the practice of freedom of speech in its sheer physical sense. They set an example and invited the people to talk and to talk freely. They encouraged the discharge of thirty-three years of unspoken words, unthought thoughts. These prolific talkers were not overly concerned with the sense of what was said as long as it was said. They inspired the people to talk and talk aloud—an activity practised hitherto only by the mosque preachers. Public oratory, which was unknown in the Islamic tradition, became a necessity in the new political education.

But it was not only speech these men set free. In addition, each became a specialist in an area of activity that it had become atrophied through years of suppression. Selim Sırrı, for example, made "movement" the keystone of his pedagogy. He believed that, above all, the nation should *move, bodily*. Like the others, he was no mere theoretician. Realizing his athletic potential, he rushed to Sweden and came back with the gospel of Swedish gymnastics, which he developed into a semi-cult. He appeared in his athletic uniform in open squares, at schools, and in the ceremony halls of the Hamidian period that he had converted into gymnasiums. Never before had a sane Turkish adult been seen like this in public. Selim Sırrı jumped, walked ropes, swam, fenced—in short, he made acrobatics, which the people had believed to be worthy only of the cheap artists in the Hamidian festivals, sound and look respectable.

Until 1908, sitting was regarded, not only as the most natural, but also the most respectable posture of man. To stand and to stand erect was a sign of disrespect, arrogance, or rebellion—son bowed before father, wife before husband, peasant before urbanite, the people before the *efendi* (master), the entire nation before the Padişah. The ex-army officer Selim Sırrı fought against this custom. He brought to education the habit of teaching people to stand up and walk erect. Although few understood the relevance of bodily movement to education or modernization, none ever hissed or attacked its prophet. Selim Sırrı not only made his gospel properly acceptable, but also succeeded in introducing it into the school programs. More amazing, he had gymnastics introduced into the curricula of the *medreses*—those institutions in which sitting was the only remaining vestige of scholastic life. Selim Sırrı waged tireless war against physical immobility for more than forty years, and if the Turkish youth today run, swim, and jump, they owe that freedom to this magician of the Meşrutiyet.

The same can be said about many other areas of contemporary Turkish life. Ismail Hakkı [Baltacıoğlu] is remembered best for his crusade against the inhibition of using the hands. He became the prophet of meaningful education in arts and crafts, not only in the primary, but also in the secondary schools. Rıza Tevfik, "the philosopher," popularized the dictum, "A sound mind in a sound body." He was an amateur wrestler and revived this old national sport as a form of entertainment as well as of exercise.

Talk, move, work, play—these were the first formulae of these empirical pedagogues, their fundamentals for the new education. Playing football, or playing on the stage—both were unbecoming to adults in the old tradition. The first English football game was played in Turkey in 1908. A number of amateur theatrical groups were formed at the same time. Such frivolity had been unknown since the days of the Tanzimat when the leading personalities had established drama clubs and written plays for them to perform. It was after 1908 also that the first Turkish actors, to be followed shortly by the first Turkish actresses, appeared on the professional stage. A National Theatre and a Conservatory of Music were established in 1914.

Unless we are blind to the meaning of the mores of medieval society, we cannot fail to regard these men as radical reformers. In fact, if the Meşrutiyet resulted in any revolutionary break with the past, it was because these men turned the scale of values upside down in an area of culture which even ambitious Islamists did not imagine could be taken over into the custody of the all-encompassing Şeriat. The new mass educators opened holes in the rock of tradition, without interference from the Islamists, and placed their dynamite there to explode the religious society which the Islamists were so carefully trying to erect upon the rock.

"Uneducating" the new generations to rid them of what they had picked up from the traditional society had to come before re-educating them. Ismail Hakkı formulated this "uneducating" as freeing the individual from the influence of the clericals, religious orders, homes, streets, coffee houses, graveyards, and beggars.[65] While the main institutions from which to be "uneducated" were religion and the family, the mass educators had a strange phobia against certain habits that they regarded as mass obsessions having no religious or cultural value. Their attitude is worth noting, as it was a manifestation of the process of social change and secularization that is apt to be overlooked because of its outward meaninglessness. One drive initiated by Ismail Hakkı may be given in illustration. He became best known through his campaign against something that would probably occur to no one under normal conditions: the tassel attached to the fez! In innumerable lectures, he ridiculed the tassel, showed it to be wasteful, unaesthetic, and, above all, utterly devoid of any function, yet stupidly carried about by everyone. At the climax of each talk he used to draw out

[65] Ismail Hakki [Baltacıoğlu], *Terbiye-i Avam* (Istanbul, 1914); *Talim ve Terbiyede Inkilâp* (Istanbul, 1914).

a pair of scissors and cut the tassel off his own fez, for which he was known until the adoption of surnames in 1935 as Püskülsüz (Tassel-less) Ismail Hakkı.

404

The tussle over the tassle deserves analysis because it is a concrete example of an aspect of the Turkish mentality peculiar to the period and almost incomprehensible to Western observers. It reflected a strange combination of common sense and sheer nonsense with a constant, almost imperceptible shift from one to the other in a manner calculated to fool and influence an audience. Its role in the last respect was to alienate the mind of the victim audience from certain traditional obsessions. The type of logic is portrayed best in the book *Efruz Bey*, but even Ömer Seyfeddin, its author, could not invent a better illustration than the crusader against the tassel. The crusade failed in its economic objective; it certainly cost Ismail Hakkı a pretty penny (and perhaps also a few others, captivated for the moment). The people did not follow Ismail Hakkı and for years he was the only Turk without a tassel. Nonetheless, this crusade had a cultural and educational meaning. It symbolized the revolt of the new education against the things that had no meaning or function—economic, religious, national, or social—and yet continued to exist simply through dogged adherence to custom. Once an innovator begins to scoff and ridicule, once he demonstrates the irrationality of a practice as insignificant as a tassel, the totality of the customs to which that practice pertains is doomed to be challenged eventually. In our particular case, Ismail Hakkı's crusade against the tassel ended some years later with the abolition of the fez.

The same thing happened with respect to a number of other customs that did not constitute a part of the Şeriat. The new pedagogues made it their business to pick out such parts of the tradition and ridicule them. Through the outwardly meaningless criticisms of these men, the people began to think about such things. As they began to think about them, they began to notice the spheres and the roles of the religious, the moral, the useful, the useless, and the ridiculous. This was the beginning of the process of revising values and institutions.

Following such impulsive, erratic, and eccentrically expressed signs of revolt against the lethargy of the tradition, came new educational views and their more or less specialized exponents. The terms pedagogy and pedagogue were heard and used for the first time. The scholar and the instructor were known previously; the pedagogue came as a recognized authority on education for which the new term *terbiye* began to be used. If the word *maârif* symbolized the era opened by Mahmud II, the term *terbiye* well represents the Meşrutiyet era, and signifies an important improvement over the first.

The new concept of *terbiye* has been the contribution of the Westernists. The father of the new pedagogy was Sâtı' (al-Husrî) who taught the idea of *fenn-i terbiye*, an art based upon the psychology of the individual (not yet conceived as child psychology).[66] To be an educator it was not enough to be a social reformer or scholar; the teacher had to be trained in the applied science of psychology. Thus, Sâtı' introduced practice-teaching in model schools attached to the Normal School. He became the promoter of professional publications, pedagogical works, and the preparation of school text-books based on pedagogical principles. These steps constituted a great advancement over the school practices of the Hamidian era.

405

For the first time teachers assumed importance while increasing in number. They began to form a professional group distinguishable from the army officers, civil servants, and clericals and from certain liberal professions. The average age of the teachers declined so that they constituted, perhaps, the youngest professional group of the time. Second only to the doctors in modern Turkish history, the teachers began to form associations and to publish professional periodicals and books.

The importance of this new professional class should not be minimized even though it never became as strong as the other groups. While less conspicuous than the others, the teachers were the first counterparts, hence competitors, of the clericals. What the clergy were to the traditional order, the teachers were to the new. The future history of Turkey, in the educational field at least, was to consist of a struggle between the *hoca* (clerical teacher) and the *muallim* (secular teacher), the first constantly retreating and the second gaining more and more ground.

The new concept of the school teacher as educator represented an important innovation and carried a number of implications for education. One consequence was to view the teacher as someone to be equipped with manual, intellectual, moral, artistic, and athletic skills. He would be a model for his community. Another was that new orientations were to be inculcated by the teachers in their

---

[66] Now a leading writer on Arab nationalism. Upon the collapse of the Ottoman Empire Sâtı' left Turkey and adopted Arab nationality and an Arab surname.

406

schools; corporal punishment would be banned; practical and manual work, physical education and art would be introduced; the schools would prepare the future generations for successful careers. A third consequence was that drawing, painting, arts and crafts, physical exercise, and singing were given a real place in the schools for the first time. Until then, such things had been regarded as undignified for an educational institution, if not contrary to religion and mores.

All these were signs of a conception of the role of education in social change as well as signs of secularization. They were meant to liberate the school from the traditions of society, even to set it at cross purposes to the society. The emphasis was on the secular, pragmatic, and civilizational role of teaching and learning.

Perhaps the best representatives of a new conception of education as a factor in the civilizational transformation of Turkey were Tevfik Fikret and his close friend Sâtı'. In line with Prince Sabahaddin, Fikret was convinced that, without removing the harmful influences of servile and parasitic intellectuals, the nation could not be led to salvation. He planned to organize an educational institution that would guide the system of education, as a prerequisite of this economic and social progress. He forwarded his idea of the New School. He explained the aim of his School to be: to educate intelligent, honest, patriotic youth. Youth should be rescued from the harmful influences of the existing environment and be educated in the new environment of the school in such a way that personal and civic virtues might be nurtured in them. The graduates would be self-dependent and would not rely upon government. Tuition would be in Turkish and English. English would be given precedence "as it was the language of a race whose liberalism and spirit of enterprise should be examples to us." French, German, and Russian were to be optional courses. Teaching and education in the New School were to be means, not ends; all ornamental, superfluous, unpractical considerations would be rejected. Crafts would be taught; physical education would be emphasized. Music, painting, and travel would constitute important parts of the program. The two ultimate professional orientations of the School would be agriculture and business.[67]

Under the Tanzimat's secular Westernism in education the French *laïque* school had been the model. The Meşrutiyet Westernists turned, as had Sabahaddin, to what they called Anglo-Saxon education.

[67] S. N. Keramet, *Fikret'in Hayat ve Eseri* (Istanbul, 1926), pp. 44-50.

The Westernist liberalism in education brought its upholders, especially Fikret, into collision with the Islamists. Its individualism, especially as represented by Sâtı‘, was challenged by the Turkists.

The Islamists were waiting for a chance to get revenge for "Old History." The most suitable pretext came when Fikret undertook the directorship of the Lycée of Galatasaray and initiated, among other changes, what has been described as "a new conception of religious education" according to which:

> Religion should be purged from all superstitious beliefs and be taught on the basis of reason and scientific knowledge while the disruption caused by the *ulema* between the world and religion, the most important cause of our social decline, should be healed.[68]

Mehmed Âkif's "Sermon," mentioned previously, not only attacked the Westernists as the grave-diggers of Islam, but also derided Fikret as the tool of the Protestant missionaries (Âkif used the word *zangoç*, the Armenian word for sexton). Fikret's retort in his *Zeyl* ("Appendix"), in which he more openly expounded his Deism, threw more fuel on the acrid fire between the Westernists and Islamists.

However, the Islamists, too, believed that the schools should educate the Turkish youth that they might eventually acquire European sciences and techniques. What they opposed was the Westernists' attempts to further a secular morality through school education. The question of the social and cultural aims of education, especially in a social environment against which the school was put as a counter-force, was not raised by the liberal educators. The question was raised following the Balkan disaster as a result of the Islamists' criticism of the new schools for their failure to inculcate Islamic morality.

The Islamists believed that the destruction of the traditional children's schools brought the destruction of one of the foundations of Islamic education. A moral collapse was inevitable. Only religion could save the society from disaster. The new schools were organized in a way to undermine Islamic values. The intermediate and higher schools had already become the battleground of reason versus faith and the hatcheries of irreligion. All education

[68] *Ibid.*, p. 54.

should be based upon the Islamic morality.[69] The demand was consistent with the Islamists' drive to make the state, legal system, etc., Islamic and yet more Islamic.

The Islamist-Westernist controversy gave Gökalp the opportunity to discuss the nature of secular morality on the one hand, and to criticize the individualist, liberal educational views of the Westernists on the other. Occupying an intermediate position between the two, he forwarded the idea of the cultural orientation to be given to the new education. The real crisis was indeed a moral crisis. The source of this crisis was indeed in the weakening of the hold of religion. However, the remedy did not lie in religious education. In a society in which religiosity was nothing but categorical imperatives for everyone, the only morality to make men good was what Gökalp called ascetic morality (*zuhdî ahlâk*) which was based on the principles of *vâcib* and *harâm* (imperatives and prohibitions). This type of morality worked well so long as the religion behind it remained as the ultimate source of moral values. But religion was no longer the source of values. That was why Turkey was facing a moral crisis; it was in a state of transition from an *ümmet* state to a state of nationhood. The religious basis of the old moral values was incapable of functioning in its old way. Therefore, those who sought to base morality on religion were unknowingly contributing to the disintegration of morality. That was why religious fanaticism and hypocrisy were found side by side; irreligiosity was man's reaction to both. Fanaticism, hypocrisy and irreligiosity were manifestations of the failure of religion to provide a basis for morality.[70]

What then would be the source or the basis of the new secular morality? Did the schools have a role in establishing it? It was in this part of his discussion that Gökalp turned from his criticism of the Islamists to jab at the Westernists. He believed that all the schools to be found in Turkey had failed to contribute to the moral

408

Gökalp

---

[69] One of the Members of Parliament said, "In order to build morality on a firm foundation in the schools it is necessary above all to base it on a sacred sanction. In order to establish morality and to develop a collective consciousness it is absolutely necessary to give the greatest emphasis to religious instruction in school programs." Another member demanded that only the Kur'an should be taught in the primary schools. Quoted by Osman Ergin, *Türkiye Maarif Tarihi* (Istanbul, 1942), IV, 1142. See pp. 1136 and 1144 for further statements by other members.

[70] Z. Gökalp, "Ahlâk Buhranı," *Yeni Mecmua*, No. 7 (Istanbul, 1918), 122-24.

reorientation of the people. More than that, they had even been sources of moral and mental confusion, if not decadence! To follow Gökalp's argument we must remember his particular distinctions between culture and civilization and his contention that the basic malady of Turkish society was an acute lack of adjustment between the two. Western civilization was defeating the institutions of Islamic civilization at every step. In the struggle between the two, the Tanzimat, in its attempt to make an adjustment, had destroyed the foundations of the national culture which had survived destruction by the Islamic civilization. There were, therefore, three types of educational institutions—the *medrese,* the foreign school, and the *mektep,* the Turkish imitation of the second.

"Talk to a Turk for ten minutes," Gökalp said, "and you can discover in which school his mentality has been molded."[71] Education in all of the schools had been penetrated by foreign civilizations; their cultural orientation was to a large extent non-Turkish. All were hostile to the Turkish culture. Each one of the three types of school, furthermore, produced men with antagonistic civilizational attachments which precluded common understanding on a cultural level. The function of the schools of all three types had been only to transmit the ready-made rules and techniques of the opposed civilizations and to ignore completely the evolution of the national culture which lingered among the uneducated outside the school. That was why they were institutions for imitation, but not for creativity. The educational problem was not, therefore, merely a matter of better techniques of teaching, more teachers equipped with modern pedagogical knowledge and skills, but rather a matter of orienting education on the basis of a new secular morality which would derive from the national culture.[72]

As an Ottomanist and Westernist, Sâtı' attacked the ideas for national education forwarded by Gökalp. The controversy between Sâtı' and Gökalp was one of the exciting fights of the period. At first it appeared that the two were sparring over pedagogical details, then a looping right of psychologism was countered by a short left of sociologism and they went into a clinch of Spencerian individualism versus Durkheim's collectivism. As the

---

[71] Emin Erişirgil, *Bir Fikir Adamının Romanı — Ziya Gökalp* (Istanbul, 1951), p. 208.

[72] Gökalp, *Turkish Nationalism,* pp. 325 ff.

410

rounds passed the styles of the two pugilists became clear: it was a liberal Ottomanist against a nationalist Turkist. Sâtı' disclosed in the long run that what he was opposing in Gökalp's arguments was the idea of nationalism. He was opposed to nationalism not simply on the basis of his individualist psychology and his liberal ideology, but for the simple reason that Turkish nationalism in education was incompatible with the multi-national composition of the Ottoman Empire. Thus, like the foreign school administrators, he would not approve of Turkish nationalism lest the non-Turkish nationalities should find their opportunities to develop their own national cultures suppressed. In the anomaly of the Ottoman Empire, the arguments of both sides, easily justifiable in themselves, represented an insoluble antinomy. The logical consequence of the position taken by Sâtı' would amount to saying that a liberal education should provide free expression for the culture of all nationalities except the Turkish, because expression of the latter would not be compatible with liberal education!

Only the historical events, the collapse of the Ottoman Empire, could solve this antinomy. Before tracing this process, we must probe further into the development of the Turkist ideology and the attempts, on the eve of World War I, to give expression to the reform policies derived from the Turkist discussions.

ALL OF THE CONTROVERSIES over the institutions of state, family, education, and economy were concerned with the social transformation (*içtimaî inkilâp*) so universally desired at the opening of the Meşrutiyet era. In their demands for programs of action, the Westernists and Islamists constituted polar opposites on almost every issue. The Turkists were between the two, sometimes representing a synthesis, and almost always gaining strength and influence.

The liberals brought nothing new to Tanzimatist secularism. But Islamist pressure for a reform which would be nothing but the implementation of an Islamic state forced the Turkists to tackle the problems of Tanzimat secularism and to offer new solutions. We must evaluate the Turkist trend less because of its ascendency in the last years of the Meşrutiyet than because of its originality and because of its legacy to Kemalist secularism.

Secularizing Reforms Through Turkist Influence

Neither the Young Ottomans nor the Young Turks had an indigenous national basis for their ideas or reforms—a class, a religious community, a race, or a nation. In the absence of a concrete group as substratum and as source of motivation and orientation, the liberals became conscious for the first time of the need for such as a group to act as a lever or, as they called it, a *nokta-i istinat*

412

(fulcrum). They became interested more in social group than in state; this was reflected in a shift of their interests to the European sociologists from the political philosophers. But the society of the Hamidian era with its Ottoman and Islamic institutions provided no fulcrum by means of which that society could be attached to Western civilization. They found the essence of Western civilization in its individualistic basis, in its economic system of private ownership, and in its freedom from governmental as well as religious authority. Only the inculcation of the principles of Western civilization could transform Ottoman society from the Oriental to the Western societal form. The fulcrum, therefore, was seen to be education. Education could transform society by liberating individuals from the yoke of tradition.

Despite the attractiveness of the liberal view of the Westernists, shown by its winning over the majority of the Young Turks during the discussions before and after 1908, it was only an intellectualist utopia. It was still devoid of social support, as was again shown by its continuous failure within the framework of a multinational non-secularized political organization.

It was the Turkists who saw that it was the people, the Turkish people, who would be the fulcrum for a transformation into nationhood.[1] And it was only indirectly, through their nationalism, that they hit upon a secularist view which gave a new note to Meşrutiyet secularism.

The word "reform" thus assumed a clearer and different meaning—it meant neither reinstating the reign of the Şeriat and establishing an Islamic State, nor mere enlightenment by imitating European education. The basic problem was one of social transformation, but not a transformation from a collectivistic system to an individualistic system. The transformation would be a change from the *ümmet* to a *millet* type of society which would inevitably involve a shift from the Eastern civilization (erroneously called Islamic or Turkish) to the modern (*asrî*, which also meant secular) civilization (erroneously conceived as Christian or European). Ziya Gökalp succeeded in replacing the unpopular term *dehrî* with the word *asrî*. The word *asrî* escaped the anathematization of the Islamists.

Two lines of action appeared open in the light of this approach: to liberate the Turkish people from the *ümmet* pattern, that is, to

[1] See Gökalp's criticism of the educational views of the liberals in *Turkish Nationalism and Western Civilization*, ed. Niyazi Berkes (London and New York, 1959), pp. 233-46.

secularize; and to provide that collectivity with new bone and flesh, that is, a new economy and technology.

The Turkists were unable to talk of the secularization of the Ottoman state because it was impossible to make it either national or secular. The difference between the Turkist and Tanzimat approaches to the problem of secularization can be illustrated best within the fields of education, law, and certain customs.

The target of, perhaps, the most intense Westernist fire was the *medrese*, which had come to be viewed as a religious institution since it had been left to the realm of matters not to be changed, following the coming of the *mektep*. While there were *medrese* revivals throughout the Islamic world, for example in Russia, India, Egypt, and Indonesia, during the last quarter of the nineteenth century, there had been in Turkey no desire to make *medreses* of *mekteps;* neither had any attempt to convert *medreses* into *mekteps* succeeded, as has been illustrated by the case of the *Dar-ul-funûn*.

If the *medrese* could not be modernizd by converting it into a secular institution, why not bring modern sciences into the *medrese*, asked both the Westernists and the Islamists of the Meşrutiyet era. Reforming the *medrese* gave to the Islamists the hope of gaining support, strengthened by European sciences, for the implementation of the Islamic state. The reform meant to the Westernists possession of the means of implementing a rational approach to religion.

Influenced by a demand for the modernization of the *medreses* from both quarters, the government took measures in 1909. One of the early *medreses*, that founded by Mehmed the Conqueror, was reopened in streamlined form.[2] The opening ceremony was attended by the Sadrazam, the Şeyhul-Islâm, the presidents of both houses of parliament, and the Minister of Education. After the opening lecture on *tafsîr*, all of them gave speeches. Stressing the deplorable state of backwardness and referring to the inclusion of modern sciences such as physics, chemistry, astronomy, geometry, and geography in the curriculum of the *medrese*, the speakers expressed their hope that the reformed institutions would lead the nation to progress. Even *İçtihad* suspended its claims that the *medreses* were incapable of reform.

One of the members of the Şeyhul-Islâm's staff proposed a reform project for the higher level of *medrese*. There would be four major faculties: (*a*) religious (*shar'i*) sciences comprising

[2] *Sırat-ı Müstakim*, No. 76 (1909).

tafsîr, *hadîth*, *kalâm*, *fiqh*, and *akhlâq*; (*b*) *hikma* (*hikmet*), comprising philosophy, mathematics, and natural sciences; (*c*) history, including also the *siyar* (the life and conduct of the Prophet); and, (*d*) languages, comprising Arabic, Persian, and Turkish.[3] Except for the absence of medical training this would be virtually a university under the Şeyhul-Islâm, standing opposite the secular university and almost a replica of the Dar-ul-funûn which the old Şeyhul-Islâm Hasan Fehmi had succeeded in destroying when it was opened under the Ministry of Education.

414

The dualism of the Tanzimat was once more endorsed officially by these measures. Once again the Westernists proved themselves unaware that in the Turkish transformation anything which became modernized ceased to be "religious," while the "religious" increasingly comprised anything that was not changing or should not change.

While such grandstand modernizing reforms were being applauded, the Şeyhul-Islâm was more interested in expanding his authority in education, law, and usages further than ever. Some of his new activities were in direct contradiction with the alleged dualist modernity. The Şeyhul-Islâm attempted to establish himself as the final authority vested with the power of control, not only over action, but even over thought. A few examples will illustrate the attempt.

The censorship department of the Hamidian administration no longer existed, but the Şeyhul-Islâm now had his own under the name of the Board of Inspection of the Şeriat Writings. The most controversial case was the battle between Abdullah Cevdet and the Islamists over his translation of Dozy's *History of Islam*.[4] Although this work was not a *shar'i* book under the jurisdiction of the board of the Şeyhul-Islâm, he exerted pressure upon the cabinet and had the book confiscated. The first Turkish translation of the Kur'an was made in 1914, but the work was confiscated before its publi-

---

[3] Şevketi, *Medaris-i Islâmiye Islahat Programı* (Istanbul, 1913).

[4] *Tarih-i Islâmiyet* (2 vols.; Cairo, 1909) was translated by Abdullah Cevdet from R. Dozy, *Essai sur l'histoire de l'Islamisme* (Paris, 1879). See *Sırat-ı Müstakim*, No. 72 (1909) and subsequent issues. See also Ebüzziya Tevfik, *Tasvir-i Efkâr*, No. 47, (1910) and Mehmet Şükrü, *Tarih-i Islâmiyet ve Mütercimi* (Istanbul, 1910). Mehmed Âkif declared Cevdet a *mulhid; Sırat-ı Müstakim*, No. 78, (1910).

cation was completed, and its further publication prohibited.[5] The teaching of evolutionism was discouraged by the arrest of a teacher of natural science on the instigation of the religious authority.[6]

The Şeyhul-Islâm not only exercised such executive powers; he also began to extend his authority over the judiciary as well as over the legislative organs by reviving an old prerogative of the Şeyhul-Islâm. According to this, a Şeyhul-Islâm's choice among the deviant opinions of the ancient *imâms* on a legal point had the force of law once it was confirmed by the ruler. Thus, the Şeyhul-Islâm began to obtain the ratification of the ruler over matters of civil law without consulting cabinet ministers or parliament.[7] In other words, the Şeyhul-Islâm tried to regain the legislative power that Hasan Fehmi had lost half a century earlier to Cevdet Paşa. His behaviour roused much criticism, but only partially effectual opposition from the government and the parliament; both claimed that the religious institution was stepping into their respective fields.

The Turkists did not believe in the feasibility of the government's attempt to modernize the *medreses* so long as the Şeyhul-Islâm sat in the cabinet, ruled the *şeriat* courts, had half the educational system under his jurisdiction, and even legislated in a particular field. The problem for them was to shift his authority to what was properly "religious." They saw the *medrese* reform not as a matter of religious reform, but as a matter of educational reform.

Gökalp prepared a memorandum for the Party of Union and Progress on the relegation of religious institutions and their men to the realm of the *diyanet* (piety).[8] This meant the severance of the Şeyhul-Islâm from politics, the *şeriat* courts, the administration of *evkaf* and, finally, the schools, because, as the highest religious authority, his main function was *iftâ*, which was incompatible with these administrative, financial, judicial, and pedagogical functions.

The main reforms carried out in 1916 in accordance with this view were: (*a*) the elimination of the Şeyhul-Islâm from the

---

[5] Osman Ergin, *Türkiye Maarif Tarihi* (Istanbul, 1943), V, p. 1611; Y. Akçura, *Türk Yurdu*, VI, No. 64 (1914), p. 2136. The idea of translating the Kur'an was discussed at length and rejected by Mustafa Sabri; see his *Dinî Mücedditler* (Istanbul, 1920), pp. 197-200.

[6] See above, pp. 379-80.

[7] See above, p. 371.

[8] Gökalp, *Turkish Nationalism*, pp. 202-14.

416

cabinet; (*b*) the transfer of the *şeriat* courts from the jurisdiction of the Şeyhul-Islâm to that of the Ministry of Justice; (*c*) the removal of the *evkaf* administration from the jurisdiction of the Şeyhul-Islâm, its complete secularization and reorganization as another financial-commercial department of the state under a cabinet minister, and the assignment of all financial matters concerning the religious institutions (mosques, medreses, etc.) to the jurisdiction of the new Ministry of *Evkaf*; and finally (*d*) the transferral of the *medreses* from the jurisdiction of the Şeyhul-Islâm to that of the Ministry of Education. The last measure was a significant step towards the complete secularization of education. It led eventually to the abolition of the *medreses*. The first measure was also a prelude to the abolition of the office of the Şeyhul-Islâm. The second prepared the ground for the eventual unification of the judiciary.

These steps constituted part of a new type of movement towards the separation of religion from the state. Religion was divested of its temporal influence in state, educational, legislational, judicial, and financial affairs. Its powers and functions were confined to the sphere of *diyanet* (as Gökalp called it), that is, to matters of piety. A department called Dar-ul Hikmet-ul Islâmiye (School of Islamic Philosophy) was founded within the office of the Şeyhul-Islâm to modernize the *kalâm*, and a specialized institution of Islamic learning (Medreset-ul Mutehassisîn) was opened. The function of these was to have been not to censor or prosecute, but to cultivate a modern understanding of Islam.

Perhaps the most important secularizing trend, the logical consequence of removing the religious authority from legislation, was to be found in the two legislative acts of the period. The first, the Law of *Şeriat* Court Procedure, promulgated in 1917, was another step towards the unification of the judicial procedure.[9] The second was the preparation of the first family code in an Islamic country.

The 1908 Revolution and, especially, the discussions on womanhood, family, marriage, and divorce stimulated the desire to revive the process of codification begun by the Tanzimat. Students of law, as well as lawyers and judges, were conscious of the insufficiency as well as shortcomings of the Mecelle as a civil code. Wrote one, "All matters relating to marriage and divorce, inheritance, wills, and guardianship were not codified and were subject to the

---

[9] The official text of the law of 12 March 1917 is in *Takvim-i Vekayi*, No. 2840, (1917).

interpretations of the *muftîs*." Everyone stressed the pressing need for the codification of a family law.[10]

The changes in the lives of women brought about by World War I, the abolition of the capitulations, the development of ideas concerning the relations between state and religion and between state and nationality facilitated the codification of the Law of Family Rights in 1917.[11]

417

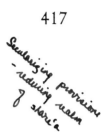

The Family Code reflected the characteristic co-existence of the secular and the religious. It incorporated provisions of Islamic, Jewish, Christian, and secular European origin. It had separate provisions for Muslims, Christians, and Jews. It codified the provisions af the ecclesiastical and customary laws. Although the Muslim marriage was basically a dissoluble contractual act and not, therefore, conceived as a sacrament, it had in time assumed the character of a customary law by not having been codified by sovereign legislators as a legal act. The Code did not bring a new system of civil law based on secular jurisprudence.

With the new Code, marriage was accepted as a legal contractual act to be registered by an authority indicated by the state even though the contracting parties were left free to practise whatever ritual or sacramental forms of marriage they wished. The law, however, removed the legally binding character of the sacramental rituals by allowing the dissolution of marriage again by a public authority. Thus, in one sense, there was a theocratization of the marriage law by the acceptance of the Muslim, Christian, and Jewish religious provisions; yet, in another sense, there was a secularization in religious affairs because an important segment of life over which the Şeriat and the church had maintained monopolistic control was given over to the sanctioning of the state and to a certain extent made a legal act. A Turkist jurist, while declaring the law to be an important step toward secularization, criticized it as not yet a civil law freed from ecclesiastical and customary provisions.[12] On the other hand, the Code of 1917 was resented by the Christians and criticized by the Islamists.

[10] Celâl Nuri, *Havayic-i Kanuniyemiz* (Istanbul, 1914); Ahmed Şuayip, *Hukuk-u İdare* (Istanbul, 1909), p. 17; Ahmed Cevad, *Bizde Kadın* (Istanbul, n.d.), p. 44.

[11] See L. Bouvat, "Le code familial Ottoman de 1917," *Revue de Monde Musulman*, XLIII (1921), 5-26; J. N. D. Anderson, *Islamic Law in the Modern World* (New York, 1959), pp. 26-27.

[12] S. Edip, "Bizde Nikâhın Şekl-i Hazırı ve Medenî Nikâh," *Türk Yurdu*, No. 154 (March 1, 1918), 126-30.

418

The Islamists' main objection to the Code was that it transferred the conclusion of the marriage contract to the authority and sanctioning power of the state. Although the state itself was yet a split-personality (one half secular and the other theocratic), the marriage contract was transferred from its theocratic half to its secular half. The scope of the *şeriat* courts was thus reduced still further; that is, there was a new and important transfer of jurisdiction from the area of the sacred to the area of the secular.

A second reason for Islamist objection was the fact that the Code recognized the right of women to initiate divorce. Even the circumscribed recognition of such a right by the provisions that a wife was entitled to divorce if the husband wished to take a second wife and the first did not consent, or if the husband violated certain conditions that the bride-to-be was allowed to have incorporated into the marriage contract, was too much for the Islamists.

The provisions of the Code about polygamy did not please the Islamists either. While the legislators had not dared abolish it entirely, the Code did erect certain obstacles to it by favouring women. According to these: (*a*) a wife could seek a divorce if she learned following marriage that her husband had a condition making marital intercourse impossible, (*b*) a bride-to-be could stipulate in the marriage contract that the husband could not enter into polygamous marriage, and (*c*) if the terms of such a marriage contract were broken, either the first or the second marriage would be dissolved automatically upon the first wife's petition.

One of the writers for *Sebil,* a professor of theology in the University of Istanbul, wrote a series of articles to show that "the rights recognized to women for divorce and against polygamy were un-Islamic, as could be shown uncontestably from the *Kitâb* (the Kur'an) and the Sunna (Prophetic Tradition)."[13] This professor also criticized the law for including some provisions from the Shâfiî and Mâlikî opinions. For him God's Law should be supreme; but it is difficult to understand from his discourse why God's Law was manifested only in the Hanafî code.

When Istanbul was occupied by the Allies in 1919, representations were made by the Christian *millets* to have the Code declared null and void. They succeeded only in having Article 156, which concerned the matters of dowry and alimony, nullified; in 1921 these matters were returned to the jurisdiction of the Christian churches. Abrogated in Turkey in 1926, the Code continued to

---

[13] See Sadreddin, "Hukuk-u Âile," *Sebil-ür Reşad,* X (1917), p. 320.

apply in Jordan and Syria until 1953 and is still applied in Lebanon and in Israel.

Parallel with this contraction of religious control within the field of law, we find a definite orientation toward the secularization of primary education. The first drive, begun in the confusion at the beginning of the period, was to replace the traditional *sibyân* schools for children by *mekteps*, that is, modern elementary schools of a parochial type. The *sibyân* schools had been the product of the abortive attempts of the Tanzimat to extend literacy. They turned out to be miniature *medreses*, producing little Kur'an reciters and industrious rote learners, where the children sat on mats or cushions (*minders*) in dank, dark cubicles, were taught to sit silently and respectfully, and were disciplined by the teacher's stick. Moving, playing, singing, talking, and laughing were the ultimate vices in the pedagogy of these schools.

Primary education assumed central importance for the first time in the Meşrutiyet period. The Ministry of Education, which previously had been concerned mainly with higher and intermediate education, competed with the Evkaf Ministry in opening *mekteps*, not only in the capital but even in the provinces. Out of this was born the policy of the full nationalization of primary education.

The secularization of the teaching staffs and the rise of the professional pedagogue and teacher have been noted in the previous chapter. Under the influence of Gökalp, through his controversies with the Westernist educationists, courses in literature, history and philosophy were introduced into secondary education. Chairs in sociology, and philosophy, and "national studies" such as literature, history, and fine arts were introduced into the new University of Istanbul. It is true that there had been new interest in philosophy in general, and in Western philosophy in particular, beginning with the Tanzimat, but philosophy had nowhere been taught and the men occupied with such frivolities were branded as *dehrî* and *zindîq*. Even towards the end of the nineteenth century, the students of a school of higher learning had risen against an attempt to introduce a course in philosophy, claiming that it would make them unbelievers. Thus, both the innovation itself and the absence of opposition to it were significant.

A number of other reforms were promoted in 1916-17 for the further separation of worldly affairs from religious traditions. Perhaps the one most significant for our subject was the step taken towards the adoption of the Western calendar. The transformation in the type of calendar used in Turkey may serve as an index to the process of secularization.

Before the nineteenth century, Ottoman Turkey, as a Muslim state, officially used the Islamic calendar called *Hijrî* (dating from the Prophet's flight from Mecca to Medina on July 19, 622 A.D. in terms of the Gregorian calendar). It is based on a lunar system, and has no method to keep the months recurring in the same solar season. Its years retrogress through all seasons once in every thirty-two and a half solar years. It was a source of inconvenience in the temporal affairs of the state, particularly in connection with fiscal matters. To overcome the difficulties, unsystematized and inaccurate traditional and local calendars were used in addition. This condition lasted in the Ottoman administration until the end of the eighteenth century.

With the disintegration of the *timar* organization, with the shift from benefice and prebend remuneration to salary payments from a public treasury, with the application of tax collection through taxation officials, and with the increase in the importance of European trade, in short, with the emergence of a new state apparatus to replace the medieval apparatus, the shortcomings of the *Hijrî* calendar for the interests of a government disposed towards increased public functions became more acute. The absence of a uniform and accurate calendar increased the difficulties inherent in a transformation from medieval to modern conditions.

From 1789 there was an increasing tendency to extend the use of solar calendars in the various departments of the state (significantly, first in the customs and then in tax-farming). It became necessary to adopt a solar calendar and to fix the beginning of the year for fiscal purposes according to a solar system. In 1790, corresponding to the year 1205 A.H., a calendar, called *Malî* (fiscal), was devised.

The fiscal year was based upon the Julian or *Rumî* (Roman) calendar (instead of the Gregorian, which had not yet been universally adopted). While it was solar in months, which were subdivisions of a solar year, these months were related to the lunar years of the *Hijrî* chronology. Thus, it was only partially connected with the religious tradition and was used in the affairs of the state as a temporal institution. The areas other than this in which the *Hijrî* chronology continued to be used began to appear as "religious" *par excellence*.

The adoption of the *Malî* calendar meant, thus, the beginning of a duality, similar to those we have observed in Chapters 4 and

6, rather than a shift from one calendar system (lunar) to another (solar). Had there been a clear differentiation between the secular and the religious, the difficulties resulting from the co-existence of solar and lunar calendars would have been confined to questions of translating from one to the other and of devising techniques for overcoming the problems of intercalation. Confusion resulted from the reform mainly because of the temporal implications of innumerable incidents dated by the *Hijrî* calendar. A further drawback resulted from the almost universal acceptance of the Gregorian system in Europe by the end of the eighteenth century (in England in 1750; in Russia only after the Bolshevik Revolution).

421

The first attempt towards a complete shift from the Islamic and Ottoman calendars to the European calendar was made in 1915. (Japan and China made the transition in 1912.) A motion made at a convention of the Party of Union and Progress stated in part,

As the lunar calendar . . . is convenient only in religious matters such as fasting and pilgrimage, but is inconvenient in social relations [*mu'âmelât*] and as the *Malî* calendar . . . has introduced several errors and difficulties of adjustment, and as our need for the European calendar is increasing day by day owing to our widening relations with the European countries, the Gregorian calendar should be adopted with necessary modifications.

This proposal was adopted by the government in 1916. The government's bill was modified by the conservative upper house (Meclis-i Âyan) which rejected the adoption of the Christian date while accepting the Gregorian, in place of the Julian, calendar. Thus, the law converted the fiscal date February 16, 1333, to March 1 of the European calendar—not 1917, but rather 1333! (In fact, the real *Hijrî* date then was Rabi ıı 28, 1335; the omission of intercalatory adjustments since the adoption of the fiscal calendar had caused a shift of two years.) The law stated that the *Hijrî* calendar would be used only for religious affairs.[14]

A very similar situation existed with regard to the telling of time. Two system of hours, one religious and beginning from sunrise and the other the mean solar system, co-existed until the official adoption in 1926 of the latter with the Greenwich clock as the standard.

Dual or multiple systems of weights and measures existed until other laws caused the standard metric system to be used for all public and official purposes.

[14] See J. Deny, "L'Adoption du calendrier grégorien en Turquie," *Revue du Monde Musulman*, XLIII (1921), 46-49.

422

The idea of reforming the script was also revived in 1912. The idea of adopting the Latin script began to be defended openly. Men like Hüseyin Cahit and Abdullah Cevdet believed that the Arabic script was incapable of any reform and, therefore, that efforts directed simply at a reform were not worth while.

The Latinizing thesis met with almost universal opposition. The chief obstacle for the Islamists was the impossibility of converting the language of a Muslim nation into a script that was nothing but 'infidel scratchings.' However, the Islamists were equally, if not more, opposed to the idea of reviving the scripts used by pre-Muslim Turks with which some of the Turkists toyed for a while. In their eyes the heathen Turks were worse than the Christian Ahl al-Kitâb. The Turkists were dissatisfied with the Arabic alphabet as it was used in Turkish. In addition to seeing the educational implications of the matter, it was they who understood the issue in historical perspective. However, the Turkists regarded the problem as being less one of script than one of simplifying the language. Only the so-called purist Turkists, who would purge Turkish of every foreign influence, became interested in reviving the script of the Orhon inscriptions or the Uygur alphabet (the first derived from the runic and the second from the Syriac scripts); this idea was never taken seriously. Those who unintentionally carried the matter to the point where adoption of the Latinized script gained considerable appeal were, in fact, the reformists. They wanted to improve the script without abandoning the use of the Arabic alphabet. They desired to overcome the differences in the Turkish and Arabic pronunciations of certain Arabic letters, and especially the confusion resulting from the traditional adaptation of the Arabic script in connection with Turkish vowels.

The reformers began with the idea of introducing invented signs to remedy the vowel problem. A number of schemes were proposed to overcome the fact that the Arabic letter *waw* carried the burden of four distinct and important vowels, *o, ö, u*, and *ü*, in addition to standing for the Turkish consonant *v* and for the English *w*, which does not exist in Turkish. Ingenious souls invented various signs to be placed above that letter to indicate the appropriate vowel sound. The more the prophets and inventors multiplied and intensified their propaganda through lectures, exhibitions, pamphlets, and demonstrations, the less the idea of improving the Arabic script appealed to the reading public.

The confusion caused by crackpot zeal inspired another group whose idea somehow created greater interest despite its greater eccentricity. This idea represented a sort of compromise with the Latinists. It consisted of using the Arabic characters as what were called non-agglutinative letters (unconnected and unmodified by positioning) and of replacing the diacritical marks by Arabic consonants to be assigned vowel values and a few invented signs that would be positioned as ordinary letters. It was believed that this invention would permit a phonetic rendering of Turkish without sacrificing the Arabic alphabet. The scheme eliminated one of the major advantages of the Arabic script—that it could be written at least as fast as a modern system of shorthand by a practised writer. On the other hand, it gave promise of minimizing what could be serious errors in reading and transcription, and of facilitating telecommunication.[15]

At first, the proposal won general interest. It even won semi-official recognition. The Minister of War issued a circular to the forces in 1914 to use this system in their intercommunications. Whatever benefit this may have had for the semi-literate non-commissioned officers, to whom a minor omission or slur in the old writing could mean the difference between attack and retreat, a worse time could not have been chosen to have the army officers re-educate themselves in the ABC's.

The controversies and inventions created a confusion characteristic of an institution entering a state of change. But so long as the language and script were regarded as matters of Islamic heritage, or of national culture, no way out was found.

Towards a National Economy

The foregoing liberalizing and secularizing measures effected by the Turkist approach to reform were to lead toward the economic advancement of the Turkish nation, which was seen more or less clearly to be the real objective.

In the degree of their ignorance concerning the nature of the economic problems of countries like Turkey, the Westernists and Islamists were on a par. If the sources for the latter were the *fiqh*

[15] A. S. Levend, *Türk Dilinde Gelişme ve Sadeleşme Safhaları* (Ankara, 1949), pp. 309-42; F. R. Unat, *Türkiyede Neşriyat Hareketleri* (Istanbul, 1939), pp. 145-46 and specimens of the proposed improved script on plates at the end.

books, those of the former were the French manuals on *l'économie politique*. Neither side understood the basic differential between an industrialized civilization and a traditionalist agrarian society.

424

Turkey's economic problems were discussed by the Westernist economists in terms of the categories of the capitalist economy and as if Turkey belonged to the same economic system. As if they had made a great discovery the Westernists said, "borrow from Europe and bring Europeans to run our economy." Typical is this statement by the economist, later the Finance Minister, of the Unionists:

The number of those . . . who would not want the coming of foreign capital to our country is less than the foreigners believe. There are certain small-scale enterprises that can be carried by the accumulated capital in the country which, of course, we would not like to have pass into the hands of foreigners. . . . Yet, in my opinion, we must accept foreigners even in such enterprises for the sake of establishing a skill, that of management and rationalization, which we lack so badly. As to important public works, these can be done only with foreign capital. . . . All countries in a state of opening themselves to civilization will inevitably stumble and fall in their new path if they seek to advance by their own forces. . . . All new countries have been able to advance only with the help of foreign capital.[16]

Cavit was the new prophet of borrowing from the European capitalists. In a series of articles on the history of the Turkish loans, he came to the conclusion, contrary to that reached by Parvus, that there was no solution to Turkey's economic recovery other than finding more and more loan capital.[17]

Meanwhile, the Islamists portrayed the economic virtues of the pious medieval trader or artisan and believed that the modern Muslim would prosper industrially and commercially with the restoration of these virtues. The Islamist literature of the period is utterly devoid of any cognizance of the real state of the peasantry, or of the working class, or of the economic conditions surrounding the entire nation. Thus, aside from the discussions of economic ethics, the Islamists had nothing to say about the ways and means of economic recovery in Turkey beyond repeating the phrase "taking sciences and industries from Europe"—as if it was as easy as importing European glue.

[16] Mehmed Cavit, "Neşriyat ve Vekayi-i Iktisadiye," *Ulûm-u Içtimaiye ve Iktisadiye Mecmuası*, II, No. 5 (May 1909), 129-30.

[17] Mehmed Cavit, in *ibid.*, II, Nos. 5-9 (1909).

If he did not bring socialism to the Turks, Parvus shattered a persistent illusion of the Turkish intellectuals. He pointed out that Turkey was not a part of the European civilization and could not become a part of it simply through volition or even by being taken into the European diplomatic concert. On the contrary, Turkey was a target of imperialistic aggression by European capitalism and well along the way to becoming an area for colonial exploitation. The economic relations between Turkey and Europe were of the nature of the relations existing between the exploited and exploiters. The major question of social revolution was not, therefore, one of a socialist revolution. This had meaning only in the capitalist countries. It was a question of national independence and economic recovery under a democracy that would turn to the people and take measures in terms of a national economy.

The Turkists were clearer on the economic aspirations for which the Turkish Revolution should stand. Probably influenced by Parvus' socialism and inspired by the economic developments of the bourgeoisie of the Turkish-speaking peoples of Russia, they developed the idea of economic nationalism and the policy of étatism in order to combat the economic bondage of the Turkish masses to the European economy and to foster the economic growth of a middle class which would be the carrier of the economic interests of the Turkish nationality within the Ottoman Empire.

After reviewing the major indices of an economic revival among the Turks in the year 1914, Akçura wrote:

The most important aspect of this economic awakening is the change we see in the mentality that despised trade and industry and believed that government and military occupations were the most worthy of an Ottoman Turk. . . . The foundation of the modern state is the bourgeois class. Contemporary prosperous states came into existence on the shoulders of the bourgeoisie, of the businessmen and bankers. The Turkish national awakening in Turkey is the beginning of the genesis of the Turkish bourgeoisie. And, if the natural growth of the Turkish bourgeoisie continues without damage or interruption, we can say that the sound establishment of the Turkish state has been guaranteed.[18]

Elsewhere Akçura clarified the economic views of the Turkists further.

[18] *Türk Yurdu*, No. 63 (April 3, 1330), 2102-3; see also Akçura, "Türklük," *Salname-i Servet-i Funûn* (1911), pp. 187-96; Akçura, "Türk Milliyetçiliğinin Iktisadî Menşelerine Dair," *Siyaset ve Iktisat* (Istanbul, 1923), pp. 141-93.

We are nationalists and democrats. . . . We believe that the real substratum of the Turkish existence is the peasant class. . . . Still, while our nationalism demands that we give the primary place to the peasantry, it equally demands that we support the growth of the Turkish bourgeoisie.

426

With the decline of the medieval trader and artisan organizations of the Turks in the Ottoman Empire under the onslaught of European capitalism and big industry, Turkish society became a crippled organism composed . . . of the classes of town gentry (eşraf), peasantry and government officials. Just as the Jews and Germans constituted the bourgeoisie in Poland, in Turkey it was the native Jews, Greeks, and Armenians who were the agents and middlemen of European capitalism, and the Levantines whose nationality and citizenship are known to no one. If the Turks fail to produce among themselves a bourgeois class by profiting from European capitalism, the chances of survival of a Turkish society composed only of peasants and officials will be very slim.[19]

Nearly all the discussants of the Union's economic policies stressed the conscious effort to promote the creation of a Turkish middle class. Turkist and pan-Turkist publications abounded with stories of the manufacturers, businessmen, oil millionaires and liberal professionals among the Russian Turks. The stories about their origins and material success were designed to dispel the two dogmas entertained by the Westernists and Islamists respectively: the Turk is incapable of economic success unless aided by Europeans; the material worldly success of the Muslim is detrimental to his salvation in the other world.

As a recent writer has put it:

The members of the central committee of the Union were convinced that democracy could not be founded and the Union would not have its fulcrum so long as the middle classes called bourgeoisie did not develop among the Turks. The First World War would provide the chance for the formation of such a social class. The capitulations had been abolished. Non-Turkish businesses could be taken under control. In their stead Turkish businessmen would be encouraged, organized, and linked by government to the state-promoted national banks.[20]

---

[19] *Türk Yurdu*, No. 140 (Aug. 12, 1333), pp. 2521-22.

[20] Emin Erişirgil, *Mehmet Âkif, Islâmcı Bir Şairin Romanı* (Ankara, 1956), pp. 328-29. See also Ahmed Emin [Yalman], *Turkey in the World War* (New Haven, 1930), p. 114; Osman Nuri [Ergin] *Mecelle-i Umûr-u Belediye* (Istanbul, 1922), I, 869.

It was under the guidance of economic Turkism following the abolition of the capitulations in 1914 that the government embarked on a series of economic measures.[21] These reforms included the initiation, not only of a policy of nationalization and Turkification in the economic institutions, but also of steps toward the secularization of these institutions by promoting banking and credit facilities, the adoption of the Gregorian calendar, and the European system of telling time.

Neither the economic nor the social consequences of these early economic reforms were harvested during the War and the following Armistice years. It is, however, certain that they were greatly responsible in giving impetus to the nationalist struggle that followed the collapse of the Ottoman Empire in 1919.

Turkist Romanticism

The conditions of World War I not only precluded the realization of the economic aspirations of the Turkists; they also fostered the romantic aspect of Turkish nationalism at the expense of its realistic aspect, both of which were implicit in the Turkists' slogan: "To the People."

The People, as Akçura defined them, were (*a*) small land-owning or landless peasants, (*b*) small artisans and shopkeepers (*esnaf*), and (*c*) wage earners and labourers.[22] These were the classes comprising the great majority of the Turks. All of them were in decline and impoverished.[23] Their economic impoverishment meant the absence of the real fulcrum of the Turkish nationality.

What was only a utopian ideal in Turkey—that is the growth of an entrepreneurial class—was a reality among the Russian Turks. The aspirations of this class weighed heavily in the formation of pan-Turkism. Pan-Turkism of the Turkish-speaking immigrants from Russia began to over-shadow the more modest To-the-People movement of the Ottoman Turkists. The real figure of the impov-

---

[21] For further details see Ahmed Emin [Yalman], *Turkey in the World War*, pp. 115 ff.

[22] Y. Akçura, *Halka Doğru* I, No. 22 (Istanbul, 1913), pp. 169-72.

[23] Parvus [Alexander Helphand], "Köylüler ve Devlet," *Türk Yurdu*, No. 9 (1912), pp. 262-63, and "Esaret-i Maliyeden Kurtulma Yolu," *ibid.*, p. 587.

erished Turk of the Ottoman Empire gave way to the imaginary ideal of the wealthy businessmen of a Turanian State extending from the Mediterranean Sea to the Chinese Wall. In the imagination of the youth, poets, and writers of prose, such illusions were more gratifying and inspiring than the realities.

Under the impact of the dark economic picture and the frustrations of European economic and political pressure, and finally of World War I, the Turkist ideology began to shift steadily from a romantic populism to grandiose schemes of pan-Turkism. The collapse, too, of pan-Islamism through the Arab uprising against the Ottoman Empire made ears more receptive to pan-Turkism. Increasingly the literary figures of Turkism turned from the discomforting reality of the Turkish people to the pre-Islamic Turkish mythology and epic. This was illustrated by the change in course of the "simple language" drive initiated by the *Genç Kalemler* (Young Pens), the originators of Ottoman Turkism, into a romantic literature devoid of any connection with the people— neither reflecting them nor ever reaching them. With this change, the respective meanings of, and the relations between, Turkism and pan-Turkism, or pan-Turanism became quite confused.

THE STRUGGLE FOR ESTABLISHMENT OF
A SECULAR NATION-STATE 1919-39

The Birth of a Nation under Fire | *chapter 15*

PAN-OTTOMANISM, pan-Islamism, and pan-Turkism collapsed together with the Ottoman Empire on October 30, 1918. Westernism, Islamism, and Turkism re-emerged after a short period of eclipse and confusion, but with important modifications. The simple reason was that the Ottoman Empire had vanished and a Turkish nation had arisen from its ashes.

The central issue around which the Turkish transformation took shape in the adoption of complete secularism has often been obscured by the dramatic political, diplomatic, and military events surrounding the rise of the Turkish Republic. The early phases in the nation's formation were conditioned by two important international opposing forces, imperialism and communism. A new Turkish nationalism and its political, economic, and cultural ideology took shape under the clashing push and pull of these two forces. Similarly, the previously romantic populism was compacted by the pressure of the two great ideologies to become the second foundation stone and leading principle of the new regime.

The core of the struggle which determined the essence of the ideology of the new regime was neither a struggle between nationalities, as in the Ottoman Empire, nor a class struggle between capitalism and communism. Once nationalism and populism were established in their new meanings, the emerging regime (1919-23) still had to face the mightiest of all challenges: the question of religion and state. Despite the misleading initial appearances, little more than simple logic was required to foresee that this would be a direct, open, and decisive battle.

After surveying the factors leading to a new conception of nationalism and populism, we shall see how the two concepts of polity, the secular state and the Islamic state, were the only contenders remaining.

432

The Tempests Stirring the Ashes

Despite ten years of Turkist agitation, very few persons could imagine the existence of a Turkish nation before the crushing Allied victory in 1918. To many, a regime of European tutelage seemed the only possible form of future existence. The ruling group in Istanbul believed that, since Great Britain controlled more Muslims than anyone else, Muslim unity under the British wing was the best alternative to an independent existence. The ideal condition would be a British protectorate over the Ottoman Caliphate, a British guarantee for the Ottoman Sultanate, and a bit of land in Anatolia for the Turks (peasants). The best expression of this conception, endorsed by the supporters of the Khilâfat Movement in India, was given later (1920) in the Treaty of Sèvres.[1] Truly no one with ordinary common sense could dream of the possibility of demanding national existence and independence on behalf of the Turkish people. Had Western imperialism been sagacious enough to impose its armistice conditions only on its own account and had the Bolshevik Revolution not challenged European imperialism, the apparently inevitable British tutelage and the establishment of a small Turkish state in a part of Anatolia probably would have been accepted all around.

In the dissolution of the Ottoman Empire, the separation of the Arab countries had no effect in spurring a Turkish national movement, because Arab national independence or, as it turned out, European mandates over the Arab territories did not endanger the existence of the Turks. On the other hand, when it was intended to wrest territories containing Greek and Armenian minorities from the Turkey of the Turks in order to expand Greece into a new Byzantine empire and in order to enlarge an independent Armenia, the clear alternatives were fight or perish. Local, spontaneous, and sporadic resistance movements sprang up in Western

---

[1] This idea was expressed indirectly both before and after the war by Mohamed Ali of India. See Maulana Mohamed Ali, *My Life: A Fragment*, ed. Afzal Iqbal (Lahore, 1944), pp. 63, 125, 133 ff., 136 f., 146, 177 f.

and Eastern Anatolia where there was actual contact with invading forces or local non-Turkish nationalist organizations. Forgetting their differences in outlook and party enmities, the local intellectuals, merchants, lawyers, doctors, teachers, landowners, and clericals formed societies for the defence of national rights (mudafaa-ı hukuk). Their aims were to protest the partition of the Turkish territories, to demand the observance of the Wilsonian principles with respect to themselves, and to pledge themselves to resist aggression and invasion.

Despite remarkable uniformity in the actions and decisions of these organizations, they were purely local or regional. The groups were neither co-ordinated nor united. They were incapable of elucidating a nationwide or positive policy. Some sought a solution in the restoration of the Şeriat, some advocated decentralization and local autonomy, and some toyed with the idea of establishing autonomous soviet republics.

The peasants, who had carried the real burden of the wars from 1913 to 1918, remained outside of these formations except when pressed directly into them by local incidents. The physical as well as economic exhaustion of the peasantry was manifest in the flight of deserting soldiers to their villages. The bulk of the peasantry was moved neither by nationalist frenzy nor by revolutionary zeal to confiscate property.

To convert this amorphous medley into a unified nationalist movement towards a dubious end was a Herculean task. No small credit for this result is owing to the new factors that brought the nationalist movement beyond the level of sporadic struggles.

First and foremost among the new factors was the direct presence of a West determined to reinstate all of the imperialistic impositions that the Union policies had tried to throw off. This factor gave anti-imperialistic colouring to the national movement. That, in turn, forced the movement to distinguish between anti-imperialism and anti-Westernism. A difficult task at best, this differentiation was complicated by the influence of communism.

The second factor was the new position of the Sultanate-Caliphate. The new ruler, Mehmed VI, known as Vahideddin, "seeing that the Nationalist' resistance to the Greeks in Anatolia was a challenge to the Principal Allied Powers and believing that the Allies were bound to prevail," turned against the nationalist movement.[2] In Allied captivity, he had better than even chances of

---

[2] Arnold J. Toynbee, *Survey of International Affairs, 1925* (London, 1927), I, 45.

434

surviving as a sultan in the same fashion as did the North African sultans under French protectorates, or the Arabian sultans under British protectorates; he had even excellent chances of presiding as Caliph over the Sunni Muslim communities of the British and French Empires in, perhaps, the not unenviable manner of the Agha Khan. Without waiting for encouragement, he took the first steps. He abolished all the reforms of the last years of the Meşrutiyet, appointed the arch-Islamist Mustafa Sabri[3] as his Şeyhul-Islâm, and inaugurated a new Hamidian period. By these acts he relieved the revolutionary reformers of the need to prove two things: that the independent national existence of the Turks was not dependent upon the existence of the Sultanate-Caliphate, and that that institution had become incompatible with national existence.

Bolshevism was the third new factor. Just as all the present-day nationalist movements directed against the West are affected by the communist ideology in one way or another, so the Turkish nationalist movement found itself affected by the Bolshevik Revolution that was taking place just around the corner. Bolshevism had far greater fascination for nations in trouble then than today. Turkey was in a far more confused and perilous situation than the majority of new nations today and, hence, more ready to emulate as well as to accept a helping hand. Also, Communist Russia had yet to become a world power and, hence, was not accused of having imperialistic designs. Above all, Russia was the only power

---

[3] See above, p. 299 and 340. In the same year that Sabri became a Şeyhul-Islâm (1919), his book entitled *Yeni Islâm Müçtehitlerinin Kıymet-i Ilmiyesi* (Istanbul, 1919) appeared. It was a refutation of the Turkists' views on Islamic reform, and perhaps the last word of the kind of orthodoxy represented by Sabri's school of thought. One of his objections was to Musa Cârullah's justification, in *Rahmet-i Ilâhiye Burhanları* (1911), of the truthfulness (*haqq* and *sawâb*) of Judaism and Christianity (and, in fact, all faiths) and of the freedom of conscience. Arguing at length against this view, Sabri said, "It seems that in this attitude of taking all religions and faiths as equally respectable and of avoiding contempt for other religions my adversary Cârullah has been fooled by that fashion of freedom of conscience current in Europe" (p. 85). According to Sabri the Jews and Christians would inevitably end in Hell because (*a*) they were not true followers of Moses or Jesus, and (*b*) since the *shari'a* of Muhammad superseded all others and was meant for all mankind, the Jews and Christians were deniers of the true law or *kâfirs*. To accept the contrary would be to deny the existence of *kufr*, of God's *rahmat*, and of Hell without which there could be no law or morality (pp. 84 ff.). The line of reasoning constituted a sad contrast with the lot of the "believers" under the occupation of the "infidels" upon whose administration Sabri's own office placed itself comfortably.

to which the Turkish nationalists had direct territorial access. A special difficulty in dealing with this factor resulted from the ambivalent attitude of the Bolshevik leaders towards the Turkish nationalist movement. This ambivalence was in itself a factor influencing Turkish nationalism.

The Turkish nationalist movement took shape, grew, and led to a new phase of social revolution under the impact of these three factors. There was, however, still another factor of great importance. The early manifestations of the popular reaction could have failed, disintegrated, or taken other directions had a nucleus of leadership not been provided by a thirty-nine-year-old general, Mustafa Kemal.

In particular, Mustafa Kemal's extraordinary personality was such a part of all the secularizing developments that almost nothing of them can be understood properly without taking it into account. It was his leadership that developed nationalism, populism, and secularism as a response to the challenges of imperialism, communism, and theocracy.

The Struggle for National Liberation

After the appearance of Mustafa Kemal's leadership in 1919, the successive congresses took decisions emphasizing the unification of the nationalist movements. They also set down the aims of the struggle for national liberation. A government was needed in place of the local councils, congresses, and partisan fighting units. In principle, this government would be the executive organ of a National Congress. The aims were unconditional national independence, the rejection of any protectorate or mandate, the rejection of exterritorial rights for foreign nationals and powers, the rejection of all special privileges for the minorities, and the acceptance of aid from any power not pursuing imperialistic objectives. A cryptic document consisting of six articles, promulgated in 1920 and known as the National Pact, added to the above: the renunciation of all territorial claims over former Ottoman territories other than those in which Turks predominated and the emphatic reaffirmation of the principle that complete independence (political and other) was to be a condition for a determined policy of Westernization. The declarations implied the wholesale liquidation of the Ottoman Empire and, with it, pan-Ottomanism, pan-Islamism and, indirectly, pan-Turanism.

436

The first divisions in the movement showed up in 1920 during the implementation of the decision to set up a government and a National Assembly at Ankara. To establish this National Assembly as a parliament when there was still a legitimate parliament at the "capital of the Ottoman Empire" was beyond the comprehension of most of the nationalist leaders until the Allied Powers did Mustafa Kemal the great service of dissolving parliament and arresting and deporting to Malta all the leading deputies whom they could catch. In this way the idea of establishing merely a permanent National Congress was transformed more easily into the idea of setting up a Supreme or Grand National Assembly to represent the nation. The Assembly convened for the first time on April 23, 1920.

There were widely differing views of the functions and authority of the Assembly. This was shown when it attempted to draw up a constitution. The ideological trends influencing its drafting as well as the discussions of policy in the Assembly are as obscure as those attending the Constitution of 1876. Just as in the earlier case, many developments were crammed into a few months; there was so much confusion, jockeying for position, and diversive activity in 1920 that nothing was published, little was recorded, and most of what was said or done could hardly be printed in the calm and certainty of later years. We may, nonetheless, understand the principal trends of thought by noting the metamorphosis that took place in the old groupings of Islamists, Westernists, and Turkists.

The scanty records show the emergence of a near mirror image of the 1908-18 picture. The clear-cut alignments had been broken because Islamism, Westernism, and Turkism had all been discredited by the outcome of the war and also because the intense clash of imperialism and communism had created new conditions. To understand the second constitutional controversy in Turkish history we must appraise briefly the new setting.

In Turkey the Russian Revolution had been favourably received, first as meaning the collapse of the Russian Empire, and later for its challenges to imperialism, its condemnation of the secret agreements concerning the partition of the Ottoman Empire, its renunciation of all Russian claims upon Turkey, and its promises to subjugated nations. This favourable reception was natural as the people had seen tangibly that their centuries-old institutions were in ruins, and the old world of which they formed a part was at an end.

While interest there undoubtedly was, this interest had limited significance. There was neither a self-conscious working class, nor a peasantry prepared to rise in the parts of unoccupied Turkey where there was political and intellectual activity. Communism was nothing but a political innovation—an object of curiosity for the masses as well as for the intellectuals. But the imperialistic pressures forced many to turn enthusiastically to the Soviets before finding out about communism.

437

The new regime in Russia was also interested in establishing contact with the national movement. Within days of his landing at Samsum (May 19, 1919), and probably between May 25 and 28, Mustafa Kemal is reported to have been met by Colonel Budyeni (the Soviet Marshal in World War II), who is believed to have come to offer help if Mustafa Kemal appeared inclined to co-operate with Russia against the imperialists.[4] Very soon the people were being addressed by the voice of the Revolution. On September 13, 1919, while the Sivas Congress was in session, a Soviet declaration was directed towards "the Toiling Workers and Peasants of Turkey."[5] Three days after the opening of the National Assembly Mustafa Kemal addressed a letter to the Soviet government proposing the establishment of diplomatic relations and military co-operation.[6] The reading of another Soviet declaration in the National Assembly on May 9, 1920, was met by enthusiastic demonstrations.[7] Two days later an official left for Moscow; the same month an unofficial Soviet envoy left Moscow for Ankara.

The earliest political and intellectual split in the movement took place at this time and was between the upholders of the "Eastern ideal" and those of the "Western ideal."[8] An excerpt from the proceedings of the National Assembly may illustrate the simple reason for this differentiation. Besim Atalay, today a well-known extremist nationalist, said:

---

[4] Husamettin Ertürk, *Iki Devrin Perde Arkası* (Istanbul, 1957), p. 531.

[5] E. H. Carr, *The Bolshevik Revolution, 1917-1923* (London, 1953), III, 245; text in J. T. Degras, *Soviet Documents on Foreign Policy* (London, 1951), pp. 164-67, and X. J. Eudin and R. C. North, *Soviet Russia and the East* (Stanford, 1957), p. 106 and the text on pp. 184-86.

[6] Carr, *The Bolshevik Revolution*, III, 248; and X. J. Eudin and R. C. North, *Soviet Russia*, pp. 106-7.

[7] Cited from *Hakimiyet-i Milliye* in *Die Welt des Islams*, V (1934), 28 and quoted by Carr, *Bolshevik Revolution*, p. 249.

[8] Halide Edib, *The Turkish Ordeal*, (London, 1928), p. 170.

438

We are at a point where two great floods are meeting. One of them
is that of the East, the cradle of faiths and religions; the other
is that of the West, the source of tyranny, oppression and aggression.
We are lost and astray between the two floods. . . . Which one
shall we join? . . . Will you remain under the bayonets of Gladstone's
sons? Or will we go to the hands of the power extended to us?
("To the East, to the East," from the floor).[9]

We can observe the conflict best in the transformation of the
terms West and East. West began to mean imperialism and East
that part of the world rising against imperialism. Although in the
past both the Islamists and the Turkists had had something in
common with such a view of the West, it became a conviction
with the spread of Bolshevism. The idea that the West was
bound to be defeated by the oppressed peoples of the East was
expounded freely.

Because of these conceptual changes, we must be chary in recognizing the Westernists of this period as radicals and the Easternists
as Islamists and conservatives. The situation was somewhat, but
not entirely, the reverse. In fact, neither the upholders of the
"Western ideal" nor the upholders of the "Eastern ideal" were
clear about their respective positions regarding the two paramount
questions of the national movement, or its political orientation and
internal regime. The problem of the political orientation of the
national movement was a matter of West versus East while that
of the internal regime was a matter of Sultanate-Caliphate versus
the people's sovereignty.

It appears that the Westernists preferred, first, to remain in
the Western camp to the extent of accepting a mandate if necessary, and second, to avoid establishing a revolutionary government.
The same men would later turn against Mustafa Kemal, particularly over the question of the abolition of the Sultanate and Caliphate.

The Easternist attitude was not better crystallized. Halide Edib,
who joined the national movement in 1920, summarized the view
of the Easternists saying:

It was an amorphous collection of ideas arising from thwarted
desires for some more congenial state of affairs which would be

[9] *T.B.M.M. Zabıt Ceridesi*, I, 258, quoted by Tarik Z. Tunaya.
*Türkiye Büyük Millet Meclisi Hükûmetinin Kuruluşu ve Siyasî
Karakteri*, reprinted from *Istanbul Üniversitesi Hukuk Fakültesi
Mecmuası*, XXIII, Nos. 3-4 (Istanbul, 1958), 20-22.

appropriate to the East. These ideas were of course very much influenced by the Russian Revolution.[10]

The Easternists and Westernists seem to have clashed first over the question of establishing a new revolutionary government. It was then rather than in connection with obtaining help from Russia that the question of the attitude to be taken towards communism arose. According to Halide Edib, the Westernists wanted to have a regime established on Western foundations and were determined not to imitate the Soviet system by which was meant, in reality, a system independent of the captive Sultan-Caliph.[11] We learn from Mustafa Kemal that the upholders of the "Western ideal" were those who wanted a National Assembly to carry out the liberation but not to establish a new regime. They wanted the existing constitutional system with its Caliphate, Sultanate and the rest to remain in the spirit of Meşrutiyet dualist secularism. They were opposed to the idea of founding a new regime based on popular sovereignty.[12]

We note, therefore, the emergence of three conceptions of the National Assembly from its very first meeting. The first understanding of the National Assembly was that it would be an institution representing the nation only for the duration of the struggle for national liberation. The second was that the National Assembly would be a continuation of the parliament of the Meşrutiyet period. (Some seem to have entertained the idea of creating a "regent sultan" or "deputy caliph" to stand in for the captive Padişah.) The third was that it would be a permanent convention representing the legislative function and executing government on behalf of the people. The third view seems to have been forwarded by the Easternists and backed by Mustafa Kemal.

439

[10] Halide Edib, *Turkish Ordeal*, p. 171. According to her Hakkı Behiç was a well-known representative of this group. It appears, however, that there was more than one who then believed in communism as the master ideology of the world to come. She mentions Hikmet [Bayur] as one who had "come very much under the influence of Marxian doctrines which he now regarded as the means of saving the world: he longed whole-heartedly to see Turkey become Bolshevist," *ibid.*, p. 173.

[11] *Ibid.*, p. 171.

[12] *Ibid.*, p. 140; see Mustafa Kemal [Atatürk],*Nutuk* (Ankara, 1927), pp. 269-71, and its English translation *Speech* (Leipzig, 1929), pp. 369-71. There are several printings of the *Nutuk;* references here are to the original 1927 edition. The translation in the quotations is mine, but I have used the published translation as a basis, correcting it as necessary.

440

The Russian regime itself came in for further attention during the discussions of the constitutional nature of the new National Assembly. According to Halide Edib, a leading representative of the Easternist view was "responsible for the first draft of the new government which Mustafa Kemal proposed to his intimate supporters and then had accepted in modified form by the National Assembly."[13] The constitution resulting from this was viewed by the Westernists as a modification of the Soviet form; we shall soon see how great that modification was.

The nature of and the motivations for the alleged communist movements and parties of the period became the subjects of much speculation and the sources of much confusion and misrepresentation later.[14] For example, communist sources claim that a genuine communism was born in Turkey out of the revolutionary desires of the working class and Turkish peasantry and that this was adulterated purposefully by Mustafa Kemal to confuse the masses so that his bourgeois nationalism could be established. Western writers have attributed Mustafa Kemal's first favouring and later persecuting communism to political expediency—a means to obtain Soviet aid. On the other hand, anti-Kemalists hint (as in the case of Halide Edib) or claim (as in the case of the anti-Kemalists of the 1940's and 1950's) that the Kemalist regime and all its reforms were inspired by communism. One need only look at a chronology of the events and the map within which the revolution operated to understand the realities.

All of the activities noted took place contemporaneously with the attempts to formulate a new constitution under the pressure of competing forces. Obtaining help from Russia came much later, when the first major crisis over the constitution had been overcome. Turkey and the Soviets concluded a treaty on March 16, 1921, in which the freedom of both sides to have their respective regimes was recognized. Actual Soviet backing of the Nationalist War came still later—after the summer of 1921.

Apart from the question of the mutual needs of the Soviets and the Turkish national movement for a political rapprochement, two views underlay the diverse "communist" movements. One was

---

[13] H. Edib, *Turkish Ordeal*, p. 170.

[14] For a list of the communist or pseudo-communist organizations then being formed see Tarik Z. Tunaya, *Türkiyede Siyasî Partiler* (Istanbul, 1952), pp. 531 f.

the view of introducing communism as the basis for the new regime; the other was the idea of utilizing communism as a model for the establishment of a new revolutionary national regime. The first would depend naturally upon the existence within Turkish society of certain forces to appropriate communism and to support and sustain it.

441

According to the Soviet writers and, following them, the Western writers, there was a widespread peasant revolutionary movement represented by the so-called Green Army.[15] In reality, the Green Army was not an expression of peasant discontent. It was organized to combat the local uprisings which seem to have come, not from peasant, but from semi-feudal reaction to the national movement. Uprisings representing this reaction had no revolutionary characteristics. One of them, led by a Şeyh Recep at Sivas, was an anti-Nationalist struggle on behalf of the Caliph. There were several others of a like nature. A certain Eşref, who led an uprising in the Eastern provinces, styled himself as the expected Mahdi and the Protector of the Şeriat. The uprisings at Düzce and Bolu, Yozgat, Zile, and Konya were instigated by the *eşraf*, *şeyhs*, and *hocas* in the name of preserving the Şeriat and Caliphate. All were anti-nationalist; none aimed at an agrarian popular revolution. The real peasant unrest was shown in the peasants' attempts to avert the burdens of another war. Their desertions threatened the dissolution of the already weak regular army far more than the Allied policy of disarming. These desertions were another factor in the creation of the Green Army. As Mustafa Kemal tells us, "It had been seen repeatedly that the reactionary rebels had

---

[15] For example, an American author, Ivar Spector, says, "Much of the deep-rooted agrarian discontent which in many parts of Turkey had resulted in spontaneous pro-Soviet demonstrations by the peasantry in 1919, found more organized expression after the establishment of the Grand National Assembly in 1920, in the formation of the Green Army, which pledged its support to the Turkish Revolution"; *The Soviet Union and the Muslim World* (revised ed.; Seattle, Wash., 1959), p. 67. According to Carr also, the "Green Army" was an expression of the peasant movement which was rooted in agrarian discontent; the "Green Army" was composed of the small and landless peasants and constituted an important part of the nationalist forces; it was fostered by Mustafa Kemal "partly because its loyalty to the nationalist cause was fervent and unquestioned, and partly because an outlet was required for the real social and agrarian discontent represented by it"; Carr, *Bolshevik Revolution*, III, 300. See M. Kemal [Atatürk], *Nutuk*, pp. 293-95; English trans., pp. 401-4.

cheated the regular forces easily by talking of the *fetvas* announced by the Padişah."[16]

442

Had the writers claiming the existence of revolutionary peasant movements taken but a glance at the then existing Turkish conditions, they would have found semi-medieval towns, desolate villages, and the war-sick townsmen and peasants of the Anatolian plateau left in the hands of the *şeyhs, hacıs* and *hocas*. There was neither a class-conscious proletariat anxious to establish soviets, nor a peasant class ready to be led by revolutionary leaders. It is true that a Turkish middle class was in the process of becoming, but it did not yet constitute a social class possessing vested interests independent of foreign and non-Turkish minority capitalism or antagonized by the working and peasant classes. At that stage all of the social classes, including the bourgeoisie, were under the threat of imperialistic subjugation. To them salvation seemed to lie, not in a class struggle, but in class solidarity and in unification into a nationality. The most urgent objective of the national movement was the organization of the struggle for national liberation.

What emerged from Mustafa Kemal's drive amidst the confused activities and organizations was the establishment of a nationalist regime with a new constitution on the basis of the sovereignty of the people as a nation. If we look at the matter in terms of these efforts, the conflicts between views and groups, the relative position of the major social classes, the pressing need to avert a civil war in order to conduct an anti-imperialistic one, and, finally, Turkey's age-old problem of modernization, we can understand why nationalism rather than communism triumphed.

In a speech before the National Assembly, Mustafa Kemal explained the new policy thus:

> The policy which we regard as clear and fully realizable is a national policy. In view of the general conditions obtaining in the world at present . . . no greater mistake could be made than that of being a utopian. . . . In order that our nation should be able to live a happy, strenuous and permanent life, it is necessary that the state should pursue an exclusively national policy. . . . When I speak of national policy, I mean it in this sense: to work within our

---

[16] M. Kemal, *Nutuk*, p. 154; see also pp. 215, 272, 308 ff. The Unionist followers of Enver Paşa were trying to convert the Green Army and the National Movement into a pan-Islamic fight against British imperialism. The Soviets seemed to have backed the movement at first, but when Mustafa Kemal purged the Green Army and took a definite stand against Enver's ambitions they dropped their support.

national boundaries for the real happiness and welfare of the nation
and the country by, above all, relying on our own strength in order
to retain our existence; not to lead the people to follow fictitious
aims of whatever nature which could only bring them misfortune;
and to expect from the civilized world treatment worthy of civilized
men, and friendship based on mutuality.[17]

"Sovereignty Belongs to the People"

We may now look at the question of establishing the new
regime. Just as we gave a somewhat detailed account of the 1876
Constitution because it was the first experiment in constitutional
government in the Islamic world, so we shall review in some detail
the establishment of the new regime as the first experiment in a
republican form of government in the Islamic world.

The Constitution and the Kemalist regime took shape in response, not only to the conflicting impacts of the forces emanating
from communism and imperialism, but also to internal conditions.
The latter played the decisive role—a role that has not often been
taken into account in understanding the resultant regime. The
Kemalists were involved in a constant struggle with the Şeriatists
and Khilâfatists from the uprisings against the national movement
until the opening of the proceedings over the Constitution.

When Mustafa Kemal drafted the invitation for elections as the
head of the committee of representatives elected by the Sivas
Congress, he and his supporters believed that what they were
doing was launching a revolution and establishing a new regime.
He says, "I had used the term 'Constituent Assembly' in my first
draft. My intention was that the elected assembly should be
authorized to change the regime right at the beginning."[18]
"Peoples' Republic" was the term he used for the kind of regime
he had in mind. But he was opposed in this attempt; and in order
to avoid the difficulty, he used the expression "an assembly with
extraordinary prerogatives." Commenting upon the views of those
who took for granted that the National Assembly was merely a
transplant of the Ottoman Parliament, he said,

[17] *Ibid.*, p. 276 English trans., p. 378-79. "In reality," Mustafa Kemal
says, this meant "acknowledging the fall of the Ottoman state and
the abolition of the Caliphate, and the creation of a new state
upon new foundations."

[18] *Ibid.*, p. 266, English trans., p. 364.

To work for the convening of the Meclis-i Meb'usan (Assembly of Deputies) in its old form and nature, with new members added to the remnants of the old, was beyond my thinking. On the contrary, I was thinking about the establishment of a permanent assembly of an entirely different nature and with entirely new authority—an assembly with which I should experience all the phases of the revolution I was planning in my mind.[19]

444

"As soon as the Assembly opened," says Mustafa Kemal, "a drive was set in motion for establishing contact and coming to a conciliation with the Sultan-Caliph."[20] The clerical members met among themselves three days before the opening of the Assembly and decided that the permission of the Sultan should be obtained before opening the Assembly. Several moderates held the same view.

Mustafa Kemal kept hammering on one idea. The Assembly would be the supreme legislative as well as executive representative of the people. No other body or person would be above it, or could claim to represent sovereignty. "Sovereignty belongs to the nation" and it would be represented by the National Assembly, he declared.

"But what about the Caliphate and the Sultanate?" the clericals and the Westernists kept asking. Mustafa Kemal answered this calmly and without hesitation:

As soon as the Sultan-Caliph is delivered from all pressure and coercion he will take his place within the frame of the legislative principles which will be determined by the Assembly.[21]

However many wholehearted supporters Mustafa Kemal had, they were numerically as nothing in the Assembly. When a committee was chosen to draft a constitutional bill in accordance with the principles laid down in the previous declarations as well as in a project Mustafa Kemal submitted following his opening speech to the Assembly on April 24, 1920, it faced the choice of declaring a republican form of government or confirming the Sultanate-Caliphate. On August 18, 1920, after four months of work, the committee produced the results of its labours. The anticipated had happened. By putting aside the directive principles and taking a direction diametrically opposed to the intentions behind calling a

[19] *Ibid.*, p. 269, English trans., p. 369.

[20] *Ibid.*, p. 276; English trans., p. 379.

[21] *Ibid.*, p. 277; English trans., p. 380.

sovereign National Assembly, the committee prepared a draft according to which the National Assembly and the government were considered to be provisional and operative only until the Sultanate-Caliphate was liberated.[22]

In the ensuing discussions the members, especially the clericals, insisted on clarifying further the intention to restore the Sultanate-Caliphate. The clericals roared protest against the proposal, suggested by their own claim that Caliphate implied Sultanate, to mention specifically the Caliphate only. They wanted both to be mentioned specifically, as they had no intention of being tricked. "These discussions went on for days and days," reported Mustafa Kemal.

One of the two clashing views was clear: the Caliphate and Sultanate existed and would exist, it maintained. And, so long as they existed, the present-day form of government had to be provisional. The kind of regime and constitution that would be introduced as soon as the Sultanate-Caliphate was liberated was known. What was to be done consisted simply of having a number of persons assembled in Ankara for the purpose of conducting the affairs of the country until the functioning of the Sultanate-Caliphate was ensured. The opposing view, on the other hand, could not be stated clearly. No one could say openly that sovereignty had passed to the people, that the Sultanate existed no longer and, as the Caliphate implied Sultanate, it too had lost its raison d'être.[23]

After thirty-seven days of inconclusive argumentation Mustafa Kemal explained to a closed session that the reigning Sultan-Caliph was a traitor and that it was an inappropriate time to argue over the Sultanate-Caliphate. "Let us not indulge in strife over the Sultanate-Caliphate in the midst of our real and urgent business. . . . This is a vast and delicate question; its solution is not a matter for these days."

After long consultations Mustafa Kemal prepared a project and submitted it on September 13, 1920. It bore the title "The Program of Populism" and contained his project of April 24, 1920, together with an enumeration of the principles of the new regime. The Assembly appointed a special committee to scrutinize the project. The resultant bill incorporated Mustafa Kemal's central thesis of national sovereignty and a people's government, as well as his view on the position of the Sultanate-Caliphate. Article 6 of his direc-

[22] *Ibid.*, p. 351; English trans., p. 479.

[23] *Ibid.*, p. 352; English trans., p. 480.

tive principles became Article 1 of the draft constitution. It read, "Sovereignty belongs unconditionally to the nation. The government is based on the principle of the people's direct rule over their own destiny."

446

The new Constitution was adopted on January 20, 1921, that is, after a five-month struggle.[24] Its adoption ended the first round of the struggle between the Kemalists and their adversaries.

Caliphate Without Sultanate?

Although a Kemalist victory, the Constitution was yet far from establishing a normal democratic government. The regime established neither Western parliamentarianism nor communist sovietism, neither an Islamic state nor a corporative system of professional representation. (A drive to introduce a system of professional representation of the peasants, artisans, liberal professions, etc. was defeated by the followers of Mustafa Kemal. The idea was previously expounded by Gökalp as an alternative to socialism.) A commitment to the Sultanate-Caliphate was avoided but a form of government was laid down which seemed to be a new form of popular government to the radicals and a provisional government established to free the Sultanate-Caliphate to the conservatives.

In Mustafa Kemal's understanding, "such a government was nothing but a People's government based on the idea of the sovereignty of the nation." Many did not anticipate its implications, but "with the passage of time, the implications of this principle came to be seen, and then conflicts and incidents ensued."[25]

Some viewed the Constitution as a party program. General Kâzım Karabekir, the future opponent of Mustafa Kemal, said:

I believe that the contents of that law should remain only as a party program in anticipation of the difficulties to be encountered in its implementation. . . . The majority of the persons making up the group supporting this Constitution are aspiring to lead the destiny of the country to a political revolution. Only a small fraction of the people would support the idea of a new regime. Supporting the new

[24] The text is in A. S. Gözübüyük and S. Kili, *Türk Anayasa Metinleri* (Ankara, 1957), pp. 85-87.

[25] M. Kemal, *Nutuk*, p. 277; English trans., p. 380.

Constitution can only be a matter of the private opinion of certain members of the Assembly.[26]

The members of the Assembly were former government officials (state and municipal administrators, educators, and army and judicial officers), members of the liberal professions (businessmen, farmers, lawyers, doctors, journalists, and engineers), clericals (*muftî, müderris, şeyh, vâiz,* and *kadı*). Only one worker had crept in. There were five Kurdish chieftains. The Assembly was fairly representative of the class and occupational structure of the country, except that the peasantry, constituting the overwhelming majority, had no representation. Several members were Khilâfatists who wanted to establish an Islamic state or Westernist constitutionalists whose objective was the retention of the constitutional monarchy associated with the attribute of caliphate.

So long as the struggle for national liberation from European imperialism was its dominant function, the Grand National Assembly rolled along with an ideology that was a mixture of Islamist anti-Westernism, nationalist populism or quasi-socialism, and conservative Westernism, all, however, garbed in anti-imperialism. There was neither an idea of making a revolution on behalf of any social class, nor the will to make radical social changes. The Assembly operated by compromise as regards social change. Despite the declared idea of national sovereignty, the Sultanate and Caliphate were still accepted as constitutionally existing institutions. Of course, the condition indicated an eventual showdown between the two portions of the Assembly, but Mustafa Kemal's policy was to postpone the struggle until it could no longer jeopardize the war.

The spirit of Şeriatism made itself felt frequently. The reactions evinced in connection with a few issues involving some degree of radicalism will illustrate the dominant temper. In one of the sessions, a doctor introduced a bill for the compulsory pre-marital medical examination of both men and women. This whipped up a storm and was rejected.[27] One of the members introduced a motion "to subjugate educational matters to the jurisdiction of the Ministry of Şeriat." (This Ministry was the creation of the new regime!) The school programs, the member felt, should be prepared by the Ministry of Education, but they would be subject to control and approval by the Ministry of Şeriat. Many of the

---

[26] Quoted in *ibid.*, p. 371; English trans., p. 505.

[27] *T.B.M.M. Zabıtları,* (reprinted in 1940), I, 149 f.; see also pp. 76, 78.

448

members approved of the idea of "subjugating all school teaching to the approval of the Committee of the Affairs of Şeriat (a new committee) in order to put an end to the *medrese*–secular school duality. One member claimed that the sole cause "of our backwardness was due to separating the world from religion" and demanded the relegation of the affairs of *evkaf*, Şeriat, justice and education to the jurisdiction of the Şeriat Committee of the Assembly. These proposals were all shelved by the supporters of Mustafa Kemal on the plea that all their time and energy should be concentrated on the struggle for national independence. The Assembly did, however, pass decrees for the opening of 465 new *medreses*—a harmless enough measure as the financial resources of the pocket Ministry of Education in Ankara were approximately nil.

In addition to its opposition to any change, even of a minor order, the Assembly was religiously tinted. In its second year (March 12, 1921), the Minister of Education reported the opening of a competition for the selection of a national anthem and added immediately that he had personally approached "our religious poet", Mehmet Âkif, begging him to write one. He then read Mehmed Âkif's poem to the Assembly. The protestations by a few members that the ideas of this poem did not represent the spirit of the nation were rejected. The members as a whole were carried away by its intense religious tenor. The poem was recited once again and was adopted with great enthusiasm as the national anthem of Turkey.[28]

The Assembly even appeared to some as the herald of the felicitous age of the Prophet. The Prohibition Law was passed in this belief (1920). Not only drinking and gambling, but also card playing and backgammon were prohibited by law. Although these laws were not passed without a struggle between the conservative and progressive sectors of the Assembly, they did pass. Furthermore, all bills had to pass the Şeriat Committee in addition to the usual parliamentary committees concerned. And the clericals had more religious "reforms" up their sleeves, such as prohibiting the unveiling of women and the wearing of luxury clothes, and even making polygamy compulsory!

All these were undoubtedly indices of the growing power of the conservative forces in the Assembly to the watchful Mustafa Kemal, who was, as yet, nothing but an ordinary general sentenced to death by the Caliph's Şeyhul-Islâm.

[28] *Ibid.*, IX, 13.

Towards the end of the first National Assembly and with the ending of the war of liberation, the conservative and reactionary elements began to increase their activities. In 1921, they were so strong that no decisions could be made without compromise. To counteract this Mustafa Kemal organized (May 10, 1921) the progressive elements into what became known as the Parliamentary Group representing the Society for the Defence of Rights. From this time onward the conservative group began to be known as the Second Group.[29] After 1921 the Second Group was outnumbered in the Assembly, but its influence increased rather than decreased. On the other hand, its members began to feel the weight of Kemal's strength and sensed the coming struggle.

Two members of the Assembly, both clericals, founded a society called Muhafaz-i-Mukaddesat Cemiyeti (Society for the Preservation of the Sacred Traditions).[30] The aim of the society, as stated in its declaration, was to fight "communism" and the tendencies imposed upon the Society for the Defence of Rights. One of the founders said:

Our aim is to preserve the rights of the Caliph-Padişah and to work
for the absolute avoidance of the republican form of government
which will create enormous harm to the country and the world
of Islam, now and in the future. It can be sensed that the Group
for the Defence of Rights, which has been formed by Mustafa Kemal
in the National Assembly, aims at replacing the Sultanate-Caliphate
with a Republican form of government.[31]

When Mustafa Kemal could no longer conceal his views of the Sultanate and Caliphate from the sensitive eyes of the reactionaries and was in distress as to how to meet a situation whose outcome he could not clearly see, British diplomacy again came to his rescue. The war was over and the Allies had invited the Sultan's government to Lausanne for peace negotiations. The British refusal to recognize the Nationalist government as the sole representative of the nation created such indignation that the conservative National Assembly was carried to a frenzy quite easily.

The mistake was fatal for the Sultanate. On October 30, 1922, the Assembly revolted against the Padişah's pretensions to represent the country at the council of peace toward the establishment

---

[29] For details see Tunaya, *Türkiyede Siyasî Partiler*, pp. 553 ff.

[30] *Ibid.*, p. 533.

[31] Reported in M. Kemal, *Nutuk*, p. 371; English trans., p. 505.

of which he had contributed nothing but harm. On November 1, 1922, Mustafa Kemal felt confident in proposing the abolition of the Sultanate. In a long speech, he gave a lucid history of the evolution of the Caliphate and Sultanate and claimed that the two could be separated as they had been separated in history, and that the second could be abolished while the first was retained. The Sultanate was nothing but temporal sovereignty and that sovereignty had been taken over by the people.

450

The proposal was given to a mixed committee of the Assembly for the preparation of a bill. In the closer atmosphere of the committee room, the national frenzy of the members subsided. The discussion was monopolized by the clerical members of the Şeriat Committee. They began a lengthy exposition of the views of the ancient jurists and theologians concerning Sultanate and Caliphate. Mustafa Kemal relates,

> They claimed by their well-known sophistry that the Sultanate could not be separated from the Caliphate. . . . Finally I took the floor and, climbing on top of the table before me, I made the following declaration: "Gentlemen, sovereignty has never been given to any nation by scholarly disputation. It is always taken by force and with coercion. . . . The Turkish nation has now taken back its usurped sovereignty by rebellion. This is a fact. The question facing us now is not whether or not this sovereignty will be left to the nation, but the simple matter of declaring that which is a fact. . . . If those who have assembled here recognize this natural fact like everyone else, all will be fine. If not, what is natural will happen anyhow, with the only difference that a few heads will probably have to be chopped off."[32]

The bill for the abolition of the Sultanate was ready in a few hours. It was read the same day in the second sitting of the Assembly and was passed amidst demonstrations.

The Child is Named Republic

The abolition of the Sultanate was far from being the end of the struggles. It was the beginning of a battle between the secularists and the Şeriatists who were gradually gaining the support of the conservative Westernists.

[32] *Ibid.*, pp. 421-22; English trans., pp. 577-78.

The abolition of Sultanate did not produce any important repercussion inside the country. The Muslims outside Turkey were not concerned with the Turks' Sultan—as the Indian Khalifâtist Mohamed Ali quaintly put it:

We were not Turkish Nationalists fighting over a little space in
which their race could breathe and live. We were Indians and
subjects of the King of England who had been at war with the
King of Turkey. . . . [33]

It was rather the Caliphate that was destined to be the object of the real battle. The clericals, the conservatives from among the nationalists, the non-Turkish Muslims and the foreign diplomats would find much in it to exploit from their respective points of view.

The last Padişah of the Ottoman dynasty was deposed as Sultan, but he was still Caliph, and on November 17, 1922, he "placed himself under British protection as the Caliph of all Muslims of the world," and left Turkey aboard the S.S. *Malaya*. The following day the Turkish National Assembly debated in closed session and the election of a new Caliph was proposed. A number of the members, according to Mustafa Kemal,

were seriously discussing the question of Caliphate. The reverend
hocas particularly were on their guard as they had found a question
very dear to their field of specialization. . . . They were speculating
about bringing the new Caliph to Ankara. He should, they said,
even be brought to the headship of the state. There was, they said,
great excitement in Turkey and all over the Islamic world about
the question of Caliphate. Serious measures should, therefore,
be taken etc., etc. Some of the speech-makers explained the necessity
of ascertaining the Caliph's attributes and prerogatives. . . . My
declaration can be summed up in the following. . . . "The Assembly
is the Assembly of the people of Turkey. Its authority extends
only and solely over the Turkish people and their destiny. It can
not appropriate to itself, by its own act, authority extending over
the entire Muslim world. The Turkish nation . . . would not trust its
own destiny to the hands of a person called Caliph. . . . The claim
that because of this there is or will be excitement in the Muslim
world is nothing but a lie. . . . The more we argue over the
matter, the less it will appear solvable. One thing can be stated
definitely; no one, even if he is called Caliph, can ever be above
the sovereign rights of the people. There is absolutely no alternative

[33] Mohamed Ali, *My Life*, p. 146.

to following this principle in deposing the escaped Caliph and electing a new one."[34]

Agreement was finally reached after long and violent discussion to depose the fugitive Caliph and elect a new one.

452

Agitations over the question of Caliphate were far from being over, however. The conservatives and the constitutionalist Westernists began to look to the new Caliph, Abdül-Mecid ('Abd al-Majîd), installed on November 18, 1922, as a possible power to check the Kemalists. The clergy, on the other hand, looked to the new Caliph as a means of making the state, thus far not declared secular, into an Islamic state. They saw themselves on the brink of the most critical and crucial event in Islamic history. The occasion would be either the last opportunity to establish a veritable Islamic state under the Caliph or a total defeat. Mustafa Kemal, too, was looking for his own chance—to proclaim the Republic.

The *ulema* of Egypt and India found a purely spiritual caliphate a thoroughly unprecedented *bid'a*. There was a good opportunity for them (whose countries were under non-Muslim rule, in the case of Egypt partly and of India altogether) to display their erudition on the uniqueness of, and to weave fantasies about, the Islamic caliphal polity. The ex-Şeyhul-Islâm, Mustafa Sabri, who had escaped to Egypt, declared from there: "The two offices are united and inseparable, both in content and in form, in the very nature of Islamic administration." He came to the conclusion that in taking political power away from the Caliphate, "the Turkish Government . . . has committed apostasy from its religion."[35] The same view was expressed in a decision published on March 24, 1924, by the Rector of Al-Azhar and by the other *ulema* of Egypt. The decision read, in part, "By this act, the Turks have introduced an innovation (*bid'a*) which is without precedent in Islam."[36]

The understanding of the *ulema* of the Caliphate in its relation to the Sultanate was in complete contradiction with that elaborated in Mustafa Kemal's speech at the Turkish National Assembly. The decision of the Egyptian *ulema* was:

[34] M. Kemal, *Nutuk*, pp. 426-27; English trans., 584-85.

[35] Quoted by Toynbee, *Survey of International Affairs*, I, 55 (from *Oriente Moderno* II, (1923), 465 f.); see pp. 52-54 for the repercussions in the Islamic world of the separation of the Sultanate and Caliphate.

[36] Full text in *ibid.*, p. 517.

The Caliphate is a general headship (*ri'asah*) in matters of religion
and of this world. Its fundamental function is to watch over the
interests of the Islamic church [*milla*] and over the administration
of the Islamic community [*ummah*].[37]

453

Not content even with believing that the Sultanate should
remain inseparable from the Caliphate in that "little space" for
which the "Nationalist Turks" had fought successfully, Mohamed
Ali was of the mind that the restoration of the Sultanate via Caliphate over the Arab territories which had revolted should be
enforced! He wrote:

As we had more than once made it clear, our sympathy with
Turkey was not political or territorial but religious, for the Sovereign
of Turkey was the successor of the Prophet and the Commander
of the Faithful. It was our religious duty to prevent the further
disintegration of the temporal power of the Khilafat which was
indispensable for the defence of our faith, to maintain the inviolability
of the sacred regions of Islam and to see that the dying injunction
of the Prophet with regard to exclusive Muslim sovereignty
over Jazirat-ul-Arab (or the Island of Arabia including Syria,
Palestine and Mesopotamia) was not disregarded.[38]

Inside Turkey also the Khilâfatists set themselves to propagate
the view that the Caliphate implied in itself the holding of temporal power. One of the clerical members of the National Assembly, Ismail Şükrü, deputy for Afyon, published a book entitled *Hilâfet-i Islâmiye ve Büyük Millet Meclisi* (The Islamic
Caliphate and the Grand National Assembly).[39] His thesis was
exactly the same as that expressed by Mustafa Sabri, Mohamed
Ali, and the Al-Azhar *ulema*. In Islam there was no spiritual office;
the Caliph was the veritable head of the Islamic community. The
Caliphate, whether it was with the Sultanate or not, was a species
of government peculiar to Islam; its function was the execution

---

[37] *Ibid.*, p. 576.

[38] Mohamed Ali, *My Life*, p. 138 f.

[39] Published in Ankara, 1923. For opposite views see Ziya Gökalp,
Turkish Nationalism and Western Civilization, ed. Niyazi Berkes
(London and New York, 1959), 223-32; H. Hulki, I. Sami, and
Rasih, *Hakimiyet-i Milliye ve Hilâfet-i Islâmiye* (Ankara, 1923);
M. Seyyid, *Hilâfet ve Hakimiyet-i Milliye* (Ankara, 1923), trans-
lated into Arabic by Abd-al-Ghanî Sanî as *Al-Khilâfah wa'as-
Saltanah al-Ummah* according to Ali Abd-al-Râziq, *Al-Islâm wa
Usûl al-Hukm* (Cairo, 1925) a work influenced by Seyyid's book
and Mustafa Kemal's ideas.

of the Şeriat "in every department of human affairs".[40] The Şeriat, as well as the religious practices of the Muslims, were null and void without a caliph invested with temporal powers.

454

In the Assembly, "the Ministry of Şeriat was becoming a supplementary organization of the Caliphate".[41] Its new Minister, Abdullah Azmi, the same man who had insisted during World War I in the Ottoman Parliament that only the Kur'an should be taught in the primary schools, declared,

My Ministry has active and important roles to play in this state whose other name is nothing but the *Khilâfet-i Islâmiye*. . . . As long as I remain in this office by your confidence, I shall see to it that they are executed.[42]

Vigorous applause by the majority of the Assembly answered this speech.

The growth of Khilâfatism at the National Assembly and in the press spurred the Kemalists to action. Mustafa Kemal, who had put forth the idea that the Caliphate could stand without the Sultanate, realized that if the Sultanate had become an anachronism for Turkey, the Caliphate was even more so for the world of Islam. "Following the abolition of the Sultanate," he says, "I accepted the abolition of the Caliphate, as it was nothing but the same personal sovereignty under another name."[43] That was, in fact, the only logical conclusion if the spiritual caliphate was rejected and the medieval conception of caliphate as the supreme rulership (*ri'asah*) was accepted. The Khilâfatists were striving to revive the Sultanate under the guise of the Caliphate. They wanted to make the Assembly the council of *meşveret* of the Caliph who would be made the head of the state.[44]

The Assembly was inspired to dissolve itself on April 1, 1923, for elections. With the exception of the extreme reactionaries, such as the founders of the Society for the Preservation of the Sacred Traditions, all nationalists, that is, all those who had joined the national liberation movement, were combined to make the

[40] See Toynbee, *Survey of International Affairs*, I, 55, for quotations from a précis of *Hilâfet-i Islâmiye* published in *Oriento Moderno*, II (1923), 585-88.

[41] *Dünya*, No. 74 (Istanbul, 1952).

[42] Kiliç Ali, *Hatıralar* (Istanbul, 1955), pp. 96-97.

[43] M. Kemal, *Nutuk*, p. 426; English trans., p. 583.

[44] *Ibid.*, p. 429; English trans., p. 588.

new People's party. The struggle between the Kemalists, the conservative element among the Westernists, and the Islamist factions would determine the future ideological course of the party.

The Kemalist faction of the People's party came out of the new elections with a slight majority. However, the elections were far from being decisive and almost all of the supporters of Khilâfatism in the previous Assembly including those who were elected on the People's party ticket, had been returned to office. Thus, the decisive battle would take place, not within the National Assembly, but within the People's party.

The necessity of facing the question of the form of government, left undecided by the Constitution of 1921, became clearer with the convening of the new National Assembly on August 2, 1923. Once the third possibility, the Sultanate as a constitutional monarchy, had been ruled out, the clear alternative was for the state to be either an Islamic state or a secular republic.

The regime which had been established under abnormal conditions and with the aim of avoiding communism, parliamentarianism, and a Sultanate monarchy all in the same breath appeared insufficient. With the abolition of the Sultanate the Khilâfatists had been given the chance to promote the establishment of a genuine theocracy by amending the Constitution. The idea of having the Caliph as the natural head of the state would be more attractive than the existing shapeless regime. Not only would the members of the Assembly be able to legitimize their representation by the sovereignty of God symbolized by the Caliph, but they would also be able to rid themselves of the dangerous domination of the revolutionary Mustafa Kemal. As F. R. Atay remarked, the Khilâfatists were now more insistent on the right of the people to delegate its sovereignty—to a religiously legitimized authority. A republican form of government was identified with atheism and communism.

In September, 1923, Mustafa Kemal appointed a special committee of his newly established People's party to draft a republican constitution. (One of the members was Ziya Gökalp.) Kemal discussed the various forms of republican government with the committee in closed sessions. The American presidential system is reported to have come in for particular attention. His contacts convinced Kemal, however, that the prevailing mood did not favour the acceptance of a new constitution. He put aside the draft of the committee. As he always believed, Article 1, which he had formulated for the first Assembly, implied nothing but a republican regime. Thus it would be sufficient merely to amend that article by adding, "Turkey is a people's state governed by a republican form of government." Complementary modifications could easily be made in Articles 3, 8, and 9.

456

The Khilâfatists were not long in giving Kemal a new opportunity. Their opposition to the Kemalist-supported cabinets was such that for weeks all the proposed lists of cabinet members failed to gain majority approval. Without ministers the Assembly was incapable of taking any vacation because, according to the Constitution, the Assembly was vested also with executive power. On October 19 Mustafa Kemal explained to a meeting of the People's party that the crisis was not a cabinet crisis but a constitutional one and that it could be overcome easily by making a slight modification in the existing Constitution, as the existing one contained no special provision on amendment procedures.

The Khilâfatists never expected Mustafa Kemal to bring up the matter so suddenly and so bluntly in a way that would make the majority feel that declaring a republican form of government was, after all, only a matter of adding a few words to the Constitution! The moment of facing the accursed word "Republic" had come.[45]

While many hesitated in confusion, the eldest member of the Assembly, Abdurrahman Şeref (1858-1925), the last official historian of the Ottoman Empire, said, "One hundred years of the Turkish transformation is giving birth to a child. Are we afraid to spell his name? Let us face it: this is Republic!" The naming of the new regime by this aged historian of the old regime was impressive indeed. A torrent of speeches choked the objections and protests of the Khilâfatists. The die was cast the same day in the Assembly. The bill declaring the establishment of the Republic was passed by evening. No time was left to the *ulema* and the lawyers to kill it in committee. The guns roaring all over Turkey at midnight of October 29-30, 1923, reverberated as tolls for a dead Caliphate.

[45] The reader should not read the last in terms of the temper of these years when Republic is proclaimed in every country after every revolution.

The Demise of the Caliphate

Still, the battle between the secularists and the Khilâfatists was far from being over. Under the amended Constitution Mustafa Kemal was elected President of a republic that was an Islamic state, because the Khilâfatists succeeded in introducing an article in the amended Constitution (absent in the Constitution of 1921) stating, "The religion of the Turkish state is Islam" (Article 2). This article became the constitutional ground of legitimacy for the Khilâfatist thesis. Nothing could have been more uncomfortable for Mustafa Kemal than to be President of an Islamic republic, just as nothing could appear more unbecoming than this to the Khilâfatists. And what about the Khalîfa? What would his place be? Should he be seen as merely a spiritual authority? Never! A Khalîfa without temporal powers meant nothing; it was an unprecedented *bid'a*, said the Azhar *ulema*, who should know if anyone did.

Mustafa Kemal probably would have tolerated the Caliphate if his concept of it had been accepted. Now he was helped by his adversaries to prove that this institution was incapable of even a spiritual function. He said:

The Caliph and the office of the Caliphate which we have maintained and safeguarded have, in reality, no raison d'être, neither in a political nor in a religious sense. The Caliphate may have a significance for us only as a historic recollection.[46]

The supporters of the Caliphate were far from accepting this *bid'a* of *bid'as*, tantamount to heresy. They maintained a fierce campaign for three months. Their stand now was not religious but constitutional and political. The Constitution needed to be re-amended to clarify the prerogatives of the Caliph. Theirs was a drive to bring the Caliphate into the Constitution on the basis of Article 2. They also claimed that the Caliphate was a matter transcending the Constitution of the Turkish Republic. It was "a link between Turkey and the Islamic world." It was "a priceless treasure" for Turkey, enabling her to obtain moral and material support from all the Muslim nations. "Unfortunately," wrote Lûfti Fikri, a famous lawyer newly elected to the presidency of

[46] M. Kemal, *Nutuk*, p. 513; English trans., p. 682.

the Istanbul Bar Association, in a published letter to the Caliph, "we [Turks] rather than the enemies of the Islamic world are the enemies of the Caliphate."[47]

458

The Kemalists became increasingly alarmed by the reports that those close to the Caliph were encouraging the delusion that he was the Ruler of all Believers. The Caliph continued to follow the court ceremony of the Padişahs; members of the dynasty continued to occupy the palaces; he staged the traditional Friday prayer processions, received delegates, sent messages to the Muslims in foreign countries, and appointed envoys to the representatives of foreign countries. A Muslim Pope was in the process of becoming.

Two incidents among several others carried Mustafa Kemal's rage to the limit. In an official communication to the government, the Caliph spoke of the inadequacy of the Caliphal Treasury and demanded an increased subvention from the Turkish state. "What is the 'Caliphal Treasury'?" Mustafa Kemal asked. "The Caliph does not and should not have a Treasury." He ordered the government representative to the Caliph to investigate whether or not such a thing existed; if so, it should be expropriated to the state treasury. "For a Caliph," he said, "no pomp and luxury, but a simple and modest life, just like human beings, is appropriate"; he ordered the dismissal of the courtiers, secretaries, councillors, etc.[48]

The second incident was another gift of British diplomacy. It became a signal for Mustafa Kemal to stage a new coup. On November 24, 1923, two Indian dignitaries, the Agha Khan and Ameer Ali, sent a letter to the Turkish government explaining the importance of the institution of the Caliphate for Sunni Muslims and inviting attention "to the very disturbing effects the present uncertain position of the Caliph-Imam is exercising among the vast populations who belong to the Sunni communion." The authors urged "the imminent necessity for maintaining the religious and moral solidarity of Islam by placing the Caliph-Imamate on a basis which would command the confidence and esteem of the Muslim nations."[49] Copies of the letter were dispatched to the editors of the Turkish newspapers which were already raging with discussions over the Caliphate.

[47] *Ibid.*, p. 502; English trans., p. 668.

[48] *Ibid.*, p. 513; English trans., p. 682.

[49] Full text in Toynbee, *Survey of International Affairs*, pp. 571 f.

More than one point in the letter could be utilized under the then existing conditions to arouse nationalist indignation against the exploitation of the Caliphate for political purposes. The fact that both the self-styled defenders of the interests of the "Sunni communion" were Shî'î, followers of those sectarians whose chief cause for dissent had been the caliphate, was one; the totally un-Muslim wording and phraseology of the letter was another. But above all, both authors were believed to have been active participants in the campaign against the Caliph's declaration of holy war (*jihâd*) during World War I.[50]

An exposé of the personal, political, and religious interests of the two petitioners provided quite enough for the Kemalists to present the incident as a frame-up having the ultimate aim of exploiting what was claimed by the Khilâfatists to be a blessing for Turkey in her relations with the Muslim world as an agency of foreign intervention in her internal temporal affairs. News reports, such as those concerning a resolution for the solution of the Caliphate question by an international body of *ulema*, passed on January 1, 1924, at the convention in India of the Jamiyatu'l-'ulamâ (Society of *Ulama*) helped the Kemalists present the threat not only as coming from the indigenous reactionaries, but also as extending to international entanglements.

The time had surely come for Mustafa Kemal to begin an open campaign against the Caliphate. His ideas, summarized in his *Speech*, are interesting for those who would compare the diametrically opposed views of two Muslim groups, the nationalists and the Khilâfatists. After explaining the unrealistic nature of the Caliphate he said:

It is easy to understand that the real intention of those who claimed that the substance of the Caliphate is temporal power was to make the people believe that the Caliphate is State and the Caliph the head of the state and, hence, in reality, the Caliph should be the head of the Turkish state. . . . I explained to the nation that for the sake of the utopia of establishing a world-wide Islamic state, the Turkish state and its handful of people cannot be subjugated to the service of a Caliph.

[50] See W. C. Smith, *Modern Islâm in India* (London, 1946), p. 198. For the Turkish view see Yusuf Hikmet Bayur, *Türkiye Devletinin Dış Siyasasi* (Istanbul, 1942), pp. 153-57. For Toynbee's opinion see *Survey of International Affairs*, p. 597.

Then he concluded:

460

> We must put an end from now on to the delusion of imagining
> ourselves the masters of the world. Enough of the calamities
> to which we have dragged the nation by our ignorance of the
> conditions of the world and our real position in it and by our
> following the fools! We cannot carry the same tragedy while
> knowing the realities.[51]

Few expected that Mustafa Kemal would dare challenge the
Caliphate or would succeed in arousing national feelings to a
higher level than that of religious zeal. The final judgment was
passed at the end of a week of strenuous struggle and discussion
in the Assembly (February 25–March 3) and following a long
speech by M. Seyyid, the Minister of Justice.[52] The bill abolishing
the Caliphate was passed on March 3, 1924.[53]

---

[51] M. Kemal, *Nutuk,* p. 433; English trans., p. 592-93.

[52] Published as *Hilâfetin Mahiyet-i Ser'iyesi* (Ankara, 1924)

[53] Toynbee, *Survey of International Affairs,* pp. 572-75.

THE TRIUMPH of the idea of a Secular state over the idea of an Islamic state produced a series of secularizing reforms within legal, educational, and cultural institutions. The first phase of these reforms was opened with the abolition of the Caliphate. Two more bills, one abolishing the Ministries of Şeriat and Evkaf, the other closing the *medreses*, unifying education under the Ministry of Education and abolishing the religious orders (*tarîqas*) and their cloisters, were passed together in the next breath. It ended with the secularization of the Constitution on November 3, 1928. The second phase lasting from then until 1938 was one in which the previous changes were supplemented, extended, and consolidated.

The Kemalist approach to the question of secularism differed radically from the approaches of the Tanzimat and Meşrutiyet. The contest of the Kemalists and Khilâfatists produced the new approach whose distinguishing feature was the introduction of a new principle of populism to replace the old notion of reforming the traditional basic institution, the Islamic Ottoman State. The Kemalist reconstruction, thus, developed as nothing but the automatic application of a new constitutional principle. This was what made it thoroughly secular as distinguished from all the movements of reform in the past.

The Principle of Populism

The Kemalist idea of the sovereignty of the people was conceived differently from both the liberal and the communist doctrines. It took shape parallel with the struggle against communism, imperialism, Sultanate and Caliphate, and was expressed in the principle of populism.

462

Populism recognized the validity of popular sovereignty to the degree circumscribed by the requirements of national unity, sovereignty, and reconstruction. It was made the cornerstone of the new political doctrine and shaped in response to the pressures of the two great rival ideologies. "Our people is composed, not of social classes with conflicting interests, but of classes whose co-existence in indispensible one to the other," was the Kemalist view of society. Turkey was understood to be confronted, not with the problem of abolishing social classes, but with the problem of creating them by abolishing the fetters inhibiting their growth and by the application of measures of economic development.

The same idea had been represented previously in another form by Ziya Gökalp. In 1918, reviewing the possible consequences of the war and the Bolshevik Revolution, he wrote:

> This great war [World War I] which shed the blood of millions of innocent men will certainly bring forth a few benefits. . . . The ideals which the war helped intensify may be summarized in two words: nationalism and populism.

Then reviewing the collapse of empires, the rise of nations, the idea of national rights to self-determination, and the question of class warfare, he said,

> Populism strives to replace the warring classes with occupational groups binding the individuals to each other with strong ties of solidarity. If we may liken society to a social organism, its real organs, those playing vital functions, are occupational groups. . . . Socialism is aiming at unattainable ends by basing itself on the class struggle. One of the post-war ideals will be populism based on the sovereignty of the occupational groups.[1]

Gökalp's idea of occupational representation was rejected by Mustafa Kemal during the constitutional discussions of 1920. The idea of rejecting class struggle and proposing populism as a union of classes was, however, taken over by Kemal. It was combined with the view that Turkey as an underdeveloped country had a problem other than that involving the economic problems of the Western civilization. Turkey's major problem involved a struggle to join Western civilization. The Turkish Revolution would mean preparing paths of development for *all* social classes.

[1] Z. Gökalp, "Halkçılık," *Yeni Mecmua*, No. 32 (Istanbul, Feb. 14, 1918), 102-4.

In his declarations on the establishment of the People's party, Kemal expressed the same idea:

The aim of a people's organization as a party is not the realization
of the interests of certain classes over against those of other classes.
The aim is rather to mobilize the entire nation, called People,
by including all classes and excluding none, in common and united
action towards genuine prosperity which is the common objective
for all.[2]

463

He explained his view over and over again at the 1923 Conference in Izmir. A speech given then by the Minister of Economy contained the first statement of the economic objective of the Kemalist thesis—economic independence and self-support. "The political revolution should be implemented by an industrial revolution." This would be achieved by entering the machine age with all possible speed; law, education and the rest would have to be placed in the service of this transition.

Kemalist Westernism

If the Economic Conference of 1923 led to anything, it was to the conclusion that the major issue to be faced was a total revolution necessitated by the relations between the developed and underdeveloped nations. An underdeveloped nation had to strive to make itself equal to the developed nations if it did not want to continue to be exploited by them. The supreme problem was, therefore, to develop the country along the lines of Western civilization.

To reach the stage achieved by the civilized nations! That became the motif of the new ideology. The reforms to be undertaken would imply nothing but a total revolution—the appropriation of Western civilization.

Mustafa Kemal opened the drive for Westernization while he was yet struggling with the Khilâfatists. Wherever he toured he emphasized the idea, "The war is over with ourselves victorious, but our real struggle for independence is to begin only now—this

[2] Mustafa Kemal's declarations on this idea will be found in *Gazi Mustafa Kemal Paşa Hazretleri Izmir Yollarında* (Ankara, 1923) and *Iktisad Esaslarımız* (Istanbul, 1940). See John Parker and Charles Smith, *Modern Turkey* (London, 1940), pp. 71-72.

is the struggle to achieve Western civilization."[3] A recurrent theme of his speeches in 1924 was the absolute determination to achieve an unconditional transformation to Western civilization and to destroy all forces of reaction. In a speech commemorating the anniversary of the War of Independence, he said,

464

> Surviving in the world of modern civilization depends upon changing ourselves. This is the sole law of any progress in the social, economic and scientific spheres of life. Changing the rules of life in accordance with the times is an absolute necessity. In an age when inventions and the wonders of science are bringing change after change in the conditions of life, nations cannot maintain their existence by age-old rotten mentalities and by tradition-worshipping. . . . Superstitions and nonsense have to be thrown out of our heads.[4]

It took determination for Kemal to preach a gospel of Westernization in the face of the anti-Westernism of the war years and he needed the prestige he had won as a national hero to get his message across. Mustafa Kemal's drive "towards the West in spite of the West" by methods contrary to Western liberalism was merely the logical consequence of his belief that the struggle for national liberation was one between advanced nations and nations that allowed themselves to be exploited by their insistence on their medievalism. The West was not a West of simply "modern sciences and techniques." In discussing the old view, F. R. Atay, one of the leading propagandists of the new view, said:

> This view was diametrically opposite to the Kemalist Revolutionary view. We were not the victims of the material superiority of the West. We were the victims of that very moral superiority which had given material superiority to the West. The West is an institution—the institution of freedom of the mind. The failure of the reactionaries was due to their identification of the "moral" with religion and their fear of our losing religion or nationality when the question of separating the world and religion was faced.[5]

Perhaps the most forceful exposition of the new Westernist view was given by Ahmed Ağaoğlu in "Three Civilizations," written while he was imprisoned on Malta. His unconditional Westernism surpassed even the radicalism of his former opponent

[3] *Gazi Mustafa Kemal Paşa Izmir Yollarında* (Ankara, 1923), pp. 22, 103-26, 79.

[4] Text in *Türk Yurdu*, No. 1 (1924).

[5] F. R. Atay, "Çankaya," *Dünya*, No. 73 (Istanbul, 1957).

Abdullah Cevdet. Every civilization, argued Ağaoğlu, constitutes a whole. The superiority of a civilization lies in its totality and not in its discrete parts. A civilization can not be fragmentized or sifted. If modern techniques and sciences have developed in Western civilization and not in others, it invites us to realize that there were congenial conditions for this in the totality of that civilization. If Western civilization is victorious over other civilizations, it is not only because of its techniques or sciences, but because of its totality, because of all of its constituent elements, because of all of its virtues and vices. And the totality of Western civilization has defeated not only the particles but again the totality of the Oriental civilizations. The warfare between the West and the Orient was one waged between two systems. Islamic civilization (the author used Islamic and Oriental interchangeably) is a system in which religion permeates everything "from clothes and furniture to schools and political institutions." The interference of religion in everything in life caused the decline of Islam, while the secularization of the West brought the superiority of its civilization. "There are now two roads for us to follow: to accept defeat and annihilation or to accept the same principles which have created contemporary Western civilization." If we want to survive, we have to secularize our view of religion, morality, social relations, and law. "This is possible only by accepting openly and unconditionally the mind as well as the behaviour of the civilization which we are bound to imitate."[6]

465

Removal of the Debris

What obstacles had to be demolished in order to free the society to borrow, to learn, and to adapt? Mustafa Kemal's declarations in 1924 and 1925 on the principle of revolutionism all stressed the incongruity of the traditional institutions with the implications of a secular polity and culture. As early as 1922 he addressed a delegation of teachers with these words,

Ideas full of irrational superstition are morbid. Social life dominated by irrational, useless, and harmful beliefs is doomed to paralysis. We must begin by purging minds and society of their very

[6] Ahmed Ağaoğlu, *Üç Medeniyet* (Ankara, 1928).

springs. . . . Our guide in political, social, and educational life will be science. . . . Progress is too difficult or even impossible for nations that insist on preserving their traditions and beliefs lacking in rational bases.[7]

466

The *şeriat* courts, the *medreses* and all *tarîqas*, their meeting places or cloisters, titles and offices, were abolished following the abolition of the Caliphate. The tombs (*türbe*) and shrines of saints were also closed. *Imâms, hocas,* and preachers were permitted to wear clerical garb only while performing their duties, and a later law, passed in 1934, prohibited the use of terms such as *hacı, hafiz,* and *molla* as religious titles in official life.

Article 9 of the Law of Associations (Cemiyetler Kanunu), promulgated in 1938, prohibited the "formation of societies based on religion, sect, and *tarîqa*." Forming societies for the purpose of religious prayer and practice was not prohibited. The same law prohibited political parties as such from engaging in religious activities and from making religious propaganda. Propaganda against the principles of secularism was prohibited by Article 163 of the Penal Code adopted in 1926. Article 241 of the same law made religious functionaries liable to prosecution for speaking derisively of the laws and public authorities in the course of their ministrations.

Opening religious schools or schools for the purpose of religious instruction was not prohibited (although no one appears to have exercised this freedom until recently). This freedom was not unlimited; the constitutional provision that every Turkish citizen had the right to free primary education and the subsequent educational laws making secular primary education compulsory to the age of twelve were active deterrents to the opening of religious schools in competition with the primary schools administered by the Ministry of Education. Further, teaching of the Arabic script in unauthorized schools was prohibited when the Latin script was adopted in 1928. Parents were free to provide religious instruction privately in out-of-school time or in collectively established classes, provided that these did not interfere with regular schooling, that they were authorized by the Ministry of

---

[7] *Atatürk'ün Maarife ait Direktifleri* (Istanbul, 1939), pp. 6-10. See also *Atatürk'ün Söylev ve Demeçleri* (2 vols.; Istanbul, 1945); *Atatürk Dedi ki* (Ankara, 1943); H. Melzig, *Atatürk'ün Başlıca Nutukları* (Istanbul, 1942); S. Omurtak [et al.] "Atatürk," *Islâm Ansiklopedisi,* I, (Istanbul, 1950), 719-804; and *Atatürk'ten Düşünceler* (Ankara, 1956).

Education, and that they were competently supervised with regard to public health and the qualifications of the instructor.[8]

These were not measures for separating the traditional institutions (not necessarily Islamic religious institutions, as none of them was a part of classical Islam) from the secular institutions in order to keep them intact beyond the sway of change. The measures were not preludes to reforming these institutions, or replacing them with better ones of a like kind. They merely removed institutions that were incompatible with the basic principles of a secular state.

467

Secularization of the Civil Law

The decisive moment in favour of secularism came in what appears to have been the greatest coup of the new period. This was, in fact, its most constructive achievement because the wheels of the society were thus put on a new track. We shall appreciate the importance of this coup better if we compare it with its two antecedents, one in the Tanzimat and the other in the Meşrutiyet period.

It was demonstrated for the third time that, if the crux of Western secularism lay in the relations between state and church, the pivot of secularization in Muslim societies lay in the secularization of law, particularly the civil law. We have seen throughout our survey how the religious institution, symbolized in Turkey by the term Şeriat, came gradually but steadily under the wave of secularization. The term had contracted finally to refer to a field that constituted the innermost core of the Şeriat—the legal relations clustering around the institution of family. The abolition of the Caliphate implied the abolition of the Şeriat as a law of the state because, once the traditional temporal and political power had been rejected, its legal basis and structure was bound to fall too.

What then would take the place of the Şeriat as a legal system? The Şeriat had already been confined to only two matters: practices carried by custom and practices and matters carried by the codification (in the Law of Family Rights of 1917) of the *fiqh* rules concerning marriage, divorce, and succession as applied in the *şeriat* courts now under the jurisdiction of the Ministry of Justice.

---

[8] See Bülent Daver, *Türkiye Cumhuriyetinde Lâyiklik* (Ankara, 1955), pp. 181-201, for further details on secularizing legislation.

468

The secular courts were already applying the Mecelle. Although both courts were now separated from the Religious Institution and secularized in this sense, neither was in accord with the legal implications of the new secular state. In addition, they created a fragmented and unco-ordinated judicial system that paralyzed the effective and speedy administration of justice.

It was in connection with such a situation that the new regime acquired a feature distinguishing it from the Tanzimat within the field of law as well as of education. The spirit of the Tanzimat secularism had been separation—the creation of a series of dichotomies. In the Kemalist regime the direction was reversed towards unification. The writings of the period abounded with criticism of the dichotomies in life, ranging from law to musical taste and personal attire.

The time had come to raise the question of the unification of the legal and judicial system. The abolition of the Caliphate gave stimulus to the clarification of the position of the new regime with respect not only to the Şeriat, but also to an aspect of the Turkish approach to secularism. At the close of his historic speech advocating the abolition of the Caliphate, the Minister of Justice, Seyyid raised the legal question with the words,

There is one point on which all jurists and legal thinkers, Eastern or Western, agree and that is the theorem that the laws of a country should be in agreement with the mores of the nation. . . . The legal system of a country is the product of its people's mores and changes only when the mores change. . . . It is not an easy task to frame laws suiting the mores of a people. Just as the West has mores and laws peculiar to itself, the East, and within that our country, have their own. . . . We are now faced with the question of determining which legal provisions are suitable and agreeable to the social conditions of our country.[9]

This, he explained, is a painstaking job because the aim is to draft laws suited to the Turkish spirit and not to adopt or borrow the codes of Germany or Switzerland in a few months.

This was a succinct formulation of the Turkist position on legal secularization, and provides us with a yardstick to see where Kemalism deviated from the Turkist view based upon Gökalp's theory of the dichotomy of culture and civilization.

Immediately before the abolition of the Caliphate the Ministry of Justice had formed a special committee to draft a new family

[9] Seyyid, *Hilâfetin Mahiyet-i Şerî'iyesi* (Ankara, 1924), pp. 60-62.

law. In his explanatory introduction to the draft presented to the National Assembly on November 27, 1923, Seyyid indicated that the draft had been prepared according to the above-mentioned juridical theorem.

469

The draft concerned marriage and divorce only. Muslims, Jews, and Christians were subjected to provisions derived separately from their religious codes. In the case of the Muslims several Shâfiî and a few Hanbalî and Mâlikî opinions were preferred to the Hanafi on the grounds that they were in better accordance with the needs of the time; for example, a guardian's marrying an insane ward, whether male or female, was prohibited according to the Shâfiî opinion. Similarly, adultery was rejected as a factor of relationship prohibiting marriage. Again in the Shâfiî opinion, coercion was accepted as making a marriage null and void. The spirit that permeated the draft was the traditional Şeriat spirit. Polygamy was neither abolished nor made subject to the consent of the first wife unless—this was the only point of deviation from the former law—a prohibition had been a condition of the first marriage. The authors' reasoning on this point was peculiar. While contending that polygamy was not an obligation but a permission and that it could be prohibited by the legislators, the committee accepted the validity of the view that polygamy obviated prostitution and contributed to the increase of population and, thus, avoided prohibiting polygamy because that "would obviate the benefits contemplated in its permissibility by the Şeriat."[10]

The draft was scrutinized and controverted during 1923 and 1924, but it was never passed by the National Assembly. Its content as well as spirit showed that the ultimate yardstick of the draft was the Şeriat, despite its claim to be a secular law based on the spirit of the national mores and a free selection of the juridical opinions of the Muslim schools of law. Opinion in the National Assembly was divided, especially with regard to the question of polygamy. The press and public took up the controversy. The poorest prospect of the draft was its complete neglect of the basic motivation—to produce a unified system of codes. Gradually the matter boiled down to a final decision between two legal systems.

Mustafa Kemal gave the first signal on March 1, 1924. He said,

The important point is to free our legal attitude, our codes, and our legal organizations immediately from principles dominating our

---

[10] *Hukuk-u Aile Kanun Lâyihası ve Esbab-i Mucibe Mezbatast*, reprinted from *T.B.M.M. Zabıt Ceridesi* (Ankara, 1923), pp. 3-22.

life that are incompatible with the necessities of the age. . . . The direction to be followed in civil law and family law should be nothing but that of Western civilization. Following the road of half measures and attachment to age-old beliefs is the gravest obstacle to the awakening of nations.[11]

470

The majority trend in 1923-24 was toward the idea of unifying all codes and legal provisions on the principles of one system, the Western legal system. It was with this in mind that Mustafa Kemal spoke at the opening of a Faculty of Law on October 5, 1925. He said there:

The Turkish Revolution signifies a transformation far broader than the word revolution suggests. . . . It means replacing an age-old political unity based on religion with one based on another tie, that of nationality. This nation has now accepted the principle that the only means of survival for nations in the international struggle for existence lies in the acceptance of the contemporary Western civilization. This nation has also accepted the principle that all of its laws should be based on secular grounds only, on a secular mentality that accepts the rule of continuous change in accordance with the change and development of life's conditions as its law. . . . The time has come to lay the legal foundations and educate new men of law satisfying the mentality and needs of our Revolution.[12]

After two years of argument the new Civil Code, adapted from the Swiss Civil Code, passed the National Assembly on February 17, 1926. The concluding remarks of the Preamble written by Mahmut Esat, the new Minister of Justice, will illustrate the dominant spirit when the Code was adopted.

The Turkish nation . . . unconditionally insisting upon all the rights which the modern age has recognized as attributed to civilized nations, has . . . by accepting this . . . law, undertaken all the responsibilities required by this code. On the day that this document . . . is promulgated, the Turkish nation will be saved from false beliefs and traditions, and the fluctuations since the Tanzimat; it will close the doors of an old civilization, and will have entered into a contemporary civilization of . . . progress.[13]

[11] *Atatürk'ün Söylev ve Demeçelri*, I, 317.

[12] Full text quoted in Osman Ergin, *Türkiye Maarif Tarihi* (Istanbul, 1943), V, 1501-4.

[13] *T.B.M.M. Zabit Ceridesi*, Session 57, 1926, vol. XXII (Ankara, 1925), pp. 267 ff.; an English translation of the code is in Lutfy Levonian, *The Turkish Press* (Athens, 1932), pp. 45-53.

The Swiss Code was framed in 1912, and stemmed from Germanic civil law. The latter had been codified in 1874-96 contemporaneously with the codification of the Mecelle, and served as the basis for the framing of the Japanese Civil Code antedating that in Turkey, and the Chinese Code postdating the Turkish one. In Turkey it was regarded as the best combination of the Roman, Germanic, and natural rights traditions of the European system of codes. Two excerpts from the Preamble answered in advance the major objections to its reception.

471

There is no fundamental difference in the needs of nations belonging to the modern family of civilization. Perpetual social and economic contacts have . . . been transforming a large civilized body of mankind into a family. . . . We must never forget that the Turkish nation has decided to accept modern civilization and its living principles without any condition or reservation. . . . If there are some points of contemporary civilization that do not seem capable of conforming to Turkish society, this is not because of the lack of capability and native capacity of the Turkish nation, but because of the medieval organization and the religious codes and institutions which abnormally surround it. . . . The Turkish nation, which is moving with determination to seize contemportary civilization and make it its own, is obliged not to make contemporary civilization conform to the Turkish nation, but to adjust its steps to the requirements of contemporary civilization at all costs. . . . The aim of law is not to maintain religious regulations, nor to maintain any other habitual customs, but to ensure political, social, economic, and national activity at all costs.

We see, therefore, that the aim of the makers of the Code was not to establish and regulate the civil relations of the people according to existing customs and mores, or religious provisions. On the contrary, it was to shape these relations according to what the makers of the Code believed they should be. Here lies the revolutionary character of the Code. Its approach differed radically from the Mecelle, as well as from the two previous family codes, in that it was not a codification bringing together different traditions for the purpose of their reconciliation, but rather one establishing a new system to the exclusion of the provisions of the religious and customary legal systems. The present-day critics of this reform point out the discrepancy between the law and reality, as if making a great discovery. Thirty years of its enforcement shows, nevertheless, that it has fulfilled and is fulfilling its main function as outlined above. The effects of the new law were felt especially in the fields pertaining to freedom of contract, private property, the integrity of the monogamous family, marriage, and divorce.

472

Above all, the Code signified the unmitigated secularization of civil life. The men of religion lost their function, not only in civil procedure, but also in the administration of the law. The idea of having civil codes and separate courts, secular or ecclesiastical, for each religious community was rejected definitively. A law promulgated on April 8, 1924, abolished the *şeriat* courts altogether (*Mahakim Teşkilâtına Ait Ahkâm Muaddil Kanun*, or Law Modifying the Provisions Concerning the Judicial Organization, Articles 8 and 10). With the promulgation of the Civil Code, the right recognized to the non-Muslim communities (Jewish, Armenian, and Greek) of being subject to separate provisions concerning civil and marital affairs by Article 42 of the Lausanne Treaty was repudiated. These communities agreed to be subject to the secular provisions of the Civil Code.

The Civil Code made marriage an entirely secular matter. It not only changed the nature of the contract, but also made it legally valid only if it was contracted by an authorized representative of the State. It divested the act of any religious significance insofar as the question of legality was concerned. Religious marriage performances were not prohibited. They were left to the inclinations of the persons concerned, after the marriage act was completed in the legal sense. Their performance or non-performance made no difference to the validity of the contract.

Similarly, the Code changed the nature of divorce radically. As a consequence of the right recognized to the husband in the marriage act by the Şeriat, he had had the greater right with respect to divorce. Although the wife, it was claimed, had a right to divorce, in practice this right had been unknown, at least in Turkey. By contrast, the husband had had unlimited freedom in matters of divorce. The Civil Code divested the husband of this prerogative. Divorce could be obtained only through a court of law. Women had the same prerogatives in divorce as men. In fact, in practice the shoe was put on the other foot. Greater facilities were provided when the complainant was the wife. This was related to another innovation. While the Şeriat law had not required that grounds be given by the husband for him to divorce his wife, the new law specified those grounds upon which divorce could be obtained. Furthermore, the examining judge was authorized to exercise discretion in terms of the counter-claims of the parties concerned. This introduced an entirely new procedural technique, the importance of which cannot be over-emphasized.

Of perhaps the greatest significance was the Code's turning the Şeriat law's permissibility for marrying four wives into a prohibition. The new Code not only abolished polygamy but also made marriage subject to a more complicated procedure, in which the most important consideration was the establishment of the bachelorhood of the intended bridegroom.

Probably the most important implication of the adoption of the Civil Code for the social and economic life of the people resulted from its effects upon the legal status of women. In addition to the effects already noted, there were the direct and indirect effects of the complete equality of men and women as regards inheritance and succession and of the recognition of a mother's equal rights to the guardianship of children. The Civil Code and the Law of Obligations, also adapted from the Swiss, introduced numerous provisions concerning ownership, contracts, financial responsibilities, mortgage, the definition of domicile, family names, etc. These superceded the relevant portions of the old Mecelle, which was discarded entirely with the promulgation of new Commercial and Penal Codes.

Another consequence of the Civil Code was the Law of Family Names adopted in 1934; still another was one that has not yet followed in the Code's place of origin: full and equal franchise for women. Women were permitted to vote and stand for election in municipal elections in 1931; a constitutional revision gave them full political rights and duties in 1934.

Extension of the Secularizing Reforms

The process of secularization initiated by the abolition of the Caliphate did not rest with revolutionizing the legal system and the areas of social and economic life. It extended, again in its new meaning, into the area of mores and informal cultural institutions. Again it came into conflict, not only with the Islamist position, but also with the Turkist position.

One of the radical changes pertained to headgear. A campaign led by Mustafa Kemal ended with the passage of the so-called Hat Law in 1925. Despite the critics' saying, "Change the head before its covering," the changing of headcovering did indeed symbolize

474

an important change in mentality for the peculiar circumstances of the Turkish case. For a century the fez had symbolized fears, superstitions, and prejudices. When a man clapped anything, however ridiculous, on his head and called it a hat, he was, in effect, declaring his freedom from all inhibitions. Wearing the veil was not prohibited by law then or since. On the other hand, measures were introduced making it disadvantageous for any but the old to remain under cover. Teachers and students could not be veiled. The families of government employees were expected to attend public functions unveiled, and public functions were organized purposely to bring out people of all types.

The emotional transformation symbolized by the adoption of the hat had numerous consequences. The critics and sceptics uniformly failed to notice these. The traumatic nature of the change made it, unconsciously, a mass reaction against the traditionalists and conservatives. It was at this time that the latter first felt themselves choked by an enveloping unseen force. For the first time they felt utterly powerless and defeated.

The turning of the iconoclastic drive against what was believed to be the area of national mores marked the beginning of the most critical stage in the Turkish transformation. This was exemplified best in an even greater step—the adoption of the Latin script.

While the Westernists had regarded the adoption of the Latin script simply as what they called a "civilizational" or technical problem, the Turkists had refrained from endorsing the idea because of their belief that the matter was one of national mores. The issue became even more touchy in the new phase for two reasons: the Latin script had been adopted by the Albanian Muslims, who were considered to have "ceded from the Ottoman Empire and from Islam"; the movement had begun also among the Turkish-speaking peoples of the Soviet Union.[14]

During the 1923 Economic Conference, a delegate had proposed the adoption of the Latin script. The idea was rejected on the several grounds that the change would turn the world of Islam against Turkey as it would signify that the Turks had accepted Christianity, that the Latin script was incapable of expressing Turkish, that all the works of centuries past would be lost, and

[14] The use of the Latin script among the Turkish-speaking nationalities of the Soviet Union was shortlived. A transition to the Cyrillic script was begun in 1937 and by 1939-40 all had shifted to it. See T. G. Winner, "Problems of Alphabetic Reform Among the Turkic Peoples of Soviet Central Asia, 1920-41," *Slavonic Review*, XXXI (London, 1952-53), 133-47.

that the change would create anarchy and even civil strife. When in 1924 a representative claimed in the National Assembly that the Arabic script was unsuited to Turkish, he was answered by a storm of protest which led to a revival of the controversy in the press.

A leading Turkist historian, Necip Âsım, wrote on this issue in 1924,

> Westernization and modernization do not by any means necessitate dropping our national traditions. It is our duty to see to it that our national structure is not damaged when changing our oriental garb and Westernizing.[15]

Turkist opinion against the Latin script increased on the eve of the international congress convened at Baku to discuss the matter. The Turkist historian, Fuad Köprülü, attended the Baku Congress and declared his opposition to the Latin script forthwith. Ayaz Ishakî, a Turkist émigré from Russia, discussed the matter at length from a nationalist point of view. While not denying the inadequacy of the Arabic script, he believed that the solution lay not in adopting the Latin script, but rather in reforming the Arabic script as it had been applied in Turkish. "However," he asked, "is the problem of script merely a matter of techniques?" Unaware of the difference between the Turkist nationalism and Kemalist nationalism, the writer believed that Kemalist Turkey could not and would not adopt the Latin script even if it was preferable for technical or civilizational reasons.[16]

Actual experiments with the Latin script began toward the end of 1927. The linguist, Cevat Emre, published a series of articles between December 1927 and May 1928, in which he made the first serious application of the Roman letters to the Turkish alphabet.[17] The attempt was based on a review of the experiments outside of Turkey. It gave considerable weight to the arguments

---

[15] Necip Âsım, "Harflerimiz," *Anadolu Mecmuası,* No. 2 (1924), 64, 66.

[16] Ayaz Ishaki, "Arap ve Latin Elifbalarını Mukayese," *Türk Yurdu,* III (Ankara, Feb. 15, 1926), 421-32. This appeared one month before the Baku Conference. See J. Castagné, *Le Congrès de Turkologie de Bakou* (Paris, 1926), concerning the proceedings of the Congress.

[17] Published in book form under the title *Muhtaç Olduğumuz Lisan Inkilâbı* (Istanbul, 1928). See also Ahmed Cevat Emre, *Atatürk'ün Inkılâp Hedefi* (Istanbul, 1956), pp. 15-20. See A. S. Levend, *Türk Dilinde Gelişme ve Sadeleşme Safhaları* (Ankara, 1949), p. 370 concerning the publications on the subject.

476

of the proponents of the Latin script. Emre's thesis was that changing the script was a matter of civilization and not of culture. The new Turkey should adopt the international script of Western civilization if it was determined to join that civilization. This was not an unprecedented move for the Turks, as they had done the same thing at least twice before, when they belonged to the pre-Islamic and Islamic civilizations. The various arguments against the change were invalid, as the family of Western civilization was composed of nations different in race, religion, and nationality.

The Committee that was finally appointed to draw up a draft alphabet and to report on a new grammer to accompany the new script recommended that ten years be taken for the transition. The two systems, the old and new, should compete with each other in publications and in the educational system.

In addition to recognizing that such a competition would be badly weighted, Mustafa Kemal was a firm believer in preventing the acceptance of yet a new duality. He opened a nationwide campaign on August 9, 1928. On November 3, 1928, a law was passed prohibiting the use of the Arabic script in all public affairs after December 1 of the same year.[18]

Among the various aspects of social life that felt, with particular intensity the impact of the secularization of government, of the family institution and certain cultural practices, was education. The Kemalist secularization of education followed a course diametrically opposed to that favoured by the Tanzimat and, to a lesser degree, Meşrutiyet reforms. The guiding principle was, as in law, unification and consolidation throughout the entire educational structure. This meant the elimination of the dichotomy between the religious and secular educational institutions and of the multiplicity in educational authority among the Muslims, non-Muslims, and foreigners. It meant, above all, the inclusion of primary education within the scope of public concern and authority and the focalization upon universal secular primary education as the basic educational policy.

As early as June 1921 Mustafa Kemal convened an educational convention in Ankara. He addressed the assembled teachers saying:

Even in these war years we must develop carefully devised programs of national education and prepare the grounds upon which our entire educational system shall operate efficiently. . . . I firmly believe that our traditional educational methods have been

[18] *Atatürkün Maarife ait Direktifleri* (Istanbul, 1939), pp. 3 f.

the most important factor in the history of our national decline. When I speak of national education I mean an education that will be free from all traditional superstitions as well as from all foreign influences, Eastern or Western, that are incompatible with our national character.[19]

In 1922 he said, "Our educational programs . . . should be in accordance with the conditions of the nation and the requirements of the age." In 1925 he said again at a teachers' convention, "Our national morality has to be nurtured and supported by civil principles and free thought."[20]

The idea of the unification of the educational system was proposed formally in the election program of 1923. In 1924 all education was given to the jurisdiction of the Ministry of Education by the Law of the Unification of Education.[21] All *medreses* were closed and in their place the Ministry of Education opened schools for the training of ministers and preachers (*imâms* and *khatîbs*). A Faculty of Divinity was also opened at the University of Istanbul.

When the clause stating that Islam was the state religion was dropped from the Constitution in 1928, the Ministry of Education took steps to drop classes in religion from the school curricula. (Already the old books on morality, ritual, etc. had been replaced by lesson books suited to the ages and understanding of the students, and the teaching of lessons in religion had been assigned to the regular classroom teachers.) Classes in religion were dropped in the urban schools in 1930; the change was effected in the village schools in 1933. In 1933 a law specifying the organization and functions of the Ministry of Education confirmed secular education and abolished earlier provisions concerning religious teaching in schools. In 1928, the teaching of Arabic and Persian was removed from the school curricula; these were left to specialized departments at the university level.

We are not here concerned with the particular problems of reform in education under the Republican regime. We only point out the emphasis placed upon the secularistic aspects of all the measures taken with respect to primary, vocational, teachers', and

[19] *Ibid.*, pp. 6-10, 17.

[20] Arnold J. Toynbee, *Survey of International Affairs, 1925* (London, 1927), I, 571 f. See also H. E. Allen, *The Turkish Transformation* (Chicago, 1935); and Daver, *Türkiye Cumhuriyetinde Lâyiklik*, pp. 124-35.

adult education, the methods and techniques of teaching, administration in general, and the content of the curricula, texts, and materials introduced.

478

The secularizing effects of the political, legal, and educational changes, as well as of the changes in the mores, upon the economic outlook and behaviour of the people deserves a fuller analysis than can be attempted here in order to evaluate the sociological consequences of the Kemalist secularism.

TWO MYTHS have sprung up and become established concerning the nature of the secularism emerging from the Kemalist Revolution. One is the belief that this secularism meant the separation of religion and state after the fashion of French laicism; the other is the belief that it was a policy of irreligion aimed at the systematic liquidation of Islam. In this chapter we shall examine the nature of this secularism together with these two contentions concerning it.

Unification versus Bifurcation

If we take Kemalist secularism as the expression of the separation of religion from state, implied in the absence of a state religion and the inclusion of secularism as a principle in the Constitution (1937)), the first contention concerning its nature would be a natural judgment. And if we believe with the Islamists that such a separation means, in the case of Islam, the abolition of religion, then the second contention would be a most valid inference. We could then join the criticism arrived at separately by the holders of these two separate views, namely, that Kemalist secularism was inconsistent, that it did not yet separate state from religion and it did not let religion have its own autonomous existence.

The Islamists, who had strongly opposed separationism when they were promoting the idea of an Islamic state, favoured the separationist interpretation of secularism following their defeat.

480

They now claimed that provisions restricting the *political* power of religion were incompatible with secularism, which implied non-interference in the affairs of religion; therefore, Kemalist secularism was not true secularism, but shoddy legitimization for the persecution of Islam. A modern secular state, said the secularist jurists on the other hand, should let religion follow its own course if the state did not intend to liquidate religion altogether. The inference was that, if Kemalist secularism did not fit one shoe, it should, perforce, fit into the other.

Yet Kemalist secularism had certain features contradicting both these judgments. It is true that certain aspects of Kemalist secularism implied political, legal, and educational restrictions upon religion while some others, such as the existence of a Department of Religious Affairs within the government and the expenditure of public funds on religious affairs, seemed to be inconsistent with a secular state. However, the seeming inconsistencies will disappear if we leave aside two pre-suppositions underlying the two judgments. Then the aspects appearing as incompatible with a doctrine of laicism (understood as a complete separation between religion and state) will prove to be, not the essence of the Kemalist secularism, but products of a process of severance, without which neither a secular state nor a non-political religion could ever come into existence on the basis of *din-u-devlet*, the legacy of medieval Islam.

The fallacy in the views of both Islamists and secularist jurists lies in the uncritical acceptance of two propositions of French laicism: that there are two institutions (Church and State), and that these ought to be separated. Our survey has shown that a development in the form of separation between religion and state took place throughout the Tanzimat and Meşrutiyet periods, and that this development was not in the direction of the severance of ties between two distinct spheres of life belonging to two distinct authorities and institutions. Rather it was one of bifurcating a whole, through a series of changes in one sector of life while another sector of life (with which religion identified itself) remained static. Every change in the first sector implied, in the second, not a re-adaptation but an opposition to the change which had been made. This increasingly became the identifying spirit of the religious sector, finally even to the extent of claiming complete superiority over the other. Its final attempt to capture the state and law failed. In consequence of this, it lost its institutional support (Khilâfat and Şeriat).

Religion was relying upon institutions that had political implications inconsistent with the basic principle of the new state; those institutions could no longer stand, even inharmoniously, side by side with the secularized sector. The abolition of the Sultanate and Caliphate was important, not in constituting the beginning, or the cause of Kemalist secularism, but in establishing for the first time in any Islamic country a state based upon the principle of popular sovereignty. It was that new principle, not a brand of secularism that had yet to mature, which necessitated the abolition of the Sultanate and Caliphate. After the abolition of the Sultanate, it became clear that the Caliphate could not co-exist with the new state by dividing up the temporal and spiritual powers. Through their insistence that a separation could not be made between the Sultanate and the Caliphate because Caliphate meant not only spiritual authority but also temporal sovereignty, the traditionalists prepared the ground for the abandonment of separationist secularism. The struggle was not over the question of separating the spiritual and temporal, but over the difference between democracy and theocracy. Either the government, laws, education, and economy would be fashioned and regulated according to the Şeriat, or all of the institutions sustaining this policy would be eradicated in order to free society from such a rule. The ascendancy of the second did not imply separating the temporal and the religious. It meant unifying dichotomous sets of laws, dichotomous institutions of education, dichotomous sets of households and many other things, including two systems of calendars and two systems of timekeeping. Education came to be the function of the state alone. Legislation completed the job of reducing the traditional authority within the institutions of family, marriage, inheritance, etc., in favour of the state. Could religion—which was not separately or independently institutionalized, but was diffused in and permeated through law, custom, and education—escape the effects of the radical changes in these fields, succeed in unifying the institutions under the secular authority, and be left "to its own course?"

The Religious Question

The Kemalist secularism cannot be designated therefore as a policy of separation. Was it then a policy of elimination? Did Kemalism launch a program of exterminating Islam from the life of the Turkish people?

Far from launching a program of extermination, the Kemalist regime took measures to promote the finding of an outlook and founding of an organization within which religion would not be destroyed as a result of having been extricated from its old shell. This unique approach to the question of secularism, was determined partly by the nature of Islam, partly by the conditions of Turkey within which Islam manifested itself, and partly by the probing of the moral question of the Revolution.

Kemalist secularism found its constitutional expression in 1928 when Article 2, stating that Islam was the religion of the state, was dropped; but nine more years were to pass before a doctrine of secularism was crystallized and secularism was introduced into the Constitution as a principle (1937). It came out gradually as an answer to the question: What is the position of Islam in a democratically conceived political community?

The question had been raised, although not directly in this form, half a century earlier by Namık Kemal. Then, it had been asked in reverse order, that is, "What is the form of democracy in an Islamically conceived community?" The answer, we know, was the Hamidian "constitutional absolutism." A democratically conceived state was found at that time to be inconceivable in Islam.

In accordance with its own principle which was accepted as a fact (without recourse to the Şeriat for legitimization), the new regime would accept the freedom of religion not because religion should be implemented as the basis of the state, but because it was the duty of the state to safeguard freedom. Freeing the conscience could be effected only when and insofar as the theocratic concept was eliminated from the body of the religious outlook.

The question boiled down, therefore, to: "Is Islam conceivable in a democratically constituted state?" Would a democracy, as a polity incompatible with theocracy, recognize the demand to subordinate it to religion (through a series of rules ranging from customs to law) as a right to be exercised on the principle of democratic freedom? The assumption of the sovereignty of the people thus implied a religious view that was not merely residual to the political principle but rather an inherent part of it.

The manner in which religion had become institutionalized in Turkey made it appear as though the question had implications for the whole social existence. Hence the two facets of the Turkish secularism, each inviting a different approach. Under the regime of popular sovereignty the religious question became one of religious enlightenment on the one hand, and, in terms of a national existence, one of moral re-integration on the other. Kemalist secularism took final shape with the interaction of these two approaches. Despite their confluences, we can best understand each by considering them separately rather than chronologically.

483

The Rationalist Approach to Religion

The first approach was based upon a view shared by Westernists and Islamists—the belief that Islam was a natural and reasonable religion. The idea of the reasonableness of Islam became a deistic conviction in Mustafa Kemal's mind. For him, the abolition of the Caliphate meant liberating Islam from its unreasonable traditional associates and preparing the ground for its emergence as a rational religion.

Mustafa Kemal had understood the role of religion in the life of the people during the strugge for national liberation. He had seen how dangerous religious fanaticism could be in moments of national disaster; he had, at the same time, felt the role of religion as a spontaneous expression of popular unity in consolidating national efforts. When on tour before the abolition of the Sultanate and Caliphate, he often went directly to the mosque, participated in the Friday prayers, and even mounted the *minbar* (pulpit) to deliver impromptu *khutbas* (sermons). His talks were not designed to arouse passions for the purpose of winning votes. Rather he openly discussed the religious reforms he had in mind for after the victory.[1] His reformism was in no small part due to the encouraging response he got at these times from the common people.

Mustafa Kemal was convinced at the same time by the deep ignorance of the interpreters of religion and, through them, of the people, that a drive for an enlightened and humanized Islam was absolutely necessary. He emphasized throughout his talks that Islam was a creed worthy of human beings; it was natural and rational; it had been corrupted by the "play-actors of religion" in the service of tyrants in order to enslave the minds of the people; it had become a religion that drew provisions for life from arbi-

---

[1] See *Gazi Mustafa Kemal Paşa Hazretleri Izmir Yollarında* (Ankara, 1923), pp. 33-34, 77, 93, 95-96.

trary interpretations of the letters of the Scriptures. In reality, Islam enjoined enlightenment and freedom; religion should preach these things for the betterment and understanding of the people. Above all the people should learn of their religion in the language they understood and without recourse to the self-styled interpreters of the "incomprehensible Book."

484

The crux of all Mustafa Kemal's experiments was not to Turkify Islam for the sake of Turkish nationalism, but to Turkify Islam for the sake of religious enlightenment. His persistent objective—the one evoking the most severe denunciations from the *ulema*, the Islamists, and the repositories of the secrets of the Arabic of the Kur'an—was to cut the ground out from under those vested interests claiming an exclusive monopoly over the understanding and interpretation of what they too claimed to be a natural and rational religion.

As early as 1923, Mustafa Kemal announced, in the name of the government, preparations for the establishment of a board of Islamic studies. The objectives would be "to study Islamic philosophy in relation to Western philosophy, to study the ritual, rational, economic, and demographic conditions of the Muslim peoples." Modernization of Islamic teachings would be sought by educating modern scholars of *ijtihâd* and *tafsîr*. The multiplicity of Islamic traditions would be recognized over against the officially supported theology that had gained exclusive sway. Islam would be approached through reason rather than tradition.

This attitude was not changed or abandoned following the promulgation of the Republic and the abolition of the Caliphate. Had the new regime merely desired the persecution of religion, it would have abandoned such projects after these two major changes. Instead, a Department of the Affairs of Piety (*Diyanet*) was constituted in 1924 to manage the administrative affairs of religion.[2] The Department of Evkaf was set up to manage the finances of the religious foundations. A Faculty of Divinity was established in the University of Istanbul for the cultivation of the new religious outlook, and schools were founded to train *imâms* and *khatîbs* (ministers and preachers) to administer religious functions in terms of the new outlook.

The new organizational apparatus was not designed to be a spiritual organization. The first article of the law instituting the Department of the Affairs of Piety distinguished the *mu'âmalât*

[2] Public Law No. 430, dated March 3, 1924.

(civil relations) from *itikadât* (beliefs) and *ibâdât* (rituals); it formally abolished the independent existence of the Şeriat as a law by putting the *mu'âmalât* under the legislative jurisdiction of the National Assembly which in 1926, by virtue of its supreme legislative authority, abolished the Şeriat as a civil law by its promulgation of the Civil Code. This same article stated that "the administration of all matters concerning the beliefs and rituals of Islam will belong to the Department of the Affairs of Piety."

485

The Department was to be an agency of public service rather than the supreme spiritual body of a religious community. Its head was to be technically qualified, and would fill the office by executive appointment upon the recognition of his competence, but holding the office would not confer upon him any extra-temporal or spiritual attributes. The department was not authorized to receive donations, and was separated from the Evkaf administration. It was given the task of translating, editing, and publishing religious works, not for the purpose of indoctrination or of making polemics, but for the purpose of supplying the public with authentic religious literature. It was barred from all direct educational functions (even the schools for the training of *imâms* and *khatîbs* fell under the jurisdiction of the Ministry of Education). Its organizational branches were headed by *muftîs* whose job was of a strictly administrative nature, such as announcing the beginning of the religious holidays (not fixed because of the Islamic lunar calendar) on the basis not, as in the past, of individual witness, but of the reports sent out by the official observatory. Issuing *fetvas* upon matters having legal implications was no longer possible.

As the founding legislation of the Department exemplifies, the objective of the new religious policy was the elimination of medieval fetters on religious expression, and the severance of all legal and political considerations from affairs of piety. Islam as *diyanet* (piety) would then be a factor of enlightenment.

The new policy aimed at providing an organization within which the believer could find ideal conditions for his religious expression, but that would authorize no one to interfere with matters of individual conscience. Freed from emotion and ambition as well as from obsolete views, practices, and superstitions, the religious strivings of the Faithful would give rebirth to "natural" Islam.

The approach was predominantly pragmatic—in line with the approach to religion of the Turks throughout their history. It did not aim at a religious doctrine, a dogma, or a theology; it remained experimental with respect to religious reform and led progressively to the further clarification of the form of secularism conceived to be best for the facilitation of a religious reform.

486

In addition to the government's activities, we must note the efforts of Mustafa Kemal as a private citizen to forward the drive for religious enlightenment. His activities were directed towards the most conspicuous aspect of everyday Islam. It seemed to him that the most obvious beginning to the rationalization of Islam lay in the matter of the language of worship. Through his appeal, leadership, and experiments (during which he evoked the admiration of not a few clericals for his knowledge and aesthetic appreciation of the Kur'an), the call to prayer (*azân*) and the sermons (*khutbas*) came to be given universally in Turkish by 1931. It is to be noted that he used neither law nor coercion to transform these simplest features of worship; in fact, the Turkish *azân* was made legally compulsory three years after his death!

To bring these aspects of Islam within the understanding of the ordinary Turkish Muslim seemed to be the prerequisite to having religion play a genuine function in social life, but this was a relatively minor concern in Mustafa Kemal's understanding of the conditions necessary for religious reform. He set his sights early upon fulfilling what he believed to be the greatest task: the translation of the Kur'an into Turkish. The drive for a rational understanding of the Kur'an, the determination to make it available to the people in their vernacular, was a logical outcome of the conviction that Islam was rational and natural. If that were so, what could be more absurd than barring the people from direct recourse to the Book, thought Mustafa Kemal. "The Turk believes in the Book," he said, "but he does not understand what it says to him. First of all, he himself must understand directly the Book that he so seeks."[3]

Until the Meşrutiyet period nothing had been done along this line except for Cevdet Paşa's reported piecemeal experiments at translation. Following 1908 the Islamists introduced the practice of providing passage translations. These were meant not to be real translations but conveyances in Turkish of the meaning. Even in this sense the translation of the whole Kur'an was avoided. The first Turkish translation of the Kur'an, made during that period,

[3] Osman Ergin, *Türkiye Maarif Tarihi* (Istanbul, 1943), V, 1633-34. On the question of Kur'an translation see pp. 1610 ff.

was confiscated by order of the Şeyhul-Islâm. The opposition of
the Islamists to translation was based on the fear that a vernacular
Scripture would draw the Turkish people away from the Arabic
original, and would ultimately lead to the establishment of an
authorized vernacular version for all purposes.

487

The Turkish Islamists' resistance to Mustafa Kemal's campaign
had been crushed by 1924.[4] The fight against translation was taken
up and carried on by the Egyptian *ulema*, who, despite their
dislike for a Turkish Caliphate, had opened a campaign against
Mustafa Kemal that became intensified when one from among
themselves, 'Ali 'Abd ar-Râziq, declared in 1925 his approval of
the abolition of the Caliphate. While the controversy raged in
Egypt over the Caliphate issue and a Caliphate Congress initiated
by the Azhar in 1925 failed in producing anything, the drive for
a translation of the Kur'an gained strength in Turkey. A full-
length translation had already appeared in 1923, but was disapproved of for its inaccuracies by the Department of the Affairs
of Piety. Its re-publication within a few years showed, however,
that there was a strong desire among the people for a translated
Kur'an. The first relatively successful full-length translation was
produced in 1924 by Hüseyin Kâzım, an associate of *İçtihad* who
had for many years defended there the idea of translating the
Kur'an. Publication began in the same year of a translation by a
former Minister of Şeriat, Mehmet Vehbi; it was accompanied by
a *tafsîr* which ran to fifteen volumes. The pace continued in 1926.
A fairly readable translation was made by Zeki Maghamiz, a
Christian Arab, and revised by I. H. Izmirli, a professor in the
Faculty of Divinity of Istanbul University. Another appeared
accompanied by an abbreviated version of an old *tafsîr*. In 1927
Izmirli made what was perhaps the most accurate translation,
although it was not readable in a literary sense. About the same
time, an anonymous translation appeared together with Cevdet
Paşa's essay on the history of the Kur'an. Such private, hasty, and
enthusiastic translation activities were discouraged after 1927.

---

[4] The question of translating the Kur'an came to be focused on the
issue of whether or not the Kur'an in the Turkish language could
be used in prayers. Among the Turkish Modernists, Ismail Hakkı
Izmirli seems to have maintained the most liberal position; see his
Introduction to his Kur'an translation *Maâni-i Kur'an* (Istanbul,
1925). Another liberal Modernist, Yusuf Ziya [Yörükân] questioned
Izmirli's position in his review of the Introduction in *Mihrab*
(Istanbul, 1925), pp. 162-64; however, he did not reject the use of
the Turkish Kur'an in prayers.

The question was then taken up by the National Assembly and Mustafa Kemal.[5]

488

The interest manifested by the people in the translations showed the importance of taking the matter more seriously under control. Private publishers were unable to produce a Turkish version that would be adequate and readable, and also possess literary value. One man was known to Mustafa Kemal as able to produce a reliable as well as literary version. The Islamist poet Mehmed Âkif had proven by his early passage translations that he would be the ideal translator. He was formally invited to assume the task upon the National Assembly's appropriation of a translation fund in 1926.

While Âkif's artistry invited him to shoulder the responsibility of fulfilling what Mustafa Kemal believed would be the greatest event of the Revolution, his Islamism called him to the duty of sabotaging the idea. From 1923, when he began to sense the future direction of Mustafa Kemal's policies, he had flirted with the Azhar *ulema*, the Manar Modernists, and their patrons, the Egyptian pashas. At first he accepted the commission, stipulating that his submission should not be regarded as a translation because he believed that the Kur'an ought not to be translated. However, an obscure *imâm's* use of Turkish for the prayers, the subsequent controversy in the press, and, especially, the reaction of Shaikh Muhammad Rashîd Ridâ, the dean of the Egyptian Modernists, disclosed to Âkif what would befall him were he to carry out his trust. The Shaikh declared the Turks' sacrilege of translating the Kur'an into their tongue as *kufr* and pronounced Kemalist Turkey heretical. According to the Shaikh, these actions were expressions of Turkish nationalism, which was another heresy. Standing upon twelve quotations from the Kur'an, which he believed showed that translating the Kur'an was heresy, the Shaikh submitted a new "masterpiece of sophistry," as Mustafa Kemal put it, for none of the quotations disclaimed translation and some, especially XLI:44, perhaps meant the contrary.[6]

---

[5] On the Turkish translations of the Kur'an after 1923 see Ergin, *Türkiye Maarif Tarihi*, V, 1611-15; G. Jaeschke, "Der Islam in der neuen Türkei," *Welt des Islams*, New series I (1951), 80. Translation activities stopped after 1935, but began again in 1950, since when several translations have appeared.

[6] Rashîd Ridâ, *Tarjamat al-Qur'ân* (Cairo, 1921-22). In this violently anti-Turkish tract, Ridâ demanded that, instead of translating the Kur'an, the Turkish government adopt Arabic as the official and compulsory language of their country to prove that the Turks

Under the Shaikh's thunderbolts, Turkey's Islamist poet wavered between his own people's remembrance of him as the greatest translator of the Kur'an and the patronage of the Egyptian pashas in whose mansions he used to winter following 1923. He settled in Egypt as the guest of his patron Abbas Halim Pasha in 1925 and refused the commission the next year. So long as Âkif remained in Egypt in protest against the Kemalist reforms, the appropriation remained in trust in the hope that the rumours of Âkif's labours were correct and that he would ultimately reverse his decision. Mustafa Kemal renewed his invitation as late as 1936 but to no avail.[7]

Here was a clear expression of Mustafa Kemal's desire for the upholders of the religious ideal to make the truths of the Kur'an freely available to the Turkish believers in the best possible literary style. Âkif's obstinate rejection of every overture in the face, not only of the several inferior translations, but also of translations into the European languages (more often read by the youth who were the main targets of the charges of irreligion) was tantamount to saying that since the Turks (like all other non-Arabs) would

---

remained Muslims. Ridâ claimed religious support for his angry and rude statements, saying that Abu Hanîfa and the Hanafî jurists prohibited the translation of the Kur'an into any non-Arabic language under any circumstances. (*Tarjamat*, pp. 19-20.) Only four years later, however, we find Ridâ the most ardent supporter of Marmeduke Pickthall's English translation. Our surprise increases when we learn from Pickthall that, when he went to Egypt to win the *ulema*'s approval, Ridâ was one of those who supplied him with evidence from Hanafî sources for the permissibility of such a translation. (Quoted in Ann Fermantle, *The Loyal Enemy*, London, 1938, p. 414.) Ridâ was a prominent Arab nationalist engaged, during and after World War I, in promoting the independence of Arab countries with British help.

[7] The only product of the assignment given to Âkif was the *tafsîr* which was intended originally to parallel the translation: Hamdi Yazır, *Hak Dini, Kur'an Dili, Yeni Mealli Türkçe Tefsir* (Istanbul, 1935-38), 8 vols. 6433 pp. This work showed no originality and its author believed that translating the Kur'an was *kufr*. On the mysterious story of Âkif's translation see Ergin, *Türkiye Maarif Tarihi*, V, 1617-18, and Emin Erişirgil, *Mehmed Akif, İslâmcı Bir Şairin Romanı* (Ankara, 1956), pp. 463-78. There is a group of Âkif admirers whose pre-occupation is to nurture an Âkif cult chiefly by exploiting the anti-Tevfik Fikret myth according to which Fikret was a traitor because he retired to an American institution. See Eşref Edib, *İnkilâp Karşısında Âkif-Fikret* (Istanbul, 1940); Fikret is portrayed there as a traitor to Turkish nationalism and Âkif as the inspirer of the Struggle for Independence.

never understand Arabic (as they had never done), it was well enough for them to be led astray by "inadequate" renderings, or to remain totally ignorant of the source of their faith.[8]

490

It was precisely the implicit thesis that there should always be a class of interpreters against which Mustafa Kemal fought. He was spurred by a determination not to allow the intervention of such a monopolistic class in the religious consciousness of the people. This was the point upon which the remaining development of the experiment with the religious question rested. Mustafa Kemal went on alone in the face of the obstinate resistance of the deposed interpreters of religion. Following long experiments, trials, and rehearsals, he initiated the recital of the Kur'an in Turkish in 1931 (repeated in 1932) and the delivery of the sermons and the call to prayer in Turkish.[9]

The Philosophical Approach

Founded in the spirit of the rational approach to the religious question, the Department of Affairs of Piety provided insight into the practicability of a religious reform in a modern secularized Muslim society. Serious and quite interesting attempts were made to prepare lesson books on religion for children; these were a continuation of the attempts during Cevdet Paşa's time to replace the fire and brimstone morality tracts by more humanized and spiritualized presentations of Islam. Perhaps the major contribution of the Department was its administration of religious personnel, publications, and events in a spirit compatible with that of the new regime. Its position with regard to religious reform remained always passive, however.

The Faculty of Divinity was initiated to serve as the springboard for the reformulation of the question on the basis of the philosophical approach. Two views competed from the beginning concerning the function of the Faculty. This is illustrated in the difference over the Faculty's name. Originally, it was to be called the Faculty of *Diniyat*. This implied an institution solely

---

[8] The failure of the Islamists in the translation drive led many to ask how men incapable of translating the Kur'an into Turkish would be able to establish an Islamic state.

[9] See Ergin, *Türkiye Maarif Tarihi*, V, 1621-37.

for the scientific study of religions. The term was rejected, as was any derivative from *kalâm* (theology). Finally, the term *Ilâhiyat* (from *ilâhî*, divine, hence, Faculty of Divinity) was coined. Despite this designation, the program and composition of the faculty were more in accordance with the idea of *diniyat*. The following groups of courses, and particularly the titles of those within the first group, will illustrate this:

    I. History of *Kalâm;* History of *Hadîth;* History of *Tafsîr;* History of *Fiqh;* History of Islam; Muslim Philosophy.

    II. Ethnology of the Muslim Peoples; Contemporary Muslim Sects; Religious History of the Turks; *Tasawwuf.*

    III. History of Religions; Philosophy of Religion; History of Philosophy; Sociology of Religion; Psychology of Religion; Aesthetics and Islamic Art; Ethics.

Those giving the first group of courses were largely former *ulema.* The third group of courses was taught by men with no specialized Islamic education. The courses of the second group were given by men falling between the two types. Although it had been decided to give the courses of the first type historically, the apologetic approach predominated and was in contrast with the scientific approach accepted in the other courses.[10]

The faculty showed more enlightened interest in the question of a religious reform than the Department of the Affairs of Piety. It supported the use of the vernacular Kur'an in worship. However, the faculty members were not in agreement on the matter of accepting officially a Turkish text and they differed on the means and methods to be used in the implementation of a religious reform. Before noting the developments that brought the faculty to an impasse on the question of a religious reform and, in turn, contributed to its reduction in status to that of an Institute of Islamic Studies following 1932, we must note the discussions in and around the faculty that constituted a turning point in the course of Turkish secularism.

A number of events culminated in 1928 in a controversy over the moral, social, and religious implications of the Kemalist re-

---

[10] M. Izzet, "Iki Yoldan Biri," *Hayat,* II, No. 33 (Istanbul, July 14, 1927), 121-22; and M. Izzett, "Dar-ul-Fununda Felsefe Dersleri," *Edebiyat Fakültesi Mecmuası,* IV (Istanbul, March-April, 1925), 121-32; Ergin, *Türkiye Maarif Tarihi* (194?), III, 1025-26.

forms.[11] The events were interpreted as symtoms of a national cultural crisis caused by the catastrophic effects of the changes. Some viewed them as pathological phenomena indicative of a social and cultural disintegration. The belief, expounded earlier by Gökalp, that secularization meant the eradication only of those features of Islam that had not been assimilated by the national culture, was being contradicted by the Revolution. Either such a national culture was an illusion, or, if it was a reality, it was incompatible with modern civilization. It was not only Islam, or medieval Islam, that was under onslaught; the national culture itself was taking a pummelling. The validity of Gökalp's distinctions between culture and civilization began to be questioned. Some began to ask whether society could survive without a national culture, or without religious faith. Mehmet Emin [Erişirgil], a professor of philosophy, wrote, for example,

490 *[492 in margin]*

We are facing a spiritual chaos. As a result of the destruction of the institutions of religion which came down from the past and which were found incompatible with national life as well as modern civilization, unrest has developed in men's souls. Up to now we have associated religion with the *medreses,* the mystic orders, and the mental attitude [he refers to the Şeriat] that governed the legal actions of the state. None of these are compatible with modern life. Nearly all of the thinking men rallied behind the struggle aimed at liberation from these traditional institutions. The sociological consequences of the struggle for national liberation and the power created by it have finally demolished all fetters. But, now we are faced with the question of religion minus these institutions and with the question of religion as a religious consciousness and as a religious experience. . . . How can we strengthen in the souls [of the people] beliefs *useful* to society? Can Islam, reshaped to fit the requirements of secular life, satisfy this need?[12]

Mehmet Izzet, the sociologist, wrote, while discussing the question of teaching religion in the secondary schools:

Every Turk today . . . feels himself in a state of ambiguity with regard to religion. This is related undoubtedly to the present-day

---

[11] Incidents of suicide, juvenile delinquency, problems of school discipline, and the conversion of four girls in a Protestant missionary school led to speculations and controversies in 1927. See *Hayat,* I, No. 14 (March 3, 1927), 261 ff.; III, Nos. 62-67 (Feb. 2-March 8, 1928), 181-3, 201-2, 205-6, 221-23, 241-42, 286; also M. A. Aynî, *Reybîlik Bedbinîlik, Lâilahîlik Nedir?* (Istanbul, 1927).

[12] *Hayat,* III, No. 66 (March 1, 1928), 261.

conditions of our society and might be a product of the rapid changes that we are undergoing, but one can claim that this condition is going to persist. . . . Then, what will be our attitude towards the old body of beliefs in a new society? Shall we give it a new position in our life by reforming and reviving these beliefs *by a new spirit?* . . . As every religious movement is a product of and supported by a social movement, what is the social movement by which the modernization of Islam might be successful, once inspired and supported by it? If we come to the conclusion that such a reform is not feasible, we must put an end to the religious instruction given in the secondary schools; this is nothing but what we may call a sort of religious gymnastics devoid of any moral and intellectual component. But we must face the problem; no society can survive without a faith. A *new* faith has to be born in the place of the old. It is true that ideas such as democracy, progress, science, have assumed today almost sacred positions. But, these have to cease being abstract concepts and must become forces capable of leading us to supreme actions by their appeal to our wills. We must search for the ways and means of translating them into forces capable of affecting the wills and capable of integrating the sentiments.[13]

Despite disagreements among themselves concerning the nature and causes of the cultural crisis, all seemed to agree that a new orientation and a new set of values and ideals were needed. They seemed to agree also that Turkish society had not yet found the source of the ideals for this new stage. There was a great need for an intellectual search for these values and ideals. The religious question, therefore, could not simply be a matter of rational enlightenment; it was also a moral question.

It was at this time that some believed a reformed Islam would provide the spiritual source to fill the moral vacuum felt to exist in the souls. A committee was formed in the faculty to prepare a preliminary report for a program of religious reform. "The aim of the religious reform envisaged," said the chairman of the committee, "would be to make religion shape the process of development now active in all other departments of life."[14]

The discussions in the committee revolved about: (*a*) the necessity for a religious reform; (*b*) the nature of that reform; (*c*) the philosophy underlying the reform; and (*d*) the measures to be taken in order to implement the reform. All agreed that a reform

---

[13] *Ibid.,* II, No. 33 (July 14, 1927), 122.

[14] Lutfy Levonian, *The Turkish Press* (Athens, 1932), p. 123; Ergin, *Türkiye Maarif Tarihi,* (1943), V, 1639-41.

was needed. There appears to have been general agreement that the reform would be a secularizing one that would bring Islam into harmony with the conditions of modern life and make it a factor in integrating national life with modern civilization. Major disagreements arose over the last two points.

494

The most daring and, from our point of interest, influential ideas were put forward by Ismail Hakki (Baltacıoğlu), the father of modern Turkish educational thought. Baltacıoğlu went much further than Mustafa Kemal in proposing changes in the manner of worship. To Baltacıoğlu, worship was an aspect of religious life that had meaning insofar as it provided aesthetic experience. The manner of worship should facilitate such experience. In addition to providing modern hygienic devices and measures in the mosques, the religious reform should include at least two major innovations: the abolition of prostration during prayer and the introduction into the mosques of instrumental music such as had constituted an integral part of Muslim mystical worship.

Baltacıoğlu's aesthetic reformism marked him as one of the worst Turkish heretics. The importance of his views lay, though, in their philosophical component. The Turkish Revolution, said he, implied two processes and two objectives. It was a movement towards making the social institutions rational; at the same time, it was a movement towards making them national in character. Being a social institution itself, religion was also going to be subjected to a transformation in these two directions. It was impossible to believe that Islam would remain bound to its old forms and conventions. Neither the theological (*kalâm*), nor the mystic (*sufî*) approach to Islam was capable of bringing forth any reform. What was really important in the face of the two-fold challenge was neither the mere translation of the Kur'an, nor the forms of the Turkish words to be used.

The important task lies in working out a philosophical view showing Islam in terms of human and permanent values. Unless the Kur'an is approached and viewed from a philosophical view of this nature, it will remain incomprehensible even when it is translated. Mere reason and logic are not enough for such an understanding.[15]

The development of thought within the faculty along the lines shown by Baltacıoğlu can be seen from the following summary. "The aim of the faculty," he wrote, "should be neither to teach

[15] Levonian, *Turkish Press*, pp. 124-26; *Millî Mecmua*, No. 110 (Istanbul, 1928); Ergin, *Türkiye Maarif Tarihi* (1943), V, 1642-44.

Islam to the people nor to propagate it; its aim should be to create and establish a religious ethos through studying religion as shown in the life of mankind and of the nation." He emphasized that a genuine religious consciousness would not exist so long as Islam was subjugated to the medieval state and scholastic reason (*'ilm*). Religious consciousness had been obliterated by the spirit of these latter which were completely foreign to itself. In the face of the liberation of Islam from the *fiqh* and *kalâm*, the religious question was, above all else, a search for, and an attempt to cultivate, genuine religious experience. Baltacıoğlu expressed his belief that Islam could "win a new lease on life" only if it underwent such a transformation. However, he said, this could never be brought about by the old *ulema*. To entrust a religious reform "to them will even be dangerous. Religious bigotry and the medieval education that we expelled from life might return in a changed guise." The *ulema* had exhausted themselves; neither *kalâm* nor *tasawwuf*, but a philosophical spirit would be the channel towards a religious ethos, universal and humanistic, to supercede the religious pathos of medieval Islam.[16]

The sum total of Baltacıoğlu's argument was that what had been believed to be a mere matter of unfolding the reasonableness of Islam implied a profound transformation in the attitude towards religion itself. The issue of consequence was the fundamental difference between the theological (*kalâm*) and philosophical outlook.

The Formalization of Secularism

The constitutional basis for the Kemalist regime was completely secularized during the discussions summarized above, in 1928, by the elimination of Article 2 of the Constitution. This was a victory for the secularists, but it neither reflected nor produced a clear and positive doctrine of secularism. That doctrine evolved to the stage where it could be given a formal expression in the revised Constitution of 1937; it continued to be clarified juridically until 1949.

Perhaps the first to recognize the practical implications of the 1923-33 experiences was Mustafa Kemal himself. He ceased to evince interest in reforming religion after 1928 and came to the

---

[16] Ismail Hakkı [Baltacıoğlu], *Terbiye* (Istanbul, 1932), pp. 157-58.

conclusion that the course of development of the religious consciousness of the people could not and should not be led by the state or by secular personalities. The religious question, thus, became a matter of free discussion within the constitutional, legal, juridical, and educational framework of a secularized state. Its discussion shifted from the theological to the philosophical level. After 1928 there was a definite decline of interest in *kalâm* (or what was called *Hikmet-i Ilâhiye*, philosophy of divinity, with reference to the unsuccessful drive to produce a modernized *kalâm*) although the moral-religious concerns of Cevdet Paşa, the old Westernists, and Turkists regained their stature from that very time. Genuine interest in philosophy developed for the first time under the impetus of the religious and moral problems of the Republic; for the first time in centuries, the study of philosophy was not equated with atheism or heresy; philosophy deposed *kalâm* just as the modern civil codes had superseded the Şeriat. According to the prevailing philosophical orientation, faith was not a truth to be proven by reason; religion had sources other than those whose interest lay in the rational explanation of the universe; those sources were not to be sought in the letters of the Scriptures; faith and reason need not, nor could they, be reconciled; the sense of moral responsibility would not be impaired by the necessary transformation in the religious consciousness.[17]

Excerpts from two text books have been chosen as illustrating well the teaching in the schools on the nature of secularism from 1928. These views survived past the reintroduction of religious instruction in the public schools in 1948, until the Kemalist secularism was challenged politically by the Ministry of Education in 1952.

The function of religion is not to provide men with knowledge but with the will and power to live. . . . The more religion leaves

---

[17] See Ergin, *Türkiye Maarif Tarihi* (1943), V, 1417; Emin [Erişirgil] in *Hayat*, III, No. 66 (March 1, 1928), 262, and III, No. 72 (April 12, 1928), 381-82. For the discussions on philosophy, science, religion, and theology see M. Şemseddin [Günaltay], *Felsefe-i Ûlâ* (İstanbul, 1923); Elmalulu Hamdi [Yazır], *Metalip ve Mezahip* (İstanbul, 1923), Introduction; Emin [Erişirgil] in *Edebiyat Fakültesi Mecmuası*, III, Nos. 2-3 (İstanbul, 1923), 164-65; Ismail Hakkı [Baltacıoğlu], *Din ve Hayat* (2nd ed.; İstanbul, 1923); Mustafa Şekip [Tunç], *Memleketimizde Felsefenin Inkişafı İçin Lâzım Gelen Şartlar* (Ankara, 1938), and *Bir Din Felsefesine Doğru* (lectures originally given in the 1930's; İstanbul, 1959). See M. Servet, "Fikir Hayatımızda Bir Muhasebe," *Hayat*, V-VI, Nos. 116-31 (Feb. 14–May 30, 1929) for a discussion of the main philosophical trends before 1930.

explanation of the events of the universe and the search for the means of influencing them to science, the more it assumes this pragmatic and moral appearance. The believer then feels God's existence above all in his own conscience; he feels Him to be the founder of a universal moral order. . . . Religion's severance from the political organization . . . has left to religious experience only the individual's conscience within which to take refuge. Then, it is faith which manifests itself as an absolute subjugation to a moral ideal that can develop in harmony with the present-day conditions of civilization and science.[18]

No society of unbelievers ever existed. . . . But in our age, there is an attitude taken to religion that did not exist previously; no one interferes in another's belief; he respects all faiths. The intolerance of previous ages has been replaced by the sentiment of tolerance. Religious tolerance, as well as tolerance in science and politics, has become the most important feature of the modern nations. . . . The state is no longer the provider of a religion nor does it have a religion. . . . With the transformation of societies into democracies, religion became separated from the state. . . . The most important factor in the secularization of the state is the evolution of science, morals, and law autonomously from the religious dogmas. And the most sublime consequence of this process is mankind's reaching toward freedom of thinking. . . . A modern state is that one which does not interfere with beliefs. . . . Equally, it does not allow anybody to interfere with the beliefs of others. . . . The modern state should punish those who would exploit religious sentiments for mundane purposes. . . . It is evident that . . . the social factors in the secularization of the state are identical with those giving rise to democracy. A democratic Turkey necessarily means a laic Turkey.[19]

The idea of having the state an organ of reform in Islam was abandoned together with the legal identification of Turkey as an Islamic state. The legislation and juridical decisions following 1928 expressed the view that there were two minimal requirements for a cultural and moral transformation based upon a rational and philosophical approach to the religious question: (1) guaranteed freedom of conscience, thought, and expression, and (2) conditions conducive to the general and creative exercise of those inalienable natural rights. The state, it was believed, should abstain from theological and philosophical controversies, from siding with any creed, and from imposing any new or old dogma, doctrine, or

[18] Mehmed Izzet, *Yeni İçtimaiyat Dersleri* (2nd ed.; Istanbul, 1928), p. 278.

[19] Necmeddin Sadak, *Sosyoloji* (Ankara, 1941), pp. 94-97.

philosophy having relevance for matters of faith. At the same time, a necessary function of the state was seen to be the active prevention and suppression of acts or movements that aimed at or tended towards the limitation of individual rights and conscience.

498

The aim of the relevant legislation was the prevention and prohibition of the exploitation of beliefs for political, pecuniary, or immoral purposes. The purpose, for example, of the elimination of religious instruction and practices from the public schools was to ensure that local or social customs would not restrict either individual or parental prerogatives with regard to religious study and practice. The refusal of the state to permit even its secular employees to interpret the religious question while in official garb was balanced by restrictions upon the rights of sectarians to propagate their creeds even while in clerical garb. Whether by unreconciled clericals or by eliminationist secularists, acts against religions, beliefs, sacred persons, institutions, objects, and properties were made criminal offenses. The historically established religions such as Christianity, Judaism, and Islam were regarded as under legal protection; acts harmful to them were conceived to be criminal offenses. One restriction placed upon the performance of religious rites was that these should not contravene the civil, criminal, or municipal codes; neither should their performance be contrary to public health, rational civic virtues, or offensive to their involuntary participants as in the case of rites performed outside of sacred precincts or private domiciles.

Three important legal limitations were placed upon religion. From these we may define the Kemalist secularism at least in a negative and indirect way—for the very concept precluded a positive formulation, especially in advance of experience.

The first limitation is expressed in Article 9 of the Law of Associations of 1938 and concerns the formation of associations on the basis of sect and order (*mezhep* and *tarikat*). Prone to misinterpretation when seen out of context, this article served to clarify the Civil Code which allowed the formation of religious associations. In consequence, to form a society of Sunnis, or Alevîs, or a Ticanî or Bektaşî sect or order was to invite lawful prosecution and sentence according to the criminal code. The restriction imposed by Article 9 did not further limit the right to form religious societies of a non-sectarian and non-exclusive nature for the purposes, for example, of collecting funds for mosque repair, of promoting piety, charity, mutual aid, interest in religions, religious literature, and similar concerns.

The second restriction was the prohibition of political associations or parties seeking particularist religious support. In terms of this restriction, a Catholic party, a Muslim party, a pan-Islamic association, and an anti-Semitic association would all be impermissible. The other side to this coin was the prohibition with respect to religion placed upon the regularly constituted political parties. Parties calling themselves by any other name were liable to closure if their constitution contained religious aims or if they engaged in religious propaganda. From about 1932 when it hit its stride until the last stages of its internal dissolution following World War II, the single party of the Kemalist regime never resorted publicly to playing on religious sentiment; rather, social and, especially, educational problems were conscientiously reformulated so as to bring out their unifying moral, cultural, or aesthetic quality.

499

The third restriction concerned a fundamental prohibition given clarification in the 1949 revision of the Penal Code and in the latter-day secularist attitude towards the Republican legal system as a whole. This restriction, stated in Article 163 of the aforesaid law, provided punishment for acts "contrary to the principle of secularism enunciated in the Constitution" and that "aim at adapting, even if partially, the basic social, or economic, or political, or legal orders of the State according to religious fundamentals and beliefs." From this it would appear that secularism was understood as nothing but the disassociation of the fundamental institutions of the state (social, economic, political, legal, and, insofar as their function was to support these, educational) from religious principles—in this case from the Şeriat.[20]

We are now in a position to understand why aspects of Kemalist secularism gave the impression that religion was under duress by the laws of the state. Religion was guaranteed freedom and protection so long as and insofar as it was not utilized to promote any social or political ideology having institutional implications. In such terms, to understand the Kemalist secularism as a matter of separating church and state is also erroneous and irrelevant. To put it in a nutshell, Kemalist secularism was nothing but rejection of the ideology of Islamic polity. The Islamist critics of this view of secularism became, ironically, the advocates of separationist secularism within the context of the Republic. Measures taken for an understanding of Islam that would not be voiced as a call to

---

[20] For a discussion of the legal aspects of the Turkish secularism see Bülent Daver, *Türkiye Cumhuriyetinde Lâyiklik* (Ankara, 1955). Çetin Özek, *Türkiyede Lâiklik* (Istanbul, 1962).

tradition, obscurantism, and reaction in times of political stress were, for them, both anti-Islamic and anti-secularist. Pretending to be true believers in "laïcisme," they opposed the secularizing legislation, not on an Islamist principle but, strangely, on the grounds of the constitutional right to free exercise of religion so that they might reassert the political ascendency of their own ideology. Resorting to democratic slogans such as "the will of the People," they were bent upon restoring a polity under which the will, sovereignty, or law of the people would become nothing but heretical concepts.[21]

500

The Secularist View of National History and Culture

The Turkish nation, whose Islamic, Ottoman, and even Turkish heritages were badly shaken, had to undergo the strains of a radical transformation in its historical consciousness. The nation's historical existence had to be reviewed and its future course had to be set in terms of the requirements of the modern world.[22] Thus, while one direction of the intellectual development stimulated by the problems of secularism was towards the philosophical discussion of religion and moral values, the other was towards the discussion of history and civilization.

The Kemalist thesis concerning the history of the Turks, distorted at home and misunderstood abroad, contained a number of historical observations that were reactions against the earlier Islamist, Ottoman, and Westernist views of Turkish history, and brought forth a new conception of Turkish nationalism that was the diametric opposite of the Turkist nationalism.

Kemalist nationalism did not separate the nation from the rest of the world. It was preoccupied primarily with discovering and formulating the affinity between Turkish history and the history of the rest of the world. It became a drive toward what had been called humanism in Turkey. Two of its features are of particular interest here. One concerned the relation of the Turk to Islam;

---

[21] For an evaluation of Turkish secularism as an experience in religious reform in Muslim countries see Wilfred C. Smith, *Islam in in Modern History* (Princeton, 1957), pp. 161-205.

[22] The earliest sign of deviating from the Turkist understanding of nationalism was given by Mehmed Izzet, *Milliyet Nazariyeleri ve Milli Hayat* (Istanbul, 1925). This is also the best work written in Turkish on the theories of nationalism.

the other the affinity of Turkey with the nations contributing to the formation of modern civilization.

Unlike the Islamist view of Turkish history, the new view took the Islamic period as only an episode in, and secondary to, the national and civilizational aspects of the Turks' history. Further, the national aspect, which was the central theme in Turkist historiography, was seen, relatively speaking, as secondary to the international character of Turkish history viewed within a vast area extending from China to Central Europe. In this framework, the Turkish people were portrayed as having been actively involved in the secular make-up of history while only passive followers within the context of religious history.

501

Kemalist historiography revealed the Turks, traditionally identified with orthodox Islam, as perhaps the only people to have had multifarious experiences with all the great religions of the world. In history, the Turks were not only distributed within the folds of the principal world religions; they were a people who had passed successively through Shamanism, Buddhism, Judaism, Christianity, Manichaeism, and Islam and carried alive in their national culture traces of all these.[23] The secularist historiography brought to attention also a fact that was either ignored or rejected previously—the Turkish national spirit had shown itself at its best within Islamic religiosity not through orthodoxy, but through the unorthodox varieties of Islam. This could be judged from the survivals of the national culture wherever and whenever non-orthodox Islam prevailed among the Turks and from the extinction of any trace of national tradition where and when orthodoxy reigned. Amazingly abundant and variegated, the mystic literature (the only literature besides the folk that may be called Turkish), heterodox sects, heretical movements, and the like became objects of interest not for the purpose of theological controversy, or to provide a nationalist basis for a religious reform, but for a secular purpose—for the recovery of the national culture.[24] The students of culture found in the songs, tales, myths, dances, previously

---

[23] See W. Barthold, "Orta Asyada Hiristiyanlık," *Türkiyat Mecmuası,* I (Istanbul, Aug., 1925), 47-100 (originally written in 1894 in Russian); M. A. Mingana, "The Early Spread of Christianity in Central Asia and the Far East," *Bulletin of the John Rylands Library,* IX (Manchester, 1925), 297-371; Fr. Psalty, "Türklerde Hiristiyanlık," *Ikinci Türk Tarih Kongresi, 1937* (Istanbul, 1943), pp. 887-95.

[24] This began to appear through researches into the literary rather than the religious history. Fuad Köprülü, *Türk Edebiyatında Ilk Mutasavvıflar* (Istanbul, 1918) has been the pioneering work.

ignored as un-Islamic, expressions strikingly akin to the spirit of modern secular culture.

It was the preoccupations with these matters that led Mustafa Kemal, known after 1934 as Atatürk, to say,

502

> I admit that man cannot do without faith, but I believe that . . .
> throughout history the Turk has respected all beliefs cherished as
> sacred, and that his religion is neither this nor that particular religion.
> All faiths are worthy of reverence to him.[25]

The obvious implication of such a deliberately bold statement was Atatürk's belief that national existence would not be dependent upon any polity based upon religion, and that the secular regime should not uphold a religious doctrine, should not view the citizen as a believer (*mu'min*), and should not attempt a religious indoctrination. Members of the Turkish nationality were *mu'mins* only as far as they themselves were concerned; they were merely citizens as far as the state was concerned. In all these respects, the Kemalist secularism contrasted sharply with the so-called Islamic ideologies.

It will be noticed here again that the secularist view lacked a positive doctrine. It continued to be far more articulate and clear when it was negative. If it is compared with the major ideologies whose combined operation upon the formation of Kemalism was described above (that is, the Islamist, communist, and liberal political ideologies), and with the later ideologies such as fascism and national socialism, Kemalism alone will be found to be lacking a political creed to be disseminated through indoctrination. This has been baffling not only to foreign observers but also to those Turks who would have preferred to be supplied with some kind of ready-made doctrine.

This lack of a doctrinal basis has inevitably been a vulnerable feature of the Kemalist secularism. The regime has been criticized by the communists for its toleration of religion, by the Islamists for its persecution of religion, and by the Western liberals for its keeping religion within the fold of state. Even a slight loss in understanding the unique constellation of factors within which Kemalist secularism took its form—a form that appears different when approached from a general and abstract doctrine—is apt to lead to the misrepresentations which we have discussed above. Because of this, Kemalism faced attacks and underwent serious tests during the years following World War II when conditions

---

[25] Quoted in Ergin, *Türkiye Maarif Tarihi* (1943), V, 1632, 1638.

in Turkey had changed. It received its heaviest attacks from chauvinist nationalism and from the Islamists. The latter raised or lowered their demands, depending upon conditions, from the restoration of the Caliphate to the reveiling of women.

From 1945 until 1960 the religious, national, and civilizational principles of the secular regime were overwhelmed by a wave of reaction that looked at times as if it were sweeping the nation back to the days of Abdül-Hamid. The governments of the 1950's gave free reign to all sorts of obscurantism under the guise of restoring the freedom of religion and in the name of democracy. These years provided laboratory check-tests of the validity and durability of a secular regime in a Muslim country. As such, the period deserves separate and detailed study. It suffices to note here, however, that Turkish secularism withstood all of the strains; it has come through its ordeal and is still one of the guiding principles of modern Turkey.

CONCLUSION

THE TRANSFORMATION of Turkey from a traditional to a secular state illustrates the complex relations between economic and technical changes and political and religious changes. For this reason it presents a valuable case history.

Since World War II, the fate of those countries which have lagged behind the West in economic development has become a matter of world-wide concern. But the problem is rarely seen in historical and cultural perspective. Economists and policy makers too often assume that such countries can develop economically through external aid while their traditional cultures remain unchanged. Yet the economic developments envisaged will be conditioned, furthered, or frustrated by traditional, as well as by new, cultural factors. Although it may seem that economic changes can create new social conditions harmonious with modern development, experience has shown that, in fact, a transformation is needed in political, social, cultural, and religious structures and values before such economic changes can be effective.

Without the breakdown of the traditional structure and attitudes, modern economic and technical aid may produce little change conducive to growth. Modern economy itself is not merely isolated pieces of technology, but a part of a cultural complex. The schemes proposed for underdeveloped countries, however, tend to take for granted the existence of those cultural conditions that accompanied the modern economic development of the West. Above all, they tend to forget that without the secularization of Western society, modern developments would not have been possible.

508

The traditional structures and institutions of all underdeveloped societies have already been affected by the impact of modern civilization. Socially and culturally this impact has been disruptive rather than constructive, and these societies are facing not merely the problems of economic advancement but also the problem of developing a new national and cultural identity. Most important to consider is the degree to which a society belonging to a disrupted traditional culture has been able to reintegrate itself, structurally as well as culturally, on a secular national basis. In most cases, the development of the new social structures and cultural orientations has required the ascendency of new political and religious concepts that are antithetical to the traditional ones. This is especially so where the "political-religious" complex has not partitioned into an identifiable or distinguishable pair.

The transformation whose course has been traced in this work is clearly that of a society forced to change under the stress of modern civilization. Turkey was geographically closer to the centres of change than any other non-Western society and was the first to feel their influence. The old polity and system of values began to disintegrate, but the reconstitution of Turkish society did not immediately follow. Despite its physical proximity to European civilization and its earlier receptiveness to it, Turkey withdrew into cultural isolation, seeking security in traditional forms. The earliest attempts at reform, in the seventeenth century, were not towards a change into something new, but towards reestablishing, reaffirming, the supremacy of the tradition of the past.

It was only in the eighteenth century, after attempts to restore the traditional institutions proved ineffective, that modernizaion and even technical development were seen as necessary conditions of reform. Even then, the desire was not for change in the basic institutions, but for an elixir to revitalize what remained as tradition. It was not until the nineteenth century that modernization became the major concern of political and intellectual efforts for reform.

When, in the nineteenth century, the changes introduced were seen clearly to affect the existing order, two tendencies appeared and crystallized. One was to reject all innovations and cling to traditional institutions, which were identified with unchangeable religious values; the other was to extricate religious values from the vicissitudes of the changing world by narrowing the scope of tradition.

These tendencies worked increasingly against one another. The attempt to limit the scope of tradition led to a greater assertion of religion over life. The association of change with external or foreign pressure made innovations seem particularly hostile to religion, which was seen as the source of all normative values, that is, as going beyond the traditional order itself. Against the external threat, religion rather than state began to seem the basis of social existence.

When, from about the middle of the nineteenth century, the state was forced by external pressures to promote change, it appeared to be the instrument of those pressures, and found itself stripped of its traditional religious legitimization. The mounting tension worked for the separation of the two intertwined elements of the traditional order, in spite of all efforts to keep state and religion side by side in a new dual relationship. Attempts to delineate the respective areas of the two produced, not a secular state with a religious organization outside it, but rather a series of divisions in the political, legal, and educational institutions, each of which manifested a religious-secular duality. In each, single fields of action could belong to the modern or the traditional pattern. The bifurcation of culture in these terms was paralleled by a distinction between the material and moral elements in the model civilization.

The constant conflicts within the divided institutions, the crises precipitated by these divisions, and the incessant accompaniment of material by non-material elements in the process of borrowing showed that the transformation was one of fundamental change. The failure of successive attempts to reform the economic, legal, and educational systems led to a demand for a new social basis.

From about the beginning of the twentieth century, one group saw hope for a new social basis in a modernized Islam, which would replace the traditional political-religious order. Believing that Islam was a secular religion, these maintained that it was capable of providing every rule of action required for accommodation with modern civilization. The economic and political failures of the secularized traditional regime, owing to the disintegration of the multi-national, multi-religious Ottoman empire into a number of nationalities, enhanced the appeal of this view. The Muslim community, however, could not itself escape disintegration into separate Muslim nationalities. Before the powerful upsurge of national movements, the fate of the state would be decisive for the fate of religion. While those who held a modern version of Islam

509

to be the basis of a modern Islamic society were developing their new totalitarian and theocratic ideology, decisive direction was given to Turkish secularism by the opposing political interests of the various Muslim national movements.

Turkish nationalism, which had remained dormant while the Ottoman Empire disintegrated into separate non-Muslim nationalities, became active only with the collapse of Islamic unity. A secular conception of national unity negated both the traditional and the "modernist" view of a state associated with or based upon religion. This negation was symbolized by the abolition of the sultanate, soon followed by the abolition of the caliphate, and the establishment of a republican form of government based upon the sovereignty of the people constituting a nation.

The national state could no longer maintain the traditional association between state and religion in the way characteristic of the traditional polity. It became instead the instrument of the real aim of the Turkish transformation—modernization and economic development. In the resultant secular state, a new arrangement was found for what were taken as *national*, *religious*, and *modern*; this was worked out within the framework of a policy of secularism which, though pursuing the same aim, differed from the varieties of Western secular regimes in its different means and different course.

glossary

THIS GLOSSARY does not contain all Turkish, Arabic or Persian words found in the text of this work. Those which are defined, analyzed, or simply given with approximate English equivalents are not included. The definitions do not necessarily give the correct etymological or lexicographical meanings; they attempt rather to convey semantic connotations in terms of the conditions in which they were used. *A.*, *T.*, *P.*, stand for Arabic, Turkish, Persian, respectively.

adalet, justice or equity; in nineteenth-century Turkish usage, just treatment of all, irrespective of creed or social standing according to enacted laws.

'adl, the A. root of the above.

adlî, legal, judicial.

adliye, secular judicial organization.

ahkâm, pl. of *hukm*, judgment, rule, provision.

ahl al-'aqd wa al-hall (A.), men invested with power to bind and loose.

ahl al-kitâb (A.), people who possess Scripture such as Jews or Christians.

ahlâk (A. *ahlâq*), ethics.

ahrar, liberals, liberal party.

511

alafranga, frankish, western, westernized, used derisively for those imitating the French manners.

alaturka, old Turkish fashion.

512

alevî, heterodox Muslim as distinguished from the *sunnî* (*q. v.*).

âlim (A. *'âlim*), a learned man. See *ulema*.

allâme (A. *'allâma*), the most learned, erudite.

âmentu (A.), "I believed", the title of a poem by Tevfik Fikret.

amîr al-mu'minîn (A.), the Commander of the Faithful, the Caliph.

'asabiyya (A.), principle of solidarity; tribalism.

'asr (A.), age.

Asr-ı Saadet, The age of felicity, the Prophet's age.

asrî, modern, secular.

avam (A. *'awâmm*), the common people.

âyan, the notables.

âya (A.), a verse of the Kur'an.

azân (A.), call to prayer.

bai'a (A.), see *bîat*.

başvekil, prime minister.

batinî, those who seek the esoteric meaning of the Kur'an (regarded heretic by the orthodox).

Bektaşî, a member of a heterodox Muslim sect named after Hajji Bektaş, who lived in Anatolia in the 13th century.

bîat, (A. *bai'a*), paying homage or allegiance.

bid'at (A. *bid'a*), innovation.

çarşaf, one or two-piece outdoor cover of women.

cemaat, a religious congregation or community; the nineteenth-century Turkish usage of this word corresponded to the European use of the term *millet* (*q. v.*)

dahrî (A.), see *dehrî*.

Dar-ul-funûn, house of sciences, university.

dehrî, materialist, secularist.

dehrîlik, materialism, secularism.

derebey, feudal chieftain.

devlet, state.

dhimmî (A.), a non-Muslim subject of a Muslim government if he belongs to a scriptural religion (see *ahl al-kitâb*).

din, religion.

din-u-devlet, a polity in which religion and state are unified.

dinsizlik, irreligion.

eşraf, local dignitaries.

evkaf, Muslim pious foundations.

faqîh (A.), a scholar of Islamic jurisprudence. See *fiqh.*

farz (A. *fard*), religious duty obligatory to every believer.

fenn-i terbiye, the science of education.

ferman, firman, imperial decree or edict.

fetva (A. *fatwâ*), authoritative opinion given by a *muftî* (*q. v.*) or *Şeyhul-Islâm* (*q. v.*)

fiqh (A.), *fikh* (T.), Islamic jurisprudence.

Frenk, western European.

ghalatât, words corrupted from their original meanings or pronunciations or spellings.

Gülhane, the name of the park where the Tanzimat Charter of 1839 was proclaimed by a ceremony.

hacı (A. *hâjji*), a person who has paid pilgrimage to Mecca.

hadîth (A.), anecdotes or sayings relating to the exemplary actions or sayings or tacit approvals of the Prophet.

hâfiz, a person who has memorized the entire Kur'an.

hanafî (A.)., *hanefî* (T.), those who adhere to the school of jurisprudence of Abû Hanîfa (A.D. 700-67)

ḥaqq (A.), *ḥak* (T.), truth.

ḥaram, prohibited, unlawful.

ḥijrî (from A. *ḥijra*, the migration of Muhammad from Mecca to Medina in September, (A.D. 622), the starting year of the Muslim calendar.

ḥikma (A.), *ḥikmet* (T.), wisdom, philosophy.

ḥoca, clerical teacher or, more commonly, a person performing some religious function who is distinguished by his gown and turban from a layman.

icma (A. ijmâ'), consensus.

içtihad (A. *ijtiḥâd*), forming an opinion on a rule of law by reasoning.

ifta (see also *fetva*), interpreting the general provisions of the law for particular cases.

ijmâ', see *icma*.

ijtiḥâd, see *içtihad*.

'ilm (T. *ilim*), knowledge, traditional knowledge, science.

imam, the prayer leader; *imâm* (A.), the head of the community of the faithful or an original founder of a school of jurisprudence.

kadıasker (from A. *qâdî' l-'askar*, military judge), Chief Justice.

kalâm, theology.

kanûn, decrees enacted by temporal rulers.

kharâbât (P.), in mystic literature, wine-shop or tavern symbolizing the convent where the novice receives the wine of love for God from the *pîr-i mughân*, the spiritual guide. See *mugh*.

Mâlikî, those who adhere to the school of law founded by Mâlik b. Anas (A.D. 710-95)

medrese (A. *madrasa*), medieval colleges where law and theology were taught predominantly.

milla, see *millet*.

millet (A. *milla*), in modern Turkish "nation", in classical Arabic, a community of faith, in 19th century diplomacy, a non-Muslim community in the Ottoman Empire.

molla or *mullah*, formerly a high-ranking judge; later any one who had some literate religious education.

muderris, a *medrese* (*q. v.*) lecturer.

mufti, a person qualified and authorized to issue a *fetva* (*q. v.*)

515

mugh (P., pl. *mughân*), Magus, a believer in the coming of a saviour in ancient Persia. Muslim mystic poets used symbolic expressions such as *pîr-i mughân* (magian saint or sage) meaning the "old man of the tavern", *mugh-beche* (magian boy) meaning the "boy-waiter of the tavern", to denote the mystic guide and the novice, respectively. See *kharâbât*.

mullah, see *molla*.

mültezim, tax-farmer.

qâdî, see *kadı*.

rahmet, mercy, compassion.

rayah (T. *raâya*, A. *ra'âyâ*), non-Muslim subjects of the 19th century Ottoman Empire; originally, peasantry.

şeyhul-Islâm (*A. shaikh al-Islâm*) the highest *muftî* (*q. v.*) before the 19th century Turkey.

şeyh (A. *shaikh*), elder, a tribal chief, a spiritual guide of a mystic order.

Shâfi'î, those who adhere to the legal doctrines of Shâfi'î (A.D. 767-820)

softa, fanatic.

sunnî, the orthodox.

tafsîr (T. *tefsir*), commentary on the Kur'an.

tasawwuf, mysticism.

ta'zîr, censure, application of a discretionary penalty.

usûl al-fiqh, the part of the Islamic jurisprudence dealing with the sources of law.

ulema (A. *ulama*, pl. of *'ilm*, *q. v.*), the order of the learned.

vâiz, preacher.

518

Pakalın, M. Z., 142, 144
Parker, J., and Smith C., 463
Parvus (Alexander Helphand), 271, 335-37, 427
Perin, C., 199
Pertussier, Charles, 77, 94
Peyssonel, M. de, 35, 60, 68
Pingaud, L., 64, 65, 67
Porter, Sir James, 28
Pressel, G. W. von, 272
Puryear, Vernon J., 138, 139

Rahmi, Hüseyin, 292
Râif, Mahmud, 80
Ramsauer, E. E., 304
Rasim, Ahmed, 156, 158, 197, 279
al-Râziq, Ali Abd, 453, 487
Reed, Howard A., 92
Refik, Ahmed, 47, 152
Reid, John, 96
Resmî, Ahmed, 57
Rifâ'a (al-Tahtâwî), 121
Rifat, Sadık, 130-32, 174
Ridâ, Rashîd, 381, 488-89
Rıza, Ahmed, 305-6
Rowland, A. L., 33

Sabah, 320
Sabit, Halim, 345, 383
Sabri, Mustafa, 299, 379, 388-89, 415, 434
Sadak, N., 497
Saib, Ahmed, 299
Said Paşa, Eginli, 244
St. Simon, 35
Salve, de, 189, 190
Sâmi, Mustafa, 129-30
Sâmi, Şemseddin, 181, 287, 296, 320
Sebil-ur-Reşat, 341, 363, 373, 374, 380, 418
Servet-i Funûn, 257, 280, 295, 296
Seton-Watson, R. W., 224, 249
Sevig, V. R., 162
Seyyid, M., 453, 460, 468-69
Sirat-ı-Mustakim, 341, 342, 348, 352, 354, 359, 360, 369, 370, 372, 380, 381, 386, 388, 389, 390, 395, 399, 413, 414
Slade, Adolphus, 93, 126
Smith, W. C., 459, 500

Sousa, N., 55
Southgate, Horatio, 138
Spector, Ivan, 441
Stephens, John, 138
Stoddard, Lothrop, 269
Suavi, Ali, 33, 208, 314, 317
Subhî, Mehmed, 48
Sumner, B. H., 244
Sungu, Ihsan, 40, 80, 107, 168, 189, 190, 204, 209, 217
Süleyman Paşa, 226, 227, 240, 242, 244, 267, 314, 317
Süssheim, K., 119
Şekip, M., 496
Şemseddin, M., 496
Şeref, Abdurrahman, 130, 132, 144, 181, 204, 456
Şevketi, Eşrefzade, 396-97, 414
Şuayip, Ahmed, 417
Şükrü, Ismail, 453
Şükrü, Mehmed, 414

Tahsin, Rıza, 112, 113, 115, 116, 120, 121, 177
Tahsin Paşa, 258
Takvim-i Vekayi, 105, 121, 126, 127, 130, 180, 184, 185, 416
Tanpınar, A. H., 34, 80, 130, 131, 132, 197, 204, 281, 317
Tansel, F. A., 196, 307, 342
Tanzimat, Ministry of Education, 144, 145, 148, 157, 163, 164, 176, 209
Tarîk, 263, 284, 299, 320
T. B. M. M. Zabıtları, 447, 469, 470
Tekin Alp (M. Cohen), 344, 358
Temo, Ibrahim, 304
Temperley, Harold, 92, 94, 126, 138, 139, 144, 149, 152, 157, 162, 202, 249
Terakki, 310
Tercüman-ı Hakikat, 257, 296
Testa, Baron de, 168
Toderini, Abbé, 41, 60
Togay, M. F., 321
Tott, Baron de, 48, 59, 68
Toynbee, Arnold, J., 12, 41, 96, 254, 270, 344, 433, 452, 454, 458, 459, 460, 477
Tunaya, Tarık Z., 204, 304, 330, 438, 440, 449
Tunç, Şekip, 496

520

526

imperialism, 69, 253, 335, 393, 432. *See also* Imperialism

industries, 129, 255, 396

institutions, 149

intervention, 143, 147, 204, 206, 208, 241

inventions, 129

languages, 35, 68, 80, 113, 118, 182, 269

life, contact with, 78

methods and techniques, 30, 42, 44-47, 59, 76, 110, 298, 303, 343, 362, 395; borrowing of, 360. *See also* Military

missions and military instructors, 73, 75, 111, 275

musicians, 122

nations, 148, 184, 394

physicians, 112

political: institutions, 80, 214; interests, 335

powers, 23, 41, 84, 96, 138, 161, 189, 206, 221, 230, 249, 260, 270, 290, 308, 312, 334, 337, 341, 356

public opinion, 64, 219

rationalism, 68

rule over Muslims, 353

sciences, 30, 49, 75, 80, 129, 181, 263, 342, 359, 393, 407, 413

scientific and technological progress, 130, 134, 178, 215, 362

statesmen, 255, 308, 335

supremacy, 221

teachers, 112

thinkers, 181, 199, 237, 291, 294, 295, 315

trade, 28, 139, 166, 420

works, 49, 59, 60, 73, 75, 78, 107, 113, 119, 128, 283, 318, 379. *See also* Sciences, Translations

Europeans, 29, 30, 32, 40, 43, 45, 53, 113, 138, 141, 166, 206, 263, 269, 349, 371, 389, 395, 426

Evkaf (*awqâf*), 62, 174, 415, 416, 448, 461, 484, 485

Evolutionism, 293, 295. *See also* Darwinism

Family and marriage, 198, 385-93 *passim*, 416, 467, 481; Law 417

Fanaticism, 79, 82, 349, 350, 351, 353, 357, 380, 382, 408, 483

Fatherland, Idea of, *see Vatan*, *also* Patriotism

Fatma Aliye, 286-87, 291

Fazıl, Mustafa, 205, 208, 232

Fehmi, Hasan, 169, 183, 191, 414, 415

Fénélon, 199, 283, 294

Fetva (*fatwâ*), 15, 16, 27, 40, 121, 127, 147, 187, 227, 229, 267, 392, 393, 442, 485

Fevzi, Halil, 185-87, 266

Fez, *see* Headgear

Fikret, Tevfik, 295, 300-2, 338-39, 406, 407, 489n.

Fikri, Lûtfi, 457

Fiqh (Islamic jurisprudence), 161, 167, 180, 187, 188, 216, 217, 218, 299, 371, 383, 384, 390, 414, 423, 467, 491, 495

Flamarion, 292

Flaubert, 292, 295

Fleury, Cardinal, 25n.

Fontenelle, 199

France, 25, 33-35, 36n., 39, 46-48, 51, 54, 64, 66, 111, 121n., 128, 130, 139, 143, 150, 177, 181, 205, 219, 224, 254, 257, 306, 309, 321, 334

Franklin, Benjamin, 41- 282

Freeman, E. A., 219, 220n.

Freemasons, 266

Free-thinkers, 84, 181, 265

French
culture and civilization, 25, 33, 52, 71, 291, 302

diplomacy, 25, 55, 64, 91, 153

government, 58

ideas, influence of, 35, 83

influence, 67, 77, 81

interests, 25, 26, 55, 59, 61, 65, 66, 67

language, 35, 75, 100, 106, 111-17, 122, 177, 181, 191, 232, 286, 380, 388, 406; influence of, 194, 276, 286, 291

literature, 116, 117, 278; influence of, 198, 279-81, 291

officers, 47, 59, 65. *See also* Military

painters, 36, 65

revolution, 71, 96, 260, 294; influence of, 83, 199

trade, 55; échelles, 55, 59n., 66

Metternich, 148
Midhat (Efendi) Ahmed, 279, 281-86, 293, 295, 296, 300, 303, 338
Midhat (Paşa), 157, 223, 226, 228-31, 233-35 *passim*, 241, 245, 248-50, 265, 308, 320
Military: institution, 25, 29, 73; instructors, 32, 58; reforms, 47, 58-60, 75, 92, 111; sciences, 32, 34, 44, 47, 59, 76; schools, *see* Schools
Mill, John Stuart, 292
Millets, 11, 12, 95, 104, 108, 145, 150, 152-54, 158, 169, 172, 179, 188, 201, 217, 221, 224, 308, 313, 318, 326, 329, 331, 334, 365, 418; system 96-98, 105, 147, 173, 189, 318. *See also* Armenians, Greeks, Catholics, Protestants
Mirabeau, 117n.
Missionaries: American, 103; Protestant, 150
Mizan, 308
Modernists, 4, 8, 349, 373, 388
Modernization, 71, 90, 134, 221, 222, 255, 263, 338, 352, 442, 475, 508, 510
Molière, 196n., 199, 294, 315
Mongols, 314, 317, 350, 351, 374
Monitorial system, 102, 103. *See also* Lancasterian Schools
Montecucculi, Raimondo, 49
Montesquieu, 199, 292, 307
Montmorency, de, 65
Muhammedan Union, 330, 341
Murad, Mehmed, 305, 307-9, 310, 321
Murad V, 223, 227-29
Muslim: countries, 41, 44, 112, 119, 222, 254, 309, 361, 363, 380, 413; medical students, 115-17; millenium, 19; nation, 220; nations, 42, 52, 83, 215, 484; rule, 52; women, 387-90 *passim;* world, 231, 253, 255, 258, 443, 449, 451, 454, 457, 459, 474
Muslims, 11, 34, 40, 43, 44, 57, 91, 94, 95, 97, 108, 114, 125, 150, 153, 208, 222, 262, 290, 296, 308, 339-43 *passim,* 374, 399, 432, 434, 445, 454, 458; constitutional rights of, 159, 227, 230, 231, 237, 239-41, 318; economic position of, 141-42, 204, 206, 395-96, 424; education of, 100-1, 104, 189, 190, 378, 476; European attitude towards, 68, 219, 312, 348-50; legal rights of, 98, 145, 162, 167, 168, 417, 469; nationalism of, 332-33, 376; of India, 125, 159, 254, 319, 327, 342, 413; of Indonesia, 159, 327, 413; of North Africa, 125, 258, 259; of Pakistan, 319; of Russia, 159, 254, 327, 413, 426, 427; and pan-Islamism, 221, 267, 268, 270; Shiî, 254.
Mustafa III, 53, 58, 64
Mustafa Fazıl Paşa, 205, 208, 232
Mültezim, 56, 73, 143
Münevver, see Intellectuals, Enlightened
Münif, Tahir, 179, 180, 181, 195, 199
Müteferrika, *see* Ibrahim Müteferrika
Mystical orders, *see* Sufî orders
Mysticism, 29, 293, 491, 492, 494

Nacharîs, Nachariya, 265, 266, 267. *See also Dehrîs,* Materialists
Naim, Ahmed, 374-76, 377, 379n., 381
Nami, Kâzım, 358
Napoleon Bonaparte, 24, 65, 67n., 75, 85, 89
National: assembly, 232, 246-48, 436, 439, 442-45, 447-52, 454-56, 469, 475, 485, 488; culture, 192, 351, 355, 365, 409, 410, 492, 501; economy, 134, 139, 335; ideals, 364; liberalism, 439, 442, 447, 454, 464, 483, 492; pact, 435; state, 367, 510; unity, 442
Nationalism, 103, 192, 202, 204, 211, 270, 313, 355, 373, 376, 410, 431, 435, 440, 442, 459; Albanian, 319; Arab, 253, 260, 269, 319, 375; Armenian, 253, 260, 312, 318; Bulgarian, 318; Circussian, 319; Greek, 103, 189; Islamic, 214, 218, 221, 231, 254, 319; Kurdish, 319; non-muslim, 89, 91, 95, 192, 321, 333; non-Turkish, 313, 321, 330, 333, 374, 433; religious, 159, 350; Roumanian, 318; Serbian, 318; Turkish, 114, 313, 318, 321, 329, 330, 333, 343, 373, 410, 427, 434, 475, 484, 488, 500, 509. *See also* Turkism, Pan-Turanism, Pan-Turkism
Nationality, idea of, 84, 198, 200, 319, 327, 331, 365, 374-77, 412
Natural rights, theory of, 210, 217

1500 copies
printed from linotype Janson
by The Runge Press Limited, Ottawa.
Typographic design by
Robert R. Reid.

The tulip pattern
on the binding is from
an Ottoman textile woven in
the sixteenth century.